Blockchain, Virtual Currencies and ICOs: Navigating the Legal Landscape

Wolters Kluwer Legal & Regulatory U.S. Editorial Staff

This publication is designed to provide accurate and authoritative information in regard to the subject matter covered. It is sold with the understanding that the publisher is not engaged in rendering legal, accounting, or other professional service. If legal advice or other expert assistance is required, the services of a competent professional person should be sought.

ISBN: 978-1-5438-0281-8

©2018 CCH Incorporated. All Rights Reserved.

2700 Lake Cook Road
Riverwoods, IL 60015
866 529 6600
www.WoltersKluwerLR.com

Printed in the United States of America

Foreword

Virtual currencies and interest in blockchain technologies took the world by storm in 2017. Over the course of that year, the price of Bitcoin surged from just under $1000 to nearly $20,000 a coin, before giving back about two thirds of those gains by the middle of 2018. That kind of volatility reflects Bitcoin's price history since it came on the stage in March 2009, when a single coin was basically worthless. Clearly, Bitcoin's growing popularity and the persistent and meteoric ascent in its value in less than a decade's time is undeniable. Likewise, interest and investment in blockchain technology, the computer-based recordkeeping infrastructure upon which Bitcoin is based, is widespread and growing. Over the past few years, the application of blockchain technology continues to expand in diverse industries including healthcare, real estate, corporate governance, supply-chain management, as well as banking and finance.

Without doubt, controversies around Bitcoin, virtual currencies, and blockchain technologies abound. Many leading business figures see Bitcoin's appreciation in value as one of the great swindles of our time and envision a precipitous crash. JP Morgan CEO Jamie Dimon has called Bitcoin "a fraud," while legendary Berkshire Hathaway CEO Warren Buffett has described Bitcoin as "rat-poison." Nevertheless, a wide swath of market participants are increasing their involvement in virtual currencies.

With this backdrop in mind, the legal and regulatory landscape has been flooded with a torrent of developments coming from regulators, law enforcement, and civil litigants alike. Beyond the deluge of information on blockchain technology and its business environment, hardly a day goes by without the release of a regulatory pronouncement or legal pleading impacting this space. As a result, legal practitioners of all stripes have struggled to keep up with an onslaught of technical and business information, and to make sense of the disparate and ever-evolving regulatory landscape.

Meanwhile regulators and law enforcement agencies continue to fight seemingly unending battles against fraudsters, hackers, and other assorted bad actors, while attempting to promote and foster technological innovations and legitimate business activities. Some areas of the cryptocurrency ecosystem remain virtually untouched by regulation, taking on a "wild wild west" veneer, while other activities may be subject to multiple regulators and a host of uncertain regulatory requirements and obligations.

While capital clearly seeks a home in the virtual currency space, for the time being it will have to interface with a crazy quilt of regulators, including the SEC, with its mission of facilitating capital formation and investor protections, the CFTC, with its oversight of fraud and manipulation in virtual currencies, various banking regulators, as well as disparate and fragmented treatment by the 50 states, which have asserted authority over virtual currency activities to various degrees.

U.S. law does not provide for direct, comprehensive federal oversight of the underlying Bitcoin or virtual currency spot markets. Commentators eyeing the legal landscape have described it as a multifaceted, multi-regulatory approach, less charitably as a hodgepodge, or even worse, a mess. *Blockchain, Virtual Currencies and ICOs: Navigating the Legal Landscape* will assist practitioners that seek to navigate the perplexing terrain of virtual currencies and cut through the fog to gain a measure of clarity with respect to the existing frameworks and central issues at play in this dynamic and challenging area.

In Chapter 1, we explore the basics of blockchain technology, virtual currencies, smart contracts, and discuss the potential impact and implications of this burgeoning technology on the legal profession.

4

Chapter 2 focuses on the various regulatory and law enforcement agencies and identifies each of their roles with respect to virtual currency regulation.

Chapter 3 surveys the SEC's involvement in virtual currencies and the role of securities laws.

Chapter 4 focuses on the CFTC's role and its approach to virtual currency regulation.

Chapter 5 explores the role of FinCEN, as well as the import of anti-money laundering regulations and know your customer requirements in the virtual currency sphere.

Chapter 6 focuses on the role of various banking regulators including the Fed, OCC, and CFPB in connection with virtual currencies.

Chapter 7 explores an assortment of state licensing, corporate governance, and enforcement issues with respect to virtual currencies.

Chapter 8 considers the current state of play and potential future directions as the virtual currency industry evolves and blockchain technologies continue to make inroads in various sectors of the economy.

July 2018

Wolters Kluwer Legal & Regulatory U.S.

EDITORIAL STAFF

Table of Contents

Detailed Table of Contents

Chapter One—Blockchain Technology

¶ 100 The Underlying Technology and its Uses

The ascent of Bitcoin and some other virtual currencies has dominated recent headlines. In 2017, Bitcoin itself saw an increase in value of 1,375 percent, climbing to just under $20,000 before giving back more than half of those gains in the first quarter of 2018. With a little less fanfare, many have also embraced the promise of blockchain technology, the digital platform underlying Bitcoin, which is viewed as having the potential to disrupt and transform business processes and solve real world problems.

Blockchain, briefly, is a decentralized peer-to-peer network of computers that relies on certain network participants to validate and log transactions on a permanent, publicly distributed ledger, as described by CFTC Chairman J. Christopher Giancarlo in testimony before Senate Banking Committee. Giancarlo also noted blockchain technology provides a solution to the age-old "double spend" problem by eliminating the need for a central authority or trusted intermediary, like a bank or other financial institution, to ensure that a party is capable of, and does, engage in a valid transaction. Giancarlo surmised "that blockchain technologies over time may come to challenge traditional market infrastructure. They are transforming the world around us, and it is no surprise that these technologies are having an equally transformative impact on US capital and derivatives markets." [Testimony of Chairman J. Christopher Giancarlo before the Senate Banking Committee, February 6, 2018.]

This chapter provides a high-level, non-technical explanation of blockchain technology, virtual currencies, and tokens. The chapter concludes by exploring the potential impact these innovations may have on the future of legal practice.

Bitcoin and its Creation

In November 2008, an anonymous person (or group of people) going by the name of Satoshi Nakamoto posted a white paper to a mailing list for cryptography experts. The storied white paper, briefly but elegantly, set forth a framework for a peer-to-peer version of electronic cash that would allow online payments to be sent directly from one party to another without going through a financial institution. [Satoshi Nakamoto, Bitcoin: A Peer-to-Peer Electronic Cash System.] In providing a vision for Bitcoin, the white paper also sets forth the basic framework for blockchain technology. [*See generally*, Paul Vigna and Michael J. Casey, *The Age of Cryptocurrency*, Ch. 2 (2015).]

With the subsequent release and implementation of the Bitcoin software in January 2009, the Bitcoin network came into existence with the creation of the first block on the chain known as the genesis block. As a result, Bitcoin became the world's first decentralized currency using peer-to-peer blockchain technology. In the process, Bitcoin became blockchain's first use case.

Distributed Ledger Technology

The terms distributed ledger technology (DLT) and blockchain are often used interchangeably. More precisely, however, blockchain is one type of DLT. "DLT is just a database that has multiple copies of the data on many nodes (computers) in the network" noted Sheppard Mullin partner James Gatto. DLT can use either a public or private network. A public network, such as the Bitcoin blockchain, is accessible to anyone who wishes to participate, and any data stored on the network is visible to all network participants in encrypted form. In contrast, private networks are permissioned, and only those parties granted access can join them. [See, Shyam Shankar, *Centralized Ledgers vs. Distributed Ledgers (Layman Understanding)*, Medium.com, July 12, 2017, https://medium.com/@shyamshankar/centralized-ledgers-vs-distributed-ledgers-layman-understanding-52449264ae23.]

Blockchain Mechanics

Blockchain is a digital ledger of transactions among multiple parties. Each transaction is represented by a set of data called a *block*. The blocks are secured and linked or *chained* with prior blocks with a cryptographic algorithm called a *hash*. By design, it is extremely difficult to modify, misrepresent, or hack once the transaction is stored.

Wolters Kluwer Vice President of Legal Markets Dean Sonderegger provided a succinct description of a basic blockchain transaction involving Bitcoin in Blockchain: the Unchangeable Game Changer [Above The Law, January 9, 2018.] He explained:

- The algorithm reads a block of data.
- The algorithm then creates a unique string or hash based on that data.
- The hash is always the same size, and small changes in the input data can lead to significant (and seemingly random) changes in the hash.

Sonderegger provides the following example concerning the addition of a block of data to a blockchain:

ABC Law firm receives 100 bitcoins

Corp 123 sends 100 bitcoins

If our hashing algorithm created an eight-character hash, a potential value for the hash for that block of data could be 0a7bz320. If we were to change the amount of Bitcoins to 200 for each part of the transaction, the hash in turn would also change and could be something such as t807gg2a. Figure 1 shows (in a simplified manner) how the hash is used to link the blocks in a blockchain.

Each block of transactions has a corresponding data header, which stores the following:

- The hash of the current block's transactions, and
- The hash of the previous block's header.

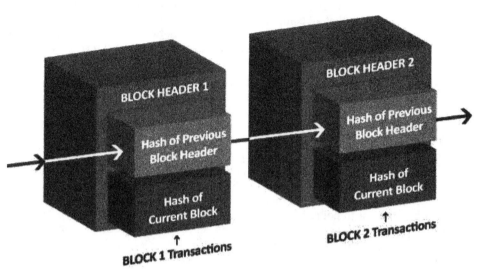

Figure 1. BLOCKCHAIN LINKING ©2018 Wolters Kluwer Legal & Regulatory, U.S.

Blockchain's arrangement of transactions in chronologically arrayed blocks allows for miners to verify the contents of the chain by comparing them to the historical ledger of transactions. Once verified, the miner will create the next block and chain it to the now-approved predecessor ledger. [Paul Vigna and Michael J. Casey, *The Age of Cryptocurrency*, Ch. 5 (2015).]

Bitcoin Miners, Immutability, and Consensus

In the Bitcoin context, miners play an important role in verifying transactions on the blockchain and securing the ledger. Essentially, Bitcoin miners contribute computing resources to verify Bitcoin transactions and hence maintain the Bitcoin blockchain. Bitcoin miners are compensated for their efforts with newly minted coins and can potentially receive transaction fees as well. The mining process also ties in closely with the two core concepts associated with blockchain—consensus and immutability.

James Gatto describes these interrelationships as follows: "*Consensus* is the process of verifying transactions before they are validated and written to the ledger. This process is done by miners or other consensus mechanisms, and *immutability* relates to once data is written to a block and the block gets filled, the system creates a hash of the block and writes the hash to the beginning of the next block—thereby chaining the blocks together. If someone goes back and changes data in a prior block, the hash will no longer match the original hash for that block, thus rendering it an invalid block. In this way, once data is written it cannot be changed and is thus referred to as immutable." As a result, blockchain's immutability feature effectively solves the double-spend problem noted in Nakamoto's white paper.

Wallets and Security Concerns

The Bitcoin blockchain employs a public-key cryptography system by which a user is assigned two keys. One key is public, which is known to the world and referred to as the Bitcoin address. The other is private and typically maintained like a private password. A wallet stores the digital credentials, which allows a user access and to transact in Bitcoin. "A Bitcoin transaction, and thus the transfer of ownership of the Bitcoins, is recorded, time-stamped, and displayed in one 'block' of the blockchain. Public-key cryptography ensures that all computers in the network have a constantly updated and verified record of all transactions within the Bitcoin network, which prevents double spending and fraud." [Jerry Brito and Andrea Castillo, Bitcoin: A Primer for Policy Makers, Ch. 2 (2016).]

Much has been said about the immutable and secure nature of blockchain technology. However, that immutability itself results in certain risks for a Bitcoin user. Once a Bitcoin transaction is completed, there is no way for it to be reversed. Unlike a credit card transaction, there are no chargebacks to merchants, and if Bitcoins are stolen, they are forever lost, unless, of course, the thief is caught.

There are a few ways for holders to lose their Bitcoin. First, a holder might share their private key with, or divulge it to, another party. If that other party then accessed the holder's wallet without authorization, the transaction would still stand. Second, if a holder's wallet is sitting on a computer connected to the internet (known as a "hot wallet") it is subject to being hacked. A holder can also simply lose or misplace his or her private key or forget where it has been stored. Wallet security remains a top concern for cryptocurrency holders. [*See generally*, Paul Vigna and Michael J. Casey, *The Age of Cryptocurrency*, Ch. 4 (2015).]

Blockchain Technology Applications

While Bitcoin and virtual realms attract significant press attention, blockchain technology is burgeoning in a host of other areas. Blockchain is being used by, or developed for, a variety of industries and sectors, including real estate, corporate records, banking and finance, trading, clearing and settlement, loan origination and securitization, records, payments processing, supply-chain management, healthcare records, and insurance.

Another expanding area using blockchain technology involves smart contracts. A smart contract, while not a legal contract per se, typically refers to a coded program that typically contains certain terms of agreement and conditions, which allow for certain provisions of a contract to be automatically executed upon notification that conditions have been fulfilled. Smart contracts are discussed in greater detail at ¶ 120 and ¶ 130.

¶ 110 Virtual Currencies

As online payment methods, virtual currencies date to the dot-com boom of the mid-1990s. The first to gain real traction was E-Gold, which launched in 1996 (it was shut down in 2009). Other online currencies of this era include Beenz, Flooz, and DigiCash. What these currencies had in common—other than names that now sound amusingly dated—is that all were centralized in a single third-party administrator.

All virtual currencies were centralized, until the Satoshi Nakamoto white paper described a "peer-to-peer electronic cash system" that relied on computational proof rather than a bank or other third-party processor, to verify transactions. Online commerce's dependence on the trusted third party came with high transaction costs and the risk of payment reversal, Nakamoto wrote. His innovation was to cut out the third party and rely on cryptographic proof, rather than trust, to verify transactions. When Bitcoin was released as open-source software in 2009, it became the first decentralized digital currency.

Bitcoin's early success speaks for itself, and it has inspired hundreds of currencies known as altcoins, many based on its software. A key Bitcoin successor is Ether, the token currency connected to the Ethereum platform. Ethereum goes beyond currency by enabling distributed computing and the deployment of smart contracts (see ¶ 120)

¶110

Defining virtual currencies and distinguishing among their attributes is a threshold issue for governments, regulators, and task forces as they analyze, regulate, and even register these new payment systems and blockchain platforms.

Defining Virtual Currency

The definition of a virtual currency varies. Purists could argue that Bitcoin is a digital currency but not a virtual currency, because it is used in the real world (as opposed to closed-system currencies that only have value with the issuing merchant). Other experts push back against the term "currency"; Chain CEO Adam Ludwin defines cryptocurrencies as "a new asset class that enable decentralized applications." [Adam Ludwin, *A Letter to Jamie Dimon* (October 16, 2017), https://blog.chain.com/a-letter-to-jamie-dimon-de89d417cb80.] This book uses the term "virtual currency," as that phrase seems to have stuck in the regulatory space.

In 2012, the European Central Bank tried to define the term "virtual currency," noting at the outset that the characteristics of currencies "might change in future, which could affect the current definition." ECB's tentative definition was "a type of unregulated, digital money, which is issued and usually controlled by its developers, and used and accepted among the members of a specific virtual community." [Virtual Currency Schemes (October 2012).] As ECB predicted, this definition quickly seemed out of date. In 2014, the Financial Action Task Force on Money Laundering (FATF) crafted a new definition of virtual currency that has gained traction among courts and regulators: "a digital representation of value that can be digitally traded and functions as (1) a medium of exchange; and/or (2) a unit of account; and/or (3) a store of value, but does not have legal tender status . . . in any jurisdiction." [Virtual Currencies: Key Definitions and Potential AML/CFT Risks (June 2014).]

The IRS adopted the FATF's definition in a 2014 notice. [*IRS Virtual Currency Guidance*, Notice 2014-21.] The SEC has also referenced the definition in enforcement actions and, notably, in the DAO Report, its strongest guidance on virtual currency issues. [*In the Matter of BTC Trading, Corp.*, Release No. 33-9685, December 8, 2014; *Report of Investigation Pursuant to Section 21(a) of the Securities Exchange Act of 1934: The DAO*, Release No. 34-81207, July 25, 2017.] The first CFTC order to hold that Bitcoin is a commodity adopted the FATF definition for its purposes. [*In the Matter of Coinflip, Inc.*, CFTC Docket No. 15-29, September 17, 2015.] In a later guidance document, however, the CFTC referenced the definition with the caveat that "this definition is not a statement of the Commission's view, and is instead offered as an aid to enhance public understanding of virtual currencies." [CFTC Primer on Virtual Currencies, October 17, 2017.]

Virtual Currency Mechanics

A user can acquire cryptocurrency by mining it, receiving it directly in a peer-to-peer transfer, or buying it on an exchange. Users keep track of their holdings by storing their private keys, used to digitally sign transactions, in a wallet. (Bitcoin is often thought of as anonymous, but because transactions include digital signatures keyed to particular users, it is more accurately described as pseudonymous. Some altcoins offer near-anonymity or other privacy protections.) Only 21 million Bitcoins will ever exist, and unknown numbers are out of circulation because the private keys have been lost.

Bitcoin works by creating incentives for users to confirm transactions through mining. Transactions are broadcast to a network of users running mining software that packages new transactions into a block and applies an algorithm, resulting in a hash. Miners add numbers to the input until the output hash falls within a range that the Bitcoin algorithm is looking for, completing a puzzle using brute force. The verified, hashed block is then added to the chain of transactions or "blockchain." The miner who found the solution is rewarded with payment in Bitcoins.

The use of cryptography to verify and record transactions places Bitcoin in a subset of virtual currency known as cryptocurrency. The algorithm adjusts so that as more miners enter the competition, it becomes more difficult to complete the verification process, ensuring that it takes about ten minutes to verify each transaction and limiting the rate at which new coins are released. This "proof-of-work" system prevents bad actors from developing a competing blockchain at a faster pace than honest miners. [Satoshi Nakamoto, Bitcoin: A Peer-to-Peer Electronic Cash System.]

The reward for solving the cryptographic puzzle halves every 210,000 blocks, or about every four years at the rate of one block per ten minutes. The reward has been 12.5 Bitcoins since the last halving in 2016; miners also receive transaction fees. Given the computing power it takes to attempt the puzzle, and the number of competitors, solo mining is akin to buying a very expensive lottery ticket. For this reason, small-scale miners pool their mining power with that of others, taking a smaller, but virtually guaranteed, payout proportional to their computing contribution.

The prevalence of pools raises concerns that Bitcoin, designed as a decentralized currency, will eventually become centralized in the hands of the most powerful mining pools. For a brief time in June 2014, the pool GHash.IO accounted for more than half of the hashing power of the entire network. [L.S., The Economist explains: How bitcoin mining works, January 20, 2015.] The pool shut down in 2016, but its dominance exposed the Bitcoin system's theoretical vulnerability to what is known as a 51-percent attack.

Forks, double-spending, and 51-percent attacks. As previously described, miners verify transactions on a blockchain-based currency by running algorithms along the entire chain and coming to a consensus about the solution. If two miners solve a block simultaneously, it creates a fork in the chain where there are temporarily two paths from the verified chain. (This use of the term "fork" should not be confused with "hard forks" in the currency's protocol that lead to the creation of an entirely new currency from that point on, such as Bitcoin and Bitcoin Cash, or Ethereum and Ethereum Classic.) An accidental fork in the chain resolves itself quickly as new blocks are added. The network adopts the longer of the two chains and abandons, or "orphans," any blocks not part of that chain. [Satoshi Nakamoto, Bitcoin: A Peer-to-Peer Electronic Cash System.]

However, a fork could also be created intentionally in a "51-percent attack," where a pool or other entity controlling over half the hashing power in the network could prevent the confirmation of legitimate transactions and reverse its own transactions, permitting it to double-spend its coins. Double-spending would quickly erode trust in Bitcoin, potentially causing the entire system to crash.

Nakamoto considered this possibility in his white paper, but concluded that the economics incentivized honest mining. "If a greedy attacker is able to assemble more CPU power than all the honest nodes, he would have to choose between using it to defraud people by stealing back his payments, or using it to generate new coins," Nakamoto wrote. "He ought to find it more profitable to play by the rules, such rules that favour him with more new coins than everyone else combined, than to undermine the system and the validity of his own wealth." [Satoshi Nakamoto, Bitcoin: A Peer-to-Peer Electronic Cash System.] But a state-sponsored or other organized actor without a profit motive could bring down the currency by amassing enough hashing power.

Bitcoin is vulnerable even to attacks by those initially holding less than half of the hashing power, as described in a paper by Cornell University researchers Ittay Eyal and

¶110

Emin Gün Sirer. In such a scenario, a pool of "selfish miners" intentionally creates a fork in the chain by keeping its discovered blocks private, eventually emerging with a longer chain that renders the public chain orphaned. The "honest miners" working on the public chain waste more resources than those on the private chain, giving them an incentive to join the selfish pool. The selfish pool can amass a majority. [Eyal, I., Sirer, E.G.: Majority is not Enough: Bitcoin Mining is Vulnerable. https://www.cs.cornell.edu/~ie53/publications/btcProcFC.pdf.]

Proof of stake. As noted above, Bitcoin (along with many altcoins) is based on proof of work, requiring significant processing before a transaction is confirmed and thus protecting the system from malicious or selfish attacks. The mining network expends tremendous energy as miners race to complete this work, and miners tend to sell virtual currency for fiat currency to pay their energy bills, depressing the price of the cryptocurrency. [Chris Mooney and Steven Mufson, Why the bitcoin craze is using up so much energy, *The Washington Post*, December 19, 2017.] An alternative to proof of work is proof of stake, which assigns transactions to miners (rather, "forgers," because they receive transaction fees instead of new coins) based on their proportionate holdings in the currency.

Ethereum plans to move from a proof-of-work system to proof of stake. Under the platform's Casper protocol, users will lock up their currency, or a portion of it, to be eligible to verify transactions. If a forger verifies incorrectly or tries to bet on both branches of a forked chain, the stake is forfeit. [Vitalik Buterin, Understanding Serenity, Part 2: Casper, December 28, 2015.]

¶ 120 Smart Contracts

The concept of a "smart contract" can, in some respects, be separated from other blockchain concepts if for no other reason than smart contracts, when conceptualized by many attorneys (but not necessarily by computer programmers), raise distinctly legal issues. It is this tension between the legal concept of a contract, or a contract with automated parts, and the programmer's concept of a contract as an electronic agent, that results in much confusion about how to define the term "smart contract." To further complicate things, a single, widely used platform places the concept of a "smart contract" within a milieu of interrelated blockchain use-cases, including tokens, decentralized applications (dapps), decentralized organizations (DOs), and decentralized autonomous organizations or DAOs (*See*, ¶ 310 for an example of a DAO in the securities regulation context). As a result, one must always keep in mind precisely which use of "smart contract" is intended—computer code that enables an electronic agent to execute a set of if-then statements or an electronic version of a paper contract with varying degrees of automated performance features.

The following discussion of smart contracts emphasizes the definitional issues that must be resolved as a pre-condition to wider use and acceptance of smart contracts as legal contracts. Smart contracts on blockchains could transform the way businesses and individuals interact with each other and how law firms counsel clients, if smart contracts are fully and securely implemented. Smart contracts hold some promise of shorter-term gains, although much of what might be achieved depends on developing a clearer definition of "smart contract" and on judicial recognition of smart contracts.

It is also necessary to examine what smart contracts can be used for in a more technical manner, including tokenization. Tokens issued via blockchains have garnered significant (if mostly negative) attention from regulators such as the Securities and Exchange Commission. Tokens issued via a blockchain frequently arise in the context of initial coin offerings (ICOs). The SEC has determined that, depending on the "facts and circumstances, including the economic realities of the transaction," these tokens must either be registered as securities or fall within an exemption to the registration requirement. This section will focus on the technical definition and implementation of tokens via a blockchain, while other sections of this book deal with the legal issues relevant to tokens in greater detail (*See*, ¶ 310 and ¶ 320).

Smart Contract Defined

"Smart contract" suggests many things to many people. On the surface, "smart contract" conjures the allure of a fully autonomous legal contract. But the current reality suggests a subtler concept. Although the concept of a smart contract has existed since the 1990s, smart contract implementation has only recently become feasible for firms and a growing number of individuals due to the development of blockchains. Bitcoin, for example, enabled virtual currencies; rival blockchains, such as Ethereum, have since enabled smart contracts. Still, the feasibility of creating smart contracts belies the difficulty of defining precisely what one is, given the lack of agreement on a universal definition.

For example, James Gatto of Sheppard, Mullin suggests that a smart contract is often is not a true contract (*i.e.*, an agreement with business operations terms and legal terms) but is more akin to computer code that implements some business logic. "It is just code that runs on the blockchain, is programmed to collect certain data and, upon the occurrence of certain events, takes actions – it enables the business logic of a contract to be automatically executed and enforced," said Gatto.

A white paper published by the Smart Contracts Alliance, an initiative of the Chamber of Digital Commerce, posited a "spectrum" of smart contracts. The CDC continuum would include contracts that consist of only computer code, contracts that have both coded and natural language components, "split" contracts written in natural language but whose performance is driven by computer code, and contracts that are written in natural language but allow for payments to be made via computer code. [Smart Contracts: 12 Use Cases for Business & Beyond, https://digitalchamber.org/wp-content/uploads/2018/02/Smart-Contracts-12-Use-Cases-for-Business-and-Beyond_Chamber-of-Digital-Commerce.pdf.]

In the following discussion, each definition falls on the "smart contracts" continuum, but each definition also emphasizes a slightly different goal of smart contracting. Although some of these definitions arise in the context of specific computing platforms, the discussion is intended to be platform-agnostic because the concept of a "smart contract" and its implementation generally raise similar technical and legal issues regardless of the chosen platform.

Nick Szabo's definition. In a forward to the CDC white paper, Nick Szabo, who is often credited as a smart contract pioneer and who also is sometimes rumored to be Bitcoin founder Satoshi Nakamoto, briefly recited the history of the smart contract from vending machines to financial contracts. Generally, Szabo said that smart contracts are designed for "objectively verifiable performances, or performances that can be automated." At present, Szabo said the best environments for using smart contracts would be the most developed blockchains and that smart contracts mostly will involve the largest financial institutions, although he suggested smart contracts may become more widely used as multiple technologies converge at what he calls "the intersection of blockchain, artificial intelligence and the Internet of Things." [Smart Contracts: 12 Use Cases for Business & Beyond, https://digitalchamber.org/wp-content/uploads/2018/02/Smart-Contracts-12-Use-Cases-for-Business-and-Beyond_Chamber-of-Digital-Commerce.pdf.]

In the mid-1990s, Szabo published a foundational paper that defined "smart contract" as a type of contract that blended cryptography with economics, law, and

¶120

business. A key component of the smart contract for Szabo is the absence of a trusted central counterparty, which a smart contract replaces with a trustless system. According to Szabo: "[a] smart contract is a computerized transaction protocol that executes the terms of a contract. The general objectives of smart contract design are to satisfy common contractual conditions (such as payment terms, liens, confidentiality, and even enforcement), minimize exceptions both malicious and accidental, and minimize the need for trusted intermediaries. Related economic goals include lowering fraud loss, arbitration and enforcement costs, and other transaction costs." [Nick Szabo, Smart Contracts (1994), http://www.fon.hum.uva.nl/rob/Courses/InformationInSpeech/ CDROM/Literature/LOTwinterschool2006/szabo.best.vwh.net/smart.contracts.html.] Szabo provided an expanded explanation of his conception of the "smart contract" a few years later. The updated white paper focuses on developing smart contracts around four contract design principles: observability, verifiability, privity, and enforceability. [Nick Szabo, Smart Contracts: Building Blocks for Digital Markets, 1996.]

Securities and Exchange Commission. The SEC cited Szabo's definition of "smart contract" in its report of investigation on The DAO. The DAO was a decentralized autonomous organization set up to solicit funding in exchange for issuing tokens that entitled token holders to vote on projects to further develop The DAO. The SEC determined that The DAO Tokens were securities under federal securities law, although the SEC opted to use The DAO report to merely warn the blockchain industry of the possible legal consequences of ICOs rather than to pursue an enforcement action against The DAO. [*Report of Investigation Pursuant to Section 21(a) of the Securities Exchange Act of 1934: The DAO*, Release No. 34-81207, July 25, 2017 (See, n. 3); *See also*, ¶ 310.]

Vitalik Buterin's definition. Vitalik Buterin, the co-founder of Ethereum, a blockchain that rivals Bitcoin and which has a built-in conception of "contract" or "smart contract," has described the smart contract as one of the "simplest form[s] of decentralized automation." Buterin offered the following definition: "a smart contract is a mechanism involving digital assets and two or more parties, where some or all of the parties put assets in and assets are automatically redistributed among those parties according to a formula based on certain data that is not known at the time the contract is initiated." [Vitalik Buterin, DAOs, DACs, DAs and More: An Incomplete Terminology Guide, https://blog.ethereum.org/2014/05/06/daos-dacs-das-and-more-an-incomplete-termi-nology-guide/.]

A computer programming perspective. "Contract" has a special meaning within the Ethereum blockchain, perhaps the blockchain most associated with smart contracts. According to the Ethereum Homestead's documentation, "[a] contract is a collection of code (its functions) and data (its state) that resides at a specific address on the Ethereum blockchain." The documentation further notes that messages can be sent between contracts, that contracts are created using high level programming languages, and that contracts are nearly Turing complete. [Ethereum Homestead Documentation, http://www.ethdocs.org/en/latest/contracts-and-transactions/contracts.html#what-is-a-contract.] Turing completeness, named after the WWII codebreaker Alan Turning, describes a programming language that can simulate any Turing machine. Turning's thesis, however, has never been proven. [See, https://en.wikipedia.org/wiki/Turing_completeness; Yale N. Patt and Sanjay J. Patel, Introduction to Computing Systems: from bits and gates to C and beyond, 2d ed., McGraw Hill Higher Education, 2004, pp. 10-11.]

Another definition of "smart contract" comes from the Ethereum white paper. There, "smart contract" means "cryptographic 'boxes' that contain value and only unlock it if certain conditions are met." The white paper also explains what a "smart contract" is not: "Note that 'contracts' in Ethereum should not be seen as something that should be 'fulfilled' or 'complied with'; rather, they are more like 'autonomous agents' that live inside of the Ethereum execution environment, always executing a specific piece of code when 'poked' by a message or transaction, and having direct control over their own ether balance and their own key/value store to keep track of persistent variables." [Ethereum white paper, https://github.com/ethereum/wiki/wiki/White-Paper.] For now, it is important to focus on the general import of these definitions; the discussion of tokens below will get into some of the details about messaging and the role that Ether, the Ethereum platform's virtual currency, plays in the context of smart contracts.

The Ethereum white paper's definition achieves several goals. For one, it provides a somewhat more technical explanation of Buterin's more general definition of a smart contract as a method for distributing digital assets. The white paper definition also is consistent with how many commentators describe the smart contract as a set of "if-then" statements. In other words, the definition suggests what is going on behind the scenes—if-then statements are being tested to determine whether they will "unlock" and allow some action to occur, for example, sending Ether from one account to multiple other accounts, provided that the sender has sufficient Ether to meet the requests.

The Ethereum yellow paper also suggests the potential ties between computer code and legal contracts: "[a]round the 1990s it became clear that algorithmic enforcement of agreements could become a significant force in human cooperation. Though no specific system was proposed to implement such a system, it was proposed that the future of law would be heavily affected by such systems. In this light, Ethereum may be seen as a general implementation of such a *crypto-law system*." [Ethereum yellow paper, https://github.com/ethereum/yellowpaper.]

One of the leading programming languages for the Ethereum blockchain, Solidity, explains that "[c]ontracts in Solidity are similar to classes in object-oriented languages." [Solidity v0.4.24 documentation, https://solidity.readthedocs.io/en/v0.4.24/contracts.html.] In brief, object-oriented programming (OOP) languages allow a programmer to create classes of objects, which have state and behavior characteristics. Classes are the building blocks in OOP languages such as Java, although there are many other OOP languages, including C++ and Python. OOP also depends on several key concepts: inheritance (how classes are related), encapsulation (keeping certain data hidden), and polymorphism (objects with multiple forms). [See, https://en.wikipedia.org/wiki/Object-oriented_programming#Objects_and_classes; https://www.techopedia.com/definition/3235/object-oriented-programming-oop; https://www.techopedia.com/definition/28106/polymorphism-general-programming; David Flanagan, Java In A Nutshell, 5th ed., O'Reilly, 2005, p. 98.]

The Ricardian contract—a bridge to the smart contract? Ian Grigg published several papers describing the Ricardian contract, a name derived from that of the British economist David Ricardo. [https://en.wikipedia.org/wiki/David_Ricardo.] Grigg's version of the Ricardian contract takes the bond as its prototype and posits that such contracts can be issued by an issuer who digitally signs a contract readable by both humans and machines and that is linked to the payment system. The Ricardian contract would use a hash for added security and to prevent a party with superior bargaining power from gradually altering the terms over time.

According to Grigg, a more precise definition of the Ricardian contract would be "[a] Ricardian Contract can be defined as a single document that is a) a contract offered by an issuer to holders, b) for a valuable right held by holders, and managed by the issuer, c) easily readable by people (like a contract on paper), d) readable by programs (parsable like a database), e) digitally signed, f) carries the keys and server information and g) allied with a unique and secure identifier." A Ricardian contract would be maintained as a text file so it could be used by other programs. The Ricardian contract also would adhere to the "rule of one contract," which Grigg described as positing a single document that is a valid contract agreed to by the parties. The goal of such a contract is for it to be accepted by courts. Grigg acknowledged that many contract law questions abound regarding the Ricardian contract and that the Ricardian contract has focused on automating "decimals" rather than evolving into a prototypical "smart contract" because, at the time he wrote, smart contracts were not in high demand and there was an open question about whether a court would accept a contract that is computer code. [Ian Grigg, The Ricardian Contract, http://iang.org/papers/ricardian_contract.html#ref_22.]

In another paper, Grigg compared and contrasted the Ricardian contract and the smart contract. According to Grigg, there is a tension between what these two contracting methods can do: The Ricardian contract is better for capturing contract semantics (words), but less capable of handling more complex code; the smart contract is good at handling computer code, but is a poor choice for capturing contract semantics. Grigg concluded by suggesting how both contract types may evolve: "[w]e can now see that the real challenge between smart contracts and Ricardian Contracts or legal documents is not to choose, but to incorporate." [Ian Grigg, On the intersection of Ricardian and Smart Contracts, February 2015.]

Smart legal contracts. The International Swaps and Derivatives Association, Inc. (ISDA) and Linklaters published a white paper that suggests a more nuanced approach to smart contracts that distinguishes between the code-based meaning of "smart contract" and the legal meaning of "smart contract." [International Swaps and Derivatives Association, Inc. (ISDA) and Linklaters, Smart Contracts and Distributed Ledger – A Legal Perspective, August 2017.] These distinctions will likely be critical to ongoing efforts to determine how much of a traditional contract can be automated.

The ISDA-Linklaters paper cited a CoinDesk op-ed article by Josh Stark in which Stark suggested that "smart contract" can be broken into components: "smart contract code" and "smart legal contract[s]." "Smart contract code" is code that resembles a smart agent or software agent, that is, a program that acts on behalf of a user or another program. Stark noted that smart contract code is recorded on the blockchain, can control blockchain assets, and can be executed by the blockchain. By contrast, a "smart legal contract" is "a way of using blockchain technology to complement, or replace, existing legal contracts." Stark had previously defined "smart contract" to mean "the use of computer code to articulate, verify and execute an agreement between parties." [Josh Stark, Making Sense of Blockchain Smart Contracts, CoinDesk, June 7, 2016; Josh Stark, How Close Are Smart Contracts to Impacting Real-World Law?, CoinDesk, April 11, 2016; See also, definition of "software agent," https://en.wikipedia.org/wiki/Software_agent.]

The ISDA-Linklaters paper also detailed a second approach, exemplified by Clack, et. al., that seeks to combine the code and contract elements discussed by Stark into a more universal definition. According to Clack, et. al.: "[a] smart contract is an automatable and enforceable agreement. Automatable by computer, although some parts may require human input and control. Enforceable either by legal enforcement of rights and obligations or via tamper-proof execution of computer code."

The Clack, et. al. definition of "smart contract" emphasizes the words "automatable" and "enforceable." By "automatable," the authors mean that some, but not necessarily all, aspects of a contract can be automated. For example, contract terms are by their nature either operational or non-operational; operational terms are more likely candidates for automation, whereas non-operational terms might not be capable of automation (or it may be undesirable to automate them).

Moreover, the authors use "enforceable" to refer to the enforceability of smart contract code and smart legal contracts by either traditional or non-traditional means. For example, smart contract code could be judged by whether the code functioned as expected in a reasonable time frame. By contrast, smart legal contracts might be enforced by traditional means such as mediation, arbitration, or in court actions. Nontraditional enforcement might include "tamper-proof" systems in which a network of computers resistant to failure could disallow "wrong performance" or "nonperformance." [Christopher D. Clack, Vikram A. Bakshi, Lee Braine, Smart Contract Templates: foundations, design landscape and research directions (August 4, 2016 and Revised March 15, 2017).]

Legislative definitions. There have been very few federal legislative proposals to define "smart contract" as compared to the small, but growing, number of states considering such definitions as updates to their versions of the Uniform Electronic Transactions Act (UETA). The following discussion briefly reviews federal law and state uniform acts. Next, the discussion compares two of the enacted state laws. The discussion concludes with a brief look at federal legislation introduced in the 113th Congress.

States are interested in adopting laws to deal with smart contracts because of concerns that the federal Electronic Signatures in Global and National Commerce Act (E-Sign Act) and the UETA, which the vast majority of states have adopted, are insufficient in their current forms to accommodate smart contracts. The E-Sign Act legalized electronic signatures and records and provides that a contract cannot be denied legal effect solely because it involved an electronic agent if the electronic agent's actions are legally attributable to the party to be bound. [15 U.S.C. § 7001, et. seq.] The UETA likewise recognized digital signatures and records and the contracts that use them. [Uniform Electronic Transactions Act, § 7.]

The UETA also provides for the use of electronic agents, a section included to address issues of intent during contract formation. [Uniform Electronic Transactions Act, § 14 and comment 1.] "Electronic agent" means "a computer program or an electronic or other automated means used independently to initiate an action or respond to electronic records or performances in whole or in part, without review or action by an individual." The relevant comment noted that the UETA was drafted to address the situation of an electronic agent that acts automatically, but it also anticipated that courts may eventually have to re-interpret "electronic agent" once advancements in artificial intelligence (sometimes called machine learning) enable autonomous electronic agents. [Uniform Electronic Transactions Act, § 2, comment 5.]

Arizona and Tennessee have enacted laws that define "smart contract," although these laws differ in some respects, which raises the question of whether those differences are semantic only or substantive. Arizona's law is typical of the changes states believe are needed to accommodate smart contracts. Arizona defines "electronic signature" and "electronic record" to include signatures and records or contracts "secured through blockchain technology." The law also recognizes that smart contracts can exist in commerce and that these contracts cannot be denied legality solely because they contain smart contract terms. The Arizona law then defines "smart contract" to mean "an event-driven program, with state, that runs on a distributed, decentralized, shared and replicated ledger and that can take custody over and instruct transfer of assets on that ledger." [Ariz. Rev. Stat. Ann. § 44-7061.]

Arizona's blockchain law is notable for several reasons. For one, the definition refers to "event-driven" programs, which appears to reference the notion that smart

¶120

contracts implement business logic through if-then statements. Second, the definition specifies that a smart contract is "with state." On the surface, this phrase is ambiguous, but it could be a reference to blockchain-enabled solutions as generally being capable of keeping track of the state of transactions that occur on a blockchain given certain inputs, in other words, a state machine. [*See*, https://www.techopedia.com/definition/16447/state-machine.] If anything should be clear from Arizona's definition of "smart contract," it is that attorneys will need to find reliable sources for definitions of technical terms because future laws and regulations are likely to use terminology that may be challenging for attorneys who do not have technology-intensive practices.

Tennessee's distributed ledger technology (DLT) law contains language similar to Arizona's blockchain law, but with a few significant differences. First, as a general matter, Tennessee defines "distributed ledger technology" such that "blockchain" is a type of DLT, a technically correct understanding of the relationship between DLT and blockchain (Arizona's definition of "blockchain" is similar but focuses on blockchain technology rather than on blockchain as one of many DLT possibilities). Arizona also noted that data on a ledger would provide a cryptographically protected, auditable, unsponsored truth, whereas Tennessee's law does not mention this aspect of DLT/blockchain technology.

Second, Tennessee's definition of "smart contract" is similar to Arizona's, but with some differences. Under Tennessee's law, "smart contract" means "an event-driven computer program, that executes on an electronic, distributed, decentralized, shared, and replicated ledger that is used to automate transactions . . . " Tennessee's definition would include transactions that involve custody and instructions to transfer assets (so does Arizona), but further specifies (Arizona does not) that the definition includes transactions that create and distribute electronic assets, synchronize information, or manage identity and user access to software. Tennessee and Arizona differ in several more ways: (1) Tennessee refers to "computer program" while Arizona refers to "program"; (2) Tennessee specifies "*electronic*, distributed, decentralized, shared, and replicated ledger" while Arizona does not use "electronic" (emphasis added); (3) Tennessee uses the word "executes" while Arizona uses "runs"; and (4) Tennessee adds the phrase "that is used to automate transactions" while Arizona has no equivalent phrase. [Tenn. Code Ann. § § 47-10-201 and 47-10-202.]

Several other states have considered changes to their laws to accommodate smart contracts. For example, a bill introduced in the Illinois General Assembly would define "smart contract" to mean "a contract stored as an electronic record which is verified by the use of a blockchain" (Illinois has not adopted the UETA, although it has similar laws). On a related note, Vermont has enacted a law that provides for the admissibility of blockchain records in court. [*See*, 12 V.S.A. § 1913; Nevada S.B. 398; Nebraska L.B. 695, Illinois H.B. 5553; Florida H.B. 1357; and California A.B. 2658.]

Lastly, Congress has not moved quickly on legislation regarding smart contracts. During the 113th Congress, Rep. Steve Stockman (R-Texas) introduced the Online Market Protection Act of 2014 to provide for a moratorium on federal and state laws and regulations pertaining to cryptocurrencies. The bill would have defined "smart contracts" to mean "cryptographically encoded agreements, often utilizing multi-signature technology, which allow for automatic or multi-party execution and public recording of transactions or property transfers when certain predetermined parameters are met." A companion bill introduced by Stockman omitted the definition of "smart contracts." [*See*, H.R. 5892 and H.R. 5777.]

The lawyer's role in smart contracting. As currently conceived, smart contracts must abide by the hornbook elements of contracting such as offer, acceptance, and consideration. But smart contracts raise many questions about how existing contract law would apply, especially as smart contracts become more autonomous. For example, what do offer, acceptance, and consideration mean in this context? How might frustration of purpose or impracticability or mistake arise under a smart contract? How would the parol evidence rule apply when interpreting a smart contract? Can a smart contract incorporate information provided by a trusted source such as an oracle?

The ISDA-Linklaters white paper discussed above noted some of the potential issues with what it calls the "internal model" where there is a "formal representation" of contract terms, perhaps rendered in an as-yet-undeveloped programming language that attorneys may need to learn. Smart contracts that fall into the "code is contract" category may present challenges due to the shortage of attorneys with knowledge of computer code and because of questions about how to deal with defects or bugs that may arise in smart contract code. [International Swaps and Derivatives Association, Inc. (ISDA) and Linklaters, Smart Contracts and Distributed Ledger – A Legal Perspective, August 2017.]

Additionally, the drafter of a smart contract may have to translate ambiguous natural language terms into code. Examples of terms that might create issues for smart contracts include "good faith," "reasonable commercial standards of fair dealing," and "reasonable," each of which is defined in the Uniform Commercial Code. These terms can leave much to the imagination, even though they are commonplace in commercial contracts. [*See*, UCC § 1-201(20) and § 1-205.]

Still another possibility is that the federal government or states may attempt to further define "smart contract." Both the federal E-Sign Act and the UETA include definitions of terms that could embrace smart contracts. The CDC, for example, has argued that the term "electronic signature" as used in the E-Sign Act and the UETA is such a term. As a result, the CDC has urged states not to adopt laws further defining "smart contract" because such laws could add to the confusion about the legality of smart contracts. [Joint Statement in Response to State "Smart Contracts" Legislation, April 2018.]

Beyond the legal contracting issues, which attorneys seem best positioned to handle, the entire concept of the law firm and legal practice more generally may become ripe for significant transformation as smart contracting evolves. An article in the Harvard Business Review noted that, based on past experience with technological break throughs, blockchain technologies may follow a similar path, with the simplest and least costly developments gaining a quick foothold to be followed years later by more difficult and costly substitutional and transformational developments (*e.g.*, autonomous smart contracts). In the case of smart contracts, the article suggested that law firms will need technological expertise to explain natural language terms and computer coded terms to clients and courts. Law firms also may need to consider transaction fees or "hosting" fees regarding smart contracts. [Marco Iansiti and Karim R. Lakhani, The Truth About Blockchain, Harvard Business Review, January-February 2017.]

An article published by a trio of attorneys from the Delaware law firm Potter Anderson Corroon LLP suggests that using smart contracts may increase the need for experienced attorneys rather than presage the obsolescence of attorneys. This is so, the article said, because attorneys will play multiple roles, including: (i) helping clients to understand when smart contracts are suitable for their business needs; (ii) working with programmers to ensure that business requirements are accurately encoded; and (iii) counseling clients on non-operational contract terms. [Matthew O'Toole, Christopher Kelly, and David Hahn, Smart Contracts Need Smart Corporate Lawyers, Potter Anderson Corroon LLP, February 7, 2018.]

Tokens, Code, and the Law

The concept of a "token" causes almost as much confusion as the term "smart contract" because of the varied meanings of the term and the potentially varied application of securities and other laws depending on how a token is structured. The discussion below will examine several definitions of "token" and summarize how the law of tokens may develop based on questions being asked about tokens today. This discussion will also provide background on one of the most widely used platforms for creating the tokens at the heart of the debate over the legality of ICOs.

What is a "token"? As a starting point, a token is simply a representation of another thing. In the blockchain context, token takes on more specific meanings. For example, one non-legal dictionary defines "utility token" as "a digital token of cryptocurrency that is issued in order to fund development of the cryptocurrency and that can be later used to purchase a good or service offered by the issuer of the cryptocurrency." [Merriam-Webster, https://www.merriam-webster.com/dictionary/utility%20token.] This definition suggests a blockchain use case often employed in ICOs, although tokenization may also involve other use cases, such as the sending of fiat currency (*e.g.,* U.S. dollars) around the world via a virtual currency token. Any definition of "token" is likely to emphasize certain aspects of tokens over others and, thus, raises the potential for ambiguity, a key challenge for lawmakers and regulators to overcome in drafting their own definitions or in applying current laws to emerging blockchain issues. But what are the legal implications of tokenization? Chapters 3 and 4 contain detailed analyses of the SEC's and the Commodity Futures Trading Commission's (CFTC's) public statements and enforcement actions regarding virtual currencies, coins, and tokens. Chapters 2, 5, and 7 discuss related tax, anti-money laundering, and state law issues.

Law meets technology. In the legal context, the debate over ICO tokens often centers on whether the tokens come first before any product or service is developed and whether the tokens can be consumed. When something like a security is tokenized, it is relatively clear that the resulting thing is a security token subject to federal and state securities laws (*See, e.g.,* ¶ 350 regarding Overstock.com's digital securities). But what about other things that can be tokenized? For example, some ICOs attempt to avoid application of the securities laws by creating utility tokens. The SEC, however, has strongly suggested that it will examine the substance of a transaction rather than its terminology; as a result, the SEC will apply long-standing tests to determine if a token is a security. [*See,* ¶ 310 and ¶ 320.]

In still other arrangements, a security and a token may be combined so the offering begins as one thing and morphs into another thing. One example of this approach is the Simple Agreement for Future Tokens (SAFT) in which the SAFT is a security but the tokens to be delivered at a later date purportedly would not be securities. The SEC has not yet directly addressed the application of securities laws to the SAFT. [The SAFT Project: Toward a Compliant Token Sale Framework, October 2, 2017, https://saft-project.com/static/SAFT-Project-Whitepaper.pdf.]

The Simple Agreement for Future Equity (SAFE) is yet another framework for funding startups. Y Combinator pioneered the SAFE, which it touts as a non-debt instrument that can replace most convertible notes. [Y Combinator, Startup Documents, http://www.ycombinator.com/documents/#safe.] The SAFE is often thought of more frequently in the context of traditional startups, although the creators of the SAFT used the SAFE as a model for their approach to ICO tokens. Sheppard Mullin's Gatto contrasted the SAFE and the SAFT. According to Gatto, the SAFE "is like convertible debt, but not debt. It enables an investor to invest money without setting a valuation and getting the actual equity when an equity round is done and using that price (less a discount) to set the price for the equity." By contrast, Gatto said the SAFT is "like a SAFE except investors get rights to tokens instead of stock."

Former CFTC Chairman Gary Gensler explored some of the open questions about tokens in a speech to the Business of Blockchain event hosted by MIT Technology Review and the MIT Media Lab. [Gary Gensler remarks at MIT Technology Review's Business of Blockchain 2018, April 23, 2018, https://www.media.mit.edu/posts/remarks-at-blockchain-event/.] Gensler said he approaches blockchain as an "optimist" and hopes the "technology succeed[s]," but he also raised several questions about ICOs of tokens, including remedies, loss recovery, and whether regulators' tools are adequately tailored to deal with DLT/blockchain issues. Gensler raised the prospect of "retroactive registration" of some ICOs that may not have complied with securities laws. This possibility has been raised before by a company that petitioned the SEC to engage in rulemaking that would allow firms to conform previous ICOs to federal securities laws while extending rescission rights to investors. [*See*, ¶ 380.]

Gensler also questioned how some token offerings are structured. For example, he asked whether a token can be designed so its focus is consumption instead of investment? Gensler also asked if a SAFT could be a viable approach (he noted that the SEC has had little to say about the SAFT). Gensler further expressed doubt that firms could devise a "security token" that could morph into another type of instrument. Lastly, Gensler raised questions about whether Ethereum and Ripple are securities. He said that a "strong case" could be made that Ethereum and Ripple violate federal securities laws. "I think there is a worthy public debate about these issues," said Gensler. With respect to Ripple, one private securities class action suit has been filed against Ripple Labs, Inc. alleging that Ripple's XRP token violates the Securities Act and California law. [*Coffey v. Ripple Labs, Inc.*, May 3, 2018.] Ripple has sought to remove the case to federal court. [*Coffey v. Ripple Labs, Inc.*, June 1, 2018.]

William Hinman, Director of the SEC's Division of Corporation Finance, in a speech to an audience at the Yahoo Finance All Markets Summit: Crypto, reiterated common themes from the SEC's guidance issued to date, specifically, that whether a token or coin is a security turns on the "economic substance" of the transaction and not the label given to the digital asset. He also suggested that decentralization is important in understanding whether a virtual currency is a security. Put another way, the analysis would look to whether a "central third party" is critical to the prospects of the enterprise. For example, Hinman said Bitcoin has a history of decentralization and that users of Bitcoin would derive negligible benefits from securities disclosure rules; Hinman also said that users of the current iteration of Etherum's virtual currency, Ether, likewise might not benefit from securities-style disclosures, although he declined to comment on whether securities laws may apply to the original effort to create Ether. But Hinman further cautioned that the legal status of a digital asset can change such that an asset functioning as a means of exchange could be re-packaged in a form that could implicate federal securities laws.

Hinman also said the SEC staff remain available to discuss virtual currency and token issues with counsel representing persons who create and promote digital assets, including potentially issuing interpretive or no-action guidance. With respect to tokens, Hinman addressed the question former CFTC Chairman Gensler had raised previously: can something that is initially a security morph into something else? For Hinman, the question should be re-phrased thus: "Can a digital asset that was originally offered in a securities offering ever be later sold in a manner that does not constitute an offering of a security?" Hinman said the answer is "likely 'no'" if the digital asset confers on its holders rights akin to financial interests. Hinman then asked if the answer is different where there is no "central enterprise" or the digital asset is used only to buy goods or services on the network it was created for? Hinman said the latter situation presents a "qualified 'yes.'" This aspect of Hinman's remarks raised the question of whether the SAFT falls within federal securities regulations. Hinman, however, said in a footnote that his remarks should not be taken as a commentary on the legal status of SAFTs. Moreover, while acknowledging that others may disagree with him, Hinman stated that "[f]rom the discussion in this speech, however, it is clear I believe a token once offered in a security offering can, depending on the circumstances, later be offered in a non-securities transaction." [William Hinman, Digital Asset Transactions: When Howey Met Gary (Plastic), June 14, 2018, https://www.sec.gov/news/speech/speech-hinman-061418.]

While the debate about how to apply federal law to tokens continues, states have also begun to address the legality of tokens. Legislation in Wyoming, for example, creates an exception to the definition of "security" for "open blockchain tokens." To fall within the exception, an open blockchain token must not be sold to an initial buyer as a financial investment, must be provided or exchangeable for goods or services (*i.e.*, a "consumptive purpose"), and the developer or seller of the token must file a notice of intent with the Wyoming secretary of state. An open blockchain token is deemed not to be sold as an investment only if: (1) the developer or seller did not market the token as a financial investment; and (2) one of four things is true: (a) the developer or seller reasonably believed the token was sold for a consumptive purpose; (b) the token's consumptive purpose is available at the time of sale and can be used at or near the time of sale; (c) the initial buyer cannot resell the token until it has a consumptive purpose if no consumptive purpose is available at the time of sale; or (d) the developer or seller takes other reasonable precautions to prevent buyers from buying the token as a financial investment. The Wyoming statute defines "open blockchain token" to include a digital unit that is (1) created in response to the verification or collection of a specified number of transactions relating to a digital ledger, by deploying computer code to a blockchain network that allows for the creation of digital tokens, or using a combination of these methods; (2) recorded in a decentralized, consensus-based ledger; and (3) capable of being traded without an intermediary or custodian of value. [Wyo. Stat. Ann. § 17-4-206 2018.]

The Wyoming law appears to be an attempt to work within the framework established by the SEC's The DAO report and a later settled administrative action in another matter, both of which suggest the SEC will look beyond labels in determining if a token is a security. Although it remains to be seen if many states will quickly adopt language that tracks the Wyoming law, at least one state has, by a narrow margin, backed away from Wyoming's attempt to clarify the law of utility tokens.

Colorado, for example, rejected a bill with language similar to the Wyoming statute. The Colorado bill passed the state's House but was subjected to a series of votes in the Senate where the bill was initially passed and then defeated by one vote. The bill closely followed Wyoming's definition of "open blockchain token" and would have defined "security" to exclude an open blockchain token that is not marketed as an investment by the developer or seller, is exchangeable for goods or services, and is not entered into for purposes of a repurchase agreement or an agreement to locate a buyer. [HB18-1426.] According to a local newspaper report, the final vote defeating the bill was influenced by the decision of the state's attorney general to oppose the bill because its language was ambiguous. [*See*, Tamara Chuang and John Frank, Colorado politicians approve — and then reject — bill to distinguish blockchain tokens from securities, Denver Post, May 9, 2018, https://www.denverpost.com/2018/05/09/colorado-bill-blockchain-technology-security/.]

Tokens on the Ethereum Platform. The following discussion addresses what many people think of as a "smart contract" when they think of DLT/blockchain technologies—the Ethereum blockchain's implementation of "smart contracts." There are other platforms, but Ethereum draws much public attention because of its frequent use in the ICO context. [*See, e.g., SEC v. Sharma*, April 2, 2018.] Ethereum's approach is to deal with "smart contracts" or "contracts" as a type of computer code that allows for the transfer of assets via the Ethereum blockchain. The assets being transferred are often tokens created for the Ethereum platform by using one of the associated Ethereum programming languages.

Note:: Much of the following discussion references the Ethereum white and yellow papers. The white paper includes code samples written using the Serpent programming language. Readers should also familiarize themselves with the Solidity programming language, which has now surpassed Serpent as one of the leading Ethereum programming languages. Ethereum founder Buterin acknowledged the decline of Serpent in a tweet. [Vitalik Buterin Twitter post, July 15, 2017, https://twitter.com/vitalikbuterin/status/886400133667201024?lang=en; See also, https://github.com/ethereum/serpent/blob/develop/README.md.]

According to the Ethereum white paper, three types of applications can be implemented on Ethereum. One type of application includes financial applications such as derivatives and sub-currencies. A second type, semi-financial applications, have both financial and non-financial aspects. The third type involves non-financial applications and can be used to conduct online voting or to create organizations whose governance is decentralized. This discussion will focus on a specific type of application called a token system. [Ethereum white paper, https://github.com/ethereum/wiki/wiki/White-Paper.]

Token systems are implemented in Ethereum by using a snippet of code called a "contract." Contracts are one of two types of Ethereum accounts: (1) "externally owned accounts" are controlled by private keys, have no code, and are used to create and sign transactions; (2) "contract accounts" are controlled by code and can be activated by messages. A token system may consist of a sub-currency or other types of value (*e.g.*, incentive points). The Ethereum white paper emphasizes that a token system, at heart, is a database whose purpose is to debit and credit accounts subject to the rule that the debited account (the sender's account) has enough Ether to fulfill the request and that the sender approved the transaction. [Ethereum white paper, https://github.com/ethereum/wiki/wiki/White-Paper.]

However, using the Ethereum platform to create contracts and tokens comes with a built-in price mechanism for executing those actions on the Ethereum blockchain. As the Ethereum white paper noted, Ether is the lifeblood of the platform and each action executed on the Ethereum blockchain incurs a "gas" cost paid in increments of Ether based on the computational intensity of the action. Contracts typically specify a gas limit and a gas price. The purpose of imposing a cost on actions on the Ethereum blockchain is to dissuade users from writing code that consumes large amounts of resources, such as running infinite loops or launching malicious attacks on the platform. [Ethereum white paper, https://github.com/ethereum/wiki/wiki/White-Paper; *See also*, Chris Dannen, Introducing Ethereum and Solidity: Foundations of Cryptocurrency and Blockchain for Beginners, Apress, 2017.]

Developers using the Ethereum platform sometimes initiate Ethereum Improvement Proposals (EIPs) or Ethereum Requests for Comment (ERCs). One such ERC, ERC 20, resulted in what today is one of the most widely used Ethereum token standards. The rationale for ERC 20 was to improve the usefulness of Ethereum smart contracts and to allow Ethereum to interact with wallets and exchanges. The ERC 20 standard contains a number of specifications for common tasks, such as checking a balance, transferring Ether, and allowing a spender to withdraw funds. [ERC 20 token standard, https://github.com/ethereum/EIPs/issues/20.]

¶120

Although it is easy to create a basic smart contract for the Ethereum platform (*e.g.*, a contract that delivers a simple message like "Hello world!"), a significant degree of programming skill is required to launch a smart contract or token as part of an ICO. The difficulty level arises from multiple sources: (i) the need to use a computer programming language (*e.g.*, Solidity); (ii) the need to install various components from GitHub, an online repository of open-source software (installation also may require basic knowledge of how to use the command line on a computer—*e.g.*, Mac OS Terminal or Microsoft PowerShell ISE); and (iii) the need to debug and test the smart contract or dapp. Experienced programmers will grasp how these steps are accomplished, while many attorneys who work outside of technical practice areas may have a steep learning curve if they want to create a contract on their own; an alternative would be to collaborate with a technical specialist.

The Ethereum platform, however, has spurred the development of tools to make some complex tasks simpler. For example, the Mist browser contains tools for inserting and deploying code. [Mist browser, https://github.com/ethereum/mist.] MetaMask provides similar tools for creating contracts and allows dapps to be run from a browser, thus, obviating the need for a full Ethereum node. [MetaMask website, https://metamask.io/.] Remix, an integrated development environment or IDE for the Solidity programming language provides a third option; Remix has an advantage over other Ethereum tools in that no installation is required to begin writing and compiling smart contracts for Ethereum in the Solidity programming language, although deployment of a smart contract involves additional steps. [Remix IDE, https://remix.ethereum.org/#optimize=false&version=soljson-v0.4.23+commit.124ca40d.js.] Tools like these often can be used to execute code on an Ethereum test network where code can be run using pretend Ether rather than incurring actual gas costs.

If one deployed a smart contract or token on, or transacted business on, the Ethereum platform, it would make sense to have a method for assessing the success of the deployment or transaction. Block explorers can provide such details. Etherscan and Etherchain are block explorers that allow one to search for transactions in Ether. Etherscan also allows one to view transactions involving tokens. In the case of a token, one can view the transaction hash, gas usage data, amount transacted, and the from and to addresses. It is even possible to view data on "uncles," those orphaned blocks that did not make it into the Ethereum blockchain during the mining process. [Etherscan website, https://etherscan.io/; Etherchain website, https://www.etherchain.org/.]

¶ 130 Impact on Legal Profession

On an almost-daily basis, lawyers are witnessing a stream of press accounts, legislative proposals, agency pronouncements, and case filings related to evolving virtual currency and blockchain regulation. As with any emerging technology, the rise of blockchain, Bitcoin, and other virtual currencies present a double-edged sword for the legal community. In one respect, blockchain's potential to disrupt and transform recordkeeping and document-authentication practices presents lawyers with a host of unique opportunities across practice areas. Opportunities have emerged for blockchain-oriented lawyers, and that trend will likely continue.

At the same time, however, challenges and risks abound. Lawyers are often called upon to render advice for cutting-edge technological products and processes never contemplated by regulatory frameworks developed decades ago. Some commentators voice concerns that blockchain's potential to eliminate intermediaries, automate processes, and replace traditional written contracts with computerized smart contracts may eliminate or drastically reduce the need for lawyers in the future.

Despite this pessimistic view, lawyers will not be going the way of the blacksmith anytime soon. In fact, in the current environment, a blockchain-savvy lawyer may be well-positioned to assist clients needing to navigate an uncertain regulatory terrain. Additionally, providing advice and representation to those seeking to adopt smart contracts or otherwise address blockchain-related issues may present opportunities to add value.

Blockchain: Legal Practices Areas

Blockchain's promise to provide a single source of truth by enabling secure, immutable, transparent and authentic records, has the potential to impact many legal practice areas and processes, which include some of the following:

Smart contracts. As noted, a smart contract is not literally a legal contract, but rather a set of code that executes actions based on the fulfillment of certain conditions. For example, "the delivery of goods" can be a satisfied condition that results in the action of "payment." Blockchain provides a decentralized ledger that stores and replicates documents and agreements. Open Law is a platform that allows for certain portions of a legal agreement to be incorporated onto the Ethereum blockchain. Integra Ledger is a company that also supports smart contracts and serves as a platform for the development of legally compliant smart contracts throughout the legal industry ecosystem.

Contract management. The immutability feature of blockchain offers potential opportunities in connection with the negation of, and version control for contracts, and other legal documents. NetDocuments is a platform that enables firms to validate document existence, details, status, and metadata via a verified and distributed digital ledger.

Document notarization. A notary public typically confirms and verifies signatures on legal documents, such as deeds and contracts. Blockchain technology can maintain and preserve these documents as part of a digital ledger. Stampery and Stampd are two companies that provide notary services online using blockchain technology in this burgeoning area.

Real estate transactions. Real estate transactions and land-title matters are another area ripe for blockchain applications. Specifically, a public blockchain ledger can keep reliable records of property titles and deeds and ownership changes as they occur. In any real estate transaction, interested parties such as purchasers, lenders, and title companies and can gain assurances that the seller actually owns the property and that title encumbrances are removed or otherwise identified and addressed prior to closing. Wolters Kluwer's Dean Sonderegger further discusses real-estate-transaction blockchain use case in an article appearing on the Above The Law website. [Dean Sonderegger, Blockchain: Building Trust in Transactions, Above The Law, January 30, 2018.]

Intellectual property. As in the real estate context, blockchain technology can provide reliable records in connection with intellectual property rights, such as trademarks, copyrights, and patents. Blockchain's immutable, secure, and transparent platform also provides a highly reliable way to track first use. Blockchain applications are also being explored to manage licensing rights and enable royalty payments for artists and musicians.

Corporate law. A move is afoot among the states to consider blockchain technology in connection with maintaining shareholder registries and other corporate records. In July 2017, the Delaware General Corporation Law was amended to allow corporations in the state to keep records, including the stock ledger, in distributed ledgers or blockchain. Wyoming enacted similar legislation in March 2018.

¶130

Criminal law—chain of custody. Chain of custody is a crucial issue in criminal law. If the chain of custody for a given evidentiary item is compromised, a criminal prosecution could be weakened or placed in jeopardy. Blockchain technology is well suited to verify chain-of-custody assertions by establishing and preserving a permanent record of the relevant evidence on the digital ledger.

Tracking criminal cases. Blockchain technology can also be used to track and share records related to criminal charges that could be used by, and shared among, law enforcement officials, prosecutors, courts, probation officers, defense attorneys, and corrections organizations. When charges are added or dropped, or a status is otherwise modified, these changes could be added to the digital ledger as well. As a result, evolutions in the use of blockchain technology could lead to overall improvements in the administration of justice.

Service of process. Efforts are already in place to use blockchain technology to secure and share data related to the service of process for parties involved in litigation.

Personal legal matters. As the ownership of Bitcoin and other digital assets becomes more commonplace throughout the general population, lawyers will need to become increasingly familiar with their involvement in the numerous garden variety legal problems people encounter. For instance, addressing cryptocurrency issues in divorce, estate planning, probate, and other property disposition scenarios already prompts many lawyers to develop a basic understanding of Bitcoin and other virtual currencies. This trend will likely continue.

Organizations Advocating for Blockchain and the Legal Industry

A number of organizations have emerged that provide a voice for the legal industry around blockchain-related issues and to advance its interests. One organization, the Global Legal Blockchain Consortium (GLBC) consists of several major law firms, corporations, and several technology vendors, including IBM. The GLBC's stated mission is to "organize and align the stakeholders in the global legal industry with regard to the use of blockchain technology to enhance the security, privacy, productivity, and interoperability of the legal technology ecosystem."

Another contingent, the Legal Industry Working Group, part of the Enterprise Ethereum Alliance (EEA), is a collaborative blockchain consortium striving to leverage open-source Ethereum technology. The group is looking to bring together "top, global law firms and leading legal minds to explore building enterprise-grade applications on Ethereum."

Finally, the Washington-based Chamber of Digital Commerce, established in 2014, is a trade association representing the digital asset and blockchain industry. Its stated mission is "to promote the acceptance and use of digital assets and blockchain-based technologies." The organization seeks to develop an environment that fosters innovation, jobs and investment in the blockchain space through education, advocacy and working closely with policymakers.

Lawyers in a Blockchain World: Threats and Opportunities

Making sense of the chaos. "As with many potential breakthrough technologies, blockchain has become subject of the hype cycle," observes Wolters Kluwer's Sonderegger. He continues: "We all may have heard that blockchain is cure for everything and will disintermediate all business processes. That's the peak of inflated expectations and it's not going to happen. I think that is behind us and it is a good time for lawyers to take practical steps to build their skills in this area." [For a discussion of the "hype cycle," see Gartner, https://www.gartner.com/technology/research/methodologies/hype-cycle.jsp.]

Sonderegger acknowledges the controversy around whether lawyers need to learn how to code, but he does not think that is necessary. Rather, he suggests lawyers become familiar with smart contract applications and protocols, noting that "traditional contracts will be around for a long time. I believe lawyers will be well-served to learn how to interact with the applications that will [] continue to be developed to provide smart contract capabilities."

Lawyers as gatekeepers. Another risk for lawyers embarking on cryptocurrency related engagements involves gatekeeper liability. In remarks before the Securities Regulation Institute in January 2018, SEC Chairman Jay Clayton indicated that the agency intends to hold gatekeepers, including lawyers, responsible for activities in connection with initial coin offerings (ICOs). The chairman observed: "To be blunt what I have seen, particularly in the ICO space, they can do better." While the SEC has not initiated enforcement proceedings against lawyers or other gatekeepers in the cryptocurrency space to date, the warning to legal professionals to proceed with due caution remains. [Jay Clayton, Opening Remarks at the Securities Regulation Institute January 22, 2018.]

Getting in early. There are certainly legal pioneers, but true blockchain and cryptocurrency legal experts are yet to emerge, given the nascent nature of the field, according to Joshua Ashley Klayman, counsel at Morrison & Foerster LLP. In a September 2017 article, she notes that, because "no one has been advising about blockchain for twenty or thirty years" (as is the case in other practice areas), "it is a great level-setter" and presents an area where a lawyer might "make a name" for himself or herself. Klayman observes that "there is so much that has not yet been determined, discovered, done . . . by anyone." She further notes: "Some of the best lawyers out there may be the ones who see the grey areas and are trying to navigate them." [Joshua Ashley Klayman, Beware of the Blockchain and Cryptocurrency "Legal Expert", September 6, 2017.]

Navigating the evolving landscape. Many governmental bodies, including the SEC, the CFTC, FinCen, a handful of banking regulators, as well as the 50 states, have staked out some turf within the virtual currency and blockchain landscape, but the extent of their authority and mandates is often less-than crystal clear, which results in an, at-best, murky jurisdictional picture. At the same time, gaping holes in regulation exist, especially with regard to the markets for Bitcoin and some other virtual currencies.

Chapter Two—Who Regulates What?

¶ 200 Securities and Exchange Commission

Established pursuant to the Securities Exchange Act of 1934, the Securities and Exchange Commission (SEC) was designed to restore investor confidence in American capital markets and establish means by which to monitor the securities industry and provide investors and markets with reliable information and rules of fair dealing. More than eight decades later, the SEC remains committed to its tripartite mission to protect investors, to maintain fair, orderly, and efficient markets, and to facilitate capital formation.

According to the SEC, the laws and rules that govern the U.S. securities industry all relate back to a simple concept: that all investors, large or small, should have access to basic information regarding an investment prior to purchase and throughout the time they continue to hold it. The SEC is concerned primarily with promoting the disclosure of important market-related information, maintaining fair dealing, and protecting against fraud; the results of these efforts are more efficient and transparent markets and facilitation of capital formation. To ensure that this objective is consistently achieved, the Commission works with market participants to learn from their experiences and keep pace with industry developments relative to existing statutes and regulations.

Among the market participants subject to SEC oversight are exchanges, brokers and dealers, investment advisers, mutual funds, transfer agents, and clearing organizations. The Commission's regulations govern these entities' business registration and registration of their securities, as well as disclosures provided to, and other interactions with, shareholders. The SEC's rules also place certain limitations on the business operations and activities subject to SEC oversight and provide for means by which to enforce the agency's rules.

As technology evolves, however, the SEC has been forced to consider ways to maintain its oversight function while remaining sufficiently flexible to encourage further developments. Commission leadership has expressed an openness to the innovations and efficiencies that could flow from blockchain technologies but continues to use the agency's oversight and enforcement powers to go after those who violate federal securities laws and SEC regulations in their cryptocurrency dealings. [Chairman's Testimony on Virtual Currencies: The Roles of the SEC and CFTC, February 6, 2018.]

Registration

The SEC is primarily charged with the regulation of securities. Section 2(a)(1) of the Securities Act defines the term "security" to mean, among other things, notes, stocks, treasury stocks, security futures, security-based swaps, bonds, debentures, evidences of indebtedness, certificates of interest or participation in a profit-sharing agreement, investment contracts, collateral trust certificates, voting trust certificates, and puts, calls, straddles or options on a security or group or index of securities. [15

U.S.C. § 77b(a)(1).] The term is designed to be broad enough to encompass novel, uncommon, or irregular instruments if they are in fact securities.

A primary means by which the SEC accomplishes its disclosure goals is the gathering of important financial and business information through the registration of securities. Under Securities Act Section 5 and the existing securities regulation regime, when companies offer and sell securities, they are required to register the offering with the Commission. [15 U.S.C. § 77e.] The disclosure requirements connected with registration of new security offerings are intended to afford potential investors an adequate basis upon which to decide whether to make an investment and to prevent misrepresentation, deceit, and other fraudulent practices in offers and sales of securities. Among other things, the Commission's registration forms call for:

- A description of the company's properties and business
- A description of the security to be offered for sale
- Information about the management of the company
- Financial statements certified by independent accountants

Civil liability may arise under Section 11 if a registration statement is false or misleading, and a person who offers or sells a security in violation of the Securities Act registration and prospectus provisions may be liable under Section 12(a)(1). [15 U.S.C. §§ 77k and 77l(a)(1).] A person who offers or sells a security by means of a communication including an untrue statement of a material fact, or omitting to state a material fact necessary to make the statements made not misleading, may be liable under Section 12(a)(2). [15 U.S.C. § 77l(a)(2).]

Exemptions from registration and prospectus requirements for certain classes of securities and types of transactions are provided under Securities Act Sections 3 and 4 and within the SEC's regulations. Among other things, exemptions may be available for:

- Banks
- Charitable and other nonprofit issuers
- Commercial paper
- Government securities
- Intrastate issues
- Security futures products
- Transactions by a person who is not an issuer, underwriter or dealer
- Private offerings
- Certain dealer and broker transactions
- Sales to accredited investors
- Crowdfunding

However, exemption from the registration and prospectus requirements does not necessarily free a security or transaction from other disclosure requirements nor provide relief from the statutory and regulatory prohibitions against fraud. [15 U.S.C. §§ 77c and 77d.]

Similarly, a security must be registered in accordance with the requirements of Exchange Act Section 12(b) if the security is to be traded on a national securities exchange. [15 U.S.C. § 78l.] Further, under Exchange Act Sections 5 and 6, a broker, dealer, or exchange may not engage in interstate commerce for the purpose of using any exchange to effect or report securities transactions without being registered with the Commission, unless an exemption applies. [15 U.S.C. §§ 78f and 78g.] Exchange Act Section 3(a) defines an "exchange" as any organization or group of persons that provides a facility to bring together buyers and sellers of securities and includes activities generally understood to be performed by a stock exchange. [15 U.S.C. § 78c.] The term "facility" includes tangible and intangible property and communications systems.

An issuer registers a security so that the security may be traded on an exchange by filing a registration statement with the exchange and filing duplicate originals with the Commission.

Under Exchange Act Section 3(a)(12), *exempted securities* include, among others:

- Government securities
- Municipal securities
- Interests in certain trust funds
- Securities issued by, or interests in, certain pooled income funds, collective trust funds, and collective investment funds
- Securities issued by, or interests in, certain church plans, companies, or accounts

Cryptocurrencies as Securities

In August 2013, in connection with a challenge to subject matter jurisdiction, the Eastern District of Texas found that Bitcoins are securities. The court applied the *Howey* test, which clarifies when an investment constitutes an "investment contract" and thus a security.

An "investment contract" is listed as a security in both the Securities Act and Exchange Act, although neither statute defines the term. In *SEC v. W.J. Howey Co.* (U.S. 1946), the U.S. Supreme Court established the test to determine whether a financial relationship constitutes an investment contract for purposes of the Securities Act.

Under *Howey*, an investment contract "means a contract, transaction or scheme" involving:

- an investment of money;
- in a common enterprise;
- with profits derived solely from the efforts of others.

Such a definition, said the Court, embodies a flexible rather than static principle, one capable of adaption to meet the varied schemes devised by those who seek the use of others' money.

Applying this test, the Texas district court noted that Bitcoins are an investment of money because the currency is accepted by some as a mode of payment. The court next found that a common enterprise existed between the company and its principal in soliciting Bitcoin loans and that the investors had an expectation of profits to be derived from their actions. As such, the court concluded, Bitcoins meet the definition of investment contract," a security under federal law. Accordingly, the court found that the defendants violated the registration provisions of the Securities Act because there was no registration statement on file. [*SEC v. Shavers*, E.D. Tex. 2013.]

Cryptocurrency and blockchain applications. Following the Texas federal court's determination, the SEC continued to enforce its registration provisions against individuals and entities dealing in cryptocurrency. For example, the Commission charged and sanctioned:

- The co-owner of two Bitcoin-related websites for unlawfully offering and selling shares in the ventures through online forums in exchange for Bitcoins without registration. [*In the Matter of Voorhees*, Release No. 33-9592, June 3, 2014.]

- The operators of "virtual exchanges" designed to allow users to list initial and secondary securities offerings for running the exchanges without SEC registration and without claiming an exemption from registration. Further, the SEC alleged that an individual respondent received transaction-based compensation for services, acted as an unregistered broker-dealer, and engaged in transactions involving unregistered securities without any relevant exemption under the Securities Act or its underlying rules.[*In the Matter of BTC Trading, Corp.*, Release No. 33-9685, December 8, 2014.]

- A company and two individuals running a financial variant of "fantasy sports" funded by users with U.S. dollars or Bitcoin for violations of Securities Act Section 5(e), which makes it unlawful to transact security-based swap transactions with non-eligible contract participants without registration, and Exchange Act Section 6(1), which makes it unlawful to effect such transactions except on a national securities exchange. [*In the Matter of Sand Hill Exchange*, Release No. 33-9809, June 17, 2015.]

The DAO

In July 2017, the SEC issued a landmark report of investigation concluding that digital tokens issued, offered, and sold by The Decentralized Autonomous Organization (The DAO) were securities subject to the federal securities laws. Similar to the Texas federal court years before, the Commission reasoned that DAO tokens were securities under the *Howey* test. The DAO invested money with a reasonable expectation of profits derived from the managerial efforts of others, and token holders' nominal voting rights did not give them meaningful control over the enterprise. The report also concluded that The DAO was required to register the offer and sale of DAO tokens unless a valid exemption applied, and the platforms that traded DAO tokens appeared to be exchanges without applicable exemptions from registration. [Report of Investigation Pursuant to Section 21(a) of the Securities Exchange Act of 1934: The DAO, Release No. 34-81207, July 25, 2017, at ¶ 1020.]

The agency opted not to bring charges against The DAO or related parties, instead releasing the report as a caution to the industry and market participants.

Beyond its particularized findings, and perhaps more importantly, the Commission's DAO report clarified some of the parameters that will be involved in the Commission's determination as to whether a particular token or other digital asset is subject to regulation and when federal securities laws apply to initial coin offerings (ICOs). With the DAO report, the SEC confirmed that issuers of DLT- or blockchain-based securities must register offers and sales of the securities with the Commission unless a valid exemption from registration applies and that platforms that provide for trading in these securities must register as national securities exchanges or operate pursuant to an exemption.

However, the Commission left open the possibility that some tokens or coins might fall outside the federal securities laws, noting that whether a transaction involves the offer and sale of a security will depend on the particular facts and circumstances involved.

ICOs

Typically, an ICO involves an opportunity for individual investors to exchange currency, such as U.S. dollars or cryptocurrencies, in return for a digital asset labeled as a coin or token.

Following the DAO report's conclusion that coins or tokens offered via ICOs can be securities that must either be registered with the Commission or subject to an exemption from registration, the SEC established a new Cyber Unit within the Division of

¶200

Enforcement to focus on violations involving DLT and blockchain technology and/or ICOs.

With regard to enforcement involving violations in connection with ICOs, several themes have emerged: unregistered securities, unregistered exchanges, and fraudulent activities. For example:

- In September 2017, the SEC brought an action against an individual that raised $300,000 from investors via ICOs alleging registration failures and numerous misrepresentations made to investors. [*SEC v. REcoin Group Foundation, LLC*, September 29, 2017; *U.S. v. Zaslavskiy*, October 27, 2017.]

- In December 2017, the SEC brought suit against a company that ran an ICO for failing to register its securities under the Securities Act and violating the antifraud provisions of both the Securities Act and the Exchange Act. [*SEC v. PlexCorps*, December 1, 2017.]

- In February 2018, the SEC brought a case against a company that allegedly ran a platform allowing users to list "assets" to be sold in initial and follow-on offerings and to be traded on a secondary market for operating an unregistered exchange and without any relevant exemption from registration. [*SEC v. Montroll*, February 21, 2018.]

SEC Chairman Jay Clayton has stressed that if a cryptocurrency, or a product tied to a cryptocurrency, is a security, its promoters cannot make offers or sales of it unless they comply with registration requirements and other applicable provisions under the federal securities laws. Further, he noted that financial products linked to underlying digital assets may be structured as securities products subject to the federal securities laws even if the underlying cryptocurrencies are not themselves securities. Simply calling something a "currency" does not mean that it is not a security, he stated. [Statement on Cryptocurrencies and Initial Coin Offerings, December 11, 2017.]

At a February 2018 Senate Banking Committee hearing, Chairman Clayton made clear his views on ICOs: "To the extent that digital assets like ICOs are securities, and I believe every ICO I have seen is a security, we have jurisdiction and our federal securities laws apply." [Chairman's Testimony on Virtual Currencies: The Roles of the SEC and CFTC, February 6, 2018.]

To date, no ICOs have been registered with the SEC, and no cryptocurrency type products have been approved for listing and trading. In addition, the SEC has not approved for listing any exchange-traded products that hold cryptocurrencies or other assets related to cryptocurrencies.

¶ 210 Commodity Futures Trading Commission

In the late 1700s in the United States, producers and merchants formed centralized commodity markets for trade in eggs, butter, vegetables, and grain; these exchanges were chiefly cash markets for "spot" delivery. Through the next century and into the early 1900s, agricultural futures trading developed in response to the need for centralized pricing and large-scale risk bearing, and the federal government began to move toward regulation. Over the decades after its passage in 1936, the Commodity Exchange Act expanded to cover additional commodities, but, in the 1970s, the value of futures trading had reached $500 billion annually and it became apparent that, to ensure the proper functioning of the futures markets and fair prices for consumers, careful supervision was necessary.

The Commodity Futures Trading Commission Act of 1974 created the Commodity Futures Trading Commission (CFTC) as an independent agency to administer the CEA and retain exclusive jurisdiction over transactions involving futures contracts and certain other commodity-related activities. The CFTC Act substantially revised the Commodity Exchange Act, including by extending the CEA's coverage to include not only previously unregulated commodities, but also all other goods and articles, and all services, rights and interests in which contracts for future delivery are presently or in the future dealt in.

After more than 40 years, the CFTC remains committed to fostering open, transparent, competitive, and financially sound markets and protecting users, consumers, and the public from fraud and manipulation and other abusive practices related to products subject to the CEA. The agency oversees a variety of individuals and organizations, including swap execution facilities (SEFs), derivatives clearing organizations (DCOs), designated contract markets (DCMs), swap data repositories, swap dealers, futures commission merchants, commodity pool operators, and other entities.

Jurisdiction

When created, the CFTC was vested with exclusive jurisdiction with respect to accounts, agreements (including commodity options), and transactions involving contracts of sale of a commodity for future delivery traded or executed on a DCM, or any other board of trade, exchange or market. Under CEA Section 1a(9), a "commodity" can be a physical commodity, such as an agricultural product (e.g., wheat, cotton) or natural resource (e.g., gold, oil) or a currency or interest rate. The definition also includes a general catchall to cover "all other goods and articles" (except, interestingly, onions and movie box office receipts) and "all services, rights, and interests in which contracts for future delivery are presently or in the future dealt in." [7 U.S.C. § 1a(9).]

The CFTC has both oversight and enforcement authority with respect to futures and other derivative products and markets, but only enforcement authority over the spot markets, where commodities themselves are actually bought and sold. As such, in terms of oversight authority over derivatives trading, the CFTC's role is broad and far reaching, including requirements for registration, trade execution and orderly trading, reporting, and recordkeeping. Prior to listing new contracts, the CEA allows DCMs to either submit a written self-certification to the CFTC that the contract complies with the CEA and CFTC regulations, including that the new contract is not readily susceptible to manipulation, or voluntarily submit the contract for Commission approval. When a DCM self-certifies a new contract, it also must determine that the offering complies with the core principles of the CEA.

In contrast, with respect to spot markets, the CFTC only has enforcement authority to police fraud and manipulation. This means the CFTC cannot impose obligations like registration on platforms or participants in the cash markets or surveillance and monitoring requirements on spot platforms and cannot otherwise require compliance with business conduct standards or other trading requirements; the agency can only investigate potential fraud and manipulation in underlying markets for commodities.

However, the Dodd-Frank Act added a provision to the CEA known as the "retail commodity provision," which provides for direct CFTC oversight if an entity offers a commodity for sale to a retail customer on a margined, leveraged, or financed basis. Thus, if borrowed funds are used to effect a transaction, then the agreement is regulated as if it were a futures transaction and becomes subject to CFTC trading and registration requirements, unless the commodity is actually delivered to the buyer within 28 days. [7 U.S.C. § 2(c)(2)(D).]

Cryptocurrencies as Commodities

In December 2014 testimony before a Senate committee, then-CFTC Chairman Timothy Massad noted the agency's view that virtual currencies are commodities, explaining that the Commission's authority extends to futures and swaps contracts in any commodity and therefore "derivative contracts based on a virtual currency represent one area" within the Commission's responsibility. [Testimony of Chairman Timothy Massad before the U.S. Senate Committee on Agriculture, Nutrition & Forestry, December 10, 2014.] Not quite a year later, the CFTC formalized its position that the term "commodity" under the CEA encompasses Bitcoin and other virtual currencies in an administrative enforcement action attacking an unregistered offering of Bitcoin options and the unregistered operation of a SEF. The definition is broad, particularly the portion covering "all services, rights, and interests in which contracts for future delivery are presently or in the future dealt in," the Commission stated. [*In the Matter of Coinflip, Inc.*, CFTC Docket No. 15-29, September 17, 2015.]

"[I]nnovation does not excuse those acting in this space from following the same rules applicable to all participants in the commodity derivatives markets," said then-CFTC Enforcement Director Aitan Goelman in a related news release. [Release No. PR7231-15, September 17, 2015.]

As commentators have elaborated: "[B]itcoins can clearly qualify as a commodity because they are articles that can be traded and made subject to futures contracts. The CFTC's authority is not over commodities themselves, however, but instead over commodity futures, which are tradable contracts to purchase or sell commodities at a certain date for a certain price." [Jerry Brito and Andrea Castillo, Bitcoin: A Primer for Policymakers (May 2016).]

As such, the CFTC's jurisdiction is generally implicated when a virtual currency is used in a derivatives contract or when there is fraud or manipulation involving a virtual currency traded in interstate commerce.

Futures and Derivative Markets Oversight; Self-Certification

Section 2(a)(1) of the CEA provides that the CFTC has exclusive jurisdiction as to accounts, agreements (including options, privileges, indemnities, bids, offers, puts, calls, advance guaranties and decline guaranties), and transactions involving contracts of sale of a commodity for future delivery, traded or executed on a contract market, or any other board of trade, exchange or market. The Commission also is authorized to prohibit or regulate leverage contracts in commodities. [7 U.S.C. § 2(a)(1).]

Over time, virtual currencies have made their way into contract markets, and the CFTC has used its exclusive jurisdiction to halt operation of a facility for trading or processing of commodity options not registered as a SEF or DCM [*In the Matter of Coinflip, Inc.*, CFTC Docket No. 15-29, September 17, 2015], to enforce laws prohibiting pre-arranged and wash trading on a derivatives platform [*In the Matter of TeraExchange LLC*, CFTC Docket No. 15-33, September 24, 2015], and to take action against an unregistered Bitcoin futures exchange [*In the Matter of BFXNA Inc.*, CFTC Docket No. 16-19, June 2, 2016]. The CFTC did, however, grant registration as a SEF and a DCO to a digital currency trading and clearing platform intending to use DLT to receive Bitcoin from, and deliver Bitcoin to, its members in connection with the option contracts traded on Bitcoin. [*In the Matter of the Application of LedgerX, LLC For Registration as a Derivatives Clearing Organization*, July 24, 2017.]

Separately, in December 2017, the Chicago Mercantile Exchange Inc. and the CBOE Futures Exchange self-certified new contracts for Bitcoin futures products and the Cantor Exchange self-certified a new contract for Bitcoin binary options under a certification process authorized by Congress and implemented by the CFTC. [Release No. 7654-17, December 1, 2017.]

The process allows DCMs to certify new products within their role as self-regulatory organizations so development of new and innovative products is not overly hindered by regulators, and the CFTC has very limited grounds for objection (mainly only fraud and/or false statements within the filing). Further, there is no provision for public input into new product self-certifications. [CFTC Backgrounder on Self-Certified Contracts for Bitcoin Products, January 2018.]

Within the limits of the self-certification process, CFTC staff has engaged with the DCMs in a voluntary "heightened review" concerning the terms and conditions of these Bitcoin futures products. The exchanges agreed to a review checklist including, among other things:

- Setting exchange large-trader reporting thresholds at five Bitcoins or less
- Entering into information-sharing agreements with spot market platforms to allow access to data
- Monitoring price settlement data from cash markets and making inquiries upon discovery of anomalies;
- Maintaining regular communication with CFTC surveillance staff on trade activities
- Coordinating product launches to enable the CFTC staff to monitor developments
- Setting substantial initial and maintenance margin for cash-settled instruments

CFTC Chairman Giancarlo has called for agency staff to consider formalized rules and heightened review requirements in connection with exchanges self-certifying new cryptocurrency-related futures contracts instead of the currently voluntary undertakings. [Remarks of Chairman J. Christopher Giancarlo to the ABA Derivatives and Futures Section Conference, Naples, Florida, January 19, 2018.]

Fraud

According to the CFTC, while its oversight authority over commodity cash markets is limited, the agency maintains general antifraud enforcement authority over virtual currency cash markets as a commodity in interstate commerce. [Release No. 7665-17, December 15, 2017.] Asserting legal authority over virtual currency in support of the CFTC's antifraud efforts and enforcing the law to halt manipulative schemes and abuses are key components in the CFTC's ability to effectively regulate these markets, the agency notes. [CFTC Backgrounder on Oversight of and Approach to Virtual Currency Futures Markets, January 4, 2018.]

In January 2018, the CFTC charged a purported cryptocurrency trader and advisor and his company with fraud in connection with purchases of and trading in virtual currencies. [*CFTC v. McDonnell*, January 18, 2018.] Along with instituting the proceeding, CFTC Director of Enforcement James McDonald issued a joint statement with his SEC counterparts. "When market participants engage in fraud under the guise of offering digital instruments—whether characterized as virtual currencies, coins, tokens or the like—the SEC and the CFTC will look beyond form, examine the substance of the activity and prosecute violations of the federal securities and commodities laws," the enforcement heads noted. [Joint Statement by SEC and CFTC Enforcement Directors Regarding Virtual Currency Enforcement Actions, January 19, 2018.]

The Eastern District of New York found that the Commission has standing to seek relief related to virtual currency fraud because virtual currencies are "commodities" under the Commodity Exchange Act. According to the court, "A 'commodity' encompasses virtual currency both in economic function and in the language of the CEA," and the CFTC has regulatory authority over commodities traded as futures and derivatives and has recently expanded its enforcement authority to fraud related to spot markets underlying the regulated derivative markets. While its regulatory oversight authority over commodity cash markets is limited, the court explained, the CFTC maintains general antifraud enforcement authority over virtual currency cash markets as a commodity in interstate commerce. Until Congress acts to clarify a system for cryptocurrency regulation, the CFTC has concurrent authority with other state and federal entities over dealings in virtual currency, the court concluded. [*CFTC v. McDonnell*, March 6, 2018, Weinstein, J.]

At present, virtual currencies are considered commodities under applicable law, and the CFTC has standing to go after potential fraudsters in connection with spot sales of virtual currencies, even if the sales do not involve a sale of futures or derivatives contracts. The CFTC intends to continue to exercise this jurisdiction to enforce the law and prosecute fraud and manipulation in markets for virtual currency derivatives and underlying spot trading. [CFTC Backgrounder on Oversight of and Approach to Virtual Currency Futures Markets, January 4, 2018, at ¶ 1050.]

Retail Commodity Transactions

The Dodd-Frank Act amended the CEA to add Section 2(c)(2)(D) to clarify the CFTC's jurisdiction over certain retail commodity transactions. The section applies to any agreement, contract, or transaction in any commodity entered into with, or offered to, a non-eligible contract participant or commercial entity on a leveraged, margined, or financed basis, requires them to be conducted on a regulated exchange, and subjects them to the CFTC's antifraud authority. However, the provision does not apply if "actual delivery" of the commodity is made within 28 days. [7 U.S.C. § 2(c)(2)(D).]

In August 2013, the CFTC issued an interpretation of the term "actual delivery" within the context of retail commodity transactions. The Commission noted that, in determining whether actual delivery has occurred within 28 days of the date that the agreement, contract, or transaction is entered into, the Commission will employ a functional approach and examine how it is marketed, managed, and performed, instead of relying solely on language used by the parties. Relevant factors will include ownership, possession, title, and physical location of the commodity purchased or sold, the nature of the relationship between the buyer, seller, and possessor of the commodity, and the manner in which the purchase or sale is recorded and completed. [Retail Commodity Transactions Under Commodity Exchange Act, August 20, 2013.]

However, in light of burgeoning interest in, and use of, virtual currencies, the CFTC issued a proposed interpretation in late 2017 setting forth its view regarding the "actual delivery" exception as it may apply to virtual currency transactions. The proposed interpretation would formally require the actual delivery of a virtual currency to a retail client within 28 days of a purchase transaction in order to avoid CFTC registration requirements by persons selling and either financing or arranging financing of the virtual currency, as well as related regulatory oversight by the Commission. The CFTC will consider "actual delivery" to have occurred when a customer can take "possession and control" of all of the cryptocurrency and use it freely no later than 28 days from the date of the initial transaction, the Commission proposes. The Commission cautions, however, that actual delivery will not have occurred when, within 28 days, virtual currency sold to a retail client is rolled, offset against, netted out, or settled in cash or virtual currency between a buyer and the offeror or counterparty seller or any person acting in concert with them. [Retail Commodity Transactions Involving Virtual Currency, December 15, 2017, at ¶ 1060.]

The Commission is reviewing comments, and a final interpretation clarifying when financed virtual currencies are "actually delivered" and when direct CFTC regulatory oversight is implicated is anticipated.

¶210

¶ 220 Financial Crimes Enforcement Network

The Financial Crimes Enforcement Network is a Treasury Department bureau established by 31 U.S.C. § 310, although it originally was created by a Treasury Department order in 1990. Its statutory duties are advising the Under Secretary of the Treasury for enforcement on matters that relate to financial intelligence and financial criminal activities; maintaining a database covering cash transactions and the movement of monetary instruments; analyzing and distributing information relating to money laundering and other financial criminal activity, terrorism, and trends in financial crimes; operating a financial crimes communication center to provide information to law enforcement agencies; assist in efforts against informal nonbank value transfer systems; help the Treasury track foreign assets; coordinate with financial intelligence units of foreign governments; and exercise Bank Secrecy Act authorities that are delegated to it by the Treasury Secretary.

It is the last of these statutory duties that brings FinCEN most directly into dealing with virtual currency. FinCEN does not actually regulate or supervise blockchain technology or virtual currency. Rather, under the Bank Secrecy Act, it regulates the virtual currency transactions in which money services businesses engage. FinCEN's focus is on how virtual currency is used.

To exercise its delegated authority, FinCEN adopted a series of regulations: 31 CFR Part 1010, which sets out general principles, and 31 CFR Parts 1020 through 1030, which apply those principles to various types of businesses, notably including money services businesses.

In the context of virtual currency, there are two types of business that are considered to be MSBs—money transmitters and some prepaid access sellers.

- A money transmitter is someone that accepts money or something that substitutes for money—such as virtual currency—and then sends that value to another person or another location.

- Prepaid access sellers are MSBs only if they sell prepaid access that can be used before the buyer's identification can be verified or they sell any single person prepaid access to more than $10,000 in a single day.

Since FinCEN only concerns itself with money transmitters and covered prepaid access sellers, those who acquire virtual currency and use it for their own purposes are not regulated. So, a Bitcoin miner or investor is not a regulated MSB, and neither is a person that buys Bitcoins and uses them to buy goods or services.

Whether FinCEN's regulations apply could be illustrated by two examples:

1. If a person who holds Bitcoin in a virtual wallet transmits that Bitcoin directly to a seller to buy a product, FinCEN is unconcerned.

2. If a person who holds Bitcoin in an account at a Bitcoin exchange website directs the website to send Bitcoin to a third party to pay for a product, the exchange website is a money transmitter that must be registered with FinCEN as an MSB and must comply with all of the relevant regulations.

FinCEN's virtual currency regulatory philosophy was explained to Congress in hearings in 2013. FinCEN Director Jennifer Shasky Calvery told the Senate's Homeland Security Committee that the bureau divided those who are active in virtual currency into three categories: users, exchangers, and administrators. Exchangers and administrators are subject to FinCEN's regulations, while users are not. [Statement of Jennifer Shasky Calvery Before the United States Senate Committee on Homeland Security and Government Affairs, November 18, 2013, at ¶ 1310.]

¶220

Shasky Calvery told the Senate that virtual currency is "a medium of exchange that operates like a currency in some environments but does not have all the attributes of real currency." It is not legal tender.

A more detailed discussion of FinCEN's regulatory philosophy can be found in ¶ 530.

¶ 230 Internal Revenue Service

Virtual currencies have grown in popularity in recent years and have emerged as a potential alternative payment method to using traditional government-issued currencies to pay for goods and services. It is widely known that the value of many virtual currencies, particularly cryptocurrencies such as Bitcoin, has risen significantly over the past year but also can fluctuate over time. As a result, the associated tax challenges have become vitally important. One of the most notable issues affecting holders of virtual currency is their tax reporting obligations.

Notice 2014-21

Due to the degree of anonymity given to users of virtual currency and the fact that certain transactions are not required to be reported to the IRS, the IRS has a particular interest in virtual currency given its parallel to traditional tax havens and the greater possibility of its use in illegal transactions. To date, the IRS has issued limited guidance on reporting exchanges of virtual currency. In March 2014, the IRS released Notice 2014-21, "Virtual Currency Guidance," which provides the agency's conclusions on certain basic tax principles concerning virtual currencies.

Currency or property? The notice begins by defining virtual currency as "a digital representation of value that functions as a medium of exchange, a unit of account, and/or a store of value," and further defines convertible virtual currency as a subset of currencies "that has an equivalent value in real currency, or that acts as a substitute for real currency." The notice limits the scope of its application to convertible virtual currencies and notes that Bitcoin is one example of a convertible virtual currency.

Notice 2014-21 provides that virtual currency is treated as property for federal income tax purposes and is not treated as currency that would be subject to rules applicable to currency transactions. However, the guidance does not address the kind of property that virtual currency should be regarded as for tax purposes. As an example, it is unclear whether virtual currency could be considered a commodity or a security. The Commodity Futures Trading Commission has already ruled that Bitcoin is a commodity for purposes of futures trading in *In re Coinflip, Inc.* (Dkt. No. 15-29) and *In re Tera Exchange LLC* (Dkt. No. 15-33). The lack of clarity from the IRS is a major concern in trying to understand the potential tax consequences of virtual currencies.

Property transactions. Because virtual currency is treated as property, the general tax principles that apply to property transactions apply to transactions using virtual currency. This means that the fair market value of virtual currency paid as wages is taxable to the employee, must be reported on a Form W-2, and is subject to federal income tax withholding, Federal Insurance Contributions Act (FICA) tax, and Federal Unemployment Tax Act (FUTA) tax.

Payments using virtual currency made to independent contractors are taxable and the self-employment tax rules apply. If a business pays $600 or more to an independent contractor, then the payee must issue a Form 1099-MISC, Miscellaneous Income, to the IRS and to the payee.

The character of gain or loss from the sale or exchange of a virtual currency depends on the nature of the virtual currency holdings in the hands of the taxpayer. For a miner, dealer, or issuer, the holding of Bitcoins would be inventory for sale in a trade or business. For investors, the notice indicates that gain or loss on the sale or exchange of virtual currencies would likely be capital gain or loss. In determining whether capital gains or losses were long term (assets held for at least one year) or short term (assets held for less than a year), the holding period of the asset begins on the day after it is acquired and ends on the date of sale or disposition.

A payment made using a virtual currency is subject to information reporting to the same extent as any other payment made in property.

The notice states that the cost basis of a unit of virtual currency received as payment for goods or services is equal to the fair market value of that unit in U.S. dollars on the date it was received. It is unclear whether virtual currency is deemed "received" on the date that it was earned or when the record ownership was transferred.

In addition to clarification on the meaning of the term "received," further guidance from the IRS would be needed on other activities and reporting requirements, such as charitable contributions of virtual currency, the tax treatment of mining costs, pooled mining activities, and the documentation establishing the cost, holding periods, and value for exchanges that do not use the U.S. dollar for virtual currency valuations.

How should gain or loss be reported? Taxpayers must report gain or loss any time they sell their virtual currency assets or exchange them for other types of property. If the fair market value of the property or cash received in exchange for the virtual currency exceeds the taxpayer's adjusted basis in the currency—which is generally defined as the original purchase price of the asset—the taxpayer has taxable gain. If the fair market value of the property or cash received in exchange for the virtual currency is less than the taxpayer's adjusted basis in the currency, the taxpayer has a loss. Code Section 1012 generally provides that a taxpayer's basis in property is its cost. Code Section 1016 sets forth the rules regarding adjustments to cost, such as commissions on the acquisition of property.

The basis of each item of property must be tracked separately and used to compute gain or loss upon its disposition. Since the ownership of virtual currencies is established through private keys, each specific purchase can be readily identified. However, tracking could be more difficult if an investor holds positions through a third-party wallet or intermediary, or when only a portion of a specific virtual currency tax lot is sold. Due to the notice's lack of specific guidance on the determination of basis, it would be prudent for a holder of virtual currency to track specific virtual currencies to manage gains and losses recognized from their disposition. It also makes the management of private key records and acquisition cost data very significant.

Applicability of tax penalties. The notice states that taxpayers may be subject to penalties for failing to comply with the tax laws. Specifically, underpayments on taxes for virtual currency transactions could be subject to accuracy-related penalties under Code Sec. 6662. In addition, failure to timely comply with the information reporting requirements for those transactions on Form 1099-MISC or Form 1099-K could give rise to penalties under Code Secs. 6721 or 6722. Relief from information reporting penalties may be available under Code Sec. 6724(a) if taxpayers demonstrate reasonable cause. However, the notice does not provide a safe harbor or penalty relief for transactions in virtual currencies that occurred or were reported before March 25, 2014—the date the notice was released.

Taxation of forks. The IRS has not issued guidance on the taxation of "hard forks." A hard fork occurs when there is a change to the software of a digital currency that creates two separate versions of the blockchain. As an example, Bitcoin Cash and Bitcoin Gold emerged after hard forks in the Bitcoin blockchain. After a hard fork takes place, the original owner of the virtual currency retains its interest in the original coin

¶230

and also has the right to use the forked coin. Due to the lack of guidance, questions remain as to whether the fork constitutes a realization event, what the basis of the new forked coin should be, and what is the character of any gain or loss recognized.

Like-kind exchanges. Under Code Sec. 1031, like-kind exchanges are transactions that allow for the disposal of an asset and the acquisition of a replacement asset within six months without immediate tax consequences. For sales prior to 2018, it is arguable that an exchange of one virtual currency for another could qualify as a non-taxable like-kind exchange. Beginning in 2018, the Tax Cuts and Jobs Act (P.L. 115-97) limited the like-kind exchange rules to real property and it is clear that like-kind treatment cannot apply to digital currency exchanges.

Increased IRS Oversight

In September 2016, the Treasury Inspector General for Tax Administration (TIGTA) issued an audit report—"As the Use of Virtual Currencies in Taxable Transactions Becomes More Common, Additional Actions Are Needed to Ensure Taxpayer Compliance"—evaluating the IRS's efforts to ensure that the use of virtual currency complies with U.S. tax laws. Although TIGTA acknowledged the issuance of guidance in Notice 2014-21 and the establishment of a Virtual Currency Issue Team, the office noted a lack of coordination between the functions responsible to identify and address potential taxpayer noncompliance issues for virtual currency transactions. TIGTA recommended in its report that the IRS develop a coordinated virtual currency strategy, provide updated guidance on the documentation requirements and tax treatments for the various uses of virtual currency, and revise third-party information reporting requirements to identify the amounts of virtual currencies used in taxable transactions.

Since the release of the report, the IRS has demonstrated an increased interest in overseeing virtual currency use. In November 2016, the IRS served a John Doe summons on the U.S.'s largest digital currency exchange Coinbase, seeking records of U.S. users who bought and sold Bitcoins between 2013 and 2015. After a challenge by anonymous users of Coinbase, the IRS narrowed the scope of the summons to seek information only for those accounts that engaged in any one transaction type (buy, sell, send, or receive) of $20,000 or more. In *U.S. v. Coinbase, Inc.*, Case No. 17-cv-01431, the federal district court for the Northern District of California issued an order in November 2017 granting the IRS petition seeking to enforce the summons, which requires the provision of the names and personally identifiable information for more than 13,000 Coinbase users.

In a March 2018 news release, IR-2018-71, the IRS reminded taxpayers that virtual currency transactions were reportable on their income tax returns similar to transactions in any other property. Taxable transactions are not limited to virtual currency sales or transactions that actually produce a profit in U.S. dollars. Virtual currency holders must consider that transactions, such as the exchange of one virtual currency for another, are taxable events and trigger tax recordkeeping requirements.

Recordkeeping. When calculating gain or loss, taxpayers should keep detailed and accurate records of their transactions and use reasonable and consistent methods. They will not receive a Form 1099 as they would for dividends and interest income. When there is missing trade information, the default position is to assume a cost basis of zero. This can cause a significant impact on taxpayers who began investing in the market when Bitcoin values were high. For example, in October 2017 when Bitcoin surpassed $6,000, having to assume a zero basis could result in a taxpayer overpaying by thousands of dollars. However, large virtual currency exchanges such as Coinbase will often keep full records of investor transactions which can be used to help its customers file their taxes.

Conclusion

The rapid expansion of virtual currency will likely have a substantial impact on the way that individuals and businesses conduct transactions in the future. Taxpayers and return preparers should pay close attention to IRS developments to ensure that they are up to date on changes that may impact virtual currency transactions.

¶ 240 Banking Regulators

The realm of federal banking regulation is led by three prudential regulators. Each of these agencies regulates and supervises specific types of banking organizations to ensure the safety and soundness of the banking system.

Office of the Comptroller of the Currency

The Office of the Comptroller of the Currency was created as a bureau of the Department of the Treasury by the National Currency Act of February 25, 1863. The National Currency Act was substantially revised in 1864, and, in 1874, it was renamed the National Bank Act.

The National Bank Act remains the authority under which the OCC and national banks operate; and the Home Owners' Loan Act of 1933 provides the basis for the operation and regulation of federal savings associations.

Regulated entities. The OCC is charged with assuring the safety and soundness of, and compliance with laws and regulations, fair access to financial services, and fair treatment of customers by the institutions and other persons subject to its jurisdiction. The OCC examines, supervises, and regulates national banks, federal branches and agencies of foreign banks, and federal savings associations to carry out this mission. The OCC also issues rules and regulations applicable to state savings associations and certain third parties that provide services to banks.

Federal branches and agencies. A federal branch is a foreign banking organization's (FBO) office licensed by the OCC to exercise such banking powers as accepting nonretail deposits and, subject to separate OCC approval, fiduciary powers. A federal agency is an FBO's office licensed by the OCC to conduct certain banking activities. The federal agency may not, however, accept deposits or exercise fiduciary powers. A federal agency primarily makes commercial loans and finances international transactions.

Comptroller of the Currency. The President, with the advice and consent of the U.S. Senate, appoints the Comptroller of the Currency to head the agency for a five-year term. The Comptroller, as head of the OCC, is responsible for all OCC programs and functions.

The Comptroller also serves as a director of the Federal Deposit Insurance Corporation and is a member of the Financial Stability Oversight Council and Federal Financial Institutions Examination Council.

Joseph M. Otting was sworn in as the 31st Comptroller of the Currency on Nov. 27, 2017.

Federal Reserve Board

The Federal Reserve Board, formally known as the Board of Governors of the Federal Reserve System, was created by the Federal Reserve Act and is the central bank of the United States. The Federal Reserve Board is commonly referred to as the Fed.

Board of Governors. The seven members of the Board of Governors are nominated by the President and confirmed by the Senate. A full term is fourteen years. One term begins every two years, on February 1 of even-numbered years. A member who serves a full term may not be reappointed. A member who completes an unexpired portion of a term may be reappointed. All terms end on their statutory date regardless of the date on which the member is sworn into office. The Chairman and the Vice Chairman of the Board are named by the President from among the members and are confirmed by the Senate. They serve a term of four years. A member's term on the Board is not affected by his or her status as Chairman or Vice Chairman.

General functions. The Fed performs five general functions to foster the effective operation of the U.S. economy and, more generally, the public interest. These five functions are:

1. conducting the nation's monetary policy to promote maximum employment, stable prices, and moderate long-term interest rates in the U.S. economy;

2. promoting the stability of the financial system and seeks to minimize and contain systemic risks through active monitoring and engagement in the U.S. and abroad;

3. promoting the safety and soundness of individual financial institutions and monitoring their impact on the financial system as a whole;

4. fostering payment and settlement system safety and efficiency through services to the banking industry and the U.S. government that facilitate U.S.-dollar transactions and payments; and

5. promoting consumer protection and community development through consumer-focused supervision and examination, research and analysis of emerging consumer issues and trends, community economic development activities, and the administration of consumer laws and regulations.

Regulated entities. By law, the Fed is responsible for supervising and regulating certain segments of the financial industry to ensure they employ safe and sound business practices and comply with all applicable laws and regulations.

Holding companies. The Fed regulates and supervises various types of holding companies.

Bank holding companies (BHCs) own or control a subsidiary bank. The bank could be a national bank, state member bank, or state nonmember bank.

Financial holding companies, which are BHCs that meet certain criteria, may own: broker-dealers engaged in securities underwriting and dealing; and business entities engaged in merchant banking, insurance underwriting, and insurance agency activities. When a financial holding company owns a subsidiary broker-dealer or insurance company, the Fed coordinates its supervisory efforts with those of the subsidiary's functional regulator.

Savings and loan holding companies directly or indirectly control either a savings association or other savings and loan holding companies. Historically, savings and loan holding companies were regulated by other agencies, but the Dodd-Frank Act transferred supervisory and regulatory responsibilities for savings and loan holding companies from the now-defunct Office of Thrift Supervision to the Fed.

State member banks. The Fed is the primary federal supervisor of state-chartered banks that have chosen to join the Federal Reserve System. Such domestically operating banks are called "state member banks."

Edge Act and agreement corporations. Edge Act and agreement corporations are U.S. financial institutions that carry out international banking and financing operations, some of which the parent banks themselves are not permitted to undertake under existing laws. These corporations, which are examined annually, may act as holding companies, provide international banking services, and finance industrial and financial projects abroad, among other activities.

Federal Deposit Insurance Corporation

The third prudential regulator is the Federal Deposit Insurance Corporation. The FDIC is an independent agency created by Congress to maintain stability and public confidence in the nation's financial system by:

- insuring deposits;

- examining and supervising financial institutions for safety and soundness and consumer protection;

- making large and complex financial institutions resolvable; and

- managing receiverships.

Insuring deposits. Deposit insurance is a fundamental component of the FDIC's role in maintaining stability and public confidence in the U.S. financial system. By promoting industry and consumer awareness of deposit insurance, the FDIC protects depositors at banks and savings associations of all sizes. When an insured depository institution fails, the FDIC ensures that the institution's customers have timely access to their insured deposits and other services.

Supervision. Although the FDIC is the insurer for all insured depository institutions in the United States, it is the primary federal supervisor only for state-chartered banks and savings institutions that are not members of the Federal Reserve System. In addition, the FDIC has statutory responsibilities for certain bank holding companies and nonbank financial companies that are designated as systemically important. The FDIC and Fed have joint responsibility for reviewing and assessing resolution plans developed by these companies that demonstrate how they would be resolved in a rapid and orderly manner under the U.S. Bankruptcy Code in the event of financial distress.

In fulfilling its supervisory responsibilities as the primary federal supervisor for state non-member banks and savings institutions, the backup supervisor for other FDIC-insured institutions, and the reviewer of resolution plans, the FDIC pursues three goals:

1. FDIC-insured institutions are safe and sound.

2. Consumers' rights are protected and FDIC-supervised institutions invest in their communities.

3. Large and complex financial institutions are resolvable in an orderly manner under bankruptcy.

Receivership management. Finally, in its capacity as a receiver for a failed bank, the FDIC assumes responsibility for efficiently recovering the maximum amount possible from the disposition of the receivership's assets and the pursuit of the receivership's claims. Funds that are collected from the sale of assets and the disposition of valid claims are distributed to the receivership's creditors according to priorities set by law.

Consumer Financial Protection Bureau

Although not a prudential regulator, the Consumer Financial Protection Bureau plays a role in the banking system as well.

Single point. The CFPB, which was created by the Dodd-Frank Act, is the single point of accountability for enforcing federal consumer financial laws and protecting consumers in the financial marketplace. Before, that responsibility was divided among several agencies, such as the OCC, Fed, FDIC, and Federal Trade Commission.

¶240

Supervisory authority. The Bureau has supervisory authority over banks, thrifts, and credit unions with assets over $10 billion, as well as their affiliates. Banks, thrifts, and credit unions that fall below the $10 billion asset threshold are supervised by the primary state or federal regulator.

The CFPB also has supervisory authority over nonbank mortgage originators and servicers, payday lenders, and private student lenders of all sizes. In addition, the regulator also supervises the larger participants of other consumer financial markets as defined by Bureau rules. These larger participants comprise the following markets: consumer reporting, consumer debt collection, student loan servicing, international money transfer, and automobile financing.

The use of examinations is one of CFPB's key tools to ensure that supervised entities comply with federal consumer financial laws.

Enforcement authority. The Bureau also has the authority to bring enforcement actions against an entity or person that the CFPB believes has violated the law. The Bureau may enforce the law by filing an action in federal district court or by initiating an administrative adjudication proceeding. Administrative proceedings are conducted by an Administrative Law Judge, who holds hearings and issues a recommended decision.

Research and reports. Finally, the CPFB studies "how consumers interact with financial products and services to help identify potential problems in the marketplace and achieve better outcomes for all."

¶ 250 Federal Trade Commission

The Federal Trade Commission (FTC) is sometimes described as the nation's consumer protection agency. However, it has both a consumer protection and a competition mission. While the agency has already used its consumer protection powers to challenge allegedly deceptive conduct involving blockchain and/or virtual currencies, it also has indicated that competition policy too could play a role in the future of the technology.

Enacted in 1914, the FTC Act established the Commission. Originally, the law empowered the Commission to go after "unfair methods of competition." In 1938, Section 5(a) of the Act, 15 U.S.C. Sec. 5(a), was amended to give the agency broad powers to prohibit "unfair or deceptive acts or practices."

In pursuing its dual mission, the FTC views itself primarily as a law enforcement agency, as opposed to a regulator. At the same time, the agency maintains and develops rules and guidance for industry, develops policy in cooperation with other federal agencies, state enforcers, and business and industry, and supports consumer education and business education programs.

In the context of blockchain and virtual currencies, the FTC has engaged in consumer protection enforcement efforts, as well as initiatives to foster agency cooperation and to develop a better understanding of the business and legal issues underlying this nascent technology.

Enforcement efforts. In its effort to protect consumers, the FTC has filed a handful of court actions aimed at allegedly deceptive conduct involving cryptocurrencies that have resulted in consent decrees. One suit, filed jointly with the State of New Jersey, involved allegations that a smartphone app developer lured consumers into downloading an app, purportedly offering free of malware, in order to load the consumers' mobile phones with malicious software to mine virtual currencies for the developer (*FTC v. Equiliv Investments*, FTC File No. 142 3144; U.S.D.C. N.J., Case No. 2:15-cv-04379-KM-JBC). Another federal court complaint alleged deceptive marketing of specialized computers designed to produce Bitcoins (*FTC v. BF Labs, Inc.*, FTC File No.

142 3058; U.S.D.C. W.D. Mo., Case No. 4:14-cv-00815-BCW). In 2018, the FTC brought its first "chain referral scheme" case involving cryptocurrency. The allegations suggested that the so-called "Bitcoin Funding Team" and "My7Network" programs, which were allegedly promoted as a means for consumers to generate income and accumulate wealth by purchasing and donating bitcoin currency to earlier "upline" participants and by recruiting others to do the same, essentially amounted to pyramid schemes (*FTC v. Dluca*, FTC File No. 172 3107; U.S.D.C. S.D. Fla., Case No. 0:18-cv-60379-KMM). In each of these actions, the FTC used traditional theories under Sec. 5 of the FTC Act to target new or novel conduct. It is likely that the agency will continue to take action against old schemes using the new technologies, as well as target new fraudulent conduct that takes a form that the FTC has yet to encounter.

Working group, public outreach. At the same time, the FTC announced its first "chain referral scheme" case in 2018, the agency disclosed the creation of an internal FTC Blockchain Working Group. In an agency blog post attributed to then-FTC Chief Technologist Neil Chilson, three primary goals were identified for the working group: (1) building on FTC staff expertise in cryptocurrency and blockchain technology through resource sharing and by hosting outside experts; (2) facilitating internal communication and external coordination on enforcement actions and other related projects; and (3) serving as an internal forum for brainstorming potential impacts on the FTC's dual missions and how to address those impacts.

The blog post also noted that cryptocurrencies and related technologies likely will affect the FTC's broader consumer protection and competition missions in at least five other ways:

1. cryptocurrency serves as a form of payment and can be used to support fraudulent conduct;

2. cryptocurrency and blockchain technology could be used as a core part of fraud efforts;

3. defendants might have cryptocurrency assets that they might have to turn over to the FTC;

4. competition advocacy might be an appropriate response, as opposed to unnecessary regulation, where cryptocurrency and blockchain technologies disrupt existing industries; and

5. blockchain technologies could address difficult consumer challenges such as micropayments, data privacy, and secure identity.

The working group is intended to enable the FTC to "continue its missions to protect consumers and promote competition in light of cryptocurrency and blockchain developments." With the skills developed at the agency, the FTC will continue hosting public forums on blockchain technology. The agency held its first such workshop in March 2017, at which FTC staff and other experts considered potential applications and consumer implications of blockchain.

"The distributed digital ledger behind blockchain promises to cut out the middleman in a number of industries and streamline a range of different transactions," said FTC Bureau of Consumer Protection Deputy Director Daniel Kaufman in opening remarks at the March 2017 forum. "It has the potential to impact an array of sectors that affect consumer's everyday lives, from payments to cross-border remittances to real estate and much more, with the promise of making transactions more efficient and secure."

With a growing list of enforcement actions and continued efforts to develop expertise, the FTC is likely to continue to be a player in the bitcoin and cryptocurrency space.

¶250

¶ 260 State Regulators

The individual states play an important role in blockchain's technological advancement and as regulators of virtual currency firms. Indeed, state licensing regimes can influence where a virtual currency business sets up shop, and several states have aggressively enforced their securities registration and antifraud rules to the point of effectively shutting down businesses operating outside these strictures. Certain states have also embraced the technological promise of distributed ledgers by permitting businesses to keep records in a blockchain or other digital format, or even doing the same with their own archives.

Specifically with regard to virtual currencies, state governments can have a significant effect on the marketplace by virtue of their regulatory authority. In virtually all states, a person or entity engaged in the business of transmitting money is required to obtain a license. The question of whether virtual currency businesses need to seek licensure under these statutes is more difficult: some state laws specifically require a license for virtual currency transmitters; other states have issued guidance clarifying that a license is not required. In the middle are states whose laws arguably could cover virtual currencies, but which have not provided guidance one way or the other.

Finally, state enforcement plays an important role in restricting virtual currency activities, particularly when it comes to initial coin offerings. As debate continues about whether various coins and tokens are securities requiring registration at the federal or state level, several states have carved out a niche for themselves as aggressive watchdogs monitoring for unlawful coin offerings. In a relatively short period of time, North Carolina, Massachusetts, and especially Texas have emerged as frontrunners in enforcing securities registration and antifraud provisions against virtual currency firms and shutting down violators.

Licensing of Exchanges

With one key exception, states have been slow to respond to the proliferation of virtual-currency exchanges. Most of these businesses are arguably subject to state money transmitter laws, which generally require a business engaged in transmitting money to apply for and obtain a license in the state. Slotting virtual currency exchanges into the existing money transmitter regime is as far as most states have gone to regulate these businesses; a few states that did not already have money transmitter laws on the books even enacted such legislation as it became clear that virtual currencies are not a passing fad.

New York is the key exception. The state took a particularly proactive approach by adopting a licensing regime specifically for virtual currency firms. When then-Superintendent Benjamin Lawsky announced the BitLicense framework in the final weeks of his tenure in 2015, he acknowledged that the Department of Financial Services instinctively thought "to shoehorn these new digital currency firms into our old money transmission rules. However, state money transmission rules date back to the civil war—when there was barely mass communication, let alone an Internet," he said. "How exactly do you set capital requirements for a 'money transmitter' that holds digital currency, which many do not even consider 'money'?" [NYDFS Announces Final Bitlicense Framework for Regulating Digital Currency Firms, June 3, 2015.]

The BitLicense framework was hit with instant criticism over its high application fee, extensive compliance requirements, and one-size-fits-all structure. Many virtual currency firms that had been operating in New York left the state during the 45-day rollout period. The criticism resurfaced when, in April 2018, the then-New York Attorney General launched the Virtual Markets Integrity Initiative, a fact-finding inquiry into the policies and practices of virtual currency trading platforms. [A.G. Schneiderman

Launches Inquiry Into Cryptocurrency "Exchanges," April 17, 2018.] The office sent questionnaires to 13 virtual currency exchanges, including some that had fled the state during the BitLicense rollout. The vocal CEO of one of these expats said that his exchange, Kraken, would not respond to the questionnaire for various reasons, including that the questionnaire amounted to a demand for free consulting work on a two-week deadline. [Kraken's Position on Regulation, Kraken Blog (April 22, 2018), https://blog.kraken.com/post/1561/krakens-position-on-regulation/.] "Ordinarily, we're happy to help government understand our business, however, this is not the way to go about it," Jesse Powell said in a social media post.

Given the backlash in response to the BitLicense framework, it is perhaps no surprise that other states have not followed New York's lead. However, Judith E. Rinearson, a partner in the New York and London offices of K&L Gates, agreed in some respects with Lawsky that the money transmitter laws are not suited to virtual currencies. As one example, she cited provisions requiring licensees to hold, in a bank account or in highly rated securities, a 100-percent reserve equal to the amount the licensee holds for others ("outstandings"). Rinearson asks rhetorically, "Should the reserve be held in cryptocurrency? Or dollars? Banks generally don't hold accounts of cryptocurrencies. But if the reserve is held in dollars, what happens if the value of the cryptocurrency goes up? The customers' funds won't be protected."

A harmonized approach to licensing virtual currency firms may be on the table. The Uniform Law Commission drafted a virtual currency statute for states' consideration that includes anti-money-laundering, cybersecurity, and recordkeeping requirements but stops short of New York's stringent rules. As a rejoinder to New York's one-size-fits-all approach, the uniform legislation offers three tiers of exemption, registration, and licensure based on business volume. [Uniform Regulation of Virtual-Currency Businesses Act (2017).] Full licensure begins at $35,000 of annual business activity, acting as a sort of sandbox for start-ups, Rinearson noted. She added that the low threshold "reflects the underlying view that all cryptocurrency companies actively serving the public really should be licensed."

ICO Registration and Enforcement

Early actions in virtual currency enforcement occurred at the federal level by the SEC and CFTC. At the end of 2017, however, as the number of ICOs and other virtual currency investments continued to grow, state securities commissioners began taking action to detect and halt unregistered virtual currency offerings and enforce antifraud provisions. States exercise dominion over offerings, such as ICOs, by requiring registration when the underlying coin or token has the properties of a security.

Securities regulation as a whole began at the state level, with 32 states having passed "blue sky" laws by 1919, well before the New-Deal-era Securities Act and Securities Exchange Act created a federal regime. At present, all the states have enacted legislation regulating the offering for sale, or sale, of corporate securities, bonds, investment contracts, and stocks. In most jurisdictions, blue sky laws are administered by a securities commission or securities commissioner in recognition of the fact that securities regulation is a full-time job for experts. U.S. regulators also joined their counterparts to the north and south by formally associating as the North American Securities Administrators Association, Inc. (NASAA) for the mutual exchange of ideas in the field of securities administration.

In addition, all jurisdictions now have enacted legislation that provides for both the licensing of dealers and salespersons and the registration of securities. The majority have adopted, or substantially adopted with modifications, the Uniform Securities Act of 1956. More recently, some states have adopted the Uniform Securities Act of 2002 in place of their previous legislation.

¶260

The effect of the state laws on virtual currency offerings means that where the underlying token, coin, or other instrument is a "security" within the state's definition (itself an utterly complicated question that is currently playing out at every level of regulation), the offering must be registered and the dealer must be authorized to conduct the offering in the state.

States did not begin enforcing these laws against ICOs until December 2017, when Texas and Massachusetts both launched sweeps of unregistered offerings and Texas brought the first state enforcement action. [*In the Matter of USI-Tech Ltd., Clifford "Cliff" Thomas and Michael "Mike" Rivera*, ENF-17-CDO-1753, December 20, 2017.] Over just a few months, the state securities regulators racked up a significant number of actions and shut down many operators. Texas's sweep has resulted in seven enforcement actions; Massachusetts obtained five consent orders in which virtual currency operators agreed to cease offerings and filed a complaint against a sixth firm. North Carolina also shut down several of the respondents identified in the other states' actions.

¶ 270 International Regulation

Like U.S. federal and state regulators, international governments have approached virtual currencies by monitoring for unregistered initial coin offerings and similar offerings; warning investors about the possibilities of fraud; and applying licensing, anti-money-laundering, and counter-terrorism requirements to those dealing in virtual currencies. Some countries have gone even further to ban the use of virtual currencies altogether, and a few have experimented with establishing their own national cryptocurrencies.

A Cautious Beginning

Very similar to the U.S. response, the international reaction to Bitcoin and other virtual currencies was initially slow and measured, ramping up as virtual currencies became more prevalent and blockchain technology became explored for a wider range of applications.

One example of this is evident in the eurozone. In February 2017, the European Securities and Markets Authority issued a report concluding that specific regulatory action on distributed ledger technology, including virtual currencies, would be premature. ESMA advised DLT supporters to be mindful of risks when designing and applying DLT solutions and promised to monitor DLT developments to assess whether they create risks not currently addressed by the EU regulatory framework. The group devoted some of the paper to that regulatory regime, specifically analyzing how DLT would map to existing rules. This includes clearing activities (governed by the European Market Infrastructure Regulation and the Markets in Financial Instruments Regulation), settlement activities (Central Securities Depositories Regulation and Settlement Finality Directive), safekeeping and recordkeeping of ownership, and reporting obligations. [*The Distributed Ledger Technology Applied to Securities Markets*, European Securities and Markets Authority, January 7, 2017.]

A year later, ESMA's 2018 supervisory convergence work program acknowledged the rapid pace of financial innovation developments across securities markets in the eurozone. ESMA said that it will analyze the emergence of instruments such as virtual currencies, new platforms like ICOs, and tools such as distributed ledger technology. ESMA also intends to analyze how market participants are embracing regulatory technology to comply with recently implemented regulations and how supervisors are deploying supervisory technology. The analysis will include increased uses of cloud computing to efficiently employ such technologies and the potential cyber risks as firms and supervisors implement the new methods. [*Supervisory Convergence Work Programme 2018*, European Securities and Markets Authority, February 7, 2018).]

In some respects, growth in the virtual currency sector is exaggerating the differences among countries' approaches: where some countries have drawn a hard line, others see an opportunity to welcome industry participants with a receptive regulatory environment. As an example, China has taken steps to crack down on virtual currency offerings and impede Bitcoin mining. Picking up the slack is Japan, once the site of the Mt. Gox Bitcoin exchange that liquidated in 2014, which has officially registered at least 16 cryptocurrency exchanges. China has banned ICOs, while Japan's Virtual Currency Act recognized Bitcoin as a form of currency. Disparate treatment among countries can lead to both regulatory and price arbitrage: from December 2017 to February 2018, Bitcoin traded at a marked premium in South Korea in part due to the government's efforts to curb speculation.

ICOs: Registration and Antifraud

One of the key areas of regulation of virtual currencies centers around ICOs and other offerings. Regulators are striving to find a balance between signaling their receptiveness to developing technologies and protecting investors from fraud. As with securities offerings generally, these interests align: securities commissions require registration to ensure that they can monitor registrants and require disclosures. Virtual currencies complicate this calculus somewhat because of their anonymity or pseudonymity.

Many countries are easing themselves in to this space by treating ICOs as securities offerings within the framework of their existing securities rules. In some cases, this approach is coupled with a regulatory sandbox that allows innovators to test their products. Other countries have specifically targeted virtual currency or token offerings with direct responses that fall along a spectrum from outright bans to tailored registration regimes.

Fitting virtual currency into existing regulations. Among the countries notable for regulating ICOs within the framework of their existing rules are Australia, Canada, the United Kingdom, Germany, and Singapore. Australia, the U.K., and Canada all have regulatory sandboxes that startups can use to test the waters under the existing regime.

Acting relatively early in September 2017, the Australian Securities & Investments Commission released guidance for issuers of ICOs. Although this guidance clarifies the existing regulation's applicability to ICOs, it signaled a willingness to engage in the new technology. "ASIC recognises that ICOs have the potential to make an important contribution to the options available to businesses to raise funds and to investment options available to investors," the information sheet (INFO 225) notes. According to the guidance, the legal status of an ICO depends on how it is structured and operated and on what rights are attached to the coin or token. Some ICOs will be subject only to the general law and consumer laws, but ICOs constituting managed investment schemes, offerings of shares, and offerings of derivatives will be governed by the Corporations Act. If the ICO or underlying coin is found to be a financial product, any platform enabling the purchase, issuance, or sale of the asset may be required to obtain a license.

Provincial governments in Canada, which does not have a federal securities regulator, have indicated a receptive approach to the emerging technology. Via a regulatory sandbox launched by the Canadian Securities Administrators, the Ontario Securities Commission granted conditional relief from registration requirements to an applicant proposing to launch an initial token offering by way of private placement. [*In the Matter of Token Funder, Inc.*, October 17, 2017.] In September 2017, the British Columbia Securities Commission registered an investment fund manager solely dedicated to cryptocurrency investments. [*B.C. Securities Commission grants landmark bitcoin investment fund manager registration*, September 6, 2017.] "We have seen from the market and from investors that there is a strong appetite for access to these kinds of investments," said Zach Masum, leader of the BCSC's Tech Team. "This first registration allows access to bitcoin investments, while providing the BCSC with unique mechanisms to monitor operations in a rapidly developing area." Indeed, Canadian regulators have been active in monitoring their markets for unregistered or fraudulent offerings and shutting down trading where appropriate. USI Tech, which was also the subject of several U.S. state enforcement actions (see ¶ 740), was barred by the securities regulators of Ontario, British Columbia, and Manitoba.

In late 2017, ESMA issued a statement to firms involved in ICOs, along with an alert to investors. [*ESMA alerts firms involved in Initial Coin Offerings (ICOs) to the need to meet relevant regulatory requirements* and *ESMA alerts investors to the high risks of Initial Coin Offerings (ICOs)*, November 13, 2017.] The statement acknowledges that some ICOs may fall outside the bounds of existing rules. "However," it continues, "where the coins or tokens qualify as financial instruments it is likely that the firms involved in ICOs conduct regulated investment activities, such as placing, dealing in or advising on financial instruments or managing or marketing collective investment schemes. Moreover, they may be involved in offering transferable securities to the public." ESMA lists the key EU rules that are likely to apply in these cases:

- The Prospectus Directive, which requires publication of a prospectus before a public offering of transferable securities or the admission to trading of such securities on a regulated market operating in the eurozone;

- The Markets in Financial Instruments Directive (MiFID), which is likely to apply to the process by which a coin or token is created, distributed or traded;

- The Alternative Investment Fund Managers Directive, which could apply to ICOs to the extent they are used to raise capital from investors in accordance with a defined investment policy; and

- The Fourth Anti-Money-Laundering Directive, which requires credit and financial institutions to carry out due diligence on customers and maintain record-keeping and other internal procedures.

The Monetary Authority of Singapore published a guide to digital token offerings that clarifies that "if a digital token constitutes a product regulated under the securities laws administered by MAS, the offer or issue of digital tokens must comply with the applicable securities laws." Such "capital market products" include "any securities, futures contracts and contracts or arrangements for purposes of leveraged foreign exchange trading." MAS will examine the structure and characteristics, including rights, of a digital token in determining if the token is a capital markets product. For example, a token can constitute a share, debenture, or unit in a collective investment scheme. The guide also discusses the extraterritorial application of Singapore's rules to certain activities and contains case studies illustrating the application of existing regulations to hypothetical offerings. [*A Guide to Digital Token Offerings*, available at *http://www.mas.gov.sg/~/media/MAS/Regulations%20and%20Financial%20Stability/Regulations%20Guidance%20and%20Licensing/Securities%20Futures%20and%20Fund%20Management/Regulations%20Guidance%20and%20Licensing/Guidelines/A%20Guide%20to%20Digital%20Token%20Offerings%20%2014%20Nov%202017.pdf.*]

Firms involved in virtual currency may also apply to use Singapore's existing regulatory sandbox for fintech innovators. Application carries the expectation that firms will already have conducted due diligence, such as testing in a lab environment and knowing the legal and regulatory requirements. If MAS approves an application, it will provide regulatory support by relaxing specific requirements for the duration of the sandbox. The entity should notify customers that it is operating in a sandbox, disclose key risks, and obtain acknowledgements from customers.

Dedicated responses to virtual currency and ICOs. Rather than fitting ICOs into existing regulations, several countries have crafted dedicated responses to virtual currencies and tokens. These approaches vary dramatically: where some governments, notably including those of China and South Korea, have instituted outright bans, others have seen an opportunity to welcome the industry to their jurisdiction with tailored regimes that elucidate the regulatory requirements. Australia was one of the first to issue specific guidance for ICOs, described above, while Gibraltar introduced the world's first—and so far only—proposals for token regulations. [*Token Regulation. Proposals for the regulation of token sales, secondary token market platforms, and investment services relating to tokens*, March 9, 2018.]

In September 2017, first China and then South Korea banned ICOs entirely. In February 2018, *China Daily* reported that China's central bank and other financial regulators are preparing a package of measures to further restrict ICOs and both domestic and international cryptocurrency trading, which will be launched "when conditions are ripe." A fintech researcher at Renmin University of China is quoted as saying, "Even though it is difficult to supervise overseas cryptocurrency trading, measures can still be taken including restriction of online trading by blocking internet accounts, shutting down web servers, forbidding illegal traders from leaving the country and enhancing coordination with overseas regulators." [Chen Jia, *China to ban initial coin offerings*, China Daily, February 6, 2018.] South Korea's ICO ban created a traffic jam but not a complete roadblock, and as a result, Bitcoin traded at a premium there until about February 2018. South Korea is reportedly considering reversing the ICO ban and instituting a registration scheme for virtual currency exchanges similar to New York's BitLicense (see ¶ 730). [Kim Yoo-chul, *Korea to allow ICOs with new regulations* The Korea Times, March 8, 2018.]

At the opposite end of the spectrum, Gibraltar crafted rules specifically tailored to ICOs. The first-of-their-kind regulations, which are still in the proposal stage, introduce the concept of an authorized sponsor responsible for compliance. The rules would not regulate technology, tokens, smart contracts, individual public offerings, or persons involved in promotion, sale, and distribution of tokens. Instead, they would regulate the promotion, sale, and distribution of tokens, the operation of secondary market platforms, and the provision of investment and ancillary services relating to tokens.

A major innovation of Gibraltar's proposals is the regime for authorizing and supervising sponsors who will be responsible for complying with the regulations. Authorized sponsors must possess appropriate, relevant knowledge and experience. They may be appointed by the Gibraltar promoter or by the organizers of the offering. Although they may delegate some of their work to others, including by outsourcing work overseas, they remain directly accountable to the Gibraltar Financial Services Commission for the actions of their delegates.

Gibraltar's regulations are meant to address a lack of regulation over token sales that are not structured as securities or debt instruments. "There are risks to the general public and to inexperienced investors, in particular, in subscribing for unregulated crowd financing instruments. Such risks are heightened where underlying products and services have yet to be built, tested and deployed, or market demand established," the proposals note. This warning echoes those issued by dozens of countries. The International Organization of Securities Commissions maintains a repository of regulators' statements on ICOs, which includes both guidance and investor alerts. Of course, these are not discrete issues: guidance may clarify that an ICO is to some extent unregulated which relates to the level of risk it poses to investors. [*Regulators' Statements on Initia*

¶270

Coin Offerings, International Organization of Securities Commissions, available at *http:// www.iosco.org/publications/?subsection=ico-statements.*]

AML and Counter-Terrorism

A separate, but certainly complementary, avenue of regulation in the virtual-currency space is via registration, licensing, or other requirements for exchanges and other firms dealing in currencies. A chief aim of these regimes is to counter money laundering and stem the flow of money to terrorist organizations. By regulating currency businesses, countries can impose anti-money-laundering and know-your-customer (AML/KYC) rules that permit the oversight of customer relationships and fund transfers.

After considering banning virtual currency exchanges entirely, South Korea shifted to banning anonymous trading. Beginning February 2018, all exchanges in South Korea must comply with KYC rules that involve real-time name verification. [Cheang Ming, *New cryptocurrency rules just came into effect in South Korea*, CNBC, January 29, 2018.]

Japan, an early situs of virtual currency trading as the onetime host of the Mt. Gox exchange, has taken a welcoming approach that recognizes virtual currency as a method of payment but requires exchanges to be licensed. The country has registered over a dozen virtual currency exchanges and shut down at least two whose policies and procedures were not up to standards. [Jake Adelstein, *Japan Shuts Down Two Cryptocurrency Exchanges But It May Be Good News For The Industry*, Forbes, March 8, 2018.] In April 2018, the licensed exchanges formed the Japanese Cryptocurrency Exchange Association, a self-regulating body whose standards and framework could be influential outside of the nation. [Samburaj Das, *Japan's 16 Licensed Cryptocurrency Exchanges Launch Self-Regulatory Body*, CNN, April 24, 2018.]

Alongside clarifications that existing rules will apply to certain ICOs (depending on their structure), the Monetary Authority of Singapore also launched consultations on new rules to address money laundering and terrorism-financing risks related to the dealing or exchange of virtual currencies for other currencies, whether virtual or fiat. Under the new payments framework, intermediaries would be required to establish policies, procedures, and controls to address these risks. [MAS Launches Second Consultation on New Regulatory Framework for Payments, November 21, 2017, available at *http://www.mas.gov.sg/News-and-Publications/Media-Releases/2017/MAS-Launches-Second-Consultation-on-New-Regulatory-Framework-for-Payments.aspx*] Similarly, Gibraltar introduced laws to regulate firms using DLT to store or transmit "value belonging to others." Among the nine regulatory principles addressed in the laws are that firms must have systems in place to prevent, detect, and disclose risks such as money laundering and terrorist financing. [*Financial Services (Distributed Ledger Technology Providers) Regulations 2017*, (LN.2017/204), October 12, 2017, available at *http:// gibraltarlaws.gov.gi/articles/2017s204.pdf.*]

In late 2017, Australia amended its Anti-Money-Laundering and Counter-Terrorism-Financing Act to expand its application to digital currencies. Prior to amendment, the Act defined "e-currency" as an electronic means of exchange backed by precious metal, bullion, or other thing prescribed by the AML/CTF rules. The law repeals this definition, substitutes a more expansive definition of "digital currency," and requires digital currency exchanges to register and be subject to expansive existing requirements, including enrolling with the Australian Transaction Reports and Analysis Centre (AUS-TRAC); implementing an AML/CTF program; identifying customers; undertaking due diligence; lodging transaction reports; and complying with recordkeeping requirements. [Anti-Money Laundering and Counter-Terrorism Financing Amendment Act 2017, No. 130, 2017.]

National Currencies

One final area of interest in the international field of virtual-currency developments is the creation by some countries of their own virtual currency. This development can have dramatic consequences for intergovernmental relations. A notable example is Venezuela, where President Nicolas Maduro attempted to evade U.S. sanctions by launching a national virtual currency, reportedly with the help of the Russian government. President Trump issued an executive order stating that "All transactions related to, provision of financing for, and other dealings in, by a United States person or within the United States, any digital currency, digital coin, or digital token, that was issued by, for, or on behalf of the Government of Venezuela on or after January 9, 2018, are prohibited." [Executive Order No. 13827, 83 Fed. Reg. 12469 (March 19, 2018).]

Estonia's own attempt to create a virtual currency, dubbed Estcoin, met a supercilious response by European Central Bank President Mario Draghi. At a September 2017 press conference, Draghi shot down the idea in a single, unequivocal sentence: "No member state can introduce its own currency; the currency of the eurozone is the euro."

¶270

Chapter Three—Securities Regulations

¶ 300 View from the Top

Top leadership at the SEC have expressed a willingness to consider the potential financial innovations and related efficiencies that may result from the further development of distributed ledger technologies (DLT) and blockchain technologies. The SEC, however, has also aggressively brought enforcement actions targeting initial coin offerings (ICOs) when such offerings appear to be offering or selling unregistered securities. Moreover, unlike the CFTC, which has allowed firms to offer Bitcoin futures, the SEC has yet to approve the listing and trading of virtual currency-based commodity-trust shares or virtual currency-themed exchange-traded funds (ETFs).

SEC Chairman Jay Clayton has struck somewhat different tones regarding virtual currencies and blockchain technologies. In February 2018 testimony before the Senate Banking Committee, Chairman Clayton divided the blockchain universe into three categories for purposes of SEC regulation. For one, the SEC lacks direct regulatory oversight of the larger cryptocurrency marketplace. Second, as Chairman Clayton and other top SEC officials have said in other contexts, the SEC remains open to the potential benefits and efficiencies that blockchain or DLT can bring to capital markets. But Chairman Clayton put ICOs in a third category of blockchain activities that can easily run afoul of federal securities laws.

With respect to blockchain regulation and enforcement, the SEC's focus has been on ICOs. At the February Senate Banking Committee hearing, Chairman Clayton made clear his views on ICOs: "To the extent that digital assets like ICOs are securities, and I believe every ICO I have seen is a security, we have jurisdiction and our federal securities laws apply." Chairman Clayton reiterated this view in reply to questioning from Sen. Mark Warner (D-Va): "ICOs that are securities offerings, we should regulate them like we regulate securities offerings. End of story."

Senate Banking Committee Chairman Mike Crapo (R-Idaho) asked both Chairman Clayton and CFTC Chairman J. Christopher Giancarlo, who also testified at the hearing, to come back to the committee with recommendations from a working group set up by the Treasury Department. Chairman Clayton mentioned that regulators, including state regulators, needed to work together to understand how best to deal with ICOs and other blockchain activities. Chairman Giancarlo explained that the Treasury working group on blockchain issues included the SEC, the CFTC, FinCEN, and the Fed. Chairman Clayton later told Sen. Warner, who had asked whether virtual currencies posed systemic risks, that he had already raised similar issues through his membership in the Financial Stability Oversight Council. The discussion of the working group first arose from Chairman Clayton's reply to a question from Sen. Crapo about the SEC's existing authorities, to which Chairman Clayton said the SEC may need new legislative authorities.

As a result, much of the SEC's evolving work on blockchain issues begins in earnest with its enforcement efforts regarding ICOs, both before and after the release of the agency's report of investigation on The DAO. Perhaps the message most often delivered by Chairman Clayton, before the Senate Banking Committee and in speeches and other public statements, is his belief that securities law gatekeepers, such as lawyers, accountants, underwriters, and dealers, have failed to exercise adequate professional skepticism regarding clients who seek to conduct ICOs. That said, however, the SEC has been actively engaged in mulling other aspects of blockchain technologies, including the listing and trading of commodity-trust shares, cryptocurrency ETFs, the issuance of digital shares, and providing guidance on the use of ICO platforms. The SEC also has been asked by private parties to consider more generalized rulemaking regarding digital assets.

¶ 310 The DAO Report: Must Initial Coin Offerings be Registered?

The SEC's report of investigation on The DAO was an effort by the agency to clarify when federal securities laws apply to ICOs. The report also served as a warning to persons who would conduct ICOs without regard for compliance with federal securities laws. As explained in The DAO report, The DAO was a decentralized autonomous organization that was intended to automate many of the functions historically carried out by traditional corporate entities. The DAO also sought investments purchased with virtual currency in exchange for DAO Tokens. Still, the organizational form of The DAO, and the intentions of its founders, were insufficient to avoid application of the federal securities laws to The DAO. [Report of Investigation Pursuant to Section 21(a) of the Securities Exchange Act of 1934: The DAO, Release No. 34-81207, July 25, 2017, Statement by the Divisions of Corporation Finance and Enforcement on the Report of Investigation on The DAO, July 25, 2017, at ¶ 1020; press release, SEC Issues Investigative Report Concluding DAO Tokens, a Digital Asset, Were Securities, July 25, 2017.]

Ultimately, the SEC chose not to bring an enforcement action against The DAO, but the report provides a road map for anyone seeking to analyze whether a particular ICO complies with federal securities laws. The Commission left open the possibility that some tokens or coins might fall outside the securities laws. Said the Commission: "Whether or not a particular transaction involves the offer and sale of a security—regardless of the terminology used—will depend on the facts and circumstances, including the economic realities of the transaction."

Virtual Organization

The DAO consisted of a German-based firm called Slock.it UG and its co-founders, who set up The DAO as a for-profit entity designed to hold assets to be determined via the issuance of DAO Tokens to investors for the purpose of using the resulting assets to fund projects. Projects were to be curated by persons selected by The DAO who would review and then "whitelist" projects for a vote by DAO Token holders. Projects were intended to produce a return on investment for DAO Token holders. DAO Tokens also could be traded on an online secondary market.

According to the Commission, The DAO was the brainchild of Slock.it's chief technology officer, Christoph Jentzsch, who explained the workings of The DAO in a white paper. The DAO was to operate using the Ethereum blockchain and the Ether (ETH) virtual currency. During a one-month period in Spring 2016, The DAO raised 12 million ETH (U.S. Dollar equivalent of $150 million) for sales of 1.15 billion DAO Tokens.

To make investments, a prospective DAO Token holder would create an Ethereum blockchain address from which they could send ETH to The DAO's Ethereum

¶310

blockchain address; DAO Tokens flowed in the opposite direction back to the holder's Ethereum blockchain address. DAO Tokens could be traded on a secondary market or on the Ethereum blockchain. DAO Tokens also could be redeemed via a DAO Entity split, which was designed to guard against a "51 percent Attack" in which an attacker could divert tokens for nefarious purposes.

With respect to proposals to fund projects, a contractor who owned at least one DAO Token and had paid an ETH deposit could submit a smart contract proposal to the Ethereum blockchain and provide details about the proposal on The DAO's website. Proposed projects were then reviewed by The DAO's curators, who ensured basic security features of the proposal and who also exercised substantial discretion over which projects made it on the "whitelist" and, thus, which projects were submitted to a vote of DAO Token holders. Holders of DAO Tokens had to approve a project by a majority vote, although each holder's vote was assigned a weight based on the number of tokens they held.

At one point, after selling DAO Tokens but before funding any projects, an unknown third party hacked The DAO and stole one-third of its assets. The DAO implemented a work-around called a hard fork, which a majority of DAO Token holders approved, and was able to restore the stolen assets to a recovery site. The remedial steps allowed DAO Token holders to recover their investment by using the recovery site to obtain ETH for DAO Tokens.

Applicable Securities Standard

The DAO report made it clear that the SEC believes that federal securities laws can apply to blockchain-enabled ICOs despite attempts by persons operating these ventures to adopt novel forms of organization or to use technology in a novel manner. The Commission reasoned that DAO Tokens were securities under the familiar *Howey* test. [*SEC v. W.J. Howey Co.*, 328 U.S. 293 (1946).] The DAO report cited the Supreme Court's re-worked version of that test: "[t]he 'touchstone' of an investment contract 'is the presence of an investment in a common venture premised on a reasonable expectation of profits to be derived from the entrepreneurial or managerial efforts of others.'"

In the context of ICOs, it is especially important for issuers to grasp the breadth of the term "security." For example, both the Securities Act and the Exchange Act define "security" with reference to numerous specific types of instruments that are deemed to be securities. Both acts also embrace the catch-all term "investment contract" as a type of security. The *Howey* test clarifies that an investment contract has three main components: (1) an investment of money; (2) a common enterprise; and (3) reasonable expectations that others' entrepreneurial or managerial efforts will generate profits. The DAO report reiterates that the *Howey* test is a flexible standard that elevates the substance of a transaction over its form. It is also important to note that not all types of instruments are evaluated using *Howey*. For example, the Supreme Court has articulated the "family resemblance" test for determining when notes are securities. [*Reves v. Ernst & Young*, 494 U.S. 56 (1990).]

Offerings Must be Registered or Exempt from Registration

The implications of applying *Howey* are significant. Securities Act Sections 5(a) and 5(c) work in tandem to make it unlawful to sell, or to offer to sell or offer to buy, any security for which there is no effective registration statement. The initial public offering process can be costly and often takes place over a period of months and sometimes years. In very general terms, the process involves filing a registration statement, typically on Form S-1, followed by a period of SEC staff comment letters directed to the issuer about specific aspects of the offering that trouble Commission staff. Towards the end of the process, there will often be a road show to be followed, eventually, by an effectiveness notice issued by the SEC on EDGAR, the electronic database where the SEC maintains issuers' public filings. One more point to remember is that, despite the intensive staff review of a proposed IPO, the SEC does not endorse securities. In fact, the beginning of a prospectus must include a Commission legend stating that neither the SEC nor any state securities commission approved or disapproved the securities or passed upon the accuracy or adequacy of disclosures contained in the prospectus and that a contrary representation is a crime. [*See*, 17 CFR 229.501.]

The federal securities laws also contain numerous registration exemptions for issuers that seek to raise capital faster and potentially at lower cost than would be possible for a company conducting a traditional IPO. These exemptions each have different requirements and are sometimes limited to accredited investors, who must satisfy income and net worth requirements. Still other requirements may include limits on the resale of securities and compliance with the SEC's bad actor disqualification provisions. Some of the most common registration exemptions include the private offering exemption, offerings conducted pursuant to Regulation A, and offerings conducted under Regulation D. Another specialized exemption exists for issuers who engage in securities-based crowdfunding under Regulation Crowdfunding. When the SEC said in The DAO report that an ICO of securities must either be registered or exempt from registration, it is these types of exemptions the agency had in mind. The following chart summarizes and compares the basic requirements for securities registration exemptions.

Exempt Offerings Compared					
Exemption	Source	Offering limit	Manner of offering	Form	Other requirements
Intrastate exemption	Securities Act § 3(a)(11). [15 U.S.C § 77c(a)(11).]	No		N/A	Offerees must reside in state. 17 CFR 230.147 is a safe harbor. 17 CFR 230.147A allows general solicitation, but sales are limited to in-state residents.
Private offering exemption	Securities Act § 4(a)(2). [15 U.S.C § 77d(a)(2).]	No	No general solicitation.	N/A	
Securities-based crowdfunding exemption	Securities Act § 4(a)(6). [15 U.S.C § 77d(a)(6).]	$1 million (periodically adjusted for inflation; currently $1,070,000)	Issuers must comply with advertising limits.	Form C	

Exempt Offerings Compared					
Exemption	Source	Offering limit	Manner of offering	Form	Other requirements
Regulation A Tier 1 exemption	17 CFR 230.251(a)(1).	$20 million ($6 million offered by affiliated selling security holders)	Testing the waters allowed with limits.	Form 1-A May utilize coordinated review program created by the North American Securities Administrators Association.	Issuer is U.S. or Canadian company and, among other things, is not an Exchange Act reporting company.
Regulation A Tier 2 exemption	17 CFR 230.251(a)(2).	$50 million ($15 million offered by affiliated selling security holders)	Testing the waters allowed with limits.	Form 1-A (State registration requirements are preempted regarding Tier 2 offerings.)	Purchasers must be qualified (17 CFR 230.256). Issuer is U.S. or Canadian company and, among other things, is not an Exchange Act reporting company.
Regulation D exemption for limited offerings and sales	17 CFR 230.504.	$5 million	Limited general solicitation.	Form D	Issuer is not an Exchange Act reporting company, investment company, or development stage company.
Regulation D unlimited offering	17 CFR 230.506(b).	No	No general solicitation.	Form D	Unlimited accredited investors; up to 35 non-accredited investors.
Regulation D unlimited offering	17 CFR 230.506(c).	No	General solicitation allowed.	Form D	Purchasers must be accredited investors and issuer must reasonably verify purchasers' status.

Note: The Commission increased the offering limit for Regulation D, Rule 504 offerings from $1 million to $5 million; the Commission also repealed Rule 505 of Regulation D, which had become redundant after the revision to Rule 504. The Commission also clarified the safe harbor for intrastate offerings and created a new exemption to allow general solicitation in some offerings. [*See*, Exemptions To Facilitate Intrastate and Regional Securities Offerings, Release No. 33-10238, October 26, 2016.] Also, Section 508 of the Economic Growth, Regulatory Relief, and Consumer Protection Act, enacted May 24, 2018, directs the SEC to amend Regulation A to remove the requirement that an issuer not be an Exchange Act reporting company immediately before the offering. [Pub. Law No. 115-174.]

The exemption for overseas transactions also may come into play for ICOs involving coins or tokens that are securities and that occur outside the U.S. For purposes of Regulation S, key terms used in Securities Act Section 5 are inapplicable to transactions in securities that occur outside the U.S. Regulation S also contains an issuer safe harbor that applies, with respect to Securities Act Section 5, to an offer or sale of securities that occurs outside the U.S. that is made in an offshore transaction where there are no direct selling efforts made in the U.S. by the issuer or its agents when certain additional requirements are satisfied. These additional requirements apply to securities that fall into one of three categories. Equity and debt securities can be treated very differently depending on which category applies: in Category 2, equity and debt are subject to a 40-day distribution compliance period; in Category 3, equity securities are subject to a one-year distribution compliance period (six months if the issuer is a reporting issuer), while debt securities are subject to a 40-day distribution compliance period. It is important to pay attention to the type of issuer because the distribution compliance period varies by the type of securities and the type of issuer. Category 1 has no distribution compliance period.

Two terms used in Regulation S deserve a closer look. For one, "offshore transaction" means an offer not made to a person in the U.S. and either (i) the buy order was originated while the buyer was outside the U.S. or the seller reasonably believes the buyer is outside the U.S.; or (ii) for purposes of the issuer and resale safe harbors, the transaction was executed via an established foreign securities exchange or via a designated offshore securities market and neither the seller nor its agents knows the transaction has been pre-arranged with a buyer in the US., respectively. The definition of offshore transaction must be read carefully because some activities are deemed not to be offshore transactions (*e.g.*, offers and sales specifically targeted at identifiable groups of U.S. citizens abroad), while other activities would either meet the definition or would not cause a transaction to fail under Regulation S. Second, "directed selling efforts" covers activities done for the purpose of, or that could be reasonably expected to have the effect of, conditioning the U.S. market for securities issued in reliance on Regulation S, including publishing advertisements in a publication with a general U.S. circulation that refers to a securities offering that relies on Regulation S (some activities, however, are deemed not to constitute directed selling activities). Regulation S contains a similar resale safe harbor. Moreover, Regulation S places limits on equity securities of domestic issuers acquired from the issuer in a transaction subject to Regulation S.

Regulation S, however, is unavailable for a transaction that is part of a plan or scheme to evade U.S. securities registration requirements, even if the transaction would technically comply with U.S. securities laws. The availability of Regulation S also does not affect the need for a person, if required, to register as a broker-dealer. The SEC also retains broad antifraud authorities that reach far beyond the scope of Regulation S. An issuer or others may, furthermore, have to comply with applicable state securities laws. [17 CFR 230.901, *et. seq.*]

Applying the *Howey* Test to The DAO

The DAO report addressed each of the *Howey* factors. First, the report said the exchange of ETH for DAO Tokens was a "contribution of value" that fell within *Howey's* requirement that there be an investment of money. According to a Tenth Circuit case cited by the report, cash is not the only possible way to invest money in an enterprise [*See, Uselton v. Comm. Lovelace Motor Freight, Inc.*, 940 F.2d 564 (10th Cir. 1991)] The report also cited the district court's decision in *Shavers*, an SEC enforcement action in which the court determined that, for purposes of a challenge to its subject matter jurisdiction, Bitcoin was money. *Shavers* is discussed more fully at ¶ 320.

¶310

Second, the report said that The DAO was a common enterprise and that investors had a reasonable expectation of profits based on The DAO's for-profit structure and its promises of a return on investment from projects. This aspect of the report provided the least analysis of any of the *Howey* factors it addressed. The report, however, emphasized the primacy of claims made in The DAO's promotional materials and the broad definition of "profits" employed by *Howey*'s more recent progeny.

The third *Howey* factor, the reasonable expectations that the entrepreneurial or managerial efforts of others will produce profits, generated some of The DAO report's most detailed analysis. Once again, the report cited The DAO's promotional materials and the reliance by investors on oversight provided by The DAO's founders and its curators. A footnote to the report also sought to debunk the notion that investors could not have an expectation of profits because The DAO would fund "projects" that may involve goods or services.

The DAO's curators played a significant role in vetting projects. For example, the curators exercised control over which projects made the whitelist. Despite DAO Token holders' ability to propose that a curator be removed, the reality was that The DAO's curators retained power over whether to allow a vote on such a proposal. Moreover, The DAO's curators cleared all projects and DAO Token holders lacked information to make informed voting decisions even though Slock.it had crated online forums for DAO Token holders. The report concluded that the large number of investors in The DAO, the dispersed nature of The DAO's investors, and the pseudonymous mode of communicating on the online forums combined to deprive The DAO's investors of any meaningful way to exert control over the entity.

Platforms

In addition to applying the definition of "security" to The DAO, the SEC's report looked briefly at the status of platforms that provided for the trading of DAO Tokens. According to the report, the platforms involved with The DAO appeared to be exchanges without an applicable exemption from registration. The SEC's Divisions of Trading and Markets and Enforcement have since issued guidance on ICO platforms. As a result, a more detailed discussion of platforms can be found at ¶ 360.

Unanswered Questions

The SEC's conclusion that The DAO Tokens were part an unregistered securities offering suggests a degree of clarity on the applicability of federal securities laws to ICOs. The fact that the matter did not result in an enforcement action can serve as a warning to those contemplating ICOs. But the report on The DAO also left open some questions about which securities laws, beyond the Securities Act registration requirements, might also apply in the context of ICOs.

Investment companies. In footnote one to The DAO report, the SEC declined to consider in detail whether The DAO was an investment company because The DAO had not begun to fund projects. Section 3 of the Investment Company Act contains a detailed definition of "investment company." [15 U.S.C. § 80a-3.] Moreover, Sections 4 and 5 of the Investment Company Act classify investment companies as face-amount certificate companies, unit investment trusts, or management companies; management companies are further subclassified as either open-end or closed-end and as either diversified or undiversified. [15 U.S.C. § § 80a-4 and 80a-5.] Section 6 of the Investment Company Act contains a number of specific exemptions from the definition of investment company; the provision also grants the Commission broad authority to exempt any person, security, or transaction (or classes of persons, securities, or transactions) from the requirements of the Investment Company Act. [15 U.S.C. § 80a-6.] Section 2 of the Investment Company Act contains a definition of "security" that includes investment contracts. [15 U.S.C. § 80a-2.] An investment company that is an open-end management investment company would initiate the registration process by filing Form N-1A with the Commission. Other registration forms apply for different types of investment companies.

Investment advisers. The SEC noted in footnote 38 to The DAO report that, because The DAO did not fund certain operations, there was no occasion for the SEC to consider whether The DAO was an investment adviser. Nevertheless, the SEC urged similar entities to consider their investment adviser status.

Section 202(a)(11) of the Investment Advisers Act defines "investment adviser" to mean a person who receives compensation as part of a business of advising others about the value of, or the advisability of buying or selling, securities. The same section excludes from this definition a variety of persons, including banks, professionals (such as attorneys), certain broker-dealers, news media outlets, nationally recognized statistical rating organizations, family offices, and any person the Commission determines should not be included in the definition. [15 U.S.C. § 80b-2(a)(11).] The Commission also has exemptive authority under Section 206A of the Investment Advisers Act. An investment adviser registers with the Commission by filing Form ADV. [15 U.S.C. § 80b-6a.]

A further issue arises because of reforms implemented via the Dodd-Frank Act that recalibrated the dividing line between investment advisers that are subject to SEC oversight and advisers that are subject to state regulations. Section 203A of the Investment Advisers Act provides that an adviser that is regulated or must be regulated by the state where its principal office and business are located cannot register with the SEC, among other things, unless it has at least $25 million in assets under management. [15 U.S.C. § 80b-3a.] Moreover, Investment Company Act Rule 203A-1 provides for switching to or from SEC registration and Rule 203A-2 contains a number of exemptions from the prohibition on SEC registration. [17 CFR 275.203A-1 and 17 CFR 275.203A-2.]

An investor can ask the promoters of an ICO if the entity issuing coins or tokens is an investment adviser. The answers to this question can be verified by accessing the SEC's Form ADV online look-up tool, which can be found at https://www.adviserinfo.sec.gov/IAPD/Default.aspx.

Regulation Crowdfunding. The DAO report noted that The DAO claimed to have been the result of an effort to create a "crowdfunding contract" for virtual currencies. That raised the question of whether The DAO would qualify for a registration exemption for securities-based crowdfunding under Securities Act Section 4(a)(6) and Regulation Crowdfunding. [15 U.S.C. § 77d(a)(6).] The DAO report cited The DAO's lack of registration as a broker-dealer or as a funding portal as two reasons why The DAO would not have satisfied Regulation Crowdfunding.

Securities-based crowdfunding is a recent capital raising option enabled by changes made in 2012 to the federal securities laws by the Jumpstart Our Business Startups (JOBS) Act. Securities-based crowdfunding allows issuers to offer securities through a streamlined process via online platforms run by either registered broker-dealers or registered funding portals. However, securities-based crowdfunding is far more complex than more common non-securities-based variants of crowdfunding. As a result, the SEC's Regulation Crowdfunding imposed a complex set of rules on securities-based crowdfunding transactions: (i) issuers are subject to reduced, but still significant, filing requirements; (ii) intermediaries such as registered broker-dealers can offer a wide variety of crowdfunding services; (iii) registered funding portals, the securities law cousins of broker-dealers, likewise must be members of the Financial Industry Regulatory Authority, Inc., (FINRA) but funding portals can offer only more limited services in exchange for lighter SEC regulation as compared to broker-dealers; and (iv) investors

¶310

are subject to strict limits on how much they can invest and crowdfunding securities are subject to resale limits. [*See,* 17 CFR 227.100, *et. seq.*]

¶ 320 SEC Enforcement

Two events stand out as setting the SEC's current tone with respect to enforcement activity related to blockchain and virtual currency matters. The first event was the release of the report of investigation on The DAO establishing that coins or tokens offered via ICOs can be securities that must either be registered with the Commission or subject to an exemption from registration. The second event was the SEC's creation of a new cyber unit within the Division of Enforcement to focus on specific enforcement priorities, including "[v]iolations involving distributed ledger technology and initial coin offerings." [SEC press release, September 25, 2017.]

Typically, an entity contemplating an ICO will issue a white paper explaining its blockchain platform and what types of virtual currency or fiat currency it will accept in exchange for coins or tokens (sometimes utility tokens). ICOs utilize a blockchain or secure DLT. The terms of an ICO may entitle buyers of coins or tokens to certain rights, such as profits, products, or voting. ICOs are often marketed via online channels such as social media websites and may even be promoted by celebrities. Some ICO coins or tokens may trade on secondary markets.

It can be helpful to examine the SEC's enforcement efforts regarding blockchain matters and ICOs both before and after The DAO report. Still, it must be remembered that the blockchain is an emerging issue for the SEC and other government regulators and that the themes that have emerged so far could change in significant ways as regulators come to terms with the blockchain era.

SEC Enforcement Before The DAO Report

Before the SEC issued its report of investigation regarding The DAO, its enforcement cases tended to address a variety of matters and lacked the current focus on ICOs. That said, firms operating in the blockchain and virtual currency space should not assume that ICO enforcement only began after The DAO report because many of the themes found in prior enforcement matters continue to arise in the SEC's more recent administrative proceedings and court cases. Those themes include the following: (i) inclusion of some cryptocurrency-denominated investments within the definition of "security"; (ii) failure to register as an exchange or to register securities; (iii) security-based swaps; and (iv) cybersecurity.

Investments denominated in virtual currencies. One of the SEC's first attempts to bring an enforcement case in the virtual currency space alleged that Trendon T. Shavers and Bitcoin Savings and Trust (BTCST) operated a Ponzi scheme in which Shavers and BTCST raised 700,000 Bitcoins ($4.5 million at then-prevailing exchange rates) from 66 investors in at least seven states. The scheme had promised a seven percent weekly return. Although Shavers returned some funds to investors, he used other funds for personal expenditures, including day-trading (at a loss), selling Bitcoin (for a gain), and to pay personal bills. [*SEC v. Shavers,* No. 13-CV-416 (E.D. Tex. 2013) (complaint).] The case prompted the SEC to issue an Investor Alert warning about the dangers of Ponzi schemes involving virtual currencies.

During the ensuing litigation, Shavers had disputed the court's subject matter jurisdiction over the case, but the court ultimately concluded that the Bitcoin-denominated investments were securities. Shavers had argued that the BTCST investments were not money and, thus, were beyond U.S. regulation; Shavers also had argued that the transactions cited by the SEC involved only Bitcoin, not money. The SEC, by contrast, argued that the BTCST investments were either investment contracts or notes subject to the federal securities laws. The court applied the *Howey* test and found that:

(i) Bitcoin is money because it can be exchanged for government-issued currencies; (ii) the relationship between Shavers and his investors exhibited the "interdependence" required by Fifth Circuit precedent to indicate the presence of a common enterprise; and (iii) investors expected Shavers to generate profits. As a result, the court found that it had subject matter jurisdiction over the case. [*SEC v. Shavers*, (E.D. Tex. 2013).]

Unregistered securities and exchanges. In one early settled administrative matter, the SEC charged that the respondent offered unregistered securities via two unregistered entities through the Global Bitcoin Stock Exchange and the MPEx platform. One offering involved 30,000 shares and raised 2,600 Bitcoin worth about $15,000. The issuing entity's business involved paying others to resend sponsored messages via social media. A second series of offerings sold 13 million shares for 50,600 Bitcoin worth about $723,000; the second offering also involved a share buyback at a stated percentage of Bitcoin per share and amounted to $3.8 million, well above the amount raised because the Bitcoin exchange rate had risen during the intervening time period. The second issuing entity operated a gaming business that paid winnings in Bitcoin.

Then-SEC Enforcement Director Andrew J. Ceresney said in a press release that the SEC would continue to enforce federal securities laws regarding unregistered offerings that involve virtual currencies. [SEC press release, June 3, 2014.] The SEC concluded that the offering violated Securities Act Sections 5(a) and 5(c). As a result, the respondent was ordered to cease and desist from violating these provisions, undertook not to participate in unregistered securities offerings involving virtual currencies for five years, and was ordered to pay disgorgement of nearly $16,000 and civil money penalties of $35,000. The respondent settled the matter without admitting or denying the SEC's findings. [*In the Matter of Erik T. Voorhees*, Release No. 33-9592, June 3, 2014.]

Another representative enforcement action from this period involved defendants who sold $19 million in shares in a virtual currency mining operation via investment contracts called "Hashlets," which consisted of the right to profit from portions of the defendants' computing power. The SEC's complaint explained that virtual currencies often are structured to provide benefits to "miners" who employ significant computing power to solve complex mathematical algorithms. The SEC charged that the defendants offered unregistered securities and that they misrepresented the nature of the mining operation (*e.g.*, that "Hashlets" were "profitable" or would never be "obsolete," that Hashlets represented actual mining activity, and that one of the businesses was engaged in mining when it was not). With respect to the investment contract character of the Hashlets, the SEC alleged that investors paid for Hashlets in U.S. dollars or Bitcoin, that investors needed only to "click-and-drag" to select "mining pools," and that investors otherwise relied on the defendants' efforts to generate profits. The SEC noted that aspects of the scheme were Ponzi-like because the defendants sometimes used investors' funds to pay off other investors. The case, filed in federal court in Connecticut, sought permanent injunctions, disgorgement, and civil money penalties. [*SEC v. Garza*, December 1, 2015.]

In yet another settled administrative action, Burnside LTC-Global and BTC Trading Corp. were operated as "virtual exchanges" designed to allow users to list initial and secondary securities offerings. BTC Trading provided a platform where persons could invest in securities offerings, with registered users being able to choose from a variety of trade types. The SEC alleged that Ethan Burnside created the exchanges without registering them with the Commission and without claiming an exemption from registration. The SEC also alleged that Burnside and BTC Trading received transaction-based compensation for their services. As a result, the SEC charged Burnside with failing to register as a broker-dealer. Moreover, Burnside had offered to buy and sell shares of LTC-Global securities and bonds of LTC-Mining securities, which, according

¶320

to the SEC, were transactions that involved unregistered securities without any relevant exemption from registration.

Burnside and BTC Trading agreed to settle the SEC's charges without admitting or denying the Commission's findings. Burnside and BTC Trading were subjected to cease and desist orders for their violations of federal securities law, Burnside for Securities Act violations, and BTC Trading for Exchange Act violations. Moreover, Burnside was ordered to pay disgorgement of $58,387 and to pay a $10,000 civil money penalty while also being subjected to associational and penny stock bars. The Commission's order explained that the amount of the civil money penalty was held to no more than $10,000 because of Burnside's cooperation with the SEC's investigation. [*In the Matter of BTC Trading, Corp.*, Release No. 33-9685, December 8, 2014.]

Regulation M. The SEC's Regulation M exists to prevent manipulative conduct in connection with the distribution of securities. Thus, Rule 101 of Regulation M prohibits certain activities by distribution participants during the restricted period; the term "distribution participant" includes underwriters and broker-dealers who agree to participate or are participating in a distribution. [17 CFR 242.100 and 17 CFR 242.101.] Rule 102 of Regulation M likewise prohibits similar conduct by issuers and selling security holders during the restricted period. [17 CFR 242.102.] Regulation M defines "distribution" as an offering of securities (it does not matter that the securities are unregistered) that is different from "ordinary trading transactions" because of the "magnitude" of the offering and any "special selling efforts and selling methods." The duration of the restricted period varies depending on whether the security has certain characteristics or involves a merger or acquisition. However, the general restricted period begins five business days before the offering price is set (or when a person becomes a distribution participant) and ends when the person's participation in the distribution is complete. [17 CFR 242.100.]

A settled administrative action prior to The DAO report involved Bitcoin Investment Trust (BIT) and SecondMarket, both units of Digital Currency Group. BIT planned to offer BIT shares to accredited investors pursuant to Regulation D. SecondMarket capitalized BIT by buying 178,000 shares for 17,800 Bitcoin. BIT then offered shares to investors in 100 share baskets. Because BIT shares were restricted shares, they were subject to resale limits. However, during the restricted period, SecondMarket bought BIT shares from shareholders and BIT bought BIT shares from SecondMarket. The SEC concluded that, for purposes of Regulation M, the BIT offering was a "distribution" because of the magnitude of sales and the sales methods employed, that BIT shares were "covered securities," and that SecondMarket was a "distribution participant." As a result, SecondMarket, acting as BIT's authorized participant, violated Rule 101 of Regulation M, and BIT violated Rule 102 of Regulation M.

The SEC imposed cease and desist orders on both BIT and SecondMarket. SecondMarket also was ordered to disgorge $53,756. In setting the penalties, the SEC said it had considered that fact that SecondMarket sought the advice of legal counsel regarding BIT's redemption program. BIT and SecondMarket neither admitted nor denied the SEC's findings. [*In the Matter of Bitcoin Investment Trust*, Release No. 34-78282, July 11, 2016.]

Trading suspensions. The SEC halted trading in at least one company's cryptocurrency-related securities before The DAO report. Specifically, the SEC took action against Sunshine Capital, Inc. because of the lack of current information about the company and because of representations the company made in a press release regarding the liquidity and value of its assets, which included a cryptocurrency called DIBCOINS. [*In the Matter of Sunshine Capital, Inc.*, File No. 500-1, April 11, 2017.]

¶320

Cryptocurrencies and security-based swaps. The SEC alleged that Sand Hill Exchange and two individuals violated the registration requirements for security-based swaps contained in Exchange Act Sections 5 and 6, as amended by the Dodd-Frank Act. Sand Hill Exchange started its business by offering a financial variant of "fantasy sports" that ultimately morphed into other forms over time. Users funded accounts with U.S. dollars or Bitcoin. One iteration of the business consisted of a "contest" in which users of the firm's website could value companies for purposes of producing a "consensus" valuation. A later variant of the firm's business model involved a game in which users bet whether companies' consensus valuations would rise or fall. Sand Hill's online marketing materials described the game variant as "a market for smart contracts on the future valuation of startups."

The SEC alleged that the contracts were security-based swaps. The respondents agreed to settle the matter without admitting or denying the Commission's findings. As a condition of the settlement, the respondents agreed to state on the firm's website that it no longer offers "smart contracts" or transactions based on actual money; Sand Hill also agreed to provide refunds to users of its website. Moreover, the SEC ordered all of the respondents to cease and desist from further violations, and Sand Hill was ordered to pay a $20,000 civil money penalty. [*In the Matter of Sand Hill Exchange*, Release No. 33-9809, June 17, 2015.]

The enforcement action also prompted an SEC Investor Alert that, among other things, noted the following: "As is the case with many types of online transactions, these websites might allow you to provide your payment or fee (or claim your prize) in Bitcoins or some other type of virtual currency. Don't be fooled—simply denominating a transaction in something other than cash does not make an otherwise illegal offer or sale of a security-based swap suddenly legal." [Investor Alert: Beware of Fantasy Stock Trading Websites Offering Real Returns, June 17, 2015.]

Ransom for customer data. In one settled administrative proceeding, Morgan Stanley Smith Barney LLC agreed to pay a $1 million civil money penalty for its violation of the safeguards rule contained in Rule 30 of Regulation S-P. [17 CFR 248.30.] The SEC had alleged that a former MSSB employee pilfered MSSB data on 730,000 customer accounts (330,000 households) and that the data had turned up on the Internet for sale in exchange for Speedcoins, a form of digital currency. The employee denied posting the data to Internet websites, but forensic analysis showed that the employee's personal server likely had been hacked by a third party who then posted the data on the Internet.

The former MSSB employee pleaded guilty to a criminal information regarding his abuse of his access to MSSB's computers and was sentenced to 36 months of probation and ordered to pay restitution of $600,000. The SEC, in its civil proceeding, also imposed associational and penny stock bars on the employee.

Although the matter is not directly involved with regulation of virtual currencies, it demonstrates the cybersecurity and related regulatory risks associated with the safekeeping of customer data and the potential that hackers may sell such data in exchange for virtual currencies or may demand ransoms to be paid in virtual currencies in exchange for returning stolen data. [*In the Matter of Morgan Stanley Smith Barney LLC*, Release No. 34-78021, June 8, 2016.]

The SEC's Focus on ICOs After The DAO Report

The report of investigation on The DAO, coupled with the creation of the Enforcement Division's cyber unit, has given the SEC's enforcement agenda a clearer emphasis on ICOs. But within this emphasis, several themes have emerged: unregistered securities, unregistered exchanges, fraud, and misappropriation of funds. Another theme that has emerged in several enforcement matters concerns the degree to which the SEC

¶320

may, at least informally, credit prompt remedial action by persons associated with ICOs the SEC believes may have violated federal securities laws. In several instances, the SEC's action has been accompanied by parallel federal criminal charges. The following discussion of post-The DAO enforcement matters is organized topically to highlight specific details about the types of charges brought by the SEC, but, in many instances, the charges touch multiple, overlapping topics.

Unregistered securities. In early December 2017, the SEC brought its first case involving an ICO after having created the Enforcement Division's cyber unit. The case against PlexCorps was filed on an emergency basis to stop a recidivist Canadian securities violator and others from defrauding investors and is typical of the SEC's ICO cases so far in that it charges multiple types of violations. The ICO allegedly raised $15 million via promised returns of 1,354 percent in fewer than 29 days. The company also allegedly falsely claimed that a "team" of experts had been secreted around the world to prevent them from being lured by competitors, the promise of developing other products, and "enormous" and "real" returns. The SEC alleged that there was no "team" beyond a skeleton crew in Canada and that at least one executive's identity was hidden from investors due to his prior securities violations.

Robert Cohen, chief of the SEC's Cyber Unit, suggested that the PlexCorps case was clearly within the unit's wheelhouse. "This first Cyber Unit case hits all of the characteristics of a full-fledged cyber scam and is exactly the kind of misconduct the unit will be pursuing." [SEC press release, December 4, 2017.] PlexCorps was charged with violating the Securities Act's registration requirements because the company neither registered its securities nor could it claim any relevant exemption from registration. PlexCorps and its executives also were charged with violating the antifraud provisions of both the Securities Act and the Exchange Act. The SEC sought a temporary restraining order and preliminary injunction, cease and desist orders, permanent injunctions, disgorgement, officer and director bars, a bar on two defendants from engaging in digital securities offerings, and civil money penalties. The SEC also obtained a court order freezing the assets of PlexCorps and two individuals. [*SEC v. PlexCorps*, December 1, 2017.]

Within days after the SEC took emergency action in the case of PlexCorps., the agency announced a significant administrative matter in which Munchee, Inc. agreed, without admitting or denying the SEC's findings, to cease and desist from violating federal securities laws regarding the company's planned utility token offering. Munchee planned to raise $15 million via sales of its MUN token to help the company develop a smartphone app that would allow users to post restaurant reviews. Munchee said it would offer a finite number of MUN tokens on the Ethereum blockchain, although initially only 45 percent of the tokens would be offered to prospective buyers and the company said it may eventually "burn" MUN to further increase the value of MUN ("burn[ing]" means to remove tokens out of circulation). Munchee also said it could increase the value of MUN by implementing a tiered system of payments for app reviews based on how much MUN the reviewer held. MUN tokens were expected to trade on secondary markets.

Munchee's white paper touted its concept for an "ecosystem" consisting of MUN payments to reviewers, advertising sales, in-app purchases, and facilitating the use of MUN to buy food at restaurants (restaurants also might reward users of Munchee's app). The white paper also mentioned the SEC's The DAO report and summarily concluded that Munchee's token offering did not present any securities issues, although, as the SEC's order noted, the white paper never explained how Munchee reached that conclusion. The Munchee app was available only in the U.S., but the MUN token offering was promoted globally via social media. Munchee and about 40 investors entered into irrevocable contracts for sale, but no MUN tokens were ever delivered and

Munchee returned proceeds to buyers. The SEC alleged that Munchee had not registered the MUN token as a security and was ineligible for any registration exemption.

The SEC's order walked through the Supreme Court's *Howey* test in the context of Munchee and quickly concluded that the planned MUN token offering was an investment contract within the definition of "security" in the Securities Act. According to the SEC, Munchee's white paper and promotional efforts via social media gave potential buyers both a reasonable expectation of profits and showed that investors would be relying on the entrepreneurial and managerial efforts of Munchee's agents. But the SEC's order went a step further and opined on the securities law status of utility tokens. Said the SEC: "Even if MUN tokens had a practical use at the time of the offering, it would not preclude the token from being a security. Determining whether a transaction involves a security does not turn on labelling—such as characterizing an ICO as involving a 'utility token'—but instead requires an assessment of 'the economic realities underlying a transaction.' All of the relevant facts and circumstances are considered in making that determination" (citation to Supreme Court precedent omitted). [*In the Matter of Munchee, Inc.*, Release No. 33-10445, December 11, 2017.]

Unregistered exchanges. The SEC brought a civil case in the federal court in Manhattan against Jon Montroll and BitFunder in which the agency made a variety of allegations, including that BitFunder was operated as an unregistered exchange and without any relevant exemption from registration. Montroll created BitFunder for the purpose of allowing users to list "assets" or "asset shares" to be sold in initial and follow-on offerings and to be traded on a secondary market. BitFunder had nearly 6,500 registered users (about half of the accounts were active) and approximately 56 asset issuers whose asset shares were listed on BitFunder, although the asset shares were not registered with the SEC. BitFunder charged transaction-based fees for certain of its services. Users were required to make deposits of Bitcoin into a wallet that Montroll controlled; withdrawals from the wallet were to be made via user request.

Montroll eventually withdrew nearly 5,000 Bitcoin from the wallet and deposited them in multiple locations. Some of the deposits were then exchanged for U.S. dollars, which Montroll then used to pay his personal expenses. The SEC said some of the other withdrawals went to locations and were used for purposes that were difficult to discern because of the pseudonymous nature of the blockchain.

As an indicator of how wide-ranging some of the SEC's cases in the blockchain space can be, the SEC also alleged that Montroll sold unregistered securities in the form of notes, which sometimes paid interest, via the BitFunder platform. Montroll told investors that the notes were a "personal loan" to be used for "personal investment purposes." The SEC, however, said Montroll used the notes to replace misappropriated Bitcoins and for his personal expenses. According to the SEC, the notes were securities that had not been registered and did not fit any applicable exemption from registration.

Moreover, the SEC alleged that Montroll failed to disclose a cyberattack on BitFunder allegedly perpetrated by BitFunder users that resulted in the theft of more than 6,000 Bitcoins. Montroll also withdrew more Bitcoins from the wallet and used portions of those withdrawals for his personal expenses. Montroll eventually closed BitFunder. [*SEC v. Montroll*, February 21, 2018).]

Fraud. Several SEC matters stand out for their allegations of securities fraud, which, in some cases, were accompanied by parallel criminal charges. Charges typically involve Exchange Act Section 10(b) and Rule 10b-5 and/or Securities Act Section 17(a). [15 U.S.C. § 77q(a); 15 U.S.C. § 78j(b); 17 CFR 240.10b-5.]

¶320

In one case, the SEC alleged that Maksim Zaslavskiy, the sole owner of two entities, REcoin and Diamond, raised $300,000 via ICOs from investors based on a scheme to convert fiat or digital currencies into tokenized currencies backed by real estate and diamonds with the expectation that the real estate or physical assets and/or the tokens would appreciate in value. The SEC claimed that the REcoin ICO investments were securities and that Zaslavskiy made numerous misrepresentations to investors, including that: (i) REcoin never bought real estate despite saying real estate backed the investments; (ii) implied that the entity raised $2.3 million but the reality was that REcoin raised only $300,000; (iii) despite claims of a team of experts, there was no team of experts and instead it was Zaslavskiy who alone ran REcoin; (iv) despite claims to use blockchain technology, REcoin investors got no digital assets; (v) although the holder of a masters of law degree, Zaslavskiy never consulted legal counsel about the legality of the REcoin offering despite claiming the offering complied with applicable laws.

As with the REcoin offering, the SEC alleged that the Diamond investments were securities. The Diamond ICO claimed that a Diamond Reserve Coin (hedged by physical assets) was available via an initial membership offering, which Zaslavskiy asserted was different from an ICO or initial public offering, distinctions the SEC alleged were a "sham." After stopping the REcoin offering because Zaslavskiy had determined a coin backed by illiquid real estate was not possible (he had previously testified that a government contract or government interference was to blame), Zaslavskiy offered REcoin investors a refund or the opportunity to invest at a discount in the Diamond ICO.

The bulk of the SEC's case against Zaslavskiy involved claims of securities fraud under Exchange Act Section 10(b) and Rule 10b-5 and under Securities Act Section 17(a). The SEC also alleged that Zaslavskiy offered to sell unregistered securities. The SEC sought temporary, preliminary and permanent injunctions, an asset freeze, repatriation of overseas assets, disgorgement, an officer and director bar, a ban on participating in digital securities offerings, and civil money penalties. Federal prosecutors in the Eastern District of New York brought related criminal charges against Zaslavskiy. [*SEC v. REcoin Group Foundation, LLC*, September 29, 2017); *U.S. v. Zaslavskiy*, October 27, 2017).]

In another case, the SEC alleged that Sohrab "Sam" Sharma and Robert Farkas raised $32 million through Centra Tech., Inc., which had issued unregistered securities via an ICO of the Centra Token, a token that was to leverage the Ethereum blockchain. The offering was expected to fund projects that would enable holders of the "Centra Card" to convert virtual currencies, some of which are not easy to spend, into U.S. dollars. The ICO also was expected to enable users to partake of a rewards program regarding Centra Tech's future earnings. The SEC alleged that Sharma and Farkas misrepresented Centra Tech's ties to major credit card companies, that the defendants boasted of fictitious executives, and that they misled investors about the potential to earn dividends. The SEC also alleged that the ICO tokens were issued without being registered and without an applicable exemption for their issuance. The SEC's complaint specifically noted that the Centra ICO had occurred after the SEC issued a report of investigation on The DAO. The SEC's case focused on alleged violations of Exchange Act Section 10(b) and Rule 10b-5, Securities Act Sections 17(a)(1)-(3), and Securities Act Sections 5(a) and 5(c). [15 U.S.C. §§ 77e(a) and 77e(c); 15 U.S.C. § 77q(a)(1)-(3); 15 U.S.C. § 78j(b); 17 CFR 240.10b-5.] As a result, the SEC sought permanent injunctions, officer and director bars, a permanent bar on the defendants' participation in any offering of digital securities, disgorgement, and civil money penalties. Federal prosecutors in Manhattan filed related criminal charges. [*SEC v. Sharma*, April 2, 2018; *U.S. v. Sharma*, March 31, 2018.]

Lastly, the SEC brought a federal court action against AirseBank and its executives over AriseBank's ICO of AriseCoin, which AriseBank had claimed raised $600 million of its $1 billion goal. AriseBank claimed to be the first "decentralized" bank with plans to offer services regarding 700 virtual currencies. AriseBank also had claimed it possessed technology to facilitate automatic trading in virtual currencies from which it would take a "broker fee." AriseBank further claimed to have a related branding deal with a major credit card issuer. The SEC alleged that AriseBank had falsely stated it had FDIC insurance and that it had a deal with the credit card company. AriseBank also allegedly failed to disclose the criminal history of an executive. Moreover, the SEC asserted that the coin offering involved unregistered securities and that no exemption from registration applied.

The SEC's complaint detailed violations of the antifraud provisions of the Securities Act and the Exchange Act. As a result, the SEC sought a range of remedies against AriseBank, including a temporary restraining order, an asset freeze, preliminary and permanent injunctions, a ban on defendants' participating in ICOs, officer and director bars, disgorgement, and civil money penalties. [*SEC v. AriseBank*, February 2, 2018 (first amended complaint).]

Trading suspensions. The SEC also has aggressively pursued trading suspensions in several matters involving ICOs. These matters have some overlap with concerns about firms that change their names or business models to reflect blockchain or coin businesses (business model changes are discussed more fully below). In one instance, the SEC temporarily suspended trading in three firms, Cherubim Interests, Inc., PDX Partners, Inc., and Victura Construction Group, Inc., after these firms announced they had acquired "AAA-rated assets from a subsidiary of a private equity investor in cryptocurrency and blockchain technology." In each instance, the SEC expressed concerns about the nature of the companies' business and the value of their assets. With respect to Cherubim, the SEC expressed further concerns about the company's delinquent periodic filings and its plans to conduct an ICO. [*In the Matter of Cherubim Interests, Inc.*, File No. 500-1, February 15, 2018; *In the Matter of PDX Partners, Inc.*, File No. 500-1, February 15, 2018; *In the Matter of Victura Construction Group, Inc.*, File No. 500-1, February 15, 2018.]

In other instances, the SEC has halted trading of the stock in firms where questions arose about the accuracy of those firms' SEC filings or other information in the marketplace or where there was unusual trading activity in the firms' stock, including the possibility of market manipulation. In one matter, the SEC noted the blockchain business of the firm's subsidiary. [*In The Matter Of UBI Blockchain Internet, Ltd.*, File No. 500-1, January 5, 2018; *In the Matter of HD View 360 Inc.*, File No. 500-1, March 1, 2018.]

In a matter involving The Crypto Company, the SEC cautioned broker-dealers, shareholders, and prospective purchasers to carefully review any information about the firm. The SEC further warned broker-dealers about making sure that they follow all the requirements of the applicable Exchange Act rule. Specifically, Rule 15c2-11 makes it unlawful for a broker-dealer to publish a quote for a security or to submit such quote for publication unless the broker-dealer's records contain information specified by the rule, and, based on the broker-dealer's review of that and other information specified by the rule, the broker-dealer reasonably believes under the circumstances that the information is materially accurate and that the information comes from reliable sources. [*In the matter of The Crypto Company*, File No.500-1, December 18, 2017; Release No. 34-82347, December 18, 2017; 17 CFR 240.15c2-11; *See also*, Initiation or Resumption of Quotations Without Specified Information, Release No. 34-29094, April 17, 1991.]

¶320

Name changes and business model pivots. Some companies have contemplated changes to their names to highlight supposed business units dealing with blockchain technology. Still other companies have acquired blockchain or coin firms in an effort to expand their business models to include more technologically focused business units. Such changes may, for example, raise questions about whether the name or business model change legitimately reflects the business being conducted by the company. SEC Chairman Clayton raised the prospect of SEC enforcement in this area during a speech in January 2018. "The SEC is looking closely at the disclosures of public companies that shift their business models to capitalize on the perceived promise of distributed ledger technology and whether the disclosures comply with the securities laws, particularly in the case of an offering," said Clayton. [Jay Clayton, Opening Remarks at the Securities Regulation Institute, January 22, 2018.]

A recent SEC case, however, suggests that business model changes could become a growing focus for the agency, although the case itself involved charges that company executives distributed unregistered, restricted stock in violation of federal securities laws. The company, which held trade receivables and payables without holding significant physical assets, obtained multiple notices of qualification for Regulation A offerings and eventually registered its securities under the Exchange Act and later was listed on Nasdaq. Then, the company acquired the right to use the trade name and website of a company described as a "blockchain-empowered solutions provider" that offered financial services tied to its Ziddu coins (but the acquired company, Ziddu.com, had no value). Following the Ziddu.com acquisition, the company's share price soared 2,662 percent within three days of the announcement of the acquisition. The immediate result of the SEC's action was to obtain a court order freezing $27 million in proceeds from allegedly unlawful stock distributions and sales. [*SEC v. Longfin Corp.*, April 4, 2018; SEC press release, April 6, 2018.] The U.S. District Court for the Southern District of New York has since granted the SEC's request for a preliminary injunction with respect to three individual defendants; a temporary restraining order was vacated regarding the company and a fourth individual defendant who lacked assets that could be frozen. [*SEC v. Longfin Corp.*, May 1, 2018, Cote, D.] The SEC's action against Longfin Corp. has spurred at least one private securities class action lawsuit alleging violations of Exchange Act Section 10(b) and Rule 10b-5 plus a controlling person claim under Exchange Act Section 20(a). [*Wei v. Longfin Corp.*, April 19, 2018.]

In yet another case, the SEC stopped an allegedly fraudulent ICO on an emergency basis. According to the SEC's complaint, the company raised $21 Million based on misrepresentations about its relationships with other companies and with the Fed. The SEC also obtained a court order freezing the company's assets and appointing a receiver. [*SEC v. Titanium Blockchain Infra-structure Services, Inc.*, May 22, 2018.]

Respondents' prompt remedial actions. Although it is difficult to infer a trend from only a few representative matters, there have been instances where it appears that the SEC exercised restraint in imposing penalties in administrative matters if the respondents had taken prompt remedial actions. The SEC has appeared to limit penalties in at least two settled administrative proceedings—one before and one after, the issuance of The DAO report.

In the more recent matter, Munchee Inc. had quickly shuttered its business after the SEC informed Munchee that its token may violate federal securities laws. Munchee had offered and sold digital tokens known as "MUN" in relation to its smartphone application that would allow users to post photographs and reviews of restaurants. The ICO was expected to raise $15 million that would be used to further develop the smartphone application. Munchee ended the ICO within hours of the SEC contacting the company during what was supposed to be day two of the ICO. The SEC ordered Munchee to cease and desist from violating federal securities laws, but it escaped the imposition of a civil penalty because of its prompt remedial actions in shutting down its ICO and returning any proceeds to investors. Munchee agreed to settle the matter without admitting or denying the SEC's findings. [*In The Matter of Munchee Inc.*, Release No. 33-10445, December 11, 2017.]

With respect to a pre-The DAO report matter regarding BTC Trading, the SEC had cited BTC Trading's failure to register the securities involved and its failure to register as an exchange. The SEC noted that BTC Trading's founder, Ethan Burnside, began to shutter two websites after the SEC contacted him. In one section of the order, the Commission acknowledged Burnside's "early and substantial assistance," which also involved the orderly shutdown of his operations, including withdrawals of Bitcoins and Litecoins by users, and his aiding Commission staff in understanding "an emerging technology." Burnside and BTC Trading were subjected to cease-and-desist orders for their violations of federal securities law, Burnside for Securities Act violations, and BTC Trading for Exchange Act violations; Burnside also was subjected to associational and penny stock bars. Moreover, Burnside was ordered to pay disgorgement of $58,387 and a $10,000 civil money penalty. The amount of the civil money penalty, however, was held to no more than $10,000 because of Burnside's cooperation with the SEC. [*In the Matter of BTC Trading, Corp.*, Release No. 33-9685, December 8, 2014.]

SEC Examination Priorities

The SEC's Office of Compliance Inspections and Examinations (OCIE) 2018 examination priorities for broker-dealers and advisers includes blockchain and ICO goals. Specifically, OCIE said it will be monitoring blockchain and ICO developments because of the potential risk to investors and the rapid growth of blockchain and ICO services provided by entities within OCIE's purview. Examinations of entities with respect to blockchain and ICO matters will focus on controls, safeguards, and risk disclosures to investors. [2018 National Exam Program Examination Priorities.] FINRA, which oversees many of the same entities as does OCIE, has publicly announced similar enforcement priorities for 2018 (See ¶ 370).

Investor Alerts and Bulletins

The SEC has issued a variety of investor alerts on virtual currencies and ICOs. A consistent theme is the need for investors to be vigilant against sales tactics intended to pressure them into making an investment in a product or service they do not fully understand. Investor alerts are available on the SEC's website at www.investor.gov.

- Investor Alert: Celebrity Endorsements (November 1, 2017).

- Investor Alert: Public Companies Making ICO-Related Claims (August 28, 2017).

- Investor Bulletin: Initial Coin Offerings (July 25, 2017).

- Investor Bulletin: Be Cautious of SAFEs in Crowdfunding (May 9, 2017).

- Investor Alert: Bitcoin and Other Virtual Currency-Related Investments (May 7, 2014).

- Investor Alert: Ponzi Schemes Using Virtual Currencies (July 23, 2013).

¶ 330 Listing of Commodity Trust Shares on Securities Exchanges

Financial technology or fintech encompasses diverse digitally driven products and services, including blockchain and digital assets such as virtual currencies. The Commission already has concluded that certain Ethereum-based tokens are securities. Moreover, the Commission may weigh in on the listing and trading of virtual currency-themed products now that the agency's Division of Trading and Markets, under its delegated authority, has disapproved a Bats BZX Exchange, Inc. (Bats BZX was later

¶330

acquired by CBOE Holdings, Inc.) proposed rule change to list and trade shares issued by the Winklevoss Bitcoin Trust. [Self-Regulatory Organizations; Bats BZX Exchange, Inc.; Order Disapproving a Proposed Rule Change, as Modified by Amendments No. 1 and 2, to BZX Rule 14.11(e)(4), Commodity-Based Trust Shares, to List and Trade Shares Issued by the Winklevoss Bitcoin Trust, Release No. 34-80206, March 10, 2017, at ¶ 1030.]

In disapproving the Bats proposal, the SEC staff noted that the applicable Exchange Act standards for the listing and trading of shares of commodity-trust exchange-traded products (ETPs) include, among other things, the requirement that the markets for the underlying commodity or derivatives on that commodity be regulated and that the exchange enter into surveillance sharing agreements with significant markets. The SEC's order said Bats could not achieve either of these requirements because the significant spot markets for Bitcoin are unregulated.

A large portion of the SEC's order reviewed the nearly 60 comment letters received on the proposed rule change, many of which emphasized that Bitcoin markets are often located overseas, can be illiquid, and may involve questionable practices, such as front-running, wash sales, and conflicts of interest regarding Bitcoin mining.

The Winklevoss Bitcoin Trust's investment goal was to track the price of Bitcoins on Gemini Trust Company's Gemini Exchange. With respect to regulatory oversight, the SEC said that, despite Bats's recitation of the CFTC's enforcement actions against Coinflip, TeraExchange, and Bitfinex, the CFTC registers spot markets only in limited instances, and the CFTC would not oversee Gemini Exchange. As for Gemini Exchange, the SEC noted that, while public comments were unclear about how much Bitcoin volume the exchange handled, it appeared to the SEC that Gemini Exchange's volume was a small part of the overall Bitcoin market.

The SEC also found fault with a white paper submitted in support of another exchange's rule proposal because it failed to account for many aspects of Bitcoin technology, such as a "hard fork" that could divide the underlying network into multiple blockchains. A footnote in the SEC's order noted that the Winklevoss Bitcoin Trust's registration statement had explained that the trust's custodian and sponsor would decide which of two resulting blockchains to use in the event of a fork. [Winklevoss Bitcoin Trust, Registration Statement (Amendment No.9), February 8, 2017.]

According to the Winklevoss Bitcoin Trust's registration statement, that choice would be made based on the "greatest cumulative computational difficulty"—*i.e.*, "the total threshold number of hash attempts required to mine all existing blocks in the respective Blockchain, accounting for potential differences in relative hash difficulty"—within the 48 hours after a hard fork. This computation would serve as a basis for transacting and valuing Bitcoins, although the creation and redemption of baskets would be halted for 24 hours before, and 48 hours after, a hard fork.

Bats has since asked the Commission to review the order disapproving of the exchange's proposal. Bats said in its petition for review that the order applied a new, "prescriptive" standard not required by the Exchange Act and argued that the potential for manipulation of Bitcoin is not as great as the SEC staff suggested. Bats also urged the Commission to review the order because of Bitcoin's novelty and the first-ever nature of the exchange's proposal. [Bats BZX Exchange, Inc., Petition for Review, March 24, 2017.]

Moreover, the SEC disapproved a similar rule change proposal by NYSE Arca, Inc. to list and trade shares of the SolidX Bitcoin Trust and has instituted proceedings to determine if yet another proposal by NYSE Arca to list and trade shares of Bitcoin Investment Trust should be approved or disapproved. [Self-Regulatory Organizations;

NYSE Arca, Inc.; Order Disapproving a Proposed Rule Change, as Modified by Amendment No. 1, Relating to the Listing and Trading of Shares of the SolidX Bitcoin Trust under NYSE Arca Equities Rule 8.201, Release No. 34-80319, March 28, 2017; Self-Regulatory Organizations; NYSE Arca, Inc.; Notice of Filing of Amendment No. 1, and Order Instituting Proceedings to Determine Whether to Approve or Disapprove a Proposed Rule Change, as Modified by Amendment No. 1, Relating to the Listing and Trading of Shares of the Bitcoin Investment Trust under NYSE Arca Equities Rule 8.201, Release No. 34-80502, April 21, 2017.] The SolidX disapproval focused on the same reasons cited for disapproving the Bats proposal: Bitcoin markets are unregulated and the exchange could not obtain the needed surveillance sharing agreements. The SEC's order instituting proceedings regarding the Bitcoin Investment Trust proposal reviews numerous disclosures in the trust's registration statement regarding Bitcoin markets and the operation of the trust.

The Forms S-1 filed by SolidX Bitcoin Trust and Bitcoin Investment Trust offer some additional details about the shares that would have been listed if the SEC had approved NYSE Arca's proposal (SolidX Bitcoin Trust has since further updated its Form S-1). [SolidX Bitcoin Trust, Registration Statement (Amendment No. 3), February 3, 2017; SolidX Bitcoin Trust, Registration Statement (Amendment No. 4), January 1, 2018.] Moreover, the NYSE Arca and Bats proposals share many features, as do the three underlying Bitcoin trusts. [Bitcoin Investment Trust, Registration Statement (Amendment No. 2), May 4, 2017.]

The Commission granted Bats's petition for review and provided the public a chance to comment on the Bats proposal to list and allow trading of shares in the Winklevoss Bitcoin Trust. [*In the Matter of Bats BZX Exchange, Inc.*, Release No. 34-80511, April 24, 2017.] Bats argued that the disapproval order should be reversed because the listing and trading of Bitcoin trust shares proposed is consistent with the federal securities laws. Bats reiterated that the Winklevoss Bitcoin Trust would offer investors an entrée into Bitcoin without the risks of direct investment in Bitcoin while also addressing the SEC's concerns about manipulation of Bitcoin markets. [Statement of Bats BZX Exchange, Inc. in Opposition to Disapproval Order, May 15, 2017.]

For example, Bats said that the basket creation/redemption feature of the Winklevoss Bitcoin Trust is an arbitrage mechanism that can hold trading prices to levels near the intraday net asset value that, when coupled with the interconnectedness of the Bitcoin market, offers a guard against manipulation, which Bats said "likely" would require global manipulation of the Bitcoin market. Bats leaned heavily on a paper authored by Craig Lewis, former SEC Chief Economist and Director of the Division of Economic and Risk Analysis. The Lewis paper was commissioned by Solid X Management LLC whose SolidX Bitcoin Trust also was the subject of an SEC disapproval order regarding listing and trading of its shares on NYSE Arca. In the paper, Lewis posited that bitcoin is less susceptible to false and misleading statements because it lacks material, nonpublic information typical of other investments, like equities. Lewis also said that the continuous nature of Bitcoin trading makes it less susceptible to manipulation of market opening and closing prices. [Craig M. Lewis, SolidX Bitcoin Trust: A Bitcoin Exchange Traded Product, February 2017; Craig M. Lewis, Supplemental Submission to SolidX Bitcoin Trust: A Bitcoin Exchange Traded Product, March 3, 2017; Statement by SolidX Management LLC Regarding Release No. 34-80511, May 15, 2017.]

Bats also disputed the SEC's finding that the CFTC would not regulate Bitcoin spot markets by noting the CFTC's antifraud and anti-manipulation authorities and the fact that the CFTC deemed Bitcoin a commodity and has granted regulatory approvals. [*In the Matter of the Application of LedgerX LLC for Registration as a Swap Execution Facility,* July 6, 2017; *In the Matter of: Order Instituting Proceedings Pursuant to TeraExchange*

LLC, CFTC Docket No. 15-33, September 24, 2015; *In the Matter of: Coinflip, Inc., d/b/a Derivabit*, CFTC Docket No. 15-29, September 17, 2015; *In the Matter of: BFXNA INC. d/b/a BITFINEX*, CFTC Docket No. 16-19, June 2, 2016.] Lastly, Bats asserted that the disapproval order imposed a new standard for approval that is inconsistent with prior similar proposals regarding commodity-trust ETPs. Specifically, Bats pointed to the order's discussion of surveillance-sharing agreements between the exchange and significant markets regarding trading of the underlying commodity (or derivatives) and that the underlying markets be regulated.

Solid X, while arguing on its own behalf, made many of the same claims about Bitcoin markets as Bats. The firm said that, to the extent the Commission alters the order of disapproval against Bats, the Commission should also reverse, modify, set aside, or remand the order of disapproval against NYSE Arca's proposal. SolidX and several other commenters also noted the changed conditions in the Bitcoin market arising from regulations imposed by the Peoples Bank of China that had the effect of reducing Chinese firms' share of the Bitcoin trading volume and increasing the volume on U.S.-dollar-denominated exchanges. Moreover, although these commenters discuss generally how a Bitcoin trust would decide what to do about a fork in the Bitcoin blockchain, the comments predate the August 2017 fork in the Bitcoin blockchain that produced a new virtual currency called Bitcoin Cash. [Statement of SolidX Management LLC, May 15, 2017, regarding File No. SR-BatsBZX-2016-30.]

It is worth noting that the SEC held out some hope for exchanges seeking to list and trade virtual currency ETP shares by noting in the Bats disapproval that the agency could reconsider the status of Bitcoin markets as they continue to develop. Moreover, the Commission has been asked by another trading venue to engage in rulemaking to more generally clarify the legal status of digital assets.

¶ 340 Exchange-Traded Funds

The SEC's Division of Investment Management issued a staff letter addressing various concerns the Division has regarding the incorporation of virtual currencies into new fund products. Overall, the Division indicated a need for an ongoing "dialogue" with the fund industry while also identifying some issues that raise questions about investor protection, especially with respect to retail investors. Among these concerns are the transparency of information about virtual currencies and their trading and valuation. "In light of these considerations, we have, at this time, significant outstanding questions concerning how funds holding substantial amounts of cryptocurrencies and related products would satisfy the requirements of the 1940 Act and its rules," said the letter.

Valuation and Other Issues

The staff letter frequently expressed concern about the volatility that seems to be inherent in some existing virtual currencies. The staff letter approaches the problem in a variety of ways, including by looking at questions about valuation, custody arrangements, the potential for arbitrage, and the possibility of market manipulation. [Division of Investment Management, Staff Letter: Engaging on Fund Innovation and Cryptocurrency-related Holdings (January 18, 2018).]

With respect to valuation, the staff letter posed six main questions:

- Will funds have adequate information to value virtual currencies and related products?

- Will funds develop policies and procedures to determine value (or fair value) of virtual currency products?

- How will funds deal with forks in a virtual currency, especially regarding the pricing of different virtual currencies and then incorporating valuation into net asset value?

- How will funds handle the inclusion of a brand new virtual currency?

- Will differences between virtual currencies impact valuation and accounting policies?

- How will funds account for possible manipulation of underlying virtual currency markets?

According to the staff letter, custodial arrangements also may pose issues for funds with investments in virtual currencies. The staff letter noted that it appeared there are currently no custodians providing services related to virtual currencies. Moreover, the custody question implies concerns about technology. For one, how would a fund validate ownership records that include private keys? When might a fund directly hold virtual currency? Also, the staff letter noted the potential cybersecurity risks regarding digital wallets.

In the case of arbitrage, the staff letter asked how an ETF would comply with the requirement that market price and NAV not materially diverge. Once again, technology raises some concerns, especially with respect to trading halts or the closing of a virtual currency exchange.

Much as the Division of Trading and Markets did when it denied applications to list and trade virtual currency-related commodity trust shares, the Investment Management Division's staff letter also addressed concerns about the possibility that underlying virtual currency markets are subject to manipulation. Specifically, the staff letter cited Chairman Clayton's December 2017 statement on cryptocurrencies in which he detailed the many potential hazards of such investments. Chairman Clayton concluded the statement by urging investors and funds to pay close attention to SEC regulations and guidance: "When advising clients, designing products and engaging in transactions, market participants and their advisers should thoughtfully consider our laws, regulations and guidance, as well as our principles-based securities law framework, which has served us well in the face of new developments for more than 80 years." [Jay Clayton, Statement on Cryptocurrencies and Initial Coin Offerings, December 11, 2017.]

Liquidity

The staff letter also addressed the issue of liquidity. By way of background, Investment Company Act Section 22(e) provides that redemption requests made to open-end funds must be paid within seven days. [15 U.S.C. § 80a-22.] The Commission's release adopting Rule 22e-4 explained that the history of the Investment Company Act was replete with references to the need for these funds to maintain a high degree of liquidity to meet redemptions, a policy that Congress embedded in Section 22(e). Moreover, the Commission's Rule 22e-4 was designed to account for newer, more complex products that may pose additional liquidity risks. [*Investment Company Liquidity Risk Management Programs*, Release No. 33-10233, October 13, 2016; *Investment Company Liquidity Risk Management Programs; Commission Guidance for In-Kind ETFs*, Release No. IC-33010, February 22, 2018 (extending compliance dates and providing guidance for in-kind ETFs); Investment Company Liquidity Risk Management Program Rules, A Small Entity Compliance Guide; Investment Company Liquidity Risk Management Programs Frequently Asked Questions.]

Rule 22e-4 applies to funds and in-kind ETFs. [17 CFR 270.22e-4.] A "fund" is a registered open-end management investment company (including separate series) that is not a money market fund or an in-kind ETF. An "in-kind ETF" is an ETF that meets redemptions by making in-kind transfers of securities, positions, and assets other than

¶340

de minimis amounts of cash and that publishes its holdings on a daily basis. An "ETF" is an open-end management investment company whose shares are listed and traded on a national securities exchange subject to an exemptive order granted or adopted by the Commission.

Under Rule 22e-4, each fund and in-kind ETF must adopt a liquidity risk management program that addresses five elements: (i) an annual review of liquidity risk; (ii) the classification of each portfolio investment into one of four buckets (highly liquid, moderately liquid, less liquid, or illiquid); (iii) the determination of a highly liquid investment minimum if the fund does not primarily hold highly liquid investments as assets; (iv) a limit on the amount of illiquid investments that are assets to no more than 15 percent of net assets; and (v) establishment of policies and procedures for making in-kind redemptions if the fund has the right to make in-kind redemptions. The rule also deals with board approvals, recordkeeping duties, and deposits into unit investment trusts. In-kind ETFs must comply with many of these requirements, but they are not required to comply with the classification or highly liquid investment minimum requirements (a footnote to the adopting release clarifies that ETFs that redeem in cash or that would not be in-kind ETFs must still comply with all elements of the liquidity risk management program).

In this context, the staff letter suggested questions regarding how funds would comply with Rule 22e-4:

- How will funds with virtual currency investments maintain adequate liquid assets to meet redemptions?
- Will virtual currency investments held as assets be classified in any bucket other than illiquid?
- Will funds be able to do market depth analysis?
- Will funds presume atypically large daily redemption amounts due to an underlying virtual currency's volatility?
- What will be the impact if funds' investments in virtual currency-related futures becomes a "substantial" segment of those markets?

Withdrawal of Registration Statements Urged

The Investment Management Division's staff letter also urged funds contemplating filing registration statements for funds that will invest in virtual currencies or related products to withdraw those registration statements. The staff letter also cautioned funds not to pursue the alternative strategy of using Securities Act Rule 485's post-effective amendment process to achieve a similar result. [17 CFR 230.485.] This latter action, the staff letter said, would be viewed "unfavorably" and could spur the staff to take action to protect investors.

Since the issuance of the staff letter, the SEC has moved forward on at least two proposals. First, NYSE Arca, Inc. had filed a proposed rule change to list and trade shares of the ProShares Bitcoin ETF and the ProShares Short Bitcoin ETF. The proposal already had been subjected to an extended review period and is now subject to proceedings to determine whether to approve or disapprove the proposal. The ProShares funds would track benchmark Bitcoin futures contracts listed and traded on the Cboe Futures Exchange and the Chicago Mercantile Exchange, although both funds may, if other investments become available, invest in other Bitcoin futures contracts or in options on Bitcoin futures contracts. The chief difference between the two ProShares funds is that the short fund would track the inverse of the benchmark Bitcoin futures contracts. The SEC said that further review was needed to address the "legal and policy" issues posed by the proposal as well as to evaluate whether the proposal satisfies the Exchange Act Rule 6(b)(5) requirement that a national securities exchange's rules be designed to prevent fraud and manipulation. [15 U.S.C. § 78f(b)5); Order Instituting Proceedings to Determine Whether to Approve or Disapprove a Proposed Rule Change to List and Trade the Shares of the ProShares Bitcoin ETF and the ProShares Short Bitcoin ETF under NYSE Arca Rule 8.200-E, Commentary .02, Release No. 34-82939, March 23, 2018.]

Likewise, the SEC instituted proceedings on whether to approve or disapprove Cboe BZX Exchange, Inc.'s proposal to list and trade shares of the GraniteShares Bitcoin ETF and the GraniteShares Short Bitcoin ETF. The long fund seeks to track Bitcoin futures contracts that are listed and traded on the Cboe Futures Exchange, Inc. while the short fund will seek returns matching the inverse of the same benchmark. [Order Instituting Proceedings to Determine Whether to Approve or Disapprove a Proposed Rule Change to List and Trade the Shares of the GraniteShares Bitcoin ETF and the GraniteShares Short Bitcoin ETF Under BZX Rule 14.11(f)(4), Trust Issued Receipts, Release No. 34-82995, April 5, 2018.]

In both the NYSE Arca and Cboe BZX proposals, the SEC sought public comment on 12 questions that broadly mirror some of the issues raised by the Division of Investment Management's staff letter. Questions common to both the NYSE Arca and Cboe BZX proposals include:

- What is the availability of OTC swaps?

- Do the funds have enough information to fair value Bitcoin futures contracts and related swaps?

- What would be the impact on the fund's NAV from potential manipulation of underlying markets?

- How would the funds respond to a fork?

- What is the potential that the funds (along with other exchange-traded products) could acquire a substantial portion of the market for Bitcoin futures contracts and related swaps?

- Do the two Bitcoin futures exchanges constitute a market of significant size?

¶ 350 Digital Securities: The Example of Overstock.com

When Overstock.com, Inc. filed its April 24, 2015 Form S-3 with the SEC, it was clear that the company's proposed issuance of digital securities would be innovative and that it might generate comments from the agency's staffers, given the planned use of rapidly developing and complex, yet potentially highly efficient, technologies to facilitate issuance of the new shares. Overstock.com's registration is an example of how one company has embraced the blockchain and DLT.

Overstock.com's Form S-3 proposed an offering of uncertificated, digital securities via DLTs more commonly associated with virtual currencies. The company said it would employ cryptography to bolster the security of the transaction. Overstock.com's Form S-3 also contained a risk factor section that described the company's potential offering of digital securities. Generally, Overstock.com said that the offering would include a "high degree of risk" and that investors could "lose all or part of []" of their investment in the securities to be offered; elsewhere, the company observed that "[d]igital securities are novel and untested . . . " The company further noted that digital securities would settle on a nearly immediate basis, rather than following the customary three-day (or T+3) settlement cycle (the SEC has since adopted a final rule enabling T+2 settlement for traditional shares).

Other risk factors highlighted by Overstock.com cover a wide range of possible risks. For one, the company's digital shares would represent a separate class of securities. Overstock.com would later refine the "separate class" language in reply to

¶350

SEC staff comment letters such that, in a registered public offering, it could pursue one of two alternatives: (i) issue new preferred stock; or (ii) reclassify its existing stock as Class A and issue new Class B stock. The digital shares would be traded on an SEC-registered broker-dealer's alternative trading system (ATS) under Regulation ATS, which would limit trading to the ATS's subscribers and also could reduce trading volume and liquidity to the point that the company's digital shares may be subject to heightened volatility and may not be capable of being sold as quickly as desired by some investors. The company noted that ATSs will use new technologies that operate in an uncertain regulatory environment. The distributed ledger involved would be public, which may hamper some investors' desired trading strategies. In order to facilitate the use of ATSs for digital shares, the private keys would initially be held by the ATSs or participating broker-dealers; this arrangement would enable investors to learn how to manage their private keys, but it also could put the private keys at risk of theft. The ATSs trading Overstock.com's digital shares also would be a closed system with potentially low trading volume, which could heighten the risk of market manipulation. Moreover, the company's digital shares could face risks from the payment systems employed, the absence of listing standards, and the lack of any ties between the price of the company's digital shares and its shares traded on national market systems (NMSs).

SEC Staff Comments on Offering

Between May and December of 2015, the SEC staff engaged in an extensive dialog with Overstock.com regarding its proposed offering of digital shares. The SEC staffs' comments focused on three key areas: the general proposition of offering digital shares; the framework to be employed; and cybersecurity and privacy issues.

General comments. The SEC staff opened with many general questions about the key features of Overstock.com's digital securities as described in several iterations of its registration statement leading up to its amended Form S-3. Overstock.com replied that it would use technologies common to virtual currencies (e.g., the Bitcoin blockchain) to validate transactions in its digital securities. For settlement reasons, Overstock.com explained that its digital securities would be traded via a closed system on an ATS in order to avoid pricing discrepancies that may result between the company's digital and traditional shares. Digital securities, for example, would not be pegged to the company's shares traded via an NMS, which means their prices could vary from the national best bid or offer. Moreover, digital shares could face additional challenges versus traditional shares due to low trading volume or poor liquidity. The use of an ATS also means there would be no minimum price or listing standards typical of NMS-traded shares.

Digital securities framework. With respect to the framework for offering digital securities, much of Overstock.com's digital securities plans remained open in some important details, but, with the effectiveness of its Form S-3, those gaps would close. In terms of how shares would be traded, Overstock.com would use the Pro Securities LLC ATS (in which Overstock.com said it holds a minority stake), while the only broker-dealer involved, DriveWealth, LLC, would use licensed technology from tZERO (Overstock.com said tZERO's name is a reference to zero settlement time or T+0) to interact with the ATS and share customer information with the issuer or its transfer agent for purposes of book entry. The purpose of the technology license is to streamline clearance and settlement, but Overstock.com's risk factors noted that this and other technologies involved are "novel and untested" regarding digital securities.

One aspect of Overstock.com's digital securities plan that drew extra scrutiny involved whether Delaware corporate law allowed the issuance of uncertificated shares that employ book entry under certain scenarios. By way of background, Section 158 of the Delaware General Corporation Law provides that a corporation's shares generally must be represented by certificates, although a company's board may provide by resolution that some or all of its stock is uncertificated. Moreover, a board resolution on uncertificated shares would not apply to certificated shares that have been issued until the certificates have been surrendered to the company. [8 Del. C. § 158.] Overall, the rights and obligations of certificated and uncertificated shareholders are identical, although the shares may be transferred differently. Leading commentators, however, have opined that certificates may eventually disappear as newer technologies are employed in the issuance of companies' shares. [*See*, Balotti and Finkelstein, Delaware Law of Corporations and Business Organizations (§ 5.19).] Overstock.com told the SEC staff that its counsel had advised that its planned issuance of uncertificated shares was allowed under Section 158 of the DGCL.

The SEC staff also flagged an item from Overstock.com's Form 10-Q. The company developed a new product called the Preborrow Assured Token (PAT), and the staff wanted to know if this product was a security. Overstock said PATs did not relate to its registration statement but were to be digital securities intended to let their holders meet Regulation SHO's locate requirements. The PATs would be issued by a special purpose entity and sold via an auction on the ATS to sophisticated investors, such as qualified institutional buyers, qualified purchasers, and accredited investors. The PATs also would rely on multiple Securities Act exemptions. The SEC also had inquired about TIGRCub digital bonds, but Overstock.com explained that this had been a test case in which its CEO purchased $500,000 of the bonds in order to demonstrate the tZERO technology.

Cybersecurity and privacy. Lastly, the SEC staff asked on several occasions how Overstock.com would deal with privacy and cybersecurity issues. In its initial reply, Overstock.com noted that the distributed ledger part of the digital shares infrastructure is public, raising at least the potential for ongoing cybersecurity and privacy worries. In one reply, the company explained that share owners would be identified in the public distributed ledger and in the proprietary ledger (a definitive ownership record). According to Overstock.com, digital securities can trade in a manner that is more secure than traditional brokerage accounts but, in any event, privacy and other risks are no greater than would be the case regarding an online brokerage account for traditional securities. Moreover, Overstock.com said there was no material risk associated with using the Bitcoin blockchain. This technology, said the company, is a mathematical validation tool that is low risk because it only has a "corroboration function."

The Rights Offering

Overtsock.com's rights offering using the tZERO technology commenced in November 2016 and experienced some issues, which prompted the company to issue a press release informing prospective investors how to best acquire the shares being offered. The rights offering closed in December 2016 with total gross proceeds nearing $10.9 million. According to Overstock.com, 126,565 of the 695,898 shares sold were blockchain-enabled shares.

Overstock.com CEO Patrick Byrne had previously likened the rights offering to the capital markets equivalent of Chuck Yeager's breaking the sound barrier during the early years of America's space program. Upon concluding the rights offering, Byrne touted the future of blockchain technology for capital markets: "In doing so, we have demonstrated to the world that there is indeed a path toward applying blockchain technology to capital markets in a way that complies with regulatory requirements and is accessible and practical for both issuers and investors. In the process, we raised a meaningful amount of capital, which Overstock can use to continue fueling our growth." [Overstock.com press release, December 15, 2016.]

Overstock.com Token/Coin Platform and ICO

Overstock.com also has been active through its subsidiaries in other aspects of the digital securities marketplace. For example, Overstock.com's Medici, Inc. subsidiary, the company's blockchain and fintech unit, recently sought to further leverage the tZERO technology for purposes of developing a platform for the trading of tokens or coins that would be considered securities under existing law. tZERO is planning its own token offering as a first step towards developing this technology. Specifically, the tZERO offering would have an expected offering size of $250 million, although the offering size could be increased to up to $300 million if demand is sufficient. On March 1, 2018, Overstock.com revealed in a Form 8-K that the SEC was investigating the token offering and that the agency had requested documents regarding the offering and tokens. [*See,* Overstock.com Form 8-K, March 1, 2018; Overstock.com Form 8-K, March 22, 2018.]

Moreover, Overstock.com shareholders have filed a putative securities class action complaint against the company regarding, in part, its planned tZERO ICO. The suit alleges that Overstock.com's stock price dropped significantly following a string of revelations about its business, including that the SEC is investigating the tZERO ICO and advisers at tZERO and that the company's Medici unit lost $22 million during the same period in which there was a major increase in the price of Bitcoin. Specifically, the complaint points to a five-month rise in Overstock.com's stock price of about 500 percent that was followed by a 4.4 percent drop after the SEC investigation was revealed, as well as a further 5.1 percent drop after the company announced a public offering of 4 million shares. One significant aspect of the shareholder suit against Overstock.com is that it asserts misrepresentations by Overstock.com itself about its business prospects and does not directly challenge the tZERO ICO. The lawsuit, filed in the federal court in Utah, seeks damages and other relief for alleged violations of Exchange Act Sections 10(b) and 20(a) and Rule 10b-5. At least one additional shareholder suit making similar allegations has been filed against Overstock.com. [*See, Morris v. Overstock.com, Inc.,* March 29, 2018; *Mahabadi v. Overstock.com, Inc.,* April 6, 2018.]

More generally, there is an open question whether ICO-related securities class actions suits might surge in light of the Supreme Court's decision in *Cyan, Inc. v. Beaver County Employees Retirement Fund.* [*Cyan, Inc. v. Beaver County Employees' Retirement Fund,* March 20, 2018, Kagan, E.] In *Cyan,* the justices held that the Securities Litigation Uniform Standards Act had not disrupted the concurrent federal-state court jurisdiction regime articulated by Congress in the Securities Act. As a result, state courts retain jurisdiction over class action suits alleging only Securities Act violations and that those suits cannot be removed to federal court. The Securities Act stands in contrast, for example, to the Exchange Act, which confers exclusive jurisdiction on federal courts. It remains to be seen how extensively the Securities Act may be used in state suits over ICOs.

Nevertheless, Ripple Labs, Inc. has become the subject of a securities class action suit filed in California alleging Securities Act and California violations. [*Coffey v. Ripple Labs, Inc.,* May 3, 2018.] Ripple has sought to remove the case from the California court to the U.S. District Court for the Northern District of California. The removal notice raises the following question: does the Supreme Court's *Cyan* opinion bar removal of a securities class action suit alleging both Securities Act and California claims if removal is instead sought under the Class Action Fairness Act? [*Coffey v. Ripple Labs, Inc.,* June 1, 2018.]

¶ 360 SEC Statement Regarding Online Platforms

The SEC's Divisions of Trading and Markets and Enforcement jointly issued a statement about online platforms that offer investors the ability to trade digital assets. Overall, the statement cautions that many of the digital assets offered for trading can be considered to be "securities," a fact that may require the online platform to be registered with the SEC, typically as a national securities exchange, an ATS, or a broker-dealer. Moreover, the statement warns prospective investors that use of the word "exchange" in a platform's name can be misleading. Platforms also may assert that they employ criteria for choosing tradable digital assets, but those criteria are not necessarily the same as listing standards for SEC-registered exchanges. Lastly, the statement observed that online platforms' use of order books or the displaying of quotes may not have the same meaning as these activities do for SEC-registered exchanges. [Divisions of Enforcement and Trading and Markets, Statement on Potentially Unlawful Online Platforms for Trading Digital Assets, March 7, 2018, at ¶ 1010.]

The overarching theme in the statement is the same as that for almost all issues regarding ICOs—is the thing being traded a security? As with other aspects of ICOs, the test remains the *Howey* standard for determining if something is an investment contract. As a result, one must continually ask if the thing being traded is an investment of money in a common enterprise where it is reasonably expected that the entrepreneurial or managerial efforts of others will generate profits.

The following discussion briefly describes the main types of SEC-registered entities the statement is concerned with: national securities exchanges, ATSs, and broker-dealers. For prospective investors in digital assets, the SEC's guidance on online platforms conjures a negative implication regarding the services and investor protections they may not receive if they do business with platforms that are not SEC-registered. For the online platforms themselves, the key takeaway is the potential that failure to register with the SEC (or to invoke an appropriate registration exemption) may result in liability for violations of the federal securities laws.

National Securities Exchanges

Under Exchange Act Sections 5 and 6, it is unlawful for a broker, dealer, or exchange to engage in interstate commerce for the purpose of using any facility of an exchange to effect securities transactions or to report securities transactions without being registered with the Commission, unless exempt from registration. [15 U.S.C. §§ 78e and 78f.] Exchange Act Section 3(a)(1) defines an "exchange" as any organization or group of persons that provides a marketplace or facility to bring together buyers and sellers of securities and includes those activities generally understood to be performed by a stock exchange. [15 U.S.C. § 78c(a)(1).] Exchange Act Section 3(a)(2) explains that a "facility" includes tangible and intangible property and communications systems. [15 U.S.C. § 78c(a)(2).] Exchange Act Rule 3b-16 expands upon the statutory definition of "exchange" by explaining that "bringing together" involves, among other things: (i) bringing together orders for securities of multiple buyers and sellers; and (ii) the use of established, non-discretionary methods by which orders interact and the buyers and sellers entering those orders agree to the terms of a trade. The rule also explains that "bringing together" does not include an association solely because it routes orders for execution or permits orders to be entered for execution against a single dealer. [17 CFR 240.3b-16.]

The SEC's statement on online platforms emphasizes some of the requirements for exchanges. Exchange Act Section 6 sets forth numerous requirements, including that an exchange must enforce compliance of its members with federal securities laws and the exchange's own rules. An exchange also must provide for the discipline of its members pursuant to fair procedures. Moreover, an exchange's rules must be designed

¶360

to, among other things, prevent fraud and manipulation. Similarly, an exchange's rules must not be designed to permit unfair discrimination between customers, issuers, or broker-dealers or seek to regulate matters unrelated to the administration of the exchange.

The SEC maintains a list of current and recently approved national securities exchanges. The list can be view by navigating to the link on the SEC's website at https://www.sec.gov/fast-answers/divisionsmarketregmrexchangesshtml.html.

Alternative Trading Systems

Exchange Act Rule 3a1-1 contains several exemptions from the statutory definition of "exchange," including for an entity that complies with Regulation ATS. [17 CFR 240.3a1-1.] The preliminary notes to Regulation ATS explain that an ATS must comply with Regulation ATS unless it is a registered national securities exchange, exempt from registration as a national securities exchange because of its limited trading volume, or it trades only government securities. ATSs are subject to federal antifraud and anti-manipulation provisions and to relevant state laws. Moreover, the requirements of Regulation ATS are in addition to other securities law provisions.

Rule 300 of Regulation ATS defines "alternative trading system" as an organization or group of persons or system that provides a marketplace or facilities for bringing together buyers and sellers of securities or otherwise performs securities functions of a stock exchange as defined in Exchange Act Rule 3b-16. [17 CFR 242.300 and 17 CFR 240.3b-16.] An ATS also must be registered with the SEC as a broker-dealer under exchange Act Section 15 and file Form ATS. [17 CFR 242.301.]

The SEC's statement on online platforms emphasizes some key features of ATSs. For example, an ATS must have reasonable policies and procedures to prevent the misuse of material, nonpublic information, keep books and records, and safeguard customers' funds and securities.

However, ATSs differ significantly from national securities exchanges with respect to policing trading by subscribers. Unlike an exchange, an ATS cannot have rules for subscriber conduct other than with respect to trading on the system. An ATS also cannot discipline subscribers except for exclusion from trading. [17 CFR 242.300.] As with exchanges, the SEC maintains a list of current ATSs at https://www.sec.gov/foia/docs/atslist.htm.

Broker-Dealers

The SEC's online platforms statement also considers the role of broker-dealers. Exchange Act Section 3(a)(4) defines "broker" as any person who is in the business of effecting transactions in securities for the account of others. [15 U.S.C. § 78c(a)(4).] The definition includes special rules for banks. Exchange Act Section 3(a)(5) defines "dealer" as any person in the business of buying and selling securities for such person's own account through a broker or otherwise; the definition excludes persons who buy or sell securities for their own account and not as part of a regular business. [15 U.S.C. § 78c(a)(5).] It should be noted that Securities Act Section 2(a)(12) contains a some-what more nuanced definition of "dealer," which, in that context, means any person who engages, either for all or part of his time, as agent, broker, or principal, in the business of offering, buying, selling, or otherwise dealing or trading in securities issued by another person. [15 U.S.C. § 77b(a)(12).] Broker-dealers must be registered with the Commission under Exchange Act Section 15. [15 U.S.C. § 78o.] Exchange Act Section 3(a)(48) defines a "registered broker or dealer" as a broker-dealer registered under the Exchange Act. [15 U.S.C. § 78c(a)(48).]

Moreover, it is important to note that the Exchange Act and the corresponding Exchange Act rules contain numerous exceptions to, and exemptions from, the broker-dealer registration requirement. Broker-dealers must also become members of FINRA. A person considering trading digital assets can check the status of anyone claiming to be a broker-dealer by accessing FINRA's BrokerCheck tool at https:// brokercheck.finra.org/.

Wallet Services

The SEC's online platforms statement mentions digital wallet services that often purport to hold digital assets. According to the SEC, however, wallet services can involve activities for which the providers must be registered with the Commission. Wallet services also can involve transactions in securities, which must either be registered with the SEC or subject to an exemption from registration.

In addition to registration as a broker-dealer, the SEC's statement notes that a wallet service provider may have to register as a transfer agent or clearing agency. Exchange Act Section 17A provides for the registration of transfer agents and clearing agencies with the Commission. Section 17A also states the congressional finding that the prompt and accurate settlement of securities transactions is necessary for the protection of investors and those who facilitate transactions on behalf of investors. [15 U.S.C. § 78q-1.] The SEC is the appropriate regulatory agency with respect to a clearing agency or transfer agent unless another regulatory agency is specified by law. [15 U.S.C § 78c(a)(34)(B).]

Transfer agents. Transfer agents are required to be registered under Exchange Act Section 17A(c)(1). [15 U.S.C. § 78q-1(c)(1).] Exchange Act Section 3(a)(25) defines "transfer agent" as any person who engages on behalf of itself or a securities issuer in certain activities, including countersigning securities upon issuance, performing the functions of a registrar, registering the transfer of securities, exchanging or converting securities, or transferring record ownership of securities via book entry. [15 U.S.C. § 78c(a)(25).]

Transfer agents are subject to Exchange Act rules on keeping books and records and to reporting requirements. Transfer agents also must comply with provisions contained in Article 8 of the Uniform Commercial Code. UCC Section 8-208(a) provides, among other things, that a person who signs a security certificate as transfer agent warrants to a purchaser for value and without notice of a particular defect that the certificate is genuine. UCC Section 8-407 also provides that, in this context, a transfer agent has the same obligations as an issuer. [Uniform Commercial Code, § 8-208(a) and § 8-407.]

Clearing agencies. Exchange Act Section 17A(b)(1) mandates that clearing agencies be registered. [15 U.S.C. § 78q-1(b)(1).] Under Exchange Act Section 3(a)(23), a "clearing agency" is any person who, among other things, acts as an intermediary in making payments or deliveries in connection with securities transactions. The statutory definition also provides a long list of entities that are excluded from the definition, including national securities exchanges, national securities associations, or broker-dealers solely because they perform certain specified activities. [15 U.S.C. § 78c(a)(23).] Upon registration, a clearing agency is a self-regulatory organization. [15 U.S.C. § 78c(a)(26).] Moreover, the Dodd-Frank Act ascribed additional duties to clearing agencies with respect to security-based swaps; the Commission implemented these regulatory mandates by adopting Exchange Act Rule 17Ad-22. [17 CFR 240.17Ad-22.]

Cybersecurity

The SEC's statement on online platforms does not discuss cybersecurity in great detail. Still, the statement suggests three questions anyone should ask before using an online platform for the purpose of storing or trading digital assets:

¶360

- How does the platform safeguard users' trading and personally identifying information?

- What are the platform's protections against cybersecurity threats, such as hacking or intrusions?

- Does the platform hold users' assets? If so, how are these assets safeguarded?

The key takeaway from the SEC's online platforms statement is that not all platforms offering services for digital assets are registered with the SEC and that they may not provide levels of security for users' personally identifiable information and stored digital assets that is comparable to what is required of SEC-registered entities. The following discussion briefly examines some of the cybersecurity requirements for SEC-registered entities.

Regulation SCI. The SEC adopted Regulation Systems Compliance and Integrity (SCI) to update and strengthen its previous guidance on data privacy and cybersecurity to meet the evolving demands of the digital world as it impacts securities transactions. Regulation SCI provides a framework for entities to engage in periodic testing of their systems and for reporting SCI events to the SEC. "SCI event" means systems disruptions, systems compliance issues, and systems intrusions. Regulation SCI also imposes special requirements for critical SCI systems, which must be capable of being resumed within two hours of a wide-scale disruption.

Under Regulation SCI, "SCI entity" includes SCI self-regulatory organizations (*e.g.*, national securities exchanges and registered clearing agencies), SCI ATSs, or certain exempt clearing agencies (*i.e.*, a clearing agency exempted by the Commission from registration under Exchange Act Section 17A, but whose exemption has conditions regarding the SEC's prior Automation Review Policy or a successor policy). An "SCI ATS" is an ATS that, during four of the preceding six calendar months, met certain trading volume thresholds requiring it to comply with Regulation SCI. But an ATS that reaches these thresholds need not comply with Regulation SCI until six months after it first crosses the relevant threshold. [*See*, 17 CFR 242.1000, *et. seq.*]

Regulation S-P. The SEC's Regulation S-P imposes notice and disclosure requirements on multiple types of SEC-registered firms with respect to consumers' nonpublic personal information. Specifically, the regulation applies to broker-dealers, investment companies, and investment advisers and their foreign equivalents that are registered with the Commission (but not to non-resident foreign firms that are not SEC-registered). [17 CFR 248.1.]

Moreover, firms subject to Regulation S-P must comply with the safeguards rule contained in Rule 30 of the regulation. Rule 30 requires each SEC-registered broker-dealer, investment company, and investment adviser subject to Regulation S-P to adopt written policies and procedures aimed at safeguarding customers' records and information. The policies and procedures must be reasonably designed to achieve specific goals regarding customer records and information, including: (i) security and confidentiality; (ii) protection against anticipated threats to security or integrity; and (iii) protection against unauthorized access that could result in substantial harm or inconvenience. [17 CFR 248.30.]

Regulation S-ID. Regulation S-ID deals with identity theft red flags. Specifically, a financial institution or creditor (as defined by the Fair Credit Reporting Act) that is a broker-dealer, investment company, or investment adviser must periodically identify covered accounts and establish an identity theft prevention program to protect these covered accounts. The program must be scaled appropriately for a firm's size, complexity, and activities. "Covered accounts" means accounts that are primarily for personal, family, or household purposes that allow multiple transactions with third parties, and other accounts for which there is a reasonably foreseeable risk to customers or to the financial institution's safety and soundness from identity theft. [17 CFR 248.201.]

¶ 370 FINRA

The Financial Industry Regulatory Authority, Inc., the SRO that oversees most activities of SEC-registered broker dealers, recently issued its 2018 examination priorities letter in which it said it would "closely monitor developments" regarding "[d]igital assets (such as cryptocurrencies) and initial coin offerings (ICOs)." FINRA said that, when digital assets or ICOs involve securities, it could examine whether firms have sufficient "supervisory, compliance and operational infrastructure" to comply with SEC and FINRA rules. [FINRA 2018 Regulatory and Examination Priorities Letter, January 8, 2018.]

FINRA also issued a report in January 2017 discussing the implications of blockchain technologies on the business of broker-dealers. The FINRA report raises many questions, such as whether DLT and blockchain technologies will truly revolutionize the securities industry or if these developments will have a more "incremental" impact. [Report on Distributed Ledger Technology: Implications of Blockchain for the Securities Industry.]

FINRA's DLT Report

As a starting point, the FINRA report posits three areas that demand additional study. First, with respect to governance, the "trustless" character of blockchain technologies raises questions about who will manage DLT systems and what risks may inhere in these systems for markets and investors. Second, operational structure will be important in several ways: (i) a DLT system must provide for access, which means there will need to be on-boarding and off-boarding requirements; (ii) validation of transactions must be done based on any of several possibilities (*e.g.*, consensus-based); (iii) assets must appear on the system in either traditional forms or tokenized forms; and (iv) DLT systems must be sufficiently transparent. Third, DLT systems must have robust security features in order to handle the possibility of cyberattacks and to maintain the security of the cryptographic keys used to access the DLT system.

A substantial portion of the FINRA report was devoted to explaining the various securities laws and regulations and FINRA rules and guidance that broker-dealers should consider when they make DLT systems a part of their business or of the services they offer to customers. The following chart is adapted from that summary and includes some additional references that were not included in the FINRA report.

Summary of FINRA and Other Rules Applicable to DLT			
Topic	Laws and Regulations	FINRA Rules	Notes
Custody of funds and securities.	Exchange Act Rules 15c3-3 and 17a-13.	Rule 4160.	The report asked who controls the DLT network and who holds the private keys.
Net capital.	Exchange Act Rule 15c3-1.	Rule 4100.	According to the report, the broker-dealer duties turn on the facts and circumstances, such as market risk and liquidity.
Books and records.	Exchange Act Rules 17a-3 and 17a-4.	Rule 4511.	Of note, said the report, is the "WORM" requirement to "write once, read many."

¶370

Summary of FINRA and Other Rules Applicable to DLT			
Topic	Laws and Regulations	FINRA Rules	Notes
Clearance and settlement.	Exchange Act Section 17A.	Rule 4311.	The SEC's guidance on online platforms mentions clearance and settlement concerns. FINRA's report also notes introducing brokers' duties in the context of carrying firms.
AML/KYC duties.	Bank Secrecy Act and customer identification program requirements (31 CFR 1023.220).	Rule 2090. Rule 3310. Notice to members 05-48.	The report noted that, even if outsourcers are used to perform some AML/KYC functions, broker-dealers still carry the responsibility of performing AML/KYC functions.
Cybersecurity/privacy and data protection.	SEC Regulation S-P. [Although not mentioned in the FINRA report, firms may also consult SEC Regulation S-ID.]	NASD Notice to members 05-49.	FINRA's report suggested that a firm understand a DLT network's policies and procedures and consider updating the firm's own policies and procedures along with training for its staff.
Trade and order reports for equity and debt securities.	[Although not mentioned in the report, see generally, the SEC's Regulation NMS.]	Rule 4550 Series. Rule 5000 Series. Rule 6100 Series. Rule 6400 Series. Rule 6700 Series.	According to the report, firms may be considering building a tokenized method for the OTC trading of NMS stocks.
Supervision and surveillance activities.		Rule 3110. Rule 3120. Notice to Members 05-48.	The report suggests that firms consider whether they have adequate access to DLT network records.
Fees, commissions, and payments.		Rule 2040. Rule 2121. Rule 2122.	The FINRA report noted that firms may need to consider what new fees they may charge for DLT-related services (*e.g.*, wallet or key management) and whether any payments will be made to persons who are not registered as broker-dealers.
Confirmations and account statements.	Exchange Act Rule 10b-10.	Rule 2232. Rule 2340.	The report noted that firms may need to consider the impact of using new DLT-related systems.
Material changes to business.		NASD Rule 1017. NASD Notice to Members 00-73.	Material business changes, the report said, may require a firm to file a Continuing Membership Application.

	Summary of FINRA and Other Rules Applicable to DLT		
Topic	Laws and Regulations	FINRA Rules	Notes
Business continuity.	[Although not mentioned by the report, firms also may consult the SEC's Regulation SCI, especially if they operate ATSs.]	Rule 4370.	The report reminded firms that business continuity is the ability to restore services following a disruption.

Source: Adapted from FINRA report titled "Distributed Ledger Technology: Implications of Blockchain for the Securities Industry" (January 2017).

The FINRA blockchain report generated 13 public comments, mostly from industry groups and a few large brokerage firms that are experimenting with DLT and blockchain services. The Securities Industry and Financial Markets Association (SIFMA), for example, observed that DLT can co-exist within the current environment for securities regulation and that DLT might be thought of as the "addition of new technology to modify existing processes." SIFMA also suggested that the creation of regulator nodes via DLT could make the gathering of market data more efficient by rendering obsolete the existing reporting framework (*e.g.*, protocols for Exchange Act Rule 10b-10 confirmations). [*See*, 17 CFR 240.10b-10.] Moreover, the Chamber of Digital Commerce noted the potential for DLT to increase efficiencies in securitization transactions by making it easier to compile loan-level data required by the SEC's Regulation AB II rulemaking. [17 CFR 229.1100, *et. seq.*]

Nasdaq, Inc. commented that regulatory language created for legacy technologies must be changed regarding requirements for the storage of information contained in records kept pursuant to Exchange Act Rules 17a-3 and 17a-4, which reference "micrographic media" (including microfilm and microfiche) and "electronic storage media" (including digital storage media or systems that, among other things, allow storage in "non-rewritable, non-erasable format"). Overall, Nasdaq said it favors more general, technologically neutral language. [*See*, 17 CFR 240.17a-3 and 240.17a-4.]

Several other commenters, however, suggested that DLT may not be the only way to increase efficiencies and lower costs associated with securities markets and securities regulations. The CFA Institute said regulators should take a "technologically agnostic" approach while ensuring that firms that employ novel technical solutions are held accountable for their compliance with existing rules. Ultimately, the CFA Institute sees DLT as a driver of efficiencies rather than of entirely new services. The CFA Institute cited the example of SWIFT, the Belgium-based financial messaging solutions provider, which recently debuted a non-DLT/blockchain product that allows for one-day settlement. For its part, SWIFT told FINRA that new developments regarding permissioned ledger technologies may allow smart contracts to permit users to access specific data sets, thus, potentially resolving current problems with the confidentiality of ledgers.

FINRA Investor Alerts

FINRA has issued multiple investor alerts on digital assets and ICOs. The alerts tend to focus on key questions, such as whether the thing being offered is a security. The investor alerts also provide some background information on important terminology, such as what constitutes a cryptocurrency or an ICO. Moreover, FINRA's investor alerts contain examples of high-pressure sales tactics and caution investors to resist these sales methods.

¶370

- Don't Fall for Cryptocurrency-Related Stock Scams (December 21, 2017).
- Initial Coin Offerings: Know Before You Invest (August 31, 2017).
- Bitcoin: More than a Bit Risky (May 7, 2014).

¶ 380 Petitions for SEC Rulemaking

Liquid M Capital, Inc. (formerly Ouisa Capital, LLC) petitioned the SEC twice to engage in rulemaking with respect to digital assets and to request that the SEC provide a form of amnesty for ICO token sales undertaken during the period before the SEC issued The DAO report. Liquid M operates an ATS that provides for the trading of digital assets, although the firm more recently said it planned to limit trading to tokens that are securities, a focus the firm sees as a growth opportunity despite the small number of tokens that are now securities. To some extent, both petitions have been superseded by The DAO report and by guidance issued by the SEC's Divisions of Trading and Markets and Enforcement regarding online platforms. Still, Liquid M sees the potential for the SEC to take actions that could further clarify the securities law status of digital assets.

In its first rulemaking petition, Liquid M asked the SEC to undertake rulemaking regarding digital assets, including by issuing a concept release to be followed by a proposed regulation, which the firm hypothetically called "Regulation DA" for Regulation Digital Assets. At the time, Liquid M saw the chief problem as one of having to rely on SEC guidance about the definition of "security" (*e.g.*, application of the *Howey* test and a small number of enforcement actions) in a manner that is heavily dependent on the facts and circumstances. Liquid M said the then-existing legal uncertainty made it costly for start-up firms to enter the market for digital assets and related services. Liquid M also asked the SEC to consider employing a regulatory sandbox in which firms could experiment with blockchain technologies without the fear of violating securities laws, provided they stay within parameters set by the SEC. [Ouisa Capital Rulemaking Petition, March 13, 2017.]

The combined effect of the SEC's The DAO report and its online platforms guidance went a long way in addressing the concerns initially raised by Liquid M, although without taking the next step to enshrine that guidance in formal notice and comment rulemaking. Liquid M's second rulemaking petition reiterated its own position that most ICO tokens are securities but also asked the SEC to further clarify the application of securities laws to these digital assets. Moreover, Liquid M urged the SEC to permit firms that conducted ICOs before The DAO report was issued to reform those token offerings to comply with federal securities laws. These reformed ICOs (what Liquid M called "retroactive registration[s]") would also give investors rescission rights. Liquid M said it worried the absence of such remedial action would raise questions about whether Liquid M, if it were to trade older tokens, could be liable for aiding and abetting Securities Act violations and whether Liquid M could be liable as a controlling person under the Exchange Act. Liquid M cited the SEC's decision to permit firms that engaged in direct-to-the-public offerings to reform those offerings as precedent for making the same allowance regarding ICO tokens. [Liquid M Capital, Inc. Rulemaking Petition, January 23, 2018.]

The SEC has now provided a variety of guidance directly to firms and investors in the blockchain space. It remains to be seen whether the SEC will pursue formal rulemaking regarding digital assets, although it is possible that a working group led by the Treasury Department that includes the SEC, the CFTC, the Fed, and FinCEN will make recommendations for regulators to clarify existing rules for blockchain technologies. For now, firms and investors will need to continue to consider the SEC's existing authorities and those of other federal and state regulators as they navigate the blockchain and virtual currency regulatory landscape.

Chapter Four—The CFTC's Approach

¶ 400 View from the Top

The CFTC has adopted a favorable, open-minded, proactive approach supportive of innovation with respect to the emerging blockchain technologies and virtual currency markets, especially when compared to the SEC. The CFTC's supportive role is demonstrated by the public statements of its leadership as well as agency undertakings. Nevertheless, the CFTC has joined the SEC, and other law enforcement authorities, in efforts to deter and prosecute fraud and market abuse, as well to promote transparency and integrity.

In particular, CFTC Chairman Giancarlo has been recognized for his forward-looking views in the virtual currency arena, and more generally has attempted to recast the agency as a 21st century regulator with the launch of its LabCFTC initiative. Nonetheless, the CFTC remains challenged to accomplish these objectives, at least in the near term: not only did Congress fail to provide appropriations for these initiatives, it instead reduced the agency's 2018 budget by $1 million.

Virtual Currencies and a New Digital Era

In testimony before the Senate Banking Committee in February 2018, Chairman Giancarlo noted, "We are entering a new digital era in world financial markets. As we saw with the development of the Internet, we cannot put the technology genie back in the bottle. Virtual currencies mark a paradigm shift in how we think about payments, traditional financial processes, and engaging in economic activity. Ignoring these developments will not make them go away, nor is it a responsible regulatory response." He added, "With the proper balance of sound policy, regulatory oversight and private sector innovation, new technologies will allow American markets to evolve in responsible ways and continue to grow our economy and increase prosperity."

The CFTC as a 21st Century Regulator

Consistent with the agency's forward-looking approach with respect to virtual currencies, CFTC leadership has frequently described the agency as a 21st century regulator. In a hearing before the House Committee on Agriculture in October 2017, Chairman Giancarlo stated, "The world is changing. Our parents' financial markets are gone. The 21st century digital transformation is well underway. And, as our markets continue to evolve, the CFTC cannot be an analog regulator in a digital age – instead we must also evolve. We must learn from the changes enveloping our world and adopt them in pursuit of our regulatory mission and the betterment of our markets."

Lab CFTC

In May 2017, the CFTC launched its LabCFTC initiative. The program serves as the focal point for Commission efforts to facilitate market-enhancing financial technology (fintech) innovation and fair competition for the benefit of the American public. LabCFTC is designed to make the CFTC more accessible to fintech innovators. It serves as a platform to inform the Commission's understanding of emerging technologies. LabCFTC will enable the CFTC to be proactive and forward-thinking as fintech applications continue to develop, and to help identify related regulatory opportunities, challenges, and, risks. At the time LabCFTC was launched, smart contracts and blockchain technology were specifically identified as breaking digital innovations that warranted further attention and consideration by the CFTC.

Budget Setback

In March 2018, the House and the Senate passed the omnibus spending bill, H.R. 1625, which reduced the CFTC's annual funding from $250 million to $249 million, well below the agency's requested appropriation of $281.5 million. As a consequence, the CFTC may lack the necessary resources to perform its duties with respect to virtual currency–related activities. The CFTC has previously stated that it had built into its 2018 Congressional budget request additional resources to strengthen its technological and econometric resources to support its ability to oversee virtual currency derivatives. Moreover, in a statement following the passage of the omnibus spending bill, CFTC Commissioner Rostin Behnam asserted that the agency will not have the resources to address challenges arising from the rapid growth of the fintech industry (among other functional areas within the agency) in a timely and adequate manner.

Kari Larsen, a regulatory attorney at Reed Smith LLP, also observes, "In recent years, the CFTC has been charged with oversight of complex swaps and cash markets, heightened reporting requirements, and greater enforcement challenges. This significant drain of resources makes it very difficult for the Commission to discharge its duties." She adds, "No doubt, the failure to apportion sufficient resources will make allocating and training staff quite difficult."

¶ 410 Agency Guidance and its Role in Educating the Consumer

Educating consumers and promoting greater public understanding has been a centerpiece of the CFTC's efforts in the virtual currency realm, consistent with the agency's core mission. Towards this end, the agency has undertaken to provide consumers, members of the investing public, and other industry participants with an ever-evolving and expanding collection of high-quality educational materials. These resources include basic primers, customer advisories, and deeper treatment of some of the regulatory issues and challenges. It appears that the CFTC intends to continue its concentrated efforts to make timely and relevant resources available to the public.

Virtual Currency Resource Materials

In December 2017, coincident with the launch of exchange-traded Bitcoin futures and options contracts, the CFTC introduced a virtual currency resource webpage. This dedicated webpage serves as a central repository for Commission-produced resources about virtual currency, with a stated goal to educate and inform the public about these assets, including the possible risks associated with investing or speculating in virtual currencies, as well as related futures products.

CFTC educational resources, including those found on the agency's virtual currency resource webpage, consist of the following:

CFTC Primer on Virtual Currencies. This primer (reproduced at ¶ 1040) provides an overview of virtual currencies and their potential use cases and helps outline the CFTC's role and oversight of virtual currencies. Moreover, it cautions investors and users of the potential risks involved with virtual currencies. The primer was produced by LabCFTC, the CFTC's fintech initiative, and is intended to educate the public with regard to emerging fintech innovations.

CFTC Backgrounder on Oversight of and Approach to Virtual Currency Futures Markets. This backgrounder (reproduced at ¶ 1050) provides clarity with regard to federal oversight of and jurisdiction over virtual currencies—the CFTC's

¶410

approach to regulation in this space. The backgrounder also summarizes the self-certification process, generally, and the self-certification of new contracts for Bitcoin futures products launched by designated contract markets (DCMs) in December 2017, as well as providing information on the CFTC's "heightened review" for virtual currency contracts. The backgrounder also explores how various constituencies may be impacted by virtual currency futures.

CFTC Backgrounder on Self-Certified Contracts for Bitcoin Product. The Chicago Mercantile Exchange Inc. (CME) and the CBOE Futures Exchange (CFE) each self-certified new contracts for Bitcoin futures products and the Cantor Exchange self-certified a new contract for Bitcoin binary options in late 2017. This fact sheet outlines the self-certification process of the CFTC, as well as the CFTC's role in oversight of virtual currencies.

CFTC Talks podcast. The Commission's podcast, CFTC Talks, is geared towards providing information about the commodity markets, futures trading, and conditions in the U.S. and abroad affecting the markets. The podcast, which is hosted by CFTC Chief Market Intelligence Officer Andrew Busch, has featured virtual currency related topics on three occasions since its inception.

- **CFTC Talks Episode 20: Roundtable with CFTC leaders on Bitcoin.** This episode features a panel of CFTC leaders discussing Bitcoin, the self-certification process of new contracts on Bitcoin, and the CFTC's role in regulating the new derivatives contracts. The panel comprises LabCFTC's Daniel Gorfine, Division of Market Oversight's Amir Zaidi, Division of Clearing and Risk's Brian Bussey, and Division of Swap Dealers and Intermediary Oversight's Matt Kulkin.

- **CFTC Talks Episode 24: With Peter Van Valkenburgh.** This episode features a discussion with Coincenter.org's Director of Research Peter Van Valkenburgh. The consensus mechanism, the key innovation underlying Bitcoin, is discussed.

- **CFTC Talks Episode 33: Chamber of Digital Commerce.** This episode features Chamber of Digital Commerce's President Perianne Boring and General Counsel Amy Davine Kim discussing the mission of the Chamber and where they see digital assets and blockchain-based technologies are heading.

Bitcoin Basics. This brochure provides fundamental information about Bitcoin, including a basic description of Bitcoin, the CFTC's jurisdiction, and how virtual currencies can be a target for fraud and for hackers. This introductory guide provides basic information about Bitcoin and its related risks.

An Introduction to Virtual Currency. This pamphlet is a quick guide to virtual currencies. It covers how virtual currencies can be purchased, why they are considered commodities, and what types of fraud can be found in the market.

Customer Advisory: Understand the Risks of Virtual Currency Trading. This customer advisory is designed to inform the public of possible risks associated with investing or speculating in virtual currencies or recently launched Bitcoin futures and options. The advisory explains that a virtual currency is a digital representation of value that functions as a medium of exchange, a unit of account, or a store of value, but it does not have legal tender status. The advisory also notes that virtual currencies are sometimes exchanged for U.S. dollars or other currencies around the world, but are not currently backed nor supported by any government or central bank, and that their value is completely derived by market forces of supply and demand. Finally, the advisory notes that virtual currencies are more volatile than traditional fiat currencies, and profits and losses related to this volatility are amplified in margined futures contracts.

Customer Advisory: Beware Virtual Currency Pump-and-Dump Schemes. This customer advisory highlights virtual currency pump-and-dump schemes that occur in the largely unregulated cash market for virtual currencies and digital tokens, and typically on platforms that offer a wide array of coin pairings for traders to buy and sell. The advisory observes that while these schemes have been around as long as the virtual currency markets themselves, the number of new virtual currency and digital coin traders has grown substantially, resulting in an increased number of potential victims or perpetrators.

Customer Advisory: Beware of "IRS Approved" Virtual Currency IRAs. This customer advisory is designed to encourage investors to be cautious of sales pitches touting "IRS approved" or "IRA approved" virtual currency retirement accounts. The advisory notes the volatility in virtual currency prices and concludes this volatility is not reduced or limited just because the virtual currencies are held in an individual retirement account (IRA) as is sometimes suggested by unscrupulous promoters.

¶ 420 Virtual Currencies as a "Commodity" under the CEA

The mission of the CFTC is to foster open, transparent, competitive, and financially sound derivatives markets. By working to avoid systemic risk, the Commission aims to protect market users and their funds, consumers, and the public from fraud, manipulation, and abusive practices related to derivatives and other products that are subject to the Commodity Exchange Act (CEA).

To ensure the integrity of US derivatives markets, the CFTC regulates derivatives market participants and activities. The agency oversees a variety of individuals and organizations which includes swap execution facilities, derivatives clearing organizations, designated contract markets, swap data repositories, swap dealers, futures commission merchants, commodity pool operators, and other entities. The CFTC also prosecutes derivative market fraud and manipulation, as well as misconduct in underlying spot markets for commodities. Congress, through the CEA [CEA Section 2(a)(1)], has granted the CFTC exclusive jurisdiction over futures, options, and swaps on commodities. In turn, the CEA defines the term "commodity" [CEA Section 1(a)(9)] very broadly to include, among other things, all goods and articles and "all services, rights, and interests in which contracts for future delivery are presently or in the future dealt in." Peculiarly, the only items specifically excluded from the definition of commodity are onions and motion picture box office receipts.

CFTC Authority and Oversight over Commodities

As a preliminary matter, it is important to recognize that the CFTC has both oversight and enforcement authority with respect to futures and other derivative products and markets, while the agency has *only* enforcement authority over the spot markets, where the commodities themselves are actually bought and sold.

This distinction is crucial. In terms of oversight authority over derivatives trading, the CFTC's role is broad and far-reaching. It includes setting requirements for registration of trading platforms or firms, trade execution, orderly trading, data reporting, and recordkeeping. In contrast, with respect to spot markets, the CFTC only has enforcement authority to police fraud and manipulation in the actual trading of commodities. Pursuant to this enforcement jurisdiction, the CFTC can investigate potential fraud and manipulation in underlying virtual cash markets.

Moreover, with respect to the spot markets for commodities, neither the CFTC nor any other federal agency has similar oversight authority. This means the CFTC cannot impose things like registration requirements on platforms or participants in the cash markets, surveillance and monitoring requirements on spot platforms, or otherwise require compliance with business conduct standards or other trading requirements.

¶420

Virtual Currencies as a "Commodity" under the CEA – an Evolving Recognition of the CFTC's authority

A chairman asserts authority over virtual currencies. In December 2014, then–CFTC Chairman Timothy Massad stated that the CFTC viewed virtual currencies as commodities in testimony before the Senate Committee on Agriculture, Nutrition and Forestry. Chairman Massad explained that although the CFTC did not have policies and procedures specific to virtual currencies like Bitcoin, the Commission's "authority extends to futures and swaps contracts in any commodity" and therefore "derivative contracts based on a virtual currency represent one area" within the Commission's responsibility.

The CFTC's position solidified through enforcement actions. In September 2015, the Commission formalized its interpretation regarding the agency's authority over virtual currencies by filing and settling an enforcement action brought against Coinflip, Inc., the owner and operator of a Bitcoin trading platform called Derivabit, which offered to connect buyers and sellers of Bitcoin option contracts.

In its order, the CFTC asserted jurisdiction over Derivabit's activities by determining that "Bitcoin and other virtual currencies are encompassed in the definition and properly defined as commodities." Based upon this finding, the CFTC found that Derivabit had illegally offered commodity options without being registered as an exchange or swap execution facility with the Commission. The *Coinflip* case represents the first time the CFTC asserted jurisdiction over contracts involving Bitcoin by recognizing that Bitcoin was a commodity. [*In the Matter of Coinflip, Inc.*, CFTC Docket No. 15-29, September 17, 2015.]

Soon thereafter, the CFTC brought two other matters further demonstrating its authority, as well as its willingness, to play a regulatory role in the virtual currency arena. The CFTC brought a case against TeraExchange LLC, and in its settlement order, the CFTC sought to prohibit wash trading and prearranged trades on a virtual currency derivatives platform. [*In the Matter of TeraExchange LLC*, CFTC Docket No. 15-33, September 24, 2015.] In 2016, the CFTC filed and settled an enforcement action against BXFNA Inc. d/b/a Bitfinex, a Bitcoin futures exchange operating in the U.S. that failed to register with the agency (see ¶ 440). [*In the Matter of BFXNA Inc.*, CFTC Docket No. 16-19, June 2, 2016.]

CFTC pursues fraud in the spot Bitcoin market. In September 2017, the CFTC filed charges against defendants Nicholas Gelfman of Brooklyn, New York, and his company, Gelfman Blueprint, Inc., in the U.S. District Court for the Southern District of New York. In this matter, the CFTC claimed the defendants were running a Bitcoin related Ponzi scheme, but the Commission's allegations regarding the defendants' handling of Bitcoin pertained to Bitcoin alone, and not futures or swaps based on Bitcoin. The complaint charged the defendants with fraud, misappropriation, and issuing false account statements. The CFTC's action is significant as it represents the agency's clearest expression that it will exercise jurisdiction over Bitcoin and cryptocurrencies when there is potential fraud, even when that fraud does not involve derivatives based on cryptocurrencies. [*CFTC v. Gelfman Blueprint, Inc.*, S.D.N.Y., September 21, 2017.]

A federal court affirms the agency's position. In 2018, the U.S. District Court for the Eastern District of New York affirmed the CFTC's position in *CFTC v. McDonnell* that virtual currencies are commodities under applicable law, and that the CFTC has standing to sue persons for fraud in connection with spot sales of virtual currencies, even where such sales do not involve the sale of futures or derivatives contracts, thereby vindicating and giving further credence to the regulatory role the CFTC has played in the virtual currency realm. [*CFTC v. McDonnell*, E.D.N.Y., January 18, 2018.]

The court's ruling specifically upheld the CFTC's authority to exercise its enforcement power over fraud to virtual currencies sold in interstate commerce and granted the CFTC an injunction against Patrick McDonnell and Cabbagetech, Corp. The CFTC charged the defendants with unlawfully soliciting customers to send money and virtual currencies for virtual currency trading advice and for the discretionary trading of virtual currencies by Mr. McDonnell.

Actual Delivery and Retail Commodity Transactions Involving Virtual Currency

Under the Dodd-Frank market reforms, Congress added to the CEA a retail commodity provision, [CEA Section 2(c)(2)(D)(i).] which provides for direct CFTC oversight if an entity offers a commodity for sale to a retail customer on a margined, leveraged, or financed basis. In other words, if borrowed funds are used to effectuate a transaction, then the agreement is regulated as if it were a futures transaction, and these contracts then become subject to CFTC requirements related to exchange trading and registration. There is an important exception to the CFTC's retail commodity jurisdiction where the commodity is actually delivered to the buyer within 28 days.

Proposed interpretation. Towards the end of 2017, the CFTC issued a proposed interpretation titled Retail Commodity Transactions Involving Virtual Currency that would formally require actual delivery of a virtual currency to a retail client within 28 days to avoid Commission registration requirements by persons selling and either financing or arranging financing of the virtual currency. The CFTC also invited public comment in connection with the proposal.

In its proposed interpretation, the CFTC said that, consistent with prior guidance involving retail transactions of tangible commodities, the CFTC will consider "actual delivery" of a virtual currency to have occurred when a customer can take "possession and control" of all of the cryptocurrency and use it freely no later than 28 days from the date of the initial transaction, and can do so without any encumbrance. This would require neither the offeror nor seller, or any person acting in concert with such persons, retaining any interest or control in the virtual currency after 28 days from the date of the transaction.

Impact of financing a transaction. Among other situations, the CFTC noted that actual delivery of a virtual currency will occur within 28 days of an initial transaction when there is a record of a sale of the relevant virtual currency, including any financed portion, on the relevant blockchain, from the seller's blockchain wallet to the buyer's blockchain wallet, or, if the transaction occurred on a matching platform, from the offeror's blockchain wallet to the purchaser's blockchain wallet—provided the purchaser's wallet is "not affiliated with or controlled by the counterparty seller or third party offeror in any manner."

The CFTC also cautioned that actual delivery will not have occurred when, within 28 days, virtual currency sold to a retail client is rolled, offset against, netted out, or settled in cash or virtual currency between a buyer and the offeror or counterparty seller or any person acting in concert with either such person.

Public comment. The comment period for the CFTC's proposed interpretation focusing on the actual delivery exception for retail virtual currency transactions came to an end in March 2018. The CFTC received a total of 96 comments, which included five comment letters from industry and trade associations, seven from industry participants, two from public interest groups, and one from a self-regulatory organization. The overwhelming majority, 81 comments, were submitted by members of the general public. It is anticipated that the CFTC will issue a final interpretation providing a clear standard when financed virtual currencies are considered actually delivered to customers, and consequently when direct CFTC regulatory oversight is implicated.

¶420

A California court ruling challenges the CFTC's actual delivery position. A California federal court dismissed an enforcement action in *CFTC v. Monex Credit Company* alleging that a precious metals company, as well as its affiliates and principals, committed fraud in connection with the financed sale of precious metals to retail customers. The court's ruling calls into question the CFTC's position regarding actual delivery and its prohibition against financing transactions. [*CFTC v. Monex Credit Company*, C.D. Cal., May 1, 2018.]

The Commission brought the action in September 2017, alleging that the Monex firms used high-pressure sales tactics to deceptively pitch leveraged precious metals trades as safe, despite causing more than $290 million in losses to retail customers over the course of almost six years.

Specifically, in its May 2018 order, the court ruled that Monex's practice of delivering precious metals to independent depositories within 28 days of their purchase by retail customers on margin fell within the "actual delivery exception" to the CFTC's authority. The court determined that the actual delivery of precious metals in financed transactions to retail persons falls outside the CFTC's authority when ownership of real metals is legally transferred to such persons within 28 days, even if the seller retains control over the commodities because of the financing beyond 28 days.

The *Monex* ruling runs directly counter to the CFTC's long-held position, which underpins its proposed interpretation for retail virtual currency transactions, that an exception to the 28-day actual delivery requirement applies where a retail customer acquires a position on a leveraged or margined basis, or financed by the offeror or counterparty (or parties acting in concert with an offeror or counterparty). In all likelihood, this decision will have important implications beyond the precious metals context. In the virtual currency realm, the case might impact cryptocurrency exchanges that would have an interest in providing financing for purchases of virtual currencies by retail customers. For the time being, the *Monex* decision represents the view of one federal court in one district of California. On May 15, 2018, that court, on its own motion, certified its dismissal order for interlocutory appeal. The district court recognized that its dismissal order involves a controlling question of law for which there is substantial ground for difference of opinion. As a result, further clarification of the issues at hand will await the appellate court's consideration of this matter.

¶ 430 Virtual Currency Swaps, Futures and Self-Certification of Bitcoin Products

A number of key developments and shifts in the regulatory landscape took place in 2017 in connection with the launch of derivative products based on virtual currencies. These changes were ushered in by the CFTC's proactive involvement and willingness to consider innovative approaches when dealing with novel Bitcoin-related products and their associated regulatory issues. During the year, the CFTC granted swap execution facility (SEF) and Designated Contract Market (DCM) status to LedgerX, an institutional trading and clearing platform for derivatives on digital currencies.

The most significant regulatory developments during the year surrounded the introduction and launch of a number of Bitcoin-related futures contracts. On December 1, 2017, the Chicago Mercantile Exchange Inc. (CME) and the CBOE Futures Exchange (CFE) self-certified new contracts for Bitcoin futures products, and the Cantor Exchange (Cantor) self-certified a new contract for Bitcoin binary options. Also on that day, CFTC Chairman J. Christopher Giancarlo proclaimed, "Bitcoin, a virtual currency, is a commodity unlike any the Commission has dealt with in the past."

Chairman Giancarlo echoed these sentiments the following month in remarks before a group of derivative and futures industry attorneys where he noted, "In the waning months of 2017, virtual currencies, especially Bitcoin, took the world by storm. The Wall Street Journal estimates that Bitcoin's value increased 1,375 percent in 2017." Giancarlo also observed that virtual currencies "are sweeping us rapidly, day-by-day, hourly, into a new future. And that torrent is bumping up against some of the established frameworks of futures regulation, including the obligation of futures exchanges to ensure that virtual currency futures are not susceptible to manipulation, and of futures clearinghouses to ensure that such products are adequately risk managed."

Although the CFTC was intimately involved with the noted DCOs and the Bitcoin-related products' self-certification process, their rapid introduction, combined with the extraordinary price volatility being experienced in the Bitcoin spot market, resulted in numerous objections from various industry participants asserting that the process denied them a meaningful opportunity to provide adequate comment or input.

Virtual Currency Swaps

In July 2017, the CFTC issued an order by a unanimous 2-0 vote granting LedgerX, LLC, a New York-based institutional trading and clearing platform for digital currencies, registration as a derivatives clearing organization (DCO) under the CEA. [Order of Registration, July 24, 2017.] In a related action, the Commission's Division of Clearing and Risk (DCR) issued a staff letter exempting LedgerX from complying with certain Commission regulations by virtue of LedgerX's unique fully collateralized clearing model. Its Bitcoin option contracts were certified in September 2017. [CFTC Letter No. 17-35, July 24, 2017.]

LedgerX's activities are considered to be significant as the company intends to use the distributed ledger technology associated with Bitcoin to receive Bitcoin from and deliver Bitcoin to its members in connection with the option contracts. LedgerX will also employ cloud-based storage to maintain many of its required books and records. Eligible participants may include registered broker-dealers, banks, futures commission merchants, qualified commodity pool entities, and qualified high-net-worth investors.

The CFTC has had prior experience with virtual currency derivatives. In October 2013, the CFTC had granted SEF registration to TeraExchange to trade Bitcoin swaps, and in November 2014, Nadex Bitcoin-based binary options were certified.

The Self-Certification of Bitcoin Futures Contracts

As noted, the CME, the CFE, and the Cantor Exchange self-certified new contracts for Bitcoin-related products on December 1, 2017. In a release, issued in January 2018, titled CFTC Backgrounder on Oversight of and Approach to Virtual Currency Futures Markets, the Commission outlined its "heightened review" process for virtual currency contracts. The backgrounder also summarized the self-certification process generally, as well as its application for new Bitcoin derivative products launched by DCMs in December 2017. The backgrounder noted the following items with regard to the self-certification process:

• The product self-certification process was deliberately designed by Congress and prior Commissions to give the initiative to DCMs to certify new products. This is consistent with a DCM's role as a self-regulatory organization and the CFTC's principles-based approach to regulation.

• This self-certification process is one that Congress promulgated and prior Commissions have implemented. Unless it is changed, the staff of the CFTC must work responsibly within the self-certification structure.

• The product self-certification process does NOT provide for public input, the creation of separate guaranty funds for clearing, or value judgments about the underlying spot market.

- There are limited grounds for the CFTC to "stay" self-certification such as filing a false statement in the certification.

- In the case of the CME and CFE self-certifications, no such grounds were evident.

- Had it even been possible, blocking self-certification would not have stemmed interest in Bitcoin or other virtual currencies nor their spectacular and volatile valuations. Instead, it would have ensured that the virtual currency spot markets continue to operate without federal regulatory surveillance for fraud and manipulation.

The CFTC asserted that it was well prepared to handle the recent self-certifications of Bitcoin futures products. The Commission further noted that CFTC staff knew that a virtual currencies market was evolving rapidly in 2017 and that the agency would likely see proposals for the launch of Bitcoin futures.

Industry Concerns and Criticism over Bitcoin Contract Self-Certifications

Soon after the CFTC gave the green light to the various exchanges for their Bitcoin-related products, Futures Industry Association (FIA) CEO Walter Lukken issued an open letter to the CFTC, saying, "We believe that the launch of new exchange-traded derivatives in cryptocurrencies deserves a healthy dialogue between regulators, exchanges, clearinghouses and the clearing firms who will be absorbing the risk of these volatile, emerging instruments during a default. Unfortunately, the launching of these innovative products through the 1-day self-certification process did not allow for proper public transparency and input."

Lukken further observed: "While we greatly appreciate the CFTC's efforts to receive additional assurances from these exchanges, we remain apprehensive with the lack of transparency and regulation of the underlying reference products on which these futures contracts are based and whether exchanges have the proper oversight to ensure the reference products are not susceptible to manipulation, fraud, and operational risk." The FIA also noted its concerns, given the extreme volatility of the underlying reference product and the novel, untested nature of the self-certified derivatives products, that clearing firms bear the brunt of the risk through guarantee fund contributions and assessment obligations, rather than the exchanges and clearinghouses who list them.

Moreover, FIA indicated the CFTC should have had public discussion on whether a separate guarantee fund for the products was appropriate or whether exchanges put additional capital in front of the clearing member guarantee fund. In addition, not all risk committees of the relevant exchanges were consulted before the certifications, per FIA's understanding. FIA said it looks forward to a "healthy public discussion" on how to improve the self-certification process in the future, as well as the CFTC's continued oversight of the emerging instruments.

Reed Smith counsel Kari Larsen sees the self-certification controversy somewhat differently. "The self-certification process is broadly applicable across futures products. The industry has said it has worked perfectly for a long time. In this instance, the exchanges worked extensively for many months before the launch. The CFTC met with all the exchange teams: risk, clearing, surveillance," she noted. "I think the FIA letter needs to be taken with a grain of salt. The exchanges were in contact with the FCM community," she added. "This whole thing got overblown, with a lot of press and media reaction thrown into the mix as well."

Heightened Review for the Self-Certification of Virtual Currency Products

Given the uniqueness of the Bitcoin-related futures products introduced by the CME and CFE, CFTC staff obtained the voluntary cooperation of the exchanges, within the limits and parameters of the current self-certification process, to engaged in a "heightened review" of the new products. In particular, this review addressed concerns that the contracts were not susceptible to price manipulation and that DCOs are properly overseeing margin requirements and related risks. The heightened review process sought to enhance the visibility and monitoring of markets for virtual currency derivatives and underlying settlement reference rates, and provide the CFTC with the means to police certain underlying spot markets for fraud and manipulation. The heightened review included seven elements:

1. Designated contract markets (DCMs) setting exchange large trader reporting thresholds at five Bitcoins or less;

2. DCMs entering into direct or indirect information sharing agreements with spot market platforms to allow access to trade and trader data;

3. DCMs agreeing to engage in monitoring of price settlement data from cash markets and identifying anomalies and disproportionate moves;

4. DCMs agreeing to conduct inquiries, including at the trade settlement and trader level when anomalies or disproportionate moves are identified;

5. DCMs agreeing to regular communication with CFTC surveillance staff on trade activities, including providing trade settlement and trader data upon request;

6. DCMs agreeing to coordinate product launches to enable the CFTC's market surveillance branch to monitor minute-by-minute developments; and

7. DCMs setting substantial initial and maintenance margin for cash-settled instruments.

CFTC Response to Industry Criticism

The CFTC's Market Risk Advisory Committee (MRAC) met later in January 2018 to further consider the new product self-certification of virtual currency products, among other topics. At the MRAC meeting, Chairman Giancarlo, while acknowledging the criticisms, addressed the self-certification process directly, noting that "it is DCMs and Designated Clearing Organizations (DCOs)—and not CFTC staff—that must solicit and address stakeholder concerns in new product self-certifications. Interested parties, especially clearing members, should indeed have an opportunity to raise appropriate concerns for consideration by regulated platforms proposing virtual currency derivatives and DCOs considering clearing new virtual currency products." [Remarks of Chairman Giancarlo before the Market Risk Advisory Committee Meeting, January 31, 2018.]

In an effort to quell some of the concerns from the clearing firm community regarding the opportunity to provide comment and input, Giancarlo also indicated that he had requested CFTC staff to add an additional element to its Review and Compliance Checklist for virtual currency product self-certifications. The revised checklist would require DCMs and Swaps Execution Facilities (SEFs) to disclose to CFTC staff what steps they have taken in their capacity as self-regulatory organizations to gather and accommodate appropriate input from concerned parties, including trading firms and FCMs.

CFTC Staff Provides Further Guidance to Clearinghouses, DCMs and SEFs

In May 2018, the CFTC's Division of Market Oversight, together with the Division of Clearing and Risk, jointly issued an advisory to registered DCOs, DCMs, and SEFs providing additional guidance for listing virtual currency derivative products. The stated

¶430

purpose for the advisory was to foster compliance with CFTC regulations, assist market participants in their efforts to design risk management programs that address the new risks imposed by virtual currency products, and ensure that market participants follow appropriate governance processes with respect to the launch of these products.

Advisory highlights. The advisory highlighted the following topic areas in the context of listing new virtual currency derivatives contracts:

- **Enhanced market surveillance.** DCMs and SEFs, as self-regulatory organizations (SROs), must establish and maintain an effective oversight program designed, among other things, to ensure that listed contracts are not readily susceptible to manipulation and to detect and prevent manipulation, price distortion, and disruptions of the delivery or cash-settlement process. The advisory further notes that as part of its review of an exchange's surveillance program, staff will assess the exchange's visibility into trader activities in the underlying spot markets.

- **Close coordination with CFTC staff.** CFTC staff expects exchanges to regularly discuss a wide range of issues related to the surveillance of virtual currency derivatives contracts, and provide surveillance information as requested by commission staff. Upon request, an exchange must also provide commission staff with data related to the settlement process referenced by the contract to enable staff to conduct its own independent surveillance

- **Large trader reporting.** Under the Commission's Large Trader Reporting System, FCMs and foreign brokers are required to file daily reports with the Commission under Part 17 of the CFTC's regulations. The reports show futures and option positions of traders with positions at or above specific reporting levels as set by the commission. With respect to any virtual currency derivative contract, staff is recommending that the exchange set the large trader reporting threshold for at five bitcoin, or the equivalent for other virtual currencies). Staff notes that this level could help facilitate surveillance of the futures and options markets by increasing an exchange's ability to focus on relevant information in the spot market.

- **Outreach to member and market participants.** Prior to listing a new contract on virtual currency, staff expects an exchange to solicit comments and views on issues relating to the listing, beyond those that relate to the contract's terms and conditions and its susceptibility to manipulation. Staff notes that consultations covering a broad scope of topics may generate information relevant to the impact of listing and clearing the new contract on members and market users.

- **DCO risk management and governance.** With regard to new product offerings, CFTC staff will review a DCO's proposed initial margin requirements to assess whether they are commensurate with the risks of the contracts, and the ability of proposed margin requirements to adequately cover potential future exposures to clearing members based on an appropriate historic time period. Commission staff also intends to seek information related to the governance process for approving a proposed contract. Moreover, staff will expect that a DCO explain its consideration of the views of clearing members in approving the proposed contract, including the DCO's response to any dissenting views regarding how the virtual currency derivatives contract will be cleared.

Commissioner Behnam comments. In a statement, Commissioner Rostin Behnan expressed his support and commended staff for issuing the advisory, noting this "is another step in providing the public with greater transparency into this process." At the same time, the commissioner observed that further and more formal action is necessary, stating, "While this staff advisory clarifies expectations, it does not equate a

¶430

change to the regulatory process. Such changes require a more fulsome and formal process, subject to Commission deliberation and public notice and comment." He added, "I look forward to continuing to explore our options, which I hope will include some parameters for determining when self-certification may not be appropriate, and for determining when such matters are appropriately brought before the Commission."

¶ 440 CFTC Enforcement Activities

After the CFTC declared that virtual currencies were a "commodity" in 2014, and subject to its oversight under the CEA (see ¶ 420), the agency has continuously deployed its enforcement resources as a central means to assert its regulatory authority in the virtual currency space. In addition to its general regulatory and enforcement jurisdiction over the virtual currency derivatives markets, the CFTC has jurisdiction to police fraud and manipulation in cash or spot markets.

As noted by Chairman Giancarlo, the agency has sought to be particularly assertive of its enforcement jurisdiction over virtual currencies. In testimony before the Senate Banking Committee in February 2018, the chairman indicated that the agency had formed an internal virtual currency enforcement task force to garner and deploy relevant expertise in this evolving asset class. The task force shares information and works cooperatively with counterparts at the SEC with similar virtual currency expertise.

The Role of the Division of Enforcement

The CFTC Division of Enforcement (DOE) is dedicated to deterring and preventing price manipulation and other disruptions of market integrity, ensuring the financial integrity of all transactions subject to the CEA, and protecting market participants from fraudulent or other abusive sales practices and misuse of customer assets. In the virtual currency realm, the DOE has been specifically tasked with policing against the following prohibited activities:

- Price manipulation of a virtual currency traded in interstate commerce;

- Pre-arranged or wash trading in an exchange-traded virtual currency swap or futures contract;

- Trading of a virtual currency futures or option contract or swap on a domestic platform or facility that has not registered with the CFTC as a SEF or DCM; and

- Certain schemes involving virtual currency marketed to retail customers, such as off-exchange financed commodity transactions with persons who fail to register with the CFTC.

The DOE and other Commission offices also coordinate various virtual currency-related matters with other governmental agencies and authorities including the SEC, FBI, Justice Department, and Financial Stability Oversight Council. The CFTC also coordinates with state entities, including state attorneys general, in addition to working with the White House, Congress, and other policy-makers.

A Survey of CFTC Enforcement Actions

The CFTC has frequently utilized its enforcement jurisdiction as means to assert its authority over virtual currency products and markets. It has been equally important for the DOE to root out fraud and "to crack down hard on those who try to abuse [virtual currency enthusiasts] with fraud and manipulation," as observed by Chairman Giancarlo. Commencing in 2015, the CFTC has brought a total of eight matters involving virtual currencies, either in the spot or derivative marketplaces. A summary of these enforcement actions follows:

¶440

In the Matter of Coinflip, Inc., d/b/a Derivabit and Francisco Riordan (September 17, 2015) - Failure to register as a SEF or DCM. The CFTC brought and simultaneously settled its first enforcement action involving virtual currencies against Coinflip, Inc. d/b/a Derivabit, a Bitcoin options trading platform operator, and its CEO, Francisco Riordan. The CFTC charged the respondents with operating a facility for the trading or processing of commodity options without having registered as a SEF or DCM, as required. The CFTC's order further found that the respondents failed to comply with the CEA or CFTC regulations applicable to swaps or conduct the activity pursuant to the CFTC's exemption for trade options. As part of the agreed order, the respondents agreed to cease and desist from further violations of the CEA and Commission regulations, and to comply with certain undertakings. No civil monetary penalty was assessed.

In the Matter of TeraExchange LLC (September 24, 2015) - Wash trading and prearranged trading in connection with a Bitcoin swap. The CFTC filed and settled a complaint against TeraExchange LLC for failing to enforce its prohibition on wash trading and prearranged trading on the SEF platform. Specifically, the CFTC order found that Tera offered a non-deliverable forward contract based on the relative value of the U.S. dollar and Bitcoin (the "Bitcoin Swap") for trading on its SEF.

On the date the subject trades occurred, the only two market participants authorized to trade on Tera's SEF entered into two transactions in the Bitcoin Swap. The transactions were for the same notional amount, price, and tenor, and had the effect of completely offsetting each other. At the time, these were the only transactions on Tera's SEF. The CFTC order required Tera to cease and desist from future violations relating to its obligations to enforce rules on trade practices, and to commit to certain remedial undertakings.

In the Matter of BFXNA Inc. d/b/a Bitfinex (June 2, 2016) - Failure to satisfy actual delivery requirements and failure to be registered as required. The CFTC filed a complaint and simultaneously settled charges against Hong Kong-based Bitcoin exchange Bitfinex for offering illegal off-exchange financed retail commodity transactions in Bitcoin and other cryptocurrencies, and for failing to register as an FCM as required by the CEA. The settlement order required Bitfinex to pay a $75,000 civil monetary penalty and to cease and desist from future violations of the CEA as charged.

Bitfinex operated an online platform for exchanging and trading cryptocurrencies, mainly Bitcoin. The order found that from April 2013 to at least February 2016, Bitfinex permitted users to borrow funds from other users on the platform in order to trade Bitcoins on a leveraged, margined, or financed basis. The order also finds that Bitfinex did not actually deliver those Bitcoins to the traders who purchased them. Instead, Bitfinex held the Bitcoins in deposit wallets that it owned and controlled.

As a result, the Commission found that these financed retail commodity transactions did not meet the exception for actual delivery and should have been executed on a registered exchange like any other futures contract. In addition, the Commission determined that Bitfinex should have been registered as an FCM (See ¶ 420).

CFTC v. Gelfman Blueprint and Nicholas Gelfman (September 21, 2017) - Charges of fraud, misappropriation, and issuing false account statements in connection with a Ponzi scheme involving Bitcoin, but no derivative products. The CFTC filed an enforcement action in the U.S. District Court for the Southern District of New York against Defendants Nicholas Gelfman, of Brooklyn, New York, and his company Gelfman Blueprint, Inc. (GBI), a New York corporation, charging them with fraud, misappropriation, and issuing false account statements in connection with solicited investments in Bitcoin.

Specifically, the CFTC's complaint alleged that from approximately January 2014 through approximately January 2016, GBI and Gelfman, the company's chief executive officer and head trader, operated a Bitcoin Ponzi scheme in which they fraudulently solicited more than $600,000 from approximately 80 persons, supposedly for placement in a pooled commodity fund that purportedly employed a high-frequency, algorithmic trading strategy, executed by defendants' computer trading program called "Jigsaw." In fact, as charged in the CFTC complaint, the strategy was fake, the purported performance reports were false, and, as is the case with all Ponzi schemes, payouts of supposed profits to GB Customers consisted of other customers' misappropriated funds. The Commission's action in this matter is significant as it indicates that the CFTC will exercise its authority over virtual currencies when fraud is involved, even if derivative instruments are not part of the fraudulent scheme.

CFTC v. My Big Coin Pay Inc. et al. (January 16, 2018) – Charges of fraud and manipulation. The CFTC filed an enforcement action in the U.S. District Court for the District of Massachusetts charging Randall Crater, Mark Gillespie, and My Big Coin Pay, Inc., a corporation based in Las Vegas, Nevada, with commodity fraud and misappropriating over $6 million from customers related to the ongoing solicitation for a virtual currency known as My Big Coin. The CFTC also obtained a restraining order freezing the assets of certain relief defendants.

Specifically, the CFTC complaint alleged that from at least January 2014 through January 2018, the defendants fraudulently solicited potential and existing MBC customers throughout the United States by making false and misleading claims and omissions about MBC's value, usage, and trade status, including representing that MBC was backed by gold. The complaint further alleged that the defendants misappropriated virtually all of the approximately $6 million they solicited from customers.

Notably, during the course of this litigation the defendants filed a motion to dismiss the CFTC's complaint claiming that it lacked jurisdiction under applicable law. The defendants argue that the CFTC may only bring an enforcement action alleging fraud in connection with the offer and sale of a commodity transacted in interstate commerce. They assert, however, that their My Big Coin virtual currency was not a commodity as defined under applicable law because it was not one of the specifically enumerated 30 commodities in the CEA's definition and it was a not a service, right or interest in which contracts for future delivery are presently or in the future dealt in. According to the defendants, solely Bitcoin qualifies as a commodity as there are currently futures contracts trading based on that virtual currency only.

CFTC v. McDonnell, Cabbagetech, Corp. d/b/a Coin Drop Markets (January 18, 2018) – Charges of fraud and misappropriation in connection with purchases and trading of Bitcoin and Litecoin. The CFTC brought an enforcement action in the U.S. District Court for the Eastern District of New York against Patrick K. McDonnell and CabbageTech, Corp. d/b/a Coin Drop Markets (CDM), a New York corporation, charging them with fraud and misappropriation in connection with purchases and trading of Bitcoin and Litecoin.

Specifically, the complaint alleged that beginning in January 2017, McDonnell and CDM engaged in a deceptive and fraudulent virtual currency scheme to induce customers to send money and virtual currencies to CDM, purportedly in exchange for real-time virtual currency trading advice and for virtual currency purchasing and trading on behalf of the customers under McDonnell's direction. The CFTC asserted that the supposedly expert, real-time virtual currency advice was never provided, and customers who provided funds to McDonnell and CDM to purchase or trade on their behalf never saw those funds again. McDonnell and CDM used their fraudulent solicitations to obtain and then simply misappropriate customer funds, according to the complaint.

¶440

This matter has particular significance as it provided a New York federal court the opportunity to affirm the CFTC's position that virtual currencies are commodities under the CEA.

CFTC v. Dillon Michael Dean and The Entrepreneurs Headquarters Limited (January 18, 2018) – Charges of fraud and misappropriation in connection with a Ponzi scheme involving binary options. The CFTC filed an enforcement action in the U.S. District Court for the Eastern District of New York against Dillon Michael Dean and his U.K.-registered company, The Entrepreneurs Headquarters Limited. The CFTC complaint charged the defendants with engaging in a fraudulent scheme to solicit Bitcoin from members of the public, misrepresenting that customers' funds would be pooled and invested in products including binary options, making Ponzi-style payments to commodity pool participants from other participants' funds, misappropriating pool participants' funds, and failing to register with the CFTC as a Commodity Pool Operator (CPO) and Associated Person of a CPO, as required.

Specifically, the complaint alleged that beginning in April 2017, defendants, who had never been registered with the CFTC in any capacity, engaged in a fraudulent scheme through which they solicited at least $1.1 million worth of Bitcoin from more than 600 members of the public. Defendants allegedly promised to convert this Bitcoin into fiat currency to invest on the customers' behalf in a pooled investment vehicle for trading commodity interests, including trading binary options on an online exchange designated as a contract market by the CFTC. Potential pool participants were solicited to invest with defendants by false claims of trading expertise and promises of high rates of return.

The complaint further alleged that, rather than convert customers' Bitcoin to fiat currency to invest in binary options contracts, as promised, defendants misappropriated their customers' funds, including by using the funds to pay other customers, in the manner of a Ponzi scheme.

Commodity Futures Trading Commission v. Kantor (April 16, 2018) - fraudulent scheme involving binary options and a virtual currency. The CFTC filed a complaint in the U.S. District Court for the Eastern District of New York charging Blake Harrison Kantor and Nathan Mullins, and the entities Blue Bit Banc, Blue Bit Analytics, Ltd., Mercury Cove, Inc., and G. Thomas Client Services, with operating a fraudulent scheme involving binary options and a virtual currency known as ATM Coin. In addition, the CFTC's complaint charges several defendants with accepting customer funds and illegally acting as FCMs without being registered with the CFTC. The complaint also alleges that the defendants acted as a common enterprise in carrying out their fraudulent scheme. The court entered a statutory restraining order freezing the assets of the defendants and a relief defendant.

The complaint alleged that beginning in April 2014, the defendants solicited potential customers through emails, phone calls, and a website to purchase illegal off-exchange binary options. Moreover, defendants falsely claimed customers' accounts would generate significant profits based upon Kantor's purported past profitable trading. Also according to the complaint, defendants misappropriated a substantial amount of the customer funds for the defendants' own personal use.

The complaint also alleged that defendants sought to cover up their misappropriation by inviting customers to transfer their binary options account balances into ATM Coin. Some customers agreed to transfer their funds into ATM Coin, and at least one customer sent additional money to defendants to purchase additional ATM Coin. Defendants then allegedly misrepresented to customers that their ATM Coin holdings were worth substantial sums of money.

¶440

¶ 450 The Role of the National Futures Association

In December 2017, around the time new Bitcoin futures products were being self-certified by the CME, CFE and the Cantor, the National Futures Association (NFA), the self-regulatory organization for the futures and derivative industry, also took certain actions relative to the introduction and launch of the new virtual currency futures contracts. First, the NFA issued its own investor advisory relative to Bitcoin. Additionally, the NFA imposed additional reporting requirements for those of its members involved with handling the new Bitcoin related products.

The Derivatives Industry's Self-Regulatory Organization

The NFA is the industrywide, self-regulatory organization for the U.S. derivatives industry and commenced its regulatory operations in 1982. Designated by the CFTC as a registered futures association, the NFA's central mission is to safeguard the integrity of the derivatives markets, protect investors and ensure members meet their regulatory responsibilities.

NFA Investor Advisory

On December 1, 2017, the NFA issued an investor advisory titled Futures on Virtual Currencies Including Bitcoin to encourage investors who are considering trading virtual currency futures to educate themselves about these products, understand their risks, and conduct due diligence before making investment decisions. The advisory noted that even though futures on virtual currencies must be traded on regulated futures exchanges, the underlying virtual currency markets may not be regulated and trading in the products involves a high level of risk. As such, the advisory urged potential traders to conduct due diligence on individuals and companies soliciting investments in futures on virtual currencies and to be aware of sales pitches promising significant returns with little risk.

Reporting Requirements for NFA Members Involved with Virtual Currencies Derivatives

In December 2017, the NFA issued notices advising FCMs, for whom the NFA serves as its designated self-regulatory organization, as well as other NFA members, that they would be subject to additional reporting requirements in the event they were involved in handling certain virtual currency transactions. The notices extended to all commodity trading advisors (CTAs), commodity pool operators (CPO) and introducing brokers (IBs).

FCMs. NFA Notice I-27 requires each FCM for which NFA is the DSRO to immediately notify NFA if the firm decides to offer its customers or non-customers the ability to trade any virtual currency futures product. The NFA noted that the obligation was ongoing, and that any FCM that did not currently intend to offer such products must notify NFA if it began offering these products. FCMs were required to email this notification to their NFA examination manager. Additionally, impacted FCMs are required to provide the following information on daily segregation reports:

- Number of customers who traded a virtual currency futures contract (including closed out positions),
- Number of non-customers who traded a virtual currency futures contract (including closed out positions), and
- Gross open virtual currency futures positions (*i.e.*, total open long positions, total open short positions).

CTAs and CPOs. NFA Notice I-17-28 similarly imposes reporting requirements upon CTAs and CPOs with respect to their trading of virtual currency products. Each CPO and CTA is required to immediately notify NFA if it executes a transaction involving any virtual currency or virtual currency derivative on behalf of a pool or managed account. Likewise, the reporting obligation is continuous in nature; any CPO or CTA that does not currently trade virtual currencies or related derivatives must notify NFA when it begins trading these products. A CPO or CTA that executes a transaction involving a virtual currency or virtual currency derivative is required to immediately notify NFA by amending the firm-level section of its annual questionnaire.

Additionally, beginning in the first quarter of 2018, CPOs and CTAs that have executed transactions involving virtual currencies or related derivatives are required to report the number of their pools or managed accounts that executed one or more transactions involving a virtual currency as well as the number of their pools or managed accounts that executed one or more transactions involving a virtual currency derivative during each calendar quarter. This information must be submitted to NFA through the firm's questionnaire no later than 15 days after the end of a quarter.

IBs. NFA Notice I-17-29 imposes similar reporting requirements upon IBs as apply to CTAs and CPOs. However, the requirements pertain only to virtual currency derivatives.

Chapter Five—FinCEN: AML and KYC Regulations

¶ 500 View from the Top

The Financial Crimes Enforcement Network is a Treasury Department bureau established by 31 U.S.C. § 310. While its principal statutory duties are the collection, analysis, and distribution of information on money laundering and other financial system abuses, both domestically and internationally, it also holds the Treasury Secretary's delegated authority to adopt regulations to implement the Bank Secrecy Act. To do so, FinCEN has adopted a series of regulations: 31 CFR Part 1010, which sets out general principles, and 31 CFR Parts 1020 through 1030, which apply those principles to various types of businesses.

FinCEN's entré into the regulation of virtual currencies is its regulations on money services businesses, found in 31 CFR Part 1022. [31 CFR Part 1022 beginning at ¶ 1170] Under these regulations, virtual currency exchangers and administrators are brought under the umbrella of money services businesses and subjected to all of the MSB regulations. Those who merely are virtual currency users are not regulated.

FinCEN Approach to Regulation

An excellent description of FinCEN's virtual currency regulatory philosophy can be found in testimony that Director Jennifer Shasky Calvery gave the Senate's Homeland Security Committee on Nov. 18, 2013. [Statement of Jennifer Shasky Calvery Before the United States Senate Committee on Homeland Security and Government Affairs, November 18, 2013, at ¶ 1310.] This testimony amounted to a tutorial on how the bureau views virtual currencies, the threats virtual currencies can pose, and the bureau's plans to mitigate those threats.

Repeating language used in earlier FinCEN guidance, Shasky Calvery described virtual currency as "a medium of exchange that operates like a currency in some environments but does not have all the attributes of real currency." Notably, it does not have the status of legal tender anywhere.

Convertible virtual currency either has an equal value in some real currency or it can be substituted for real currency, she continued. Also, convertible virtual currency can be either centralized or decentralized.

Then there is cryptocurrency. According to Shasky Calvery, cryptocurrency relies on cryptographic software protocols both to create the currency and to track and validate ownership transfers. Bitcoin is a cryptographic decentralized virtual currency.

Shasky Calvery also used two diagrams to demonstrate the difference between a centralized and a decentralized virtual currency, using Liberty Reserve (discussed under FinCEN Enforcement below) as an example of a centralized virtual currency and Bitcoin as an example of decentralized virtual currency:

Ex. 1

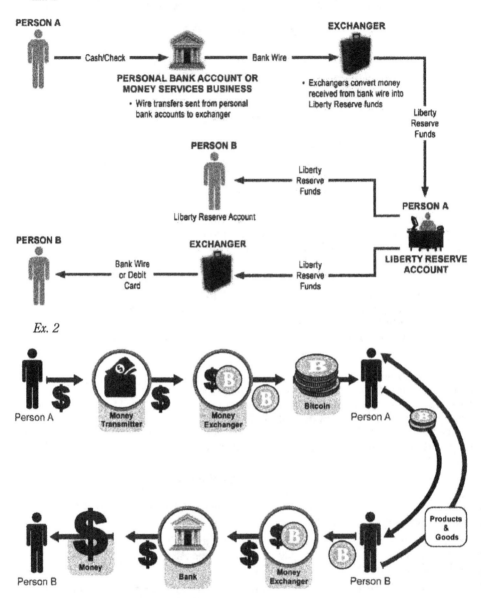

Ex. 2

The Director told the senators that virtual currency can have legitimate uses, but then listed a number of reasons why it might be preferable to real currency for illicit purposes. These included anonymity, simple global access, low costs, the absence of anyone who can maintain information on users and report suspicious activities, and an ability to exploit weaknesses in national regulatory schemes.

FinCEN's MSB definition rule (76 *Federal Register* 43585, July 21, 2011) was the agency's effort to eliminate at least some of these advantages by requiring that information be collected and, if appropriate, reported to law enforcement agencies. Since that final rule, and another rule on prepaid access (76 *Federal Register* 45403, July 29, 2011),

¶500

were adopted, the bureau has focused its efforts on using guidance and advisory opinions to explain its regulatory and enforcement priorities.

¶ 510 Overview of Money Laundering and Related Regulations

The source of FinCEN's authority to adopt regulations that apply to virtual currency is the Bank Secrecy Act, 12 U.S.C. § 1951 through 12 U.S.C. § 1959 and 31 U.S.C. § 5311 through 31 U.S.C. § 5328. The Treasury Department's authority to adopt regulations to implement these statutes has been delegated to the bureau.

FinCEN relied on that delegated authority when it adopted the regulations that impose on MSBs requirements for suspicious activity reporting, currency transaction reporting, anti-money laundering programs that include know-your-customer aspects, and Travel Rule compliance.

Bank Secrecy Act Sections

Several BSA sections are significant to FinCEN's authority and virtual currency.

First, 31 U.S.C. § 5312 defines "financial institution." Under this section, "financial institution" includes many businesses other than banks, thrifts, and credit unions. The following are defined as "financial institutions":

- issuers, redeemers, and cashiers of traveler's checks, checks, money orders, or similar instruments (31 U.S.C. § 5312(2)(K));

- precious metals, stones, and jewelry dealers (31 U.S.C. § 5312(2)(N)); and

- any other business the Treasury deems to be similar to such a business (31 U.S.C. § 5312(2)(Y)). [31 U.S.C. § 5312 at ¶ 1070.]

Second, 31 U.S.C. § 5318 allows FinCEN to require that financial institutions make Suspicious Activity Reports, implement anti-money laundering programs, and establish know-your-customer regimes. [31 U.S.C. § 5318 at ¶ 1080.]

Third, 31 U.S.C. § 5330 defines what is a money transmitting business and allows FinCEN to create registration requirements for these businesses. [31 U.S.C. § 5330 at ¶ 1090.]

FinCEN Regulations

As noted earlier, the regulations that cover virtual currency begin with 31 CFR Part 1010 (beginning at ¶ 1100). This CFR Part lays out general rules on compliance programs, recordkeeping and reporting, and exemptions for all financial institutions. Subsequent CFR Parts, 31 CFR Part 1020 through 31 CFR Part 1030, apply the general rules to specific types of businesses, incorporating many rules by reference and supplying some specific replacements or augmentations.

Rules relevant to virtual currency are found mainly in 31 CFR Part 1022 (beginning at ¶ 1170), which addresses money services businesses. In addition, FinCEN found it necessary in one advisory opinion, FIN-2015-R001, to interpret the rules for dealers in precious metals, stones, and jewels, which are in 31 CFR Part 1027 (beginning at ¶ 1220).

All financial institutions are required to:

- establish anti-money laundering programs, which include assessments of their risk of exposure to money laundering and also customer identification programs [31 CFR 1010.210; for MSBs, 31 CFR 1022.210];

- make Currency Transaction Reports [31 CFR 1010.310 through 31 CFR 1010.314; for MSBs, 31 CFR 1022.310 through 31 CFR 1022.314];

- make Suspicious Activity Reports [31 CFR 1022.320;

- report the receipt of more than $10,000 in currency received "in the course of a trade or business" that was not the subject of a CTR [31 CFR 1010.330; for MSBs, 31 CFR 1022.330]; and

- maintain required records, including those relevant to the Funds Travel Rule [31 CFR 1010.410].

Financial institutions that qualify as MSBs must register with FinCEN. The bureau has noted that compliance with its regulations is an obligation that is independent of the registration requirement.

What is an MSB? The important question then is what businesses must satisfy these requirements? In other words, what is an MSB?

FinCEN's regulation, 31 CFR 1010.100, lists seven categories of MSBs. However, most of those do not apply in the case of virtual currencies. For example, a dealer in foreign exchange will not be using virtual currency because virtual currency, under FinCEN's definitions, is not legal tender in any nation. In fact, there are two categories of MSBs that are relevant to virtual currency: money transmitters and prepaid access sellers. [31 CFR 1010.100 at ¶ 1100.]

A money transmitter is a person that accepts "currency, funds, or other value that substitutes for currency" and then transmits the value to another person or another location by any means. "Other value that substitutes for currency" covers virtual currency. "Any means" should be understood to mean *any* means—using an informal value transfer network, or a Federal Reserve Bank, or anything in between is covered.

The regulation adds that whether a person is a money transmitter is determined by the specific facts and circumstances.

There are six specific exceptions. A person is not a money transmitter if that person:

1. only provides computer or network access services that are used by a money transmitter;

2. acts as a payment processer to facilitate buying or paying for goods or services, using a clearance and settlement system, under an agreement with the seller or creditor;

3. operates a clearance and settlement system, or otherwise acts as an intermediary, between financial institutions that are subject to the BSA;

4. physically transports currency, documents, "or other value that substitutes for currency," and is in the business of doing so, as long as the ownership of the item does not change (the "physically transports" requirement seemingly would exclude any application to virtual currency);

5. provides prepaid access (this is not the same as being a seller of prepaid access); or

6. accepts and transmits funds as part of the sale of goods or services—other than money transmission services—by that person. [31 CFR 1010.100 at ¶ 1100.]

Prepaid access. Prepaid access sellers generally are not MSBs. There are two exceptions. If the prepaid access can be used before the buyer's identification can be verified, or if the seller sells any single person prepaid access to more than $10,000 in a single day, the seller is an MSB. The latter provision is subject to a safe harbor if the seller has policies and procedures reasonably adapted to avoid such a sale, which presumably would protect a company from mistakes or misdeeds by properly trained employees. [31 CFR 1010.100 at ¶ 1100.]

¶510

If a company is a money transmitter or prepaid access seller under the regulation, it must satisfy the MSB obligations.

Exemptions. There are three exemptions from the MSB definition. "Money services business" does not include:

1. a U.S. or foreign bank;

2. a U.S. entity that is registered with and supervised by the Securities and Exchange Commission or the Commodities Futures Trading Commission, or a foreign entity engaged in activities similar to the activities of such a person; or

3. an individual who engages in MSB-type activities infrequently and not for profit. [31 CFR 1010.100 at ¶ 1100.]

MSB Compliance Requirements

As noted earlier, MSBs are required to meet the BSA requirements that apply to all financial institutions. These requirements cover operations, record retention, and reporting.

AML programs. MSBs must have anti-money laundering programs, and an MSB's program must include an assessment of its particular risk of exposure to money laundering. The program must be written, and the MSB must produce it for inspection on request.

FinCEN's regulation sets out specific required elements. These include that the program must have policies, procedures, and internal controls that are reasonably designed to ensure compliance with the regulation, including:

- obtaining and verifying customer identification information;

- designating a BSA compliance officer;

- training all appropriate employees; and

- securing a periodic review of the program, which may not be carried out by the BSA officer. [31 CFR 1022.210].

Special know-your-customer provisions apply to MSBs that are prepaid access sellers.

CTRs. MSBs must file Currency Transaction Reports (see generally, 31 CFR 1010.310 through 31 CFR 1010.314, as the regulations specifically for MSBs simply incorporate the regulations for financial institutions). This requires the MSB to report any person's currency transactions that total more than $10,000 in a single banking day. [31 CFR 1010.311 and 31 CFR 1010.313.] Transactions with commercial banks need not be reported. [31 CFR 1010.315.]

The MSB must obtain identifying information from the customer before it completes any reportable transaction, and that information is to be verified in an acceptable manner. Necessary information includes the person's name and address, and the identity, account number, and Social Security or taxpayer identification number of any person on whose behalf the transaction is taking place. [31 CFR 1010.312.]

Currency transactions. In addition to filing CTRs, MSBs must report the receipt of more than $10,000 in currency in a single transaction or two or more related transactions in the course of their business activities. The identity of the person from whom the currency was received must be ascertained and verified. Transactions on which CTRs were filed need not be reported under this section.

A report must be made if the MSB receives currency from one person for the benefit of a third party. [31 CFR 1010.320 at ¶ 1160.]

SARs. MSBs must file Suspicious Activity Reports as required by 31 CFR 1022.320. An SAR must be filed on "any suspicious transaction relevant to a possible violation of law or regulation" if it involves assets of at least $2,000 and the MSB has reason to suspect that the transaction:

- involves or is intended to launder the proceeds of illegal activity;

- is intended to avoid the filing of a CTR or other regulatory requirement; or

- involves the MSB in facilitating criminal activity.

An SAR and all supporting documentation are to be retained for at least five years. SARs, and any information that would reveal that an SAR has been filed, are confidential and may be revealed only as the regulation explicitly permits. [31 CFR 1022.320 at ¶ 1190.]

Travel Rule. MSBs must maintain records needed to satisfy the Funds Travel Rule. This requires the MSB to collect and retain described information on covered transactions of more than $3,000, including information that would identify the person who initiates the transaction and the person who receives the funds. [31 CFR 1010.410.]

Quick reference guides. FinCEN has provided MSBs with two quick reference guides to help them comply with these obligations:

- *A Quick Reference Guide for Money Services Businesses—Bank Secrecy Act Requirements* (at www.fincen.gov/sites/default/files/shared/ bsa_en_bank_reference.pdf).

- *A Quick Reference Guide for Money Services Businesses—Reporting Suspicious Activity* (at www.fincen.gov/sites/default/files/shared/ rsa_en_report_reference.pdf).

In addition, the bureau has published a longer guide on MSB obligations: *Money Laundering Prevention—A Money Services Business Guide* (at www.fincen.gov/sites/ default/files/guidance/msb_prevention_guide.pdf).

MSB Guidance

FIN-2013-G001 was issued by FinCEN in 2013 to clarify how it intended to enforce the regulations it adopted in 2011. In that guidance, which focused on convertible virtual currency such as Bitcoin, the bureau explained the distinctions between virtual currency users, who are not MSBs and thus not subject to the regulations, and virtual currency exchangers and administrators, who are money transmitters under the regulation. [FIN-2013-G001, March 18, 2013, at ¶ 1240.]

According to the guidance:

- A "user" is a person that obtains virtual currency and uses it to buy goods or services or otherwise for its own benefit.

- An "exchanger" is a person that engages in the business of exchanging virtual currency for real currency, funds, or other virtual currency.

- An "administrator" is a person that engages in the business of issuing virtual currency and that has the authority to withdraw that virtual currency from circulation.

An exchanger or administrator that either accepts and transmits convertible virtual currency or buys and sells convertible virtual currency is a money transmitter, the guidance says. It is important to remember that FinCEN primarily is concerned with what the person does with virtual currency it has obtained, not with how it obtained the currency.

¶510

The guidance then applied the bureau's regulatory principles to three types of activities: brokers and dealers in e-currencies and e-precious metals; centralized convertible virtual currencies (*i.e.*, those with administrators); and de-centralized convertible currencies (*i.e.*, those without administrators).

E-currency and e-precious metals are digital certificates of ownership of real currency or real precious metal, with the underlying assets being held by the broker or dealer that distributed the certificate. These digital certificates are a form of virtual currency, the guidance says. If the broker or dealer accepts and transmits funds solely to accomplish a purchase or sale of the underlying currency or metal for a customer, it is not a money transmitter; it would be protected by exception No. 6 (above).

However, if the customer's funds are transferred between the customer and a person that is not a party to the transaction, the exception does not apply and the broker or dealer is a money transmitter. The guidance provides, as examples, allowing a third party to put funds into the customer's account to pay for a purchase, transferring value from one customer's account to another's, or closing out a customer's position and transferring the proceeds to a third party.

The guidance also makes clear that the same result is reached whether the broker or dealer deals in real currency or metals or e-currency or e-metals. Either way, the person is a money transmitter that must register as an MSB and meet the relevant requirements.

If a convertible virtual currency has a centralized repository, the administrator is a money transmitter if it allows the transfer of value from one person to another or from one location to another, the guidance says. Since FinCEN views two accounts of the same person to be two locations, transferring value from an account at one institution to an account at another would make the administrator a money transmitter, even if the same person owns both accounts.

Additionally, an exchanger that used access to the administrator's services to accept the virtual currency and transfer it to another person would be a money transmitter, according to FIN-2013-G001. This could happen if the exchanger accepts real currency from a virtual currency buyer and transmits it to the administrator to fund the buyer's account. That would constitute transmission to another location.

Alternatively, it could happen if the exchanger accepts currency from a user and then internally credits the user with a portion of the exchanger's account at the administrator's, then transmits that internal credit as directed by the user. That would constitute transmission to another person.

In the case of a decentralized convertible virtual currency that a person can obtain by its own efforts, such as by mining Bitcoin, the use of the currency determines the result, the guidance says. A person that creates the currency, i.e. mines the Bitcoin, and then uses it to obtain goods or services, whether real or virtual, is a user, not a money transmitter. However, if that person sells the virtual currency to another, it is a money transmitter.

And, probably rather obviously, if a person accepts decentralized convertible virtual currency from another and transmits it to a third party as part of a transfer of currency, funds, or value, the person is a money transmitter.

FIN-2013-G001 also clarified two other virtual currency-related situations. First, the guidance said, accepting or transmitting virtual currency is not providing or selling prepaid access "because prepaid access is limited to real currencies." Second, a person that exchanges virtual currency for real currency, or vice versa, is not a dealer in foreign exchange. Only a person that exchanges the legal tender of two countries is a dealer in foreign exchange. [FIN-2013-G001, March 18, 2013, at ¶ 1240.]

¶510

¶ 520 Administrative Rulings

To date, FinCEN has issued six administrative rulings addressing virtual currency-related activities. The most recent of those was issued in mid-2015, which could indicate that the industry now understands what the bureau is looking for.

FIN-2014-R001—Bitcoin mining. A company that mines Bitcoins would not be a money transmitter as long as it used the Bitcoins to buy goods and services for its own use, converted them to real currency in order to make such purchases or pay existing debts, or transferred ownership of the Bitcoins to the company's owner, FinCEN said in FIN-2014-R001. The company would be a user of virtual currency, not an exchanger or administrator. [FIN-2014-R001, January 30, 2014, at ¶ 1250.]

According to the ruling, whether the Bitcoin was bought or mined, "The label applied to a particular process of obtaining a virtual currency is not material to the legal characterization under the BSA of the process or of the person engaging in the process to send that virtual currency or its equivalent value to any other person or place." Rather, what matters is "what the person uses the convertible virtual currency for, and for whose benefit."

The company could pass the Bitcoin on to its owner as a legitimate distribution to its shareholders, the ruling continued.

The bureau did warn the company that a transfer to a third party at the direction of a person who sold goods or services to the company could constitute money transmission.

FIN-2014-R002—virtual currency investment software. A company that created software to be used in its own purchases of virtual currency as part of its virtual currency investment strategy would not be a money services business, according to FinCEN in FIN-2014-R002. The software, which would not be sold to any third parties, would provide a platform on which sellers would offer their virtual currency to the company and receive payment in real currency. The company would sell its virtual currency on an exchange, not through the proprietary software. [FIN-2014-R002, January 30, 2014, at ¶ 1260.]

Creating software and making it available to sellers would not make the company a money transmitter, the bureau first said. It would not constitute the acceptance and transmission of value.

Since the company intended that its virtual currency activities would be only for its own account and its own investment purposes, it would not be in the business of exchanging virtual currency for real currency, FinCEN continued. However, any transfers made by the company to third parties at the direction of its counterparties, creditors, or owners could constitute money transmission, the bureau warned.

The bureau also noted that providing services to third parties that included accepting and transmitting virtual currency, or exchanging virtual currency for real currency or other virtual currency, could be money transmission activities that would make the company an MSB.

FIN-2014-R007—renting currency mining systems. A company that rented its virtual currency mining system to other persons would not be a money transmitter, FinCEN decided in FIN-2014-R007. [FIN-2014-R007, April 29, 2014, at ¶ 1270.]

According to the ruling, the company had developed a computer system that it used to mine cryptocurrency. The company would rent its proprietary system to other persons for periods of anywhere between 24 hours and 30 days in exchange for rent payments based only on the length of the rental. The renter would furnish necessary information to the company, which would input the information into the system. Any

¶520

cryptocurrency that was mined would be owned solely by the renter; the company would not have access to the cryptocurrency and would neither receive nor transmit cryptocurrency for the renter.

Under such an arrangement, the company would not be acting as an exchanger, FinCEN determined, since it did not exchange virtual currency for another type of currency, either real or virtual. Neither would it be an administrator, since it did not issue virtual currency and did not have the authority to redeem virtual currency.

The company would not be a money transmitter, the bureau continued. Renting computer systems was not covered by the regulation; in fact, a person that only provided delivery, communication, or network access services to money transmitters was explicitly exempt from being deemed to be a money transmitter.

FIN-2014-R011—virtual currency trading platforms. A company that created and operated a convertible virtual currency trading and booking platform would be a money transmitter, FinCEN determined in FIN-2014-R011. In the process of reaching the decision, the bureau considered and rejected several exemption claims raised by the company. [FIN-2014-R011, October 27, 2014, at ¶ 1280.]

The company told FinCEN that it intended to create a trading system that would match offers to sell or buy convertible virtual currency in exchange for real currency. The trading system would be matched by individual book accounts in which buyers and sellers could deposit funds or virtual currency to cover their transactions.

Transactions would not take place directly between buyers and sellers. Rather, persons wishing to buy or sell would submit orders to the company, which would attempt to match the orders. If a match was found, the company would buy the currency from the seller and then sell it to the buyer; the buyer and seller would not be identified to each other. The company told FinCEN that it would not permit transfers between accounts, funding of accounts by third parties, or transfers from accounts to third parties.

The company claimed that any of three separate reasons exempted it from begin required to register as an MSB:

1. It was functioning similarly to a securities or commodity exchange, and there was no money transfer between it and anyone other than the buyers and sellers.

2. Any money transmission that was occurring either was integral to the company's business activities or was covered by the payment processor exemption.

3. The company was a user, not an exchanger or administrator.

FinCEN rejected all of the claims.

As far as FinCEN was concerned, any similarity between the company's trading platform and a securities or commodities exchange was irrelevant. As the bureau put it, "FinCEN's guidance issued on a product or service under one set of specific facts and circumstances should only be relied upon when applied to another product or service that shares the same specific facts and circumstances."

That a transaction was completed only if there was a match also was said to be irrelevant. There was no "element of conditionality" in the definition of money transmission. It was enough that the company accepted real or virtual currency from one person, for transmission to another person, under predetermined conditions.

The separation of each buy/sell transaction into two transactions, each between the company and a third party, did not change FinCEN's analysis. In fact, it weakened the company's argument. Each trade actually comprised two money transmissions, the first between the company and the seller and the second between the company and the buyer.

The money transmissions were not eligible for the exemption relating to transmissions that were integral to the company's services (31 CFR 1010.100(ff)(5)(F)), the bureau then said. The company's plans failed to meet one of the three criteria for the exemption because the money transmission was not a necessary part of a non-money transmission service. Instead, "money transmission is the sole purpose of the Company's System."

The company also would not qualify for the payment processor exemption (31 CFR 1010.100(ff)(5)(B)). The trading platform would fail to satisfy two of the four criteria for that exemption: it would not receive payment as a seller or creditor from a debtor or buyer for non-money transmission services, and it was not operating through a clearing and settlement system that was open only to financial institutions that were subject to regulation under the BSA.

The company would be engaged in money transmission and would not be protected by any of the regulatory exemptions, FinCEN said.

The company also was an exchanger of virtual currency, not just a user, the bureau concluded. How the transactions were funded was not the issue, according to the ruling. Whether the company acted as a broker, matching buy and sell offers, or as a dealer, buying and selling using its own virtual currency reserve, it would be a money transmitter.

FIN-2014-R012—virtual currency payment system. A company that intended to create a payment system that would allow hotels in Latin America to be paid in virtual currency rather than in the legal tender of their own countries would be a money transmitter, according to FinCEN in FIN-2014-R012. The system was intended to help the hotels manage the overseas customer foreign exchange risk that resulted from national currency controls and high levels of inflation. [FIN-2014-R012, October 27, 2014, at ¶ 1290.]

The company's plan was that hotel customers making a reservation would pay on a website using a credit card. However, the payment would not go directly to the hotel; rather, it would be routed to the company, which would exchange it for the appropriate amount in Bitcoin and transfer that to the hotel. The Bitcoin would come from the company's reserve that it had accumulated through its own market purchases from exchangers, not from a contemporaneous exchange.

The company tried to convince FinCEN that it would not be a virtual currency exchanger because it would pay the hotels from its own previously purchased stock of Bitcoin rather than making an exchange for each transaction. As a fallback, the company tried to convince the bureau that it was exempt from the MSB registration regulations. FinCEN disagreed with both arguments.

As it had in FIN-2014-R002, the bureau said that the company's plan to use its own reserve of Bitcoin rather than buy Bitcoin to complete each individual reservation payment transaction was irrelevant. The company would be in the business of accepting a customer's real currency and converting it into virtual currency for delivery to a hotel. That would make the company an exchanger and, therefore, a money transmitter.

The company's exemption claims also failed. The company would not benefit from the payment processor exemption because it would not be working through a clearing and settlement system that was open only to BSA-regulated companies. It was ineligible for the exemption protecting transmissions that were integral to providing its services because money transmission was the sole purpose of the company's activities. Money transmission was not essential to the performance of a non-money transmission service.

¶520

FIN-2015-R001—negotiable certificates of precious metal ownership. A company need not carry out transactions in money-type virtual currency to be considered a money transmitter, as a precious metals broker, dealer, and investor learned. FIN-2015-R001 is instructive because, while Bitcoin was only tangentially involved, the consistency of FinCEN's interpretation of its regulations was demonstrated. [FIN-2015-R001, August 14, 2015, at ¶ 1300.]

The ruling said the company engaged in three relevant activities:

1. It provided Internet-based precious metals brokerage services.

2. It bought and sold precious metals for its own account.

3. It held precious metals in custody for buyers, opening a digital wallet for each customer and issuing a freely transferable digital certificate of ownership that linked to that customer's wallet on the Bitcoin ledger. This arrangement let the customer enter into transactions with the metals held by the company in the same way it could trade or exchange Bitcoin.

The third described activity made the company a convertible virtual currency administrator, and thus an MSB that was required to register with FinCEN, the bureau said.

The company-issued digital certificate of ownership allowed the unrestricted transfer of value from one customer to another, according to the ruling. As a result, the company was allowing a transfer of value that went beyond what was necessary to execute a purchase or sale of precious metals. Since the company actually issued the digital certificate, it was the administrator. In this case, the digital certificate of ownership was a virtual currency.

Dealers in precious metals, stones, or jewels can be financial institutions under FinCEN regulations if their business activities exceed a $50,000-per-year threshold. The bureau told the company that if it met that test it would be an MSB that was subject to registration and compliance duties.

Summary

The take-away is that FinCEN has been very consistent in the principles it uses to analyze whether a company is an MSB.

First among these principles is that how a company acquired the virtual currency it owns is not significant. What matters is whether the virtual currency is used by the company for its own benefit—to buy goods or services, pay debts, make an investment, or make a distribution to shareholders—or is transmitted to another person. If the former, the person is a user of virtual currency and not an MSB.

On the other hand, a company that exchanges virtual currency for other value, or vice versa, and then transmits the end result to another person is an exchanger. Unless one of the narrowly construed exemptions applies, such a person will be deemed to be a money transmitter, and thus an MSB. In deciding whether there is an exchange, FinCEN will look past the labels and examine the reality of the totality of the transaction.

Of importance is that the exemption from being deemed to be a money transmitter for a company that accepts and transmits funds as part of the sale of services by that company requires that the service in question be something other than money transmission.

¶ 530 FinCEN Enforcement

Since amending its regulations to assert control over MSBs and virtual currency, FinCEN and the Treasury Department have been involved in three significant enforcement actions, against Liberty Reserve, Ripple Labs, Inc., and BTC-e. The Ripple Labs and BTC-e matters were enforcement actions by Treasury or FinCEN; the Liberty Reserve action saw FinCEN proposing the imposition of BSA special measures in conjunction with a Justice Department criminal prosecution.

Ripple Labs

In 2015 Ripple Labs Inc., and its wholly-owned subsidiary XRP II, LLC, became the first virtual currency company penalized by FinCEN for acting as an unregistered MSB. In coordinated settlement agreements with the bureau and the U.S. Attorney for the Northern District of California, the company agreed to pay a civil penalty of $700,000, which was partially satisfied by a $450,000 criminal forfeiture, for failing to register as an MSB, failing to implement an effective anti-money laundering program, and failing to file appropriate Suspicious Activity Reports. According to FinCEN, the virtual currency offered by Ripple Labs was the second largest cryptocurrency by market capitalization at the time. Only Bitcoin was larger.

The settlement included an agreed Statement of Facts and Violations in which the company conceded it had violated the BSA. Given that enforcement action settlements in the financial services industry routinely do not include admissions of responsibility, this was unusual.

According to the agreed statement of facts, Ripple Labs offered virtual currency exchange services for its own convertible virtual currency, XRP. XRP was "pre-mined," meaning that it had been completely generated before Ripple Labs began selling it in exchange for real currency. In an affidavit filed in other litigation, Ripple Labs even described itself as a currency exchange service that provided virtual currency transaction services.

Among the BSA compliance failures that Ripple Labs admitted, were failing to have:

- an appropriate anti-money laundering program;
- adequate BSA compliance policies and procedures;
- a designated BSA compliance officer;
- any anti-money laundering training programs;
- a complete anti-money laundering risk assessment; or
- any independent review of its practices and procedures.

The company also failed to file SARs on some suspicious transactions. Three of these were detailed in the statement of facts. In one, the company waived its know-your-customer practices in order to keep a customer. In two others, the company rejected transactions because of concerns that something was improper but still failed to file SARs.

BTC-e

BTC-e, also known as Canton Business Corporation, in 2017 became the first non-U.S. MSB to be sanctioned by FinCEN. The bureau assessed a $110 million civil penalty against BTC-e, and an additional $12 million penalty against Russian national Alexander Vinnick. Vinnick also was the subject of an indictment obtained by the U.S. Attorney for the Northern District of California (as of early 2018, this criminal prosecution remains pending).

BTC-e was described by FinCEN as "an internet-based, foreign-located money transmitter" that carried out exchanges of both real and virtual currency. The company was said to be one of the world's largest virtual currency exchanges, transacting in Bitcoin, Litecoin, Namecoin, Novacoin, Peercoin, Ethereum, and Dash, and some of those transactions had buyers, sellers, or both in the United States.

¶530

According to FinCEN, BTC-e did not collect any information that would enable it to identify its customers, asking only for a username, password, and email address. The company "embraced the pervasive criminal activity conducted at the exchange." In fact, its customer services personnel advised customers how to process and gain access to the proceeds of illegal drug sales on the dark net.

Further, the company processed transactions in funds that had been stolen from Bitcoin exchange Mt. Gox and the proceeds of various ransomeware attacks.

Liberty Reserve

Liberty Reserve, a web-based money transfer system with more than one million users worldwide, operated one of the world's largest and most widely used digital currencies, which could be used to send and receive payments to and from people all over the world. Liberty Reserve users were required to make any deposits or withdrawals through the use of third-party "exchangers," by which the company avoided collecting any information about its users through banking transactions or other activity that would create a financial paper trail. At its peak in late 2012, it handled a transactional volume of over $300 million per month, a significant portion of which came from users in the United States. Liberty Reserve ultimately grew into a financial hub for cybercriminals around the world who used it to amass, distribute, store, and launder criminal proceeds.

By May 2013, when it was shut down as a result of the government's criminal investigation, Liberty Reserve had more than 5.5 million user accounts worldwide and had processed more than 78 million financial transactions with a combined value of over $8 billion.

Enforcement proceedings. Liberty Reserve and seven of its principals, including founder Arthur Budovsky, were charged in federal court with running a $6 billion money laundering scheme and operating an unlicensed money transmitting business. According to the U.S. Attorney's Office, Liberty Reserve and its principals allowed criminals involved in Internet investment schemes called high-yield investment programs (HYIPs), which Budovsky allegedly knew to be online Ponzi schemes, to operate. Budovsky designed Liberty Reserve to appeal to criminals, setting up the business with weak anti-money laundering controls and allowing users to move money anonymously through Liberty Reserve's system, regardless of the volume or origin of the funds, the government alleged.

Budovsky was arrested in Spain in May 2013 and extradited to the United States in October 2014. He pleaded guilty to one count of conspiring to commit money laundering in January 2016 and was sentenced to 20 years in prison for his role in running Liberty Reserve's massive money laundering enterprise.

The Treasury Department named Liberty Reserve as "a financial institution of primary money laundering concern" under Section 311 of the USA PATRIOT Act. In connection with this determination, FinCEN proposed to prohibit covered U.S. financial institutions from opening or maintaining accounts for foreign banks used to process transactions involving Liberty Reserve and require covered financial institutions to apply special due diligence to the accounts to guard against any transactions involving Liberty Reserve and found Liberty Reserve appeared "designed to facilitate money laundering and illicit finance."

FinCEN did not participate in the enforcement action against the company, but it did exercise another of its regulatory authorities—the imposition of special anti-money laundering measures under the BSA. BSA Section 311 gives FinCEN the authority to find that a foreign financial institution is an institution "of primary money laundering concern" and require that domestic financial institutions take special measures to protect the U.S. financial system. [31 U.S.C. § 5318A.]

After making the required finding, FinCEN proposed a rule that would have imposed the "fifth special measure," prohibiting U.S. financial institutions from maintaining correspondent or pass-through accounts for Liberty Reserve (78 *Federal Register* 34008, June 6, 2013). This essentially would have cut Liberty Reserve off from the U.S. financial system.

Since the Treasury Department's criminal prosecution was successful in closing Liberty Reserve, the special measure became unnecessary. The proposal eventually was withdrawn (81 *Federal Reserve* 9039, Feb. 24, 2016).

BSA special measures. The ability to impose the BSA special measures against non-U.S. MSBs remains in effect. They can be imposed not only against a non-U.S. financial institution but also against a specific type of transaction that has been found to be of primary money laundering concern.

FinCEN proposed imposing the fifth special measure against Liberty Reserve. The other four special measures are, in order:

1. requiring U.S. financial institutions to collect and report information on transactions with a non-U.S. MSB;

2. requiring U.S. financial institutions to collect information on the beneficial ownership of a foreign financial institution's non-U.S. account holder;

3. requiring U.S. financial institutions to identify and gather know-your-customer information on customers of a foreign financial institution that can use a pass-through account opened for the foreign institution; and

4. requiring U.S. financial institutions to identify and gather know-your-customer information on customers of a foreign financial institution that can use a correspondent account opened for the foreign institution.

These special measures give FinCEN the ability to take some action against foreign MSBs, or other foreign financial institutions, that are not subject to its enforcement authority or to broader U.S. jurisdiction.

Silk Road

While FinCEN had no involvement in the Silk Road enforcement actions, the company's operations and the resulting legal consequences are instructive.

Now-defunct Silk Road was an online black market best known as a platform for selling illegal products and services and illegal Bitcoin use. Operated on the Tor network (a special network of computers on the Internet designed to conceal true IP addresses), thousands of users were able to browse the site anonymously and securely, and Silk Road accepted only Bitcoin payments to make use of its anonymity. Each Silk Road user had to have an account with an associated Silk Road Bitcoin address, and the addresses were stored on wallets maintained on servers. A user had to obtain Bitcoins and then send them to the associated address to make purchases. To complete a transaction, the Bitcoins were transferred to a Silk Road escrow account and finally to the Silk Road Bitcoin address of the seller.

Alleged Silk Road owner and operator Ross Ulbricht did not directly sell items in the exchanges but profited from the illegal activities taking place on his website through commissions. According to the Federal Bureau of Investigation, Silk Road facilitated over one million transactions resulting in approximately $1.2 billion in sales and $80 million in commissions.

¶530

Several federal agencies worked together for more than two years to uncover the individual behind Silk Road. In October 2013, the FBI was finally able to shut down the site and arrest Ulbricht. The FBI seized the Bitcoins stored on the Silk Road site in connection with a previously filed civil action seeking the forfeiture of the Silk Road website and all of its assets, including Bitcoins, allegedly used to facilitate money laundering. Federal agents ultimately seized over 173,000 Bitcoins in connection with the matter, worth millions of dollars.

Criminal proceedings. Ulbricht was charged with counts of engaging in a continuing criminal enterprise, money laundering, computer hacking, and conspiracy to traffic narcotics. In February 2015, he was found guilty on charges of money laundering, computer hacking, and narcotics trafficking. Ulbricht was sentenced to life imprisonment without the possibility of parole and ordered to forfeit $183 million.

In May 2017, a Second Circuit panel denied Ulbricht's appeal, rejecting his arguments concerning unconstitutional searches and involvement of corrupt federal agents and affirming his conviction and life sentence. "The fact that Ulbricht operated the site from behind a computer, rather than in person like a more prototypical drug kingpin, does not make his crime less serious or less dangerous [, and] while a life sentence for selling drugs alone would give pause, we would be hard put to find such a sentence beyond the bounds of reason for drug crimes of this magnitude," the panel stated. Noting Silk Road's trafficking in other illegal goods and services beyond drugs (*i.e.* counterfeit documents, stolen credit cards, hacking tools and attacks, assassinations, sex trafficking, espionage, etc.), the Second Circuit concluded that a life sentence was within the range of reasonable decisions that the district court could have reached.

NOTE: To date, more than 100 other individuals have been arrested in connection with Silk Road.

¶ 540 Congressional Response

Congress has seemed to have little inclination to intrude into FinCEN's handling of virtual currencies and MSBs. No legislation has affected the bureau's 2013 final rules on MSBs and prepaid access.

Several virtual currency-related bills have been introduced in the 115th Congress (2017-2018), but most have focused on national security concerns, i.e. the potential for the use of virtual currency to fund terrorism. Most of the bills have not progressed since they were introduced and assigned to the committee with jurisdiction.

Perhaps the most virtual currency-focused of these bills is the Combating Money Laundering, Terrorist Financing, and Counterfeiting Act of 2017 (S. 1241). This bipartisan bill would expand the BSA definition of "financial institution" to include virtual currency exchanges, issuers and redeemers of prepaid access and digital currency, and virtual currency tumblers—persons or systems that combine and mix cryptocurrency to attempt to create anonymity that blockchain technology ledgers prevent. The definition of "monetary instruments" would be expanded to include prepaid access devices. Also, operating an unregistered MSB would become a federal felony.

Hearings were held in the Senate Judiciary Committee on the bill in November 2017, six months after it was introduced in the Senate by committee chair Chuck Grassley (R-Iowa) and ranking member Dianne Feinstein (D-Calif). However, as of April 2018, there has been no further action.

Testimony at a House Financial Services Financial Institutions and Consumer Credit Subcommittee hearing on April 27, 2018, could point to possible House of Representatives legislation. The hearing, titled "Implementation of FinCEN's Customer Due Diligence Rule—Financial Institution Perspective," offered a critique of the bureau's beneficial owner identification efforts [31 CFR 1010.210; for MSBs, 31 CFR 1022.210].

The witnesses agreed that the beneficial owner identification requirements have the potential to provide useful information to law enforcement agencies. However, they complained about certain specific aspects of those requirements. For example, they argued that:

- Compliance with the rule is burdensome and expensive, but not well-tailored to the objectives of the BSA.

- Banks are required to ensure the information they receive is accurate, but they do not have the tools or guidance they need to make that judgment.

- Financial institutions should not be required to confirm beneficial ownership each time a customer opens a new account.

- Regulatory agencies other than FinCEN should not be able to impose additional requirements.

- The determination of beneficial ownership should be based on ownership of or control over the funds, not on corporate officer titles.

They also complained that FinCEN's efforts to explain the requirements, such as by issuing questions and answers, are inadequate. In fact, those efforts might be exacerbating financial institutions' uncertainty by making demands that go beyond the rule.

In addition, at least one of the witnesses, Clearing House Association President Greg Baer, asserted that none of the FinCEN guidance can be binding unless it first is subject to a notice and comment period (in apparent reliance on a Government Accountability Office opinion relating to the Consumer Financial Protection Bureau's bulletin on indirect automobile lending and the Equal Credit Opportunity Act). Compliance with the FAQs should not be considered mandatory, he said; moreover, FinCEN should not be able to revise its examination manual substantively without notice and comment.

Several witnesses supported the Counter Terrorism and Illicit Finance Act as a path to resolving some of their concerns. This is a 2017 legislative proposal drafted by Representatives Steve Pearce (R-NM) and Blaine Luetkemeyer (R-Mo) that was the subject of a Nov. 29, 2017, subcommittee hearing but apparently has yet to be formally introduced in the House.

Chapter Six—Banking and Other Financial Regulations

¶ 600 View from the Top

In the realm of innovation, such as blockchain technology or financial technology ("fintech"), a number of perspectives apply with respect to banking regulators.

For the Office of the Comptroller of the Currency, it is "Responsible Innovation" which means "the use of new or improved financial products, services and processes to meet the evolving needs of consumers, businesses, and communities in a manner that is consistent with sound risk management and is aligned with the bank's overall business strategy."

On the other hand, the Federal Reserve Board has a "public policy interest in understanding and monitoring the development of innovations that could affect the structural design and functioning of financial markets," most notably "the safety and efficiency of the [nation's] payment system."

Finally, the Consumer Financial Protection Bureau is tasked with ensuring that consumers are adequately protected when encountering product innovation.

The following sections will explore how each of these agencies is meeting its specific perspectives.

¶ 610 Fed Research

According to the "The Federal Reserve System Purposes & Functions," the Federal Reserve Board, since its creation in 1913, "performs several key functions to maintain the integrity of the payment system. These functions help keep cash, check, and electronic transactions moving reliably through the U.S. economy on behalf of consumers, businesses, and others participating in the economy."

In general, the Fed is responsible for developing regulations and supervisory policies for elements of the payment system that fall within its jurisdiction; and the 12 Federal Reserve Banks help supervise entities under the Fed's jurisdiction pursuant to these regulations and policies.

Also, the Fed conducts research on a wide range of topics related to the design and activities of payment, clearing, and settlement (PCS) systems. The Fed has also used its role as a leader and catalyst in facilitating collaboration among industry stakeholders to identify, develop, and implement improvements in the end-to-end speed, safety, and efficiency of U.S. payments.

Digital innovations in finance, loosely known as fintech, have garnered a great deal of attention across the financial industry and how it affects PCS systems.

Distributed ledger technology (DLT) is one such innovation that has been cited as a means of transforming PCS processes, including how funds are transferred and how securities, commodities, and derivatives are cleared and settled. DLT is a term that has been used by the industry in a variety of ways and so does not have a single definition. In the strictest sense, a distributed ledger is a type of database that is shared across nodes in a network. One specific type of distributed ledger is a blockchain, which adds changes to the database via a series of blocks of transactional data that are chronologically and cryptographically linked to one another.

Fed Interest in Distributed Ledger Technology

Given the fact that in 2015, the U.S. PCS systems processed approximately 600 million transactions per day, valued at over $12.6 trillion, the Fed has a public policy interest in understanding and monitoring the development of innovations that could affect the structural design and functioning of financial markets.

In its 103rd Annual Report, the Fed provided background on steps being taken to better understand the implication of DLT on the payment, clearing, and settlement processes. As a preliminary step, a team of Federal Reserve staff held discussions with a broad range of parties that are interested in, participate in, or are otherwise contributing to the evolution of DLT.

The research team presented its findings in a December 2016 working paper titled "Distributed ledger technology in payments, clearing, and settlement." The working paper examined how DLT might be used in the area of payments, clearing, and settlement and identifies both the opportunities and challenges facing its practical implementation and possible long-term adoption.

Potential to transform. As noted in the working paper, the industry believes DLT has the potential to transform several areas in financial markets, including cross-border payments; post-trade processing of securities, commodities, and derivatives; and areas that are heavily paper-based, such as syndicated loans and trade finance. At the same time, however, a number of challenges to development and adoption remain, including technological hurdles, governance issues, and risk-management considerations.

Still in its infancy. The working paper also noted that the industry's understanding and application of DLT to financial market structures is still in its infancy, and stakeholders are taking a variety of approaches towards its development. At this stage, it is difficult to predict how DLT will figure into the future of payments as the industry continues to explore a range of possible uses.

Fed Position Explained

Although the 2016 working paper was "a dip of a toe in the water," a number of Fed Governors have further articulated the Fed's position on the use of DLT.

Risks thoroughly understood and managed. Prior to the release of the working paper, Governor Lael Brainard emphasized that while the Fed seeks to facilitate innovation in fintech, the Fed also must ensure that "risks are thoroughly understood and managed." Speaking at the Institute of International Finance Blockchain Roundtable, Brainard stated that federal regulators "should seek to analyze the implications of technology developments through constructive and timely engagement." Moreover, regulators should be "prepared to make the necessary regulatory adjustments if their safety and integrity is proven" and their potential benefits are "found to be in the public interest."

Focusing on DLT, Brainard noted that "it provides a credible way to transfer an asset without the need for trust in intermediaries or counterparties, much like a physical cash transaction." She added that distributed ledger technologies can reduce costs, provide faster processing, improve efficiencies, and enhance "financial transparency" in the payment, clearing, and settlement processes.

In a later 2016 speech at the Institute of International Finance Annual Meeting Panel on Blockchain in Washington, D.C., Brainard discussed the latest oversight efforts by the Fed regarding distributed ledger technology.

¶610

She provided a few examples of the use cases that the Fed has explored in its discussions with industry stakeholders in order to illustrate the potential of distributed ledger technologies to improve payments, clearing, and settlement, as well as the considerations that are important in assessments of benefits and risks. At the time of her speech, Brainard noted that much of the industry was at a "proof of concept" stage of development.

Finally, appearing at the Yale Law School Center for the Study of Corporate Law, now-Fed Chairman Jerome H. Powell noted that the Fed and other central banks have adopted broad public policy objectives to guide the development and oversight of the payments system. At the Fed, Powell states, they have identified efficiency and safety as the "most fundamental" objectives. The payments system must be innovative, while also addressing risks, supporting financial stability, and maintaining public confidence, according to Powell. He stated that "Safe payment systems are built from proven technology and operate reliably and with integrity."

Costs for upgrading and streamlining. Touching on DLT, Powell observed that work by the financial industry has focused on the development of "permissioned" systems. Issues include whether finality of settlement is to be determined by a central trusted party or by a majority of participants, and whether participants are able to view information on other parties' transactions. Another issue, according to Powell, is the costs for upgrading and streamlining payment, clearing, settlement, and related functions with DLT. Technical issues including whether a particular version of DLT will work for the intended purpose are still being explored, stated Powell, and issues of reliability, scalability, and security remain. Powell also stated that governance and risk management is critical, as well as the legal issues surrounding and supporting DLT.

¶ 620 Special National Bank Charter

Recognizing that the financial services industry in the United States is undergoing rapid technological change aimed at meeting evolving consumer and business expectations and need, the Office of the Comptroller of the Currency has developed an initiative that will provide the means to develop new or improved financial products, services, and processes to meet the evolving needs of consumers, businesses, and communities, while also being consistent with sound risk management and is aligned with the bank's overall business strategy.

Ultimately, the OCC envisions the development of a new special purpose national bank (SPNB) charter that financial technology companies or fintech companies could operate under to bring their products and services to market.

"Responsible Innovation"

The genesis of the OCC's "Responsible Innovation" initiative can be found in a speech given by Thomas J. Curry, who served as the Comptroller of the Currency from 2012 through 2017, at an August 2015 conference sponsored by the Federal Home Loan Bank of Chicago, entitled "Leading Toward the Future; Ideas and Insight for a New Era."

In his remarks, Curry noted "[n]ew approaches that meet the needs of an evolving marketplace are the lifeblood of our nation's economy, and it's our job as a regulator to support and even encourage innovation that helps bank customers." He also expressed concern over the perception that it is too difficult to get new ideas through the regulatory approval process. Curry further emphasized that it is important that regulators "view new ideas with an open mind and not dismiss them."

White Paper

The next step taken by the OCC in its "Responsible Innovation" initiative was the March 2016 publication of a whitepaper entitled "Supporting Responsible Innovation in the Federal Banking System: An OCC Perspective." ["Supporting Responsible Innovation in the Federal Banking System: An OCC Perspective," March 2016, at ¶ 1320.]

The whitepaper discussed the principles that would guide the development of the agency's framework for evaluating new and innovative financial products and services. The framework built upon the OCC's mission, first advanced by Comptroller of the Currency Curry, to ensure that national banks and federal savings associations:

- operate in a safe and sound manner;
- provide fair access to financial services;
- treat customers fairly, and
- comply with applicable laws and regulations.

Guiding principles. The OCC also established a set of guiding principles in formulating its innovation framework. The eight principles are:

1. support responsible innovation;

2. foster an internal culture receptive to responsible innovation;

3. leverage agency experience and expertise;

4. encourage responsible innovation that provides fair access to financial services and fair treatment of consumers;

5. further safe and sound operations through effective risk management;

6. encourage banks of all sizes to integrate responsible innovation into their strategic planning;

7. promote ongoing dialogue through formal outreach; and

8. collaborate with other regulators.

OCC Framework

Following the release of its March 2016 guiding principles, the OCC then released its "Recommendations and Decisions for Implementing a Responsible Innovation Framework," which was to be the blueprint that the agency will use to support the ability of national banks and federal savings associations to fulfill their role of providing financial services to consumers, businesses, and their communities through responsible innovation that is safe and sound, consistent with applicable law, and protective of consumer rights. ["Recommendations and Decisions for Implementing a Responsible Innovation Framework," October 2016, at ¶ 1330.]

Office of Innovation. As part of its framework, the OCC established the Office of Innovation in order to improve the agency's ability to identify, understand, and respond to financial innovation affecting the federal banking system. Among other things, the Office of Innovation was to: 1) serve as a central point of contact and facilitate responses to inquiries and requests; 2) monitor the evolving financial services landscape; and 3) collaborate with domestic and international regulators.

Recommendations. Besides the establishment of the Office of Innovation, the framework also provided that the OCC should:

- establish an outreach and technical assistance program;
- conduct awareness and training activities;
- encourage coordination and facilitation;
- establish an innovation research function; and

¶620

- promote interagency collaboration.

Outreach and technical assistance. The framework calls on the OCC to develop a wide-reaching outreach program that enables the agency to maintain a broad understanding of industry trends as well as the needs of consumers of financial services from all stakeholder perspectives. It was noted that the innovation outreach strategy can leverage existing agency avenues for outreach with banks and community and consumer groups. A formal outreach program for nonbanks would need to be developed.

Awareness and training activities. To build an effective awareness and training program to ensure adequate evaluation and supervision of new products, services, and processes by a well-informed staff, the framework recommends:

- improved staff awareness of industry innovations and developing trends;

- the creation of additional training content necessary to evaluate and understand industry innovations; and

- broadening and increasing OCC expertise in areas related to innovation.

Coordination and facilitation. Given that inquiries and requests related to innovation may be new and potentially novel, it is important that the OCC have well-coordinated, consistent, and timely responses wherever possible. To achieve this goal, the framework recommends that the OCC should:

- improve the timeliness and transparency of its decision-making; and

- develop and implement an optional program for OCC participation in bank-run pilots.

Innovation research function. To address the rapid and dramatic advances in fintech, the OCC needs to improve its ability to identify and understand trends and innovations in the financial services industry. The framework envisions the OCC should:

- develop a research function within the Office of Innovation to analyze how innovation affects individual banks, bank segments, and the federal banking system as a whole; and

- use research and dialogue with industry, consumer, and community groups to inform policy and guidance.

Promote interagency collaboration. Finally, to promote collaboration, the framework calls on the OCC to:

- leverage existing interagency channels at both the domestic and international levels; and

- develop an OCC-led information-sharing group.

SPNB Paper. The next piece of OCC's Responsible Innovation initiative was the December 2016 release of a paper, entitled "Exploring Special Purpose National Bank Charters for Fintech Companies" (SPNB Paper) that discussed several important issues associated with the approval of a national bank charter. ["Exploring Special Purpose National Bank Charters for Fintech Companies," December 2016, at ¶ 1340.]

At the time of the paper's release, Comptroller of Currency Curry noted that "no topic in banking and finance has drawn more interest than innovative financial technology." He added that the OCC *"will* move forward with chartering financial technology companies that offer bank products and services and meet our high standards and chartering requirements."

The paper discussed:

- features and attributes of a national bank charter;

- baseline supervisory expectations; and
- the chartering process.

Charter's features and attributes. The paper noted that an SPNB has the same status and attributes under federal law as a full-service national bank. An SPNB's activities are limited by either its articles of association or through OCC-imposed conditions for approving the charter.

If a fintech were to be granted a SPNB charter, it would also be required to become a member of the Federal Reserve System by subscribing for the stock of the appropriate Federal Reserve Bank. This would allow the fintech company to avail itself of the discount rate on loans it receives from its regional Federal Reserve Bank's lending facility

Baseline supervisory expectations. For any entity seeking a national charter, there are a number of baseline supervisory expectations that it is presumed to follow. These baseline expectations stress the importance of:

- a detailed business plan;
- governance;
- capital;
- liquidity;
- compliance risk management;
- financial inclusion; and
- recovery and resolution planning.

A business plan should be comprehensive, reflecting in-depth planning by the organizers, board of directors, and management; and clearly articulate why the entity is seeking a national bank charter and provide significant detail about the proposed bank's activities.

The governance structure for any proposed special purpose national bank needs to be commensurate with the risk and complexity of its proposed products, services, and activities.

Also, minimum and ongoing capital levels need to be commensurate with the risk and complexity of the proposed activities including on- and off-balance sheet activities.

As with capital, minimum and ongoing liquidity—both operating and contingent obligations—for an SPNB need to be commensurate with the risk and complexity of the proposed activities. In assessing the liquidity position of a proposed bank, the OCC considers a proposed bank's access to funds as well as its cost of funding.

An applicant seeking an SPNB charter will also be expected to demonstrate a culture of compliance that includes a top-down, enterprise-wide commitment to understanding and adhering to applicable laws and regulations and to operating consistently with OCC supervisory guidance.

Although a fintech company seeking an SPNB charter would not be subject to the Community Reinvestment Act unless it accepted deposits that were insured by the FDIC, the OCC expects an applicant seeking an SPNB charter that engages in lending activities to demonstrate a commitment to financial inclusion that supports fair access to financial services and fair treatment of customers. The nature of the commitment would depend on the entity's business model and the types of loan products or services it intends to provide.

Finally, the OCC expects business plans to articulate specific financial or other risk triggers that would prompt the board and management's determination to unwind the

¶620

operation in an organized manner. These strategies must provide a comprehensive framework for evaluating the financial effects of severe stress that may affect an entity and options to remain viable under such stress. The business plan must address material changes in the institution's size, risk profile, activities, complexity, and external threats, and be integrated into the entity's overall risk governance framework. Plans must be specific to that entity, aligned with the entity's other plans, and coordinated with any applicable parent or affiliate planning.

Chartering process. The OCC's standard process for reviewing and making decisions about charter applications would apply to applications from fintech companies for an SPNB charter. The established charter policies and procedures are set forth in 12 CFR Part 5 and the "Charters" booklet of the *Comptroller's Licensing Manual.*

The chartering process consists of four stages:

• The prefiling stage which provides potential applicants the opportunity to engage with the OCC in formal and informal meetings to discuss their proposal, the chartering process, and application requirements.

• The filing stage is the point in the process in which the organizers submit the application.

• The review and evaluation stage allows the OCC to conduct background and field investigations, and review and analyze the application to determine whether the proposed bank: (1) has a reasonable chance of success; (2) will be operated in a safe and sound manner; (3) will provide fair access to financial services; (4) will ensure compliance with laws and regulations; (5) will promote fair treatment of customers; and (6) will foster healthy competition.

• The decision stage, which includes three phases: (1) the preliminary conditional approval phase, when the OCC decides whether to grant preliminary conditional approval; (2) the organization phase, when the bank raises capital, prepares for opening, and the OCC conducts a preopening examination; and (3) the final approval phase, when the OCC decides whether the bank has met the requirements and conditions for opening.

Draft Supplement

The final piece of the OCC's initiative to charter a fintech company as an SPNB was the March 2017 release of a draft Supplement to its current *Comptroller's Licensing Manual* which addresses the unique factors that must be considered in evaluating special purpose applications.

The draft Supplement applies specifically to the OCC's consideration of applications from fintech companies to charter an SPNB and does not apply to other types of special purpose banks described in the current *Comptroller's Licensing Manual.*

Under the draft Supplement to the *Licensing Manual*, a special purpose national bank would be defined as a national bank that either pays checks (or makes other similar transfers, such as using debit cards) or lends money. Accepting deposits will not be permitted, and the banks will not be covered by the FDIC.

The draft Supplement noted that the OCC uses "its existing chartering standards and procedures as the basis for processing applications for all national banks" and that the publication "describes the OCC's approach to key aspects of the chartering process for fintech companies." However, the draft Supplement cautioned, "It is not a comprehensive guide to all of the procedures and requirements relevant to filing an application for an SPNB charter."

Initial steps. The draft Supplement provides the initial steps that a fintech company should take toward an SPNB charter. These steps include:

- Initial contact with the OCC through the agency's Office of Innovation.

- Prefiling meetings with the OCC in which the fintech company provides information on its business plan, as well as any novel policy or legal issues and any unique aspects of the charter application.

- Activities of the proposed SPNB that include bank-permissible activities core banking activities.

- Filing procedures which include the publication of a notice of its charter in the community in which the proposed SPNB will be located as soon as possible before or after the filing date.

Chartering standards. As with any charter application, the OCC is guided by the following principles:

- maintaining a safe and sound banking system;

- encouraging a national bank to provide fair access to financial services by helping to meet the credit needs of its entire community;

- ensuring compliance with laws and regulations; and

- promoting fair treatment of customers, including efficiency and better service.

The OCC's regulations and policies also set forth additional considerations, including whether the proposed bank can reasonably be expected to achieve and maintain profitability and whether approving its charter will foster healthy competition.

The OCC will not approve proposals that are contrary to OCC policy or other established public policy. For example, proposals to provide financial products and services that have predatory, unfair, or deceptive features or that pose undue risk to consumer protection, compliance, or safety and soundness would be inconsistent with the OCC's chartering standards and will not be approved.

In evaluating an SPNB charter application, the OCC will consider, among other things, whether the proposed bank:

- has organizers and management with appropriate skills and experience;

- has adequate capital to support the projected volume and type of business and proposed risk profile;

- has a business plan that articulates a clear path and a timeline to profitability; and

- includes in its business plan, if applicable, a financial inclusion plan that has an appropriate description of the proposed goals, approach, activities, and milestones for serving the relevant market and community.

The OCC will also coordinate, as appropriate, with other regulators with jurisdiction over the proposed SPNB, to facilitate simultaneous consideration of any applications or approvals that may be required by those regulators.

Receiverships Rule

An additional piece to the OCC's fintech chartering initiative was the issuance of the December 2016 final rule governing receiverships for national banks that are not insured by the FDIC. [81 *Federal Register* 92594, December 20, 2016, at ¶ 1370.]

The final rule incorporated the framework set forth in the National Bank Act for the Comptroller to appoint a receiver for an uninsured bank and clarified certain powers held by the receiver, as well as describing the receiver's duties in winding up the affairs of the uninsured bank.

¶620

The OCC issued the final rule to address a regulatory gap and provide clarity to market participants about how uninsured banks will be treated in receivership.

During the regulatory process, two commenters expressed concerns related to the receivership framework. These commenters expressed concern that the earlier-established legal regime for receiverships under the NBA and associated judicial precedent does not include select elements subsequently created for insured depository institutions, and questioning if it might not be as effective outside the trust bank sphere in application to the receivership of special purpose national banks engaged in fintech activities.

OCC Further Explains Innovation Process

Given the somewhat quick succession of documents that the OCC released regarding its Responsible Innovation initiative and the chartering of fintech companies, the agency released its OCC Summary of Comments and Explanatory Statement: Special Purpose National Bank Charters for Financial Technology Companies in March 2017. The Explanatory Statement addressed key issues raised by commenters and explained the OCC's decision to issue its draft Supplement for public comment. [OCC Summary of Comments and Explanatory Statement: Special Purpose National Bank Charters for Financial Technology Companies, March 2017, at ¶ 1350.]

Responding to comments on its SPNB Paper, the OCC emphasized that it will be guided by three principles when issuing an SPNB charter to a fintech company:

1. There will be no "inappropriate commingling of banking and commerce."

2. Products with predatory features and unfair or deceptive acts and practices will not be permitted.

3. There will be no "light touch" supervision. Special purpose national banks will be expected to meet the same standards as all other national banks.

Specifically, the OCC said that fintech banks will be subject to leverage and risk-based capital standards. However, "alternative approaches"—meaning heightened requirements—might be needed to determine appropriate capital requirements because these banks are expected to have comparatively few on-balance sheet exposures.

Criticism and Challenges

Despite the deliberative process that the OCC took to get to the point where it is ready to accept charter applications from fintech companies, a number of stakeholders have criticized the OCC for its initiative. There have also been two court challenges seeking to stop the OCC from issuing an SPNB charter to any fintech company.

Criticism of the OCC's initiative has been lodged by a wide spectrum of stakeholders.

Congressional concerns. Senators Sherrod Brown (D-Ohio) and Jeff Merkley (D-Ore) wrote to the OCC expressing concerns that a new federal charter for fintech firms could weaken consumer protections, limit competition, and threaten financial stability.

The senators also raised concerns that the granting of a national charter, or as they termed it an "alternative charter" for fintech companies, could encourage charter shopping in order to avoid unfavorable state and federal laws. The letter also addressed the issue of financial inclusion, that is, federal efforts toward a more inclusive banking system for the underbanked. Brown and Merkley queried whether "[p]roviding a more favorable charter to companies engaged only in narrow lines of bank services would have a detrimental impact on the consumers who are supposed to benefit from financial innovation." They observed, "It is unclear to us how the OCC's proposal, which would normalize the delivery of a la carte services by non-depository firms, aligns with the goal of providing the underbanked with access to a full range of 'safe, secure, and affordable banking services.'"

Finally, the senators expressed concern that the OCC's granting of an alternative charter would undermine the separation of banking and commerce and that preserving that separation is important for "several important reasons." Brown and Merkley cited the possibility that large commercial firms could acquire alternative charters and offer preferential treatment to their own financial services products to lock customers or manufacturers into uncompetitive rates and terms by relying on the market power of their commercial platforms.

Unlawful and invalid nature. The Conference of State Bank Supervisors submitted a comment letter [at ¶ 1360] reiterating its opposition to the OCC's proposal to issue a special charter for fintech companies. The CSBS called the OCC's proposal an "unprecedented expansion" of the agency's chartering authority and that it amounted to an end run around Congress. The letter also noted that the proposal would stifle innovation while activities-based state licensing encourages and enables financial innovation. Furthermore, the CSBS stated that the OCC's proposal poses dangerous consequences stemming from the preemption of state laws. Finally, as part of its letter, the CSBS provided a Legal and Policy Assessment that provided "a more in-depth discussion of the unlawful and invalid nature of a special purpose national nonbank charter."

Primary line of defense. A group of 250 consumer advocacy organizations, led by Americans for Financial Reform and the Center for Responsible Lending, expressed strong opposition to the OCC's proposal. The groups were concerned that the proposal would enable lenders to avoid state interest rate caps, other state protections, and state oversight. The groups' letter noted, "State laws often operate as the primary line of defense for consumers and small businesses; thus, the proposal puts them at great risk."

Highly problematic. Maria T. Vullo, Superintendent of the New York Department of Financial Services, voiced her opposition to the proposal noting that "using the term 'fintech' to potentially sweep all nonbank financial services companies not authorized under the National Bank Act into a new regulatory regime is highly problematic."

The NYDFS letter added that:

- the creation of a national charter is likely to stifle rather than encourage innovation;

- a national charter would encourage large "too big to fail" institutions, permitting a small number of technology-savvy firms to dominate different types of financial services;

- the recent financial crisis demonstrated that lax regulation on the federal level is devastating for our financial system and consumers;

- the proposal could permit companies to engage in regulatory arbitrage and avoid important state consumer protection laws, such as strong usury protections; and

- state regulators are experienced and better equipped to regulate cash-intensive nonbank financial service companies.

More thoughtful deliberation. A comment letter by Robin L. Wiessmann, Secretary of the Pennsylvania Department of Banking and Securities, called on the OCC to address three concerns:

- the broad application and ambiguity of the term "fintech;"

- the need by the OCC to have an adequate regulatory scheme in place before approving charters; and

¶620

• the possible federal preemption of existing state consumer protection laws.

Weismann concluded her letter that the OCC proposal required "more thoughtful deliberation about the intended and unintended consequences that will result from such an apparent departure from the OCC's current policy and scope of supervision."

Due caution. Although the Consumer Bankers Association supported "any effort to enhance the ability of banks to innovate in order to better serve U.S. consumers with products and services appropriate for the rapidly changing financial services environment," it could not "yet support the inclusion of fintech companies into the federal banking system." In its comment letter, the CBA noted that the OCC needed to provide more clarity about the regulatory and supervisory framework that will be applied to the fintech companies. The trade association recommended that the OCC utilize its new Office of Innovation and Responsible Innovation Framework to conduct a thorough study of the fintech sector to provide sufficient information to evaluate the need for and public benefits of a fintech charter.

New chartering rules. The Independent Community Bankers Association also expressed "strong concerns about issuing SPNB charters to fintech companies without spelling out clearly the supervision and regulation that these chartered institutions and their parent companies would be subject to." In its comment letter, the ICBA called on the OCC to issue new chartering rules, pursuant to the Administrative Procedure Act and in consultation with the other agencies, that clearly spell out the agency's expectations for capital, liquidity, supervision, and examination, and addresses whether these new institutions will have direct access to the Federal Reserve's clearing and payment system and its discount window. The OCC must ensure that these new institutions are subject to the same supervision and regulation to which community banks are subject.

Many difficult questions. Although the American Bankers Association expressed support for an SPNB charter for fintech companies, as long as existing rules are applied evenly and fairly, and with effective oversight, the trade group noted that "answers to many difficult questions should be made before granting any special purpose charter, including how to ensure that regulations and consumer protection are applied evenly; what protections must be in place to preserve existing laws regarding the separation of banking and commerce; and how would enforcement of operating agreements be accomplished." The ABA also urged the OCC to work with other agencies "carefully and cooperatively" before any new charter is approved to assure that no current policy lines are directly or inadvertently moved as a consequence of this action.

Concerns with draft Supplement. Commenting on the OCC's release of the draft Supplement to its *Licensing Manual,* the CSBS urged Congress to "weigh in" against the issue of OCC non-bank charters.

The ICBA reiterated its concerns about the agency's proposal to grant SPNB charters to fintech companies. The letter advised that the OCC should rescind its draft Supplement and request specific congressional authorization to grant fintech charters.

Finally, the Consumer Bankers Association contended that the OCC "has not provided a clear rationale or justification for offering a national bank charter to fintech companies, and the standards and conditions for granting these charters have yet to be fully developed." It urged the OCC to conduct an in-depth study of the fintech sector. After such study, if the OCC still concluded that the public would benefit from a fintech charter, the CBA said it will ask the agency to issue a formal charter proposal for public notice and comment.

Legal challenges. To date, both the CSBS and the New York Department of Financial Services have filed lawsuits seeking to block the OCC from chartering any fintech company as an SPNB. The CSBS filed suit in April 2017 and the NYDFS in May 2017.

The CSBS's complaint alleged that the OCC's claimed authority to create charters for a broad variety of nonbank financial services providers, regardless of whether they might be thought of as fintech companies exceeded the agency's authority under the National Bank Act. The complaint also alleged that the OCC intended, as part of the chartering process, to negotiate a secret agreement with each company about which federal banking laws will be applied to it, thereby creating significant preemption issues.

The NYDFS lawsuit, which was filed in the U.S. District Court for the Southern District of New York, alleged that "[t]he Fintech Charter Decision is lawless, ill-conceived, and destabilizing of financial markets that are properly and most effectively regulated by New York State." The NYDFS complaint also alleged that the proposed fintech charter would injure the NYDFS monetarily, since its operating expenses are funded by assessments levied by the OCC on New York licensed financial institutions. According to the NYDFS, every non-depository financial firm that receives an SPNB charter from the OCC in place of a New York license deprives the NYDFS of crucial resources that are necessary to fund its regulatory function.

The district court in the NYDFS lawsuit ruled that the NYDFS's purported injuries were too future-oriented and speculative to confer standing. Similarly, the claims were unripe because they are "contingent on future events that may never occur."

The district court in the CSBS lawsuit reached a similar conclusion. It noted that any potential harm to state banking regulators was speculative and tenuous.

Future of the OCC's Initiative

The start of a new presidential administration in January 2017, tied with the departure of Thomas Curry as the Comptroller of the Currency, has slowed the OCC's Responsible Innovation initiative.

Need to proceed cautiously. In one of his last speeches as Comptroller of the Currency, Curry addressed a fintech and innovation conference at Northwestern University' Kellogg School of Management. Curry spoke about the OCC's decision to grant special licenses for fintech charters and of the opposition to this plan. "Early on in this process, we recognized that our regulatory instinct has been to say no and to be too risk averse. Over the last two years, we've worked very hard to take a more open approach, while still maintaining appropriate caution to prevent reckless and bad behavior." However, he also stressed the need to proceed cautiously. "We have to be open to responsible innovation but we cannot compromise the integrity of the banking system or allow untested products to result in unintended consumer harm, or unfairness in accessing financial products or services, or non-compliance with laws or regulations."

"Out of the shadows." Following Curry's departure, Keith Noreika became Acting Comptroller of the Currency. In a July 2017 speech, at the Exchequer Club in Washington, D.C., Noreika defended the OCC's position in favor of granting national charters to fintech companies, noting that these charters were part of the natural evolution of banking, a way to prevent stagnation of the system. Noreika advocated bringing fintechs "out of the shadows" and "into a well-established supervisory and regulatory regime that will promote their safety and soundness and allow the federal banking system and its customers to benefit from their inclusion." He also offered assurance that neither states nor consumers will be left powerless in the wake of nationally chartered fintechs, citing the Dodd-Frank Act and the limits on the OCC's application of federal preemption in *Barnett Bank*.

"Exaggerated" concerns. Speaking at Georgetown University's Institute of International Economic Law's Fintech Week in October 2017, Noreika called concerns over

¶620

an inappropriate mixing of banking and commerce "exaggerated." He noted that the initiative to charter nondepository fintech companies remained a work in progress. Noreika also refuted assertions that the OCC is considering granting charters to nonfinancial companies as unwarranted fears. He concluded with a call for "a constructive discussion of where commerce and banking coexist successfully today and where else it may make sense in the future."

"Not yet settled." Since becoming the 31st Comptroller of the Currency in November 2017, Joseph Otting has been somewhat silent on his agency's Responsible Innovation initiative.

An April 24, 2018, Advisory issued by David F. Freeman, Jr., Christopher L. Allen, Robert C. Azarow, A. Patrick Doyle, Howard L. Hyde, Michael A. Mancusi, Brian C. McCormally, Michael B. Mierzewski, and Kevin M. Toomey of the law firm Arnold Porter noted that "Otting is not yet settled on issuing special-purpose charters to fintech companies, but expects to have a position within the next 60-90 days." The Arnold Porter Advisory added, "Otting is likely taking into consideration the possibility of litigation if a decision is made to offer national charters to fintech companies, and an affirmative decision would likely have an implementation delay unless the OCC and the various state regulators can come to a mutual agreement regarding national charters."

¶ 630 CFPB Regulation of Digital Wallets

When it was established by the Dodd-Frank Act, the Consumer Financial Protection Bureau was given the authority to carry out a broad group of consumer financial protection laws. These core laws are referred to as the "enumerated consumer laws."

One of those laws, the Electronic Fund Transfer Act (EFTA) establishes the basic rights, liabilities, and responsibilities of consumers who use electronic fund transfer and remittance transfer services and of financial institutions or other persons that offer these services. The EFTA is implemented by Reg E—Electronic Funds Transfer (12 CFR Part 1005).

CFPB's Prepaid Rule

In November 2016, the CFPB issued amendments to Regulation E that created tailored provisions governing disclosures, limited liability and error resolution, and periodic statements, and added new requirements regarding the posting of account agreements. These amendments have been referred to as the Prepaid Rule.

Prepaid Accounts

One feature of the Prepaid Rule was the addition of the term "prepaid account" to the definition of "account" in Regulation E. The Bureau included prepaid products within the scope of the EFTA and Regulation E on the belief that there were gaps in the existing federal regulatory regimes that caused certain prepaid products not to receive full consumer protections.

For purposes of the Prepaid Rule, certain products that meet one of the following two criteria are deemed to be prepaid accounts.

Marketed or labeled. A product that is marketed or labeled as "prepaid" and is redeemable upon presentation at multiple, unaffiliated merchants for goods and services or usable at ATMs is deemed to be a prepaid account under Regulation E.

Load that and pay. The second type of product that is a prepaid account under Regulation E must meet a three prong-test:

    1. it is issued on a prepaid basis in a specified amount or is capable of being loaded with funds after issuance;

2. its primary function is to conduct transactions with multiple, unaffiliated merchants for goods or services, to conduct transactions at ATMs, or to conduct person-to-person (P2P) transfers; and

3. it is not a checking account, a share draft account, or a negotiable order of withdrawal (NOW) account.

Digital Wallets

One type of product that meets the new definition of prepaid account is a digital wallet.

Important funding source. In its Prepaid Rule, the CFPB noted that a 2015 survey by the Federal Reserve Board suggested that digital wallets serve as an important funding source for mobile payments, that is, consumer payment for goods and services using mobile phones. The survey reported that 15 percent of mobile payment users reported that they used an account at a non-financial institution such as PayPal to fund their payments. The Fed's survey was updated in 2016 which found that the percentage of mobile payment users reported that they used an account at a non-financial institution appeared to have held steady at 16 percent.

Pass-through vehicle for funds. To satisfy the regulatory definition of prepaid account, the prepaid product cannot merely act as a pass-through vehicle. For example, if a digital wallet is only capable of storing a consumer's payment credentials for other accounts but is incapable of having funds stored on it, then the digital wallet is not a prepaid account. However, if a product allows a consumer to transfer funds, which can be stored before the consumer designates a destination for the funds, the product satisfies the definition of prepaid account in Regulation E.

Chilling innovation. During the regulatory process, some commenters expressed concern that the CFPB's rulemaking would have defined prepaid accounts broadly to include digital wallets and other emerging products, thereby chilling innovation in the payments market.

In the preamble to the Prepaid Rule, the Bureau addressed this concern noting that it:

1. carefully evaluated the benefits and costs of extending Regulation E to digital wallets;

2. recognized that there is some need for tailoring of particular provisions for prepaid accounts in certain circumstances; and

3. believed that there is substantial value to both consumers and financial institutions in promoting consistent treatment where it is logical and appropriate across products.

Explicit exemption. Also during the regulatory process, a digital wallet provider argued for an explicit exemption for digital wallets, which it defined as a card, code, or other device that is capable of accessing two or more payment credentials for purposes of making payment for goods and services at multiple unaffiliated merchants.

The commenter asserted digital wallets are used primarily to access payment credentials, not funds; and to the extent digital wallets store funds, such funds are almost always loaded onto the wallets as a result of a P2P transaction, not because the accountholder purposefully loads the wallet with funds for future use. The commenter further contended that digital wallets do not present the same risks as prepaid accounts—specifically, digital wallets charge lower fees than general-purpose reloadable cards and do not offer overdraft features.

¶630

The Bureau was not convinced by the commenter's argument that digital wallets used in this fashion are fundamentally dissimilar to other types of prepaid accounts. The CFPB noted that, to the extent that digital wallets are used to access funds the consumer has deposited into the account in advance, digital wallets operate very much like a prepaid account.

Same protections. The CFPB concluded that consumers who use digital wallets for financial transactions deserve the same protections as consumers who use other prepaid accounts. The Bureau observed that, as with other prepaid accounts, a consumer's digital wallet could fall victim to erroneous or fraudulent transactions.

Regulation Z Protections

The Prepaid Rule also made amendments to Regulation Z (12 CFR Part 1026) regarding overdraft credit features that may be offered in conjunction with prepaid accounts. These overdraft credit features impact digit wallets.

Hybrid prepaid-credit card. Generally, a prepaid account number that can access a digital wallet would be a hybrid prepaid-credit card if it meets the conditions set forth in 12 CFR 1026.61(a).

For instance, a prepaid account number that can access a digital wallet is a hybrid prepaid-credit card where it can be used from time to time to access a covered separate credit feature offered by the prepaid account issuer, its affiliate, or its business partner in the course of authorizing, settling, or otherwise completing a transaction conducted with the prepaid account number to obtain goods or services, obtain cash, or conduct person-to-person transfers.

On the other hand, a prepaid account number that can access a digital wallet is not subject to Regulation Z's hybrid prepaid-credit card provisions if:

- credentials stored in the prepaid account that access a "non-covered separate credit feature" that is not offered by the prepaid account issuer, its affiliate, or its business partner, even if the prepaid account number can access those credentials in the course of authorizing, settling, or otherwise completing a transaction conducted with the prepaid account number to obtain goods or services, obtain cash, or conduct P2P transfers; or

- credentials stored in the prepaid account that access a "non-covered separate credit feature" where the prepaid account number cannot access those credentials in the course of authorizing, settling, or otherwise completing a transaction conducted with the prepaid account number to obtain goods or services, obtain cash, or conduct P2P transfers, even if such credit feature is offered by the prepaid account issuer, its affiliate, or its business partner.

A "non-covered separate credit feature" is defined as a separate credit feature that does not meet the two conditions set forth in 12 CFR 1026.61(a)(2)(i). The two conditions in 12 CFR 1026.61(a)(2)(i) are:

- the prepaid card can be used from time to time to access credit from the credit feature in the course of authorizing, settling, or otherwise completing transactions conducted with the card to obtain goods or services, obtain cash, or conduct P2P transfers; and

- the credit feature is offered by the prepaid account issuer, its affiliate, or its business partner. The hybrid prepaid-credit card can access both the covered credit feature and the asset feature of the prepaid account, and is a credit card under Regulation Z with respect to the covered separate credit feature.

Overdraft credit feature. Therefore, a prepaid card issuer that offers an overdraft credit feature accessible by a hybrid prepaid-credit card must structure that overdraft feature as a separate credit feature, not as a negative balance to a prepaid account.

Negative balances generally are banned, but an exception permits them if:

1. the prepaid card cannot access credit from a covered separate credit feature accessible by a hybrid prepaid-credit card;

2. the prepaid account issuer has a general policy and practice of declining transactions that will result in a negative balance; and

3. the prepaid account issuer does not generally charge credit-related fees.

A 2018 amendment to the Prepaid Rule broadened the exception to permit a negative balance even if a covered separate credit feature offered by a business partner is attached to the prepaid account as long as the other conditions are satisfied.

The Prepaid Rule generally requires prepaid account issuers to structure an overdraft credit feature accessible by a hybrid prepaid-credit card as a separate credit feature, not as a negative balance to a prepaid account. Therefore, under the Prepaid Rule, an overdraft credit feature should only be structured as a negative balance on a prepaid account if the issuer has a policy and practice of declining to authorize certain transactions as described above and does not impose certain credit-related fees on the asset feature of the prepaid account.

Chapter Seven—State Licensing, Corporate Governance, and Enforcement

¶ 700 View from the Top

Corporations are beginning to see ways to implement blockchain technology, and states are searching for ways to facilitate blockchain business as well as crack down on fraud. For example, Bank of America may be considering use of blockchain technology to enhance its data sharing systems with a blockchain, according to a recently released patent application describing a permissioned blockchain that would securely record and authenticate personal and business data. The Blockchain Research Institute is investigating more ways that blockchain could transform retail transactions, transportation and manufacturing processes, and even health care, particularly with regard to digitized medical records that could be shared across providers. As McDermott Will & Emery partner Lee Schneider noted: "Anything can be put on an immutable blockchain ledger. It is a powerful thing and can blow your mind."

Companies also could benefit from increased efficiencies in corporate governance activities like shareholder voting. Addressing the Council of Institutional Investors at a conference in late 2017, Vice Chancellor J. Travis Laster lauded distributed ledger technology as the "plunger" that would "fix the proxy plumbing." Moreover, according to SEC Commissioner Kara Stein, blockchain and DLT may help companies identify and reach their shareholder bases more effectively.

Relatedly, some state governments have begun to consider how to use technology to create and maintain more accurate records and simplify interactions with members of the public. Several states are actively considering using blockchain technology in elections, in tracking real estate transactions and maintaining records, and even centralizing identifying data for purposes of government assistance programs. As Illinois Chief Information Officer and Department of Innovation & Technology Acting Secretary Kirk Lonbom noted, "Blockchain can play a key role in creating a highly efficient, hyperconnected and secure government, which translates into better services for our citizens."

Even as developments in blockchain technology are helping states shore up their own records and allow corporations to do the same, state securities regulators are concerned about fraud and investor vulnerability in the virtual currency space.

The membership organization for state and provincial securities commissioners, the North American Securities Administrators Association (NASAA), expressed concerns about Bitcoin and other virtual currencies in early 2018. The organization had previously identified ICOs and cryptocurrency-related investments as "emerging investor threats" for 2018. NASAA President Joseph Borg, who is also Alabama's securities overseer, said, "Cryptocurrencies and investments tied to them are high-risk products with an unproven track record and high price volatility." Other concerns around virtual currency identified in the NASAA alert are:

- A lack of robust regulatory oversight or FDIC insurance;
- Susceptibility to cybersecurity breaches or hacks; and
- A lack of recourse should the virtual currency disappear.

Fraud. Two states in particular have taken the lead on rooting out unregistered and fraudulent virtual currency offerings. As Secretary of the Commonwealth of Massachusetts, William Galvin issued his own warning about "Bitcoin mania." Comparing Bitcoin to the tulip mania of the 1600s, Secretary Galvin expressed the opinion that Bitcoin is "just the latest in a history of speculative bubbles that most often burst, leaving the average investors with a worthless product." His office's warning came just three days after Bitcoin futures began trading on the Chicago Board Options Exchange, and it betrayed some skepticism about this development, noting that the new listing "gives Bitcoin an air of legitimacy." Massachusetts conducted a sweep of virtual currency offerings that has led to six enforcement actions or consent orders to date.

Texas's securities commissioner also acted quickly in this space. An April 2018 release notes, "Texas was the first state securities regulator to enter an order against a cryptocurrency firm and has entered the most orders of any state regulator." The state seems less skittish about virtual currency itself than Secretary Galvin, and the release was careful to note that the state is only regulating offerings, not the underlying currencies themselves. "There is a lot of hype surrounding cryptocurrencies, but the companies offering investments are often not disclosing all the information investors need to make an informed decision," Securities Commissioner Travis J. Iles said. "Investors risk giving their hard-earned money to anonymous promoters hiding behind websites who have no intention of making good on their promises."

Despite an interest in protecting constituents' investments, the Texas authority has not been shy about pursuing an unregistered or fraudulent offering to the point that the virtual currency's market value evaporates. The April release notes that after the state entered a cease-and-desist order against a virtual currency firm called BitConnect (an action echoed by the state's counterpart in North Carolina), "the value of the company's own cryptocurrency, called BitConnect Coin, fell from $2.6 billion to nearly zero."

State Licensure. Another way states have claimed dominion over virtual currency firms is by requiring them to obtain a license. Most states that have taken this approach require licensure through their existing money transmitter laws. In 2013, the New York Department of Financial Services launched an inquiry with the goal of developing a comprehensive licensing regime for virtual currency firms. Two years later, in mid-2015, NYDFS released the final BitLicense framework. It imposes anti-money-laundering requirements and requires companies to develop policies and procedures, including on cybersecurity, and to retain certain records.

As part of the Department's outreach, then-Superintendent Benjamin Lawsky solicited questions and unofficial comments on the proposal via a February 2014 Reddit AMA ("ask me anything"). A common picture emerged from the questions: participants in the AMA were concerned about licensing being too stringent, particularly in terms of anti-money-laundering and know-your-customer requirements. Lawsky acknowledged that the rules had to balance requiring diligence and transparency with avoiding burdensome compliance costs. "Any regulations we issue for virtual currency firms will have to be carefully tailored with this in mind," he said.

Nevertheless, it was clear that Lawsky was especially focused on money laundering and terrorism concerns. One commenter asked why anti-money-laundering rules were such a high priority given a calculation by a former Federal Reserve Governor, Lawrence Lindsey, that the ratio of guilty verdicts to currency-transaction reports is less than 1:100,000. Lawsky clarified that NYDFS is a regulator, not a prosecutor, but added:

> However, we do have an obligation to help ensure the integrity of the financial system and as part of that to prevent money laundering. It is worth repeating that without massive money laundering it is very hard for terrorism to thrive. So we see our anti-money laundering (AML) work as one of

¶700

our more important obligations. Now that doesn't mean we should be undertaking unreasonable and/or ineffective means to find and address money laundering. But the Know Your Customer (KYC) rules we have for banks are important. The key is finding the most effective methods to root out and deter money laundering without having an overbearing impact on those who are just trying to use the system legally and without driving firms out of business with extraordinary compliance costs.

Superintendent Lawsky also explained why the state wanted to act early in the virtual currency space. "We do think that regulatory clarity could have many benefits for [virtual currency] businesses," he said. "At the same time, we want to move carefully and not go so fast that we fail to see the unintended consequences of the framework." When the final BitLicense framework was released the following year, firms did react negatively, with many ceasing operations in the state—although several sought and obtained a license or charter.

This appears to have been a warning bell for other regulators contemplating licensing requirements. When the Uniform Law Commission drafted a uniform virtual currencies law for states to consider adopting, it countered the BitLicense's one-size-fits-all approach with "a unique, three-tiered structure" with varying layers of regulation depending on a firm's activity. As Coin Center put it in endorsing the model act, "The model law is meticulously drafted . . . Careful parsing easily reveals who *does* need to get a license, who *does not*, and what a licensee must do to protect their customers. This certainty is lacking in most existing state money transmission laws and the New York BitLicense." However, the Bitcoin Foundation spoke out against the act, arguing that the proposed statute would discourage innovation and add to legal uncertainty within state regulations. [Uniform Regulation of Virtual-Currency Businesses Act, §§ 103, 202, 203, and 207, at ¶ 1400.]

¶ 710 Corporate Governance; Government Applications

Potential uses of distributed ledger technology and blockchains go beyond cryptocurrency trading and transactions and could potentially change the way companies engage in corporate governance and government agencies conduct administrative activities. Many financial institutions, including exchanges, are considering how these technologies could be used to increase efficiencies and streamline corporate processes and record-keeping activities while increasing transparency and accuracy. Specifically, industry participants are considering how DLT could be used to record and track trade execution and settlement, asset ownership, trading value, as well as maintain corporate records. Many are also evaluating the potential use of the technology to increase proxy voting accuracy and accounting transparency.

Simultaneously, state government agencies are exploring the possibility of implementing DLT- or blockchain-based record systems to guard against data breaches and create efficiencies in information gathering and record maintenance. Delaware and Illinois have led the way in exploring the potential application of these technologies to facilitate more secure methods by which residents can interact with government entities and to increase internal administrative efficiencies by creating paperless records arguably more accurate and less vulnerable to manipulation. Other states have begun to follow suit in considering the use of DLT and blockchain in areas ranging from voting procedures to real estate transactions and related records.

Corporate Governance

Virtual currencies are only one application of blockchain technology. While lawmakers and regulators remain cautious about potential threats of fraud and investor exploitation, many are optimistic about the potential for innovation, transparency, and accuracy. Corporate governance could change dramatically under DLT and blockchain, in both positive and negative ways. Commenters have suggested that use of these technologies could lower costs while increasing efficiencies but decrease privacy and adversely affect businesses' decision-making processes. Despite the potential drawbacks, several states have decided to move forward with specific efforts to enable automated recordkeeping and data storage with blockchain technology, and certain other states have noted that their laws do not prohibit maintenance of records with DLT or blockchain technology.

Beyond creation and maintenance of corporate records, some commentators have suggested that blockchain technology could be used in connection with a variety of other corporate governance matters. In addition to recording and tracking transactions on exchanges, the technology could be used to increase transparency by making executive compensation more traceable for investors and highlighting trading activities of executives and directors. Further, the technology could assist in ensuring accurate accounting and auditing and increasing transparency of share ownership and valuation, as well as in corporate affairs generally. Others have noted that blockchain technology could serve to simplify the annual meeting process and ensure accuracy in shareholder voting.

Record maintenance

Nevada. In June 2017, Nevada enacted legislation to clarify the definition of "blockchain technology" and to recognize it as a type of electronic record for the purposes of the Uniform Electronic Transactions Act, which governs the use of electronic signatures, contracts, and records in most states. In addition to prohibiting local governments from taxing and/or licensing blockchain use, the language of the legislation also permits data from a blockchain to be introduced in "proceedings." [S.B. 398, 79th Leg., Reg. Sess. (Nev. 2017).]

According to State Senator Ben Kieckhefer (R-Reno), the bill helps "ensure the State keeps pace with technological advancements" and provides a legal framework for people using blockchain technology so they're not operating in a legal gray area.

Delaware. In July 2017, in an effort to continue to attract corporations to the state and curb costly recordkeeping errors, Delaware governor John Carney signed a law to allow Delaware corporations to keep records in distributed ledgers or blockchain. The law, which passed overwhelmingly in the state legislature, expressly permits corporations to use networks of electronic databases in the creation and maintenance of records, including the stock ledger.

The method also resolves ownership inconsistencies between corporate and securities laws, as Delaware confers rights on the direct, record owners of shares while some federal securities laws require that listed securities be depository-eligible and indirectly owned. In the 2017 Dole Food class-action litigation, where class members filed facially eligible claims to over 49 million Dole shares despite the fact that the company had only 37 million shares outstanding, Vice Chancellor Laster wrote: "Distributed ledger technology offers a potential technological solution by maintaining multiple, current copies of a single and comprehensive stock ownership ledger." The legislation also explicitly allows certain communications to shareholders to be delivered via DLT. [S.B. 69, 149th Gen. Assem., Reg. Sess. (Del. 2017).]

Wyoming. In the last year, Wyoming has considered a series of bills designed to entice cryptocurrency and blockchain organizations to do business in the state. Of the five bills recently signed into law, three relax Wyoming's regulations concerning cryptocurrency and two amend the state's corporation law to facilitate blockchain and cryptocurrency innovation and development.

¶710

In March 2018, Wyoming enacted legislation to update the state's Business Corporations Act to allow corporations to create, maintain, and store corporate records on a blockchain in order to minimize the resources expended and errors associated with physical record maintenance. Specifically, the legislation authorizes corporations to use "distributed or electronic networks or databases" for records, to use data addresses associated with private keys to identify shareholders, and to accept shareholder votes if signed by a network signature corresponding with a data address. [H.B. 101, 64th Leg., Budg. Sess. (Wyo. 2018).]

Tennessee. Also in March 2018, Tennessee enacted legislation recognizing the legal validity of blockchain technology using a distributed, decentralized, shared, and replicated ledger with data protected with cryptography that is immutable and auditable. Specifically, the unanimously passed legislation declares that:

- A signature secured through blockchain technology is an electronic signature;

- Blockchain records or contracts are electronic records; and

- Any person using blockchain technology to secure information has the same ownership rights to the information as he or she had before securing the information. [S.B. 1662, 110th Gen. Assem., Reg. Sess. (Tenn. 2018).]

Arizona. In April 2018, Arizona enacted legislation to allow companies to hold and share data using blockchain technology. While Arizona law already authorizes the use of blockchain in commerce and recognizes the validity of signatures and records in connection with blockchain technology, the change goes a step further to preemptively permit businesses to use the technology in new and innovative ways. [H.B. 2603, 53rd Leg., 2d Reg. Sess. (Ariz. 2018).]

"This is permissive, it's not a shall it's a may," said State Rep. Jeff Weninger (R-Chandler).

Separately, the Arizona legislature passed HB 2601 to acknowledge "virtual coins" as digital representations of value that can be digitally traded and function as a medium of exchange or store of value. The legislation also provides a framework for regulation of "virtual coin offerings" that involve the use of virtual coins falling under the definition of a "security." In addition, the legislature approved HB 2602 to prevent municipalities and counties from restricting mining-like activities in a residence, reserving decision-making authority concerning these activities to state government. Arizona Governor Doug Ducey signed the bills on April 12, 2018. [H.B. 2601 and 2602, 53rd Leg., 2d Reg. Sess. (Ariz. 2018).]

Other governance uses

Some think of blockchain technology as nothing more than a means of data storage, but the accurate, transparent, and immutable nature of the technology could transform the exchange of information by eliminating the need for, and costs associated with, the use of an intermediary. Possible areas of use for blockchain technology and DLT could include shareholder voting and proposal submission, accounting and auditing activities, and various means by which to increase transparency for investors and regulators.

Voting and proposals. Shareholder voting can be ambiguous and sometimes inaccurate, particularly in large companies with diverse ownership. A proxy contest can be a tedious process involving identification of stockholders, assessing likelihood of success, and maintaining lines of communication with shareholders. All of these processes require substantial resources. While proxy voting addresses concerns surrounding the reaching of quorums, studies have documented problems with corporate elections, including inexact voter lists, incomplete ballot distribution, and inaccurate tabulation of votes. [*See e.g.*, Marcel Kahan & Edward B. Rock, *The Hanging Chads of Corporate Voting*, GEORGETOWN L.J. 96 (2008).] Imprecise vote tabulation under current procedures particularly affects the outcome of close corporate elections, which often end up decided in favor of management. [David Yermack, *Corporate Governance and Blockchains*, REVIEW OF FINANCE (November 2016), *available at* https://academic.oup.com/rof/article/21/1/7/2888422.]

The main problems with the chains of intermediaries in share ownership and the current proxy voting system involve transparency, verification, and identification—three of the main benefits associated with blockchain technology. [Anne Lafarre & Christoph Van der Elst, *Blockchain Technology for Corporate Governance and Shareholder Activism*, European Corporate Governance Institute (ECGI) - Law Working Paper No. 390/2018 (March 2018), *available at* SSRN: https://ssrn.com/abstract=3135209 or http://dx.doi.org/10.2139/ssrn.3135209.] Blockchain technology and DLT could improve proxy voting in publicly traded companies to avoid clerical errors and other inaccuracies in the voting process by allowing shareholders to participate in and observe the voting process as it occurs. Commenters have noted that, if companies are able to verify shareholder identity and shareholders can vote in a secure and authenticated fashion, then corporations will be able to create an increasingly democratic governance culture.

A corporation is generally entitled to rely exclusively on the stock ledger to determine the record holders entitled to vote. [Balotti, Finkelstein and Williams, *Delaware Law of Corporations and Business Organizations* §9.5.] According to Lewis Cohen and Soraya Ghebleh of Hogan Lovells, a distributed stock ledger, accessible only to permissioned parties, that automatically updates in a verifiable fashion upon a change in ownership, could provide for a transparent and accountable "trustless intermediary" and eliminate the inefficiencies of manual authorization and verification involved in stock ledger updates.

Accessible and current ownership records could also facilitate communications between the company and its investors while simultaneously increasing transparency and reducing the costs associated with paper-based transactions. The enhanced speed, transparency, and accuracy of blockchain voting could motivate shareholders to more frequently participate in corporate governance generally and demand votes on more topics and with greater frequency. Further, blockchain voting would facilitate faster, more precise vote tabulation and aid in resolving ambiguities about the outcomes of close elections while potentially reducing the use of empty voting practices by investors borrowing shares to temporarily acquire voting rights without economic exposure to related cash flow rights.

From a practical standpoint, voting via blockchain could be implemented by allocating to eligible voting shareholders vote tokens in proportion to their voting power and allowing them to transmit their respective votes to addresses on the blockchain, which would then be registered on the ledger. In 2017, in conjunction with several industry participants, Broadridge and AST successfully completed pilots testing blockchain-enabled proxy voting and vote tabulation.

According to several of the largest central securities depositories (CSDs), blockchain technology could not only assist in verifying ownership, voting authentication, and voting rights allocation, but also could play a role throughout the entirety of the annual meeting process, including meeting notification and management, proxy assignments, and final reviews by auditors and regulators. Further, in a private blockchain, the company and qualifying shareholders could place proposals on the blockchain, and smart contracting could be used to make sure all rules and access rights and limitations are contained in the blockchain as appropriate constraints.

¶710

Shareholders would then be immediately notified and be able to cast votes in a much shorter period.

Business operations. On May 30, 2018, Vermont Governor Phil Scott signed into law a bill permitting Vermont-based limited liability companies to use blockchain technology for a material part of their business operations. The law, effective July 1, 2018, allows LLCs to become blockchain-based limited liability companies (BBLLCs) by so specifying in their articles of organization. [S.269, L. 2018.]

A BBLLC may be entirely or partly governed by blockchain technology. The operating agreement should set forth a summary of the BBLLC's mission and purpose; whether the BBLLC's consensus ledger or database will be fully or partially decentralized and fully or partially public or private; voting procedures; proposals to upgrade software systems and amend the operating agreement; protocols addressing system security breaches or other unauthorized actions affecting the blockchain technology's integrity; and the rights and obligations of each participant group within the BBLLC.

The law defines "blockchain" as "a cryptographically secured, chronological, and decentralized consensus ledger or consensus database maintained via Internet, peer-to-peer network, or other interaction." It also defines "virtual currency" as "a digital representation of value that is used as a medium of exchange, unit of account, or store of value and is not legal tender, whether or not denominated in legal tender."

Accounting. Some have suggested that a firm could post all of its transactions on a public blockchain. More recently, David Yermack of the NYU Stern School of Business opined that a firm could permanently record all routine accounting data, with a time stamp, which would prevent alteration or manipulation, including practices such as back-dating sales contracts or amortizing operating expenses. With this application, any shareholder could aggregate a firm's transactions into income statement and balance sheet data without having to wait for quarterly financial statements. While acknowledging that this process could result in proprietary information becoming available to outsiders, Yermack noted that it could also increase shareholders' trust in the integrity of a company's data and minimize reliance on auditors to verify the accuracy of books and records.

Further, according to Yermack, real-time blockchain accounting could allow stakeholders to more readily spot a transaction that implies a conflict of interest without the potential of management determining that it does not meet the standard for required disclosure.

One commenter suggested that, to avoid improper use of confidential information, access to records could be limited only to those with access to SEC disclosures, although this could frustrate the very purpose of the complete transparency of blockchain. Further, even though back-dating may not be feasible, forward-dating could still be used by keeping a parallel accounting system. Managerial evasion would still be possible, particular in connection with voluntary blockchain reporting mechanisms. In light of transition costs and potential misuse, blockchain accounting could be "utopic and impracticable." [Fiammetta S. Piazza, *Bitcoin and the Blockchain as Possible Corporate Governance Tools: Strengths and Weaknesses*, 5 PENN. ST. J.L. & INT'L AFF. 262.]

General transparency. More generally, blockchain technology not only could lead to lower costs and greater efficiencies, but also could foster a culture of increased transparency. Shareholders typically rely on the board of directors and official disclosures and are themselves not able to verify the veracity of company information. Real-time access and secure communications via blockchain could reduce the need for burdensome disclosure requirements and give shareholders the ability to communicate directly with management.

Yermack notes that blockchain technology also could render executive compensation more easily traceable and quantifiable for average investors, as opposed to the information provided in disclosures to the SEC, but suggests that the availability of such information could undermine the use of equity-based compensation by hindering executives' trade leverage. Commenters have also noted that it is possible that registration of shares on a blockchain could lead to shareholder overreaction to managerial moves made in accordance with sound business judgment.

To achieve its potential, blockchain technology must be scalable, and a critical mass of stakeholders must be willing to move forward to further develop the technology. Lowering the cost of certain corporate governance functions could lead to improvements in liquidity and have a positive impact on market structure as a whole. However, the practical implementation of these changes will require consensus across market participants and company executives.

State Governments

Separate from, or perhaps in connection with, companies' potential use of blockchain technology and DLT to enhance corporate governance, some state governments have begun to consider how to use the technology to keep more accurate records and simplify interactions with members of the public. Delaware and Illinois are charting the course in considering potential applications of these technologies to facilitate more secure government interactions and increase efficiencies while minimizing fraud and other malicious activities. And other states are following their lead.

Delaware. Delaware green-lighted the use of blockchain technology by companies registered in the state and began moving toward creating a hospitable regulatory environment and infrastructure appropriate for use of a distributed stock ownership ledger in 2017. Before this, as part of the Delaware Blockchain Initiative, former Governor Markell also committed the state government to the use of the technology by partnering with New York-based blockchain company Symbiont to store public archives on a distributed ledger, making the state among the first to embrace the technology for its own activities.

However, in 2018, the state appeared to slow its pace on blockchain adoption to further consider how a new approach would affect companies and shareholders. According to Deputy Secretary of State Kristopher Knight, state agencies have an obligation to not "haphazardly advance ideas that could disrupt Delaware's grip on its corporate franchise business." While Delaware could see gains with blockchain, the government must also consider potential costs, he said.

This move could potentially delay companies' consideration and adoption of blockchain, as a corporate blockchain for state filings would only work if it can be connected to a state filing system.

Illinois. In January 2018, the Illinois Blockchain and Distributed Ledger Task Force provided a final report to the state's General Assembly. Under HJR 25, among other things, the Task Force was directed to study:

- Opportunities and risks associated with using the technologies;

- Projects in other jurisdictions that Illinois could consider, and

- How Illinois law could be modified to support the technologies.

The report, the first official Illinois report to be certified in a public blockchain, suggests that blockchain technology and DLT can lead to a smarter, cheaper, and safer way to administer government. [Illinois Blockchain and Distributed Ledger Task Force, Final Report to the General Assembly, January 31, 2018, at ¶ 1390.]

¶710

The Task Force found that blockchain technology could facilitate increased security in interactions with government and maintenance of paperless records while enhancing data accuracy and cybersecurity protections for Illinois residents. The report pointed out that blockchain technology addresses data reconciliation by requiring network participants to share data points, eliminating the need to reconcile entries, and standardizes data and transaction formats across users. The permanent and persistent storage function of blockchain technology ensures immutability and data integrity, which could aid in forensic analysis, legal discovery proceedings, and regulatory oversight, while reducing costs for the state.

According to the report, computational power, scalability, and performance could raise challenges as ledger size increases. Substantial resources also could be involved in updating legacy systems and existing operations and facilitating interactions among varying protocols, but blockchain technology could simplify management of information and enable government agencies to access and use data while maintaining privacy and security.

To determine eligibility for government services, various pieces of data are used to verify a person's identity and assets. Often this information is stored in separate databases across agencies. The Illinois task force noted that a digital identity model based on DLT could be used to consolidate disparate data and enable citizens to share relevant information with government to access public services as necessary, making government entities verifiers of identity as opposed to custodians of information.

In addition to distribution of government benefits, the report suggested that the government could use blockchain technology to create marketplaces for tasks such as waste management, recycling services, or snow removal, to manage disaster recovery distributions, and to improve visibility of tax credits.

The report offered eight legislative proposals related to public recording, recordkeeping, and modernization of property laws to take advantage of blockchain technology. It also noted the availability the Task Force's database of over 200 public-sector blockchain and DLT projects around the world to provide an overview of how government entities at various levels are employing blockchain technology in their governing efforts.

Colorado. In January 2018, Colorado introduced Colorado SB 86, which would require annual assessments by state entities to consider the benefits and costs of blockchain technology and evaluate whether it could be used to reduce fraud and to protect computer systems from cyberattacks. The bill notes that attempts to breach Colorado government records reached between 6 million and 8 million per day in 2017. The bill directs Colorado's Chief Information Security Officer to specifically "develop and maintain a series of metrics to identify, assess, and monitor each public agency data system for its platform descriptions, vulnerabilities, risks, liabilities, appropriate employee access control, and the benefits and costs of adopting encryption and distributed ledger technologies."

New York. New York introduced AB 8792 and AB 8793 to provide for consideration of the use of blockchain technology to protect voter records and election results and to establish a task force to study and report on the potential implementation of blockchain technology in connection with state recordkeeping, information storage, and service delivery. Separately, New York is considering a bill to establish a task force to study the potential impact of a state-issued cryptocurrency.

Virginia. Joint resolution HJR 153 introduced in the Virginia legislature in January 2018 similarly would establish a subcommittee charged to study the potential implementation of blockchain technology in state recordkeeping, information storage, and service delivery.

With regard to other state blockchain activities, the Georgia and Illinois legislatures have introduced bills to require their respective tax authorities to accept cryptocurrencies for payment of taxes and license fees. Arizona recently adopted legislation allowing taxpayers to satisfy income tax liability using a virtual currency payment gateway, such as Bitcoin, Litecoin, or other recognized cryptocurrency using an electronic peer-to-peer system.

West Virginia is testing a mobile blockchain voting solution for military service member residents in two counties who are unable to vote in person in a primary election. Its objective is to offer a voting solution that is straightforward and more secure than currently available systems. If the pilot is successful, the state will expand the program to more counties in the November general election.

Despite state zeal for implementing uses of blockchain technology and DLT, time and money remain common barriers to implementation. As Mark Calem of KPMG noted: "States have funding challenges, and agencies have to focus on getting their core mission done. So while automation can help . . . they just don't have the wherewithal to do that."

¶ 720 Licensing

The response of most states to regulating the virtual currency space has been to absorb this emerging technology into existing laws whereby they license and regulate entities engaged in transmitting money. Some states have amended their money transmitter laws to expressly include virtual currencies in the definition of money, while others rely on definitions broad enough to pick up such transactions without specifically identifying virtual currencies. States that take this approach risk an adverse ruling should courts disagree, as when a Florida court held that transactions in Bitcoin were not money transfers. In response, Florida's legislature shored up its statute to specifically prohibit the laundering of virtual currencies. Still other states have issued guidance clarifying that virtual currencies are *not* money for purposes of their money transmitter acts.

New York is the only state to have enacted a separate licensing regime specifically for virtual currency firms. In remarks concurrent with the release of the final framework, known as the BitLicense, then-Superintendent of Financial Services Benjamin M. Lawsky acknowledged that some members of his department had an instinct "to shoehorn these new digital currency firms into our old money transmission rules. However, state money transmission rules date back to the Civil War—when there was barely mass communication, let alone an Internet." Response to the new framework has been mixed: a number of firms fled the state after release of the final rules, which include a $5,000 application fee and substantial governance requirements. However, the state has granted a license to three virtual currency firms and a charter to two others.

In an effort to harmonize the approach among states, the Uniform Law Commission developed the Uniform Regulation of Virtual-Currency Businesses Act. In February 2018, the American Bar Association approved the draft law, which has been introduced in three states. In light of criticism of the one-size-fits-all approach taken in New York, the model law creates three separate tiers of regulation based on a company's earnings.

State Money Transmitter Laws

Most states have responded to the emergence of virtual currencies in the framework of their existing money transmitter laws. All states except Montana have one, and most are longstanding laws developed to protect customers who contracted with a

¶720

financial intermediary, such as Western Union. Nevertheless, the laws' definitions are often broad enough to pick up less-traditional avenues of transfer, even including transactions in virtual currency. Money transmitter laws require those whose activities fall within the definition to obtain a license from the state. This typically means paying initial and annual fees, posting a bond, maintaining a minimum net worth, and submitting to examinations by the licensing body.

As New York's then-Superintendent of Financial Services Benjamin M. Lawsky observed when explaining why his state took a different approach, some of these money transmitter laws date back to the Civil War. The development of each law by each state, sometimes over centuries, means that each state has a different approach when it comes to the regulation of a form of currency that by its nature has no borders.

Some states have rested on their existing definitions of the transmission of money, which may be phrased broadly enough as to subsume virtual currency transfers. Indeed, until 2016, South Carolina did not have a money transmission law, but despite having been drafted in a post-Bitcoin age, the law does not specifically reference virtual currencies. It defines "money" as "a medium of exchange that is authorized or adopted by the United States or a foreign government" and broadly defines "monetary value" as "a medium of exchange, whether or not redeemable in money." [A266, L. 2016.] "Money transmission" means "selling or issuing payment instruments, stored value, or receiving money or monetary value for transmission." New Mexico also enacted its first money transmissions act in 2016. The law does not mention virtual currencies specifically, and its definitions are similar to those of South Carolina. [Ch. 88, L. 2016.]

Broad definitions may seem like a wise approach given that virtual currencies are still evolving and many are struggling to understand the existing technology, much less predict what will happen in the near future. On the other hand, an overly broad definition can lead to regulatory uncertainty, leaving those who transact in virtual currencies unclear as to whether they need to apply for licensure as a money transmitter. To alleviate this concern, some states have issued guidance clarifying the scope of their licensing requirements. These states include Illinois, Kansas, Tennessee, and Texas. [Illinois Department of Financial and Professional Regulation Digital Currency Regulatory Guidance, June 13, 2017; Kansas Office of the State Bank Commissioner Guidance Document MT 2014-01, June 6, 2014; Tennessee Department of Financial Institutions, Memo Re: Regulatory Treatment of Virtual Currencies Under the Tennessee Money Transmitter Act, December 16, 2015; Texas Department of Banking Supervisory Memorandum 1037, April 3, 2014.]

Via no-action relief, the Idaho Department of Finance wrote that "an exchanger that sells its own inventory of virtual currency is generally not considered a virtual currency transmitter under the Idaho Money Transmitters Act. Alternatively, an exchanger that holds customer funds while arranging a satisfactory buy/sell order with a third party, and transmits virtual currency and fiat currency between buyer and seller, will typically be considered a virtual currency transmitter." [Idaho Department of Finance no-action letter, recipient redacted, July 26, 2016.]

A criminal case in Florida is a cautionary tale of failing to consider virtual currencies as part of the statutory definition. The court dismissed prosecutors' case against a Bitcoin seller for unlawfully operating a "money services business, to wit a money transmitter." The sale of Bitcoin did not fall under the plain meaning of the statute because the defendant was yielding a profit on the spread of Bitcoin akin to a day trader in stocks, rather than receiving a commission or fee for transmitting the virtual currency. "Nothing in our frame of references allows us to accurately define or describe Bitcoin," the court lamented, adding that the Florida legislature may choose to regulate virtual currency in the future. [*Florida v. Espinoza*, July 22, 2016, Pooler, T.] The money transmitters law still does not claim dominion over virtual currency, although the legislature did amend its anti-money-laundering statute to specifically define virtual currency and prohibit its laundering.

Finally, other states have amended their money transmitters laws to expressly regulate virtual currency transmitters. For example, on the heels of South Carolina's new money transmitters law, North Carolina replaced its existing law with a new money transmitters act that specifically defines "money transmission" as including "maintaining control of virtual currency on behalf of others." [N.C.G.S. § § 53-208.41 et seq.]

New York BitLicense

In June 2015, the New York Department of Financial Services announced the release of the final BitLicense framework for regulating digital currency firms. The announcement marked the culmination of a two-year-long inquiry during which the NYDFS held public hearings, published two drafts of proposed rules for comment, and engaged with the community on social media, notably including a Reddit AMA ("ask me anything") hosted by then-Superintendent Benjamin Lawsky. The proposals received over 3,500 comments, not including the 1,200 responses to the AMA.

License required. Under the final framework, a BitLicense is required for anyone engaging in any of the following activities involving New York State or persons that reside, are located, have a place of business, or are conducting business in New York:

- Transmitting virtual currency;
- Storing, holding, or maintaining custody or control of virtual currency on behalf of others;
- Buying and selling virtual currency as a customer business;
- Performing exchange services as a customer business; or
- Controlling, administering, or issuing a virtual currency.

Application fee. There is a non-refundable $5,000 fee to apply for a BitLicense. (The application form is reproduced at ¶ 1380.)

Regulatory overlap. An entity chartered under the New York Banking Law need not apply for a BitLicense, but must receive the prior approval of the Department to engage in virtual currency business activity.

Some companies may need both a money transmitter license and a BitLicense, but applicants can cross-satisfy many application requirements in order to avoid unnecessary duplication.

On-ramp. The BitLicense framework provides the superintendent discretion to grant a conditional two-year license after a comprehensive evaluation of, among other things, an applicant's business model and the risks it presents. The license is available only to applicants that do not satisfy all of the regulatory requirements upon licensing.

Capital requirements. The licensee must maintain capital in an amount and form that the superintendent determines is sufficient based on an assessment of the specific risks applicable to each licensee. A non-exclusive list of factors the superintendent may consider is included in the final regulations. [23 NYCRR 200.8(a).]

Custody and protection of assets. A BitLicense holder must also maintain a surety bond or trust account, denominated in U.S. dollars, in such form and amount as is acceptable to the superintendent. To the extent a licensee stores, holds, or maintains custody or control of virtual currency on behalf of another person, the licensee must hold virtual currency of the same type and amount. Licensees are prohibited from selling, transferring, or encumbering customer assets, including virtual currency, except at the direction of the customer.

¶720

Anti-money-laundering requirements. Licensees must conduct an initial risk assessment and establish an anti-money-laundering (AML) program based on the results. The program must, at a minimum:

- Provide for a system of internal controls, policies, and procedures designed to ensure ongoing compliance with AML laws, rules, and regulations;
- Provide for independent compliance testing conducted by qualified internal personnel;
- Designate a qualified individual or individuals responsible for coordinating and monitoring day-to-day compliance with the AML program; and
- Provide ongoing personnel training.

The AML program must include a written policy reviewed and approved by the board of directors or equivalent body. Each licensee must maintain records of all virtual currency transactions and notify the NYDFS if one person makes a transfer or series of transfers exceeding $10,000 in one day. As part of this program, the licensee must maintain a customer identification program.

Each licensee that is not subject to suspicious activity reporting requirements under federal law must file reports of transactions that indicate a possible violation of law or regulation within 30 days from detecting the possible violation. Licensees that are already required to file Suspicious Activity Reports with FinCEN are not required to file separately with the NYDFS.

Other provisions. The final regulations also list requirements in the event a licensee contemplates a material change to its business or a change in control. Licensees are also required to maintain certain books and records, submit quarterly financial statements, and submit to examinations at least every other year. Licensees must establish and maintain cybersecurity programs designed to identify risks, protect their systems, detect intrusions, respond to cybersecurity events, and restore normal operations and services. The rules restrict advertising and require certain disclosures to customers.

Response. Companies that were already providing virtual currency services in New York were given 45 days to apply for a BitLicense. A number of companies instead left the state in a move that became known as the "Bitcoin exodus." Explaining its decision to cease operations in New York, the Bitcoin exchange Kraken wrote, "While we're sure that the protection from New York law enforcement is valuable, it comes at a price that exceeds the market opportunity of servicing New York residents." That price, according to Kraken, includes the compliance cost itself coupled with a lack of a guarantee of support from New York banks; a lack of a guarantee of enforcement against unlicensed competitors; and burdens and restrictions on global operations. In April 2018, Kraken's CEO announced that the firm would not respond to a 34-point request for information from the then-New York Attorney General. In a blog post, Kraken opined that, among other things, the two-week deadline is unreasonable and that the letter amounted to a request for free consulting work.

Other businesses stayed put, however. NYDFS granted the first virtual currency charter to itBit Trust Company in May 2015 and the first BitLicense to Circle Internet Financial in September 2015, followed closely by the granting of a charter to the Winklevoss twins' Gemini cryptocurrency exchange. BitLicenses have also been granted to Ripple affiliate XRP II; Coinbase; and bitFlyer USA. The XRP press release notes that as of June 13, 2016, NYDFS had received 26 BitLicense applications.

Still, criticism of the BitLicense has not waned; NYDFS was named in a lawsuit by a firm that was denied a license and now challenges NYDFS's authority to regulate virtual currencies. In February 2018, two Democratic state senators, including Banking Committee Chair Jesse E. Hamilton, III, convened a roundtable to discuss virtual currency regulation in the state, with a particular focus on the future of the BitLicense.

The Uniform Regulation of Virtual-Currency Businesses Act

A model law could bring clarity and uniformity to the virtual currency landscape while avoiding overly burdensome regulation. The National Conference of Commissioners on Uniform State Laws drafted the Uniform Regulation of Virtual-Currency Businesses Act (at ¶ 1400) in part to avoid the one-size-fits-all approach taken by New York. The model law received the conference's approval in July 2017 and the American Bar Association's in February 2018. It has been introduced in three states: Connecticut (HB 5496), Hawaii (SB 2129, deferred), and Nebraska (LB 987).

Under the URVCBA, "virtual currency" is a digital representation of value that is used as a medium of exchange, unit of account, or store of value and is not legal tender. The definition was kept technology-neutral to encompass as many types of virtual currency as possible, while excluding merchants' rewards programs or equivalent on online game platforms. The act only regulates companies that assume "control" of a client's virtual currency.

The URVCBA has a three-tier structure based on business activity level. Those doing less than $5,000 of virtual-currency business in a year are exempt from registration or other regulation. Those with business activity between $5,000 and $35,000 must register, but are not required to obtain a license. This functions as a "regulatory sandbox" to allow companies to focus on innovation in the early stage of development. Finally, companies with activity levels greater than $35,000 annually must be licensed. The act also contemplates licensure by reciprocity, either through the Nationwide Multistate Licensing System and Registry or otherwise on a bilateral or multilateral basis.

Otherwise, the model act contains some elements similar to the BitLicense regime. For example, the URVCBA requires licensees and provisional registrants to issue disclosures to potential customers. In addition, all virtual-currency businesses regulated by the Act must establish specific policies and compliance programs to guard against fraud, cyber threats, and money laundering or financing of terrorist activity. Applicants must deposit a surety bond or other security and maintain a minimum net worth—the model act suggests $25,000—along with sufficient unencumbered reserves as agreed to by the state. Licensees also agree to submit to examinations and are subject to enforcement measures and remedies, including civil penalties.

¶ 730 State Enforcement

Early actions in virtual currency enforcement occurred at the federal level by the SEC and CFTC. At the end of 2017, however, as initial coin offerings and other virtual currency investments grew, state securities commissioners began taking action to detect and halt unregistered virtual currency offerings and enforce antifraud violations. In just a short period of time, the securities regulators in Texas and Massachusetts signaled vigilance in the virtual currency space, each conducting a sweep for unregistered offerings in December 2017. Texas's sweep has resulted in seven enforcement actions; Massachusetts obtained five consent orders in which virtual currency operators agreed to cease offerings and filed a complaint against a sixth firm.

The state regulators' work has complemented that of the federal agencies. The association of state regulators, the North American Securities Administrators Association, echoed some of the concerns of the SEC and CFTC when it issued a warning about speculation in cryptocurrency during the price fluctuations of late 2017. "Investors should go beyond the headlines and hype to understand the risks associated with investments in cryptocurrencies, as well as cryptocurrency futures contracts and other

¶730

financial products where these virtual currencies are linked in some way to the underlying investment," said NASAA President Joe Borg in the news release.

SEC Chairman Jay Clayton and Commissioners Kara M. Stein and Michael S. Piwowar commended NASAA for its release, noting that many promoters of ICOs and other cryptocurrency-related investments are not following federal or state securities laws. "The SEC and state securities regulators are pursuing violations, but we again caution you that, if you lose money, there is a substantial risk that our efforts will not result in a recovery of your investment," the commissioners advised.

Texas

The Texas State Securities Board carved out an early role for itself as a watchdog in the area of virtual currency enforcement. On December 18, 2017, staff in the Enforcement Division began a four-week sweep of investment offerings by promotors who appeared to be illegally soliciting Texas investors. The 32 resulting investigations led to seven enforcement actions against virtual currency promotors, the most of any state regulator, according to an April 10, 2018, news release from enforcement staff. Among the findings of the investigations, summarized in a report issued concurrently with the news release, are:

- No promoters were registered to sell securities in Texas, a violation of the Texas Securities Act;

- Thirty promoters were broadly using websites, social media, and online advertising to market to Texans;

- Seven promoters were offering securities tied to a new cryptocurrency;

- At least five promoters all but ignored investing risks by guaranteeing returns, some as high as 40 percent per month;

- Only 11 promoters provided potential investors with a physical address, leaving investors with little recourse if they lost their money; and

- Six of the offerings involved payment of a commission to investors who recruited new investors into the scheme.

Enforcement staff continues to investigate offerings uncovered during the four-week sweep. The Division had opened approximately 60 investigative files related to investment programs as of the issuance of the report.

USI-Tech. On December 20, 2017, Texas became the first state to issue an administrative order against a cryptocurrency promoter when it ordered Dubai-based USI-Tech Limited to stop soliciting Texas residents to invest in a Bitcoin mining venture that had promised triple-digit returns in targeted Craigslist advertisements.

USI-Tech had two U.S.-based sales agents, in Maryland and California; neither was registered to sell securities in Texas, and the investment was not registered in Texas. The agents' websites promoted the mining investment, claiming that it "derives its value from [USI-Tech's] nonexclusive interest in a series of Bitcoin mining contracts," and promised a 1 percent daily return.

The USI-Tech website said that, while the returns did not depend on the value of Bitcoin, its Bitcoin platform "consistently provides returns of up to 150 percent per year." Both the company and the sales agents were telling potential investors that per the FTC, the mining contracts were "certified legal products in the USA." However, the Texas State Securities Board, not the FTC, regulates the registration of the mining investment as a security in Texas.

The agents also allegedly attempted to mislead the public by claiming that USI-Tech had a "binding legal opinion" from a law firm stating the company is "a legal business in good standing." The Texas Securities Commissioner alleged violations of State Securities Board rules, including a failure to disclose:

- Information about the facilities used to mine bitcoins, the costs of mining Bitcoins, and whether the firm had successfully mined Bitcoins;

- The terms of the contracts and an explanation of USI-Tech's "non-exclusive interest" in mining contracts; and

- Information about whether the company's financial condition is strong enough to provide a 1 percent daily return.

The North Carolina Secretary of State also issued, on February 16, 2018, a temporary cease-and-desist order barring USI-Tech from offering unregistered securities, acting as an unregistered securities dealer, and engaging in fraud. The order became final on April 6. [*In the Matter of USI-Tech Limited*, File No. 18 ADM 002, April 6, 2018.]

Bitconnect. On January 4, 2018, the Texas Securities Commissioner ordered the British firm BitConnect to cease marketing a purported $4 billion cryptocurrency program to Texas residents. The emergency cease-and-desist order alleged that BitConnect was fraudulently offering unregistered securities in violation of the Texas Securities Act. [*In the Matter of BitConnect*, Order No. ENF-18-CDO-1754, January 4, 2018.]

BitConnect's now-defunct website described the firm as an "open source all in one bitcoin and crypto community platform designed to provide multiple investment opportunities." The company claimed that it had introduced 9.4 million "BitConnect Coins" into the marketplace, with a total market capitalization of $4.1 billion. One of BitConnect's investment opportunities, the "BitConnect Lending Program," allegedly represented that investors could earn returns of up to 40 percent interest per month. Under the program, investors would purchase BitConnect coins using Bitcoin, a more established cryptocurrency, and then "lend" their funds out for investment by a "BitConnect Trading Bot."

The Commissioner alleged that BitConnect touted its unregistered investment programs as a "safe way to earn a high rate of return," despite offering no information concerning the algorithms used by the Trading Bot or how the programs would generate returns for investors. The order also alleged that BitConnect intentionally failed to disclose the identity of its principals, the physical address of its place of business, or its financial condition.

On January 9, 2018, North Carolina also blocked BitConnect from operating cryptocurrency-based investment programs. The North Carolina securities officials found that the firm's investment programs were unregistered securities. Regulators also found that BitConnect encouraged members of the investing public to act as unregistered salespeople by selling the instruments in violation of the Securities Act. Secretary of State Elaine F. Marshall clarified, "We are not condemning cryptocurrencies as a whole. We are targeting this specific investment scheme." She added that her agency, which also issued an investor alert on cryptocurrency schemes, will continue to investigate schemes promising returns that appear "too good to be true." [*In the Matter of BitConnect*, File No. 17 SEC 091, January 9, 2018.]

In particular, the state's cease-and-desist order found that that BitConnect was not registered as a dealer or salesman of securities in North Carolina, made misrepresentations, and omitted the disclosure of material facts when offering these investments in the state. Some of the company's misrepresentations included the following:

- BitConnect Coin is the investment tool investors need to jump start their financial security;

¶730

- Investors can "secure their future by gaining quick profit growth for tomorrow that is practical and attainable";

- The investment ensures "financial freedom is available and investors can start today. Store and invest wealth and earn substantial interest and investment"; and

- Investors who purchase BitConnect Coin are purchasing "an interest bearing asset with 120 percent return per year. It is that simple."

In the wake of the states' actions, BitConnect announced on its website that it was shutting down its exchange and lending operation. The announcement cited the two cease-and-desist orders from Texas and North Carolina as "a hindrance for the legal continuation of the platform." BitConnect also attributed the shutdown to "continuous bad press" that "made community members uneasy and created a lack of confidence in the platform" as well as distributed denial of service (DDoS) attacks that destabilized the platform and "created more panic inside the community." If the company was seeking to mitigate panic by shutting down, it backfired: a week later, it was named in a twelve-count private class action complaint that alleged investors' holdings dropped by 90 percent when the business abruptly shuttered.

R2B Coin. Several weeks after the BitConnect action, on January 26, 2018, the Texas Securities Commissioner issued yet another emergency cease-and-desist order to bar an offshore cryptocurrency offering. The commissioner alleged that Hong Kong-based R2B Coin fraudulently offered unregistered securities to Texas residents by, among other things, representing that its eponymous cryptocurrency "will never go down in value" while failing to disclose the calculations or analysis behind its price projections. The commissioner also alleged that R2B Coin misled potential investors about the possibility that the company will list its stock on a major stock exchange and that investors will be able to trade their tokens for stock. [*In the Matter of R2B Coin*, ENF-18-CDO-1756, January 24, 2018.]

The order stated that the company is offering investors the opportunity to invest in "R2B Coin" tokens through the firm's website during a "pre-trade sales period" expected to last between three and four months. By means of the website, a series of conference calls, and other solicitations through "affiliates," R2B Coin allegedly represented to investors that "you can get in for hundreds of bucks and make thousands of dollars" and "the faster you buy the more you will make." While R2B Coin determines the price of the tokens during the pre-trade sales period, the order alleged that R2B Coin intentionally failed to disclose the basis it used to set the price and that buyers or sellers on the free market may later set a price that is different from the price set by R2B Coin.

The order also alleged that R2B Coin has misleadingly represented that the distributor of the tokens, Williams Corp. Ltd., is a "licensed global firm" and a "licensed securities dealer" based in Hong Kong and Dubai. The order noted that that the representations concerning registration were deceptive because R2B Coin was not disclosing either the name of the agency issuing a license to Williams Corp. or the nature of that license. Williams Corp. has never been registered to sell securities in Texas, according to the order.

DavorCoin. On February 3, 2018, Texas's fourth emergency action hit DavorCoin, a cryptocurrency lending program that represents that its "core team members are mostly bankers and engineers from EU countries." DavorCoin said that an investor lending the platform $30,000 worth of davorcoin may earn $15,390 in the first month of the program and $107,217 after 120 days. DavorCoin did not provide any details about how it would generate those profits and did not disclose the identity of its principals or its place of business, citing tax and regulation risks. Texas's enforcement release posits that DavorCoin stepped up marketing after BitConnect shut down. [*In the Matter of DavorCoin*, ENF-18-CDO-1757, February 2, 2018.]

Investors in Crypto. In the state's first action against an onshore entity, and the first by consent, the CEO of an Austin-area cryptocurrency investment firm agreed to stop offering securities for sale in Texas until the firm complied with state registration requirements. The February 15 order found that the CEO of Investors in Crypto LLC was offering unregistered securities in various cryptocurrency trading programs and investment portfolios and marketing them on social media and an online forum. [*In the Matter of Investors of Crypto LLC*, ENF-18-CDO-1759, February 15, 2018.]

LeadInvest. The Texas State Securities Board cracked down on another purported cryptocurrency offering on March 5, 2018. The regulator's emergency cease-and-desist order barring LeadInvest from securities dealings in Texas alleged that the firm fraudulently solicited investors to participate in a "green energy Bitcoin mining farm buildout in Ireland" and a "fiat currency lending program" at unrealistic returns. LeadInvest also misappropriated a photo taken in 2005 of former solicitors general and Supreme Court Justice Ruth Bader Ginsburg and represented those individuals as constituting its "CodeOfEthics [sic] Association." [*In the Matter of LeadInvest*, ENF-18-CDO-1760, Feb 26, 2018.]

Financial Freedom Club. On April 5, 2018, Commissioner Iles entered an emergency cease-and-desist order against a convicted felon who offered investments in an unregistered cryptocurrency trading program that purportedly delivered returns of 8 percent per week. The order alleged that the individual, who controlled Orlando-based Financial Freedom Club Inc., concealed criminal fraud convictions from investors. According to the allegations, the individual told potential investors that he would refer to profit payments as a "commission" to avoid securities laws. The scheme also involved New York-based 911MoneyStore Inc. Investors were told that they would receive an invoice for a gold watch that they would never receive so that, should the investment "go bad," they could request a chargeback from their credit or debit card issuer.

Massachusetts

Texas is not the lone star of cryptocurrency enforcement; as noted above, North Carolina has also pursued some of the same virtual currency firms, and Massachusetts has taken action to root out fraudulent and unregistered offerings. Secretary of the Commonwealth William F. Galvin, who oversees the Massachusetts Securities Division, issued a warning about "Bitcoin mania" on December 13, 2017. "Going back to the 1600s with tulip mania to the present Bitcoin craze, chasing the next best thing will, more often than not, end in disaster for the average investor," Galvin said. "Bitcoin is just the latest in a history of speculative bubbles that most often burst, leaving the average investors with a worthless product." The warning came just three days after the Chicago Board Options Exchange (CBOE) began trading Bitcoin futures.

On January 17, 2018, the Enforcement Section of the Massachusetts Securities Division filed a complaint charging a Massachusetts resident with running an unregistered initial coin offering in tokens of a Cayman Islands company known only as "Caviar." While the respondents represented that Caviar tokens are not available for sale to U.S. citizens, the Caviar website's screening procedures were inadequate to prevent the sale of tokens to U.S. residents, and at least two such sales occurred. [*In the Matter of Caviar*, No. E-2017-0120, January 17, 2018.]

On March 27, 2018, the Massachusetts Securities Division censured five companies and ordered them, by consent, to permanently desist from selling unregistered or non-exempt securities in the state:

¶730

1. 18Moons, Inc., a children's programming company, planned to offer up to 100 million in planet kid coins to potential purchasers in late 2017 but ceased operations upon receiving a Division subpoena on January 25, 2018; [*In the Matter of 18Moons, Inc.*, No. E-2018-0010, March 27, 2018.]

2. Across Platforms, Inc., d/b/a ClickableTV, planned to initially offer up to $100 million ClickableTV tokens, with a hard cap of $27.5 million, on March 1, 2018, but stopped the offering upon receiving a Division subpoena on February 7, 2018; [*In the Matter of Across Platforms, Inc. d/b/a ClickableTV*, No. E-2018-0016, March 27, 2018.]

3. Mattervest, Inc., used Twitter to provide potential customers with links to a weekly newsletter listing the latest investment pool deals but ceased operations when it received an inquiry letter from the Division on January 31, 2018; [*In the Matter of Mattervest, Inc.*, No. E-2018-0011, March 27, 2018.]

4. Pink Ribbon ICO, a publicly traded company on the blockchain that supports women and families facing financial burdens from cancer, stated on its Facebook page an intent to trade $5 million coins on the open market, but took down the page after receiving a Division inquiry letter on February 2, 2018; [*In the Matter of Pink Ribbon ICO*, No. E-2018-0029, March 27, 2018.]

and

5. Sparkco Inc., d/b/a Librium ICO, planned to expand its existing freelance platform operations by pre-selling its services through an initial cryptographic token offering on December 8, 2017. The company, however, postponed the offering indefinitely upon receiving a Division subpoena on February 5, 2018. [*In the Matter of Sparkco, Inc. d/b/a Librium*, No. E-2018-0017, March 27, 2018.]

The enforcement actions resulted from a sweep of unregistered cryptocurrency transactions beginning in mid-December 2017. The Division determined that the unregistered, non-exempt coin offerings fell within the definitions of "security" and "investment contract" of the Massachusetts Securities Act and rules.

Chapter Eight—Conclusion

¶ 800   The Current State of Play
¶ 810   Future Directions

¶ 800 The Current State of Play

"Blockchain is here to stay," according to Jay Baris, a partner at Shearman & Sterling. The challenge is, however, "How do you apply legal standards developed 80 years ago, in the early days of television, to distributed ledger technology, which was beyond imagination back then?"

Blockchain's ability to record information with a high level of security makes it useful for many assets and transactions. For example, U.S. and non-U.S. jurisdictions have investigated the use of blockchain to record real property chains of ownership, and smart contracts have the potential to provide both reliability and simplicity for many transactions. In April 2018, a coffee roaster announced plans to allow customers to scan a QR symbol and gain access to all of the information on their coffee, from farm to bag, using blockchain. One can imagine myriad similar uses, such as tracking the ownership of a motor vehicle, recording the supply chain of manufactured goods, or displaying the provenance of a bottle of single barrel bourbon.

Virtual currency, however, is burdened by its perceived association with nefarious actors and their illicit activities. There also is the ongoing concern that the value of any virtual currency is based on the "greater fool theory." Companies raising funds through initial coin offerings, for example, face the challenge of showing that their offered tokens have a valuable function beyond moving from digital wallet to digital wallet at progressively higher prices. (At the May 2018 Berkshire Hathaway shareholders' meeting, Warren Buffet referred to Bitcoin as "probably rat poison squared," according to CNBC.)

Virtual currency's continued survival may, in the end, be based on whether it offers enough value to society for national governments to permit its continued existence in the face of its potential for harm. After all, it is questionable whether governments will permit a medium of exchange to flourish if its only perceived use is to pay for illegal transactions and launder money.

As an example, in 2016 the government of India withdrew its 500 and 1,000 rupee notes from circulation in an effort to stop the use of large-denomination currency for evading taxes and completing illicit transactions. After taking such a step, would the government look favorably on the existence of virtual currency that can replace the withdrawn real currency and possibly nullify the effort? In fact, in 2018 the Reserve Bank of India did ban the financial institutions it regulates from providing services to anyone who deals in or exchanges virtual currency.

The People's Republic of China's central bank also has moved to block virtual currency trading. The central bank of Denmark has not gone that far, but its head, Lars Rohde, has described Bitcoin as "deadly" and told investors "don't come crying to us" if they are defrauded. Yet both institutions see great potential in blockchain.

However, the needed benefits might well exist. In fact, according to Judith E. Rinearson, a partner at K&L Gates LLP, most people don't understand the benefits that virtual currencies can offer. For example, the ability to "tokenize" a virtual currency can allow faster and cheaper transfers of funds between persons who are using different fiat currencies. Virtual currencies can facilitate moving funds to persons who are subject to repressive governments, she says, and they can provide "a guaranteed source of funds when Fiat currencies are not available."

Rinearson also notes that "One interesting [thing] about cryptocurrencies is that they are not fully anonymous, and that the transactions can often be tracked and monitored." This feature could alleviate some concerns over illicit activities.

U.S. regulators seem to be more open-minded than those of some other nations. While a number of U.S. regulators have acted against the use, or abuse, of virtual currencies in ways that threaten to aid illegal activities or defraud investors, there so far has been no significant push in the United States to ban legitimate virtual currency trading activities. Of course, that is not the same as saying there are no concerns.

So, how might these concerns be addressed?

¶ 810 Future Directions

One of the challenges of writing a book on blockchain technology and virtual currency in 2018 is the rapidly shifting landscape. Numerous regulatory agencies are feeling their way across that shifting landscape in an effort to discern, as Chapter 2 is titled, "Who Regulates What?" With that uncertainty, including the potential for turf battles over issues such as whether any given virtual currency is a security, a commodity, or neither, forecasting developments in regulation becomes a daunting task.

One thing seems to be reasonably clear, however—the U.S. government has shown little to no inclination to interfere with the development of blockchain technology. Instead, the focus has been on how one aspect of blockchain—virtual currency—is used, or misused, and how its use should be regulated.

Blockchain technology. Blockchain-related undertakings will continue to attract attention and investment across a wide range of industry sectors and businesses. While smaller scale and retail investors have been dominant in Bitcoin and virtual currency markets thus far, this might be changing. Future growth may well be fueled by increased involvement by large financial institutions and institutional investors. In the virtual currency space, large exchanges like the Intercontinental Exchange, Nasdaq, and a New York Stock Exchange affiliate, apparently don't want to miss out. They have all recently announced their intentions to establish virtual currency exchanges. Other trusted names, like Goldman Sachs, Barclays, Nomura, and JP Morgan also have raised their stakes in various virtual currency ventures. Moreover, players in the blockchain space are becoming increasingly knowledgeable and sophisticated.

Bitcoin's arrangement around proof-of-work has led to criticisms about energy consumption and a search for alternatives for transaction verification. New altcoins, tokens, and other enterprises using blockchain technology are likely to follow Ethereum's lead of transitioning to proof-of-stake methods. As distributed ledger technology continues to evolve, regulators will need to settle on working definitions of "virtual currency" and other key terms.

The future may bring additional clarity about the precise meaning of the term "smart contract." Today, multiple definitions of "smart contract" are commonplace, and it remains too easy to conflate legal and computer programming concepts. State lawmakers have made early attempts to achieve greater clarity, but the legal and blockchain industries still must determine the extent to which traditional legal concepts realistically can be automated.

As for tokens, it will be important to watch how regulators ultimately treat Ethereum and Ripple. A decision, for example, that Ethereum and/or Ripple are securities could have a significant impact on the blockchain marketplace.

Securities and Exchange Commission. As the Securities and Exchange Commission begins to apply its existing regulations to emerging distributed ledger and blockchain technologies, the Commission and its staff may eventually cross several regulatory thresholds. First, SEC Chairman Jay Clayton has indicated that the agency will continue to crack down on fraudulent initial coin offerings, for which the chairman places much blame on securities law gatekeepers, such as attorneys. It remains to be seen whether the SEC will focus its ICO enforcement efforts in a significant way on these gatekeepers.

For now, those contemplating ICOs, and those who would provide platforms that support ICOs, should carefully evaluate whether planned offerings involve a security. The answer to this single question is often the entry point to the entirety of federal securities law and is one of the touchstones for the SEC's use of its enforcement powers. Prospective investors in ICOs and other securities products with virtual currency components should continue to ask probing questions of those who promote these investments with an eye to the many warnings contained in the SEC's numerous Investor Alerts.

Second, the SEC may decide whether innovative fund products, such as virtual currency-themed commodity trusts and exchange traded funds, will be allowed to offer investors a path to investing in virtual currencies. The SEC has questioned whether underlying virtual currency markets are susceptible to manipulation and whether these markets are sufficiently transparent. These concerns motivated the SEC's previous decisions to deny exchanges' applications to list and trade virtual currency-themed products.

Similar concerns also prompted the SEC to issue guidance on online platforms and ETFs. The SEC has instituted proceedings on whether to approve or disapprove several exchange proposals in this area. Its decisions may help to clarify further the extent to which the agency will allow funds to offer products that promise to open virtual currency markets to a wide range of investors.

Commodity Futures Trading Commission. It may be unlikely that the CFTC will play a dominant role in the future of virtual currency regulation given stringent budgetary restraints and other demands imposed on the agency. Still, the CFTC is well positioned to make important future contributions based its ongoing endeavors in the virtual currency space, its continuous enforcement efforts over the spot Bitcoin and other virtual currency markets, and its regulatory authority over futures and derivatives for Bitcoin and other cryptocurrencies. Commission leadership, while acknowledging a resource-challenged environment, has demonstrated a willingness to partner with and compliment the efforts of other regulators and law enforcement agencies in the cryptocurrency space. As noted earlier, the CFTC's budget was cut by $1 million for FY 2018, notwithstanding several years of flat funding and its request for a $31.5 million funding increase.

The CFTC continues to cooperate with state regulators. The CFTC and individual state securities commissions entered into a groundbreaking Memorandum of Understanding (MOU) in May 2018 at a meeting of NASAA (Northern American Securities Administrators Association). The MOU is designed to focus the parties' collective resources to better uphold the law, including with respect to virtual currencies fraud and enforcement. Chairman J. Christopher Giancarlo, stated, "This MOU will establish protocols and procedures, for the access, use, and confidentiality of information and treatment of non-public information in the course of law enforcement."

Among other things, the MOU creates a framework for cooperation that will result in leveraging of resources to support enforcement actions, enhancing the impact of enforcement efforts and their deterrent effect, preventing the duplication of efforts by multiple authorities, and encouraging the development of consistent and clear governmental responses to violations of the Commodity Exchange Act. He added, "We applaud

NASAA on a new program being announced today. It complements the CFTC's on-going virtual currency investigations with NASAA members."

In addition, CFTC Commissioner Brian Quintenz noted that the CFTC has continued to work closely with the SEC in bringing civil enforcement actions against fraud, market manipulation, and disruptive trading involving virtual currency in remarks made before the FIA Law and Compliance conference in May 2018. Quintenz, along with fellow Commissioner Rostin Behnam, both pointed to efforts between CFTC and SEC to harmonize the agencies' rules, as well as to further coordinate and cooperate in connection with future enforcement undertakings. Virtual currency markets will likely see the results of any such CFTC-SEC joint efforts down the line.

Internationally, the CFTC and the United Kingdom's Financial Conduct Authority (FCA) entered into a cooperation arrangement on financial technology innovation in February 2018. The arrangement focuses on information-sharing with regard to financial technology (fintech) market trends and developments. This includes blockchain and digital ledger technologies. The arrangement commits the regulators to collaborate and support innovative firms through each other's fintech initiatives – LabCFTC for the CFTC and FCA Innovate for the FCA.

Despite these cooperative arrangements, the CFTC's ability to discharge its obligations with respect to virtual currency regulation and oversight, to say nothing of it playing a leading role in the virtual currency realm, remain in some doubt. In remarks before an industry association, CFTC Commissioner Brian Quintenz warned that if the CFTC does not get a significant funding increase for FY 2019, the agency may be forced to cut staff and may have trouble meeting its core market surveillance and enforcement missions. The commissioner candidly observed, "Staff's ability to conduct regular risk, compliance, and cybersecurity examinations will be curtailed; enforcement efforts to police fraud and manipulation—particularly in the cryptocurrency spot markets—will be strained."

Banking regulators. What lies ahead for the initiatives started by the Office of the Comptroller of the Currency, Federal Reserve Board, and Consumer Financial Protection Bureau is a big question mark.

Although the OCC under the leadership of Thomas Curry was moving ahead with the steps needed to charter fintech companies as special purpose national banks, the OCC under the current leadership of Joseph Otting seems tepid. Also, even though the OCC has beaten back legal challenges to its SPNB chartering initiative by the New York Department of Financial Services and the Conference of State Bank Supervisors as premature, those legal challenges could return if and when the OCC issues an SPNB charter to a fintech company.

The Fed's research on the use distributed ledger technology for the nation's payment systems is still in its nascent stages with no timeline for when, or even if, DLT would be implemented.

Finally, the CFPB's coverage of digital wallets under its Prepaid Rule could be in jeopardy given the current climate in Washington. The Republican-held Congress has been actively using the Congressional Review Act to eliminate a number of Obama-era regulations, and the Prepaid Rule could fall to such an initiative or be modified by a CFPB rulemaking.

Financial Crimes Enforcement Network. The Financial Crimes Enforcement Network seems to be satisfied with the framework it has created around the regulation of money services businesses and money transmitters. FIN-2013-G001 remains the best expression of what the bureau thinks and what it wants from those involved in the

¶810

virtual currency economy. [FIN-2013-GOO1, March 18, 2013, at https://www.fincen.gov/statutes_regs/guidance/pdf/FIN-2013-G001.pdf.]

Put simply, those who use virtual currency to buy goods or services for their own use, to pay their own bills, or to make investments for their own accounts, are virtual currency users who are not subject to FinCEN's regulations. Those who exchange virtual currency for real currency, funds, or other virtual currency, or who engage in the business of issuing virtual currency and have the authority to redeem that virtual currency, are exchangers or administrators, respectively. Such companies must register with FinCEN as money services businesses and comply with the full panoply of regulatory requirements.

Principally, FinCEN focusses on what you do with the virtual currency you hold, not on how you came to hold it. There is no indication that point of view will change in the foreseeable future.

However, there might be some clouds on the horizon for the bureau's beneficial ownership identification and verification requirements. Some of the objections raised by financial institutions, especially those related to who is considered to be a beneficial owner and whether the rule as it stands effectively carries out the Bank Secrecy Act, may result in some adjustments.

Rinearson suggests that FinCEN should take a look at methods of identification beyond just Social Security Numbers and dates of birth. She also would like the bureau to monitor how states enforce federal anti-money laundering laws, saying "In my view, some of the states are way off in their understanding of federal AML laws."

State regulator activities. In the realm of state licensure, there are three main frameworks: the controversial BitLicense regime adopted in New York, the varied money transmitter laws existing in nearly all states, and a uniform law tailored specifically toward virtual currencies.

Rinearson says that the industry welcomes advances that would ease compliance burdens while reducing fraud risks. The fact that the uniform law has been introduced in three states demonstrates interest, and she believes it eventually will be enacted in at least some states. Many industry participants would like to see reciprocity agreements among states so that they only need to obtain a single license, she adds. "Having a single federal license that preempts state licensing would be another option favored by many fintechs."

On BitLicense, Rinearson observes that although the framework does impose some burdens, "the companies that took the time and resources to get their BitLicense are among the most respected and successful in the crypto space." She says that she is hearing from more companies interested in applying for the license and while the state may work on making the BitLicense more user-friendly, she doubts the regime will be rescinded entirely.

Corporate governance. Potential uses of DLT and blockchain go beyond cryptocurrency trading and transactions; they could change the way companies engage in corporate governance and the way government agencies conduct administrative activities. Corporations are beginning to see new and innovative ways to harness the benefits of blockchain technology, and states are searching for ways to facilitate blockchain business as well as to detect and prevent fraud.

Companies could benefit from increased efficiencies in corporate governance activities, such as shareholder voting using blockchain technology and/or DLT, and the technology could provide a means to make and keep accurate shareholder records and communicate with shareholder bases more effectively. Industry participants are considering how DLT could be used to record and track trade execution and settlement, asset ownership, and trading value, as well as to maintain corporate records. Many also are evaluating the potential use of the technology to increase proxy voting accuracy and accounting transparency.

Several state governments are considering how to use blockchain technology and DLT to keep more accurate records and create efficiencies in interactions with the public. Pending legislation in state legislatures could change the way state agencies evaluate how technology could be used to reduce fraud and protect systems from cyberattacks, as well as to protect voter records and ensure accurate election results. It also is likely states will move forward with further efforts concerning the potential implementation of blockchain technology in state recordkeeping, information storage, and service delivery. However, system upgrades and financial constraints will remain important considerations in potential implementation.

Even as companies and state governments are considering the potential of blockchain technology and DLT to create and maintain accurate records more efficiently, state securities regulators remain concerned about fraud and investor protection, particularly with regard to virtual currencies.

Internal Revenue Service. Where there is income, there is the Internal Revenue Service. The IRS concluded in Notice 2014-21 that the receipt of Bitcoins and other cryptocurrencies is taxable. The issuance of a subpoena in *U.S. v. Coinbase, Inc.*, Case No. 17-cv-01431 (N.D. Cal., 2017), indicates that the IRS likely is actively investigating whether taxpayers are underreporting income related to cryptocurrency activities.

It should be noted that the enforcement order in *Coinbase* demonstrates that the IRS can issue summonses to other virtual currency exchanges. It also means that miners, investors, and others who use and exchange virtual currencies should be aware that the IRS can obtain information that could be used to enforce compliance of tax reporting and payments concerning virtual currency.

Due to limited guidance issued by the IRS, there are significant federal tax questions regarding virtual currencies. Until further guidance is available, taxpayers should consider keeping detailed and accurate records of their transactions and should likely take a conservative approach in gray areas.

Appendix A—Federal Laws

¶1000 Electronic Signatures in Global and National Commerce Act

Title 15, United States Code, Chapter 96

General rule of validity

In general

Sec. 7001 (a) [Electronic Signatures in Global and National Commerce Act, Sec. 101] Notwithstanding any statute, regulation, or other rule of law (other than this title [I] and title II), with respect to any transaction in or affecting interstate or foreign commerce—

(1) a signature, contract, or other record relating to such transaction may not be denied legal effect, validity, or enforceability solely because it is in electronic form; and

(2) a contract relating to such transaction may not be denied legal effect, validity, or enforceability solely because an electronic signature or electronic record was used in its formation.

Preservation of rights and obligations

(b) This title [I] does not—

(1) limit, alter, or otherwise affect any requirement imposed by a statute, regulation, or rule of law relating to the rights and obligations of persons under such statute, regulation, or rule of law other than a requirement that contracts or other records be written, signed, or in nonelectronic form; or

(2) require any person to agree to use or accept electronic records or electronic signatures, other than a governmental agency with respect to a record other than a contract to which it is a party.

Consumer disclosures

(c) (1) CONSENT TO ELECTRONIC RECORDS. Notwithstanding subsection (a), if a statute, regulation, or other rule of law requires that information relating to a transaction or transactions in or affecting interstate or foreign commerce be provided or made available to a consumer in writing, the use of an electronic record to provide or make available (whichever is required) such information satisfies the requirement that such information be in writing if—

(A) the consumer has affirmatively consented to such use and has not withdrawn such consent;

(B) the consumer, prior to consenting, is provided with a clear and conspicuous statement—

(i) informing the consumer of (I) any right or option of the consumer to have the record provided or made available on paper or in nonelectronic form, and (II) the right of the consumer to withdraw the consent to have the record provided or made available in an electronic form and of any conditions, consequences (which may include termination of the parties' relationship), or fees in the event of such withdrawal;

(ii) informing the consumer of whether the consent applies (I) only to the particular transaction which gave rise to the obligation to provide the record, or (II) to identified categories of records that may be provided or made available during the course of the parties' relationship;

(iii) describing the procedures the consumer must use to withdraw consent as provided in clause (i) and to update information needed to contact the consumer electronically; and

(iv) informing the consumer (I) how, after the consent, the consumer may, upon request, obtain a paper copy of an electronic record, and (II) whether any fee will be charged for such copy;

(C) the consumer—

(i) prior to consenting, is provided with a statement of the hardware and software requirements for access to and retention of the electronic records; and

(ii) consents electronically, or confirms his or her consent electronically, in a manner that reasonably demonstrates that the consumer can access information in the electronic form that will be used to provide the information that is the subject of the consent; and

(D) after the consent of a consumer in accordance with subparagraph (A), if a change in the hardware or software requirements needed to access or retain electronic records creates a material risk that the consumer will not be able to access or retain a subsequent electronic record that was the subject of the consent, the person providing the electronic record—

(i) provides the consumer with a statement of (I) the revised hardware and software requirements for access to and retention of the electronic records, and (II) the right to withdraw consent without the imposition of any fees for such withdrawal and without the imposition of any condition or consequence that was not disclosed under subparagraph (B)(i); and

(ii) again complies with subparagraph (C).

(2) OTHER RIGHTS.—

(A) PRESERVATION OF CONSUMER PROTECTIONS. Nothing in this title [I] affects the content or timing of any disclosure or other record required to be provided or made available to any consumer under any statute, regulation, or other rule of law.

(B) VERIFICATION OR ACKNOWLEDGMENT. If a law that was enacted prior to this Act expressly requires a record to be provided or made available by a specified method that requires verification or acknowledgment of receipt, the record may be provided or made available electronically only if the method used provides verification or acknowledgment of receipt (whichever is required).

(3) EFFECT OF FAILURE TO OBTAIN ELECTRONIC CONSENT OR CONFIRMATION OF CONSENT. The legal effectiveness, validity, or enforceability of any contract executed by a consumer shall not be denied solely because of the failure to obtain electronic consent or confirmation of consent by that consumer in accordance with paragraph (1)(C)(ii).

(4) PROSPECTIVE EFFECT. Withdrawal of consent by a consumer shall not affect the legal effectiveness, validity, or enforceability of electronic records provided or made available to that consumer in accordance with paragraph (1) prior to implementation of the consumer's withdrawal of consent. A consumer's withdrawal of consent shall be effective within a reasonable period of time after receipt of the withdrawal by the provider of the record. Failure to comply with paragraph (1)(D) may, at the election of the consumer, be treated as a withdrawal of consent for purposes of this paragraph.

(5) PRIOR CONSENT. This subsection does not apply to any records that are provided or made available to a consumer who has consented prior to the effective date of this title [I] to receive such records in electronic form as permitted by any statute, regulation, or other rule of law.

(6) ORAL COMMUNICATIONS. An oral communication or a recording of an oral communication shall not qualify as an electronic record for purposes of this subsection except as otherwise provided under applicable law.

Retention of contracts and records

(d)(1) ACCURACY AND ACCESSIBILITY. If a statute, regulation, or other rule of law requires that a contract or other record relating to a transaction in or affecting interstate or foreign commerce be retained, that requirement is met by retaining an electronic record of the information in the contract or other record that—

(A) accurately reflects the information set forth in the contract or other record; and

(B) remains accessible to all persons who are entitled to access by statute, regulation, or rule of law, for the period required by such statute, regulation, or rule of law, in a form that is capable of being accurately reproduced for later reference, whether by transmission, printing, or otherwise.

(2) EXCEPTION. A requirement to retain a contract or other record in accordance with paragraph (1) does not apply to any information whose sole purpose is to enable the contract or other record to be sent, communicated, or received.

(3) ORIGINALS. If a statute, regulation, or other rule of law requires a contract or other record relating to a transaction in or affecting interstate or foreign commerce to be provided, available, or retained in its original form, or provides consequences if the contract or other record is not provided, available, or retained in its original form, that statute, regulation, or rule of law is satisfied by an electronic record that complies with paragraph (1).

(4) CHECKS. If a statute, regulation, or other rule of law requires the retention of a check, that requirement is satisfied by retention of an electronic record of the information on the front and back of the check in accordance with paragraph (1).

¶1000   §7001

Accuracy and ability to retain contracts and other records

(e) Notwithstanding subsection (a), if a statute, regulation, or other rule of law requires that a contract or other record relating to a transaction in or affecting interstate or foreign commerce be in writing, the legal effect, validity, or enforceability of an electronic record of such contract or other record may be denied if such electronic record is not in a form that is capable of being retained and accurately reproduced for later reference by all parties or persons who are entitled to retain the contract or other record.

Proximity

(f) Nothing in this title affects the proximity required by any statute, regulation, or other rule of law with respect to any warning, notice, disclosure, or other record required to be posted, displayed, or publicly affixed.

Notarization and acknowledgment

(g) If a statute, regulation, or other rule of law requires a signature or record relating to a transaction in or affecting interstate or foreign commerce to be notarized, acknowledged, verified, or made under oath, that requirement is satisfied if the electronic signature of the person authorized to perform those acts, together with all other information required to be included by other applicable statute, regulation, or rule of law, is attached to or logically associated with the signature or record.

Electronic agents

(h) A contract or other record relating to a transaction in or affecting interstate or foreign commerce may not be denied legal effect, validity, or enforceability solely because its formation, creation, or delivery involved the action of one or more electronic agents so long as the action of any such electronic agent is legally attributable to the person to be bound.

Insurance

(i) It is the specific intent of the Congress that this title [I]and title II apply to the business of insurance.

Insurance agents and brokers

(j) An insurance agent or broker acting under the direction of a party that enters into a contract by means of an electronic record or electronic signature may not be held liable for any deficiency in the electronic procedures agreed to by the parties under that contract if—

(1) the agent or broker has not engaged in negligent, reckless, or intentional tortious conduct;

(2) the agent or broker was not involved in the development or establishment of such electronic procedures; and

(3) the agent or broker did not deviate from such procedures.

Exemption to preemption

In general

Sec. 7002(a) [Electronic Signatures in Global and National Commerce Act, Sec. 102] State statute, regulation, or other rule of law may modify, limit, or supersede the provisions of section 101 [15 USC 7001] with respect to State law only if such statute, regulation, or rule of law—

(1) constitutes an enactment or adoption of the Uniform Electronic Transactions Act as approved and recommended for enactment in all the States by the National Conference of Commissioners on Uniform State Laws in 1999, except that any exception to the scope of such Act enacted by a State under section 3(b)(4) of such Act shall be preempted to the extent such exception is inconsistent with this title [I] or title II, or would not be permitted under paragraph (2)(A)(ii) of this subsection; or

(2)(A) specifies the alternative procedures or requirements for the use or acceptance (or both) of electronic records or electronic signatures to establish the legal effect, validity, or enforceability of contracts or other records, if—

(i) such alternative procedures or requirements are consistent with this title [I] and title II; and

(ii) such alternative procedures or requirements do not require, or accord greater legal status or effect to, the implementation or application of a specific technology or technical specification for performing the functions of creating, storing, generating, receiving, communicating, or authenticating electronic records or electronic signatures; and

(B) if enacted or adopted after the date of the enactment of this Act, makes specific reference to this Act.

Exceptions for actions by states as market participants

(b) Subsection (a)(2)(A)(ii) shall not apply to the statutes, regulations, or other rules of law governing procurement by any State, or any agency or instrumentality thereof.

Prevention of circumvention

(c) Subsection (a) does not permit a State to circumvent this title [I] or title II through the imposition of nonelectronic delivery methods under section 8(b)(2) of the Uniform Electronic Transactions Act.

Specific exceptions

Excepted requirements

Sec. 7003(a) [Electronic Signatures in Global and National Commerce Act, Sec. 103] The provisions of section 101 [15 USC 7001] shall not apply to a contract or other record to the extent it is governed by—

(1) a statute, regulation, or other rule of law governing the creation and execution of wills, codicils, or testamentary trusts;

(2) a State statute, regulation, or other rule of law governing adoption, divorce, or other matters of family law; or

(3) the Uniform Commercial Code, as in effect in any State, other than sections 1-107 and 1-206 and Articles 2 and 2A.

Additional exceptions

(b) The provisions of section 101 [15 USC 7001] shall not apply to—

(1) court orders or notices, or official court documents (including briefs, pleadings, and other writings) required to be executed in connection with court proceedings;

(2) any notice of—

(A) the cancellation or termination of utility services (including water, heat, and power);

(B) default, acceleration, repossession, foreclosure, or eviction, or the right to cure, under a credit agreement secured by, or a rental agreement for, a primary residence of an individual;

(C) the cancellation or termination of health insurance or benefits or life insurance benefits (excluding annuities); or

(D) recall of a product, or material failure of a product, that risks endangering health or safety; or

(3) any document required to accompany any transportation or handling of hazardous materials, pesticides, or other toxic or dangerous materials.

Review of exceptions

(c)(1) EVALUATION REQUIRED. The Secretary of Commerce, acting through the Assistant Secretary for Communications and Information, shall review the operation of the exceptions in subsections (a) and (b) to evaluate, over a period of 3 years, whether such exceptions continue to be necessary for the protection of consumers. Within 3 years after the date of enactment of this Act [June 30, 2003], the Assistant Secretary shall submit a report to the Congress on the results of such evaluation.

(2) DETERMINATIONS. If a Federal regulatory agency, with respect to matter within its jurisdiction, determines after notice and an opportunity for public comment, and publishes a finding, that one or more such exceptions are no longer necessary for the protection of consumers and eliminating such exceptions will not increase the material risk of harm to consumers, such agency may extend the application of section 101 [15 USC 7001] to the exceptions identified in such finding.

Applicability to federal and state governments

Filing and access requirements

Sec. 7004(a) [Electronic Signatures in Global and National Commerce Act, Sec. 104] Subject to subsection (c)(2), nothing in this title [I]limits or supersedes any requirement by a Federal regulatory agency, self-regulatory organization, or State regulatory agency that records be filed with such agency or organization in accordance with specified standards or formats.

Preservation of existing rulemaking authority

(b)(1) USE OF AUTHORITY TO INTERPRET. Subject to paragraph (2) and subsection (c), a Federal regulatory agency or State regulatory agency that is responsible for rulemaking under any other statute may interpret section 101 [15 USC 7001] with respect to such statute through—

(A) the issuance of regulations pursuant to a statute; or

(B) to the extent such agency is authorized by statute to issue orders or guidance, the issuance of orders or guidance of general applicability that are publicly available and published (in the Federal Register in the case of an order or guidance issued by a Federal regulatory agency).

This paragraph does not grant any Federal regulatory agency or State regulatory agency authority to issue regulations, orders, or guidance pursuant to any statute that does not authorize such issuance.

(2) LIMITATIONS ON INTERPRETATION AUTHORITY. Notwithstanding paragraph (1), a Federal regulatory agency shall not adopt any regulation, order, or guidance described in paragraph (1), and a State regulatory agency is preempted by section 101 [15 USC 7001] from adopting any regulation, order, or guidance described in paragraph (1), unless—

(A) such regulation, order, or guidance is consistent with section 101 [15 USC 7001];

(B) such regulation, order, or guidance does not add to the requirements of such section; and

(C) such agency finds, in connection with the issuance of such regulation, order, or guidance, that—

(i) there is a substantial justification for the regulation, order, or guidance;

(ii) the methods selected to carry out that purpose—

(I) are substantially equivalent to the requirements imposed on records that are not electronic records; and

(II) will not impose unreasonable costs on the acceptance and use of electronic records; and

(iii) the methods selected to carry out that purpose do not require, or accord greater legal status or effect to, the implementation or application of a specific technology or technical specification for performing the functions of creating, storing, generating, receiving, communicating, or authenticating electronic records or electronic signatures.

(3) PERFORMANCE STANDARDS.—

(A) ACCURACY, RECORD INTEGRITY, ACCESSIBILITY. Notwithstanding paragraph (2)(C)(iii), a Federal regulatory agency or State regulatory agency may interpret section 101(d) [15 USC 7001(d)] to specify performance standards to assure accuracy, record integrity, and accessibility of records that are required to be retained. Such performance standards may be specified in a manner that imposes a requirement in violation of paragraph (2)(C)(iii) if the requirement (i) serves an important governmental objective; and (ii) is substantially related to the achievement of that objective. Nothing in this paragraph shall be construed to grant any Federal regulatory agency or State regulatory agency authority to require use of a particular type of software or hardware in order to comply with section 101(d) [15 USC 7001(d)].

(B) PAPER OR PRINTED FORM. Notwithstanding subsection (c)(1), a Federal regulatory agency or State regulatory agency may interpret section 101(d) [15 USC 7001(d)]to require retention of a record in a tangible printed or paper form if—

(i) there is a compelling governmental interest relating to law enforcement or national security for imposing such requirement; and

(ii) imposing such requirement is essential to attaining such interest.

(4) EXCEPTIONS FOR ACTIONS BY GOVERNMENT AS MARKET PARTICIPANT. Paragraph (2)(C)(iii) shall not apply to the statutes, regulations, or other rules of law governing procurement by the Federal or any State government, or any agency or instrumentality thereof.

Additional limitations

(c)(1) REIMPOSING PAPER PROHIBITED. Nothing in subsection (b) (other than paragraph (3)(B) thereof) shall be construed to grant any Federal regulatory agency or State regulatory agency authority to impose or reimpose any requirement that a record be in a tangible printed or paper form.

(2) CONTINUING OBLIGATION UNDER GOVERNMENT PAPERWORK ELIMINATION ACT. Nothing in subsection (a) or (b) relieves any Federal regulatory agency of its obligations under the Government Paperwork Elimination Act (title XVII of Public Law 105-277).

Authority to exempt from consent provision

(d)(1) IN GENERAL. A Federal regulatory agency may, with respect to matter within its jurisdiction, by regulation or order issued after notice and an opportunity for public comment, exempt without condition a specified category or type of record from the requirements relating to consent in section 101(c) [15 USC 7001(c)] if such exemption is necessary to eliminate a substantial burden on electronic commerce and will not increase the material risk of harm to consumers.

(2) PROSPECTUSES. Within 30 days after the date of enactment of this Act, the Securities and Exchange Commission shall issue a regulation or order pursuant to paragraph (1) exempting from section 101(c) [15 USC 7001(c)] any records that are required to be provided in order to allow advertising, sales literature, or other information concerning a security issued by an investment company that is registered under the Investment Company Act of 1940, or concerning the issuer thereof, to be excluded from the definition of a prospectus under section 2(a)(10)(A) of the Securities Act of 1933 [15 USC 77b(a)(10(A)].

Electronic letters of agency

(e) The Federal Communications Commission shall not hold any contract for telecommunications service or letter of agency for a preferred carrier change, that otherwise complies with the Commission's rules, to be legally ineffective, invalid, or unenforceable solely because an electronic record or electronic signature was used in its formation or authorization.

Studies

Delivery

Sec. 7005(a) [Electronic Signatures in Global and National Commerce Act, Sec. 105] Within 12 months after the date of the enactment of this Act [June 30, 2001], the Secretary of Commerce shall conduct an inquiry regarding the effectiveness of the delivery of electronic records to consumers using electronic mail as compared with delivery of written records via the United States Postal Service and private express mail services. The Secretary shall submit a report to the Congress regarding the results of such inquiry by the conclusion of such 12-month period.

Study of electronic consent

(b) Within 12 months after the date of the enactment of this Act [June 30, 2001], the Secretary of Commerce and the Federal Trade Commission shall submit a report to the Congress evaluating any benefits provided to consumers by the procedure required by section 101(c)(1)(C)(ii) [15 USC 7001(c)(1)(C)(ii)]; any burdens imposed on electronic commerce by that provision; whether the benefits outweigh the burdens; whether the absence of the procedure required by section 101(c)(1)(C)(ii) [15 USC 7001(c)(1)(C)(ii)] would increase the incidence of fraud directed against consumers; and suggesting any revisions to the provision deemed appropriate by the Secretary and the Commission. In conducting this evaluation, the Secretary and the Commission shall solicit comment from the general public, consumer representatives, and electronic commerce businesses.

Definitions

Sec. 7006 [Electronic Signatures in Global and National Commerce Act, Sec. 106] For purposes of this title [I]:

(1) CONSUMER. The term "consumer" means an individual who obtains, through a transaction, products or services which are used primarily for personal, family, or household purposes, and also means the legal representative of such an individual.

(2) ELECTRONIC. The term "electronic" means relating to technology having electrical, digital, magnetic, wireless, optical, electromagnetic, or similar capabilities.

(3) ELECTRONIC AGENT. The term "electronic agent" means a computer program or an electronic or other automated means used independently to initiate an action or respond to electronic records or performances in whole or in part without review or action by an individual at the time of the action or response.

(4) ELECTRONIC RECORD. The term "electronic record" means a contract or other record created, generated, sent, communicated, received, or stored by electronic means.

(5) ELECTRONIC SIGNATURE. The term "electronic signature" means an electronic sound, symbol, or process, attached to or logically associated with a contract or other record and executed or adopted by a person with the intent to sign the record.

(6) FEDERAL REGULATORY AGENCY. The term "Federal regulatory agency" means an agency, as that term is defined in section 552(f) of title 5, United States Code.

(7) INFORMATION. The term "information" means data, text, images, sounds, codes, computer programs, software, databases, or the like.

(8) PERSON. The term "person" means an individual, corporation, business trust, estate, trust, partnership, limited liability company, association, joint venture, governmental agency, public corporation, or any other legal or commercial entity.

(9) RECORD. The term "record" means information that is inscribed on a tangible medium or that is stored in an electronic or other medium and is retrievable in perceivable form.

(10) REQUIREMENT. The term "requirement" includes a prohibition.

(11) SELF-REGULATORY ORGANIZATION. The term "self-regulatory organization" means an organization or entity that is not a Federal regulatory agency or a State, but that is under the supervision of a Federal regulatory agency and is authorized under Federal law to adopt and administer rules applicable to its members that are enforced by such organization or entity, by a Federal regulatory agency, or by another self-regulatory organization.

(12) STATE. The term "State" includes the District of Columbia and the territories and possessions of the United States.

(13) TRANSACTION. The term "transaction" means an action or set of actions relating to the conduct of business, consumer, or commercial affairs between two or more persons, including any of the following types of conduct—

(A) the sale, lease, exchange, licensing, or other disposition of (i) personal property, including goods and intangibles, (ii) services, and (iii) any combination thereof; and

(B) the sale, lease, exchange, or other disposition of any interest in real property, or any combination thereof.

Transferable records

Definitions

Sec. 7021 (a) [Electronic Signatures in Global and National Commerce Act, Sec. 201] For purposes of this section:

(1) TRANSFERABLE RECORD. The term "transferable record" means an electronic record that—

(A) would be a note under Article 3 of the Uniform Commercial Code if the electronic record were in writing;

(B) the issuer of the electronic record expressly has agreed is a transferable record; and

(C) relates to a loan secured by real property.

A transferable record may be executed using an electronic signature.

(2) OTHER DEFINITIONS. The terms "electronic record", "electronic signature", and "person" have the same meanings provided in section 106 of this Act [15 USC 7006].

Control

(b) A person has control of a transferable record if a system employed for evidencing the transfer of interests in the transferable record reliably establishes that person as the person to which the transferable record was issued or transferred.

Conditions

(c) A system satisfies subsection (b), and a person is deemed to have control of a transferable record, if the transferable record is created, stored, and assigned in such a manner that—

(1) a single authoritative copy of the transferable record exists which is unique, identifiable, and, except as otherwise provided in paragraphs (4), (5), and (6), unalterable;

(2) the authoritative copy identifies the person asserting control as—

(A) the person to which the transferable record was issued; or

(B) if the authoritative copy indicates that the transferable record has been transferred, the person to which the transferable record was most recently transferred;

(3) the authoritative copy is communicated to and maintained by the person asserting control or its designated custodian;

(4) copies or revisions that add or change an identified assignee of the authoritative copy can be made only with the consent of the person asserting control;

(5) each copy of the authoritative copy and any copy of a copy is readily identifiable as a copy that is not the authoritative copy; and

(6) any revision of the authoritative copy is readily identifiable as authorized or unauthorized.

Status as holder

(d) Except as otherwise agreed, a person having control of a transferable record is the holder, as defined in section 1-201(20) of the Uniform Commercial Code, of the transferable record and has the same rights and defenses as a holder of an equivalent record or writing under the Uniform Commercial Code, including, if the applicable statutory requirements under section 3-302(a), 9-308, or revised section 9-330 of the Uniform Commercial Code are satisfied, the rights and defenses of a holder in due course or a purchaser, respectively. Delivery, possession, and endorsement are not required to obtain or exercise any of the rights under this subsection.

Obligor rights

(e) Except as otherwise agreed, an obligor under a transferable record has the same rights and defenses as an equivalent obligor under equivalent records or writings under the Uniform Commercial Code.

Proof of control

(f) If requested by a person against which enforcement is sought, the person seeking to enforce the transferable record shall provide reasonable proof that the person is in control of the transferable record. Proof may include access to the authoritative copy of the transferable record and related business records sufficient to review the terms of the transferable record and to establish the identity of the person having control of the transferable record.

UCC references

(g) For purposes of this subsection, all references to the Uniform Commercial Code are to the Uniform Commercial Code as in effect in the jurisdiction the law of which governs the transferable record.

Principles governing the use of electronic signatures in international transactions

Promotion of electronic signatures

Sec. 7031 (a) [Electronic Signatures in Global and National Commerce Act, Sec. 301]

(1) REQUIRED ACTIONS. The Secretary of Commerce shall promote the acceptance and use, on an international basis, of electronic signatures in accordance with the principles specified in paragraph (2) and in a manner consistent with section 101 [15 USC 7001]. The Secretary of Commerce shall take all actions necessary in a manner consistent with such principles to eliminate or reduce, to the maximum extent possible, the impediments to commerce in electronic signatures, for the purpose of facilitating the development of interstate and foreign commerce.

(2) PRINCIPLES. The principles specified in this paragraph are the following:

(A) Remove paper-based obstacles to electronic transactions by adopting relevant principles from the Model Law on Electronic Commerce adopted in 1996 by the United Nations Commission on International Trade Law.

¶1000   §7031

(B) Permit parties to a transaction to determine the appropriate authentication technologies and implementation models for their transactions, with assurance that those technologies and implementation models will be recognized and enforced.

(C) Permit parties to a transaction to have the opportunity to prove in court or other proceedings that their authentication approaches and their transactions are valid.

(D) Take a nondiscriminatory approach to electronic signatures and authentication methods from other jurisdictions.

Consultation

(b) In conducting the activities required by this section, the Secretary shall consult with users and providers of electronic signature products and services and other interested persons.

Definitions

(c) As used in this section, the terms "electronic record" and "electronic signature" have the same meanings provided in section 106 of this Act [15 USC 7006].

Appendix B—SEC Materials

¶1010 Statement on Potentially Unlawful Online Platforms for Trading Digital Assets

Divisions of Enforcement and Trading and Markets

March 7, 2018

Online trading platforms have become a popular way investors can buy and sell digital assets, including coins and tokens offered and sold in so-called Initial Coin Offerings ("ICOs"). The platforms often claim to give investors the ability to quickly buy and sell digital assets. Many of these platforms bring buyers and sellers together in one place and offer investors access to automated systems that display priced orders, execute trades, and provide transaction data.

A number of these platforms provide a mechanism for trading assets that meet the definition of a "security" under the federal securities laws. If a platform offers trading of digital assets that are securities and operates as an "exchange," as defined by the federal securities laws, then the platform must register with the SEC as a national securities exchange or be exempt from registration. The federal regulatory framework governing registered national securities exchanges and exempt markets is designed to protect investors and prevent against fraudulent and manipulative trading practices.

Considerations for Investors Using Online Trading Platforms

To get the protections offered by the federal securities laws and SEC oversight when trading digital assets that are securities, investors should use a platform or entity registered with the SEC, such as a national securities exchange, alternative trading system ("ATS"), or broker-dealer.

The SEC staff has concerns that many online trading platforms appear to investors as SEC-registered and regulated marketplaces when they are not. Many platforms refer to themselves as "exchanges," which can give the misimpression to investors that they are regulated or meet the regulatory standards of a national securities exchange. Although some of these platforms claim to use strict standards to pick only high-quality digital assets to trade, the SEC does not review these standards or the digital assets that the platforms select, and the so-called standards should not be equated to the listing standards of national securities exchanges. Likewise, the SEC does not review the trading protocols used by these platforms, which determine how orders interact and execute, and access to a platform's trading services may not be the same for all users. Again, investors should not assume the trading protocols meet the standards of an SEC-registered national securities exchange. Lastly, many of these platforms give the impression that they perform exchange-like functions by offering order books with updated bid and ask pricing and data about executions on the system, but there is no reason to believe that such information has the same integrity as that provided by national securities exchanges.

In light of the foregoing, here are some questions investors should ask before they decide to trade digital assets on an online trading platform:

- Do you trade securities on this platform? If so, is the platform registered as a national securities exchange (see our link to the list below)?

- Does the platform operate as an ATS? If so, is the ATS registered as a broker-dealer and has it filed a Form ATS with the SEC (see our link to the list below)?

- Is there information in FINRA's BrokerCheck ® about any individuals or firms operating the platform?

- How does the platform select digital assets for trading?

- Who can trade on the platform?

- What are the trading protocols?

- How are prices set on the platform?

- Are platform users treated equally?

- What are the platform's fees?

- How does the platform safeguard users' trading and personally identifying information?

- What are the platform's protections against cybersecurity threats, such as hacking or intrusions?

- What other services does the platform provide? Is the platform registered with the SEC for these services?

- Does the platform hold users' assets? If so, how are these assets safeguarded?

Resources for Investors

Investor.gov Spotlight on Initial Coin Offerings and Digital Assets

Chairman Jay Clayton Statement on Cryptocurrencies and Initial Coin Offerings

Chairman Jay Clayton's Testimony on Virtual Currencies: The Roles of the SEC and CFTC

Report of Investigation Pursuant to Section 21(a) of the Securities and Exchange Act of 1934: The DAO

Investors can find a list of SEC-registered national securities exchanges here: List of Active National Securities Exchanges

Investors can find a list of ATSs that have filed a Form ATS with the SEC here: List of Active Alternative Trading Systems

Considerations for Market Participants Operating Online Trading Platforms

A platform that trades securities and operates as an "exchange," as defined by the federal securities laws, must register as a national securities exchange or operate under an exemption from registration, such as the exemption provided for ATSs under SEC Regulation ATS. An SEC-registered national securities exchange must, among other things, have rules designed to prevent fraudulent and manipulative acts and practices. Additionally, as a self-regulatory organization ("SRO"), an SEC-registered national securities exchange must have rules and procedures governing the discipline of its members and persons associated with its members, and enforce compliance by its members and persons associated with its members with the federal securities laws and the rules of the exchange. Further, a national securities exchange must itself comply with the federal securities laws and must file its rules with the Commission.

An entity seeking to operate as an ATS is also subject to regulatory requirements, including registering with the SEC as a broker-dealer and becoming a member of an SRO. Registration as a broker-dealer subjects the ATS to a host of regulatory requirements, such as the requirement to have reasonable policies and procedures to prevent the misuse of material non-public information, books and records requirements, and financial responsibility rules, including, as applicable, requirements concerning the safeguarding and custody of customer funds and securities. The overlay of SRO membership imposes further regulatory requirements and oversight. An ATS must comply with the federal securities laws and its SRO's rules, and file a Form ATS with the SEC.

Some online trading platforms may not meet the definition of an exchange under the federal securities laws, but directly or indirectly offer trading or other services related to digital assets that are securities. For example, some platforms offer digital wallet services (to hold or store digital assets) or transact in digital assets that are securities. These and other services offered by platforms may trigger other registration requirements under the federal securities laws, including broker-dealer, transfer agent, or clearing agency registration, among other things. In addition, a platform that offers digital assets that are securities may be participating in the unregistered offer and sale of securities if those securities are not registered or exempt from registration.

In advancing the SEC's mission to protect investors, the SEC staff will continue to focus on platforms that offer trading of digital assets and their compliance with the federal securities laws.

Consultation with Securities Counsel and the SEC Staff

We encourage market participants who are employing new technologies to develop trading platforms to consult with legal counsel to aid in their analysis of federal securities law issues and to contact SEC staff, as needed, for assistance in analyzing the application of the federal securities laws.In particular, staff providing assistance on these matters can be reached at FinTech@sec.gov.

Resources for Market Participants

Regulation of Exchanges and Alternative Trading Systems

Select Commission Enforcement Actions

SEC v. Jon E. Montroll and Bitfunder

In re BTC Trading, Corp. and Ethan Burnside

SEC v. REcoin Group Foundation, LLC et al.

SEC v. PlexCorps et al.

In re Munchee, Inc.

SEC v. AriseBank et al.

¶ 1020 Report of Investigation Pursuant to Section 21(a) of the Securities Exchange Act of 1934: The DAO

SECURITIES AND EXCHANGE COMMISSION

SECURITIES EXCHANGE ACT OF 1934

Release No. 81207 / July 25, 2017

I. Introduction and Summary

The United States Securities and Exchange Commission's ("Commission") Division of Enforcement ("Division") has investigated whether The DAO, an unincorporated organization; Slock.it UG ("Slock.it"), a German corporation; Slock.it's co-founders; and intermediaries may have violated the federal securities laws. The Commission has determined not to pursue an enforcement action in this matter based on the conduct and activities known to the Commission at this time.

As described more fully below, The DAO is one example of a Decentralized Autonomous Organization, which is a term used to describe a "virtual" organization embodied in computer code and executed on a distributed ledger or blockchain. The DAO was created by Slock.it and Slock.it's co-founders, with the objective of operating as a for-profit entity that would create and hold a corpus of assets through the sale of DAO Tokens to investors, which assets would then be used to fund "projects." The holders of DAO Tokens stood to share in the anticipated earnings from these projects as a return on their investment in DAO Tokens. In addition, DAO Token holders could monetize their investments in DAO Tokens by reselling DAO Tokens on a number of web-based platforms ("Platforms") that supported secondary trading in the DAO Tokens.

After DAO Tokens were sold, but before The DAO was able to commence funding projects, an attacker used a flaw in The DAO's code to steal approximately one-third of The DAO's assets. Slock.it's co-founders and others responded by creating a work-around whereby DAO Token holders could opt to have their investment returned to them, as described in more detail below.

The investigation raised questions regarding the application of the U.S. federal securities laws to the offer and sale of DAO Tokens, including the threshold question whether DAO Tokens are securities. Based on the investigation, and under the facts presented, the Commission has determined that DAO Tokens are securities under the Securities Act of 1933 ("Securities Act") and the Securities Exchange Act of 1934 ("Exchange Act").[1] The Commission deems it appropriate and in the public interest to issue this report of investigation ("Report") pursuant to Section 21(a) of the Exchange Act[2] to advise those who would use a Decentralized Autonomous Organization ("DAO Entity"), or other distributed ledger or blockchain-enabled means for capital raising, to take appropriate steps to ensure compliance with the U.S. federal securities laws. All securities offered and sold in the United States must be registered with the Commission or must qualify for an exemption from the registration requirements. In addition, any entity or person engaging in the activities of an exchange must register as a national securities exchange or operate pursuant to an exemption from such registration.

This Report reiterates these fundamental principles of the U.S. federal securities laws and describes their applicability to a new paradigm—virtual organizations or capital raising entities that use distributed ledger or blockchain technology to facilitate capital raising and/or investment and the related offer and sale of securities. The automation of certain functions through this technology, "smart contracts,"[3] or computer code, does not remove conduct from the purview of the U.S. federal securities laws.[4] This Report also serves to

---

[1] This Report does not analyze the question whether The DAO was an "investment company," as defined under Section 3(a) of the Investment Company Act of 1940 ("Investment Company Act"), in part, because The DAO never commenced its business operations funding projects. Those who would use virtual organizations should consider their obligations under the Investment Company Act.

[2] Section 21(a) of the Exchange Act authorizes the Commission to investigate violations of the federal securities laws and, in its discretion, to "publish information concerning any such violations." This Report does not constitute an adjudication of any fact or issue addressed herein, nor does it make any findings of violations by any individual or entity. The facts discussed in Section II, infra, are matters of public record or based on documentary records. We are publishing this Report on the Commission's website to ensure that all market participants have concurrent and equal access to the information contained herein.

[3] Computer scientist Nick Szabo described a "smart contract" as:

a computerized transaction protocol that executes terms of a contract. The general objectives of smart contract design are to satisfy common contractual conditions (such as payment terms, liens, confidentiality, and even enforcement), minimize exceptions both malicious and accidental, and minimize the need for trusted intermediaries. Related economic goals include lowering fraud loss, arbitrations and enforcement costs, and other transaction costs.

See Nick Szabo, *Smart Contracts*, 1994, http://www.virtualschool.edu/mon/Economics/SmartContracts.html.

[4] See SEC v. C.M. Joiner Leasing Corp., 320 U.S. 344, 351 (1943) ("[T]he reach of the [Securities] Act does not stop with the obvious and commonplace. Novel, uncommon, or irregular devices, whatever they appear to be, are also reached if it be proved as matter of fact that they were widely offered or dealt in under terms or courses of dealing which established their character in commerce as 'investment contracts,' or as 'any interest or instrument commonly known as a

stress the obligation to comply with the registration provisions of the federal securities laws with respect to products and platforms involving emerging technologies and new investor interfaces.

II. Facts

A. *Background*

From April 30, 2016 through May 28, 2016, The DAO offered and sold approximately 1.15 billion DAO Tokens in exchange for a total of approximately 12 million Ether ("ETH"), a virtual currency[5] used on the Ethereum Blockchain.[6] As of the time the offering closed, the total ETH raised by The DAO was valued in U.S. Dollars ("USD") at approximately $150 million.

The concept of a DAO Entity is memorialized in a document (the "White Paper"), authored by Christoph Jentzsch, the Chief Technology Officer of Slock.it, a "Blockchain and IoT [(internet-of-things)] solution company," incorporated in Germany and co-founded by Christoph Jentzsch, Simon Jentzsch (Christoph Jentzsch's brother), and Stephan Tual ("Tual").[7] The White Paper purports

to describe "the first implementation of a [DAO Entity] code to automate organizational governance and decision making."[8] The White Paper posits that a DAO Entity "can be used by individuals working together collaboratively outside of a traditional corporate form. It can also be used by a registered corporate entity to automate formal governance rules contained in corporate bylaws or imposed by law." The White Paper proposes an entity—a DAO Entity—that would use smart contracts to attempt to solve governance issues described as inherent in traditional corporations.[9] As described, a DAO Entity purportedly would supplant traditional mechanisms of corporate governance and management with a blockchain such that contractual terms are "formalized, automated and enforced using software."[10]

B. *The DAO*

"The DAO" is the "first generation" implementation of the White Paper concept of a DAO Entity, and it began as an effort to create a "crowdfunding contract" to raise "funds to grow [a] company in the crypto space."[11] In November 2015, at an Ethereum Developer Conference in London,

---

(Footnote Continued)

'security'."); *see also Reves v. Ernst & Young*, 494 U.S. 56, 61 (1990) ("Congress' purpose in enacting the securities laws was to regulate investments, in whatever form they are made and by whatever name they are called.").

[5] The Financial Action Task Force defines "virtual currency" as:

a digital representation of value that can be digitally traded and functions as: (1) a medium of exchange; and/or (2) a unit of account; and/or (3) a store of value, but does not have legal tender status (i.e., when tendered to a creditor, is a valid and legal offer of payment) in any jurisdiction. It is not issued or guaranteed by any jurisdiction, and fulfils the above functions only by agreement within the community of users of the virtual currency. Virtual currency is distinguished from fiat currency (a.k.a. "real currency," "real money," or "national currency"), which is the coin and paper money of a country that is designated as its legal tender; circulates; and is customarily used and accepted as a medium of exchange in the issuing country. It is distinct from e-money, which is a digital representation of fiat currency used to electronically transfer value denominated in fiat currency.

FATF Report, Virtual Currencies, Key Definitions and Potential AML/CFT Risks, FINANCIAL ACTION TASK FORCE (June 2014), http://www.fatf-gafi.org/media/fatf/documents/reports/Virtual-currency-key-definitions-and-potential-aml-cft-risks.pdf.

[6] Ethereum, developed by the Ethereum Foundation, a Swiss nonprofit organization, is a decentralized platform that runs smart contracts on a blockchain known as the Ethereum Blockchain.

[7] Christoph Jentzsch released the final draft of the White Paper on or around March 23, 2016. He introduced his concept of a DAO Entity as early as November 2015 at an Ethereum Developer Conference in London, as a medium to raise funds for Slock.it, a German start-up he co-founded in September 2015. Slock.it purports to create technology that embeds smart contracts that run on the Ethereum Blockchain into real-world devices and, as a result, for example, permits anyone to rent, sell or share physical objects in a decentralized way. *See* SLOCK.IT, https://slock.it/.

[8] Christoph Jentzsch, *Decentralized Autonomous Organization to Automate Governance Final Draft – Under Review*, https://download.slock.it/public/DAO/WhitePaper.pdf.

[9] *Id.*

[10] *Id.* The White Paper contained the following statement:

A word of caution, at the outset: the legal status of [DAO Entities] remains the subject of active and vigorous debate and discussion. Not everyone shares the same definition. Some have said that [DAO Entities] are autonomous code and can operate independently of legal systems; others have said that [DAO Entities] must be owned or operate[d] by humans or human created entities. There will be many use cases, and the DAO [Entity] code will develop over time. Ultimately, how a DAO [Entity] functions and its legal status will depend on many factors, including how DAO [Entity] code is used, where it is used, and who uses it. This paper does not speculate about the legal status of [DAO Entities] worldwide. This paper is not intended to offer legal advice or conclusions. Anyone who uses DAO [Entity] code will do so at their own risk.

Id.

[11] Christoph Jentzsch, *The History of the DAO and Lessons Learned*, SLOCK.IT BLOG (Aug. 24, 2016), https://blog.slock.it/the-history-of-the-dao-and-lessons-learned-d06740f8cfa5#.5o62zo8uv. Although The DAO has been described as a "crowdfunding contract," The DAO would not have met the requirements of Regulation Crowdfunding, adopted under Title III of the Jumpstart Our Business Startups (JOBS) Act of 2012 (providing an exemption from registration for certain crowdfunding), because, among other things, it was not a broker-dealer or a funding portal registered with the SEC and the Financial Industry Regulatory Authority ("FINRA"). *See Regulation Crowdfunding: A Small Entity Compliance Guide for Issuers*, SEC (Apr. 5, 2017) https://www.sec.gov/info/smallbus/secg/rccomplianceguide-051316.htm; *Updated Investor Bulletin: Crowdfunding for Investors*, SEC (May 10, 2017), https://www.sec.gov/oiea/investor-alerts-bulletins/ib_crowdfunding-.html.

Christoph Jentzsch described his proposal for The DAO as a "for-profit DAO [Entity]," where participants would send ETH (a virtual currency) to The DAO to purchase DAO Tokens, which would permit the participant to vote and entitle the participant to "rewards."[12] Christoph Jentzsch likened this to "buying shares in a company and getting . . . dividends."[13] The DAO was to be "decentralized" in that it would allow for voting by investors holding DAO Tokens.[14] All funds raised were to be held at an Ethereum Blockchain "address" associated with The DAO and DAO Token holders were to vote on contract proposals, including proposals to The DAO to fund projects and distribute The DAO's anticipated earnings from the projects it funded.[15] The DAO was intended to be "autonomous" in that project proposals were in the form of smart contracts that exist on the Ethereum Blockchain and the votes were administered by the code of The DAO.[16]

On or about April 29, 2016, Slock.it deployed The DAO code on the Ethereum Blockchain, as a set of pre-programmed instructions.[17] This code was to govern how The DAO was to operate.

To promote The DAO, Slock.it's co-founders launched a website ("The DAO Website"). The DAO Website included a description of The DAO's intended purpose: "To blaze a new path in business for the betterment of its members, existing simultaneously nowhere and everywhere and operating solely with the steadfast iron will of unstoppable code."[18] The DAO Website also described how The DAO operated, and included a link through which DAO Tokens could be purchased. The DAO Website also included a link to the White Paper, which provided detailed information about a DAO Entity's structure and its source code and, together with The DAO Website, served as the primary source of promotional materials for The DAO. On The DAO Website and elsewhere, Slock.it represented that The DAO's source code had been reviewed by "one of the world's leading security audit companies" and "no stone was left unturned during those five whole days of security analysis."[19]

Slock.it's co-founders also promoted The DAO by soliciting media attention and by posting almost daily updates on The DAO's status on The DAO and Slock.it websites and numerous online forums relating to blockchain technology. Slock.it's co-founders used these posts to communicate to the public information about how to participate in The DAO, including: how to create and acquire DAO Tokens; the framework for submitting proposals for projects; and how to vote on proposals. Slock.it also created an online forum on The DAO Website, as well as administered "The DAO Slack" channel, an online messaging platform in which over 5,000 invited "team members" could discuss and exchange ideas about The DAO in real time.

1. DAO Tokens

In exchange for ETH, The DAO created DAO Tokens (proportional to the amount of ETH paid) that were then assigned to the Ethereum Blockchain address of the person or entity remitting the ETH. A DAO Token granted the Token holder certain voting and ownership rights. According to promotional materials, The DAO would earn profits by funding projects that would provide DAO Token holders a return on investment. The various promotional materials disseminated by Slock.it's co-founders touted that DAO Token holders would receive "rewards," which the White Paper defined as, "any [ETH] received by a DAO [Entity] generated from projects the DAO [Entity] funded." DAO Token holders would then vote to either use the rewards to fund new projects or to distribute the ETH to DAO Token holders.

From April 30, 2016 through May 28, 2016 (the "Offering Period"), The DAO offered and sold DAO Tokens. Investments in The DAO were made "pseudonymously" (i.e., an individual's or entity's pseudonym was their Ethereum Blockchain address). To purchase a DAO Token offered for sale by The DAO, an individual or entity sent ETH from their Ethereum Blockchain address to an Ethereum Blockchain address associated with The DAO. All of the ETH raised in the

---

[12] *See* Slockit, *Slock.it DAO demo at Devcon1: IoT + Blockchain,* YOUTUBE (Nov. 13, 2015), https://www.youtube.com/watch?v=49wHQoJxYPo.

[13] *Id.*

[14] *See* Jentzsch, *supra* note 8.

[15] *Id.* In theory, there was no limitation on the type of project that could be proposed. For example, proposed "projects" could include, among other things, projects that would culminate in the creation of products or services that DAO Token holders could use or charge others for using.

[16] *Id.*

[17] According to the White Paper, a DAO Entity is "activated by deployment on the Ethereum [B]lockchain. Once deployed, a [DAO Entity's] code requires 'ether' [ETH] to engage in transactions on Ethereum. Ether is the digital fuel that powers the Ethereum Network." The only way to update or alter The DAO's code is to submit a new proposal for voting and achieve a majority consensus on that proposal. *See*

Jentzsch, *supra* note 8. According to Slock.it's website, Slock.it gave The DAO code to the Ethereum community, noting that:

> The DAO framework is [a] side project of Slock.it UG and a gift to the Ethereum community. It consisted of a definitive whitepaper, smart contract code audited by one of the best security companies in the world and soon, a complete frontend interface. All free and open source for anyone to re-use, it is our way to say 'thank you' to the community.

SLOCK.IT, https://slock.it. The DAO code is publicly-available on GitHub, a host of source code. *See The Standard DAO Framework, Inc., Whitepaper,* GITHUB, https://github.com/slockit/DAO.

[18] The DAO Website was available at https://daohub.org.

[19] Stephen Tual, *Deja Vu DAO Smart Contracts Audit Results,* SLOCK.IT BLOG (Apr. 5, 2016), https://blog.slock.it/deja-vu-dai-smart-contracts-audit-results-d26bc088e32e.

offering as well as any future profits earned by The DAO were to be pooled and held in The DAO's Ethereum Blockchain address. The token price fluctuated in a range of approximately 1 to 1.5 ETH per 100 DAO Tokens, depending on when the tokens were purchased during the Offering Period. Anyone was eligible to purchase DAO Tokens (as long as they paid ETH). There were no limitations placed on the number of DAO Tokens offered for sale, the number of purchasers of DAO Tokens, or the level of sophistication of such purchasers.

DAO Token holders were not restricted from re-selling DAO Tokens acquired in the offering, and DAO Token holders could sell their DAO Tokens in a variety of ways in the secondary market and thereby monetize their investment as discussed below. Prior to the Offering Period, Slock.it solicited at least one U.S. web-based platform to trade DAO Tokens on its system and, at the time of the offering, The DAO Website and other promotional materials disseminated by Slock.it included representations that DAO Tokens would be available for secondary market trading after the Offering Period via several platforms. During the Offering Period and afterwards, the Platforms posted notices on their own websites and on social media that each planned to support secondary market trading of DAO Tokens.[20]

In addition to secondary market trading on the Platforms, after the Offering Period, DAO Tokens were to be freely transferable on the Ethereum Blockchain. DAO Token holders would also be permitted to redeem their DAO Tokens for ETH through a complicated, multi-week (approximately 46-day) process referred to as a DAO Entity "split."[21]

2. Participants in The DAO

According to the White Paper, in order for a project to be considered for funding with "a DAO [Entity]'s [ETH]," a "Contractor" first must sub-

mit a proposal to the DAO Entity. Specifically, DAO Token holders expected Contractors to submit proposals for projects that could provide DAO Token holders returns on their investments. Submitting a proposal to The DAO involved: (1) writing a smart contract, and then deploying and publishing it on the Ethereum Blockchain; and (2) posting details about the proposal on The DAO Website, including the Ethereum Blockchain address of the deployed contract and a link to its source code. Proposals could be viewed on The DAO Website as well as other publicly-accessible websites. Per the White Paper, there were two prerequisites for submitting a proposal. An individual or entity must: (1) own at least one DAO Token; and (2) pay a deposit in the form of ETH that would be forfeited to the DAO Entity if the proposal was put up for a vote and failed to achieve a quorum of DAO Token holders. It was publicized that Slock.it would be the first to submit a proposal for funding.[22]

ETH raised by The DAO was to be distributed to a Contractor to fund a proposal only on a majority vote of DAO Token holders.[23] DAO Token holders were to cast votes, which would be weighted by the number of tokens they controlled, for or against the funding of a specific proposal. The voting process, however, was publicly criticized in that it could incentivize distorted voting behavior and, as a result, would not accurately reflect the consensus of the majority of DAO Token holders. Specifically, as noted in a May 27, 2016 blog post by a group of computer security researchers, The DAO's structure included a "strong positive bias to vote YES on proposals and to suppress NO votes as a side effect of the way in which it restricts users' range of options following the casting of a vote."[24]

Before any proposal was put to a vote by DAO Token holders, it was required to be reviewed by one or more of The DAO's "Curators." At the time of the formation of The DAO, the Curators were a group of individuals chosen by Slock.it.[25] Accord-

---

[20] The Platforms are registered with FinCEN as "Money Services Businesses" and provide systems whereby customers may exchange virtual currencies for other virtual currencies or fiat currencies.

[21] According to the White Paper, the primary purpose of a split is to protect minority shareholders and prevent what is commonly referred to as a "51% Attack," whereby an attacker holding 51% of a DAO Entity's Tokens could create a proposal to send all of the DAO Entity's funds to himself or herself.

[22] It was stated on The DAO Website and elsewhere that Slock.it anticipated that it would be the first to submit a proposal for funding. In fact, a draft of Slock.it's proposal for funding for an "Ethereum Computer and Universal Sharing Network" was publicly-available online during the Offering Period.

[23] DAO Token holders could vote on proposals, either by direct interaction with the Ethereum Blockchain or by using an application that interfaces with the Ethereum Blockchain. It was generally acknowledged that DAO Token holders needed some technical knowledge in order to submit a vote,

and The DAO Website included a link to a step-by-step tutorial describing how to vote on proposals.

[24] By voting on a proposal, DAO Token holders would "tie up" their tokens until the end of the voting cycle. *See* Jentzsch, *supra* note 8 at 8 ("The tokens used to vote will be blocked, meaning they can not [sic] be transferred until the proposal is closed."). If, however, a DAO Token holder abstained from voting, the DAO Token holder could avoid these restrictions; any DAO Tokens not submitted for a vote could be withdrawn or transferred at any time. As a result, DAO Token holders were incentivized either to vote yes or to abstain from voting. *See* Dino Mark et al., *A Call for a Temporary Moratorium on The DAO*, HACKING, DISTRIBUTED (May 27, 2016, 1:35 PM), http://hackingdistributed.com/2016/05/27/dao-call-for-moratorium/.

[25] At the time of the DAO's launch, The DAO Website identified eleven "high profile" individuals as holders of The DAO's Curator "Multisig" (or "private key"). These individuals all appear to live outside of the United States. Many of them were associated with the Ethereum Foundation, and The DAO Website touted the qualifications and trustworthiness of these individuals.

¶1020

ing to the White Paper, the Curators of a DAO Entity had "considerable power." The Curators performed crucial security functions and maintained ultimate control over which proposals could be submitted to, voted on, and funded by The DAO. As stated on The DAO Website during the Offering Period, The DAO relied on its Curators for "failsafe protection" and for protecting The DAO from "malicous [sic] actors." Specifically, per The DAO Website, a Curator was responsible for: (1) confirming that any proposal for funding originated from an identifiable person or organization; and (2) confirming that smart contracts associated with any such proposal properly reflected the code the Contractor claims to have deployed on the Ethereum Blockchain. If a Curator determined that the proposal met these criteria, the Curator could add the proposal to the "whitelist," which was a list of Ethereum Blockchain addresses that could receive ETH from The DAO if the majority of DAO Token holders voted for the proposal.

Curators of The DAO had ultimate discretion as to whether or not to submit a proposal for voting by DAO Token holders. Curators also determined the order and frequency of proposals, and could impose subjective criteria for whether the proposal should be whitelisted. One member of the group chosen by Slock.it to serve collectively as the Curator stated publicly that the Curator had "complete control over the whitelist ... the order in which things get whitelisted, the duration for which [proposals] get whitelisted, when things get unwhitelisted ... [and] clear ability to control the order and frequency of proposals," noting that "curators have tremendous power."[26] Another Curator publicly announced his subjective criteria for determining whether to whitelist a proposal, which included his personal ethics.[27] Per the White Paper, a Curator also had the power to reduce the voting quorum requirement by 50% every other week. Absent action by a Curator, the quorum could be reduced by 50% only if no proposal had reached the required quorum for 52 weeks.

3. Secondary Market Trading on the Platforms

During the period from May 28, 2016 through early September 2016, the Platforms became the preferred vehicle for DAO Token holders to buy and sell DAO Tokens in the secondary market

using virtual or fiat currencies. Specifically, the Platforms used electronic systems that allowed their respective customers to post orders for DAO Tokens on an anonymous basis. For example, customers of each Platform could buy or sell DAO Tokens by entering a market order on the Platform's system, which would then match with orders from other customers residing on the system. Each Platform's system would automatically execute these orders based on pre-programmed order interaction protocols established by the Platform.

None of the Platforms received orders for DAO Tokens from non-Platform customers or routed its respective customers' orders to any other trading destinations. The Platforms publicly displayed all their quotes, trades, and daily trading volume in DAO Tokens on their respective websites. During the period from May 28, 2016 through September 6, 2016, one such Platform executed more than 557,378 buy and sell transactions in DAO Tokens by more than 15,000 of its U.S. and foreign customers. During the period from May 28, 2016 through August 1, 2016, another such Platform executed more than 22,207 buy and sell transactions in DAO Tokens by more than 700 of its U.S. customers.

4. Security Concerns, The "Attack" on The DAO, and The Hard Fork

In late May 2016, just prior to the expiration of the Offering Period, concerns about the safety and security of The DAO's funds began to surface due to vulnerabilities in The DAO's code. On May 26, 2016, in response to these concerns, Slock.it submitted a "DAO Security Proposal" that called for the development of certain updates to The DAO's code and the appointment of a security expert.[28] Further, on June 3, 2016, Christoph Jentzsch, on behalf of Slock.it, proposed a moratorium on all proposals until alterations to The DAO's code to fix vulnerabilities in The DAO's code had been implemented.[29]

On June 17, 2016, an unknown individual or group (the "Attacker") began rapidly diverting ETH from The DAO, causing approximately 3.6 million ETH—1/3 of the total ETH raised by The DAO offering—to move from The DAO's Ethereum Blockchain address to an Ethereum Blockchain address controlled by the Attacker

---

[26] Epicenter, *EB134 – Emin Gün Sirer And Vlad Zamfir: On A Rocky DAO*, YouTube (June 6, 2016), https://www.youtube.com/watch?v=ON5GhIQdFU8.

[27] Andrew Quentson, *Are the DAO Curators Masters or Janitors?*, The Coin Telegraph (June 12, 2016), https://cointelegraph.com/news/are-the-dao-curators-masters-or-janitors.

[28] *See* Stephan Tual, *Proposal #1-DAO Security, Redux*, Slock.it Blog (May 26, 2016), https://blog.slock.it/both-our-proposals-are-now-out-voting-starts-saturday-morning-ba322d6d3aea. The unnamed security expert would "act as the first point of contact for security disclosures, and continually monitor, pre-empt and avert any potential attack vectors

The DAO may face, including social, technical and economic attacks." *Id.* Slock.it initially proposed a much broader security proposal that included the formation of a "DAO Security" group, the establishment of a "Bug Bounty Program," and routine external audits of The DAO's code. However, the cost of the proposal (125,000 ETH), which would be paid from The DAO's funds, was immediately criticized as too high and Slock.it decided instead to submit the revised proposal described above. *See* Stephan Tual, *DAO.Security, a Proposal to guarantee the integrity of The DAO*, Slock.it Blog (May 25, 2016), https://blog.slock.it/dao-security-a-proposal-to-guarantee-the-integrity-of-the-dao-3473899ace9d.

[29] *See TheDAO Proposal_ID 5*, Etherscan, https://etherscan.io/token/thedao-proposal/5.

(the "Attack").[30] Although the diverted ETH was then held in an address controlled by the Attacker, the Attacker was prevented by The DAO's code from moving the ETH from that address for 27 days.[31]

In order to secure the diverted ETH and return it to DAO Token holders, Slock.it's co-founders and others endorsed a "Hard Fork" to the Ethereum Blockchain. The "Hard Fork," called for a change in the Ethereum protocol on a going forward basis that would restore the DAO Token holders' investments as if the Attack had not occurred. On July 20, 2016, after a majority of the Ethereum network adopted the necessary software updates, the new, forked Ethereum Blockchain became active.[32] The Hard Fork had the effect of transferring all of the funds raised (including those held by the Attacker) from The DAO to a recovery address, where DAO Token holders could exchange their DAO Tokens for ETH.[33] All DAO Token holders who adopted the Hard Fork could exchange their DAO Tokens for ETH, and avoid any loss of the ETH they had invested.[34]

III. Discussion

The Commission is aware that virtual organizations and associated individuals and entities increasingly are using distributed ledger technology to offer and sell instruments such as DAO Tokens to raise capital. These offers and sales have been referred to, among other things, as "Initial Coin Offerings" or "Token Sales." Accordingly, the Commission deems it appropriate and in the public interest to issue this Report in order to stress that the U.S. federal securities law may apply to various activities, including distributed ledger technology, depending on the particular facts and circumstances, without regard to the form of the organization or technology used to effectuate a particular offer or sale. In this Report, the Commission considers the particular facts and circumstances of the offer and sale of DAO Tokens to demonstrate the application of existing U.S. federal securities laws to this new paradigm.

A. *Section 5 of the Securities Act*

The registration provisions of the Securities Act contemplate that the offer or sale of securities to the public must be accompanied by the "full and fair disclosure" afforded by registration with the Commission and delivery of a statutory prospectus containing information necessary to enable prospective purchasers to make an informed investment decision. Registration entails disclosure of detailed "information about the issuer's financial condition, the identity and background of management, and the price and amount of securities to be offered . . . ." *SEC v. Cavanagh*, 1 F. Supp. 2d 337, 360 (S.D.N.Y. 1998), *aff'd*, 155 F.3d 129 (2d Cir. 1998). "The registration statement is designed to assure public access to material facts bearing on the value of publicly traded securities and is central to the Act's comprehensive scheme for protecting public investors." *SEC v. Aaron*, 605 F.2d 612, 618 (2d Cir. 1979) (citing *SEC v. Ralston Purina Co.*, 346 U.S. 119, 124 (1953)), *vacated on other grounds*, 446 U.S. 680 (1980). Section 5(a) of the Securities Act provides that, unless a registration statement is in effect as to a security, it is unlawful for any person, directly or indirectly, to engage in the offer or sale of securities in interstate commerce. Section 5(c) of the Securities Act provides a similar prohibition against offers to sell, or offers to buy, unless a registration statement has been filed. Thus, both Sections 5(a) and 5(c) of the Securities Act prohibit the unregistered offer or sale of securities in interstate commerce. 15 U.S.C. § 77e(a) and (c). Violations of Section 5 do not require scienter. *SEC v. Universal Major Indus. Corp.*, 546 F.2d 1044, 1047 (2d Cir. 1976).

B. *DAO Tokens Are Securities*

1. Foundational Principles of the Securities Laws Apply to Virtual Organizations or Capital Raising Entities Making Use of Distributed Ledger Technology

Under Section 2(a)(1) of the Securities Act and Section 3(a)(10) of the Exchange Act, a security includes "an investment contract." *See* 15 U.S.C. §§ 77b-77c. An investment contract is an investment of money in a common enterprise with a reasonable expectation of profits to be derived from the entrepreneurial or managerial efforts of others. *See SEC v. Edwards*, 540 U.S. 389, 393 (2004); *SEC v. W.J. Howey Co.*, 328 U.S. 293, 301 (1946); *see also United Housing Found., Inc. v. Forman*, 421 U.S. 837, 852-53 (1975) (The "touchstone" of an investment contract "is the presence of an investment in a common venture premised on a reasonable expectation of profits to be derived from the entrepreneurial or managerial efforts of others."). This definition embodies a *"flexible rather than a static principle,* one that is capable of adaptation to meet the countless and variable schemes devised by those who seek the use of the money of others on the promise of profits." *Howey*, 328 U.S. at 299 (emphasis added). The test "permits the fulfillment of the statutory purpose of compelling full and fair disclosure relative to the issuance of 'the many types of instruments that in our commercial world fall within the

---

[30] *See* Stephan Tual, *DAO Security Advisory: live updates*, SLOCK.IT BLOG (June 17, 2016), https://blog.slock.it/dao-security-advisory-live-updates-2a0a42a2d07b.

[31] *Id.*

[32] A minority group, however, elected not to adopt the new Ethereum Blockchain created by the Hard Fork because to do so would run counter to the concept that a blockchain is

immutable. Instead they continued to use the former version of the blockchain, which is now known as "Ethereum Classic."

[33] *See* Christoph Jentzsch, *What the 'Fork' Really Means*, SLOCK.IT BLOG (July 18, 2016), https://blog.slock.it/what-the-fork-really-means-6fe573ac31dd.

[34] *Id.*

ordinary concept of a security.'" *Id.* In analyzing whether something is a security, "form should be disregarded for substance," *Tcherepnin v. Knight*, 389 U.S. 332, 336 (1967), "and the emphasis should be on economic realities underlying a transaction, and not on the name appended thereto." *United Housing Found.*, 421 U.S. at 849.

2. Investors in The DAO Invested Money

In determining whether an investment contract exists, the investment of "money" need not take the form of cash. *See, e.g., Uselton v. Comm. Lovelace Motor Freight, Inc.*, 940 F.2d 564, 574 (10th Cir. 1991) ("[I]n spite of *Howey's* reference to an 'investment of money,' it is well established that cash is not the only form of contribution or investment that will create an investment contract.").

Investors in The DAO used ETH to make their investments, and DAO Tokens were received in exchange for ETH. Such investment is the type of contribution of value that can create an investment contract under *Howey. See SEC v. Shavers*, No. 4:13-CV-416, 2014 WL 4652121, at *1 (E.D. Tex. Sept. 18, 2014) (holding that an investment of Bitcoin, a virtual currency, meets the first prong of *Howey*); *Uselton*, 940 F.2d at 574 ("[T]he 'investment' may take the form of 'goods and services,' or some other 'exchange of value'.") (citations omitted).

3. With a Reasonable Expectation of Profits

Investors who purchased DAO Tokens were investing in a common enterprise and reasonably expected to earn profits through that enterprise when they sent ETH to The DAO's Ethereum Blockchain address in exchange for DAO Tokens. "[P]rofits" include "dividends, other periodic payments, or the increased value of the investment." *Edwards*, 540 U.S. at 394. As described above, the various promotional materials disseminated by Slock.it and its co-founders informed investors that The DAO was a for-profit entity whose objective was to fund projects in exchange for a return on investment.[35] The ETH was pooled and available to The DAO to fund projects. The projects (or "contracts") would be proposed by Contractors. If the proposed contracts were whitelisted by Curators, DAO Token holders could vote on whether The DAO should fund the proposed contracts. Depending on the terms of each particular contract, DAO Token holders stood to share in potential profits from the contracts. Thus, a reasonable investor would have been motivated, at least in part, by the prospect of profits on their investment of ETH in The DAO.

4. Derived from the Managerial Efforts of Others

a. The Efforts of Slock.it, Slock.it's Co-Founders, and The DAO's Curators Were Essential to the Enterprise

Investors' profits were to be derived from the managerial efforts of others—specifically, Slock.it and its co-founders, and The DAO's Curators. The central issue is "whether the efforts made by those other than the investor are the undeniably significant ones, those essential managerial efforts which affect the failure or success of the enterprise." *SEC v. Glenn W. Turner Enters., Inc.*, 474 F.2d 476, 482 (9th Cir. 1973). The DAO's investors relied on the managerial and entrepreneurial efforts of Slock.it and its co-founders, and The DAO's Curators, to manage The DAO and put forth project proposals that could generate profits for The DAO's investors.

Investors' expectations were primed by the marketing of The DAO and active engagement between Slock.it and its co-founders with The DAO and DAO Token holders. To market The DAO and DAO Tokens, Slock.it created The DAO Website on which it published the White Paper explaining how a DAO Entity would work and describing their vision for a DAO Entity. Slock.it also created and maintained other online forums that it used to provide information to DAO Token holders about how to vote and perform other tasks related to their investment. Slock.it appears to have closely monitored these forums, answering questions from DAO Token holders about a variety of topics, including the future of The DAO, security concerns, ground rules for how The DAO would work, and the anticipated role of DAO Token holders. The creators of The DAO held themselves out to investors as experts in Ethereum, the blockchain protocol on which The DAO operated, and told investors that they had selected persons to serve as Curators based on their expertise and credentials. Additionally, Slock.it told investors that it expected to put forth the first substantive profit-making contract proposal—a blockchain venture in its area of expertise. Through their conduct and marketing materials, Slock.it and its co-founders led investors to believe that they could be relied on to provide the significant managerial efforts required to make The DAO a success.

Investors in The DAO reasonably expected Slock.it and its co-founders, and The DAO's Curators, to provide significant managerial efforts after The DAO's launch. The expertise of The DAO's creators and Curators was critical in monitoring the operation of The DAO, safeguarding investor funds, and determining whether proposed contracts should be put for a vote. Investors had little choice but to rely on their expertise. At the time of the offering, The DAO's protocols had already

---

[35] That the "projects" could encompass services and the creation of goods for use by DAO Token holders does not change the core analysis that investors purchased DAO To-

kens with the expectation of earning profits from the efforts of others.

been pre-determined by Slock.it and its co-founders, including the control that could be exercised by the Curators. Slock.it and its co-founders chose the Curators, whose function it was to: (1) vet Contractors; (2) determine whether and when to submit proposals for votes; (3) determine the order and frequency of proposals that were submitted for a vote; and (4) determine whether to halve the default quorum necessary for a successful vote on certain proposals. Thus, the Curators exercised significant control over the order and frequency of proposals, and could impose their own subjective criteria for whether the proposal should be whitelisted for a vote by DAO Token holders. DAO Token holders' votes were limited to proposals whitelisted by the Curators, and, although any DAO Token holder could put forth a proposal, each proposal would follow the same protocol, which included vetting and control by the current Curators. While DAO Token holders could put forth proposals to replace a Curator, such proposals were subject to control by the current Curators, including whitelisting and approval of the new address to which the tokens would be directed for such a proposal. In essence, Curators had the power to determine whether a proposal to remove a Curator was put to a vote.[36]

And, Slock.it and its co-founders did, in fact, actively oversee The DAO. They monitored The DAO closely and addressed issues as they arose, proposing a moratorium on all proposals until vulnerabilities in The DAO's code had been addressed and a security expert to monitor potential attacks on The DAO had been appointed. When the Attacker exploited a weakness in the code and removed investor funds, Slock.it and its co-founders stepped in to help resolve the situation.

b. DAO Token Holders' Voting Rights Were Limited

Although DAO Token holders were afforded voting rights, these voting rights were limited. DAO Token holders were substantially reliant on the managerial efforts of Slock.it, its co-founders, and the Curators.[37] Even if an investor's efforts help to make an enterprise profitable, those efforts do not necessarily equate with a promoter's significant managerial efforts or control over the enterprise. See, e.g., Glenn W. Turner, 474 F.2d at 482 (finding that a multi-level marketing scheme was an investment contract and that investors relied on the promoter's managerial efforts, despite the fact that investors put forth the majority of the

labor that made the enterprise profitable, because the promoter dictated the terms and controlled the scheme itself); Long v. Shultz, 881 F.2d 129, 137 (5th Cir. 1989) ("An investor may authorize the assumption of particular risks that would create the possibility of greater profits or losses but still depend on a third party for all of the essential managerial efforts without which the risk could not pay off."). See also generally SEC v. Merchant Capital, LLC, 483 F.3d 747 (11th Cir. 2007) (finding an investment contract even where voting rights were provided to purported general partners, noting that the voting process provided limited information for investors to make informed decisions, and the purported general partners lacked control over the information in the ballots).

The voting rights afforded DAO Token holders did not provide them with meaningful control over the enterprise, because (1) DAO Token holders' ability to vote for contracts was a largely perfunctory one; and (2) DAO Token holders were widely dispersed and limited in their ability to communicate with one another.

First, as discussed above, DAO Token holders could only vote on proposals that had been cleared by the Curators.[38] And that clearance process did not include any mechanism to provide DAO Token holders with sufficient information to permit them to make informed voting decisions. Indeed, based on the particular facts concerning The DAO and the few draft proposals discussed in online forums, there are indications that contract proposals would not have necessarily provide enough information for investors to make an informed voting decision, affording them less meaningful control. For example, the sample contract proposal attached to the White Paper included little information concerning the terms of the contract. Also, the Slock.it co-founders put forth a draft of their own contract proposal and, in response to questions and requests to negotiate the terms of the proposal (posted to a DAO forum), Slock.it founder explained that the proposal was intentionally vague and that it was, in essence, a take it or leave it proposition not subject to negotiation or feedback. See, e.g., SEC v. Shields, 744 F.3d 633, 643-45 (10th Cir. 2014) (in assessing whether agreements were investment contracts, court looked to whether "the investors actually had the type of control reserved under the agreements to obtain access to information necessary to protect, manage, and control their investments at the time they purchased their interests.").

---

[36] DAO Token holders could put forth a proposal to split from The DAO, which would result in the creation of a new DAO Entity with a new Curator. Other DAO Token holders would be allowed to join the new DAO Entity as long as they voted yes to the original "split" proposal. Unlike all other contract proposals, a proposal to split did not require a deposit or a quorum, and it required a seven-day debating period instead of the minimum two-week debating period required for other proposals.

[37] Because, as described above, DAO Token holders were incentivized either to vote yes or to abstain from voting, the

results of DAO Token holder voting would not necessarily reflect the actual view of a majority of DAO Token holders.

[38] Because, in part, The DAO never commenced its business operations funding projects, this Report does not analyze the question whether anyone associated with The DAO was an "[i]nvestment adviser" under Section 202(a)(11) of the Investment Advisers Act of 1940 ("Advisers Act"). See 15 U.S.C. § 80b-2(a)(11). Those who would use virtual organizations should consider their obligations under the Advisers Act.

Second, the pseudonymity and dispersion of the DAO Token holders made it difficult for them to join together to effect change or to exercise meaningful control. Investments in The DAO were made pseudonymously (such that the real-world identities of investors are not apparent), and there was great dispersion among those individuals and/or entities who were invested in The DAO and thousands of individuals and/or entities that traded DAO Tokens in the secondary market—an arrangement that bears little resemblance to that of a genuine general partnership. *Cf. Williamson v. Tucker*, 645 F.2d 404, 422-24 (5th Cir. 1981) ("[O]ne would not expect partnership interests sold to large numbers of the general public to provide any real partnership control; at some point there would be so many [limited] partners that a partnership vote would be more like a corporate vote, each partner's role having been diluted to the level of a single shareholder in a corporation.").[39] Slock.it did create and maintain online forums on which investors could submit posts regarding contract proposals, which were not limited to use by DAO Token holders (anyone was permitted to post). However, DAO Token holders were pseudonymous, as were their posts to the forums. Those facts, combined with the sheer number of DAO Token holders, potentially made the forums of limited use if investors hoped to consolidate their votes into blocs powerful enough to assert actual control. This was later demonstrated through the fact that DAO Token holders were unable to effectively address the Attack without the assistance of Slock.it and others. The DAO Token holders' pseudonymity and dispersion diluted their control over The DAO. *See Merchant Capital*, 483 F.3d at 758 (finding geographic dispersion of investors weighing against investor control).

These facts diminished the ability of DAO Token holders to exercise meaningful control over the enterprise through the voting process, rendering the voting rights of DAO Token holders akin to those of a corporate shareholder. *Steinhardt Group, Inc. v. Citicorp.*, 126 F.3d 144, 152 (3d Cir. 1997) ("It must be emphasized that the assignment of nominal or limited responsibilities to the participant does not negate the existence of an investment contract; where the duties assigned are so narrowly circumscribed as to involve little real choice of action . . . a security may be found to exist . . . . [The] emphasis must be placed on economic reality.") (citing *SEC v. Koscot Interplanetary, Inc.*, 497 F.2d 473, 483 n. 14 (5th Cir. 1974)).

By contract and in reality, DAO Token holders relied on the significant managerial efforts provided by Slock.it and its co-founders, and The DAO's Curators, as described above. Their efforts, not those of DAO Token holders, were the "undeniably significant" ones, essential to the overall success and profitability of any investment into The DAO. *See Glenn W. Turner*, 474 F.2d at 482.

C. Issuers Must Register Offers and Sales of Securities Unless a Valid Exemption Applies

The definition of "issuer" is broadly defined to include "every person who issues or proposes to issue any security" and "person" includes "any unincorporated organization." 15 U.S.C. § 77b(a)(4). The term "issuer" is flexibly construed in the Section 5 context "as issuers devise new ways to issue their securities and the definition of a security itself expands." *Doran v. Petroleum Mgmt. Corp.*, 545 F.2d 893, 909 (5th Cir. 1977); *accord SEC v. Murphy*, 626 F.2d 633, 644 (9th Cir. 1980) ("[W]hen a person [or entity] organizes or sponsors the organization of limited partnerships and is primarily responsible for the success or failure of the venture for which the partnership is formed, he will be considered an issuer . . . .").

The DAO, an unincorporated organization, was an issuer of securities, and information about The DAO was "crucial" to the DAO Token holders' investment decision. *See Murphy*, 626 F.2d at 643 ("Here there is no company issuing stock, but instead, a group of individuals investing funds in an enterprise for profit, and receiving in return an entitlement to a percentage of the proceeds of the enterprise.") (citation omitted). The DAO was "responsible for the success or failure of the enterprise," and accordingly was the entity about which the investors needed information material to their investment decision. *Id.* at 643-44.

During the Offering Period, The DAO offered and sold DAO Tokens in exchange for ETH through The DAO Website, which was publicly-accessible, including to individuals in the United States. During the Offering Period, The DAO sold approximately 1.15 billion DAO Tokens in exchange for a total of approximately 12 million ETH, which was valued in USD, at the time, at approximately $150 million. Because DAO Tokens were securities, The DAO was required to register the offer and sale of DAO Tokens, unless a valid exemption from such registration applied.

---

[39] The Fifth Circuit in *Williamson* stated that:

A general partnership or joint venture interest can be designated a security if the investor can establish, for example, that (1) an agreement among the parties leaves so little power in the hands of the partner or venture that the arrangement in fact distributes power as would a limited partnership; or (2) the partner or venturer is so inexperienced and unknowledgeable in business affairs that he is incapable of intelligently exercising his partnership or venture

powers; or (3) the partner or venturer is so dependent on some unique entrepreneurial or managerial ability of the promoter or manager that he cannot replace the manager of the enterprise or otherwise exercise meaningful partnership or venture powers.

Williamson, 645 F.2d at 424 & n.15 (court also noting that, "this is not to say that other factors could not also give rise to such a dependence on the promoter or manager that the exercise of partnership powers would be effectively precluded.").

Moreover, those who participate in an unregistered offer and sale of securities not subject to a valid exemption are liable for violating Section 5. *See, e.g., Murphy*, 626 F.2d at 650-51 ("[T]hose who ha[ve] a necessary role in the transaction are held liable as participants.") (citing *SEC v. North Am. Research & Dev. Corp.*, 424 F.2d 63, 81 (2d Cir. 1970); *SEC v. Culpepper*, 270 F.2d 241, 247 (2d Cir. 1959); *SEC v. International Chem. Dev. Corp.*, 469 F.2d 20, 28 (10th Cir. 1972); *Pennaluna & Co. v. SEC*, 410 F.2d 861, 864 n.1, 868 (9th Cir. 1969)); *SEC v. Softpoint, Inc.*, 958 F. Supp 846, 859-60 (S.D.N.Y. 1997) ("The prohibitions of Section 5 . . . sweep[] broadly to encompass 'any person' who participates in the offer or sale of an unregistered, non-exempt security."); *SEC v. Chinese Consol. Benevolent Ass'n.*, 120 F.2d 738, 740-41 (2d Cir. 1941) (defendant violated Section 5(a) "because it engaged in selling unregistered securities" issued by a third party "when it solicited offers to buy the securities 'for value'").

D. A System that Meets the Definition of an Exchange Must Register as a National Securities Exchange or Operate Pursuant to an Exemption from Such Registration

Section 5 of the Exchange Act makes it unlawful for any broker, dealer, or exchange, directly or indirectly, to effect any transaction in a security, or to report any such transaction, in interstate commerce, unless the exchange is registered as a national securities exchange under Section 6 of the Exchange Act, or is exempted from such registration. *See* 15 U.S.C. § 78e. Section 3(a)(1) of the Exchange Act defines an "exchange" as "any organization, association, or group of persons, whether incorporated or unincorporated, which constitutes, maintains, or provides a market place or facilities for bringing together purchasers and sellers of securities or for otherwise performing with respect to securities the functions commonly performed by a stock exchange as that term is generally understood . . . ." 15 U.S.C. § 78c(a)(1).

Exchange Act Rule 3b-16(a) provides a functional test to assess whether a trading system meets the definition of exchange under Section 3(a)(1). Under Exchange Act Rule 3b-16(a), an organization, association, or group of persons shall be considered to constitute, maintain, or provide "a marketplace or facilities for bringing together purchasers and sellers of securities or for otherwise performing with respect to securities the functions commonly performed by a stock exchange," if such organization, association, or group of persons: (1) brings together the orders for securities of multiple buyers and sellers; and (2) uses established, non-discretionary methods (whether by providing a trading facility or by setting rules) under which such orders interact with each other, and the buyers and sellers entering such orders agree to the terms of the trade.[40]

A system that meets the criteria of Rule 3b-16(a), and is not excluded under Rule 3b-16(b), must register as a national securities exchange pursuant to Sections 5 and 6 of the Exchange Act[41] or operate pursuant to an appropriate exemption. One frequently used exemption is for alternative trading systems ("ATS").[42] Rule 3a1-1(a)(2) exempts from the definition of "exchange" under Section 3(a)(1) an ATS that complies with Regulation ATS,[43] which includes, among other things, the requirement to register as a broker-dealer and file a Form ATS with the Commission to provide notice of the ATS's operations. Therefore, an ATS that operates pursuant to the Rule 3a1-1(a)(2) exemption and complies with Regulation ATS would not be subject to the registration requirement of Section 5 of the Exchange Act.

The Platforms that traded DAO Tokens appear to have satisfied the criteria of Rule 3b-16(a) and do not appear to have been excluded from Rule 3b-16(b). As described above, the Platforms provided users with an electronic system that matched orders from multiple parties to buy and sell DAO Tokens for execution based on non-discretionary methods.

IV. Conclusion and References for Additional Guidance

Whether or not a particular transaction involves the offer and sale of a security—regardless of the terminology used—will depend on the facts and circumstances, including the economic realities of the transaction. Those who offer and sell securi-

---

[40] *See* 17 C.F.R. § 240.3b-16(a). The Commission adopted Rule 3b-16(b) to exclude explicitly certain systems that the Commission believed did not meet the exchange definition. These systems include systems that merely route orders to other execution facilities and systems that allow persons to enter orders for execution against the bids and offers of a single dealer system. *See* Securities Exchange Act Rel. No. 40760 (Dec. 8, 1998), 63 FR 70844 (Dec. 22, 1998) (Regulation of Exchanges and Alternative Trading Systems) ("Regulation ATS"), 70852.

[41] 15 U.S.C. § 78e. A "national securities exchange" is an exchange registered as such under Section 6 of the Exchange Act. 15 U.S.C. § 78f.

[42] Rule 300(a) of Regulation ATS promulgated under the Exchange Act provides that an ATS is:
any organization, association, person, group of persons, or system: (1) [t]hat constitutes, maintains, or

provides a market place or facilities for bringing together purchasers and sellers of securities or for otherwise performing with respect to securities the functions commonly performed by a stock exchange within the meaning of [Exchange Act Rule 3b-16]; and (2) [t]hat does not: (i) [s]et rules governing the conduct of subscribers other than the conduct of subscribers' trading on such [ATS]; or (ii) [d]iscipline subscribers other than by exclusion from trading.

Regulation ATS, *supra* note 40, Rule 300(a).

[43] *See* 17 C.F.R. § 240.3a1-1(a)(2). Rule 3a1-1 also provides two other exemptions from the definition of "exchange" for any ATS operated by a national securities association, and any ATS not required to comply with Regulation ATS pursuant to Rule 301(a) of Regulation ATS. *See* 17 C.F.R. §§ 240.3a1-1(a)(1) and (3).

ties in the United States must comply with the federal securities laws, including the requirement to register with the Commission or to qualify for an exemption from the registration requirements of the federal securities laws. The registration requirements are designed to provide investors with procedural protections and material information necessary to make informed investment decisions. These requirements apply to those who offer and sell securities in the United States, regardless whether the issuing entity is a traditional company or a decentralized autonomous organization, regardless whether those securities are purchased using U.S. dollars or virtual currencies, and regardless whether they are distributed in certificated form or through distributed ledger technology. In addition, any entity or person engaging in the activities of an exchange, such as bringing together the orders for securities of multiple buyers and sellers using established non-discretionary methods under which such orders interact with each other and buyers and sellers entering such orders agree upon the terms of the trade, must register as a national securities exchange or operate pursuant to an exemption from such registration.

To learn more about registration requirements under the Securities Act, please visit the Commission's website Registration Under the Securities Act of 1933. To learn more about the Commission's registration requirements for investment companies, please visit the Commission's website Investment Company Registration and Regulation Package. To learn more about the Commission's registration requirements for national securities

exchanges, please visit the Commission's website National Securities Exchanges. To learn more about alternative trading systems, please see the Regulation ATS adopting release Release No. 34-40760.

For additional guidance, please see the following Commission enforcement actions involving virtual currencies:

- *SEC v. Trendon T. Shavers and Bitcoin Savings and Trust*, Civil Action No. 4:13-CV-416 (E.D. Tex., complaint filed July 23, 2013)

- *In re Erik T. Voorhees*, Rel. No. 33-9592 (June 3, 2014)

- *In re BTC Trading, Corp. and Ethan Burnside*, Rel. No. 33-9685 (Dec. 8, 2014)

- *SEC v. Homero Joshua Garza, Gaw Miners, LLC, and ZenMiner, LLC (d/b/a Zen Cloud)*, Civil Action No. 3:15-CV-01760 (D. Conn., complaint filed Dec. 1, 2015)

- *In re Bitcoin Investment Trust and SecondMarket, Inc.*, Rel. No. 34-78282 (July 11, 2016)

- *In re Sunshine Capital, Inc.*, File No. 500-1 (Apr. 11, 2017)

And please see the following investor alerts:

- *Bitcoin and Other Virtual Currency-Related Investments* (May 7, 2014)

- *Ponzi Schemes Using Virtual Currencies* (July 2013)

By the Commission.

¶ 1030 Order Disapproving Listing and Trading of Winklevoss Bitcoin Trust

SECURITIES AND EXCHANGE COMMISSION

(Release No. 34-80206; File No. SR-BatsBZX-2016-30)

March 10, 2017

Self-Regulatory Organizations; Bats BZX Exchange, Inc.; Order Disapproving a Proposed Rule Change, as Modified by Amendments No. 1 and 2, to BZX Rule 14.11(e)(4), Commodity-Based Trust

Shares, to List and Trade Shares Issued by the Winklevoss Bitcoin Trust

Bats BZX Exchange ("Exchange" or "BZX") has filed a proposed rule change to list and trade shares of the Winklevoss Bitcoin Trust.[1] When an

---

[1] The Exchange filed notice of the proposed rule change on June 30, 2016, and the Commission published the notice in the *Federal Register* on July 14, 2016. *See* Exchange Act Release No. 78262 (July 8, 2016), 81 FR 45554 (July 14, 2016) ("Notice"). On August 23, 2016, the Commission designated a longer period within which to act on the proposed rule change. *See* Exchange Act Release No. 78653 (Aug. 23, 2016), 81 FR 59256 (Aug. 29, 2016). On October 12, 2016, the Commission instituted proceedings under Section 19(b)(2)(B) of the Securities Exchange Act of 1934 ("Exchange Act"), 15 U.S.C. 78s(b)(2)(B), to determine whether to approve or disapprove the proposed rule change. *See* Exchange Act Release No. 79084 (Oct. 12, 2016), 81 FR 71778 (Oct. 18, 2016). On October 20, 2016, the Exchange filed Amendment No. 1 to the proposed rule change, replacing the original filing in its entirety, and Amendment No. 1 was published for comment in the *Federal Register* on November 3, 2016. *See* Exchange Act Release No. 79183 (Oct. 28, 2016), 81 FR 76650 (Nov. 3, 2016) ("Amendment No. 1"). On January 4, 2017, the Commission

designated a longer period for Commission action on the proposed rule change. *See* Exchange Act Release No. 79725 (Jan. 4, 2017), 82 FR 2425 (Jan. 9, 2017) (designating March 11, 2017, as the date by which the Commission must either approve or disapprove the proposed rule change). On February 22, 2017, the Exchange filed Amendment No. 2 to the proposed rule change ("Amendment No. 2"). Amendment No. 2 further modified the Exchange's proposal by (a) changing the size of a creation and redemption basket from 10,000 shares to 100,000 shares, (b) changing the bitcoin value of a share from 0.1 bitcoin to 0.01 bitcoin, and (c) changing the Exchange's representation about the number of shares outstanding at the commencement of trading from 100,000 shares to 500,000 shares. Because Amendment No. 2 does not materially alter the substance of the proposed rule change, Amendment No. 2 is not subject to notice and comment. Amendment No. 2 is available on the Commission's website at *https://www.sec.gov/comments/sr-batsbzx-2016-30/batsbzx201630-1594698-132357.pdf*.

exchange makes such a filing,[2] the Commission must determine whether the proposed rule change is consistent with the statutory provisions, and the rules and regulations, that apply to national securities exchanges.[3] The Commission must approve the filing if it finds that the proposed rule change is consistent with these legal requirements, and it must disapprove the filing if it does not make such a finding.[4]

As discussed further below, the Commission is disapproving this proposed rule change because it does not find the proposal to be consistent with Section 6(b)(5) of the Exchange Act, which requires, among other things, that the rules of a national securities exchange be designed to prevent fraudulent and manipulative acts and practices and to protect investors and the public interest.[5] The Commission believes that, in order to meet this standard, an exchange that lists and trades shares of commodity-trust exchange-traded products ("ETPs") must, in addition to other applicable requirements, satisfy two requirements that are dispositive in this matter. First, the exchange must have surveillance-sharing agreements with significant markets for trading the underlying commodity or derivatives on that commodity. And second, those markets must be regulated.[6]

Based on the record before it, the Commission believes that the significant markets for bitcoin are unregulated. Therefore, as the Exchange has not entered into, and would currently be unable to enter into, the type of surveillance-sharing agreement that has been in place with respect to all previously approved commodity-trust ETPs—agreements that help address concerns about the potential for fraudulent or manipulative acts and

practices in this market—the Commission does not find the proposed rule change to be consistent with the Exchange Act.

I. DESCRIPTION OF THE PROPOSAL

The Exchange proposes to list and trade shares ("Shares") of the Winklevoss Bitcoin Trust ("Trust") as Commodity-Based Trust Shares under BZX Rule 14.11(e)(4).[7] Details regarding the proposal and the Trust can be found in Amendments No. 1 and 2 to the proposal,[8] and in the registration statement for the Trust,[9] but the salient aspects of the proposal are described below.[10]

The Trust would hold only bitcoins as an asset,[11] and the bitcoins would be in the custody of, and secured by, the Trust's custodian, Gemini Trust Company LLC ("Custodian"), which is a limited-liability trust company chartered by the State of New York and supervised by the New York State Department of Financial Services ("NYSDFS").[12] Gemini Trust Company is also an affiliate of Digital Asset Services LLC, the sponsor of the Trust ("Sponsor").[13] The Trust would issue and redeem the Shares only in "Baskets" of 100,000 Shares and only to Authorized Participants, and these transactions would be conducted "in-kind" for bitcoin only.[14]

The investment objective of the Trust would be for the Shares to track the price of bitcoins on the Gemini Exchange, which is a digital-asset exchange owned and operated by the Gemini Trust Company.[15] The Net Asset Value ("NAV") of the Trust would be calculated each business day, based on the clearing price of that day's 4:00 p.m. ET Gemini Exchange Auction, a two-sided auction

---

[2] Such filings are made under Section 19(b)(1) of the Exchange Act, 15 U.S.C. 78s(b)(1), and Exchange Act Rule 19b-4, 17 CFR 240.19b-4.

[3] See Exchange Act Section 19(b)(2)(C), 15 U.S.C. 78s(b)(2)(C).

[4] See id.

[5] 15 U.S.C. 78f(b)(5).

[6] As discussed below, infra note 96 and accompanying text, the significant markets relating to the commodity-trust ETPs approved to date have been well-established regulated futures markets for the underlying commodity.

[7] See BZX Rule 14.11(e)(4)(C) (permitting the listing and trading of "Commodity-Based Trust Shares," defined as a security (a) that is issued by a trust that holds a specified commodity deposited with the trust; (b) that is issued by such trust in a specified aggregate minimum number in return for a deposit of a quantity of the underlying commodity; and (c) that, when aggregated in the same specified minimum number, may be redeemed at a holder's request by the trust, which will deliver to the redeeming holder the quantity of the underlying commodity). Other national securities exchanges that list and trade shares of commodity-trust ETPs have similar rules. See, e.g., NYSE Arca Equities Rule 8.201 (permitting the listing and trading of Commodity-Based Trust Shares) and Nasdaq Rule 5711(d) (permitting the listing and trading of Commodity-Based Trust Shares). Commodity-trust ETPs differ from exchange-traded funds ("ETFs") in a number of ways, including that they hold as an asset a single commodity,

rather than a portfolio of multiple securities, and that they are not regulated under the Investment Company Act of 1940.

[8] See Amendments No. 1 and 2, supra note 1.

[9] See Registration Statement on Form S-1, as amended, dated February 8, 2017 (File No. 333-189752) ("Registration Statement"). The Exchange represents in the proposed rule change that the Registration Statement will be effective as of the date of any offer and sale pursuant to the Registration Statement.

[10] The proposed rule change describes the ETP's underlying bitcoin asset as a "digital asset" and as a "commodity." See Amendment No. 1, supra note 1, 81 FR at 76652 & n.21, and describes the ETP as a Commodity-Based Trust. For a purpose of considering this proposal, this order describes bitcoin as a "digital asset" and a "commodity."

[11] Bitcoin is a digital asset that is issued by, and transmitted through, the decentralized, open-source protocol of the peer-to-peer bitcoin computer network that hosts the public transaction ledger, known as the "Blockchain," on which all bitcoins are recorded. The bitcoin network source code includes the protocols that govern the creation of bitcoin and the cryptographic system that secures and verifies bitcoin transactions. See id. at 76652.

[12] See id. at 76651–52.

[13] See id. at 76651.

[14] See id. at 76664–65. See also Amendment No. 2, supra note 1.

[15] See Amendment No. 1, supra note 1, 81 FR at 76652.

open to all Gemini Exchange customers.[16] The Intraday Indicative Value of the Trust would be calculated and disseminated by the Sponsor, every 15 seconds during the Exchange's regular trading session, based on the most-recent Gemini Exchange Auction price.[17]

The Exchange represents that it has entered into a comprehensive surveillance-sharing agreement with the Gemini Exchange.[18]

II. SUMMARY OF COMMENT LETTERS

The comment period closed on November 25, 2016. As of March 8, 2017, the Commission had received 59 comment letters on the proposed rule change.[19] Many of these letters address the nature and uses of bitcoin;[20] the state of development of bitcoin as a digital asset;[21] the inherent value of, and risks of investing in, bitcoin;[22] the desire of investors to gain access to bitcoin through an ETP;[23] the appropriate measures for the Trust to secure its bitcoin holdings against theft or loss;[24] whether the Trust should insure its bitcoin holdings against theft or loss;[25] the

---

[16] *See id.* In the event that the Sponsor determines that the Gemini Exchange Auction price, because of extraordinary circumstances, is "not an appropriate basis for evaluation of the Trust's bitcoin on a given Business Day," the Exchange's proposal provides that the Sponsor may use other specified criteria to value the holdings of the Trust. *See id.* at 76664.

[17] *See id.* at 76666.

[18] *See id.* at 76668. As discussed below, *infra* Section III.B.3, the Commission does not believe that this agreement is sufficient to form the basis for approving this proposed rule change.

[19] *See* Letters from Robert D. Miller, VP Technical Services, RKL eSolutions (July 11, 2016) ("R.D. Miller Letter"); Jorge Stolfi, Full Professor, Institute of Computing UNICAMP (July 13, 2016) ("Stolfi Letter"); Guillaume Lethuillier (July 26, 2016) ("Lethuillier Letter"); Michael B. Casey (July 31, 2016) ("Casey Letter"); Erik A. Aronesty, Sr. Software Engineer, Bloomberg LP (Aug. 2, 2016) ("Aronesty Letter"); Dan Anderson (Aug. 27, 2016) ("R. Miller Letter"); Robert Miller (Oct. 12, 2016) ("R. Miller Letter"); Lysle Shaw-McMinn, O.D. (Oct. 13, 2016) ("McMinn Letter"); Nils Neidhardt (Oct. 13, 2016) ("Neidhardt Letter"); Dana K. Barish (2 letters; Oct. 13, 2016) ("Barish Letter" and "Barish Letter II"); Xin Lu (Oct. 13, 2016) ("Xin Lu Letter"); Rodger Delehanty (Oct. 14, 2016) ("Delehanty Letter"); Dylan (Oct. 14, 2016) ("Dylan Letter"); Dana K. Barish (Oct. 14, 2016) ("Barish Letter III"); Dana K. Barish (2 letters; Oct. 15, 2016) ("Barish Letter IV" and "Barish Letter V"); Jorge Stolfi, Full Professor, Institute of Computing UNICAMP (Nov. 1, 2016) ("Stolfi Letter II"); Michael B. Casey (Nov. 5, 2016) ("Casey Letter II"); Anonymous (Nov. 8, 2016) ("Anonymous Letter"); Chris Burniske, Blockchain Products Lead, ARK Investment Management LLC (Nov. 8, 2016) ("ARK Letter"); Colin Keeler (Nov. 14, 2016) ("Keeler Letter"); Robert S. Tull, (Nov. 14, 2016) ("Tull Letter"); Mark T. Williams (Nov. 15, 2016) ("Williams Letter"); Anonymous (Nov. 21, 2016) ("Anonymous Letter II"); XBT OPPS Team (Nov. 21, 2016) ("XBT Letter"); Anonymous (Nov. 22, 2016) ("Anonymous Letter III"); Ken Maher (Nov. 22, 2016) ("Maher Letter"); Kyle Murray, Assistant General Counsel, Bats Global Markets, Inc. (Nov. 25, 2016) ("Bats Letter"); Colin Baird (Nov. 26, 2016) ("Baird Letter"); Scott P. Hall (Jan. 5, 2017) ("Hall Letter"); Suzanne H. Shatto (Jan. 24, 2017) ("Shatto Letter"); Joshua Lim and Dan Matuszewski, Treasury & Trading Operations, Circle Internet Financial, Inc. (Feb. 3, 2017) ("Circle Letter"); Zachary J. Herbert (Feb. 10, 2017) ("Herbert Letter"); Thomas Fernandez (Feb. 12, 2017) ("Fernandez Letter"); Diego Tomaselli (Feb. 17, 2017) ("Tomaselli Letter"); Hans Christensen (Feb. 20, 2017) ("Christensen Letter"); Jake Kim (Feb. 22, 2017) ("Kim Letter"); Andrea Dalla Val (Mar. 4, 2017) ("Dalla Val Letter"); Josh Barraza (Mar. 6, 2017) ("Barraza Letter"); Chad Rigsby (Mar. 6, 2017) ("Rigsby Letter"); Michael Lee (Mar. 6, 2017) ("Lee Letter"); Fabrizio Marchionne (Mar. 6, 2017) ("Marchionne Letter"); Ben Elron (Mar. 6, 2017) ("Elron Letter"); Patrick Miller (Mar. 6, 2017) ("P. Miller Letter"); Phil Chronakis (Mar. 6, 2017) ("Chronakis Letter"); Situation

Letter (Mar. 6, 2017) ("Situation Letter"); Steven Swiderski (Mar. 6, 2017) ("Swiderski Letter"); Marcia Paneque (Mar. 6, 2017) ("Paneque Letter"); Jeremy Nootenboom (Mar. 6, 2017) ("Nootenboom Letter"); Alan Struna (Mar. 6, 2017) ("Struna Letter"); Mike Johnson (Mar. 6, 2017) ("Johnson Letter"); Anonymous (Mar. 7, 2017) ("Anonymous Letter IV"); Brian Bang (Mar. 7, 2017) ("Bang Letter"); Anthony Schulte (Mar. 7, 2017) ("Schulte Letter"); Melissa Whitman (Mar. 8, 2017) ("Whitman Letter"); Harold Primm (Mar. 8, 2017) ("Primm Letter"); Shad (Mar. 8, 2017) ("Shad Letter"); Anonymous (Mar. 8, 2017) ("Anonymous Letter V"). All comments on the proposed rule change are available on the Commission's website at: *https://www.sec.gov/comments/sr-batsbzx-2016-30/ batsbzx201630.shtml.*

[20] *See, e.g.,* Stolfi Letter, *supra* note 19; Stolfi Letter II, *supra* note 19; Chronakis Letter, *supra* note 19.

[21] *See, e.g.,* Stolfi Letter II, *supra* note 19; Barish Letter IV, *supra* note 19; ARK Letter, *supra* note 19; Lee Letter, *supra* note 19; Chronakis Letter, *supra* note 19; Struna Letter, *supra* note 19; Johnson Letter, *supra* note 19; Anonymous Letter IV, *supra* note 19; Whitman Letter, *supra* note 19; Anonymous Letter V, *supra* note 19.

[22] *See, e.g.,* Stolfi Letter, *supra* note 19; Stolfi Letter II, *supra* note 19; Shatto Letter, *supra* note 19; Lethuillier Letter, *supra* note 19; Delehanty Letter, *supra* note 19; Xin Lu Letter, *supra* note 19; Neidhardt Letter, *supra* note 19; XBT Letter, *supra* note 19; Williams Letter, *supra* note 19; ARK Letter, *supra* note 19; Kim Letter, *supra* note 19; Dalla Val Letter, *supra* note 19; Paneque Letter, *supra* note 19; Lee Letter, *supra* note 19; Chronakis Letter, *supra* note 19; Struna Letter, *supra* note 19; Johnson Letter, *supra* note 19; Whitman Letter, *supra* note 19; Primm Letter, *supra* note 19; Anonymous Letter V, *supra* note 19.

[23] *See, e.g.,* R.D. Miller Letter, *supra* note 19; R. Miller Letter, *supra* note 19; Hall Letter, *supra* note 19; Keeler Letter, *supra* note 19; Lethuillier Letter, *supra* note 19; McMinn Letter, *supra* note 19; Herbert Letter, *supra* note 19; Fernandez Letter, *supra* note 19; Tomaselli Letter, *supra* note 19; Circle Letter, *supra* note 19; Baird Letter, *supra* note 19; Stolfi Letter, *supra* note 19; Anderson Letter, *supra* note 19; P. Miller Letter, *supra* note 19; Swiderski Letter, *supra* note 19; Situation Letter, *supra* note 19; Paneque Letter, *supra* note 19; Nootenboom Letter, *supra* note 19; Chronakis Letter, *supra* note 19.

[24] *See, e.g.,* Barish Letter, *supra* note 19; Barish Letter IV, *supra* note 19; Neidhardt Letter, *supra* note 19; Dylan Letter, *supra* note 19; Keeler Letter, *supra* note 19; Casey Letter, *supra* note 19; Aronesty Letter, *supra* note 19; ARK Letter, *supra* note 19; Tull Letter, *supra* note 19; Stolfi Letter, *supra* note 19; Stolfi Letter II, *supra* note 19; McMinn Letter, *supra* note 19; Lethuillier Letter, *supra* note 19; Delehanty Letter, *supra* note 19; Tull Letter II, *supra* note 19; Anonymous Letter, *supra* note 19; Bats Letter, *supra* note 19; Struna Letter, *supra* note 19.

[25] *See, e.g.,* Anonymous Letter, *supra* note 19; Tull Letter, *supra* note 19; Lethuillier Letter, *supra* note 19; Aronesty

blockchain treatment of positions in the Shares, including short positions or derivative positions;[26] the potential conflicts of interest related to the affiliations among the Sponsor, the Custodian, and the Gemini Exchange;[27] the proposed valuation method for the Trust's holdings;[28] or the legitimacy or enhanced regulatory protection that Commission approval of the proposed ETP might confer upon bitcoin as a digital asset.[29] Ultimately, however, comments on these topics do not bear on the basis for the Commission's decision to disapprove the proposal. Accordingly, the Commission will summarize and address the comments that relate to the susceptibility of bitcoin or the Shares to fraudulent or manipulative acts and practices, including the need for surveillance-sharing agreements with significant, regulated markets for trading in bitcoin or derivatives on bitcoin.

A. *Comments Regarding The Worldwide Market for Bitcoin*

Several commenters note that the majority of bitcoin trading occurs on exchanges outside the United States. One commenter claims that most daily trading volume is conducted on poorly capitalized, unregulated exchanges located outside the United States and that these non-U.S. exchanges and their practices significantly influence the price discovery process.[30] Another commenter states that the biggest and most-influential bitcoin exchange is located outside U.S. jurisdiction.[31]

One commenter states that, since 2013, the price of bitcoin has been defined mostly by the major Chinese exchanges, whose volumes dwarf those of exchanges outside China. According to the commenter, those exchanges are not regulated or audited, and are suspected of engaging in unethical practices like front-running, wash trades, and trading with insufficient funds. The commenter interprets pricing data from these Chinese exchanges to mean that the price of bitcoin is defined entirely by speculation, without any ties to fundamentals.[32] Another commenter also observes that Chinese markets drive much of the volume in the bitcoin markets and that the bitcoin/Chinese Yuan (BTC/CNY) quote is apt to trade at a significant premium to the bitcoin/U.S. dollar (BTC/USD) quote. The commenter points out that large arbitrage opportunities would not exist for long in efficient markets, but they do persist in bitcoin markets.[33]

One commenter claims that a sizeable number of traders and owners of bitcoin do not desire to trade in a well-regulated environment for reasons including tax evasion, evading capital controls, and money laundering. This commenter also states that U.S. exchanges do not offer products such as fee-free trading, margin trading, or options, which drive traffic to the top non-U.S. exchanges. The commenter claims that, because trade is now sparse on regulated U.S. exchanges including Gemini, arbitrage will not occur efficiently or proportionally to mitigate manipulation from the dominant unregulated bitcoin exchanges. This commenter also claims that several Chinese exchanges actively engage in bitcoin mining operations, creating a conflict of interest, and notes that these exchanges are unaudited and unaccountable.[34] Another commenter also claims that the Chinese exchanges that account for the bulk of trading are subject to little regulatory oversight and that existing know-your-customer or identity-verification measures are lax and can be easily bypassed.[35]

One commenter states that the market for bitcoin, by trade volume, is very shallow. This commenter notes that the majority of bitcoin is hoarded by a few owners or is out of circulation. The commenter also notes that ownership concentration is high, with 50 percent of bitcoin in the hands of fewer than 1,000 people, and that this high ownership concentration creates greater market liquidity risk, as large blocks of bitcoin are difficult to sell in a timely and market efficient manner. This commenter claims that daily trade volume is only a small fraction of total bitcoin

---

(Footnote Continued)

Letter, *supra* note 19; Delehanty Letter, *supra* note 19; XBT Letter, *supra* note 19; ARK Letter, *supra* note 19; Anonymous Letter III, *supra* note 19; Bats Letter, *supra* note 19.

[26] *See, e.g.*, Anonymous Letter, *supra* note 19; Tull Letter, *supra* note 19.

[27] *See, e.g.*, XBT Letter, *supra* note 19; Tull Letter, *supra* note 19; Stolfi Letter II, *supra* note 19; ARK Letter, *supra* note 19; Anonymous Letter II, *supra* note 19; Bats Letter, *supra* note 19.

[28] *See, e.g.*, McMinn Letter, *supra* note 19; Bats Letter, *supra* note 19; Delehanty Letter II, *supra* note 19; Dylan Letter, *supra* note 19; ARK Letter, *supra* note 19; Anonymous Letter II, *supra* note 19; Circle Letter, *supra* note 19.

[29] *See, e.g.*, Stolfi Letter, *supra* note 19; Circle Letter, *supra* note 19; Kim Letter, *supra* note 19; Delehanty Letter, *supra* note 19; Baird Letter, *supra* note 19; Anonymous Letter, *supra* note 19; Keeler Letter, *supra* note 19; Dalla Val Letter, *supra* note 19; Elron Letter, *supra* note 19; P. Miller Letter, *supra* note 19; Marchionne Letter, *supra* note 19; Situation Letter, *supra* note 19; Paneque Letter, *supra* note 19; Nootenboom

Letter, *supra* note 19; Chronakis Letter, *supra* note 19; Johnson Letter, *supra* note 19; Bang Letter, *supra* note 19; Primm Letter, *supra* note 19.

[30] *See* Williams Letter, *supra* note 19, at 2.

[31] *See* Anonymous Letter IV, *supra* note 19.

[32] *See* Stolfi Letter II, *supra* note 19.

[33] *See* ARK Letter, *supra* note 19, at 5.

[34] *See* Maher Letter, *supra* note 19; *see also* Johnson Letter, *supra* note 19; Anonymous Letter IV, *supra* note 19. According to the Exchange, "bitcoin mining" refers to the process of adding a set of transaction records (a "block") to bitcoin's "blockchain"—its public ledger of past transactions. *See* Amendment No. 1, *supra* note 1, 81 FR at 76655. The Exchange states that "[b]itcoin miners engage in a set of prescribed complex mathematical calculations in order to add a block to the blockchain and thereby confirm bitcoin transactions included in that block's data. Miners that are successful in adding a block to the blockchain are automatically awarded a fixed number of bitcoins for their efforts." *Id.*

[35] *See* Maher Letter, *supra* note 19.

¶1030

mined.[36] This commenter also states that several fundamental flaws make bitcoin a dangerous asset class to force into an exchange traded structure, including shallow trade volume, extreme hoarding, low liquidity, hyper price volatility, a global web of unregulated bucket-shop exchanges, high bankruptcy risk, and oversized exposure to trading in countries where there is no regulatory oversight.[37] This commenter believes that lack of regulation and consumer protection also increase the chance and incentives for market price manipulation and states that approving the ETP before structural protections and controls are firmly in place would put investors at undue risk.[38]

The Exchange, in its comment letter, asserts that bitcoin is resistant to manipulation, arguing that the increasing strength and resilience of the global bitcoin marketplace serve to reduce the likelihood of price manipulation and that arbitrage opportunities across globally diverse marketplaces allow market participants to ensure approximately equivalent pricing worldwide.[39]

The Exchange further asserts, in its comment letter, that the Commodity Futures Trading Commission ("CFTC") has designated bitcoin as a commodity and is "broadly responsible for the integrity" of U.S. bitcoin spot markets.[40] The Exchange acknowledges that the CFTC has not yet brought any enforcement actions based on the anti-manipulation provisions of the Commodity Exchange Act, but notes that the CFTC has issued orders against U.S. and non-U.S. bitcoin exchanges for engaging in other activity prohibited by the Commodity Exchange Act. The Exchange's comment letter states that a regulatory framework for providing oversight and deterring market manipulation therefore currently exists in the U.S.[41]

Finally, the Commission notes a paper that was submitted with respect to a similar proposed rule change,[42] arguing that bitcoin is relatively uncorrelated with other assets, enabling investors to construct more efficient portfolios,[43] and that, as a general matter, the underlying market for bitcoin is inherently resistant to manipulation.[44] The author of the paper posits that the underlying bitcoin market is not susceptible to manipulation because (a) there is no inside information related to earn-

ings, revenue, corporate actions, or new sources of supply; (b) the asset is not subject to the dissemination of false or misleading information; (c) each bitcoin market is an independent entity, so that a demand for liquidity does not necessarily propagate across other exchanges; (d) a substantial over-the-counter ("OTC") market provides additional liquidity and absorption of shocks; (e) there is no market-close pricing event to manipulate; (f) the market is not subject to "spoofing" or other high-frequency-trading tactics; (g) order books on exchanges worldwide are publicly visible and available through APIs (application program interfaces); and (h) it is unlikely that any one person could obtain a dominant market share.[45] The author also asserts that listing the shares on a national securities exchange and a shift from OTC trading to trading on exchanges would make the overall bitcoin market more transparent.[46]

B. Comments Regarding the Gemini Exchange

Several commenters discuss the Gemini Exchange's low trading volumes[47] and one commenter claims that of all the exchanges Gemini has the worst pricing.[48] Another commenter asserts that there is a significant risk that the nominal ETP share price will be manipulated by relatively small trades that manipulate the bitcoin price at that exchange.[49] This commenter notes that, while U.S.-based bitcoin exchanges are subjected to stricter regulations and auditing for the holding of client accounts, the trading itself seems to occur in a regulatory vacuum and seems impossible to audit effectively.[50] This commenter expresses concerns regarding the Gemini Exchange Spot Price,[51] noting that the nominal price of the Shares under the proposal is supposed to be tied to the market price of bitcoins at the Gemini Exchange, which is closely tied to the ETP proponents.[52]

One commenter claims that among U.S.-dollar bitcoin exchanges, Gemini has a 3% share and its liquidity measured by order book depth is significantly lower than several other exchanges. The commenter notes that it is possible that after the launch of an ETP, Gemini's liquidity and volume

---

[36] *See* Williams Letter, *supra* note 19, at 1–2.

[37] *See id.* at 1.

[38] *See id.*, at 2–3.

[39] *See* Bats Letter, *supra* note 19, at 2.

[40] *See id.* at 3.

[41] *See id.*

[42] Craig M. Lewis, "SolidX Bitcoin Trust: A Bitcoin Exchange Traded Product" (Feb. 2017) (analysis commissioned by SolidX Management LLC and submitted to comment file SR-NYSEArca-2016-101) ("Lewis Paper"). A supplemental submission related to this paper was submitted on March 3, 2017. Craig M. Lewis, "Supplemental Submission to SolidX Bitcoin Trust: A Bitcoin Exchange Traded Product" (Mar. 3, 2017) ("Lewis Paper II").

[43] *See* Lewis Paper, *supra* note 42, at 3, 11–15.

[44] *See id.* at 5–8.

[45] *See* Lewis Paper, *supra* note 42, at 5–6, 8–9; Lewis Paper II, *supra* note 42, at 2. The Commission notes that the Lewis Paper made additional assertions directed to the particular structure and pricing mechanism of another proposed bitcoin-based commodity-trust ETP, and the Commission does not address those arguments in this order.

[46] *See* Lewis Paper, *supra* note 42, at 7.

[47] *See, e.g.*, Maher Letter, *supra* note 19; Stolfi Letter, *supra* note 19; Anonymous Letter II, *supra* note 19.

[48] *See* Anonymous Letter II, *supra* note 19.

[49] *See* Stolfi Letter, *supra* note 19.

[50] *See* Stolfi Letter II, *supra* note 19.

[51] *See* Stolfi Letter, *supra* note 19.

[52] *See id.*

will increase, but claims that the nature of bitcoin trading that leads to the concentration of volume and liquidity outside of U.S. borders makes any significant future increase unlikely.[53] This commenter also observes that while Gemini is a regulated U.S. exchange, it does not operate in a vacuum. The commenter claims that the global landscape of many unregulated bitcoin exchanges exerts huge influence on the Gemini Exchange and consequently on the Winklevoss ETP.[54]

One commenter states that exchanges other than Gemini are not subject to the same level of oversight and that, if the ETP were based on some broad measure of weighted prices across different exchanges, then completely unregulated actors might be able to exercise undue influence on the ETP valuation price.[55]

One commenter states that the Gemini Exchange Auction could be an improvement over other bitcoin pricing mechanisms, but asserts that the auction has not improved volume. The commenter claims that the Gemini Exchange has the lowest liquidity of the three exchanges in the United States and is one of the least-liquid of all exchanges that trade bitcoin for U.S. dollars.[56] The commenter observes that the auction data show that traders in the auction are taking advantage of the discounted auction price. The commenter notes that the daily two-sided auction process was designed to maximize price discovery and reduce price volatility that could be the result of momentum pricing, but asks what measures have been put in place to address traders who take advantage of the discounted auction price. The commenter also notes that while other financial products sometimes have auctions to determine price, an auction on a stock exchange does not require money to be deposited in advance with the exchange to be in the auction. The commenter notes that, by contrast, the Gemini Exchange requires dollars or bitcoin to be deposited before participation. The commenter believes that this is a problem because the Gemini auction is limited and "warped" and has failed on at least two occasions.[57]

One commenter claims that there are more robust ways to value the Trust's holdings than using the spot price of a single exchange, such as the Gemini Exchange. The commenter notes that bitcoin trades on a number of exchanges around the world and that most of these exchanges can be considered isolated liquidity pools, which are more vulnerable to manipulation or security breach than the broader market.[58] The com-

menter also notes that the Gemini Exchange typically processes less than 10% of the total volume in the bitcoin/U.S. dollar pair and states that an index of the most reliable exchanges should be constructed to value the Trust's holdings. The commenter questions whether using only the Gemini Exchange's spot price could serve to incentivize Authorized Participants and other market participants to direct traffic and flow to Gemini, at the expense of best execution.[59]

Another commenter takes a different view on the merits of single versus multiple price sources. This commenter notes that bitcoin spot prices diverge across exchanges due to various factors and that some exchanges may suffer from lack of oversight and a lack of transparency or fairness. The commenter claims that these facts strengthen the case for an investment product that does not rely on the spot price of less-credible exchanges to value its holdings and instead relies on the spot price on the Gemini Exchange, which is subject to substantive regulation of its exchange activity and custody of assets by the NYSDFS. This commenter also notes that, while leveraged trading on some other exchanges has historically sparked excessive price volatility and instability, Gemini does not offer such products and would be able to serve as a trusted, regulated spot exchange for institutional market participants driving the arbitrage mechanism that ensures efficient pricing between the spot price and the Shares. The commenter claims that the Gemini Exchange has the potential for more-robust price discovery as liquidity is concentrated on that exchange.[60]

One commenter states that there is an inherent trade-off to using one exchange versus an average of several exchanges, some of which may be less scrupulous. The commenter acknowledges that manipulation is a legitimate concern, but notes that it is not uncommon to see a very small number of physical trades determine the base price for a much larger paper market.[61]

Other commenters view the risk of manipulation as more significant. One commenter notes that it would be surprising if illegal and manipulative practices did not occur, since they would be easy to implement, impossible to detect, perfectly legal, and extremely lucrative.[62] This commenter also states that the Gemini Exchange Auction closing volumes have been low and have shown a slight decreasing trend since the inception of the auction. The commenter notes that, with low volumes, it seems possible to manipulate the NAV by entering suitable bids or asks in the Gemini

---

[53] See Maher Letter, *supra* note 19 (noting that the market is very concentrated and is controlled by a small group of exchanges operating in China, three of which represented 96% of all bitcoin trade volume over a six-month period, and noting that the Gemini Exchange had a 0.07% share of bitcoin volume worldwide during that period, with a 3% share of USD-exchange volume).

[54] See id.

[55] See Delehanty Letter, *supra* note 19.

[56] See Anonymous Letter II, *supra* note 19.

[57] See id.

[58] See ARK Letter, *supra* note 19, at 8.

[59] See id. at 8–9.

[60] See Circle Letter, *supra* note 19, at 2.

[61] See Delehanty Letter, *supra* note 19.

[62] See Stolfi Letter II, *supra* note 19.

Exchange Auction.[63] Another commenter agrees that bitcoin traders can manipulate trading on Gemini Exchange because of its low trading volumes and notes that the Trust's documentation states that momentum pricing of bitcoin has resulted, and may continue to result, in speculation regarding future appreciation in the value of bitcoin, making the price of bitcoin more volatile.[64] The commenter states that the value of bitcoin may therefore be more likely to fluctuate due to changing investor confidence in future appreciation in the Gemini Exchange Auction price, which could adversely affect an investment in the Shares.[65] According to another commenter, in this unregulated environment, price manipulation and front-running of large buy or sell orders can happen and well-connected customers can gain preferential treatment in order execution.[66]

The Exchange, in its comment letter, notes that the Gemini Exchange Auction typically already transacts a volume greater than the proposed creation basket size for the Trust, and would likely support the needs of Authorized Participants to engage in basket creation or redemption. The Exchange claims that the global bitcoin marketplace has the potential to provide even more liquidity and to be a source of bitcoin for basket creation and hedging. The Exchange also notes that all intraday order-book and trade information on the Gemini Exchange is publicly available through various electronic formats and is also redistributed by various online aggregators, and that, with the launch of the proposed Trust, the Sponsor must make important pricing data available in real time.[67]

The Exchange acknowledges in its comment letter that less-liquid markets, such as the market for bitcoin, may be more easily manipulated, but claims that these concerns are mitigated with respect to the Shares and the trading on the Gemini Exchange. The Exchange notes that the Gemini Exchange Auction price is based on an extremely similar mechanism to the one leveraged for the Exchange's own Opening and Closing Auctions and allows full and transparent participation from all Gemini Exchange participants in the price discovery process. The Exchange states that the auction process leverages mechanics which have proven over the years to be robust and effective on the Exchange and other national listing exchanges in both liquid and illiquid securities alike. The Exchange notes that, because the time of the Gemini Exchange Auction coincides with the Exchange's Closing Auction, efficient real-time arbitrage between the closing price of the Trust and the Gemini Exchange Auction price will be prevalent and will lead to resilient and effective pricing of both the Trust and the underlying bitcoin asset, leading to convergence between the Trust's closing price and its NAV.[68] The Exchange states that the Gemini Exchange Auction price typically deviates very little from the prevailing price on other bitcoin exchanges, and the Exchange presents statistics to show that this price is consistent with other pricing sources.[69]

C. Comments on the Derivatives Markets for Bitcoin

One commenter claims that the bitcoin markets are not yet efficient and attributes this inefficiency, in part, to the nascent state of the bitcoin derivatives market. This commenter notes that derivatives provide investors more ways to hedge against bitcoin's potential price movements, introduce more volume and liquidity, and generally give the markets more points of information about bitcoin's future prospects, leading to tighter bid/ask spreads. The commenter claims that most derivatives activity within the bitcoin markets is offered by entities outside of the purview of U.S. regulators.[70] This commenter notes that, within the United States, one market offers bitcoin forwards, but no one currently offers regulated bitcoin futures. The commenter states that bitcoin options offered by regulated U.S. entities may come next, but that as of now there are none. The commenter observes that the lack of a robust and regulated derivatives market means that market participants do not have a broad basket of tools at their disposal, making hedging difficult and keeping away many market makers that provide significant liquidity to traditional capital markets. The commenter claims that, while derivative products may be in development, a full suite of investor tools that will drive market efficiency and eliminate price disparities is likely at least a couple of years away.[71] The commenter also notes that without a robust derivatives market for institutional investors to short the underlying asset, or otherwise hedge their positions, there likely would be little counterbalance to the new demand generated by the ETP, and that Authorized Participants could then have trouble sourcing bitcoin and hedging their positions, stalling the creation process.[72] The commenter concludes that it would be premature to launch a bitcoin ETP because bitcoin markets are not liquid enough to support an open-end fund, and because an ecosystem of institutional-grade infrastructure players is not yet available to support such a product.[73]

One commenter disagrees with assertions linking inefficient bitcoin markets to nascent derivatives markets, stating that no evidence has been

---

[63] See id.

[64] See Anonymous Letter II, supra note 19.

[65] See id.

[66] See Williams Letter, supra note 19, at 2.

[67] See Bats Letter, supra note 19, at 9.

[68] See id. at 7–8.

[69] See id. at 8–9.

[70] See ARK Letter, supra note 19, at 5–6.

[71] See id. at 6.

[72] See id. at 13–14.

[73] See id. at 2.

provided regarding the would-be effect of derivatives on the bitcoin market. The commenter claims that the assertion assumes that bitcoin pricing is inefficient, which the commenter claims is not the case. The commenter also claims that the assertion assumes that the lack of a derivatives market causes pricing to be inefficient, instead stating that there is direct evidence that many securities trade successfully and efficiently on U.S. and non-U.S. exchanges despite not having a direct derivatives market.[74] The commenter also disagrees with the claim that, absent a robust derivatives market, there would be little counterbalance to the new demand generated by the ETP, stating that it is impossible to predict the success or failure of the ETP. The commenter notes that Authorized Participants may be able to source bitcoin from China.[75]

Another commenter claims that there are several bitcoin futures markets that have a significant impact on the spot price along with several OTC markets, such as the one recently launched by the Gemini Exchange, that also offer liquidity.[76]

The author of the paper submitted with respect to a similar proposal states that one of the key differences between bitcoin and other commodities is the lack of a liquid and transparent derivatives market and that, although there have been nascent attempts to establish derivatives trading in bitcoin, bitcoin derivatives markets are not at this time sufficiently liquid to be useful to Authorized Participants and market makers who would like to use derivatives to hedge exposures.[77] The author claims that, for physical commodities that are not traded on exchanges, the presence of a liquid derivatives market is a necessary condition, but claims that for digital assets like bitcoin, derivatives markets are not necessary because price discovery occurs on the OTC market and exchanges instead.[78]

III. DISCUSSION AND COMMISSION FINDINGS

A. *Overview*

Under Section 19(b)(2)(C) of the Exchange Act, the Commission must approve the proposed rule change of a self-regulatory organization ("SRO") if the Commission finds that the proposed rule change is consistent with the requirements of the Exchange Act and the applicable rules and regulations thereunder.[79] If it is unable to make such a finding, the Commission must disapprove the proposed rule change.[80] Additionally, under Rule 700(b)(3) of the Commission's Rules of Practice, the "burden to demonstrate that a proposed rule change is consistent with the Exchange Act and the rules and regulations issued thereunder . . . is on the self-regulatory organization that proposed the rule change."[81]

After careful consideration, and for the reasons discussed in greater detail below, the Commission does not believe that the proposed rule change, as modified by Amendments No. 1 and 2, is consistent with the requirements of the Exchange Act and the applicable rules and regulations thereunder.[82] Specifically, the Commission does not find that the proposed rule change is consistent with Section 6(b)(5) of the Exchange Act—which requires that the rules of a national securities exchange be designed, among other things, to prevent fraudulent and manipulative acts and practices and to protect investors and the public interest[83]—because the Commission believes that significant markets for bitcoin are unregulated and that, therefore, the Exchange has not entered into, and would currently be unable to enter into, the type of surveillance-sharing agreement that helps address concerns about the potential for fraudulent or manipulative acts and practices in

---

[74] *See* Anonymous Letter III, *supra* note 19. Several commenters also assert that regulation by the Exchange of activity in the ETP could substitute for a lack of regulation in underlying or derivatives markets. *See, e.g.,* Baird Letter, *supra* note 19; Keeler Letter, *supra* note 19; Marchionne Letter, *supra* note 19; Bang Letter, *supra* note 19.

[75] *See* Anonymous Letter III, *supra* note 19.

[76] *See* Dylan Letter, *supra* note 19, at 1.

[77] *See* Lewis Paper, *supra* note 42, at 8.

[78] *See id.*

[79] 15 U.S.C 78s(b)(2)(C)(i).

[80] 15 U.S.C. 78s(b)(2)(C)(ii).

[81] 17 CFR 201.700(b)(3). The description of a proposed rule change, its purpose and operation, its effect, and a legal analysis of its consistency with applicable requirements must all be sufficiently detailed and specific to support an affirmative Commission finding. *Id.* Any failure of a self-regulatory organization to provide the information elicited by Form 19b-4 may result in the Commission not having a sufficient basis to make an affirmative finding that a proposed rule change is consistent with the Exchange Act and the rules and regulations issued thereunder that are applicable to the self-regulatory organization. *Id.*

[82] In disapproving the proposed rule change, as modified by Amendments No. 1 and 2, the Commission has considered its impact on efficiency, competition, and capital formation. *See* 15 U.S.C. 78c(f); *see also* notes 42–46 & 115–118 and accompanying text. The Commission notes that, according to the Exchange, the Sponsor believes that the Shares will represent a cost-effective and convenient means of gaining investment exposure to bitcoin similar to a direct investment in bitcoin, allowing investors to more effectively implement strategic and tactical asset allocation strategies that use bitcoin, with lower cost than that associated with the direct purchase, storage, and safekeeping of bitcoin. *See* Amendment No. 1, *supra* note 1, 81 FR at 76662; *see also* Lewis Paper, *supra* note 42, at 3, 11–16 (asserting that a bitcoin-based ETP would enable ordinary investors to construct more efficient portfolios). Regarding competition, the Exchange has asserted that approval of the proposed rule change "will enhance competition among market participants, to the benefit of investors and the marketplace." Amendment No. 1, *supra* note 1, 81 FR at 76669. The Commission recognizes that the Exchange asserts these economic benefits, but, for the reasons discussed throughout, the Commission must disapprove the proposed rule change because it is not consistent with the Exchange Act.

[83] 15 U.S.C. 78f(b)(5).

the market for the Shares. Accordingly, the Commission disapproves the proposed rule change.[84]

B. *Analysis*

1. *Commodity-Trust ETPs and Surveillance-Sharing Agreements*

The Exchange proposes to list and trade the Shares under BZX Rule 14.11(e)(4), which governs the listing of Commodity-Based Trust Shares.[85] In this regard, the proposal is similar to many past proposals to list and trade shares of ETPs holding precious metals,[86] assets that individuals could otherwise obtain directly (for example, in the form of bullion coins), but at the cost of having to secure those holdings.[87] The Commission analyzes this proposal under the standards it has applied to previous commodity-trust ETPs.

A key consideration for the Commission in determining whether to approve or disapprove a proposal to list and trade shares of a new commodity-trust ETP is the susceptibility of the shares or the underlying asset to manipulation. This consideration flows directly from the requirement in Section 6(b)(5) of the Exchange Act that a national securities exchange's rules must be designed "to prevent fraudulent and manipulative acts and practices" and "to protect investors and the public interest."[88]

Since at least 1990, the Commission has expressed the view that the ability of a national securities exchange to enter into surveillance-sharing agreements "furthers the protection of investors and the public interest because it will enable the [e]xchange to conduct prompt investigations into possible trading violations and other regulatory improprieties."[89] The Commission has

also long held that surveillance-sharing agreements are important in the context of exchange listing of derivative security products, such as equity options. In 1994, the Commission stated:

As a general matter, the Commission believes that the existence of a surveillance sharing agreement that effectively permits the sharing of information between an exchange proposing to list an equity option and the exchange trading the stock underlying the equity option is necessary to detect and deter market manipulation and other trading abuses. In particular, the Commission notes that surveillance sharing agreements provide an important deterrent to manipulation because they facilitate the availability of information needed to fully investigate a potential manipulation if it were to occur. These agreements are especially important in the context of derivative products based on foreign securities because they facilitate the collection of necessary regulatory, surveillance and other information from foreign jurisdictions.[90]

With respect to ETPs, when approving in 1995 the listing and trading of one of the first commodity-linked ETPs—a commodity-linked exchange-traded note—on a national securities exchange, the Commission continued to emphasize the importance of surveillance-sharing agreements, noting that the listing exchange had entered into surveillance-sharing agreements with each of the futures markets on which pricing of the ETP would be based and stating that "[t]hese agreements should help to ensure the availability of information necessary to detect and deter potential manipulations and other trading abuses, thereby making [the commodity-linked notes] less readily susceptible to manipulation.[91]

---

[84] The Commission's disposition of the Exchange's proposed rule change is independent of, and serves a fundamentally different purpose than, any Commission actions with respect to the Securities Act of 1933 registration statement of the Trust.

[85] The Commission notes that in settled actions the CFTC has designated bitcoin as a commodity and has asserted jurisdiction over the trading of at least certain derivatives on bitcoin, as well as certain leveraged or margined retail transactions in bitcoin. *See In re Coinflip, Inc., d/b/a Derivabit, and Francisco Riordan*, CFTC Docket No. 15-29, 2015 WL 5535736 (CFTC Sept. 17, 2015) (Order Instituting Proceedings Pursuant to Sections 6(c) and 6(d) of the Commodity Exchange Act, Making Findings and Imposing Remedial Sanctions ("Coinflip Settlement Order")), available at *http://www.cftc.gov/idc/groups/public/@lrenforcementactions/documents/legalpleading/enfcoinfliprorder09172015.pdf*.

[86] *See, e.g.,* streetTRACKS Gold Shares, Exchange Act Release No. 50603 (Oct. 28, 2004), 69 FR 64614 (Nov. 5, 2004) (SR-NYSE-2004-22) (order approving the listing and trading of shares of commodity-trust ETP holding physical gold bullion).

[87] *See* Amendment No. 1, *supra* note 1, 81 FR at 76662 ("The Sponsor believes that investors will be able to more effectively implement strategic and tactical asset allocation strategies that use bitcoin by using the Shares instead of directly purchasing and holding bitcoin, and for many investors, transaction costs related to the Shares will be lower than those associated with the direct purchase, storage and safekeeping of bitcoin.").

[88] 15 U.S.C. 19f(b)(5).

[89] *See* Exchange Act Release No. 27877 (Apr. 4, 1990), 55 FR 13344 (Apr. 10, 1990) (SR-NYSE-90-14).

[90] Exchange Act Release No. 33555 (Jan. 31, 1994), 59 FR 5619 (Feb. 7, 1994) (SR-Amex-93-28) (order approving listing of options on American Depositary Receipts). The Commission further stated that, "[b]ecause of the additional leverage provided by an option on an ADR, the Commission generally believes that having a comprehensive surveillance sharing agreement in place, between the exchange where the ADR option trades and the exchange where the foreign security underlying the ADR primarily trades, will ensure the integrity of the marketplace. The Commission further believes that the ability to obtain relevant surveillance information, including, among other things, the identity of the ultimate purchasers and sellers of securities, is an essential and necessary component of a comprehensive surveillance sharing agreement." Id., 59 FR at 5621.

[91] *See* Exchange Act Release No. 35518 (Mar. 21, 1995), 60 FR 15804 (Mar. 27, 1995) (SR-Amex-94-30). In that matter, the Commission noted that the listing exchange had comprehensive surveillance-sharing agreements with all of the exchanges upon which the futures contracts overlying the notes traded and was able to obtain market surveillance information, including customer identity information, for transactions occurring on NYMEX and other futures exchanges. *See id.*, 60 FR at 15806 n.21. *See also* Exchange Act Release No. 36885 (Feb. 26, 1996), 61 FR 8315, n.17 (Mar. 4, 1996) (SR-Amex-95-50) (approving the exchange listing and trading of

In 1998, in adopting Exchange Act Rule 19b-4(e)[92] to permit the generic listing and trading of certain new derivatives securities products—including ETPs—the Commission again emphasized the importance of the listing exchange's ability to obtain from underlying markets, through surveillance-sharing agreements (called information-sharing agreements in the release), the information necessary to detect and deter manipulative activity. Specifically, in adopting rules governing the generic listing of new derivatives securities products, the Commission stated that the Rule 19b-4(e) procedures would "enable the Commission to continue to effectively protect investors and promote the public interest" and stated that:

It is essential that the SRO have the ability to obtain the information necessary to detect and deter market manipulation, illegal trading and other abuses involving the new derivative securities product. Specifically, there should be a comprehensive ISA [information-sharing agreement] that covers trading in the new derivative securities product and its underlying securities in place between the SRO listing or trading a derivative product and the markets trading the securities underlying the new derivative securities product. Such agreements provide a necessary deterrent to manipulation because they facilitate the availability of information needed to fully investigate a manipulation if it were to occur.[93]

The Commission, in the NDSP Adopting Release, also stressed the importance of these surveillance-sharing agreements comprehensively covering trading in the underlying assets. In the case of a product overlying domestic securities, the Commission said that the exchange listing a derivative securities product should ensure that it was either a common member of the Intermarket Surveillance Group with, or had entered into an information-sharing agreement with, each market trading each underlying security.[94] Further, the Commission stated that:

For a new derivative securities product overlying an instrument with component securities from several countries, the Commission recognizes that it may not be practical in all instances to secure comprehensive ISAs with all of the relevant foreign markets. Foreign countries' securities or ADRs that are not subject to a comprehensive ISA should not represent a significant percentage of the weight of such an underlying instrument."[95]

Consistent with these statements, for the commodity-trust ETPs approved to date for listing and trading, there have been in every case well-established, significant, regulated markets for trading futures on the underlying commodity—gold, silver, platinum, palladium, and copper—and the ETP listing exchange has entered into surveillance-sharing agreements with, or held Intermarket Surveillance Group membership in common with, those markets.[96]

(Footnote Continued)

Commodity Indexed Securities, and noting (a) that through the comprehensive surveillance-sharing agreements, the listing exchange was able to obtain market surveillance information, including customer identity information, for transactions occurring on NYMEX and COMEX and that, through the Intermarket Surveillance Group information-sharing agreement, the listing exchange was able to obtain, upon request, surveillance information with respect to trades effected on the London Metal Exchange, including client identity information and (b) that, if a different market were utilized for purposes of calculating the value of a designated futures contract, the listing exchange had represented that it would ensure that it entered into a surveillance-sharing agreement with respect to the new relevant market). The Commission has made similar statements about surveillance-sharing agreements with respect to the listing and trading of stock-index, currency, and currency-index warrants. See, e.g., Exchange Act Release No. 36166 (Aug. 29, 1995), 60 FR 46660 (Sept. 7, 1995) (SR-PSE-94-28) (approving a proposal to adopt uniform listing and trading guidelines for stock-index, currency, and currency-index warrants).Specifically, the Commission noted that "a surveillance sharing agreement should provide the parties with the ability to obtain information necessary to detect and deter market manipulation and other trading abuses" and stated that the Commission "generally requires that a surveillance sharing agreement require that the parties to the agreement provide each other, upon request, information about market trading activity, clearing activity, and the identity of the ultimate purchasers for securities." Id., 60 FR at 46665 n.35. In addition, the Commission stated that "[t]he ability to obtain relevant surveillance information, including, among other things, the identity of the ultimate purchasers and sellers of securities, is an essential and necessary component

of a comprehensive surveillance sharing agreement." Id., 60 FR at 46665 n.36.

[92] 17 CFR 240.19b-4(e).

[93] Amendment to Rule Filing Requirements for Self-Regulatory Organizations Regarding New Derivative Securities Products, Exchange Act Release No. 40761 (Dec. 8, 1998), 63 FR 70952, 70959 (Dec. 22, 1998) (File no. S7-13-98) ("NDSP Adopting Release").

[94] See id., 63 FR at 70959. The Commission further noted that "if a new SRO trades component securities underlying a new derivative securities product and is not a member of the ISG, the SRO seeking to list and trade such new derivative securities product pursuant to Rule 19b-4(e) should enter into a comprehensive ISA with the non-ISG SRO. Conversely, if a new SRO seeks to list and trade a new derivative securities product pursuant to Rule 19b-4(e) and is not a member of the ISG, such SRO should enter into a comprehensive ISA with each SRO that trades securities underlying the new derivative securities product." See id., 63 FR at 70959, n.99.

[95] See id., 63 FR at 70959.

[96] See streetTRACKS Gold Shares, Exchange Act Release No. 50603 (Oct. 28, 2004), 69 FR 64614 (Nov. 5, 2004) (SR-NYSE-2004-22) (approval order notes the New York Stock Exchange's representation that "the most significant gold futures exchanges are the COMEX division of the NYMEX and the Tokyo Commodity Exchange"); iShares COMEX Gold Trust, Exchange Act Release No. 51058 (Jan. 19, 2005), 70 FR 3749 (Jan. 26, 2005) (SR-Amex-2004-38) (approval order notes the American Stock Exchange's representation that "the most significant gold futures exchanges are the COMEX division of the NYMEX and the Tokyo Commodity Exchange"); iShares Silver Trust, Exchange Act Release No. 53521 (Mar. 20, 2006), 71 FR 14967 (Mar. 24, 2006) (SR-Amex-2005-72) (approval

¶1030

The Exchange represents that its existing surveillance measures, which focus on trading in the Shares, are sufficient to support the proposed rule change. Specifically, the Exchange represents that its surveillance procedures are adequate to properly monitor the trading of the Shares on the Exchange during all trading sessions and to deter and detect violations of Exchange rules and the applicable federal securities laws.[97] The Exchange further represents that trading of the Shares through the Exchange will be subject to the Exchange's surveillance procedures for derivative products, including Commodity-Based Trust Shares, and that the Exchange may obtain information regarding trading in the Shares through the Intermarket Surveillance Group, from other

members or affiliates of that group, or from exchanges with which the Exchange has a surveillance-sharing agreement.[98] In addition, the Exchange notes that it has entered into a comprehensive surveillance-sharing agreement with the Gemini Exchange and represents that it may obtain information about bitcoin transactions, trades, and market data from the Gemini Exchange (and from any bitcoin exchanges with which the Exchange enters into a surveillance-sharing agreement in the future), as well as certain additional information that is publicly available through the Blockchain. Moreover, several commenters assert that regulation by the Exchange of activity in the ETP could substitute for a lack of regulation in underlying or derivatives markets.[99]

(Footnote Continued)

order notes the American Stock Exchange's representation that "the most significant silver futures exchanges are the COMEX and the Tokyo Commodity Exchange"); ETFS Gold Trust, Exchange Act Release No. 59895 (May 8, 2009), 74 FR 22993 (May 15, 2009) (SR-NYSEArca-2009-40) (accelerated approval order notes NYSE Arca's representation that the COMEX is one of the "major world gold markets"); ETFS Silver Trust, Exchange Act Release No. 59781 (Apr. 17, 2009), 74 FR 18771 (Apr. 24, 2009) (SR-NYSEArca-2009-28) (accelerated approval order notes NYSE Arca's representation that "the most significant silver futures exchanges are the COMEX . . . and the Tokyo Commodity Exchange"); ETFS Palladium Trust, Exchange Act Release No. 60971 (Nov. 9, 2009), 74 FR 59283 (Nov. 17, 2009) (SR-NYSEArca-2009-94) (notice of proposed rule change includes NYSE Arca's representation that "the most significant palladium futures exchanges are the NYMEX and the Tokyo Commodity Exchange" and that "NYMEX is the largest exchange in the world for trading precious metals futures and options"); ETFS Platinum Trust, Exchange Act Release No. 60970 (Nov. 9, 2006), 74 FR 59319 (Nov. 17, 2009) (SR-NYSEArca-2009-95) (notice of proposed rule change includes NYSE Arca's representation that "the most significant palladium futures exchanges are the NYMEX and the Tokyo Commodity Exchange" and that "NYMEX is the largest exchange in the world for trading precious metals futures and options"); Sprott Physical Gold Trust, Exchange Act Release No. 61236 (Dec. 23, 2009), 75 FR 170 (Jan. 4, 2010) (SR-NYSEArca-2009-113) (notice of proposed rule change includes NYSE Arca's representation that the COMEX is one of the "major world gold markets"); Sprott Physical Silver Trust, Exchange Act Release No. 63043 (Oct. 5, 2010), 75 FR 62615 (Oct. 12, 2010) (SR-NYSEArca-2010-84) (accelerated approval order notes NYSE Arca's representation that the COMEX is one of the "major world silver markets"); ETFS Precious Metals Basket Trust, Exchange Act Release No. 62402 (Jun. 29, 2010), 75 FR 39292 (July 8, 2010) (SR-NYSEArca-2010-56) (notice of proposed rule change includes NYSE Arca's representation that "the most significant gold, silver, platinum and palladium futures exchanges are the COMEX and the TOCOM"); ETFS White Metals Basket Trust, Exchange Act Release No. 62620 (July 30, 2010), 75 FR 47655 (Aug. 6, 2010) (SR-NYSEArca-2010-71) (notice of proposed rule change includes NYSE Arca's representation that "the most significant silver, platinum and palladium futures exchanges are the COMEX and the TOCOM"); ETFS Asian Gold Trust, Exchange Act Release No. 63267 (Nov. 8, 2010), 75 FR 69494 (Nov. 12, 2010) (SR-NYSEArca-2010-95) (notice of proposed rule change includes NYSE Arca's representation that "the most significant gold futures exchanges are the COMEX and the Tokyo Commodity Exchange" and that "COMEX is the largest exchange in the world for trading precious metals futures and options"); Sprott Physical Platinum and Palladium Trust, Exchange Act

Release No. 68101 (Oct. 24, 2012), 77 FR 65732 (Oct. 30, 2012) (SR-NYSEArca-2012-111) (accelerated approval order notes NYSE Arca's representation that "[f]utures on platinum and palladium are traded on two major exchanges: The New York Mercantile Exchange . . . and Tokyo Commodities Exchange"); APMEX Physical—1 oz. Gold Redeemable Trust, Exchange Act Release No. 66627 (Mar. 20, 2012), 77 FR 17539 (Mar. 26, 2012) (SR-NYSEArca-2012-18) (notice of proposed rule change cross-references the proposed rule change to list and trade shares of the ETFS Gold Trust, in which NYSE Arca represented that the COMEX is one of the "major world gold markets"); JPM XF Physical Copper Trust, Exchange Act Release No. 68440 (Dec. 14, 2012), 77 FR 75468 (Dec. 20, 2012) (SR-NYSEArca-2012-28) (approval order notes NYSE Arca's representation that "[a] majority of copper derivatives trading occurs on three exchanges: The LME, the Commodity Exchange, Inc. . . . and the Shanghai Futures Exchange"); iShares Copper Trust, Exchange Act Release No. 68973 (Feb. 22, 2013), 78 FR 13726 (Feb. 28, 2013) (SR-NYSEArca-2012-66) (approval order notes NYSE Arca's representation that "the LME is the longest standing exchange trading copper futures, with the greatest number of open copper futures and options contracts"); First Trust Gold Trust, Exchange Act Release No. 69847 (Jun. 25, 2013), 78 FR 39399 (July 1, 2013) (SR-NYSEArca-2013-61) (notice of proposed rule change cross-references the proposed rule change to list and trade shares of the ETFS Gold Trust, in which NYSE Arca represented that the COMEX is one of the "major world gold markets"); Merk Gold Trust, Exchange Act Release No. 71038 (Dec. 11, 2013), 78 FR 76367 (Dec. 17, 2013) (SR-NYSEArca-2013-137) (notice of proposed rule change cross-references the proposed rule change to list and trade shares of the ETFS Gold Trust, in which NYSE Arca represented that the COMEX is one of the "major world gold markets"); Long Dollar Gold Trust, Exchange Act Release No. 79518 (Dec. 9, 2016), 81 FR 90876 (Dec. 15, 2016) (SR-NYSEArca-2016-84) (accelerated approval order notes NYSE Arca's representation that "[t]he most significant gold futures exchange is COMEX, part of the CME Group, Inc., which began to offer trading in gold futures contracts in 1974").

[97] *See* Amendment No. 1, *supra* note 1, 81 FR at 76668.

[98] *See id.*

[99] *See, e.g.*, Baird Letter, *supra* note 19 (stating that, if the U.S. were to approve an ETP and bring regulatory standards and oversight to cryptocurrencies, investors would not see major problems as they did with the Bitfinex and Mt. Gox hacks and that, if the ETP were not approved, investors would be forced to use those less-than-ideal exchanges); Keeler Letter, *supra* note 19 (stating that the alternative to a regulated ETP is investors having to purchase bitcoin at unregulated exchanges lacking SEC oversight); Bang Letter, *supra* note 19 (stating that disapproval of the ETP would create a

The Commission views the Exchange's proposed surveillance procedures regarding the Shares themselves as necessary, but not sufficient in light of the discussion below noting that the Exchange has not entered into, and would currently be unable to enter into, surveillance-sharing agreements with significant, regulated markets for trading either bitcoin itself or derivatives on bitcoin.[100] Moreover, the Commission does not accept the premise, suggested by some commenters, that regulation of trading in the Shares is a sufficient and acceptable substitute for regulation in the spot or derivatives markets related to the underlying asset.[101] Absent the ability to detect and deter manipulation of the Shares—through surveillance sharing with significant, regulated markets related to the underlying asset—the Commission does not believe that a national securities exchange can meet its Exchange Act obligations when listing shares of a commodity-trust ETP.

The Commission continues to believe that surveillance-sharing agreements between the exchange listing shares of a commodity-trust ETP and significant, regulated markets related to the underlying asset provide a "necessary deterrent to manipulation."[102] To the extent there is some question as to the degree to which bitcoin is subject to manipulation, moreover, surveillance-sharing agreements with significant, regulated markets relating to bitcoin would help answer that question and address instances of such manipulation. Therefore, the Commission's analysis of the Exchange's proposal examines whether regulated markets of significant size exist—in either bitcoin or derivatives on bitcoin—with which the Ex-

change has, or could enter into, a surveillance-sharing agreement.

2. The Worldwide Spot Market for Bitcoin

With respect to spot bitcoin trading outside the United States, the information in the Exchange's proposal and from commenters demonstrates that the bulk of bitcoin trading occurs in non-U.S. markets where there is little to no regulation governing trading,[103] and thus no meaningful governmental market oversight designed to detect and deter fraudulent and manipulative activity.[104] The Exchange notes in its comment letter that only a minority of the global spot bitcoin exchanges are subject to any regulatory regime.[105] Additionally, the Commission notes that no bitcoin spot market is currently a member of the Intermarket Surveillance Group.[106]

With respect to trading in the United States, the Exchange asserts that the CFTC is broadly responsible for the integrity of bitcoin spot markets and that, therefore, a regulatory framework for providing oversight and deterring market manipulation currently exists in the United States.[107] The Exchange's conclusion about the state of regulation in the U.S. market for bitcoin, however, is not supported by the facts the Exchange presents.

Although the CFTC can bring enforcement actions against manipulative conduct in spot markets for a commodity, spot markets are not required to register with the CFTC, unless they offer leveraged, margined, or financed trading to retail customers.[108] In all other cases, including the Gemini Exchange, the CFTC does not set standards for, approve the rules of, examine, or otherwise regulate bitcoin spot markets.[109] The

---

(Footnote Continued)

more risky environment for investors, who will not have the option of investing through regulated exchanges).

[100] See infra Section III.B.

[101] See, e.g., Anderson Letter, supra note 19; Baird Letter, supra note 19; Keeler Letter, supra note 19; Marchionne Letter, supra note 19; Bang Letter, supra note 19.

[102] NDSP Adopting Release, supra note 93, 63 FR at 70959.

[103] See Bats Letter, supra note 19, at 2–3 (noting that only a minority of global bitcoin exchanges are fully regulated for their fiduciary and custodial activities); Stolfi Letter II, supra note 19 (remarking that, since 2013, the price of bitcoin has been defined mostly by the major Chinese exchanges, whose volumes dwarf those of exchanges outside China, which are not regulated or audited, and which are suspected of unethical practices like front-running, wash trades, and trading with insufficient funds); ARK Letter, supra note 19, at 11–12 (noting that over 90% of bitcoin spot trading volume occurs in the BTC/CNY pair, where there is little regulatory oversight and transparency); Maher Letter, supra note 19 (explaining that the Chinese bitcoin exchanges fall under little oversight by any regulatory entities); Williams Letter, supra note 19, at 1 (noting that, among several fundamental flaws that make bitcoin a dangerous asset class to force into an ETP structure, specific risks include the "global web of unregulated bucket shop exchanges" and the "oversized exposure to trading in countries where there is no regulatory oversight, such as China"); Lee Letter, supra note 19 (noting that there is cur-

rently no regulation or oversight for the worldwide market of exchanges).

[104] See supra notes 31–38 and accompanying text. The Commission also notes that, while the Exchange represents that it can obtain information about bitcoin trading made publicly available through the Blockchain, see Amendment No. 1, supra note 1, 81 FR at 76668, this information identifies parties to a transaction only by a pseudonymous public-key address.

[105] See Bats Letter, supra note 19, at 2–3 (noting that only a minority of global bitcoin exchanges are fully regulated for their fiduciary and custodial activities, and naming Gemini Trust Company LLC and itBit Trust Company LLC, as the only two exchange operators that are subject to substantive regulation, each overseen by the NYSDFS).

[106] See http://www.isgportal.com (listing the current members and affiliate members of the Intermarket Surveillance Group).

[107] See Bats Letter, supra note 19, at 3.

[108] Commodity Exchange Act Section 2(c)(2)(D), 7 U.S.C. 2(c)(2)(D). See also Commodity Exchange Act Section 2(c)(2)(A), 7 U.S.C. 2(c)(2)(A) (defining CFTC jurisdiction to specifically cover contracts of sale of a commodity for future delivery (or options on such contracts), or an option on a commodity (other than foreign currency or a security or a group or index of securities), that is executed or traded on an organized exchange).

[109] The Gemini Exchange is not registered with the CFTC.

Exchange notes in its comment letter that the CFTC has brought several bitcoin-related enforcement actions against bitcoin-related entities,[110] but the actions cited by the Exchange do not demonstrate that a regulatory framework for providing oversight and deterring market manipulation currently exists for the bitcoin spot market. Rather, the cited enforcement actions have involved either (a) the failure of an entity to register with the CFTC before trading derivatives on bitcoin or offering leveraged, margined, or financed bitcoin trading to retail customers,[111] or (b) the facilitation of wash trades in bitcoin swaps by a swap execution facility registered with the CFTC.[112]

Some commenters believe that bitcoin markets can be manipulated.[113] The Exchange agrees, in its comment letter, that "less liquid markets, such as the market for bitcoin, may be more manipulable," but asserts that the strength and resilience of the global bitcoin market serve to reduce the likelihood of manipulation.[114] Additionally, the author of the paper submitted with respect to a similar proposal for a bitcoin-based ETP asserts that, for several reasons, the underlying market for bitcoin is not susceptible to manipulation.[115]

The Commission does not believe that the record supports a finding that the unique properties of bitcoin and the underlying bitcoin market are so different from the properties of other commodities and commodity futures markets that they justify a significant departure from the standards applied to previous commodity-trust ETPs. While the Exchange and the author of the paper submit that arbitrage across bitcoin markets will help to keep worldwide bitcoin prices aligned with one another, hindering manipulation,[116] neither provides data regarding how long pricing disparities may persist before they are arbitraged away, and one commenter specifically noted that large arbitrage opportunities persist in bitcoin markets.[117]

The Commission also believes that the paper's discussion of the possible sources of manipulation is incomplete and does not form a basis to find that bitcoin cannot be manipulated—or to find, by implication, that no surveillance-sharing agreement is necessary between an exchange listing shares of a bitcoin-based ETP and significant markets trading bitcoin or bitcoin derivatives. For example, while there is no inside information related to the earnings or revenue of bitcoin, there may be material non-public information related to the actions of regulators with respect to bitcoin; regarding order flow, such as plans of market participants to significantly increase or decrease their holdings in bitcoin; regarding new sources of demand, such as new ETPs that would hold bitcoin; or regarding the decision of a bitcoin-based ETP with respect to how it would respond to a "fork" in the blockchain, which would create two different, non-interchangeable types of bitcoin.[118]

Moreover, the manipulation of asset prices, as a general matter, can occur simply through trading activity that creates a false impression of supply or demand, whether in the context of a closing auction or in the course of continuous trading, and does not require formal linkages among markets (such as consolidated quotations or routing requirements) or the complex quoting behavior associated with high-frequency trading.[119] Finally, while it may or may not be possible to acquire a dominant position in the bitcoin market as a whole, it might be quite possible to acquire a position large enough to temporarily move the price on a single, less-liquid bitcoin trading market, even if OTC markets exist that are capable of absorbing liquidity shocks.

3. The Gemini Exchange

The Exchange represents that it has entered into a comprehensive surveillance-sharing agreement with the Gemini Exchange with respect to trading of the bitcoin asset underlying the Trust and that the Gemini Exchange is supervised by

---

[110] Bats Letter, *supra* note 19, at 3.

[111] See *Coinflip Settlement Order, supra* note 85; *In re BFXNA Inc.*, d/b/a Bitfinex, CFTC Docket No. 16-19 (CFTC June 2, 2016) (Order Instituting Proceedings Pursuant to Sections 6(c) and 6(d) of the Commodity Exchange Act, Making Findings and Imposing Remedial Sanctions ("BFXNA Settlement Order")), *available at http://www.cftc.gov/idc/groups/public/@lrenforcementactions/documents/legalpleading/enfbfxnaorder060216.pdf.*

[112] See *In re TeraExchange LLC*, CFTC Docket No. 15-33, 2015 WL 5658082 (CFTC Sept. 24, 2015) (Order Instituting Proceedings Pursuant to Sections 6(c) and 6(d) of the Commodity Exchange Act, Making Findings and Imposing Remedial Sanctions ("TeraExchange Settlement Order")), *available at http://www.cftc.gov/idc/groups/public/@lrenforcementactions/documents/legalpleading/enfteraexchangeorder92415.pdf.*

[113] See *supra* notes 34–38 and accompanying text.

[114] See *supra* notes 39–41 and accompanying text.

[115] See *Lewis Paper, supra* note 42; *see also supra* notes 42–46 and accompanying text.

[116] See *Bats Letter, supra* note 19, at 2; *Lewis Paper, supra* note 42, at 6–7.

[117] See *ARK Letter, supra* note 19, at 5.

[118] For example, as described in the Trust's Registration Statement, *supra* note 9, in the event the Bitcoin Network undergoes a "hard fork" into two blockchains, the Custodian and the Sponsor will determine which of the resulting blockchains to use as the basis for the assets of the Trust and, under certain circumstances, will have discretion to determine which blockchain is "most likely to be supported by a majority of users or miners." *Id.* at 113. *See also* Lee Letter, *supra* note 19; Johnson Letter, *supra* note 19; Schulte Letter, *supra* note 19; Anonymous Letter IV, *supra* note 19; Anonymous Letter V, *supra* note 19. The decision of the Custodian and Sponsor to support one resulting blockchain over another could have a material effect on the relative value of the bitcoins in each of the blockchains.

[119] The Commission notes that, even if transparent order books and transaction reports on bitcoin markets would by definition include the quoting or trading activity of a person attempting to manipulate the market, along with the activity of all other market participants, such information could not, by itself, definitively establish in real time which activity represented bona fide trading interest and which represented an intent to manipulate.

the NYSDFS.[120] Additionally, the Exchange states in its comment letter that it "agrees that less liquid markets, such as the market for bitcoin, may be more manipulable, but believes that . . . such concerns are mitigated as it relates to the Shares of the Trust and trading activity on the Gemini Exchange."[121] As explained below, however, the Commission does not believe this surveillance-sharing agreement to be sufficient, because the Gemini Exchange conducts only a small fraction of the worldwide trading in bitcoin, and because the Gemini Exchange is not a "regulated market" comparable to a national securities exchange or to the futures exchanges that are associated with the underlying assets of the commodity-trust ETPs approved to date.[122]

Commenters disagree on whether the Gemini Exchange conducts a significant volume of trading in bitcoin and whether trading on the Gemini Exchange is susceptible to manipulation. The Exchange promotes the Gemini Exchange as one of the top three bitcoin exchanges in the United States,[123] and some commenters believe that the Gemini Exchange conducts sufficient volume to support the Winklevoss Bitcoin Trust.[124] Other commenters, however, question these assertions, some noting that the vast majority of bitcoin trading, including trading denominated in U.S. dollars

("USD") occurs on unregulated exchanges outside the United States.[125]

The information currently available demonstrates that the Gemini Exchange does not, at this time, trade a significant volume of bitcoin relative to the overall market for the asset.[126]

Instead, bitcoin trading on the Gemini Exchange represents a small percentage of overall bitcoin trading. For example, calculations using statistics from *data.bitcoinity.org*,[127] show that, in the six months preceding February 28, 2017, trading on the Gemini Exchange accounted for just 0.07% of all worldwide bitcoin trading, and 5.16% of the much-smaller bitcoin-USD market worldwide.[128]

Moreover, self-reported statistics from the Gemini Exchange show that volume in the Gemini Exchange Auction is small relative to daily trading in bitcoin and to the number of bitcoin in a creation or redemption basket for the Trust. As of February 28, 2017, the average daily volume in the Gemini Exchange Auction, since its inception on September 21, 2016, has been 1195.72 bitcoins, compared to average daily worldwide volume of approximately 3.4 million bitcoins in the six months preceding February 28, 2017. Also, as of February 28, 2017, the median number of bitcoins

---

[120] *See* Amendment No. 1, *supra* note 1, 81 FR at 76660, 76668.

[121] *See* Bats Letter, *supra* note 19. at 7–8.

[122] *See supra* note 96.

[123] *See* Amendment No. 1, *supra* note 1, 81 FR at 76659; Bats Letter, *supra* note 19, at 7–8. *But see* Anonymous Letter II, *supra* note 19 ("There are only three exchanges in the United States. Gemini has the lowest liquidity of the three and is one of the least liquid exchanges of all exchanges that trade bitcoin for US dollars.").

[124] *See* McMinn Letter, *supra* note 19 (stating that trading volume on the Gemini Exchange is sufficient, and that manipulation of these Shares, while possible, would equally be possible for other exchange-traded funds); Delehanty Letter (concluding that trading volume in the recent Gemini bitcoin daily auctions seemed "to be of reasonable size"); *see also* Circle Letter, *supra* note 19, at 2 (noting that the Gemini Exchange would also have the potential for more robust price discovery as liquidity is concentrated on the exchange).

[125] *See* ARK Letter, *supra* note 19, at 7–8 (noting that Gemini typically processes less than 10% of the total volume in the bitcoin-USD market); Williams Letter, *supra* note 19, at 2 (noting that most daily trading volume is conducted outside the U.S. and that 90% of bitcoin trading volume occurs in China); Stolfi Letter, *supra* note 19 (concluding that the Gemini Exchange "has relatively low liquidity and trade volume" and that "[t]here seems to be a significant risk that the nominal ETF share price will be manipulated, by relatively small trades that manipulate the bitcoin price at that exchange"); Stolfi Letter II, *supra* note 19 (concluding that the auction closing volume on the Gemini Exchange has shown a decreasing trend since its inception and is now under $1 million USD during work days, and considerably less during weekends, and that "[w]ith such low volume, it seems possible to manipulate the NAV value by entering suitable bids or asks in the auction"); Stolfi Letter II, *supra* note 19 (noting that, since 2013, the price of bitcoin has been defined mostly by the major Chinese exchanges, whose volumes dwarf those of exchanges outside China); Maher Letter, *supra* note 19

(characterizing volume on the Gemini Exchange as "sparse"); Anonymous Letter II, *supra* note 19 (asserting that "anyone who trades bitcoin can manipulate trading on the Gemini Exchange because it has no volume," and further stating that Gemini Exchange has the worst pricing and the lowest trade volume in comparison to other exchanges); Anonymous Letter IV, *supra* note 19 (claiming that Gemini has "the lowest trading volume of known exchanges" and that "[t]here is evidence that markets have been manipulated by the exchanges for years").

[126] *See* Williams Letter, *supra* note 19, at 2 (stating that most daily trading volume in bitcoin is conducted on poorly capitalized, unregulated bucket shop exchanges located outside of the U.S., such as in China, Singapore, Hong Kong, and Bulgaria, and asserting that these non-U.S. exchanges and their practices significantly influence the price discovery process); ARK Letter, *supra* note 19, at 11–12 (stating that the average daily trading volume for bitcoin over the last year has been around $1 billion and that over 90% of that volume occurs in the bitcoin-Chinese Yuan pair where there is little regulatory oversight and transparency); Maher Letter, *supra* note 19 (stating that BTC-E is one of the earliest bitcoin exchanges with a reputation for the least transparency and is often associated with laundering of stolen or illicitly-obtained bitcoin, but that it had shown three times the market share of volume as Gemini in the last six months); Stolfi Letter II, supra note 19 (noting that, since 2013, the price of bitcoin has been defined mostly by the major Chinese exchanges, whose volumes dwarf those of exchanges outside China).

[127] Because bitcoin trading activity is dispersed across markets, many of which are unregulated, and OTC transactions worldwide, there is no centralized, regulatory data source for bitcoin trading statistics. Accordingly, the Commission's analysis of worldwide trading activity must use unofficial sources that purport to gather and disseminate trading data.

[128] One commenter provides similar statistics comparing worldwide bitcoin trading volume to the Gemini Exchange bitcoin trading volume. *See supra* note 53 and accompanying text.

traded in the Gemini Exchange Auction on a business day (when a creation or redemption request might be submitted to the Trust) has been just 1,061.99 bitcoins,[129] barely larger than the 1,000 bitcoins in a creation or redemption basket.[130]

Additionally, 88.2% of the business-day auctions were for fewer than 2,000 bitcoins—equivalent to two creation or redemption baskets—suggesting that creation or redemption activity on the Gemini Exchange might dwarf other trading.

Regarding the regulation of the Gemini Exchange, the Exchange notes in its proposed rule change that the Gemini Trust Company is supervised by the NYSDFS, asserting that the Gemini Trust Company is one of only two bitcoin exchange operators in the world subject to substantive regulation. The Commission, however, does not believe that the record supports a finding that the Gemini Exchange is a "regulated market" comparable to a national securities exchange or to the futures exchanges that are associated with the underlying assets of the commodity-trust ETPs approved to date.

The Exchange represents that the Gemini Trust Company is subject to capitalization, anti-money-laundering compliance, consumer protection, and cybersecurity requirements set forth by the NYSDFS.[131] Commission regulation of the securities markets includes similar elements, but national securities exchanges are also, among other things, required to have rules that are "designed to prevent fraudulent and manipulative acts and practices, to promote just and equitable principles of trade, to foster cooperation and coordination with persons engaged in regulating, clearing, settling, processing information with respect to, and facilitating transactions in securities, to remove impediments to and perfect the mechanism of a free and open market and a national market system, and, in general, to protect investors and the public interest."[132] Moreover, national securities exchanges are subject to Commission oversight of, among other things, their governance, membership qualifications, trading rules, disciplinary procedures, recordkeeping, and fees.[133] Designated Contract Markets (commonly called "futures markets") registered with and regulated by

the CFTC must comply with, among other things, a similarly comprehensive range of regulatory principles and must file rule changes with the CFTC.[134]

4. The Market for Derivatives on Bitcoin

As noted above,[135] the commodity-trust ETPs previously approved by the Commission for listing and trading have had—in lieu of significant, regulated spot markets—significant, well-established, and regulated futures markets that were associated with the underlying commodity and with which the listing exchange had entered into a surveillance-sharing agreement.

One commenter states that there are several bitcoin futures markets that have a significant impact on the spot price, but this commenter did not identify any regulated futures market.[136] Another commenter describes the state of derivatives markets for bitcoin as "nascent."[137]

The Exchange also describes the current derivative markets for bitcoin as "[n]ascent."[138] The Exchange notes that certain types of options, futures contracts for differences, and other derivative instruments are available in certain jurisdictions, but that many of these are not available in the United States and that they generally are not regulated "to the degree that U.S. investors expect derivatives instruments to be regulated."[139] The Exchange notes that the CFTC has approved the registration of TeraExchange LLC as a swap execution facility ("SEF") and that, on October 9, 2014, TeraExchange announced that it had hosted the first executed bitcoin swap traded on a CFTC-regulated platform.[140] Further, the Exchange notes that the CFTC has temporarily registered another SEF that would trade swaps on bitcoin.[141]

The Commission acknowledges that TeraExchange, a market for swaps on bitcoin, has registered with the CFTC, but the Exchange's description of trading activity on that market fails to note that the very activity it cites was the subject of an enforcement action by the CFTC. The CFTC found that TeraExchange had improperly arranged for participants to make prearranged,

---

[129] Although the Gemini Exchange conducts an auction on each calendar day, in order to better represent auction volume for days on which creations or redemptions might occur in the Shares, the calculation of average and median auction volume excludes auctions that occurred on weekends and days on which the U.S. equities markets are closed.

[130] See Amendment No. 2, supra note 1 (setting size of creation unit at 100,000 shares, with the value of a share at 0.01 BTC, making content of a creation unit 1,000 BTC).

[131] See Amendment No. 1, supra note 1, 81 FR at 76658–59.

[132] 15 U.S.C. 78f(b)(5).

[133] Section 6 of the Exchange Act, 15 U.S.C. 78f, requires national securities exchanges to register with the Commission and requires an exchange's registration to be approved by the Commission, and Section 19(b) of the Exchange Act, 15 U.S.C. 78s(b), requires national securities exchanges to file proposed rule changes with the Commission.

[134] See, e.g., Designated Contract Markets (DCMs), U.S. Commodity Futures Trading Commission, available at http://www.cftc.gov/IndustryOversight/TradingOrganizations/DCMs/index.htm.

[135] See supra note 96 and accompanying text.

[136] See Dylan Letter, supra note 19, at 1 (identifying OKCoin, BitVC, and Bitmex as three of the largest overseas bitcoin futures markets). See also ARK Letter, supra note 19, at 6 (stating that most derivatives activity within the bitcoin markets is conducted by unregulated entities).

[137] See ARK Letter, supra note 19, at 5.

[138] See Amendment No. 1, supra note 1, 81 FR at 76661.

[139] See id.

[140] See id. See also ARK Letter, supra note 19, at 6 (noting that TeraExchange offers bitcoin forwards).

[141] See Amendment No. 1, supra note 1, 81 FR at 76661.

offsetting "wash" transactions of the same price, notional amount, and tenor and then issued a press release "to create the impression of actual trading in the Bitcoin swap."[142] Neither the Exchange nor any commenter provides evidence of meaningful trading volume in bitcoin derivatives on any regulated marketplace. Thus, the Commission believes that the bitcoin derivatives markets are not significant, regulated markets related to bitcoin with which the Exchange can enter into a surveillance-sharing agreement.

One commenter, and the author of the paper submitted with respect to a similar rule filing, assert that the existence of bitcoin derivative markets is not a necessary condition for a bitcoin ETP.[143] The key requirement the Commission is applying here, however, is not that a futures or derivatives market is required for every ETP, but that—when the spot market is unregulated—there must be significant, regulated derivatives markets related to the underlying asset with which the Exchange can enter into a surveillance-sharing agreement.

C. *Basis for Disapproval*

The Commission has, in past approvals of commodity-trust ETPs, emphasized the importance of surveillance-sharing agreements between the national securities exchange listing and trading the ETP, and significant markets relating to the underlying asset.[144] Such agreements, which are a necessary tool to enable the ETP-listing exchange to detect and deter manipulative conduct, enable the exchange to meet its obligation under Section 6(b)(5) of the Exchange Act to have rules that are designed to prevent fraudulent and manipulative acts and practices and to protect investors and the public interest.[145]

As described above, the Exchange has not entered into a surveillance-sharing agreement with a significant, regulated, bitcoin-related market. The Commission also does not believe, as discussed above, that the proposal supports a finding that the significant markets for bitcoin or derivatives on bitcoin are regulated markets with which the Exchange can enter into such an agreement. Therefore, as the Exchange has not entered into, and would currently be unable to enter into, the type of surveillance-sharing agreement that has been in place with respect to all previously approved commodity-trust ETPs, the Commission does not find the proposed rule change to be consistent with the Exchange Act and, accordingly, disapproves the proposed rule change.

The Commission notes that bitcoin is still in the relatively early stages of its development and that, over time, regulated bitcoin-related markets of significant size may develop.[146] Should such markets develop, the Commission could consider whether a bitcoin ETP would, based on the facts and circumstances then presented, be consistent with the requirements of the Exchange Act.

IV. CONCLUSION

For the reasons set forth above, the Commission does not find that the proposed rule change, as modified by Amendment Nos. 1 and 2, is consistent with the requirements of the Exchange Act and the rules and regulations thereunder applicable to a national securities exchange, and in particular, with Section 6(b)(5) of the Exchange Act.

IT IS THEREFORE ORDERED, pursuant to Section 19(b)(2) of the Exchange Act, that the proposed rule change (SR-BatsBZX-2016-30), as modified by Amendments No. 1 and 2, be, and it hereby is, disapproved.

For the Commission, by the Division of Trading and Markets, pursuant to delegated authority.[147]

Eduardo A. Aleman

Assistant Secretary

---

[142] *See* TeraExchange Settlement Order, *supra* note 112.

[143] *See* Anonymous Letter III, *supra* note 19, at 2; Lewis Paper, *supra* note 42, at 8.

[144] *See supra* note 96 and accompanying text.

[145] 15 U.S.C. 78f(b)(5).

[146] The Exchange notes, for example, that the CME and the ICE recently announced bitcoin pricing indexes. *See* Amendment No. 1, *supra* note 1, 81 FR at 76666. In the future, regulated futures or derivative markets might begin to trade products based on these indexes.

[147] 17 CFR 200.30-3(a)(12).

Appendix C—CFTC Materials

¶ 1040 A CFTC Primer on Virtual Currencies
October 17, 2017

Please note that LabCFTC cannot and will not provide legal advice. If you have specific questions regarding your activities and whether they conform to legal or regulatory requirements, you should consult with a qualified lawyer or appropriate expert. LabCFTC has no independent authority or decision-making power, and cannot independently provide, or create an expectation for, legal or regulatory relief. Communications from LabCFTC shall not create estoppel against CFTC or other enforcement actions. Any formal requests for relief must be addressed by relevant CFTC staff or, as necessary, by the Commission. LabCFTC will work with entities on such requests with the appropriate offices through established processes.

This primer format is intended to be an educational tool regarding emerging FinTech innovations. It is not intended to describe the official policy or position of the CFTC, or to limit the CFTC's current or future positions or actions. The CFTC does not endorse the use or effectiveness of any of the financial products in this presentation. It is organized as follows:

☐ Overview
　–What is a Virtual Currency?
　–Bitcoin and Related Technologies
　–Potential Uses of Virtual Currencies and Blockchain Technologies
☐ The Role of the CFTC
　–The CFTC's Mission
　–Sample Permitted and Prohibited Activities
　–ICOs, Virtual Tokens, and CFTC Oversight
☐ Risks of Virtual Currencies
　–Operational Risks
　–Speculative Risks
　–Cybersecurity Risks
　Fraud and Manipulation Risks

OVERVIEW OF VIRTUAL CURRENCIES
What is a Virtual Currency?

☐ Although precise definitions offered by others are varied, an IRS definition provides us with a general idea:

–"Virtual currency is a digital representation of value that functions as **a medium of exchange, a unit of account, and/or a store of value.**

–In some environments, it operates like 'real' currency . . . but it **does not have legal tender status** [in the U.S.].

–Virtual currency that has an equivalent value in real currency, or that acts as a substitute for real currency, is referred to as 'convertible' virtual currency. **Bitcoin is one example of a convertible virtual currency.**

–Bitcoin can be digitally traded between users and can be purchased for, or exchanged into, U.S. dollars, Euros, and other real or virtual currencies."[†]

What is Bitcoin?

[†] IRS Notice 2014-21, available at https://www.irs.gov/businesses/small-businesses-self-employed/virtual-currencies (emphasis added). Please note that this definition is not a statement of the Commission's view, and is instead offered as an aid to enhance public understanding of virtual currencies. We further note that one prominent type of virtual currency is cryptocurrency. Cryptocurrency has been described as "an electronic payment system based on cryptographic proof instead of trust, allowing any two willing parties to transact directly with each other without the need for a trusted third party." Satoshi Nakamoto, Bitcoin: A Peer-to-Peer Electronic

☐ Bitcoin is currently the largest convertible virtual currency by market capitalization (close to $72 billion in August 2017)[†]

☐ Bitcoin was created in 2008 by a person or group that used the name "Satoshi Nakamoto," with the belief that:

"[w]hat is needed is an electronic payment system based on cryptographic proof instead of trust, allowing any two willing parties to transact directly with each other without the need for a trusted third party."

☐ Bitcoin:

–Is "pseudonymous" (or partially anonymous) in that an individual is identified by an alpha-numeric public key/address;

–Relies on cryptography (and unique digital signatures) for security based on public and private keys and complex mathematical algorithms;

–Runs on a decentralized peer-to-peer network of computers and "miners" that operate on open-source software and do "work" to validate and irrevocably log transactions on a permanent public distributed ledger visible to the entire network;

–Solves the lack of trust between participants who may be strangers to each other on a public ledger through the transaction validation work noted in the sub-bullet above; and

–Enables the transfer of ownership without the need for a trusted, central intermediary.

What is the Difference between Public and Private Ledger Systems?

☐ Certain virtual currencies operate on public distributed ledger systems that capture "blocks" of transactions – there is no inherent trust in this decentralized system.

–Virtual currencies create an economic incentive for dispersed, independent, computers, or groups of computers, around the world to confirm transactions and perform verifiable "work" (that creates consensus) to publish a new block of transactions on the public ledger in exchange for a payment of the applicable virtual currency.

☐ Private / permissioned distributed ledger networks typically have some degree of trust between participants.

–Private ledger systems allow a network of known participants to share transaction information between themselves more efficiently.

–While cryptography and consensus may still be involved in private ledger systems, these systems do not necessarily involve a virtual currency that may serve as the economic incentive for miner or validator participation in public networks.

Sample Potential Use Cases of Virtual Currencies

☐ Store of Value

–Like precious metals, many virtual currencies are a "non-yielding" asset (meaning they do not pay dividends or interest), but they may be more fungible, divisible, and portable

–Limited or finite supply of virtual currencies may contrast with 'real' (fiat) currencies

☐ Trading

–Trading in virtual currencies may result in capital gains or losses

–Note that trading in virtual currencies may involve significant speculation and volatility risk (see Virtual Currency Risks section below)

☐ Payments and Transactions

–Some merchants and online stores are accepting virtual currencies in exchange for physical and digital goods (i.e., payments)

(Footnote Continued)

Cash System (Oct. 31, 2008), available at https:// bitcoin.org/bitcoin.pdf.

[†] Paul Vigna, *Bitcoin, Valued Like a Cool Blue Chip, Trading Like a Hot Small Cap*, Wall Street Journal (Aug. 29, 2017), available at https://blogs.wsj.com/moneybeat/ 2017/08/28/bitcoin-valued-like-a-blue-chip-trading-like-a-small-cap/. It is important to note that there are many other virtual currencies with sizeable market capitalizations that are built upon various Blockchain technologies, but may have different characteristics or functionalities than Bitcoin, including Ethereum (or Ether), Litecoin, and Ripple.

–Some public Blockchain systems rely on the payment of fees in virtual currency form in order to power the network and underlying transactions

☐ Transfer / Move Money

–Domestic and international money transfer (e.g., remittances) in order to increase efficiencies and potentially reduce related fees

Sample Potential Use Cases of Blockchain/DLT Technology

Blockchain, or distributed ledger technology,[*] underpins many virtual currencies, but can also be used within private, permissioned ledger systems – versions of public and private systems may be used by:

☐ Financial Institutions

–Trading & Payment Platforms / Clearing and Settlement

–Regulatory Reporting, Compliance & Audit

–Know Your Customer (KYC) / Anti-Money Laundering (AML)

–Repurchase Agreement Transactions ("Repos," i.e., short-term borrowing of securities)

☐ Governments

- –General Records Management
- –Title & Ownership Records Management (e.g., real property deeds and title transfer)
- –Regulatory Reporting and Oversight

☐ Cross-Industry

–Smart Contracts (i.e., self executing agreements)

–Resource / Asset Sharing Agreements (e.g., allowing rental of a personal car left behind during a vacation or allowing rental of excess computer or data storage)

–Digital Identity (e.g., proof of identity when entering into a contract)

THE ROLE OF THE CFTC

The CFTC's Mission

☐ The mission of the CFTC is to foster open, transparent, competitive, and financially sound markets. By working to avoid systemic risk, the Commission aims to protect market users and their funds, consumers, and the public from fraud, manipulation, and abusive practices related to derivatives and other products that are subject to the Commodity Exchange Act (CEA).

☐ To foster the public interest and fulfill its mission, the CFTC will act:

–To deter and prevent price manipulation or any other disruptions to market integrity;

–To ensure the financial integrity of all transactions subject to the CEA and the avoidance of systemic risk;

–To protect all market participants from fraudulent or other abusive sales practices and misuse of customer assets; and

–To promote responsible innovation and fair competition among boards of trade, other markets, and market participants.

☐ Responsible innovation is market-enhancing.

Virtual Currencies are Commodities

☐ The definition of "commodity" in the CEA is broad.

–It can mean a physical commodity, such as an agricultural product (e.g., wheat, cotton) or natural resource (e.g., gold, oil).

–It can mean a currency or interest rate.

–The CEA definition of "commodity" also includes "all services, rights, and interests . . . in which contracts for future delivery are presently or in the future dealt in."

---

[*] *See generally* Marco Iansiti and Karim R. Lakhani, *The Truth About Blockchain*, Harvard Business Review (Jan-Feb 2017), available at https://hbr.org/2017/01/the- truth-about-blockchain (for a general overview of how a public Blockchain works).

☐ The CFTC first found that Bitcoin and other virtual currencies are properly defined as commodities in 2015.‡

☐ The CFTC has oversight over futures, options, and derivatives contracts.

☐ The CFTC's jurisdiction is implicated when a virtual currency is used in a derivatives contract, or if there is fraud or manipulation involving a virtual currency traded in interstate commerce.

• Beyond instances of fraud or manipulation, the CFTC generally does not oversee "spot" or cash market exchanges and transactions involving virtual currencies that do not utilize margin, leverage, or financing.

Examples of Permitted Activities

☐ TeraExchange, LLC, a Swap Execution Facility ("SEF") registered with the CFTC, entered in to the virtual currency market in 2014 by listing a Bitcoin swap for trading. Trading on a SEF platform is limited to "eligible contract participants," a type of sophisticated trader, which includes various financial institutions and persons, with assets above specified statutory minimums.

☐ North American Derivatives Exchange Inc. ("NADEX"), a designated contract market ("DCM"), listed binary options based on the Tera Bitcoin Price Index from November 2014 to December 2016. Retail customers may trade on NADEX.

☐ LedgerX, LLC ("LedgerX") registered with the CFTC as a SEF and Derivative Clearing Organization ("DCO") in July 2017. It plans to list digital currency options.

Examples of Prohibited Activities‡

☐ Price manipulation of a virtual currency traded in interstate commerce.

☐ Pre-arranged or wash trading in an exchange-traded virtual currency swap or futures contract.

☐ A virtual currency futures or option contract or swap traded on a domestic platform or facility that has not registered with the CFTC as a SEF or DCM.

☐ Certain schemes involving virtual currency marketed to retail customers, such as off-exchange financed commodity transactions with persons who fail to register with the CFTC.

ICOs, Virtual Tokens, and CFTC Oversight

☐ The Securities and Exchange Commission ("SEC") recently released a report about an Initial Coin Offering or "ICO" (the "DAO Report").‡

☐ The DAO Report explains that "The DAO" is an example of a "Decentralized Autonomous Organization," which is a "virtual" organization embodied in computer code and executed on a distributed ledger or blockchain.

☐ Investors exchanged Ether, a virtual currency, for virtual DAO "Tokens" to fund projects in which the investors would share in anticipated earnings. DAO Tokens could be resold on web-based platforms.

☐ Based on the facts and circumstances, the SEC determined that DAO Tokens are "securities" under the federal securities laws.

☐ There is no inconsistency between the SEC's analysis and the CFTC's determination that virtual currencies are commodities and that virtual tokens may be commodities or derivatives contracts depending on the particular facts and circumstances.

–The CFTC looks beyond form and considers the actual substance and purpose of an activity when applying the federal commodities laws and CFTC regulations

RISKS OF VIRTUAL CURRENCIES

Virtual Currencies Have Risks

---

‡ See, In the Matter of: Coinflip, Inc., d/b/a Derivabit, and Francisco Riordan, CFTC Docket No. 15-29, available at http://www.cftc.gov/idc/groups/public/@lrenforce-mentactions/documents/legalpleading/enfcoinfliprorder09172015.pdf.

‡ Please note that this is not an exhaustive list of prohibited activities.

‡ See Release No. 81207, Report of Investigation Pursuant to Section 21(a) of the Securities Exchange Act of 1934: The DAO, available at https://www.sec.gov/litigation/investreport/34-81207.pdf.

☐ While virtual currencies have potential benefits, this emerging space also involves various risks, including:

    –Operational Risks

    –Cybersecurity Risks

    –Speculative Risks

    –Fraud and Manipulation Risks

☐ Virtual currencies are relatively unproven and may not perform as expected (for example, some have questioned whether public distributed ledgers are in fact immutable).

☐ Investors and users of virtual currencies should educate themselves about these and other risks before getting involved.

Virtual Currency: Operational Risk

☐ *Conduct extensive research before giving any money or personal information to a virtual currency platform.*

☐ The virtual currency marketplace is comprised of many different platforms where you can convert one type of virtual currency into another or into real currency, if offered.

☐ Many of these platforms are not subject to the supervision which applies to regulated exchanges. For example, if they engage in only certain spot or cash market transactions and do not utilize margin, leverage, or financing, they may be subject to federal and state money transmission and anti-money laundering laws, but they do not have to follow all the rules that regulated exchanges operate under.

☐ Some virtual currency platforms may be missing critical system safeguards and customer protection related systems; without adequate safeguards, customers may lose some or all of their virtual assets.

Virtual Currency: Cybersecurity Risk

☐ *Keep your property in safe accounts and carefully verify digital wallet addresses.*

☐ Some platforms may "commingle" (mix) customer assets in shared accounts (at a bank for real currency or a digital wallet for virtual currency). This may affect whether or how you can withdraw your currency.

☐ Depending on the structure and security of the digital wallet, some may be vulnerable to hacks, resulting in the theft of virtual currency or loss of customer assets.

    –If a bad actor gains access to your private key, it can take your virtual currency with limited or no recourse

☐ When transferring virtual currency, be sure to confirm the destination wallet address, even when using "copy and paste." It is possible for hackers to change digital wallet addresses on your computer.

Virtual Currency: Speculative Risk

☐ *Only invest what you are willing and able to lose.*

☐ The virtual currency marketplace has been subject to substantial volatility and price swings.

☐ An individual or coordinated group trading a large amount of virtual currency at once could affect the price, depending on the overall amount of trading in the marketplace.

☐ Periods of high volatility with inadequate trade volume may create adverse market conditions, leading to harmful effects such as customer orders being filled at undesirable prices.

☐ Some advertisements promise guaranteed returns – this can be a common tactic with fraudulent schemes.

Virtual Currency: Fraud & Manipulation Risk

☐ *Carefully research the platform you want to use, and pay close attention to the fee structure and systems safeguards.*

☐ Unregistered virtual currency platforms may not be able to adequately protect against market abuses by other traders.

    –For example, recent news articles discuss potential "spoofing" activity and other manipulative behavior that can negatively affect prices

¶1040

☐ Some virtual currency platforms may be selling you virtual currency directly from their own account – these types of transactions may give the platform unfair advantages and sometimes resemble fraudulent "bucket shop" schemes.

☐ There is also a risk of Ponzi schemers and fraudsters seeking to capitalize on the current attention focused on virtual currencies.

¶ 1050 CFTC Backgrounder on Oversight of and Approach to Virtual Currency Futures Markets

January 4, 2018

This backgrounder provides clarity regarding federal oversight of and jurisdiction over virtual currencies; the CFTC's approach to regulation of virtual currencies; the self-certification process generally, as well as specifically regarding the recent self-certification of new contracts for bitcoin futures products by designated contract markets (DCMs); background on the CFTC's "heightened review" for virtual currency contracts; and a discussion of the constituencies the CFTC believes could be impacted by virtual currency futures.

Federal and State Oversight of Virtual Currencies

US law does not provide for direct, comprehensive Federal oversight of underlying Bitcoin or virtual currency spot markets. As a result, US regulation of virtual currencies has evolved into a multifaceted, multi-regulatory approach:

- **State Banking** regulators oversee certain US and foreign virtual currency spot exchanges largely through state money transfer laws.

- The **Internal Revenue Service (IRS)** treats virtual currencies as property subject to capital gains tax.

- The **Treasury's Financial Crimes Enforcement Network (FinCEN)** monitors Bitcoin and other virtual currency transfers for anti-money laundering purposes.

- The **Securities and Exchange Commission (SEC)** takes increasingly strong action against unregistered initial coin offerings.

The **CFTC** also has an important role to play. In 2014, the CFTC declared virtual currencies to be a "commodity" subject to oversight under its authority under the Commodity Exchange Act (CEA).[1]

Since then, the CFTC has taken action against unregistered Bitcoin futures exchanges (BitFinex),[2] enforced the laws prohibiting wash trading and prearranged trades on a derivatives platform,[3] issued proposed guidance on what is a derivative market and what is a spot market in the virtual currency context,[4] issued warnings about valuations and volatility in spot virtual currency markets,[5] and addressed a virtual currency Ponzi scheme.[6]

CFTC Approach to Responsible Regulation of Virtual Currencies

The CFTC seeks to promote responsible innovation and development that is consistent with its statutory mission to foster open, transparent, competitive and financially sound derivative trading markets and to prohibit fraud, manipulation and abusive practices in connection with derivatives and other products subject to the CEA. The CFTC believes that the responsible regulatory response to virtual currencies involves the following:

1) **Consumer Education**. Amidst the wild assertions, bold headlines, and shocking hyperbole, there is a need for greater public understanding.

2) **Asserting Legal Authority**. Asserting legal authority over virtual currency derivatives in support of the CFTC's anti-fraud and manipulation efforts, including in underlying spot markets, is a key component in the CFTC's ability to effectively regulate these markets.

---

[1] Testimony of CFTC Chairman Timothy Massad before the U.S. Senate Committee on Agriculture, Nutrition and Forestry (Dec. 10, 2014), http://www.cftc.gov/PressRoom/SpeechesTestimony/opamassad-6.

[2] *In re* BXFNA Inc. d/b/a Bitfinex, Dkt. No. 16-19 (CFTC June 2, 2016), http://www.cftc.gov/idc/groups/public/@lrenforcementactions/documents/legalpleading/enfbfxnaorder060216.pdf.

[3] *In re* TeraExchange LLC, Dkt. No. 15-33 (CFTC Sept. 24, 2015), http://www.cftc.gov/idc/groups/public/@lrenforcementactions/documents/legalpleading/enfteraexchangeorder92415.pdf.

[4] CFTC, Retail Commodity Transactions Involving Virtual Currency, 82 Fed. Reg. 60335 (Dec. 20, 2017), www.gpo.gov/fdsys/pkg/FR-2017-12-20/pdf/2017-27421.pdf.

[5] CFTC, A CFTC Primer on Virtual Currencies (Oct. 17, 2017), http://www.cftc.gov/idc/groups/public/documents/file/labcftcprimercurrencies100417.pdf.

[6] On September 21, 2017, the CFTC filed a complaint in federal court in the Southern District of New York against Nicholas Gelfman and Gelfman Blueprint, Inc., *see* http://www.cftc.gov/idc/groups/public/@lrenforcementactions/documents/legalpleading/enfgelfmancomplaint09212017.pdf.

3) **Market Intelligence.** Gaining the ability to monitor markets for virtual currency derivatives and underlying settlement reference rates through the gathering of trade and counterparty data will provide regulatory and enforcement insights into those markets.

4) **Robust Enforcement.** In addition to its general regulatory and enforcement jurisdiction over the virtual currency derivatives markets, the CFTC has jurisdiction to police fraud and manipulation in cash or spot markets. The CFTC intends to continue to exercise this jurisdiction to enforce the law and prosecute fraud, abuse, manipulation or false solicitation in markets for virtual currency derivatives and underlying spot trading.

5) **Government-wide Coordination.** The CFTC actively coordinates its approach to Bitcoin and other virtual currencies with other Federal regulators, including the Securities and Exchange Commission (SEC), Federal Bureau of Investigation (FBI), Justice Department and Financial Stability Oversight Council (FSOC). The CFTC also coordinates with state entities, including state Attorneys General, in addition to working with the White House, Congress and other policy-makers.

Virtual Currency Self-Certifications

On Friday, December 1, 2017, the Chicago Mercantile Exchange Inc. (CME) and the CBOE Futures Exchange (CFE) self-certified new contracts for bitcoin futures products and the Cantor Exchange self-certified a new contract for bitcoin binary options.

- The product self-certification process was deliberately designed by Congress and prior Commissions to give the initiative to DCMs to certify new products. This is consistent with a DCM's role as a self-regulatory organization (SRO) and the CFTC's principles-based approach to regulation.

- This self-certification process is one that Congress promulgated and prior Commissions have implemented. Unless it is changed, the staff of the CFTC must work responsibly within the self-certification structure.

- It is notable that the product self-certification process does NOT provide for public input, the creation of separate guaranty funds for clearing, or value judgments about the underlying spot market.[7]

- There are limited grounds for the CFTC to "stay" self-certification such as filing a false statement in the certification.[8]

- In the case of the CME and CFE self-certifications, no such grounds were evident.

- Had it even been possible, blocking self-certification would not have stemmed interest in Bitcoin or other virtual currencies nor their spectacular and volatile valuations. Instead, it would have ensured that the virtual currency spot markets continue to operate without federal regulatory surveillance for fraud and manipulation.

The CFTC was well prepared to handle the recent self-certifications of Bitcoin futures products. CFTC staff knew that a virtual currencies market was evolving rapidly in 2017 and that the agency would likely see proposals for the launch of Bitcoin futures.

- The CFTC has past experience with virtual currency derivatives, such as TeraExchange swaps,[9] Nadex binary options,[10] and LedgerX options.[11]

- CME created the Bitcoin Reference Rate in December 2016. CFE approached the CFTC in July 2017.

---

[7] CEA section 5c(c)(1); 7 U.S.C. 7a-2(c); and 17 C.F.R. 40.2.

[8] *See* 17 C.F.R. 40.2(c). There are a few other limited avenues to provide additional time for consideration, such as the statutory requirement for special steps when a Systematically Important Derivatives Clearing Organization (SIDCO) proposes rule changes that could materially affect the nature or level of risk undertaken. But, there was no such finding of materiality of new Bitcoin futures, given market size. Also, this would not have applied to CFE contracts, which are not cleared by a SIDCO. An-other avenue would have required the CFTC to adopt a rule though regular order and require DCM adoption. For a variety of reasons, that was not feasible.

[9] TeraExchange was registered as a swap execution facility (SEF) in October 2013 and its Bitcoin swaps were certified on September 11, 2014.

[10] Nadex's Bitcoin options were certified on November 26, 2014.

[11] LedgerX was registered as a SEF in July 2017 and its Bitcoin options were certified on September 19, 2017.

- The CFTC built into its 2018 Congressional budget request[12] additional resources to strengthen its technological and econometric resources to support its ability to oversee virtual currency derivatives.

Although CFTC staff did not dictate the firm date for CME and CFE listing Bitcoin futures, the exact timing of these issues in 2017 did not affect the self-certification process.

Background on "Heightened Review" for Virtual Currency Self-Certifications

Within the limits and parameters of the current self-certification process, CFTC staff has engaged in a "heightened review" with the DCMs and worked collaboratively through several drafts of the terms and conditions of these Bitcoin futures products to address issues. At the heart of the CFTC's heightened review is extensive visibility and monitoring of markets for virtual currency derivatives and underlying settlement reference rates. Virtual currency self-certification under heightened review means that the CFTC not only has clear legal authority, but now also will have the means to police certain underlying spot markets for fraud and manipulation.

Heightened review includes:

1) derivatives clearing organizations (DCOs) setting substantially high initial[13] and maintenance margin for cash-settled Bitcoin futures;

2) DCMs setting large trader reporting thresholds at five bitcoins or less;

3) DCMs entering direct or indirect information sharing agreements with spot market platforms to allow access to trade and trader data;

4) DCM monitoring of data from cash markets with respect to price settlements and other Bitcoin prices more broadly, and identifying anomalies and disproportionate moves in the cash markets compare to the futures markets;

5) DCMs agreeing to engage in inquiries, including at the trade settlement level when necessary;

6) DCMs agreeing to regular coordination with CFTC surveillance staff on trade activities, including providing the CFTC surveillance team with trade settlement data upon request; and

7) DCMs coordinating product launches so that the CFTC's market surveillance branch can carefully monitor minute-by-minute developments.

The CFTC expects that any registered entity seeking to list a virtual currency derivative product would follow the same process, terms and conditions.

Constituencies Impacted By Self-Certification of Virtual Currency Futures

While engaged in this heightened review, the CFTC identified three constituencies impacted by virtual currency futures:

- **Market Participants and Consumers.** The CFTC seeks to look out for virtual currency market participants and consumers through the CFTC's educational efforts, such as the CFTC Virtual Currency Primer,[14] CFTC Bitcoin consumer advisory,[15] the CFTC market advisory,[16] the CFTC Dedicated bitcoin webpage,[17] the CFTC analysis of Bitcoin spot market data,[18] and CFTC weekly publication of Bitcoin futures "Commitment of Traders" data.[19]

Market participants and consumers are also protected through DCOs greatly increasing initial margin levels and efforts by the National Futures Association (NFA), in conjunction with the CFTC, to direct NFA members to heighten customer protection.[20] Finally, the CFTC will work to

---

[12] The CFTC's FY 2018 budget request was submitted on May 23, 2017.

[13] In the case of CME and CFE Bitcoin futures, the initial margin was ultimately set at 47 percent and 44 percent, respectively. By way of comparison that is more than ten times the margin required for CME corn futures product.

[14] *See supra* note 9.

[15] CFTC Customer Advisory: Understand the Risks of Virtual Currency Trading (Dec. 15, 2017), http://www.cftc.gov/idc/groups/public/@customerprotection/documents/file/customeradvisory_urvct121517.pdf.

[16] CFTC, Statement on Self-Certification of Bitcoin Products by CME, CFE and Cantor Exchange (Dec. 1, 2017), http://www.cftc.gov/PressRoom/PressReleases/pr7654-17.

[17] CFTC, Bitcoin, http://www.cftc.gov/Bitcoin/index.htm.

[18] *See supra* note 8.

[19] CFTC, Commitments of Traders, http://www.cftc.gov/MarketReports/CommitmentsofTraders/index.htm.

[20] *See* NFA, Investor Advisory—Futures on Virtual Currencies Including Bitcoin (Dec. 1, 2017), https://

protect consumers through its ongoing enforcement activities, including those against virtual currency Ponzi schemes[21] and unregistered futures exchanges.[22]

- **Public Interest.** The CFTC looks to protect the public interest in regard to virtual currencies through its formation of a virtual currency task team, including recruitment of greater virtual currency expertise, its establishment of "heightened review" of virtual currency futures, its assertive enforcement against fraud and manipulation in Bitcoin and other virtual currency and its providing legal certainty to CFTC anti-fraud and manipulation jurisdiction over spot markets. In fact, without the self-certification of Bitcoin futures products, the CFTC's surveillance of virtual currency spot trading markets would be practically impossible and legally challengeable.

- **DCO Clearing Members.** The CFTC recognizes that major global banks and brokerages that are DCO clearing members are able to look after their own commercial interests by choosing not to trade virtual currency futures (as some have done), requiring substantially higher initial margins (as many have done), and through their active participation in DCO risk committees. One clearing member called for the CFTC to force DCOs to establish a separate clearing system for virtual currencies.[23] However, as noted above, the CFTC's "hands were tied" by statute from requiring a separate clearing system or guaranty fund for Bitcoin futures. Where separate guaranty funds have been used by DCOs in the past, they have come about through independent negotiations between clearing members and DCOs, not by CFTC action.

It is important to note that there is no provision in statute or regulation for public input into new product self-certifications. Neither statute nor rule would have prevented CME and CFE from launching their new products before public hearings could have been called. Even if the CFTC could have held public hearings or requested public input, it is unlikely that the outcome would have changed, as the CFTC staff found no basis to determine their filings to be inconsistent with the CEA or CFTC regulations.

Independent from the self-certification process, the CFTC and its advisory committees have the ability to call hearings. Both the Market Risk Advisory Committee (MRAC) and the Technology Advisory Committee (TAC) will hold hearings this month, to allow clearing members, alongside the virtual currency futures trading platforms and appropriate representatives of the public interest, to discuss the process of self-certification of new products, such as virtual currencies, and, more broadly, the challenges and opportunities of virtual currencies for CFTC regulated derivatives and underlying spot markets.

(Footnote Continued)

www.nfa.futures.org/investors/investor-advisory.html; NFA, Additional Reporting Requirements Regarding Virtual Currency Futures Products for FCMs for Which NFA is the DSRO (Dec. 6, 2017), https:// www.nfa.futures.org/news/new-sNotice.asp?ArticleID=4973; NFA, Additional Reporting Requirements For IBs That Solicit or Accept Orders in Virtual Currency Products (Dec. 14, 2017), https:// www.nfa.futures.org/news/new-sNotice.asp?ArticleID=4975; NFA, Additional Reporting Requirements for CPOs and CTAs That Trade Virtual Currency Products (Dec. 14, 2017), https://

www.nfa.futures.org/news/ newsNotice.asp?ArticleID=4974.

[21] *See supra* note 10.

[22] *In re* Coinflip, Inc., Dkt. No. 15-29 (CFTC Sept. 17, 2015), http://www.cftc.gov/idc/groups/public/ @lrenforcementactions/documents/legalpleading/ enfcoinfliprorder09172015.pdf.

[23] Chloe Aiello, Keep Bitcoin Away From the Real Economy, Says Billionaire 'Father of High Speed Trading,' cnbc.com (Nov. 15, 2017), https://www.cnbc.com/ 2017/11/15/thomas-peterffy-keep-bitcoin-away-from-the-real-economy.html.

¶ 1060 Retail Commodity Transactions Involving Virtual Currency

COMMODITY FUTURES TRADING COMMISSION

17 CFR Part 1

RIN 3038-AE62

AGENCY: Commodity Futures Trading Commission.

ACTION: Proposed interpretation; request for comment.

SUMMARY: The Commodity Futures Trading Commission (the "Commission" or "CFTC") is issuing this proposed interpretation of the term "actual delivery" as set forth in a certain provision of the Commodity Exchange Act ("CEA") pursuant to the Dodd-Frank Wall Street Reform and Consumer Protection Act (the "Dodd-Frank Act"). Specifically, this proposed interpretation is being issued to inform the public of the Commission's views as to the meaning of actual delivery within the specific context of retail commodity transactions in virtual currency. The Commission requests comment on this proposed interpretation and further invites comment on specific questions related to the Commission's treatment of virtual currency transactions.

DATES: Comments must be received on or before March 20, 2018.

ADDRESSES: You may submit comments, identified by RIN 3038-AE62, by any of the following methods:

• *CFTC website: http://comments.cftc.gov.* Follow the instructions for submitting comments through the Comments Online process on the website.

• *Mail:* Christopher Kirkpatrick, Secretary of the Commission, Commodity Futures Trading Commission, Three Lafayette Center, 1155 21st Street NW, Washington, DC 20581.

• *Hand Delivery/Courier:* Same as Mail, above.

• *Federal eRulemaking Portal: http://www.regulations.gov.* Follow the instructions for submitting comments.

Please submit your comments using only one method.

All comments must be submitted in English or, if not, accompanied by an English translation. Comments will be posted as received to *http://*

www.cftc.gov. You should submit only information that you wish to make available publicly. If you wish the Commission to consider information that you believe is exempt from disclosure under the Freedom of Information Act ("FOIA"),[1] a petition for confidential treatment of the exempt information may be submitted according to the procedures established in Commission Regulation 145.9.[2]

The Commission reserves the right, but shall have no obligation, to review, pre-screen, filter, redact, refuse or remove any or all of your submission from *http://www.cftc.gov* that it may deem to be inappropriate for publication, such as obscene language. All submissions that have been redacted or removed that contain comments on the merits of the interpretation will be retained in the public comment file and will be considered as required under the Administrative Procedure Act and other applicable laws, and may be accessible under FOIA.

FOR FURTHER INFORMATION CONTACT: Philip W. Raimondi, Special Counsel, (202) 418-5717, *praimondi@cftc.gov;* or David P. Van Wagner, Chief Counsel, (202) 418-5481, *dvanwagner@cftc.gov;* Office of the Chief Counsel, Division of Market Oversight, Commodity Futures Trading Commission, 1155 21st Street NW, Washington, DC 20581.

SUPPLEMENTARY INFORMATION:

I. Background

With certain exceptions, the CFTC has been granted exclusive jurisdiction over commodity futures, options, and all other derivatives that fall within the definition of a swap.[3] Further, the Commission has been granted general anti-fraud and anti-manipulation authority over "any swap, or a contract of sale of any commodity in interstate commerce, or for future delivery on or subject to the rules of any registered entity."[4] The Commission's mission is to foster open, transparent, competitive and financially sound markets; and protect the American public from fraudulent schemes and abusive practices in those markets and products over which it has been granted jurisdiction.

Pursuant to CEA section 2(c)(2)(D),[5] the marketplace for "retail commodity transactions" is one such area over which the Commission has been granted explicit oversight authority.[6] CEA section

---

[1] 5 U.S.C. 552.

[2] 17 CFR 145.9. Commission regulations referred to herein are found at 17 CFR chapter I.

[3] 7 U.S.C. 2(a)(1)(A). The CFTC shares its swap jurisdiction in certain aspects with the Securities and Exchange Commission ("SEC"). *See* 7 U.S.C. 2(a)(1)(C).

[4] 7 U.S.C. 9(1).

[5] 7 U.S.C. 2(c)(2)(D).

[6] The authority provided to the Commission by CEA section 2(c)(2)(D) is in addition to, and independent from, the

jurisdiction over contracts of sale of a commodity for future delivery and transactions subject to regulation pursuant to CEA section 19 that the CEA has historically granted to the Commission. It is also in addition to, and independent from, the jurisdiction over swaps granted to the Commission by the Dodd-Frank Act. Further, the authority granted under CEA section 2(c)(2)(D) is in addition to, and independent of, the Commission's ability to bring enforcement actions for fraud or manipulation in connection with swaps, contracts of sale of any commodity in interstate commerce, or for future delivery on or subject to the rules of any registered entity. 7 U.S.C. 9(1), 9(3), 13(a)(2); 17 CFR 180.1, 180.2.

2(c)(2)(D) applies to any agreement, contract or transaction in any commodity that is entered into with, or offered to (even if not entered into with), a person that is neither an eligible contract participant[7] nor an eligible commercial entity[8] ("retail") on a leveraged or margined basis, or financed by the offeror, the counterparty or a person acting in concert with the offeror or counterparty on a similar basis.[9] CEA section 2(c)(2)(D) further provides that such an agreement, contract or transaction is subject to CEA sections 4(a),[10] 4(b),[11] and 4b[12] "as if the agreement, contract or transaction was a contract of sale of a commodity for future delivery."[13] The statute, however, excepts certain transactions from its application. In particular, CEA section 2(c)(2)(D)(ii)(III)(aa)[14] excepts a contract of sale that "results in actual delivery within 28 days or such other longer period as the Commission may determine by rule or regulation based upon the typical commercial practice in cash or spot markets for the commodity involved."[15] If no exception is applicable, these retail transactions are "commodity interests" subject to Commission regulations together with futures, options, and swaps.[16] Under this authority, the Commission regulates retail commodity transactions, with the exception of contracts of sale that result in actual delivery within 28 days.[17]

The Dodd-Frank Act added CEA section 2(c)(2)(D) to address certain judicial uncertainty involving the Commission's regulatory oversight capabilities. The Commission has long held that certain speculative commodity transactions involving leverage or margin may have indicia of futures contracts, subjecting them to Commission oversight.[18] However, judicial decisions emerged that called into question the Commission's oversight over certain leveraged retail transactions in currencies and other commodities.[19] In 2008, Congress addressed this judicial uncertainty by providing the Commission with more explicit authority over retail foreign currency transactions in CEA section 2(c)(2)(C).[20] These new statutory provisions established a two-day actual delivery exception for such transactions.[21] Two years later, Congress provided the Commission with explicit oversight authority over all other "retail commodity transactions" in CEA section 2(c)(2)(D).[22] As noted, these new statutory provisions established an exception for instances when actual delivery of the commodity occurs within 28 days.[23]

In connection with its retail commodity transaction oversight, the Commission previously issued a proposed interpretation of the term "actual delivery" in the context of CEA section 2(c)(2)(D), accompanied by a request for comment.[24] In that interpretation, the Commission provided several examples of what may and may not satisfy the actual delivery exception. After reviewing public comments, the Commission issued a final interpretation in 2013 (the "2013 Guidance").[25]

The 2013 Guidance explained that the Commission will consider evidence "beyond the four corners of contract documents" to assess whether actual delivery of the commodity occurred.[26] The Commission further noted that it will "employ a functional approach and examine how the agreement, contract, or transaction is marketed, managed, and performed, instead of relying solely on language used by the parties in the agreement, contract, or transaction."[27] The 2013 Guidance also included a list of relevant factors the Commission will consider in an actual delivery determina-

---

[7] 7 U.S.C. 1a(18).

[8] 7 U.S.C. 1a(17); *see also* 7 U.S.C. 2(c)(2)(D)(iv).

[9] 7 U.S.C. 2(c)(2)(D)(i).

[10] 7 U.S.C. 6(a) (prohibiting the off-exchange trading of futures transactions by U.S. persons unless the transaction is conducted on or subject to the rules of a designated contract market).

[11] 7 U.S.C. 6(b) (permitting foreign boards of trade registered with the Commission with the ability to provide direct access to U.S. persons).

[12] 7 U.S.C. 6b (prohibiting fraudulent conduct in connection with any contract of sale of any commodity in interstate commerce, among other things).

[13] 7 U.S.C. 2(c)(2)(D)(iii).

[14] 7 U.S.C. 2(c)(2)(D)(ii)(III)(aa).

[15] The Commission has not adopted any regulations permitting a longer actual delivery period for any commodity pursuant to this statute. Accordingly, the 28-day actual delivery period remains applicable to all commodities, while retail foreign currency transactions remain subject to a 2-day actual delivery period pursuant to CEA section 2(c)(2)(C).

[16] 17 CFR 1.3(yy).

[17] In addition, certain commercial transactions and securities are excepted pursuant to CEA section 2(c)(2)(D)(ii).

[18] *See In re Stovall*, CFTC Docket No. 75-7 [1977-1980 Transfer Binder] Comm. Fut. L. Rep. (CCH) ¶ 20,941, at

23,777 (CFTC Dec. 6, 1979) (applying traditional elements of a futures contract to a purported cash transaction).

[19] *See, e.g., CFTC v. Zelener*, 373 F.3d 861 (7th Cir. 2004); *CFTC v. Erskine*, 512 F.3d 309 (6th Cir. 2008).

[20] *See* Food, Conservation and Energy Act of 2008, Public Law 110-246, 122 Stat. 1651 (2008).

[21] 7 U.S.C. 2(c)(2)(C)(i)(II)(bb)(AA).

[22] *See* Dodd-Frank Wall Street Reform and Consumer Protection Act of 2010, Public Law 111-203, 124 Stat. 1376 (2010); *see also Hearing to Review Implications of the CFTC v. Zelener Case Before the Subcomm. on General Farm Commodities and Risk Management of the H. Comm. on Agriculture*, 111th Cong. 52-664 (2009) (statement of Rep. Marshall, Member, H. Comm. on Agriculture) ("If in substance it is a futures contract, it is going to be regulated. It doesn't matter how clever your draftsmanship is."); 156 Cong. Rec. S5,924 (daily ed. July 15, 2010) (statement of Sen. Lincoln) ("Section 742 corrects [any regulatory uncertainty] by extending the Farm Bill's *'Zelener* fraud fix' to retail off-exchange transactions in *all* commodities.") (emphasis added).

[23] 7 U.S.C. 2(c)(2)(D)(ii)(III)(aa).

[24] Retail Commodity Transactions Under Commodity Exchange Act, 76 FR 77670 (Dec. 14, 2011).

[25] Retail Commodity Transactions Under Commodity Exchange Act, 78 FR 52426 (Aug. 23, 2013).

[26] *Id.* at 52,428.

[27] *Id.*

tion[28] and again provided examples[29] of what may and may not constitute actual delivery. As per the 2013 Guidance, the only satisfactory examples of actual delivery involve transfer of title and possession of the commodity to the purchaser or a depository acting on the purchaser's behalf.[30] Among other things, mere book entries and certain instances where a purchase is "rolled, offset, or otherwise netted with another transaction" do not constitute actual delivery.[31]

Within a year after the 2013 Guidance was released, the Eleventh Circuit issued an opinion affirming a preliminary injunction obtained by the Commission in CFTC v. Hunter Wise Commodities, LLC.[32] Hunter Wise further reinforced the Commission's interpretation of actual delivery in the 2013 Guidance. Specifically, the Eleventh Circuit recognized that delivery "denotes a transfer of possession and control."[33] Indeed, "[i]f 'actual delivery' means anything, it means something other than simply 'delivery,' for we must attach meaning to Congress's use of the modifier 'actual.'"[34] Accordingly, the Court stated that actual delivery "denotes '[t]he act of giving real and immediate possession to the buyer or the buyer's agent" and constructive delivery does not suffice.[35] Notably, the Eleventh Circuit found that its own holding harmonized with the 2013 Guidance and recognized that the legislative history behind CEA section 2(c)(2)(D) also "complements" its decision.[36]

Soon after the Hunter Wise decision, the Commission established that virtual currency is a commodity as that term is defined by CEA section 1a(9).[37] Subsequently, the Commission brought its first enforcement action against a platform that offered virtual currency transactions to retail customers on a leveraged, margined, or financed basis without registering with the Commission.[38] In the Bitfinex settlement order, the Commission

found that the virtual currency platform violated CEA sections 4(a) and 4d because the unregistered entity "did not actually deliver bitcoins purchased from them" as prescribed within the actual delivery exception.[39] Rather, the entity "held the purchased bitcoins in bitcoin deposit wallets that it owned and controlled."[40]

After Bitfinex, the Commission received requests for guidance with regard to the meaning of the actual delivery exception in the specific context of virtual currency transactions. Accordingly, the Commission has decided to issue this proposed interpretation and seek public comment. The Commission is issuing this proposed interpretation to inform the public of the Commission's views as to the meaning of the term "actual delivery" in the context of virtual currency and to provide the public with guidance on how the Commission intends to assess whether any given retail commodity transaction in virtual currency (whereby an entity or platform offers margin trading or otherwise facilitates[41] the use of margin, leverage, or financing arrangements for their retail market participants) results in actual delivery, as the term is used in CEA section 2(c)(2)(D)(ii)(III)(aa).[42] The Commission requests comment generally on this proposed interpretation and further invites comment on specific questions, as outlined within this release.

II. Commission Interpretation of Actual Delivery for Virtual Currency

A. Virtual Currency as a Commodity

As noted previously, the Commission considers virtual currency to be a commodity,[43] like many other intangible commodities that the Commission has recognized over the course of its existence (e.g., renewable energy credits and emission allowances, certain indices, and certain debt in-

---

[28] "Relevant factors in this determination include the following: Ownership, possession, title, and physical location of the commodity purchased or sold, both before and after execution of the agreement, contract, or transaction, including all related documentation; the nature of the relationship between the buyer, seller, and possessor of the commodity purchased or sold; and the manner in which the purchase or sale is recorded and completed." 78 FR at 52428.

[29] In the 2013 Guidance, Examples 1 and 2 illustrate circumstances where actual delivery is made, while Examples 3, 4 and 5 illustrate circumstances where actual delivery is not made. In setting forth the examples, the Commission made clear that they are non-exclusive and were intended to provide the public with guidance on how the Commission would apply the interpretation. 78 FR at 52427-28.

[30] Id.

[31] Id.

[32] CFTC v. Hunter Wise Commodities, LLC, et al., 749 F.3d 967 (11th Cir. 2014) (hereinafter, Hunter Wise).

[33] 749 F.3d at 978-79, (citing Black's Law Dictionary 494 (9th ed. 2009)).

[34] 749 F.3d at 979.

[35] Id.

[36] 749 F.3d at 977.

[37] In re Coinflip, Inc., d/b/a Derivabit, and Francisco Riordan, CFTC Docket No. 15-29, 2015 WL 5535736, [Current Transfer Binder] Comm. Fut. L. Rep. (CCH) ¶ 33,538 (CFTC Sept. 17, 2015) (consent order); In re TeraExchange LLC, CFTC Docket No. 15-33, 2015 WL 5658082, [Current Transfer Binder] Comm. Fut. L. Rep. (CCH) ¶ 33,546 (CFTC Sept. 24, 2015) (consent order).

[38] In re BFXNA INC. d/b/a BITFINEX, CFTC Docket No. 16-19 (June 2, 2016) (consent order) (hereinafter, Bitfinex).

[39] Id.

[40] Id.

[41] Specifically, CEA section 2(c)(2)(D)(i) captures any such retail commodity transaction "entered into, or offered . . . on a leveraged or margined basis, or financed by the offeror, the counterparty, or a person acting in concert with the offeror or counterparty on a similar basis."

[42] 7 U.S.C. 2(c)(2)(D)(ii)(III)(aa).

[43] In re Coinflip, Inc., d/b/a Derivabit, and Francisco Riordan, CFTC Docket No. 15-29, 2015 WL 5535736, [Current Transfer Binder] Comm. Fut. L. Rep. (CCH) ¶ 33,538 (CFTC Sept. 17, 2015) (consent order); In re TeraExchange LLC, CFTC Docket No. 15-33, 2015 WL 5658082, [Current Transfer Binder] Comm. Fut. L. Rep. (CCH) ¶ 33,546 (CFTC Sept. 24, 2015) (consent order).

struments, among others).[44] Indeed, since their inception, virtual currency structures were proposed as digital alternatives to gold and other precious metals.[45] As a commodity, virtual currency is subject to applicable provisions of the CEA and Commission regulations.

The Commission interprets the term virtual currency broadly. In the context of this interpretation, virtual or digital currency:[46] Encompasses any digital representation of value (a "digital asset") that functions as a medium of exchange, and any other digital unit of account that is used as a form of a currency (*i.e.*, transferred from one party to another as a medium of exchange); may be manifested through units, tokens, or coins, among other things; and may be distributed by way of digital "smart contracts," among other structures.[47] However, the Commission notes that it does not intend to create a bright line definition at this time given the evolving nature of the commodity and, in some instances, its underlying public distributed ledger technology ("DLT" or "blockchain").

B. The Commission's Interest in Virtual Currency

The Commission recognizes that certain virtual currencies and their underlying blockchain technologies have the potential to yield notable advancements in applications of financial technology ("FinTech"). Indeed, as part of its efforts to facilitate beneficial FinTech innovation and help ensure market integrity, the Commission launched the LabCFTC initiative.[48] This initiative provides the Commission with a platform to engage the FinTech community and promote market-enhancing innovation in furtherance of improving the

quality, resiliency, and competitiveness of the markets overseen by the Commission. As such, the Commission is closely following the development and continuing evolution of blockchain technologies and virtual currencies.

Moreover, since virtual currency can serve as an underlying component of derivatives transactions, the Commission maintains a close interest in the development of the virtual currency marketplace generally. As a practical matter, virtual currency, by virtue of its name, represents a digital medium of exchange for goods and services, similar to fiat currency.[49] Over time, numerous centralized platforms have emerged as markets to convert virtual currency into fiat currency or other virtual currencies. These platforms provide a place to immediately exchange one commodity for another "on the spot."

Some of these centralized platforms also attempt to cater to those that wish to speculate on the price movements of a virtual currency against other currencies. For example, a speculator may purchase virtual currency using borrowed money in the hopes of covering any outstanding balance owed through profits from favorable price movements in the future. This interpretation is specifically focused on such "retail commodity transactions," whereby an entity or platform: (i) Offers margin trading or otherwise facilitates[50] the use of margin, leverage, or financing arrangements for their retail market participants; (ii) typically to enable such participants to speculate or capitalize on price movements of the commodity—two hallmarks of a regulated futures marketplace.[51]

---

[44] *See generally* Further Definition of "Swap," "Security-Based Swap," and "Security-Based Swap Agreement"; Mixed Swaps; Security-Based Swap Agreement Recordkeeping, 77 FR 48208 at 48233 (Aug. 13, 2012) (discussing application of the swap forward exclusion to intangible commodities).

[45] Nick Szabo, *Bit gold*, Unenumerated (Dec. 27, 2008), *http://unenumerated.blogspot.com/2005/12/bit-gold.html*.

[46] The Commission uses the term "virtual currency" and "digital currency" interchangeably for purposes of this proposed interpretation. However, the Commission acknowledges that the two terms may have certain practical differences in other contexts. For example, one view is that "digital currency" includes fiat currencies, while "virtual currency" does not. *See* The Financial Action Task Force [FATF], *Virtual Currencies: Key Definitions and Potential AML/CFT Risks*, at 4 (June 27, 2014), *http://www.fatf-gafi.org/media/fatf/documents/reports/Virtual-currency-key-definitions-and-potential-aml-cft-risks.pdf*. Further, this interpretation is not intended to encompass transactions otherwise covered by CEA section 2(c)(2)(C) and related Commission regulations.

[47] One prominent type of virtual currency is cryptocurrency. Cryptocurrency is described as "an electronic payment system based on cryptographic proof instead of trust, allowing any two willing parties to transact directly with each other without the need for a trusted third party." Satoshi Nakamoto, *Bitcoin: A Peer-to-Peer Electronic Cash System* (Oct. 31, 2008), *https://bitcoin.org/bitcoin.pdf*. Transactions are represented by a hash or "chain of digital signatures," which takes into account the previous owner and the next owner. Given the lack of a centralized authority, transaction verification is "pub-

licly announced" in a transparent ledger "system for participants to agree on a single history" of transactions. *Id.* Each transaction moves from one digital wallet to another, recognized as "nodes" on a distributed ledger network. This structure represents one form of DLT or blockchain technology, which underlies bitcoin—a widely traded virtual currency.

[48] *See* Press Release, Commodity Futures Trading Commission, CFTC Launches LabCFTC as Major FinTech Initiative (May 17, 2017), *http://www.cftc.gov/PressRoom/PressReleases/pr7558-17*.

[49] Michael J. Casey and Paul Vigna, *Bitcoin and the Digital-Currency Revolution*, The Wall Street Journal (Jan. 23, 2015), *https://www.wsj.com/articles/the-revolutionary-power-of-digital-currency-1422035061* ("Once inside the coffee shop, you will open your wallet's smartphone app and hold its QR code reader up to the coffee shop's device" to buy a cup of coffee).

[50] As noted earlier, CEA section 2(c)(2)(D)(i) captures any such retail transaction "entered into, or offered . . . on a leveraged or margined basis, or financed by the offeror, counterparty, or a person acting in concert with the offeror or counterparty on a similar basis." The Commission views any financing arrangements facilitated, arranged, or otherwise endorsed by the offeror or counterparty to satisfy this statutory definition for purposes of this interpretation.

[51] *See, e.g.*, *CFTC v. Int'l Foreign Currency, Inc.*, 334 F. Supp. 2d 305, 310 (E.D.N.Y. 2004) (listing elements typically found in a futures contract); *In re Stovall*, CFTC Docket No. 75-7 [1977-1980 Transfer Binder] Comm. Fut. L. Rep. (CCH) ¶ 20,941, at 23,777 (CFTC Dec. 6, 1979) (describing how futures contracts, being traded on margin, "are entered into

Beyond their practical and speculative functions, the emergence of these nascent markets has also been negatively marked by a variety of retail customer harm that warrants the Commission's attention, including, among other things, flash crashes and other market disruptions,[52] delayed settlements,[53] alleged spoofing,[54] hacks,[55] alleged internal theft,[56] alleged manipulation,[57] smart contract coding vulnerabilities,[58] bucket shop arrangements and other conflicts of interest.[59] These types of activities perpetrated by bad actors can inhibit market-enhancing innovation, undermine market integrity, and stunt further market development.

C. Actual Delivery of Virtual Currency

As underscored by its efforts to engage the FinTech community, the Commission emphasizes that it does not intend to impede market-enhancing innovation or otherwise harm the evolving virtual currency marketplace with this interpretation. To the contrary, the Commission believes this interpretation can help advance a healthy ecosystem and support further market-enhancing innovation. Additionally, the Commission takes seriously its goal of protecting U.S. retail market participants engaged in the virtual currency marketplace that falls within the Commission's jurisdiction—as it would with respect to retail market participants trading in any other retail commodity

marketplace that falls within its jurisdiction. The Commission drafted this interpretation with such a balance in mind.

As discussed above, a retail commodity transaction may be excepted from CEA section 2(c)(2)(D) (and thus not subject to CEA sections 4(a), 4(b), and 4b) if actual delivery of the commodity occurs within 28 days of the transaction.[60] The longstanding Model State Commodity Code also contains an exception from its "commodity contract" regulation when physical settlement occurs within 28 days.[61] However, the Model State Commodity Code provides for the ability to lengthen *or shorten* its 28-day physical delivery exception time period, while CEA section 2(c)(2)(D) only provides the Commission with the ability to lengthen its actual delivery exception time period.[62] Therefore, absent Congressional action, the Commission is unable to reduce the actual delivery exception period for speculative, leverage-based retail commodity transactions in virtual currency. The one-size-fits-all 28 day delivery period in CEA section 2(c)(2)(D) may not properly account for innovation or customary practice in certain cash markets, such as virtual currency transactions that would presumably take much less than 28 days to deliver to a purchaser in a typical spot transaction.[63] Without the application of CEA section 2(c)(2)(D), retail market participants that transact on platforms offering

---

(Footnote Continued)

primarily for the purpose of assuming or shifting the risk of change in value of commodities, rather than for transferring ownership of the actual commodities."); David J. Gilberg, *Regulation of New Financial Instruments Under the Federal Securities and Commodities Laws*, 39 Vand. L. Rev. 1599, 1603-04, n.14 (1986) (typically, futures "traders are interested only in obtaining cash payments of price differentials, not actual commodities").

[52] *See, e.g.*, Paul Vigna, *Virtual Currencies Bitcoin and Ether Wrap Up a Wild Quarter*, The Wall Street Journal, Jul. 3, 2017, at B6 (describing a recent flash crash affecting the price of virtual currency Ether, caused by "a multimillion-dollar sell order" that subsequently "sparked a cascade of stop-loss orders"); Paul Vigna, *BitBeat: Bitcoin Price Drops on Block-Size Debate, 'Flash Crash,'* The Wall Street Journal (Aug. 20, 2015), http://blogs.wsj.com/moneybeat/2015/08/20/bitbeat-bitcoin-price-drops-on-block-size-debate-flash-crash/ ("bitcoin's speculative traders love this kind of stuff [margin trading]; these guys could easily give Wall Street's casino hotshots a run for their money").

[53] Paul Vigna, *Virtual Currencies Bitcoin and Ether Wrap Up a Wild Quarter*, The Wall Street Journal, Jul. 3, 2017, at B6 ("[t]here were delays of hours and even days.").

[54] Lionel Laurent, *Bitcoin Wrestles With Spoofy the Trader*, Bloomberg Gadfly (Aug. 7, 2017), https://www.bloomberg.com/gadfly/articles/2017-08-07/bitcoin-has-a-spoofy-problem.

[55] *See, e.g.*, Paul Vigna and Gregor Stuart Hunter, *Bitcoin Sinks After Exchange Reports Hack*, The Wall Street Journal (Aug. 3, 2016), http://www.wsj.com/articles/bitcoin-sinks-after-exchange-reports-hack-1470195727; Nathaniel Popper and Rachel Abrams, *Apparent Theft Rattles the Bitcoin World*, N.Y. Times, Feb. 25, 2014, at B1; Alex Hern, *A History of Bitcoin Hacks*, The Guardian (Mar. 18, 2014), http://www.theguardian.com/technology/2014/mar/18/history-of-bitcoin-hacks-alternative-currency.

[56] Jessica Lipscomb, *Cryptsy Founder Paul Vernon Disappeared, Along With Millions of His Customers' Cash*, Miami New Times (Jun. 28, 2016), http://www.miaminewtimes.com/news/cryptsy-founder-paul-vernon-disappeared-along-with-millions-of-his-customers-cash-8557571.

[57] Izabella Kaminska, *When OTC markets backfire, bitcoin edition*, Financial Times—Alphaville (Mar. 8, 2017), https://ftalphaville.ft.com/2017/03/08/2185731/when-otc-markets-backfire-bitcoin-edition.

[58] Matthew Leising, *The Ether Thief*, Bloomberg Markets Magazine (Jun. 13, 2017), https://www.bloomberg.com/features/2017-the-ether-thief/ (while not technically an event specific to any one platform, this hack illustrates an event that dramatically affected the price and status of a virtual currency traded on such platforms).

[59] *See, e.g.*, Vitalik Buterin, *Bitfinex: Bitcoinica Rises From The Grave*, Bitcoin Magazine (Nov. 22, 2012), http://bitcoinmagazine.com/articles/bitfinex-bitcoinica-rises-from-the-grave-1353644122; Matt Levine, *How A Bank Should Be?*, Bloomberg View (Mar. 11, 2015), https://www.bloomberg.com/view/articles/2015-03-11/how-should-a-bank-be- ("Just because you mumble the word 'blockchain' doesn't make otherwise illegal things legal"); Matt Levine, *Bitcoin Bucket Shop Kicks Bucket*, Bloomberg View (Jun. 19, 2015), https://www.bloomberg.com/view/articles/2015-06-19/bitcoin-bucket-shop-kicks-bucket.

[60] 7 U.S.C. 2(c)(2)(D)(ii)(III)(aa).

[61] *See* Model State Commodity Code section 1.01(e), [1984-1986 Transfer Binder] Comm. Fut. L. Rep. (CCH) ¶ 22,568 (Apr. 5, 1985).

[62] To date, the Commission has not chosen to extend the 28-day actual delivery period in any instance.

[63] Notably, Congress provided a 2-day actual delivery exception for retail foreign currency transactions. *See* 7 U.S.C. 2(c)(2)(C)(i)(II)(bb)(AA).

speculative transactions in virtual currency (involving margin, leverage, or other financing) will not be afforded many of the protections that flow from registration under the CEA. Despite the statutory limitations, the Commission will utilize its current statutory authority as best it can to prevent fraud in retail commodity transactions involving virtual currency.

The Commission, in interpreting the term actual delivery for the purposes of CEA section 2(c)(2)(D)(ii)(III)(aa), will continue to follow the 2013 Guidance and "employ a functional approach and examine how the agreement, contract, or transaction is marketed, managed, and performed, instead of relying solely on language used by the parties in the agreement, contract, or transaction."[64]

Further, the Commission will continue to assess all relevant factors[65] to aid in such an actual delivery determination. More specifically, the Commission's view of when "actual delivery" has occurred within the context of virtual currency requires:

(1) A customer having the ability to: (i) Take possession and control of the entire quantity of the commodity, whether it was purchased on margin, or using leverage, or any other financing arrangement, and (ii) use it freely in commerce (both within and away from any particular platform) no later than 28 days from the date of the transaction;

(2) The offeror and counterparty seller (including any of their respective affiliates or other persons acting in concert with the offeror or counterparty seller on a similar basis)[66] not retaining any interest in or control over any of the commodity purchased on margin, leverage, or other financing arrangement at the expiration of 28 days from the date of the transaction.[67]

Consistent with the 2013 Guidance, a sham delivery does not constitute actual delivery for purposes of this interpretation. The offeror and counterparty seller, including their agents, must retain no interest or control whatsoever in the

virtual currency acquired by the purchaser at the expiration of 28 days from the date of entering into the transaction. Indeed, in its simplest form, actual delivery of virtual currency connotes the ability of a purchaser to utilize the virtual currency purchased "on the spot" to immediately purchase goods or services with the currency elsewhere.

In the context of an "actual delivery" determination in virtual currency, physical settlement of the commodity must occur. A cash settlement or offset mechanism, as described in Example 4 below, will not satisfy the actual delivery exception of CEA section 2(c)(2)(D). The distinction between physical settlement and cash settlement in this context is akin to settlement of a spot foreign currency transaction at a commercial bank or hotel in a foreign nation—the customer receives physical foreign currency, not U.S. dollars. As mentioned, such physical settlement must occur within 28 days from the date on which the "agreement, contract, or transaction is entered into" to constitute "actual delivery."[68]

Consistent with the interpretation above, the Commission provides the following non-exclusive examples to further clarify the meaning of actual delivery in the virtual currency context:

Example 1: Actual delivery of virtual currency will have occurred if, within 28 days of entering into an agreement, contract, or transaction, there is a record on the relevant public distributed ledger network or blockchain of the transfer of virtual currency, whereby the entire quantity of the purchased virtual currency, including any portion of the purchase made using leverage, margin, or other financing, is transferred from the counterparty seller's blockchain wallet[69] to the purchaser's blockchain wallet, the counterparty seller retains no interest in or control over the transferred commodity, and the counterparty seller has transferred title[70] of the commodity to the purchaser. When a matching platform or other third party offeror acts as an intermediary, the virtual currency's public distributed ledger must reflect the purchased virtual currency transferring

---

[64] 78 FR at 52428.

[65] This list includes, but is not limited to "[o]wnership, possession, title, and physical location of the commodity purchased or sold, both before and after execution of the agreement, contract, or transaction, including all related documentation; the nature of the relationship between the buyer, seller, and possessor of the commodity purchased or sold; and the manner in which the purchase or sale is recorded and completed." *Id.*

[66] The Commission recognizes that the offeror of the transaction and the ultimate counterparty may be two separate entities or may be the same. For example, the Commission would consider as the offeror of the transaction a virtual currency platform that makes the transaction available to the retail customer or otherwise facilitates the transaction. That virtual currency platform could also be considered a counterparty to the transaction if, for example, the platform itself took the opposite side of the transaction or the purchaser of the virtual currency enjoyed privity of contract solely with the platform rather than the seller. Additionally,

the Commission recognizes that some virtual currency platforms may provide a purchaser with the ability to source financing or leverage from other users or third parties. The Commission would consider such third parties or other users to be acting in concert with the offeror or counterparty seller on a similar basis.

[67] Among other things, the Commission may look at whether the offeror or seller retain any ability to access or withdraw any quantity of the commodity purchased from the purchaser's account or wallet.

[68] 78 FR at 52427.

[69] The source of the virtual currency is provided for purposes of this example. However, the focus of this analysis remains on the actions that would constitute actual delivery of the virtual currency to the purchaser.

[70] For purposes of this interpretation, title may be reflected by linking an individual purchaser with proof of ownership of the particular wallet or wallets that contain the purchased virtual currency.

from the counterparty seller's blockchain wallet to the third party offeror's blockchain wallet and, separately, from the third party offeror's blockchain wallet to the purchaser's blockchain wallet, provided that the purchaser's wallet is not affiliated with or controlled by the counterparty seller or third party offeror in any manner.

Example 2: Actual delivery will have occurred if, within 28 days of entering into a transaction: (1) The counterparty seller has delivered the entire quantity of the virtual currency purchased, including any portion of the purchase made using leverage, margin, or financing, into the possession of a depository (*i.e.*, wallet or other relevant storage system) other than one owned, controlled, or operated by the counterparty seller (including any parent companies, partners, agents, affiliates, and others acting in concert with the counterparty seller)[71] that has entered into an agreement with the purchaser to hold virtual currency as agent for the purchaser without regard to any asserted interest of the offeror, the counterparty seller, or persons acting in concert with the offeror or counterparty seller on a similar basis; (2) counterparty seller has transferred title of the commodity to the purchaser; (3) the purchaser has secured full control over the virtual currency (*i.e.*, the ability to immediately remove the full amount of purchased commodity from the depository); and (4) no liens (or other interests of the offeror, counterparty seller, or persons acting in concert with the offeror or counterparty seller on a similar basis) resulting from the use of margin, leverage, or financing used to obtain the entire quantity of the commodity purchased will continue forward at the expiration of 28 days from the date of the transaction.

Example 3: Actual delivery will *not* have occurred if, within 28 days of entering into a transaction, a book entry is made by the offeror or counterparty seller purporting to show that delivery of the virtual currency has been made to the purchaser, but the counterparty seller or offeror has *not*, in accordance with the methods described in Example 1 or Example 2, actually delivered the entire quantity of the virtual currency purchased, including any portion of the purchase made using leverage, margin, or financing, and transferred title to that quantity of the virtual currency to the purchaser, regardless of whether the agreement, contract, or transaction between the purchaser and offeror or counterparty seller purports to create an enforceable obligation[72] to deliver the commodity to the purchaser.

Example 4: Actual delivery will *not* have occurred if, within 28 days of entering into a transac-

tion, the agreement, contract, or transaction for the purchase or sale of virtual currency is rolled, offset against, netted out, or settled in cash or virtual currency (other than the purchased virtual currency) between the purchaser and the offeror or counterparty seller (or persons acting in concert with the offeror or counterparty seller).

III. Request for Comment

The Commission requests comment from the public regarding the Commission's proposed interpretation of "actual delivery" in the context of virtual currency and further invites comments on specific questions related to the Commission's treatment of virtual currency transactions. The Commission encourages all comments including background information, actual market examples, best practice principles, expectations for the possible impact on further innovation, and estimates of any asserted costs and expenses. Specifically, the Commission requests comment on the following questions:

Question 1: As noted in this proposed interpretation, the Commission is limited in its ability to shorten the length of the actual delivery exception period for retail commodity transactions in virtual currency—which presumably take much less than 28 days to deliver to a purchaser. Would a 2-day actual delivery period, such as the actual delivery exception in CEA section 2(c)(2)(C), more accurately apply to such transactions in virtual currency? Would another actual delivery period be more appropriate? What additional information should the Commission consider in determining an appropriate actual delivery exception period for retail commodity transactions in virtual currency? If the Commission were to decide that a shorter actual delivery exception period would be more appropriate in the context of virtual currency, should the Commission engage Congress to consider an adjustment to CEA section 2(c)(2)(D)'s the actual delivery exception? For example, should the Commission seek that Congress amend CEA section 2(c)(2)(D)'s actual delivery exception to be more aligned with the broader delivery period adjustment language in the Model State Commodity Code?

Question 2: With respect to the Commission's proposed interpretation, are there additional examples the Commission should consider in satisfaction of the "actual delivery" exception to CEA section 2(c)(2)(D)?

Question 3: The Commission is concerned about offerors of virtual currency retail commodity transactions that may be subject to conflicts of interest, including situations such as an offeror or

---

[71] The Commission recognizes that an offeror could act in concert with both the purchaser and the counterparty seller in the ordinary course of business if it intermediates a transaction. It is not intended that such activity would prevent an offeror from associating with a depository, as otherwise allowed by this example.

[72] This "enforceable obligation" language is provided in reference to an exception to CEA section 2(c)(2)(D) that is limited by its terms to a commercial transaction involving two commercial entities with a pre-existing line of business in the commodity at issue that is separate and distinct from the business of engaging in a retail commodity transaction. *See* 7 U.S.C. 2(c)(2)(D)(ii)(III)(bb).

its principals taking the opposite side of a customer transaction, either directly or through an affiliated liquidity provider or market maker. These arrangements may, in certain circumstances, resemble bucket shops.[73] How should the Commission evaluate such circumstances if a platform seeks to avail itself of the actual delivery exception? Are there any additional factors that the Commission should consider in its determination of whether the "actual delivery" exception is available?

Question 4: As noted above, CEA sections 4(a), 4(b), and 4b apply to retail commodity transactions "as if" the transaction was a futures contract.[74] Therefore, absent an exception, a retail commodity transaction must be offered on or subject to the rules of a designated contract market ("DCM").[75] Separately, an entity soliciting or accepting orders for retail commodity transactions and accepting money, securities, or property (or extending credit in lieu thereof) to margin, guarantee, or secure such transactions must register with the Commission as a futures commission merchant ("FCM").[76] As a result of these requirements, the Commission recognizes that certain entities or platforms will choose not to offer virtual currency retail commodity transactions. This business decision is not unique to any particular commodity. However, as noted earlier, the Commission does not intend to stifle innovation. Rather, it is acting to protect U.S. retail customers regarding transactions that fall within its jurisdiction. Therefore, the Commission requests comments as to what factors may be relevant to consider regarding the Commission's potential use of its exemptive authority under CEA section 4(c)[77] in this regard. For example, please note any advantages and disadvantages regarding the potential to establish a distinct registration and compliance regime for entities that seek to offer retail commodity transactions in virtual currency. Why would such treatment be uniquely warranted[78] in the context of virtual currency? Please also note any other issues that the Commission should consider regarding such an analysis. What other alternatives should the Commission consider instead of establishing a distinct registration and compliance regime?

Question 5: In Example 2, the Commission sets forth a proposed set of facts that permits actual delivery to a depository instead of the purchaser. What should the Commission consider in further clarifying the meaning of "depository" for purposes of this interpretation? For example, could the depository maintain certain licenses or regis-

trations in order to qualify for this example? In addition, should the Commission further prohibit the depository from being owned or operated by the offeror (including any offeror parent company, partner, agent, and other affiliates)? Please note any factors the Commission should consider in making this determination (such as the effect of contractual agreements between the depository and the offeror).

Question 6: Example 2 also requires the purchaser to secure full control over the virtual currency once it is deposited in a depository in order for the fact pattern to constitute actual delivery. The Commission requests comment regarding what types of circumstances would ensure a purchaser has obtained "full control" of the commodity. For example, is possession of a unique key or other credentials that allow full access and ability to transfer virtual currency sufficient to provide full control? Similarly, how should the Commission view full control by a user in light of commonly used cybersecurity techniques and money transmitter procedures otherwise required by law?

Question 7: Example 2 also requires that no liens resulting from the use of margin, leverage, or financing used to obtain the entire quantity of the commodity purchased by the buyer continue forward at the expiration of 28 days from the date of the transaction. The Commission requests comment regarding circumstances under which a lien would be considered terminated for purposes of this interpretation. For example, are there circumstances where the Commission should consider allowing "forced sale" scenarios, whereby the purchased virtual currency is used to satisfy any resulting liens from the retail commodity transaction, while still interpreting the transaction as having resulted in actual delivery to the purchaser? Should the Commission consider other types of lien scenarios or interests, such as those liens that would not provide a right to repossession of the commodity?

Question 8: As noted above, the status of "title" is one of the factors the Commission considers in an actual delivery determination for retail commodity transactions.[79] In Examples 1 and 2, this interpretation notes that "title" may be reflected by linking an individual purchaser with proof of ownership of the particular wallet or wallets that contain the purchased virtual currency. What additional examples, if any, should the Commission consider to address the status of "title" for the purposes of an actual delivery determination?

---

[73] Vitalik Buterin, *Bitfinex: Bitcoinica Rises From The Grave*, Bitcoin Magazine (Nov. 22, 2012), *http://bitcoinmagazine.com/articles/bitfinex-bitcoinica-rises-from-the-grave-1353644122* (describing a bucket shop arrangement whereby a platform "steps in and acts as the counterparty to some of its users," creating "perverse incentives").

[74] 7 U.S.C. 2(c)(2)(D)(iii).

[75] 7 U.S.C. 6(a).

[76] 7 U.S.C. 1a(28); 7 U.S.C. 6d(a).

[77] 7 U.S.C. 6(c).

[78] Arguably, beyond the distributed ledger technologies, entities offering virtual currency retail commodity transactions operate in a similar manner to any other entity offering retail commodity transactions online.

[79] *See* 78 FR at 52428.

¶1060

Question 9: While this interpretation is solely focused on the actual delivery exception to CEA section 2(c)(2)(D), the Commission recognizes other exceptions may be available.[80] Specifically, the Commission recognizes that the SEC recently issued a statement regarding the application of federal securities laws to certain initial coin offerings ("ICOs").[81] Depending on their use, the tokens or units issued in an ICO may be commodities, commodity options, derivatives, or otherwise fall within the Commission's virtual currency definition described in this interpretation. However, any such tokens that are deemed securities (and trade in a manner that qualifies as a retail commodity transaction) would be excepted from the retail commodity transaction definition pursuant to section 2(c)(2)(D)(ii)(II) of the Act. Are there concerns with the scope of this exception with regard to retail commodity transactions?

What factors should the Commission consider if it were to issue further guidance regarding this exception?

Issued in Washington, DC, on December 15, 2017 by the Commission.

Christopher J. Kirkpatrick,

Secretary of the Commission.

Appendix to Retail Commodity Transactions Involving Virtual Currency—Commission Voting Summary

On this matter, Chairman Giancarlo and Commissioners Quintenz and Behnam voted in the affirmative. No Commissioner voted in the negative.

[FR Doc. 2017-27421 Filed 12-19-17; 8:45 am]

BILLING CODE **6351-01**-P

---

[80] *See generally* 7 U.S.C. 2(c)(2)(D)(ii).

[81] Report of Investigation Pursuant to Section 21(a) of the Securities Exchange Act of 1934: The DAO, Exchange Act Release No. 81207 (Jul. 25, 2017).

¶1060

Appendix D—FinCEN Materials

¶1070 Bank Secrecy Act Sec. 5312(a)

Sec. 5312(a) Definitions and application

[Act of September 13, 1982, Sec. 1 (Bank Secrecy Act)] In this subchapter [II]—

(1) "financial agency" means a person acting for a person (except for a country, a monetary or financial authority acting as a monetary or financial authority, or an international financial institution of which the United States Government is a member) as a financial institution, bailee, depository trustee, or agent, or acting in a similar way related to money, credit, securities, gold, or a transaction in money, credit, securities, or gold.

(2) "financial institution" means—

(A) an insured bank (as defined in section 3(h) of the Federal Deposit Insurance Act (12 U.S.C. 1813(h)));

(B) a commercial bank or trust company;

(C) a private banker;

(D) an agency or branch of a foreign bank in the United States;

(E) any credit union;

(F) a thrift institution;

(G) a broker or dealer registered with the Securities and Exchange Commission under the Securities Exchange Act of 1934 (15 U.S.C. 78a et seq.);

(H) a broker or dealer in securities or commodities;

(I) an investment banker or investment company;

(J) a currency exchange;

(K) an issuer, redeemer, or cashier of travelers' checks, checks, money orders, or similar instruments;

(L) an operator of a credit card system;

(M) an insurance company;

(N) a dealer in precious metals, stones, or jewels;

(O) a pawnbroker;

(P) a loan or finance company;

(Q) a travel agency;

(R) a licensed sender of money or any other person who engages as a business in the transmission of funds, including any person who engages as a business in an informal money transfer system or any network of people who engage as a business in facilitating the transfer of money domestically or internationally outside of the conventional financial institutions system;

(S) a telegraph company;

(T) a business engaged in vehicle sales, including automobile, airplane, and boat sales;

(U) persons involved in real estate closings and settlements;

(V) the United States Postal Service;

(W) an agency of the United States Government or of a State or local government carrying out a duty or power of a business described in this paragraph;

(X) a casino, gambling casino, or gaming establishment with an annual gaming revenue of more than $1,000,000 which—

(i) is licensed as a casino, gambling casino, or gaming establishment under the laws of any State or any political subdivision of any State; or

(ii) is an Indian gaming operation conducted under or pursuant to the Indian Gaming Regulatory Act other than an operation which is limited to class I gaming (as defined in section 4(6) of such Act);".

(Y) any business or agency which engages in any activity which the Secretary of the Treasury determines, by regulation, to be an activity which is similar to, related to, or a substitute for any activity in which any business described in this paragraph is authorized to engage; or

(Z) any other business designated by the Secretary whose cash transactions have a high degree of usefulness in criminal, tax, or regulatory matters.

(3) "monetary instruments" means—

(A) United States coins and currency; and

(B) as the Secretary may prescribe by regulation, coins and currency of a foreign country, travelers' checks, bearer negotiable instruments, bearer investment securities, bearer securities, stock on which title is passed on delivery, and similar material; and

(C) as the Secretary of the Treasury shall provide by regulation for purposes of sections 5316 and 5333, checks, drafts, notes, money orders, and other similar instruments which are drawn on or by a foreign financial institution and are not in bearer form.

(4) NONFINANCIAL TRADE OR BUSINESS.—The term "nonfinancial trade or business" means any trade or business other than a financial institution that is subject to the reporting requirements of section 5313 and regulations prescribed under such section.

(5) "person", in addition to its meaning under section 1 of title 1, includes a trustee, a representative of an estate and, when the Secretary prescribes, a governmental entity.

(6) "United States" means the States of the United States, the District of Columbia, and, when the Secretary prescribes by regulation, the Commonwealth of Puerto Rico, the Virgin Islands, Guam, the Northern Mariana Islands, American Samoa the Trust Territory of the Pacific Islands, a territory or possession of the United States, or a military or diplomatic establishment.

[Definitions in this subchapter]

(b) In this subchapter [II]—

(1) "domestic financial agency" and "domestic financial institution" apply to an action in the United States of a financial agency or institution.

(2) "foreign financial agency" and "foreign financial institution" apply to an action outside the United States of a financial agency or institution.

Additional definitions

(c) For purposes of this subchapter [II], the following definitions shall apply:

(1) CERTAIN INSTITUTIONS INCLUDED IN DEFINITION.—The term "financial institution" (as defined in subsection (a)) includes the following:

(A) Any futures commission merchant, commodity trading advisor, or commodity pool operator registered, or required to register, under the Commodity Exchange Act.

¶1080 Bank Secrecy Act Sec. 5318(a)

Sec. 5318(a) General powers of Secretary

[Act of September 13, 1982, Sec. 1 (Bank Secrecy Act)] The Secretary of the Treasury may (except under section 5315 of this title [31] and regulations prescribed under section 5315)—

(1) except as provided in subsection (b)(2), delegate duties and powers under this subchapter [II] to an appropriate supervising agency and the United States Postal Service;

(2) require a class of domestic financial institutions or nonfinancial trades or businesses to maintain appropriate procedures to ensure compliance with this subchapter [II] and regulations prescribed under this subchapter [II] or to guard against money laundering;

(3) examine any books, papers, records, or other data of domestic financial institutions or nonfinancial trades or businesses relevant to the recordkeeping or reporting requirements of this subchapter [II];

(4) summon a financial institution or nonfinancial trade or business, an officer or employee of a financial institution or nonfinancial trade or business (including a former officer or employee), or any person having possession, custody, or care of the reports and records required under this subchapter [II], to appear before the Secretary of the Treasury or his delegate at a time and place named in the summons and to produce such books, papers, records, or other data, and to give testimony, under oath, as may be relevant or material to an investigation described in subsection (b);

(5) exempt from the requirements of this subchapter [II] any class of transactions within any State if the Secretary determines that—

(A) under the laws of such State, that class of transactions is subject to requirements substantially similar to those imposed under this subchapter; and

(B) there is adequate provision for the enforcement of such requirements;

(6) rely on examinations conducted by a State supervisory agency of a category of financial institution, if the Secretary determines that—

(A) the category of financial institution is required to comply with this subchapter [II] and regulations prescribed under this subchapter [II]; or

(B) the State supervisory agency examines the category of financial institution for compliance with this subchapter and regulations prescribed under this subchapter [II]; and

(7) prescribe an appropriate exemption from a requirement under this subchapter [II] and regulations prescribed under this subchapter [II]. The Secretary may revoke an exemption under this paragraph or paragraph (5) by actually or constructively notifying the parties affected. A revocation is effective during judicial review.

Limitations on summons power

(b) (1) SCOPE OF POWER.—The Secretary of the Treasury may take any action described in paragraph (3) or (4) of subsection (a) only in connection with investigations for the purpose of civil enforcement of violations of this subchapter, section 21 of the Federal Deposit Insurance Act, section 411 of the National Housing Act, or chapter 2 of Public Law 91-508 (12 U.S.C. 1951 et seq.) or any regulation under any such provision.

(2) AUTHORITY TO ISSUE.—A summons may be issued under subsection (a) (4) only by, or with the approval of, the Secretary of the Treasury or a supervisory level delegate of the Secretary of the Treasury.

Administrative aspects of summons

(c) (1) PRODUCTION AT DESIGNATED SITE.—A summons issued pursuant to this section may require that books, papers, records, or other data stored or maintained at any place be produced at any designated location in any State or in any territory or other place subject to the jurisdiction of the United States not more than 500 miles distant from any place where the financial institution or nonfinancial trade or business operates or conducts business in the United States.

(2) FEES AND TRAVEL EXPENSES.—Persons summoned under this section shall be paid the same fees and mileage for travel in the United States that are paid witnesses in the courts of the United States.

(3) NO LIABILITY FOR EXPENSES.—The United States shall not be liable for any expense, other than an expense described in paragraph (2), incurred in connection with the production of books, papers, records, or other data under this section.

Service of summons

(d) Service of a summons issued under this section may be by registered mail or in such other manner calculated to give actual notice as the Secretary may prescribe by regulation.

Contumacy or refusal

(e) (1) REFERRAL TO ATTORNEY GENERAL.—In case of contumacy by a person issued a summons under paragraph (3) or (4) of subsection (a) or a refusal by such person to obey such summons, the Secretary of the Treasury shall refer the matter to the Attorney General.

(2) JURISDICTION OF COURT.—The Attorney General may invoke the aid of any court of the United States within the jurisdiction of which—

(A) the investigation which gave rise to the summons is being or has been carried on;

(B) the person summoned is an inhabitant; or

(C) the person summoned carries on business or may be found,

to compel compliance with the summons.

(3) COURT ORDER.—The court may issue an order requiring the person summoned to appear before the Secretary or his delegate to produce books, papers, records, and other data, to give testimony as may be necessary to explain how such material was compiled and maintained, and to pay the costs of the proceeding.

(4) FAILURE TO COMPLY WITH ORDER.—Any failure to obey the order of the court may be punished by the court as a contempt thereof.

(5) SERVICE OF PROCESS.—All process in any case under this subsection may be served in any judicial district in which such person may be found.

§5318(e) ¶1080

Written and signed statement required

(f) No person shall qualify for an exemption under subsection (a)(5) unless the relevant financial institution or nonfinancial trade or business prepares and maintains a statement which—

(1) describes in detail the reasons why such person is qualified for such exemption; and

(2) contains the signature of such person.

Reporting of suspicious transactions

(g)(1) IN GENERAL.—The Secretary may require any financial institution, and any director, officer, employee, or agent of any financial institution, to report any suspicious transaction relevant to a possible violation of law or regulation.

(2) NOTIFICATION PROHIBITED.—

(A) IN GENERAL.—If a financial institution or any director, officer, employee, or agent of any financial institution, voluntarily or pursuant to this section or any other authority, reports a suspicious transaction to a government agency—

(i) neither the financial institution, director, officer, employee, or agent of such institution (whether or not any such person is still employed by the institution), nor any other current or former director, officer, or employee of, or contractor for, the financial institution or other reporting person, may notify any person involved in the transaction that the transaction has been reported; and

(ii) no current or former officer or employee of or contractor for the Federal Government or of or for any State, local, tribal, or territorial government within the United States, who has any knowledge that such report was made may disclose to any person involved in the transaction that the transaction has been reported, other than as necessary to fulfill the official duties of such officer or employee.

(B) DISCLOSURES IN CERTAIN EMPLOYMENT REFERENCES.—

(i) RULE OF CONSTRUCTION.—Notwithstanding the application of subparagraph (A) in any other context, subparagraph (A) shall not be construed as prohibiting any financial institution, or any director, officer, employee, or agent of such institution, from including information that was included in a report to which subparagraph (A) applies—

(I) in a written employment reference that is provided in accordance with section 18(w) of the Federal Deposit Insurance Act [12 USC 1828(w)]in response to a request from another financial institution; or

(II) in a written termination notice or employment reference that is provided in accordance with the rules of a self-regulatory organization registered with the Securities and Exchange Commission or the Commodity Futures Trading Commission, except that such written reference or notice may not disclose that such information was also included in any such report, or that such report was made.

(ii) INFORMATION NOT REQUIRED.—Clause (i) shall not be construed, by itself, to create any affirmative duty to include any information described in clause (i) in any employment reference or termination notice referred to in clause (i).

(3) LIABILITY FOR DISCLOSURES.—

(A) IN GENERAL.—Any financial institution that makes a voluntary disclosure of any possible violation of law or regulation to a government agency or makes a disclosure pursuant to this subsection or any other authority, and any director, officer, employee, or agent of such institution who makes, or requires another to make any such disclosure, shall not be liable to any person under any law or regulation of the United States, any constitution, law, or regulation of any State or political subdivision of any State, or under any contract or other legally enforceable agreement (including any arbitration agreement), for such disclosure or for any failure to provide notice of such disclosure to the person who is the subject of such disclosure or any other person identified in the disclosure.

(B) RULE OF CONSTRUCTION.—Subparagraph (A) shall not be construed as creating—

(i) any inference that the term "person", as used in such subparagraph, may be construed more broadly than its ordinary usage so as to include any government or agency of government; or

(ii) any immunity against, or otherwise affecting, any civil or criminal action brought by any government or agency of government to enforce any constitution, law, or regulation of such government or agency.

¶1080   §5318(f)

(4) SINGLE DESIGNEE FOR REPORTING SUSPICIOUS TRANSACTIONS.—

(A) IN GENERAL.—In requiring reports under paragraph (1) of suspicious transactions, the Secretary of the Treasury shall designate, to the extent practicable and appropriate, a single officer or agency of the United States to whom such reports shall be made.

(B) DUTY OF DESIGNEE.—The officer or agency of the United States designated by the Secretary of the Treasury pursuant to subparagraph (A) shall refer any report of a suspicious transaction to any appropriate law enforcement, supervisory agency, or United States intelligence agency for use in the conduct of intelligence or counterintelligence activities, including analysis, to protect against international terrorism.

(C) COORDINATION WITH OTHER REPORTING REQUIREMENTS.—Subparagraph (A) shall not be construed as precluding any supervisory agency for any financial institution from requiring the financial institution to submit any information or report to the agency or another agency pursuant to any other applicable provision of law.

Anti-money laundering programs

(h) (1) IN GENERAL.—In order to guard against money laundering through financial institutions, each financial institution shall establish anti-money laundering programs, including, at a minimum—

(A) the development of internal policies, procedures, and controls;

(B) the designation of a compliance officer;

(C) an ongoing employee training program; and

(D) an independent audit function to test programs.

(2) REGULATIONS.—The Secretary of the Treasury, after consultation with the appropriate Federal functional regulator (as defined in section 509 of the Gramm-Leach-Bliley Act) [15 U.S.C. 6809], may prescribe minimum standards for programs established under paragraph (1), and may exempt from the application of those standards any financial institution that is not subject to the provisions of the rules contained in part 103 of title 31, of the Code of Federal Regulations, or any successor rule thereto, for so long as such financial institution is not subject to the provisions of such rules.

(3) CONCENTRATION ACCOUNTS.—The Secretary may prescribe regulations under this subsection that govern maintenance of concentration accounts by financial institutions, in order to ensure that such accounts are not used to prevent association of the identity of an individual customer with the movement of funds of which the customer is the direct or beneficial owner, which regulations shall, at a minimum—

(A) prohibit financial institutions from allowing clients to direct transactions that move their funds into, out of, or through the concentration accounts of the financial institution;

(B) prohibit financial institutions and their employees from informing customers of the existence of, or the means of identifying, the concentration accounts of the institution; and

(C) require each financial institution to establish written procedures governing the documentation of all transactions involving a concentration account, which procedures shall ensure that, any time a transaction involving a concentration account commingles funds belonging to 1 or more customers, the identity of, and specific amount belonging to, each customer is documented.

Due diligence for United States private banking and correspondent bank accounts involving foreign persons

(i) (1) IN GENERAL.—Each financial institution that establishes, maintains, administers, or manages a private banking account or a correspondent account in the United States for a non-United States person, including a foreign individual visiting the United States, or a representative of a non-United States person shall establish appropriate, specific, and, where necessary, enhanced, due diligence policies, procedures, and controls that are reasonably designed to detect and report instances of money laundering through those accounts.

(2) ADDITIONAL STANDARDS FOR CERTAIN CORRESPONDENT ACCOUNTS.—

(A) IN GENERAL.—Subparagraph (B) shall apply if a correspondent account is requested or maintained by, or on behalf of, a foreign bank operating—

(i) under an offshore banking license; or

(ii) under a banking license issued by a foreign country that has been designated—

(I) as noncooperative with international antimoney laundering principles or procedures by an intergovernmental group or organization of which the United States is a member, with which designation the United States representative to the group or organization concurs; or

(II) by the Secretary of the Treasury as warranting special measures due to money laundering concerns.

(B) POLICIES, PROCEDURES, AND CONTROLS.—The enhanced due diligence policies, procedures, and controls required under paragraph (1) shall, at a minimum, ensure that the financial institution in the United States takes reasonable steps—

(i) to ascertain for any such foreign bank, the shares of which are not publicly traded, the identity of each of the owners of the foreign bank, and the nature and extent of the ownership interest of each such owner;

(ii) to conduct enhanced scrutiny of such account to guard against money laundering and report any suspicious transactions under subsection (g); and

(iii) to ascertain whether such foreign bank provides correspondent accounts to other foreign banks and, if so, the identity of those foreign banks and related due diligence information, as appropriate under paragraph (1).

(3) MINIMUM STANDARDS FOR PRIVATE BANKING ACCOUNTS.—If a private banking account is requested or maintained by, or on behalf of, a non-United States person, then the due diligence policies, procedures, and controls required under paragraph (1) shall, at a minimum, ensure that the financial institution takes reasonable steps—

(A) to ascertain the identity of the nominal and beneficial owners of, and the source of funds deposited into, such account as needed to guard against money laundering and report any suspicious transactions under subsection (g); and

(B) to conduct enhanced scrutiny of any such account that is requested or maintained by, or on behalf of, a senior foreign political figure, or any immediate family member or close associate of a senior foreign political figure, that is reasonably designed to detect and report transactions that may involve the proceeds of foreign corruption.

(4) DEFINITIONS.—For purposes of this subsection, the following definitions shall apply:

(A) OFFSHORE BANKING LICENSE.—The term "offshore banking license" means a license to conduct banking activities which, as a condition of the license, prohibits the licensed entity from conducting banking activities with the citizens of, or with the local currency of, the country which issued the license.

(B) PRIVATE BANKING ACCOUNT.—The term "private banking account" means an account (or any combination of accounts) that—

(i) requires a minimum aggregate deposits of funds or other assets of not less than $1,000,000;

(ii) is established on behalf of 1 or more individuals who have a direct or beneficial ownership interest in the account; and

(iii) is assigned to, or is administered or managed by, in whole or in part, an officer, employee, or agent of a financial institution acting as a liaison between the financial institution and the direct or beneficial owner of the account.

Prohibition on United States correspondent accounts with foreign shell banks

(j)(1) IN GENERAL.—A financial institution described in subparagraphs (A) through (G) of section 5312(a)(2) (in this subsection referred to as a "covered financial institution") shall not establish, maintain, administer, or manage a correspondent account in the United States for, or on behalf of, a foreign bank that does not have a physical presence in any country.

(2) PREVENTION OF INDIRECT SERVICE TO FOREIGN SHELL BANKS.—A covered financial institution shall take reasonable steps to ensure that any correspondent account established, maintained, administered, or managed by that covered financial institution in the United States for a foreign bank is not being used by that foreign bank to indirectly provide banking services to another foreign bank that does not have a physical presence in any country. The Secretary of the Treasury shall, by regulation, delineate the reasonable steps necessary to comply with this paragraph.

(3) EXCEPTION.—Paragraphs (1) and (2) do not prohibit a covered financial institution from providing a correspondent account to a foreign bank, if the foreign bank—

(A) is an affiliate of a depository institution, credit union, or foreign bank that maintains a physical presence in the United States or a foreign country, as applicable; and

(B) is subject to supervision by a banking authority in the country regulating the affiliated depository institution, credit union, or foreign bank described in subparagraph (A), as applicable.

(4) DEFINITIONS.—For purposes of this subsection—

(A) the term "affiliate" means a foreign bank that is controlled by or is under common control with a depository institution, credit union, or foreign bank; and

(B) the term "physical presence" means a place of business that—

(i) is maintained by a foreign bank;

(ii) is located at a fixed address (other than solely an electronic address) in a country in which the foreign bank is authorized to conduct banking activities, at which location the foreign bank—

(I) employs 1 or more individuals on a full-time basis; and

(II) maintains operating records related to its banking activities; and

(iii) is subject to inspection by the banking authority which licensed the foreign bank to conduct banking activities.

Bank records related to anti-money laundering programs

(k) (1) DEFINITIONS.—For purposes of this subsection, the following definitions shall apply:

(A) APPROPRIATE FEDERAL BANKING AGENCY.—The term "appropriate Federal banking agency" has the same meaning as in section 3 of the Federal Deposit Insurance Act (12 U.S.C. 1813).

(B) INCORPORATED TERM.—The term "correspondent account" has the same meaning as in section 5318A(e)(1)(B).

(2) 120-HOUR RULE.—Not later than 120 hours after receiving a request by an appropriate Federal banking agency for information related to anti-money laundering compliance by a covered financial institution or a customer of such institution, a covered financial institution shall provide to the appropriate Federal banking agency, or make available at a location specified by the representative of the appropriate Federal banking agency, information and account documentation for any account opened, maintained, administered or managed in the United States by the covered financial institution.

(3) FOREIGN BANK RECORDS.—

(A) SUMMONS OR SUBPOENA OF RECORDS.—

(i) IN GENERAL.—The Secretary of the Treasury or the Attorney General may issue a summons or subpoena to any foreign bank that maintains a correspondent account in the United States and request records related to such correspondent account, including records maintained outside of the United States relating to the deposit of funds into the foreign bank.

(ii) SERVICE OF SUMMONS OR SUBPOENA.—A summons or subpoena referred to in clause (i) may be served on the foreign bank in the United States if the foreign bank has a representative in the United States, or in a foreign country pursuant to any mutual legal assistance treaty, multilateral agreement, or other request for international law enforcement assistance.

(B) ACCEPTANCE OF SERVICE.—

(i) MAINTAINING RECORDS IN THE UNITED STATES.—Any covered financial institution which maintains a correspondent account in the United States for a foreign bank shall maintain records in the United States identifying the owners of such foreign bank and the name and address of a person who resides in the United States and is authorized to accept service of legal process for records regarding the correspondent account.

(ii) LAW ENFORCEMENT REQUEST.—Upon receipt of a written request from a Federal law enforcement officer for information required to be maintained under this paragraph, the covered financial institution shall provide the information to the requesting officer not later than 7 days after receipt of the request.

(C) TERMINATION OF CORRESPONDENT RELATIONSHIP.—

(i) TERMINATION UPON RECEIPT OF NOTICE.—A covered financial institution shall terminate any correspondent relationship with a foreign bank not later than 10 business days after receipt of written notice from the Secretary or the Attorney General (in each case, after consultation with the other) that the foreign bank has failed—

(I) to comply with a summons or subpoena issued under subparagraph (A); or

(II) to initiate proceedings in a United States court contesting such summons or subpoena.

(ii) LIMITATION ON LIABILITY.—A covered financial institution shall not be liable to any person in any court or arbitration proceeding for terminating a correspondent relationship in accordance with this subsection.

(iii) FAILURE TO TERMINATE RELATIONSHIP.—Failure to terminate a correspondent relationship in accordance with this subsection shall render the covered financial institution liable for a civil penalty of up to $10,000 per day until the correspondent relationship is so terminated.

Identification and verification of accountholders

(l)(1) IN GENERAL.—Subject to the requirements of this subsection, the Secretary of the Treasury shall prescribe regulations setting forth the minimum standards for financial institutions and their customers regarding the identity of the customer that shall apply in connection with the opening of an account at a financial institution.

(2) MINIMUM REQUIREMENTS.—The regulations shall, at a minimum, require financial institutions to implement, and customers (after being given adequate notice) to comply with, reasonable procedures for—

(A) verifying the identity of any person seeking to open an account to the extent reasonable and practicable;

(B) maintaining records of the information used to verify a person's identity, including name, address, and other identifying information; and

(C) consulting lists of known or suspected terrorists or terrorist organizations provided to the financial institution by any government agency to determine whether a person seeking to open an account appears on any such list.

(3) FACTORS TO BE CONSIDERED.—In prescribing regulations under this subsection, the Secretary shall take into consideration the various types of accounts maintained by various types of financial institutions, the various methods of opening accounts, and the various types of identifying information available.

(4) CERTAIN FINANCIAL INSTITUTIONS.—In the case of any financial institution the business of which is engaging in financial activities described in section 4(k) of the Bank Holding Company Act of 1956 [12 U.S.C. 1843(k)] (including financial activities subject to the jurisdiction of the Commodity Futures Trading Commission), the regulations prescribed by the Secretary under paragraph (1) shall be prescribed jointly with each Federal functional regulator (as defined in section 509 of the Gramm-Leach-Bliley Act, including the Commodity Futures Trading Commission) appropriate for such financial institution.

(5) EXEMPTIONS.—The Secretary (and, in the case of any financial institution described in paragraph (4), any Federal agency described in such paragraph) may, by regulation or order, exempt any financial institution or type of account from the requirements of any regulation prescribed under this subsection in accordance with such standards and procedures as the Secretary may prescribe.

(6) EFFECTIVE DATE.—Final regulations prescribed under this subsection shall take effect before the end of the 1-year period beginning on the date of enactment of the International Money Laundering Abatement and Financial Anti-Terrorism Act of 2001.

Applicability of rules

(m) Any rules promulgated pursuant to the authority contained in section 21 of the Federal Deposit Insurance Act (12 U.S.C. 1829b) shall apply, in addition to any other financial institution to which such rules apply, to any person that engages as a business in the transmission of funds, including any person who engages as a business in an informal money transfer system or any network of people who engage as a business in facilitating the transfer of money domestically or internationally outside of the conventional financial institutions system.

Reporting of certain cross-border transmittals of funds

(n)(1) IN GENERAL.—Subject to paragraphs (3) and (4), the Secretary shall prescribe regulations requiring such financial institutions as the Secretary determines to be appropriate to report to the Financial Crimes Enforcement Network certain cross-border electronic transmittals of funds, if the Secretary determines that reporting of such transmittals is reasonably necessary to conduct the efforts of the Secretary against money laundering and terrorist financing.

(2) LIMITATION ON REPORTING REQUIREMENTS.—Information required to be reported by the regulations prescribed under paragraph (1) shall not exceed the information required to be retained by the reporting financial institution pursuant to section 21 of the Federal Deposit Insurance Act [12 USC 1829b] and the regulations promulgated thereunder, unless—

¶1080   §5318(l)

(A) the Board of Governors of the Federal Reserve System and the Secretary jointly determine that a particular item or items of information are not currently required to be retained under such section or such regulations; and

(B) the Secretary determines, after consultation with the Board of Governors of the Federal Reserve System, that the reporting of such information is reasonably necessary to conduct the efforts of the Secretary to identify cross-border money laundering and terrorist financing.

(3) FORM AND MANNER OF REPORTS.—In prescribing the regulations required under paragraph (1), the Secretary shall, subject to paragraph (2), determine the appropriate form,

(4) FEASIBILITY REPORT.—

(A) IN GENERAL.—Before prescribing the regulations required under paragraph (1), and as soon as is practicable after the date of enactment of the Intelligence Reform and Terrorism Prevention Act of 2004, the Secretary shall submit a report to the Committee on Banking, Housing, and Urban Affairs of the Senate and the Committee on Financial Services of the House of Representatives that—

(i) identifies the information in cross-border electronic transmittals of funds that may be found in particular cases to be reasonably necessary to conduct the efforts of the Secretary to identify money laundering and terrorist financing, and outlines the criteria to be used by the Secretary to select the situations in which reporting under this subsection may be required;

(ii) outlines the appropriate form, manner, content, and frequency of filing of the reports that may be required under such regulations;

(iii) identifies the technology necessary for the Financial Crimes Enforcement Network to receive, keep, exploit, protect the security of, and disseminate information from reports of cross-border electronic transmittals of funds to law enforcement and other entities engaged in efforts against money laundering and terrorist financing; and

(iv) discusses the information security protections required by the exercise of the Secretary's authority under this subsection.

(B) CONSULTATION.—In reporting the feasibility report under subparagraph (A), the Secretary may consult with the Bank Secrecy Act Advisory Group established by the Secretary, and any other group considered by the Secretary to be relevant.

(5) REGULATIONS.—

(A) IN GENERAL.—Subject to subparagraph (B), the regulations required by paragraph (1) shall be prescribed in final form by the Secretary, in consultation with the Board of Governors of the Federal Reserve System, before the end of the 3-year period beginning on the date of enactment of the National Intelligence Reform Act of 2004.

(B) TECHNOLOGICAL FEASIBILITY.—No regulations shall be prescribed under this subsection before the Secretary certifies to the Congress that the Financial Crimes Enforcement Network has the technological systems in place to effectively and efficiently receive, keep, exploit, protect the security of, and disseminate information from reports of cross-border electronic transmittals of funds to law enforcement and other entities engaged in efforts against money laundering and terrorist financing.

¶1090 Bank Secrecy Act Sec. 5330(a)

Sec. 5330(a) Registration with Secretary if the Treasury required

[Riegle Community Development and Regulatory Improvement Act of 1994, Sec. 408(b) (Bank Secrecy Act)]

(1) IN GENERAL.—Any person who owns or controls a money transmitting business shall register the business (whether or not the business is licensed as a money transmitting business in any State) with the Secretary of the Treasury not later than the end of the 180-day period beginning on the later of—

(A) the date of enactment of the Money Laundering Suppression Act of 1994; or

(B) the date on which the business is established.

(2) FORM AND MANNER OF REGISTRATION.—Subject to the requirements of subsection (b), the Secretary of the Treasury shall prescribe, by regulation, the form and manner for registering a money transmitting business pursuant to paragraph (1).

(3) BUSINESSES REMAIN SUBJECT TO STATE LAW.—This section shall not be construed as superseding any requirement of State law relating to money transmitting businesses operating in such State.

(4) FALSE AND INCOMPLETE INFORMATION.—The filing of false or materially incomplete information in connection with the registration of a money transmitting business shall be considered as a failure to comply with the requirements of this subchapter [II].

Contents of registration

(b) The registration of a money transmitting business under subsection (a) shall include the following information:

(1) The name and location of the business.

(2) The name and address of each person who—

(A) owns or controls the business;

(B) is a director or officer of the business; or

(C) otherwise participates in the conduct of the affairs of the business.

(3) The name and address of any depository institution at which the business maintains a transaction account (as defined in section 19(b)(1)(C) of the Federal Reserve Act).

(4) An estimate of the volume of business in the coming year (which shall be reported annually to the Secretary).

(5) Such other information as the Secretary of the Treasury may require.

Agents of money transmitting businesses

(c)(1) MAINTENANCE OF LISTS OF AGENTS OF MONEY TRANSMITTING BUSINESSES.—Pursuant to regulations which the Secretary of the Treasury shall prescribe, each money transmitting business shall—

(A) maintain a list containing the names and addresses of all persons authorized to act as an agent for such business in connection with activities described in subsection (d)(1)(A) and such other information about such agents as the Secretary may require; and

(B) make the list and other information available on request to any appropriate law enforcement agency.

(2) TREATMENT OF AGENT AS MONEY TRANSMITTING BUSINESS.—The Secretary of the Treasury shall prescribe regulations establishing, on the basis of such criteria as the Secretary determines to be appropriate, a threshold point for treating an agent of a money transmitting business as a money transmitting business for purposes of this section.

Definitions

(d) For purposes of this section, the following definitions shall apply:

(1) MONEY TRANSMITTING BUSINESS.—The term "money transmitting business" means any business other than the United States Postal Service which—

(A) provides check cashing, currency exchange, or money transmitting or remittance services, or issues or redeems money orders, travelers' checks, and other similar instruments or any other person who engages as a business in the transmission of funds, including any person who engages as a business in an informal money transfer system or any network of people who engage as a business in facilitating the transfer of money domestically or internationally outside of the conventional financial institutions system;

(B) is required to file reports under section 5313; and

(C) is not a depository institution (as defined in section 5313(g)).

(2) MONEY TRANSMITTING SERVICE.—The term "money transmitting service" includes accepting currency or funds denominated in the currency of any country and transmitting the currency or funds, or the value of the currency or funds, by any means through a financial agency or institution, a Federal reserve bank or other facility of the Board of Governors of the Federal Reserve System, or an electronic funds transfer network.

Civil penalty for failure to comply with registration requirements

(e)(1) IN GENERAL.—Any person who fails to comply with any requirement of this section or any regulation prescribed under this section shall be liable to the United States for a civil penalty of $5,000 for each such violation.

(2) CONTINUING VIOLATION.—Each day a violation described in paragraph (1) continues shall constitute a separate violation for purposes of such paragraph.

(3) ASSESSMENTS.—Any penalty imposed under this subsection shall be assessed and collected by the Secretary of the Treasury in the manner provided in section 5321 and any such assessment shall be subject to the provisions of such section.

¶ 1100

31 CFR § 1010.100 General definitions.

When used in this chapter and in forms prescribed under this chapter, where not otherwise distinctly expressed or manifestly incompatible with the intent thereof, terms shall have the meanings ascribed in this subpart. Terms applicable to a particular type of financial institution or specific part or subpart of this chapter are located in that part or subpart. Terms may have different meanings in different parts or subparts.

(a) *Accept.* A receiving financial institution, other than the recipient's financial institution, accepts a transmittal order by executing the transmittal order. A recipient's financial institution accepts a transmittal order by paying the recipient, by notifying the recipient of the receipt of the order or by otherwise becoming obligated to carry out the order.

(b) *At one time.* For purposes of § 1010.340 of this part, a person who transports, mails, ships or receives; is about to or attempts to transport, mail or ship; or causes the transportation, mailing, shipment or receipt of monetary instruments, is deemed to do so "at one time" if:

(1) That person either alone, in conjunction with or on behalf of others;

(2) Transports, mails, ships or receives in any manner; is about to transport, mail or ship in any manner; or causes the transportation, mailing, shipment or receipt in any manner of;

(3) Monetary instruments;

(4) Into the United States or out of the United States;

(5) Totaling more than $10,000;

(6) (i) On one calendar day; or

(ii) If for the purpose of evading the reporting requirements of § 1010.340, on one or more days.

(c) *Attorney General.* The Attorney General of the United States.

(d) *Bank.* Each agent, agency, branch or office within the United States of any person doing business in one or more of the capacities listed below:

(1) A commercial bank or trust company organized under the laws of any State or of the United States;

(2) A private bank;

(3) A savings and loan association or a building and loan association organized under the laws of any State or of the United States;

(4) An insured institution as defined in section 401 of the National Housing Act;

(5) A savings bank, industrial bank or other thrift institution;

(6) A credit union organized under the law of any State or of the United States;

(7) Any other organization (except a money services business) chartered under the banking laws of any state and subject to the supervision of the bank supervisory authorities of a State;

(8) A bank organized under foreign law;

(9) Any national banking association or corporation acting under the provisions of section 25(a) of the Act of Dec. 23, 1913, as added by the Act of Dec. 24, 1919, ch. 18, 41 Stat. 378, as amended (12 U.S.C. 611-32).

(e) *Bank Secrecy Act.* The Currency and Foreign Transactions Reporting Act, its amendments, and the other statutes relating to the subject matter of that Act, have come to be referred to as the Bank Secrecy Act. These statutes are codified at 12 U.S.C. 1829b, 12 U.S.C. 1951-1959, 18 U.S.C. 1956, 18 U.S.C. 1957, 18 U.S.C. 1960, and 31 U.S.C. 5311-5314 and 5316-5332 and notes thereto.

(f) *Beneficiary.* The person to be paid by the beneficiary's bank.

(g) *Beneficiary's bank.* The bank or foreign bank identified in a payment order in which an account of the beneficiary is to be credited pursuant to the order or which otherwise is to make payment to the beneficiary if the order does not provide for payment to an account.

(h) *Broker or dealer in securities.* A broker or dealer in securities, registered or required to be registered with the Securities and Exchange Commission under the Securities Exchange Act of 1934, except persons who register pursuant to section 15(b)(11) of the Securities Exchange Act of 1934.

(i) *Business day.* As used in this chapter with respect to banks, business day means that day, as normally communicated to its depository customers, on which a bank routinely posts a particular transaction to its customer's account.

(j) *Commodity.* Any good, article, service, right, or interest described in section 1a(4) of the Commodity Exchange Act ("CEA"), 7 U.S.C. 1a(4).

(k) *Common carrier.* Any person engaged in the business of transporting individuals or goods for a fee who holds himself out as ready to engage in such transportation for hire and who undertakes to do so indiscriminately for all persons who are prepared to pay the fee for the particular service offered.

(l) *Contract of sale.* Any sale, agreement of sale, or agreement to sell as described in section 1a(7) of the CEA, 7 U.S.C. 1a(7).

(m) *Currency.* The coin and paper money of the United States or of any other country that is designated as legal tender and that circulates and is customarily used and accepted as a medium of exchange in the country of issuance. Currency includes U.S. silver certificates, U.S. notes and Federal Reserve notes. Currency also includes official foreign bank notes that are customarily used and accepted as a medium of exchange in a foreign country.

(n) *Deposit account.* Deposit accounts include transaction accounts described in paragraph (ccc) of this section, savings accounts, and other time deposits.

¶1100   31 CFR § 1010.100

(o) *Domestic*. When used herein, refers to the doing of business within the United States, and limits the applicability of the provision where it appears to the performance by such institutions or agencies of functions within the United States.

(p) *Established customer*. A person with an account with the financial institution, including a loan account or deposit or other asset account, or a person with respect to which the financial institution has obtained and maintains on file the person's name and address, as well as taxpayer identification number (*e.g.*, social security or employer identification number) or, if none, alien identification number or passport number and country of issuance, and to which the financial institution provides financial services relying on that information.

(q) *Execution date*. The day on which the receiving financial institution may properly issue a transmittal order in execution of the sender's order. The execution date may be determined by instruction of the sender but cannot be earlier than the day the order is received, and, unless otherwise determined, is the day the order is received. If the sender's instruction states a payment date, the execution date is the payment date or an earlier date on which execution is reasonably necessary to allow payment to the recipient on the payment date.

(r) *Federal functional regulator*.

(1) The Board of Governors of the Federal Reserve System;

(2) The Office of the Comptroller of the Currency;

(3) The Board of Directors of the Federal Deposit Insurance Corporation;

(4) The Office of Thrift Supervision;

(5) The National Credit Union Administration;

(6) The Securities and Exchange Commission; or

(7) The Commodity Futures Trading Commission.

(s) *FinCEN*. FinCEN means the Financial Crimes Enforcement Network, a bureau of the Department of the Treasury.

(t) *Financial institution*. Each agent, agency, branch, or office within the United States of any person doing business, whether or not on a regular basis or as an organized business concern, in one or more of the capacities listed below:

(1) A bank (except bank credit card systems);

(2) A broker or dealer in securities;

(3) A money services business as defined in paragraph (ff) of this section;

(4) A telegraph company;

(5)(i) *Casino*. A casino or gambling casino that: Is duly licensed or authorized to do business as such in the United States, whether under the laws of a State or of a Territory or Insular Possession of the United States, or under the Indian Gaming Regulatory Act or other Federal, State, or tribal law or arrangement affecting Indian lands (including, without limitation, a casino operating on the assumption or under the view that no such authorization is required for casino operation on Indian lands); and has gross annual gaming revenue in excess of $1 million. The term includes the principal headquarters and every domestic branch or place of business of the casino.

(ii) For purposes of this paragraph (t)(5), "gross annual gaming revenue" means the gross gaming revenue received by a casino, during either the previous business year or the current business year of the casino. A casino or gambling casino which is a casino for purposes of this chapter solely because its gross annual gaming revenue exceeds $1,000,000 during its current business year, shall not be considered a casino for purposes of this chapter prior to the time in its current business year that its gross annual gaming revenue exceeds $1,000,000.

(iii) Any reference in this chapter, other than in this paragraph (t)(5) and in paragraph (t)(6) of this section, to a casino shall also include a reference to a card club, unless the provision in question contains specific language varying its application to card clubs or excluding card clubs from its application;

(6)(i) *Card club*. A card club, gaming club, card room, gaming room, or similar gaming establishment that is duly licensed or authorized to do business as such in the United States, whether under the laws of a State, of a Territory or Insular Possession of the United States, or of a political subdivision of any of the foregoing, or under the Indian Gaming Regulatory Act or other Federal, State, or tribal law or arrangement affecting Indian lands (including, without limitation, an establishment operating on the assumption or under the view that no such authorization is required for operation on Indian lands for an establishment of such type), and that has gross annual gaming revenue in excess of $1,000,000. The term includes the principal headquarters and every domestic branch or place of business of the establishment. The term "casino," as used in this chapter shall include a reference to "card club" to the extent provided in paragraph (t)(5)(iii) of this section.

(ii) For purposes of this paragraph (t)(6), "gross annual gaming revenue" means the gross revenue derived from or generated by customer gaming activity (whether in the form of per-game or per-table fees, however computed, rentals, or otherwise) and received by an establishment, during either the establishment's previous business year or its current business year. A card club that is a financial institution for purposes of this chapter solely because its gross annual revenue exceeds $1,000,000 during its current business year, shall not be considered a financial institution for purposes of this chapter prior to the time in its current business year when its gross annual revenue exceeds $1,000,000;

(7) A person subject to supervision by any state or Federal bank supervisory authority;

(8) A futures commission merchant;

(9) An introducing broker in commodities; or

(10) A mutual fund.

(11) An investment adviser.

31 CFR § 1010.100   ¶1100

(u) *Foreign bank.* A bank organized under foreign law, or an agency, branch or office located outside the United States of a bank. The term does not include an agent, agency, branch or office within the United States of a bank organized under foreign law.

(v) *Foreign financial agency.* A person acting outside the United States for a person (except for a country, a monetary or financial authority acting as a monetary or financial authority, or an international financial institution of which the United States Government is a member) as a financial institution, bailee, depository trustee, or agent, or acting in a similar way related to money, credit, securities, gold, or a transaction in money, credit, securities, or gold.

(w) *Funds transfer.* The series of transactions, beginning with the originator's payment order, made for the purpose of making payment to the beneficiary of the order. The term includes any payment order issued by the originator's bank or an intermediary bank intended to carry out the originator's payment order. A funds transfer is completed by acceptance by the beneficiary's bank of a payment order for the benefit of the beneficiary of the originator's payment order. Electronic fund transfers as defined in section 903(7) of the Electronic Fund Transfer Act (15 U.S.C. 1693a(7)), as well as any other funds transfers that are made through an automated clearinghouse, an automated teller machine, or a point-of-sale system, are excluded from this definition.

(x) *Futures commission merchant.* Any person registered or required to be registered as a futures commission merchant with the Commodity Futures Trading Commission ("CFTC") under the CEA, except persons who register pursuant to section 4f(a)(2) of the CEA, 7 U.S.C. 6f(a)(2).

(y) *Indian Gaming Regulatory Act.* The Indian Gaming Regulatory Act of 1988, codified at 25 U.S.C. 2701-2721 and 18 U.S.C. 1166-68.

(z) *Intermediary bank.* A receiving bank other than the originator's bank or the beneficiary's bank.

(aa) *Intermediary financial institution.* A receiving financial institution, other than the transmittor's financial institution or the recipient's financial institution. The term intermediary financial institution includes an intermediary bank.

(bb) *Introducing broker-commodities.* Any person registered or required to be registered as an introducing broker with the CFTC under the CEA, except persons who register pursuant to section 4f(a)(2) of the CEA, 7 U.S.C. 6f(a)(2).

(cc) *Investment security.* An instrument which:

(1) Is issued in bearer or registered form;

(2) Is of a type commonly dealt in upon securities exchanges or markets or commonly recognized in any area in which it is issued or dealt in as a medium for investment;

(3) Is either one of a class or series or by its terms is divisible into a class or series of instruments; and

(4) Evidences a share, participation or other interest in property or in an enterprise or evidences an obligation of the issuer.

(dd) *Monetary instruments.* (1) Monetary instruments include:

(i) Currency;

(ii) Traveler's checks in any form;

(iii) All negotiable instruments (including personal checks, business checks, official bank checks, cashier's checks, third-party checks, promissory notes (as that term is defined in the Uniform Commercial Code), and money orders) that are either in bearer form, endorsed without restriction, made out to a fictitious payee (for the purposes of § 1010.340), or otherwise in such form that title thereto passes upon delivery;

(iv) Incomplete instruments (including personal checks, business checks, official bank checks, cashier's checks, third-party checks, promissory notes (as that term is defined in the Uniform Commercial Code), and money orders) signed but with the payee's name omitted; and

(v) Securities or stock in bearer form or otherwise in such form that title thereto passes upon delivery.

(2) Monetary instruments do not include warehouse receipts or bills of lading.

(ee) [Reserved]

(ff) *Money services business.* A person wherever located doing business, whether or not on a regular basis or as an organized or licensed business concern, wholly or in substantial part within the United States, in one or more of the capacities listed in paragraphs (ff)(1) through (ff)(7) of this section. This includes but is not limited to maintenance of any agent, agency, branch, or office within the United States.

(1) *Dealer in foreign exchange.* A person that accepts the currency, or other monetary instruments, funds, or other instruments denominated in the currency, of one or more countries in exchange for the currency, or other monetary instruments, funds, or other instruments denominated in the currency, of one or more other countries in an amount greater than $1,000 for any other person on any day in one or more transactions, whether or not for sameday delivery.

(2) *Check casher.* (i) In general. A person that accepts checks (as defined in the Uniform Commercial Code), or monetary instruments (as defined at § 1010.100(dd)(1)(ii), (iii), (iv), and (v)) in return for currency or a combination of currency and other monetary instruments or other instruments, in an amount greater than $1,000 for any person on any day in one or more transactions.

(ii) *Facts and circumstances; Limitations.* Whether a person is a check casher as described in this section is a matter of facts and circumstances. The term "check casher" shall not include:

(A) A person that sells prepaid access in exchange for a check (as defined in the Uniform

Commercial Code), monetary instrument or other instrument;

(B) A person that solely accepts monetary instruments as payment for goods or services other than check cashing services;

(C) A person that engages in check cashing for the verified maker of the check who is a customer otherwise buying goods and services;

(D) A person that redeems its own checks; or

(E) A person that only holds a customer's check as collateral for repayment by the customer of a loan.

(3) *Issuer or seller of traveler's checks or money orders.* A person that

(i) Issues traveler's checks or money orders that are sold in an amount greater than $1,000 to any person on any day in one or more transactions; or

(ii) Sells traveler's checks or money orders in an amount greater than $1,000 to any person on any day in one or more transactions.

(4) *Provider of prepaid access—*

(i) *In general.* A provider of prepaid access is the participant within a prepaid program that agrees to serve as the principal conduit for access to information from its fellow program participants. The participants in each prepaid access program must determine a single participant within the prepaid program to serve as the provider of prepaid access.

(ii) *Considerations for provider determination.* In the absence of registration as the provider of prepaid access for a prepaid program by one of the participants in a prepaid access program, the provider of prepaid access is the person with principal oversight and control over the prepaid program. Which person exercises "principal oversight and control" is a matter of facts and circumstances. Activities that indicate "principal oversight and control" include:

(A) Organizing the prepaid program;

(B) Setting the terms and conditions of the prepaid program and determining that the terms have not been exceeded;

(C) Determining the other businesses that will participate in the prepaid program, which may include the issuing bank, the payment processor, or the distributor;

(D) Controlling or directing the appropriate party to initiate, freeze, or terminate prepaid access; and

(E) Engaging in activity that demonstrates oversight and control of the prepaid program.

(iii) *Prepaid program.* A prepaid program is an arrangement under which one or more persons acting together provide(s) prepaid access. However, an arrangement is not a prepaid program if:

(A) It provides closed loop prepaid access to funds not to exceed $2,000 maximum value that can be associated with a prepaid access device or vehicle on any day;

(B) It provides prepaid access solely to funds provided by a Federal, State, local, Territory and Insular Possession, or Tribal government agency;

(C) It provides prepaid access solely to funds from pre-tax flexible spending arrangements for health care and dependent care expenses, or from Health Reimbursement Arrangements (as defined in 26 U.S.C. 105(b) and 125) for health care expenses; or

(D) *(1)* It provides prepaid access solely to:

(i) Employment benefits, incentives, wages or salaries; or

(ii) Funds not to exceed $1,000 maximum value and from which no more than $1,000 maximum value can be initially or subsequently loaded, used, or withdrawn on any day through a device or vehicle; and

(2) It does not permit:

(i) Funds or value to be transmitted internationally;

(ii) Transfers between or among users of prepaid access within a prepaid program; or

(iii) Loading additional funds or the value of funds from non-depository sources.

(5) *Money transmitter.* (i) *In general.*

(A) A person that provides money transmission services. The term "money transmission services" means the acceptance of currency, funds, or other value that substitutes for currency from one person *and* the transmission of currency, funds, or other value that substitutes for currency to another location or person by any means. "Any means" includes, but is not limited to, through a financial agency or institution; a Federal Reserve Bank or other facility of one or more Federal Reserve Banks, the Board of Governors of the Federal Reserve System, or both; an electronic funds transfer network; or an informal value transfer system; or

(B) Any other person engaged in the transfer of funds.

(ii) *Facts and circumstances; Limitations.* Whether a person is a money transmitter as described in this section is a matter of facts and circumstances. The term "money transmitter" shall not include a person that only:

(A) Provides the delivery, communication, or network access services used by a money transmitter to support money transmission services;

(B) Acts as a payment processor to facilitate the purchase of, or payment of a bill for, a good or service through a clearance and settlement system by agreement with the creditor or seller;

(C) Operates a clearance and settlement system or otherwise acts as an intermediary solely between BSA regulated institutions. This includes but is not limited to the Fedwire system, electronic funds transfer networks, certain registered clearing agencies regulated by the Securities and Exchange Commission ("SEC"), and derivatives clearing organizations, or other clearinghouse arrangements established by a financial agency or institution;

(D) Physically transports currency, other monetary instruments, other commercial paper, or other value that substitutes for currency as a person primarily engaged in such business, such as an armored car, from one person to the same person at another location or to an account belonging to the same person at a financial institution, provided that the person engaged in physical transportation has no more than a custodial interest in the currency, other monetary instruments, other commercial paper, or other value at any point during the transportation;

(E) Provides prepaid access; or

(F) Accepts and transmits funds only integral to the sale of goods or the provision of services, other than money transmission services, by the person who is accepting and transmitting the funds.

(6) *U.S. Postal Service.* The United States Postal Service, except with respect to the sale of postage or philatelic products.

(7) *Seller of prepaid access.* Any person that receives funds or the value of funds in exchange for an initial loading or subsequent loading of prepaid access if that person:

(i) Sells prepaid access offered under a prepaid program that can be used before verification of customer identification under § 1022.210(d)(1)(iv); or

(ii) Sells prepaid access (including closed loop prepaid access) to funds that exceed $10,000 to any person during any one day, and has not implemented policies and procedures reasonably adapted to prevent such a sale.

(8) *Limitation.* For the purposes of this section, the term "money services business" shall not include:

(i) A bank or foreign bank;

(ii) A person registered with, and functionally regulated or examined by, the SEC or the CFTC, or a foreign financial agency that engages in financial activities that, if conducted in the United States, would require the foreign financial agency to be registered with the SEC or CFTC; or

(iii) A natural person who engages in an activity identified in paragraphs (ff)(1) through (ff)(5) of this section on an infrequent basis and not for gain or profit.

(gg) *Mutual fund.* An "investment company" (as the term is defined in section 3 of the Investment Company Act (15 U.S.C. 80a-3)) that is an "open-end company" (as that term is defined in section 5 of the Investment Company Act (15 U.S.C. 80a-5)) that is registered or is required to register with the Commission under section 8 of the Investment Company Act (15 U.S.C. 80a-8).

(hh) *Option on a commodity.* Any agreement, contract, or transaction described in section 1a(26) of the CEA, 7 U.S.C. 1a(26).

(ii) *Originator.* The sender of the first payment order in a funds transfer.

(jj) *Originator's bank.* The receiving bank to which the payment order of the originator is issued if the originator is not a bank or foreign bank, or the originator if the originator is a bank or foreign bank.

(kk) *Payment date.* The day on which the amount of the transmittal order is payable to the recipient by the recipient's financial institution. The payment date may be determined by instruction of the sender, but cannot be earlier than the day the order is received by the recipient's financial institution and, unless otherwise prescribed by instruction, is the date the order is received by the recipient's financial institution.

(ll) *Payment order.* An instruction of a sender to a receiving bank, transmitted orally, electronically, or in writing, to pay, or to cause another bank or foreign bank to pay, a fixed or determinable amount of money to a beneficiary if:

(1) The instruction does not state a condition to payment to the beneficiary other than time of payment;

(2) The receiving bank is to be reimbursed by debiting an account of, or otherwise receiving payment from, the sender; and

(3) The instruction is transmitted by the sender directly to the receiving bank or to an agent, funds transfer system, or communication system for transmittal to the receiving bank.

(mm) *Person.* An individual, a corporation, a partnership, a trust or estate, a joint stock company, an association, a syndicate, joint venture, or other unincorporated organization or group, an Indian Tribe (as that term is defined in the Indian Gaming Regulatory Act), and all entities cognizable as legal personalities.

(nn) *Receiving bank.* The bank or foreign bank to which the sender's instruction is addressed.

(oo) *Receiving financial institution.* The financial institution or foreign financial agency to which the sender's instruction is addressed. The term receiving financial institution includes a receiving bank.

(pp) *Recipient.* The person to be paid by the recipient's financial institution. The term recipient includes a beneficiary, except where the recipient's financial institution is a financial institution other than a bank.

(qq) *Recipient's financial institution.* The financial institution or foreign financial agency identified in a transmittal order in which an account of the recipient is to be credited pursuant to the transmittal order or which otherwise is to make payment to the recipient if the order does not provide for payment to an account. The term recipient's financial institution includes a beneficiary's bank, except where the beneficiary is a recipient's financial institution.

(rr) *Secretary.* The Secretary of the Treasury or any person duly authorized by the Secretary to perform the function mentioned.

(ss) *Security.* Security means any instrument or interest described in section 3(a)(10) of the Securities Exchange Act of 1934, 15 U.S.C. 78c(a)(10).

(tt) *Self-regulatory organization:*

(1) Shall have the same meaning as provided in section 3(a)(26) of the Securities Exchange Act of 1934 (15 U.S.C. 78c(a)(26)); and

¶1100   31 CFR § 1010.100

(2) Means a "registered entity" or a "registered futures association" as provided in section 1a(29) or 17, respectively, of the Commodity Exchange Act (7 U.S.C. 1a(29), 21).

(uu) *Sender.* The person giving the instruction to the receiving financial institution.

(vv) *State.* The States of the United States and, wherever necessary to carry out the provisions of this chapter, the District of Columbia.

(ww) *Prepaid access.* Access to funds or the value of funds that have been paid in advance and can be retrieved or transferred at some point in the future through an electronic device or vehicle, such as a card, code, electronic serial number, mobile identification number, or personal identification number.

(xx) *Structure (structuring).* For purposes of § 1010.314, a person structures a transaction if that person, acting alone, or in conjunction with, or on behalf of, other persons, conducts or attempts to conduct one or more transactions in currency, in any amount, at one or more financial institutions, on one or more days, in any manner, for the purpose of evading the reporting requirements under § § 1010.311, 1010.313, 1020.315, 1021.311 and 1021.313 of this chapter. "In any manner" includes, but is not limited to, the breaking down of a single sum of currency exceeding $10,000 into smaller sums, including sums at or below $10,000, or the conduct of a transaction, or series of currency transactions at or below $10,000. The transaction or transactions need not exceed the $10,000 reporting threshold at any single financial institution on any single day in order to constitute structuring within the meaning of this definition.

(yy) *Taxpayer Identification Number.* Taxpayer Identification Number ("TIN") is defined by section 6109 of the Internal Revenue Code of 1986 (26 U.S.C. 6109) and the Internal Revenue Service regulations implementing that section (*e.g.,* social security number or employer identification number).

(zz) *Territories and Insular Possessions.* The Commonwealth of Puerto Rico, the United States Virgin Islands, Guam, the Commonwealth of the Northern Mariana Islands, and all other territories and possessions of the United States other than the Indian lands and the District of Columbia.

(aaa) [Reserved]

(bbb) *Transaction.* (1) Except as provided in paragraph (bbb)(2) of this section, transaction means a purchase, sale, loan, pledge, gift, transfer, delivery, or other disposition, and with respect to a financial institution includes a deposit, withdrawal, transfer between accounts, exchange of currency, loan, extension of credit, purchase or sale of any stock, bond, certificate of deposit, or other monetary instrument, security, contract of sale of a commodity for future delivery, option on any contract of sale of a commodity for future delivery, option on a commodity, purchase or redemption of any money order, payment or order for any money remittance or trans-

fer, purchase or redemption of casino chips or tokens, or other gaming instruments or any other payment, transfer, or delivery by, through, or to a financial institution, by whatever means effected.

(2) For purposes of § § 1010.311, 1010.313, 1020.315, 1021.311, 1021.313, and other provisions of this chapter relating solely to the report required by those sections, the term "transaction in currency" shall mean a transaction involving the physical transfer of currency from one person to another. A transaction which is a transfer of funds by means of bank check, bank draft, wire transfer, or other written order, and which does not include the physical transfer of currency, is not a transaction in currency for this purpose.

(ccc) *Transaction account.* Transaction accounts include those accounts described in 12 U.S.C. 461(b)(1)(C), money market accounts and similar accounts that take deposits and are subject to withdrawal by check or other negotiable order.

(ddd) *Transmittal of funds.* A series of transactions beginning with the transmittor's transmittal order, made for the purpose of making payment to recipient of the order. The term includes any transmittal order issued by the transmittor's financial institution or an intermediary financial institution intended to carry out the transmittor's transmittal order. The term transmittal of funds includes a funds transfer. A transmittal of funds is completed by acceptance by the recipient's financial institution of a transmittal order for the benefit of the recipient of the transmittor's transmittal order. Electronic fund transfers as defined in section 903(7) of the Electronic Fund Transfer Act (15 U.S.C. 1693a(7)), as well as any other funds transfers that are made through an automated clearinghouse, an automated teller machine, or a point-of-sale system, are excluded from this definition.

(eee) *Transmittal order.* The term transmittal order includes a payment order and is an instruction of a sender to a receiving financial institution, transmitted orally, electronically, or in writing, to pay, or cause another financial institution or foreign financial agency to pay, a fixed or determinable amount of money to a recipient if:

(1) The instruction does not state a condition to payment to the recipient other than time of payment;

(2) The receiving financial institution is to be reimbursed by debiting an account of, or otherwise receiving payment from, the sender; and

(3) The instruction is transmitted by the sender directly to the receiving financial institution or to an agent or communication system for transmittal to the receiving financial institution.

(fff) *Transmittor.* The sender of the first transmittal order in a transmittal of funds. The term transmittor includes an originator, except where the transmittor's financial institution is a financial institution or foreign financial agency other than a bank or foreign bank.

(ggg) *Transmittor's financial institution.* The receiving financial institution to which the transmittal order of the transmittor is issued if the transmittor is not a financial institution or foreign financial agency, or the transmittor if the transmittor is a financial institution or foreign financial agency. The term transmittor's financial institution includes an originator's bank, except where the originator is a transmittor's financial institution other than a bank or foreign bank.

(hhh) *United States.* The States of the United States, the District of Columbia, the Indian lands (as that term is defined in the Indian Gaming Regulatory Act), and the Territories and Insular Possessions of the United States.

(iii) *U.S. person.* (1) A United States citizen; or

(2) A person other than an individual (such as a corporation, partnership or trust), that is established or organized under the laws of a State or the United States. Non-U.S. person means a person that is not a U.S. person.

(jjj) *U.S. Postal Service.* The United States Postal Service, except with respect to the sale of postage or philatelic products.

(kkk) *Closed loop prepaid access.* Prepaid access to funds or the value of funds that can be used only for goods or services in transactions involving a defined merchant or location (or set of locations), such as a specific retailer or retail chain, a college campus, or a subway system.

(lll) *Loan or finance company.* A person engaged in activities that take place wholly or in substantial part within the United States in one or more of the capacities listed below, whether or not on a regular basis or as an organized business concern. This includes but is not limited to maintenance of any agent, agency, branch, or office within the United States. For the purposes of this paragraph (lll), the term "loan or finance company" shall include a sole proprietor acting as a loan or finance company, and shall not include: A bank, a person registered with and functionally regulated or examined by the Securities and Exchange Commission or the Commodity Futures Trading Commission, any government sponsored enterprise regulated by the Federal Housing Finance Agency, any Federal or state agency or authority administering mortgage or housing assistance, fraud prevention or foreclosure prevention programs, or an individual employed by a loan or finance company or financial institution under this part. A loan or finance company is not a financial institution as defined in the regulations in this part at 1010.100(t).

(1) *Residential mortgage lender or originator.* A residential mortgage lender or originator includes:

(i) *Residential mortgage lender.* The person to whom the debt arising from a residential mortgage loan is initially payable on the face of the evidence of indebtedness or, if there is no such evidence of indebtedness, by agreement, or to whom the obligation is initially assigned at or immediately after settlement. The term "residential mortgage lender" shall not include an individual who finances the sale of the individual's own dwelling or real property.

(ii) *Residential mortgage originator.* A person who accepts a residential mortgage loan application or offers or negotiates terms of a residential mortgage loan.

(iii) *Residential mortgage loan.* A loan that is secured by a mortgage, deed of trust, or other equivalent consensual security interest on:

(A) A residential structure that contains one to four units, including, if used as a residence, an individual condominium unit, cooperative unit, mobile home or trailer; or

(B) Residential real estate upon which such a structure is constructed or intended to be constructed.

(2) [Reserved]

(mmm) *Housing government sponsored enterprise.* (1) A "housing government sponsored enterprise" is one of the following "Regulated Entities" under 12 U.S.C. 4502(20) subject to the general supervision and regulation of the Federal Housing Finance Agency (FHFA):

(i) The Federal National Mortgage Association;

(ii) The Federal Home Loan Mortgage Corporation; or

(iii) Each Federal Home Loan Bank.

(2) The term "housing government sponsored enterprise" does not include any "Entity-Affiliated Party," as defined in 12 U.S.C. 4502(11).

(nnn) *Investment adviser.*

¶ 1110
31 CFR § 1010.200 General.

Each financial institution (as defined in 31 U.S.C. 5312(a)(2) or (c)(1)) should refer to Subpart B of its Chapter X Part for any additional program requirements. Unless otherwise indicated, the program requirements contained in this Subpart B apply to all financial institutions (as defined in 31 U.S.C. 5312(a)(2) or (c)(1)).

¶ 1120
31 CFR § 1010.205 Exempted anti-money laundering programs for certain financial institutions.

(a) *Exempt financial institutions.* Subject to the provisions of paragraphs (c) and (d) of this section, the following financial institutions (as defined in 31 U.S.C. 5312(a)(2) or (c)(1)) are exempt from the requirement in 31 U.S.C. 5318(h)(1) concerning the establishment of anti-money laundering programs:

(1) An agency of the United States Government, or of a State or local government, carrying out a duty or power of a business described in 31 U.S.C. 5312(a)(2); and

(2) [Reserved]

¶1110   31 CFR § 1010.200

(b) *Temporary exemption for certain financial institutions.* (1) Subject to the provisions of paragraphs (c) and (d) of this section, the following financial institutions (as defined in 31 U.S.C. 5312(a)(2) or (c)(1)) are exempt from the requirement in 31 U.S.C. 5318(h)(1) concerning the establishment of anti-money laundering programs:

(i) Pawnbroker;

(ii) Travel agency;

(iii) Telegraph company;

(iv) Seller of vehicles, including automobiles, airplanes, and boats;

(v) Person involved in real estate closings and settlements;

(vi) Private banker;

(vii) Commodity pool operator;

(viii) Commodity trading advisor; or

(ix) Investment company.

(2) Subject to the provisions of paragraphs (c) and (d) of this section, a bank (as defined in § 1010.100(d)) that is not subject to regulation by a Federal functional regulator (as defined in § 1010.100(r)) is exempt from the requirement in 31 U.S.C. 5318(h)(1) concerning the establishment of anti-money laundering programs.

(3) Subject to the provisions of paragraphs (c) and (d) of this section, a person described in § 1010.100(t)(7) is exempt from the requirement in 31 U.S.C. 5318(h)(1) concerning the establishment of anti-money laundering programs.

(c) *Limitation on exemption.* The exemptions described in paragraph (b) of this section shall not apply to any financial institution that is otherwise required to establish an anti-money laundering program by this chapter.

(d) *Compliance obligations of deferred financial institutions.* Nothing in this section shall be deemed to relieve an exempt financial institution from its responsibility to comply with any other applicable requirement of law or regulation, including title 31 of the U.S.C. and this chapter.

¶ 1130

31 CFR § 1010.210 Anti-money laundering programs.

Each financial institution (as defined in 31 U.S.C. 5312(a)(2) or (c)(1)) should refer to Subpart B of its Chapter X Part for any additional anti-money laundering program requirements.

¶ 1140

31 CFR § 1010.220 Customer identification program requirements.

Each financial institution (as defined in 31 U.S.C. 5312(a)(2) or (c)(1)) should refer to Subpart B of its Chapter X Part for any additional customer identification program requirements.

¶ 1150

31 CFR § 1010.230 Beneficial ownership requirements for legal entity customers.

(a) *In general.* Covered financial institutions are required to establish and maintain written procedures that are reasonably designed to identify and verify beneficial owners of legal entity customers and to include such procedures in their anti-money laundering compliance program required under 31 U.S.C. 5318(h) and its implementing regulations.

(b) *Identification and verification.* With respect to legal entity customers, the covered financial institution's customer due diligence procedures shall enable the institution to:

(1) Identify the beneficial owner(s) of each legal entity customer at the time a new account is opened, unless the customer is otherwise excluded pursuant to paragraph (e) of this section or the account is exempted pursuant to paragraph (h) of this section. A covered financial institution may accomplish this either by obtaining a certification in the form of appendix A of this section from the individual opening the account on behalf of the legal entity customer, or by obtaining from the individual the information required by the form by another means, provided the individual certifies, to the best of the individual's knowledge, the accuracy of the information; and

(2) Verify the identity of each beneficial owner identified to the covered financial institution, according to risk-based procedures to the extent reasonable and practicable. At a minimum, these procedures must contain the elements required for verifying the identity of customers that are individuals under § 1020.220(a)(2) of this chapter (for banks); § 1023.220(a)(2) of this chapter (for brokers or dealers in securities); § 1024.220(a)(2) of this chapter (for mutual funds); or § 1026.220(a)(2) of this chapter (for futures commission merchants or introducing brokers in commodities); provided, that in the case of documentary verification, the financial institution may use photocopies or other reproductions of the documents listed in paragraph (a)(2)(ii)(A)(1) of § 1020.220 of this chapter (for banks); § 1023.220 of this chapter (for brokers or dealers in securities); § 1024.220 of this chapter (for mutual funds); or § 1026.220 of this chapter (for futures commission merchants or introducing brokers in commodities). A covered financial institution may rely on the information supplied by the legal entity customer regarding the identity of its beneficial owner or owners, provided that it has no knowledge of facts that would reasonably call into question the reliability of such information.

(c) *Account.* For purposes of this section, *account* has the meaning set forth in § 1020.100(a) of this chapter (for banks); § 1023.100(a) of this chapter (for brokers or dealers in securities); § 1024.100(a) of this chapter (for mutual funds); and § 1026.100(a) of this chapter (for futures commission merchants or introducing brokers in commodities).

(d) *Beneficial owner.* For purposes of this section, *beneficial owner* means each of the following:

(1) Each individual, if any, who, directly or indirectly, through any contract, arrangement, understanding, relationship or otherwise, owns 25 percent or more of the equity interests of a legal entity customer; and

(2) A single individual with significant responsibility to control, manage, or direct a legal entity customer, including:

(i) An executive officer or senior manager (*e.g.*, a Chief Executive Officer, Chief Financial Officer, Chief Operating Officer, Managing Member, General Partner, President, Vice President, or Treasurer); or

(ii) Any other individual who regularly performs similar functions.

(3) If a trust owns directly or indirectly, through any contract, arrangement, understanding, relationship or otherwise, 25 percent or more of the equity interests of a legal entity customer, the beneficial owner for purposes of paragraph (d)(1) of this section shall mean the trustee. If an entity listed in paragraph (e)(2) of this section owns directly or indirectly, through any contract, arrangement, understanding, relationship or otherwise, 25 percent or more of the equity interests of a legal entity customer, no individual need be identified for purposes of paragraph (d)(1) of this section with respect to that entity's interests.

Note to paragraph (d). The number of individuals that satisfy the definition of "beneficial owner," and therefore must be identified and verified pursuant to this section, may vary. Under paragraph (d)(1) of this section, depending on the factual circumstances, up to four individuals may need to be identified. Under paragraph (d)(2) of this section, only one individual must be identified. It is possible that in some circumstances the same person or persons might be identified pursuant to paragraphs (d)(1) and (2) of this section. A covered financial institution may also identify additional individuals as part of its customer due diligence if it deems appropriate on the basis of risk.

(e) *Legal entity customer.* For the purposes of this section:

(1) *Legal entity customer.* means a corporation, limited liability company, or other entity that is created by the filing of a public document with a Secretary of State or similar office, a general partnership, and any similar entity formed under the laws of a foreign jurisdiction that opens an account.

(2) *Legal entity customer.* does not include:

(i) A financial institution regulated by a Federal functional regulator or a bank regulated by a State bank regulator;

(ii) A person described in § 1020.315(b)(2) through (5) of this chapter;

(iii) An issuer of a class of securities registered under section 12 of the Securities Exchange Act of 1934 or that is required to file reports under section 15(d) of that Act;

(iv) An investment company, as defined in section 3 of the Investment Company Act of 1940, that

is registered with the Securities and Exchange Commission under that Act;

(v) An investment adviser, as defined in section 202(a)(11) of the Investment Advisers Act of 1940, that is registered with the Securities and Exchange Commission under that Act;

(vi) An exchange or clearing agency, as defined in section 3 of the Securities Exchange Act of 1934, that is registered under section 6 or 17A of that Act;

(vii) Any other entity registered with the Securities and Exchange Commission under the Securities Exchange Act of 1934;

(viii) A registered entity, commodity pool operator, commodity trading advisor, retail foreign exchange dealer, swap dealer, or major swap participant, each as defined in section 1a of the Commodity Exchange Act, that is registered with the Commodity Futures Trading Commission;

(ix) A public accounting firm registered under section 102 of the Sarbanes-Oxley Act;

(x) A bank holding company, as defined in section 2 of the Bank Holding Company Act of 1956 (12 U.S.C. 1841) or savings and loan holding company, as defined in section 10(n) of the Home Owners' Loan Act (12 U.S.C 1467a(n));

(xi) A pooled investment vehicle that is operated or advised by a financial institution excluded under paragraph (e)(2) of this section;

(xii) An insurance company that is regulated by a State;

(xiii) A financial market utility designated by the Financial Stability Oversight Council under Title VIII of the Dodd-Frank Wall Street Reform and Consumer Protection Act of 2010;

(xiv) A foreign financial institution established in a jurisdiction where the regulator of such institution maintains beneficial ownership information regarding such institution;

(xv) A non-U.S. governmental department, agency or political subdivision that engages only in governmental rather than commercial activities; and

(xvi) Any legal entity only to the extent that it opens a private banking account subject to § 1010.620 of this chapter.

(3) The following legal entity customers are subject only to the control prong of the beneficial ownership requirement:

(i) A pooled investment vehicle that is operated or advised by a financial institution not excluded under paragraph (e)(2) of this section; and

(ii) Any legal entity that is established as a nonprofit corporation or similar entity and has filed its organizational documents with the appropriate State authority as necessary.

(f) *Covered financial institution.* For the purposes of this section, *covered financial institution* has the meaning set forth in § 1010.605(e)(1) of this chapter.

(g) *New account.* For the purposes of this section, *new account* means each account opened at a covered financial institution by a legal entity customer on or after the applicability date.

¶1150   31 CFR § 1010.230

(h) *Exemptions.*

(1) Covered financial institutions are exempt from the requirements to identify and verify the identity of the beneficial owner(s) set forth in paragraphs (a) and (b)(1) and (2) of this section only to the extent the financial institution opens an account for a legal entity customer that is:

(i) At the point-of-sale to provide credit products, including commercial private label credit cards, solely for the purchase of retail goods and/or services at these retailers, up to a limit of $50,000;

(ii) To finance the purchase of postage and for which payments are remitted directly by the financial institution to the provider of the postage products;

(iii) To finance insurance premiums and for which payments are remitted directly by the financial institution to the insurance provider or broker;

(iv) To finance the purchase or leasing of equipment and for which payments are remitted directly by the financial institution to the vendor or lessor of this equipment.

(2) *Limitations on Exemptions.* (i) The exemptions identified in paragraphs (h)(1)(ii) through (iv) of this section do not apply to transaction accounts through which a legal entity customer can make payments to, or receive payments from, third parties.

(ii) If there is the possibility of a cash refund on the account activity identified in paragraphs (h)(1)(ii) through (iv) of this section, then beneficial ownership of the legal entity customer must be identified and verified by the financial institution as required by this section, either at the time of initial remittance, or at the time such refund occurs.

(i) *Recordkeeping.* A covered financial institution must establish procedures for making and maintaining a record of all information obtained under the procedures implementing paragraph (b) of this section.

(1) *Required records.* At a minimum the record must include:

(i) For identification, any identifying information obtained by the covered financial institution pursuant to paragraph (b) of this section, including without limitation the certification (if obtained); and

(ii) For verification, a description of any document relied on (noting the type, any identification number, place of issuance and, if any, date of issuance and expiration), of any non-documentary methods and the results of any measures undertaken, and of the resolution of each substantive discrepancy.

(2) *Retention of records.* A covered financial institution must retain the records made under paragraph (i)(1)(i) of this section for five years after the date the account is closed, and the records made under paragraph (i)(1)(ii) of this section for five years after the record is made.

(j) *Reliance on another financial institution.* A covered financial institution may rely on the performance by another financial institution (including an affiliate) of the requirements of this section with respect to any legal entity customer of the covered

financial institution that is opening, or has opened, an account or has established a similar business relationship with the other financial institution to provide or engage in services, dealings, or other financial transactions, provided that:

(1) Such reliance is reasonable under the circumstances;

(2) The other financial institution is subject to a rule implementing 31 U.S.C. 5318(h) and is regulated by a Federal functional regulator; and

(3) The other financial institution enters into a contract requiring it to certify annually to the covered financial institution that it has implemented its anti-money laundering program, and that it will perform (or its agent will perform) the specified requirements of the covered financial institution's procedures to comply with the requirements of this section.

APPENDIX A: to § 1010.230: Certification Regarding Beneficial Owners of Legal Entity Customers

I. GENERAL INSTRUCTIONS

What is this form?

To help the government fight financial crime, Federal regulation requires certain financial institutions to obtain, verify, and record information about the beneficial owners of legal entity customers. Legal entities can be abused to disguise involvement in terrorist financing, money laundering, tax evasion, corruption, fraud, and other financial crimes. Requiring the disclosure of key individuals who own or control a legal entity (i.e., the beneficial owners) helps law enforcement investigate and prosecute these crimes.

Who has to complete this form?

This form must be completed by the person opening a new account on behalf of a legal entity with any of the following U.S. financial institutions: (i) a bank or credit union; (ii) a broker or dealer in securities; (iii) a mutual fund; (iv) a futures commission merchant; or (v) an introducing broker in commodities.

For the purposes of this form, a **legal entity** includes a corporation, limited liability company, or other entity that is created by a filing of a public document with a Secretary of State or similar office, a general partnership, and any similar business entity formed in the United States or a foreign country. **Legal entity** does not include sole proprietorships, unincorporated associations, or natural persons opening accounts on their own behalf.

What information do I have to provide?

This form requires you to provide the name, address, date of birth and Social Security number (or passport number or other similar information, in the case of Non-U.S. Persons) for the following individuals (*i.e.*, the **beneficial owners**):

(i) Each individual, if any, who owns, directly or indirectly, 25 percent or more of the equity interests of the legal entity customer (e.g., each natural person that owns 25 percent or more of the shares of a corporation); **and**

(ii) An individual with significant responsibility for managing the legal entity customer (*e.g.*, a Chief Executive Officer, Chief Financial Officer, Chief Operating Officer, Managing Member, General Partner, President, Vice President, or Treasurer).

The number of individuals that satisfy this definition of "beneficial owner" may vary. Under section (i), depending on the factual circumstances, up to four individuals (but as few as zero) may need to be identified. Regardless of the number of individuals identified under section (i), you must provide the identifying information of one individual under section (ii). It is possible that in some circumstances the same individual might be identified under both sections (e.g., the President of Acme, Inc. who also holds a 30% equity interest). Thus, a completed form will contain the identifying information of at least one individual (under section (ii)), and up to five individuals (i.e., one individual under section (ii) and four 25 percent equity holders under section (i)).

The financial institution may also ask to see a copy of a driver's license or other identifying document for each beneficial owner listed on this form.

II. CERTIFICATION OF BENEFICIAL OWNER(S)

Persons opening an account on behalf of a legal entity must provide the following information:

a. Name and Title of Natural Person Opening Account:

_____

b. Name, Type, and Address of Legal Entity for Which the Account is Being Opened:

_____

c. The following information for each individual, if any, who, directly or indirectly, through any contract, arrangement, understanding, relationship or otherwise, owns 25 percent or more of the equity interests of the legal entity listed above:

Name	Date of Birth	Address (Residential or Business Street Address)	For U.S. Persons: Social Security Number	For Non-U.S. Persons: Social Security Number, Passport Number and Country of Issuance, or other similar identification number[1]

[1] In lieu of a passport number, Non-U.S. Persons may also provide a Social Security Number, an alien identification card number, or number and country of issuance of any other government-issued document evidencing nationality or residence and bearing a photograph or similar safeguard.

(If no individual meets this definition, please write "Not Applicable.")

d. The following information for one individual with significant responsibility for managing the legal entity listed above, such as:

■ *An executive officer or senior manager (e.g., Chief Executive Officer, Chief Financial Officer, Chief Operat-* ing Officer, Managing Member, General Partner, President, Vice President, Treasurer); or

■ *Any other individual who regularly performs similar functions.*

(If appropriate, an individual listed under section (c) above may also be listed in this section (d)).

Name/Title	Date of Birth	Address (Residential or Business Street Address)	For U.S. Persons: Social Security Number	For Non-U.S. Persons: Social Security Number, Passport Number and Country of Issuance, or other similar identification number[1]

I, _____(name of natural person opening account), hereby certify, to the best of my knowledge, that the information provided above is complete and correct.

Signature: _ Date: _____

Legal Entity Identifier _____ (Optional)

¶1150   **31 CFR § 1010.230**

¶ 1160

31 CFR § 1010.320 Reports of suspicious transactions.

Each financial institution (as defined in 31 U.S.C. 5312(a)(2) or (c)(1)) should refer to subpart C of its financial institution part in this Chapter for any additional suspicious transaction reporting requirements.

¶ 1165

31 CFR § 1010.410 Records to be made and retained by financial institutions.

Each financial institution shall retain either the original or a copy or reproduction of each of the following:

(a) A record of each extension of credit in an amount in excess of $10,000, except an extension of credit secured by an interest in real property, which record shall contain the name and address of the person to whom the extension of credit is made, the amount thereof, the nature or purpose thereof, and the date thereof;

(b) A record of each advice, request, or instruction received or given regarding any transaction resulting (or intended to result and later canceled if such a record is normally made) in the transfer of currency or other monetary instruments, funds, checks, investment securities, or credit, of more than $10,000 to or from any person, account, or place outside the United States.

(c) A record of each advice, request, or instruction given to another financial institution or other person located within or without the United States, regarding a transaction intended to result in the transfer of funds, or of currency, other monetary instruments, checks, investment securities, or credit, of more than $10,000 to a person, account or place outside the United States.

(d) A record of such information for such period of time as the Secretary may require in an order issued under § 1010.370(a), not to exceed five years.

(e) *Nonbank financial institutions.* Each agent, agency, branch, or office located within the United States of a financial institution other than a bank is subject to the requirements of this paragraph (e) with respect to a transmittal of funds in the amount of $3,000 or more:

(1) *Recordkeeping requirements.* (i) For each transmittal order that it accepts as a transmittor's financial institution, a financial institution shall obtain and retain either the original or a microfilm, other copy, or electronic record of the following information relating to the transmittal order:

(A) The name and address of the transmittor;

(B) The amount of the transmittal order;

(C) The execution date of the transmittal order;

(D) Any payment instructions received from the transmittor with the transmittal order;

(E) The identity of the recipient's financial institution;

(F) As many of the following items as are received with the transmittal order:[1]

(1) The name and address of the recipient;

(2) The account number of the recipient; and

(3) Any other specific identifier of the recipient; and

(G) Any form relating to the transmittal of funds that is completed or signed by the person placing the transmittal order.

(ii) For each transmittal order that it accepts as an intermediary financial institution, a financial institution shall retain either the original or a microfilm, other copy, or electronic record of the transmittal order.

(iii) For each transmittal order that it accepts as a recipient's financial institution, a financial institution shall retain either the original or a microfilm, other copy, or electronic record of the transmittal order.

(2) *Transmittors other than established customers.* In the case of a transmittal order from a transmittor that is not an established customer, in addition to obtaining and retaining the information required in paragraph (e)(1)(i) of this section:

(i) If the transmittal order is made in person, prior to acceptance the transmittor's financial institution shall verify the identity of the person placing the transmittal order. If it accepts the transmittal order, the transmittor's financial institution shall obtain and retain a record of the name and address, the type of identification reviewed, and the number of the identification document (*e.g.,* driver's license), as well as a record of the person's taxpayer identification number (*e.g.,* social security or employer identification number) or, if none, alien identification number or passport number and country of issuance, or a notation in the record of the lack thereof. If the transmittor's financial institution has knowledge that the person placing the transmittal order is not the transmittor, the transmittor's financial institution shall obtain and retain a record of the transmittor's taxpayer identification number (*e.g.,* social security or employer identification number) or, if none, alien identification number or passport number and country of issuance, if known by the person placing the order, or a notation in the record of the lack thereof.

(ii) If the transmittal order accepted by the transmittor's financial institution is not made in person, the transmittor's financial institution shall obtain and retain a record of the name and address of the person placing the transmittal order, as well as the person's taxpayer identification number (*e.g.,* social security or employer identification number) or, if none, alien identification number or passport number

---

[1] For transmittals of funds effected through the Federal Reserve's Fedwire funds transfer system by a domestic broker or dealers in securities, only one of the items is required to be retained, if received with the transmittal order, until such time as the bank that sends the order to the Federal Reserve Bank completes its conversion to the expanded Fedwire message format.

and country of issuance, or a notation in the record of the lack thereof, and a copy or record of the method of payment (*e.g.*, check or credit card transaction) for the transmittal of funds. If the transmittor's financial institution has knowledge that the person placing the transmittal order is not the transmittor, the transmittor's financial institution shall obtain and retain a record of the transmittor's taxpayer identification number (*e.g.*, social security or employer identification number) or, if none, alien identification number or passport number and country of issuance, if known by the person placing the order, or a notation in the record of the lack thereof.

(3) *Recipients other than established customers.* For each transmittal order that it accepts as a recipient's financial institution for a recipient that is not an established customer, in addition to obtaining and retaining the information required in paragraph (e) (1) (iii) of this section:

(i) If the proceeds are delivered in person to the recipient or its representative or agent, the recipient's financial institution shall verify the identity of the person receiving the proceeds and shall obtain and retain a record of the name and address, the type of identification reviewed, and the number of the identification document (*e.g.*, driver's license), as well as a record of the person's taxpayer identification number (*e.g.*, social security or employer identification number) or, if none, alien identification number or passport number and country of issuance, or a notation in the record of the lack thereof. If the recipient's financial institution has knowledge that the person receiving the proceeds is not the recipient, the recipient's financial institution shall obtain and retain a record of the recipient's name and address, as well as the recipient's taxpayer identification number (*e.g.*, social security or employer identification number) or, if none, alien identification number or passport number and country of issuance, if known by the person receiving the proceeds, or a notation in the record of the lack thereof.

(ii) If the proceeds are delivered other than in person, the recipient's financial institution shall retain a copy of the check or other instrument used to effect payment, or the information contained thereon, as well as the name and address of the person to which it was sent.

(4) *Retrievability.* The information that a transmittor's financial institution must retain under paragraphs (e) (1) (i) and (e) (2) of this section shall be retrievable by the transmittor's financial institution by reference to the name of the transmittor. If the transmittor is an established customer of the transmittor's financial institution and has an account used for transmittals of funds, then the information also shall be retrievable by account number. The information that a recipient's financial institution must retain under paragraphs (e) (1) (iii) and (e) (3) of this section shall be retrievable by the recipient's financial institution by reference to the name of the recipient. If the recipient is an established customer of the recipient's financial institution and has an account used for transmittals of funds, then the information also shall be retrievable by account number. This information

need not be retained in any particular manner, so long as the financial institution is able to retrieve the information required by this paragraph, either by accessing transmittal of funds records directly or through reference to some other record maintained by the financial institution.

(5) *Verification.* Where verification is required under paragraphs (e) (2) and (e) (3) of this section, a financial institution shall verify a person's identity by examination of a document (other than a customer signature card), preferably one that contains the person's name, address, and photograph, that is normally acceptable by financial institutions as a means of identification when cashing checks for persons other than established customers. Verification of the identity of an individual who indicates that he or she is an alien or is not a resident of the United States may be made by passport, alien identification card, or other official document evidencing nationality or residence (*e.g.*, a foreign driver's license with indication of home address).

(6) *Exceptions.* The following transmittals of funds are not subject to the requirements of this section:

(i) Transmittals of funds where the transmittor and the recipient are any of the following:

(A) A bank;

(B) A wholly-owned domestic subsidiary of a bank chartered in the United States;

(C) A broker or dealer in securities;

(D) A wholly-owned domestic subsidiary of a broker or dealer in securities;

(E) A futures commission merchant or an introducing broker in commodities;

(F) A wholly-owned domestic subsidiary of a futures commission merchant or an introducing broker in commodities;

(G) The United States;

(H) A state or local government; or

(I) A Federal, State or local government agency or instrumentality; or

(J) A mutual fund; and

(K)

(ii) Transmittals of funds where both the transmittor and the recipient are the same person and the transmittor's financial institution and the recipient's financial institution are the same broker or dealer in securities.

(f) Any transmittor's financial institution or intermediary financial institution located within the United States shall include in any transmittal order for a transmittal of funds in the amount of $3,000 or more, information as required in this paragraph (f):

(1) A transmittor's financial institution shall include in a transmittal order, at the time it is sent to a receiving financial institution, the following information:

(i) The name and, if the payment is ordered from an account, the account number of the transmittor;

(ii) The address of the transmittor, except for a transmittal order through Fedwire until such time as the bank that sends the order to the Federal

¶1165   31 CFR § 1010.410

Reserve Bank completes its conversion to the expanded Fedwire format;

(iii) The amount of the transmittal order;

(iv) The execution date of the transmittal order;

(v) The identity of the recipient's financial institution;

(vi) As many of the following items as are received with the transmittal order:[2]

(A) The name and address of the recipient;

(B) The account number of the recipient;

(C) Any other specific identifier of the recipient; and

(vii) Either the name and address or numerical identifier of the transmittor's financial institution.

(2) A receiving financial institution that acts as an intermediary financial institution, if it accepts a transmittal order, shall include in a corresponding transmittal order at the time it is sent to the next receiving financial institution, the following information, if received from the sender:

(i) The name and the account number of the transmittor;

(ii) The address of the transmittor, except for a transmittal order through Fedwire until such time as the bank that sends the order to the Federal Reserve Bank completes its conversion to the expanded Fedwire format;

(iii) The amount of the transmittal order;

(iv) The execution date of the transmittal order;

(v) The identity of the recipient's financial institution;

(vi) As many of the following items as are received with the transmittal order:[3]

(A) The name and address of the recipient;

(B) The account number of the recipient;

(C) Any other specific identifier of the recipient; and

(vii) Either the name and address or numerical identifier of the transmittor's financial institution.

(3) *Safe harbor for transmittals of funds prior to conversion to the expanded Fedwire message format.* The following provisions apply to transmittals of funds effected through the Federal Reserve's Fedwire funds transfer system or otherwise by a financial institution before the bank that sends the order to the Federal Reserve Bank or otherwise completes its conversion to the expanded Fedwire message format.

(i) *Transmittor's financial institution.* A transmittor's financial institution will be deemed to be in compliance with the provisions of paragraph (f)(1) of this section if it:

(A) Includes in the transmittal order, at the time it is sent to the receiving financial institution, the information specified in paragraphs (f)(1)(iii) through (v), and the information specified in paragraph (f)(1)(vi) of this section to the extent that such information has been received by the financial institution, and

(B) Provides the information specified in paragraphs (f)(1)(i), (ii) and (vii) of this section to a financial institution that acted as an intermediary financial institution or recipient's financial institution in connection with the transmittal order, within a reasonable time after any such financial institution makes a request therefor in connection with the requesting financial institution's receipt of a lawful request for such information from a Federal, State, or local law enforcement or financial regulatory agency, or in connection with the requesting financial institution's own Bank Secrecy Act compliance program.

(ii) *Intermediary financial institution.* An intermediary financial institution will be deemed to be in compliance with the provisions of paragraph (f)(2) of this section if it:

(A) Includes in the transmittal order, at the time it is sent to the receiving financial institution, the information specified in paragraphs (f)(2)(iii) through (f)(2)(vi) of this section, to the extent that such information has been received by the intermediary financial institution; and

(B) Provides the information specified in paragraphs (f)(2)(i), (ii) and (vii) of this section, to the extent that such information has been received by the intermediary financial institution, to a financial institution that acted as an intermediary financial institution or recipient's financial institution in connection with the transmittal order, within a reasonable time after any such financial institution makes a request therefor in connection with the requesting financial institution's receipt of a lawful request for such information from a Federal, State, or local law enforcement or regulatory agency, or in connection with the requesting financial institution's own Bank Secrecy Act compliance program.

(iii) *Obligation of requesting financial institution.* Any information requested under paragraph (f)(3)(i)(B) or (f)(3)(ii)(B) of this section shall be treated by the requesting institution, once received, as if it had been included in the transmittal order to which such information relates.

(4) *Exceptions.* The requirements of this paragraph (f) shall not apply to transmittals of funds that are listed in paragraph (e)(6) of this section or § 1020.410(a)(6) of this chapter.

---

[2] For transmittals of funds effected through the Federal Reserve's Fedwire funds transfer system by a financial institution, only one of the items is required to be included in the transmittal order, if received with the sender's transmittal order, until such time as the bank that sends the order to the Federal Reserve Bank completes its conversion to the expanded Fedwire message format.

[3] For transmittals of funds effected through the Federal Reserve's Fedwire funds transfer system by a financial institution, only one of the items is required to be included in the transmittal order, if received with the sender's transmittal order, until such time as the bank that sends the order to the Federal Reserve Bank completes its conversion to the expanded Fedwire message format.

¶ 1170

31 CFR § 1022.100 Definitions.

Refer to § 1010.100 of this Chapter for general definitions not noted herein.

¶ 1180

31 CFR § 1022.311 Filing obligations.

Refer to § 1010.311 of this Chapter for reports of transactions in currency filing obligations for money services businesses.

¶ 1190

31 CFR § 1022.320 Reports by money services businesses of suspicious transactions.

(a) *General.* (1) Every money services business described in § 1010.100(ff)(1), (3), (4), (5), (6), and (7) of this chapter, shall file with the Treasury Department, to the extent and in the manner required by this section, a report of any suspicious transaction relevant to a possible violation of law or regulation. Any money services business may also file with the Treasury Department, by using the form specified in paragraph (b)(1) of this section, or otherwise, a report of any suspicious transaction that it believes is relevant to the possible violation of any law or regulation but whose reporting is not required by this section.

(2) A transaction requires reporting under the terms of this section if it is conducted or attempted by, at, or through a money services business, involves or aggregates funds or other assets of at least $2,000 (except as provided in paragraph (a)(3) of this section), and the money services business knows, suspects, or has reason to suspect that the transaction (or a pattern of transactions of which the transaction is a part):

(i) Involves funds derived from illegal activity or is intended or conducted in order to hide or disguise funds or assets derived from illegal activity (including, without limitation, the ownership, nature, source, location, or control of such funds or assets) as part of a plan to violate or evade any Federal law or regulation or to avoid any transaction reporting requirement under Federal law or regulation;

(ii) Is designed, whether through structuring or other means, to evade any requirements of this chapter or of any other regulations promulgated under the Bank Secrecy Act; or

(iii) Serves no business or apparent lawful purpose, and the reporting money services business knows of no reasonable explanation for the transaction after examining the available facts, including the background and possible purpose of the transaction.

(iv) Involves use of the money services business to facilitate criminal activity.

(3) To the extent that the identification of transactions required to be reported is derived from a review of clearance records or other similar records of money orders or traveler's checks that have been sold or processed, an issuer of money orders or traveler's checks shall only be required to report a transaction or pattern of transactions that involves or aggregates funds or other assets of at least $5,000.

(4) The obligation to identify and properly and timely to report a suspicious transaction rests with each money services business involved in the transaction, provided that no more than one report is required to be filed by the money services businesses involved in a particular transaction (so long as the report filed contains all relevant facts). Whether, in addition to any liability on its own for failure to report, a money services business that issues the instrument or provides the funds transfer service involved in the transaction may be liable for the failure of another money services business involved in the transaction to report that transaction depends upon the nature of the contractual or other relationship between the businesses, and the legal effect of the facts and circumstances of the relationship and transaction involved, under general principles of the law of agency.

(b) *Filing procedures.* (1) *What to file.* A suspicious transaction shall be reported by completing a Suspicious Activity Report ("SAR"), and collecting and maintaining supporting documentation as required by paragraph (c) of this section.

(2) *Where to file.* The SAR shall be filed in a central location to be determined by FinCEN, as indicated in the instructions to the SAR.

(3) *When to file.* A money services business subject to this section is required to file each SAR no later than 30 calendar days after the date of the initial detection by the money services business of facts that may constitute a basis for filing a SAR under this section. In situations involving violations that require immediate attention, such as ongoing money laundering schemes, the money services business shall immediately notify by telephone an appropriate law enforcement authority in addition to filing a SAR. Money services businesses wishing voluntarily to report suspicious transactions that may relate to terrorist activity may call FinCEN's Financial Institutions Hotline at 1-866-556-3974 in addition to filing timely a SAR if required by this section.

(c) *Retention of records.* A money services business shall maintain a copy of any SAR filed and the original or business record equivalent of any supporting documentation for a period of five years from the date of filing the SAR. Supporting documentation shall be identified as such and maintained by the money services business, and shall be deemed to have been filed with the SAR. A money services business shall make all supporting documentation available to FinCEN or any Federal, State, or local law enforcement agency, or any Federal regulatory authority that examines the money services business for compliance with the Bank Secrecy Act, or any State regulatory authority administering a State law that requires the money services business to comply with the Bank Secrecy Act or otherwise authorizes the State authority to ensure that the money services business complies with the Bank Secrecy Act.

(d) *Confidentiality of SARs.* A SAR, and any information that would reveal the existence of a SAR, are confidential and shall not be disclosed except as authorized in this paragraph (d). For purposes of this paragraph (d) only, a SAR shall include any suspicious activity report filed with FinCEN pursuant to any regulation in this chapter.

(1) *Prohibition on disclosures by money services businesses.* (i) *General rule.* No money services business, and no director, officer, employee, or agent of any money services business, shall disclose a SAR or any information that would reveal the existence of a SAR. Any money services business, and any director, officer, employee, or agent of any money services business that is subpoenaed or otherwise requested to disclose a SAR or any information that would reveal the existence of a SAR, shall decline to produce the SAR or such information, citing this section and 31 U.S.C. 5318(g)(2)(A)(i), and shall notify FinCEN of any such request and the response thereto.

(ii) *Rules of Construction.* Provided that no person involved in any reported suspicious transaction is notified that the transaction has been reported, this paragraph (d)(1) shall not be construed as prohibiting:

(A) The disclosure by a money services business, or any director, officer, employee, or agent of a money services business, of:

(1) A SAR, or any information that would reveal the existence of a SAR, to FinCEN or any Federal, State, or local law enforcement agency, or any Federal regulatory authority that examines money services business for compliance with the Bank Secrecy Act, or any State regulatory authority administering a State law that requires the money services business to comply with the Bank Secrecy Act or otherwise authorizes the State authority to ensure that the money services business complies with the Bank Secrecy Act; or

(2) The underlying facts, transactions, and documents upon which a SAR is based, including but not limited to, disclosures to another financial institution, or any director, officer, employee, or agent of a financial institution, for the preparation of a joint SAR.

(B) The sharing by a money services business, or any director, officer, employee, or agent of the money services business, of a SAR, or any information that would reveal the existence of a SAR, within the money services business's corporate organizational structure for purposes consistent with Title II of the Bank Secrecy Act as determined by regulation or in guidance.

(2) *Prohibition on disclosures by government authorities.* A Federal, State, local, territorial, or Tribal government authority, or any director, officer, employee, or agent of any of the foregoing, shall not disclose a SAR, or any information that would reveal the existence of a SAR, except as necessary to fulfill official duties consistent with Title II of the Bank Secrecy Act. For purposes of this section, "official duties" shall not include the disclosure of a SAR, or any information that would reveal the existence of a SAR, in response to a request for disclosure of non-public information or a request for use in a private legal proceeding, including a request pursuant to 31 CFR 1.11.

(e) *Limitation on liability.* A money services business, and any director, officer, employee, or agent of any money services business, that makes a voluntary disclosure of any possible violation of law or regulation to a government agency or makes a disclosure pursuant to this section or any other authority, including a disclosure made jointly with another institution, shall be protected from liability to any person for any such disclosure, or for failure to provide notice of such disclosure to any person identified in the disclosure, or both, to the full extent provided by 31 U.S.C. 5318(g)(3).

(f) *Compliance.* Money services businesses shall be examined by FinCEN or its delegatees for compliance with this section. Failure to satisfy the requirements of this section may be a violation of the Bank Secrecy Act and of this chapter.

(g) *Applicability date.* This section applies to transactions occurring after December 31, 2001.

¶ 1200

31 CFR § 1022.380 Registration of money services businesses.

(a) *Registration requirement.* (1) *In general.* Except as provided in paragraph (a)(3) of this section, relating to agents, and except for sellers of prepaid access as defined in § 1010.100(ff)(7) of this chapter to the extent that they are not already agents, each money services business (whether or not licensed as a money services business by any State) must register with FinCEN. Each provider of prepaid access must identify each prepaid program for which it is the provider of prepaid access. Each money services business must, as part of its registration, maintain a list of its agents as required by 31 U.S.C. 5330 and this section. This section does not apply to the United States Postal Service, to agencies of the United States, of any State, or of any political subdivision of a State.

(2) *Foreign-located Money Services Business.* Each foreign-located person doing business, whether or not on a regular basis or as an organized or licensed business concern, in the United States as a money services business shall designate the name and address of a person who resides in the United States and is authorized, and has agreed, to be an agent to accept service of legal process with respect to compliance with this chapter, and shall identify the address of the location within the United States for records pertaining to paragraph (b)(1)(iii) of this section.

(3) *Agents.* A person that is a money services business solely because that person serves as an agent of another money services business, see § 1010.100(ff) of this Chapter, is not required to register under this section, but a money services business that engages in activities described in § 1010.100(ff) of this Chapter both on its own behalf and as an agent

for others must register under this section. For example, a supermarket corporation that acts as an agent for an issuer of money orders and performs no other services of a nature and value that would cause the corporation to be a money services business, is not required to register; the answer would be the same if the supermarket corporation served as an agent both of a money order issuer and of a money transmitter. However, registration would be required if the supermarket corporation, in addition to acting as an agent of an issuer of money orders, cashed checks or exchanged currencies (other than as an agent for another business) in an amount greater than $1,000 in currency or monetary or other instruments for any person on any day, in one or more transactions.

(4) *Agency status.* The determination whether a person is an agent depends on all the facts and circumstances.

(b) *Registration procedures.* (1) *In general.* (i) A money services business must be registered by filing such form as FinCEN may specify with FinCEN (or such other location as the form may specify). The information required by 31 U.S.C. 5330(b) and any other information required by the form must be reported in the manner and to the extent required by the form.

(ii) A branch office of a money services business is not required to file its own registration form. A money services business must, however, report information about its branch locations or offices as provided by the instructions to the registration form.

(iii) A money services business must retain a copy of any registration form filed under this section and any registration number that may be assigned to the business at a location in the United States and for the period specified in § 1010.430(d) of this Chapter.

(2) *Registration period.* A money services business must be registered for the initial registration period and each renewal period. The initial registration period is the two-calendar-year period beginning with the calendar year in which the money services business is first required to be registered. However, the initial registration period for a money services business required to register by December 31, 2001 (see paragraph (b)(3) of this section) is the two-calendar year period beginning 2002. Each two-calendar-year period following the initial registration period is a renewal period.

(3) *Due date.* The registration form for the initial registration period must be filed on or before the end of the 180-day period beginning on the day following the date the business is established. The registration form for a renewal period must be filed on or before the last day of the calendar year preceding the renewal period.

(4) *Events requiring re-registration.* If a money services business registered as such under the laws of any State experiences a change in ownership or control that requires the business to be re-registered under State law, the money services business must also be re-registered under this section. In addition, if there is a transfer of more than 10 percent of the voting power or equity interests of a money services business (other than a money services business that must report such transfer to the Securities and Exchange Commission), the money services business must be re-registered under this section. Finally, if a money services business experiences a more than 50-per cent increase in the number of its agents during any registration period, the money services business must be re-registered under this section. The registration form must be filed not later than 180 days after such change in ownership, transfer of voting power or equity interests, or increase in agents. The calendar year in which the change, transfer, or increase occurs is treated as the first year of a new two-year registration period.

(c) *Persons required to file the registration form.* Under 31 U.S.C. 5330(a), any person who owns or controls a money services business is responsible for registering the business; however, only one registration form is required to be filed for each registration period. A person is treated as owning or controlling a money services business for purposes of filing the registration form only to the extent provided by the form. If more than one person owns or controls a money services business, the owning or controlling persons may enter into an agreement designating one of them to register the business. The failure of the designated person to register the money services business does not, however, relieve any of the other persons who own or control the business of liability for the failure to register the business. See paragraph (e) of this section, relating to consequences of the failure to comply with 31 U.S.C. 5330 or this section.

(d) *List of agents.* (1) *In general.* A money services business must prepare and maintain a list of its agents. The initial list of agents must be prepared by January 1, 2002, and must be revised each January 1, for the immediately preceding 12 month period; for money services businesses established after December 31, 2001, the initial agent list must be prepared by the due date of the initial registration form and must be revised each January 1 for the immediately preceding 12-month period. The list is not filed with the registration form but must be maintained at the location in the United States reported on the registration form under paragraph (b)(1) of this section. Upon request, a money services business must make its list of agents available to FinCEN and any other appropriate law enforcement agency (including, without limitation, the examination function of the Internal Revenue Service in its capacity as delegee of Bank Secrecy Act examination authority). Requests for information made pursuant to the preceding sentence shall be coordinated through FinCEN in the manner and to the extent determined by FinCEN. The original list of agents and any revised list must be retained for the period specified in § 1010.430(d) of this Chapter.

(2) *Information included on the list of agents.* (i) *In general.* Except as provided in paragraph (d)(2)(ii) of this section, a money services business must include the following information with respect to each agent on the list (including any revised list) of its agents—

(A) The name of the agent, including any trade names or doing-business-as names;

(B) The address of the agent, including street address, city, state, and ZIP code;

(C) The telephone number of the agent;

(D) The type of service or services (money orders, traveler's checks, check sales, check cashing, currency exchange, and money transmitting) the agent provides;

(E) A listing of the months in the 12 months immediately preceding the date of the most recent agent list in which the gross transaction amount of the agent with respect to financial products or services issued by the money services business maintaining the agent list exceeded $100,000. For this purpose, the money services gross transaction amount is the agent's gross amount (excluding fees and commissions) received from transactions of one or more businesses described in § 1010.100(ff) of this Chapter;

(F) The name and address of any depository institution at which the agent maintains a transaction account (as defined in 12 U.S.C. 461(b)(1)(C)) for all or part of the funds received in or for the financial products or services issued by the money services business maintaining the list, whether in the agent's or the business principal's name;

(G) The year in which the agent first became an agent of the money services business; and

(H) The number of branches or subagents the agent has.

(ii) *Special rules.* Information about agent volume must be current within 45 days of the due date of the agent list. The information described by paragraphs (d)(2)(i)(G) and (d)(2)(i)(H) of this section is not required to be included in an agent list with respect to any person that is an agent of the money services business maintaining the list before the first day of the month beginning after February 16, 2000 so long as the information described by paragraphs (d)(2)(i)(G) and (d)(2)(i)(H) of this section is made available upon the request of FinCEN and any other appropriate law enforcement agency (including, without limitation, the examination function of the Internal Revenue Service in its capacity as delegee of Bank Secrecy Act examination authority).

(e) *Consequences of failing to comply with 31 U.S.C. 5330 or the regulations thereunder.* It is unlawful to do business without complying with 31 U.S.C. 5330 and this section. A failure to comply with the requirements of 31 U.S.C. 5330 or this section includes the filing of false or materially incomplete information in connection with the registration of a money services business. Any person who fails to comply with any requirement of 31 U.S.C. 5330 or this section shall be liable for a civil penalty of $5,000 for each violation. Each day a violation of 31 U.S.C. 5330 or this section continues constitutes a separate violation. In addition, under 31 U.S.C. 5320, the Secretary of the Treasury may bring a civil action to enjoin the violation. See 18 U.S.C. 1960 for a criminal penalty for failure to comply with the registration requirements of 31 U.S.C. 5330 or this section.

(f) *Applicability date.* This section is applicable as of September 20, 1999. Registration of money services businesses under this section will not be required prior to December 31, 2001.

¶1210

31 CFR § 1022.410 Additional records to be made and retained by dealers in foreign exchange.

(a)(1) After July 7, 1987, each dealer in foreign exchange shall secure and maintain a record of the taxpayer identification number of each person for whom a transaction account is opened or a line of credit is extended within 30 days after such account is opened or credit line extended. Where a person is a non-resident alien, the dealer in foreign exchange shall also record the person's passport number or a description of some other government document used to verify his identity. Where the account or credit line is in the names of two or more persons, the dealer in foreign exchange shall secure the taxpayer identification number of a person having a financial interest in the account or credit line. In the event that a dealer in foreign exchange has been unable to secure the identification required within the 30-day period specified, it shall nevertheless not be deemed to be in violation of this section if:

(i) It has made a reasonable effort to secure such identification, and

(ii) It maintains a list containing the names, addresses, and account or credit line numbers of those persons from whom it has been unable to secure such identification, and makes the names, addresses, and account or credit line numbers of those persons available to the Secretary as directed by him.

(2) The 30-day period provided for in paragraph (a)(1) of this section shall be extended where the person opening the account or credit line has applied for a taxpayer identification or social security number on Form SS-4 or SS-5, until such time as the person maintaining the account or credit line has had a reasonable opportunity to secure such number and furnish it to the dealer in foreign exchange.

(3) A taxpayer identification number for an account or credit line required under paragraph (a)(1) of this section need not be secured in the following instances:

(i) Accounts for public funds opened by agencies and instrumentalities of Federal, state, local or foreign governments,

(ii) Accounts for aliens who are—

(A) Ambassadors, ministers, career diplomatic or consular officers, or

(B) Naval, military or other attaches of foreign embassies, and legations, and for members of their immediate families,

(iii) Accounts for aliens who are accredited representatives to international organizations which are entitled to enjoy privileges, exemptions, and immunities as an international organization under the International Organizations Immunities Act of December 29, 1945 (22 U.S.C. 288), and for the members of their immediate families,

(iv) Aliens temporarily residing in the United States for a period not to exceed 180 days,

(v) Aliens not engaged in a trade or business in the United States who are attending a recognized college or any training program, supervised or conducted by any agency of the Federal Government, and

(vi) Unincorporated subordinate units of a tax exempt central organization which are covered by a group exemption letter.

(b) Each dealer in foreign exchange shall retain either the original or a microfilm or other copy or reproduction of each of the following:

(1) Statements of accounts from banks, including paid checks, charges or other debit entry memoranda, deposit slips and other credit memoranda representing the entries reflected on such statements;

(2) Daily work records, including purchase and sales slips or other memoranda needed to identify and reconstruct currency transactions with customers and foreign banks;

(3) A record of each exchange of currency involving transactions in excess of $1000, including the name and address of the customer (and passport number or taxpayer identification number unless received by mail or common carrier) date and amount of the transaction and currency name, country, and total amount of each foreign currency;

(4) Signature cards or other documents evidencing signature authority over each deposit or security account, containing the name of the depositor, street address, taxpayer identification number (TIN) or employer identification number (EIN) and the signature of the depositor or of a person authorized to sign on the account (if customer accounts are maintained in a code name, a record of the actual owner of the account);

(5) Each item, including checks, drafts, or transfers of credit, of more than $10,000 remitted or transferred to a person, account or place outside the United States;

(6) A record of each receipt of currency, other monetary instruments, investment securities and checks, and of each transfer of funds or credit, or more than $10,000 received on any one occasion directly and not through a domestic financial institution, from any person, account or place outside the United States;

(7) Records prepared or received by a dealer in the ordinary course of business, that would be needed to reconstruct an account and trace a check in excess of $100 deposited in such account through its internal recordkeeping system to its depository institution, or to supply a description of a deposited check in excess of $100;

(8) A record maintaining the name, address and taxpayer identification number, if available, of any person presenting a certificate of deposit for payment, as well as a description of the instrument and date of transaction;

(9) A system of books and records that will enable the dealer in foreign exchange to prepare an accurate balance sheet and income statement.

(c) This section does not apply to banks that offer services in dealing or changing currency to their customers as an adjunct to their regular service.

¶ 1220

31 CFR § 1027.210 Anti-money laundering programs for dealers in precious metals, precious stones, or jewels.

(a) *Anti-money laundering program requirement.* (1) Each dealer shall develop and implement a written anti-money laundering program reasonably designed to prevent the dealer from being used to facilitate money laundering and the financing of terrorist activities through the purchase and sale of covered goods. The program must be approved by senior management. A dealer shall make its anti-money laundering program available to the Department of Treasury through FinCEN or its designee upon request.

(2) To the extent that a retailer's purchases from persons other than dealers and other retailers exceeds the $50,000 threshold contained in § 1027.100(b)(2)(i), the anti-money laundering compliance program required of the retailer under this paragraph need only address such purchases.

(b) *Minimum requirements.* At a minimum, the anti-money laundering program shall:

(1) Incorporate policies, procedures, and internal controls based upon the dealer's assessment of the money laundering and terrorist financing risks associated with its line(s) of business. Policies, procedures, and internal controls developed and implemented by a dealer under this section shall include provisions for complying with the applicable requirements of the Bank Secrecy Act (31 U.S.C. 5311 *et seq.*), and this chapter.

(i) For purposes of making the risk assessment required by paragraph (b)(1) of this section, a dealer shall take into account all relevant factors including, but not limited to:

(A) The type(s) of products the dealer buys and sells, as well as the nature of the dealer's customers, suppliers, distribution channels, and geographic locations;

(B) The extent to which the dealer engages in transactions other than with established customers or sources of supply, or other dealers subject to this rule; and

(C) Whether the dealer engages in transactions for which payment or account reconciliation is routed to or from accounts located in jurisdictions that have been identified by the Department of State as a sponsor of international terrorism under 22 U.S.C. 2371; designated as non-cooperative with international anti-money laundering principles or procedures by an intergovernmental group or organization of which the United States is a member and with which designation the United States representative or organization concurs; or designated by the Secretary of the Treasury pursuant to 31 U.S.C. 5318A as warranting special measures due to money laundering concerns.

(ii) A dealer's program shall incorporate policies, procedures, and internal controls to assist the dealer in identifying transactions that may involve use of the dealer to facilitate money laundering or terrorist financing, including provisions for making reasonable inquiries to determine whether a transaction involves money laundering or terrorist financing, and for refusing to consummate, withdrawing from, or terminating such transactions. Factors that may indicate a transaction is designed to involve use of the dealer to facilitate money laundering or terrorist financing include, but are not limited to:

(A) Unusual payment methods, such as the use of large amounts of cash, multiple or sequentially numbered money orders, traveler's checks, or cashier's checks, or payment from third parties;

(B) Unwillingness by a customer or supplier to provide complete or accurate contact information, financial references, or business affiliations;

(C) Attempts by a customer or supplier to maintain an unusual degree of secrecy with respect to the transaction, such as a request that normal business records not be kept;

(D) Purchases or sales that are unusual for the particular customer or supplier, or type of customer or supplier; and

(E) Purchases or sales that are not in conformity with standard industry practice.

(2) Designate a compliance officer who will be responsible for ensuring that:

(i) The anti-money laundering program is implemented effectively;

(ii) The anti-money laundering program is updated as necessary to reflect changes in the risk assessment, requirements of this chapter, and further guidance issued by the Department of the Treasury; and

(iii) Appropriate personnel are trained in accordance with paragraph (b)(3) of this section.

(3) Provide for on-going education and training of appropriate persons concerning their responsibilities under the program.

(4) Provide for independent testing to monitor and maintain an adequate program. The scope and frequency of the testing shall be commensurate with the risk assessment conducted by the dealer in accordance with paragraph (b)(1) of this section. Such testing may be conducted by an officer or employee of the dealer, so long as the tester is not the person designated in paragraph (b)(2) of this section or a person involved in the operation of the program.

(c) *Implementation date.* A dealer must develop and implement an anti-money laundering program that complies with the requirements of this section on or before the later of January 1, 2006, or six months after the date a dealer becomes subject to the requirements of this section.

¶ 1230

31 CFR § 1027.410 Recordkeeping.
Refer to § 1010.410 of this Chapter.

¶ 1240 Application of FinCEN's Regulations to Persons Administering, Exchanging, or Using Virtual Currencies

Department of the Treasury

Financial Crimes Enforcement Network

Guidance

FIN-2013-G001

Issued: March 18, 2013

Subject: Application of FinCEN's Regulations to Persons Administering, Exchanging, or Using Virtual Currencies

The Financial Crimes Enforcement Network ("FinCEN") is issuing this interpretive guidance to clarify the applicability of the regulations implementing the Bank Secrecy Act ("BSA") to persons creating, obtaining, distributing, exchanging, accepting, or transmitting virtual currencies.[1] Such persons are referred to in this guidance as "users," "administrators," and "exchangers," all as defined below.[2] A user of virtual currency is *not* an MSB under FinCEN's regulations and therefore is not subject to MSB registration, reporting, and recordkeeping regulations. However, an administrator or exchanger *is* an MSB under FinCEN's regulations, specifically, a money transmitter, unless a limitation to or exemption from the definition applies to the person. An administrator or exchanger is not a provider or seller of prepaid access, or a dealer in foreign exchange, under FinCEN's regulations.

Currency vs. Virtual Currency

FinCEN's regulations define currency (also referred to as "real" currency) as "the coin and paper money of the United States or of any other country that [i] is designated as legal tender and that [ii] circulates and [iii] is customarily used and accepted as a medium of exchange in the country of issuance."[3] In contrast to real currency, "virtual" currency is a medium of exchange that operates like a currency in some environments, but does not have all the attributes of real currency. In

particular, virtual currency does not have legal tender status in any jurisdiction. This guidance addresses "convertible" virtual currency. This type of virtual currency either has an equivalent value in real currency, or acts as a substitute for real currency.

Background

On July 21, 2011, FinCEN published a Final Rule amending definitions and other regulations relating to money services businesses ("MSBs").[4] Among other things, the MSB Rule amends definitions of dealers in foreign exchange (formerly referred to as "currency dealers and exchangers") and money transmitters. On July 29, 2011, FinCEN published a Final Rule on Definitions and Other Regulations Relating to Prepaid Access (the "Prepaid Access Rule").[5] This guidance explains the regulatory treatment under these definitions of persons engaged in virtual currency transactions.

Definitions of User, Exchanger, and Administrator

This guidance refers to the participants in generic virtual currency arrangements, using the terms "user," "exchanger," and "administrator."[6] A *user* is a person that obtains virtual currency to purchase goods or services.[7] An *exchanger* is a person engaged as a business in the exchange of virtual currency for real currency, funds, or other virtual currency. An *administrator* is a person engaged as a business in issuing (putting into circulation) a virtual currency, and who has the authority to redeem (to withdraw from circulation) such virtual currency.

Users of Virtual Currency

A user who obtains convertible virtual currency and uses it to purchase real or virtual goods or services is *not* an MSB under FinCEN's regula-

---

[1] FinCEN is issuing this guidance under its authority to administer the Bank Secrecy Act. *See* Treasury Order 180-01 (March 24, 2003). This guidance explains only how FinCEN characterizes certain activities involving virtual currencies under the Bank Secrecy Act and FinCEN regulations. It should not be interpreted as a statement by FinCEN about the extent to which those activities comport with other federal or state statutes, rules, regulations, or orders.

[2] FinCEN's regulations define "person" as "an individual, a corporation, a partnership, a trust or estate, a joint stock company, an association, a syndicate, joint venture, or other unincorporated organization or group, an Indian Tribe (as that term is defined in the Indian Gaming Regulatory Act), and all entities cognizable as legal personalities." 31 CFR § 1010.100(mm).

[3] 31 CFR § 1010.100(m).

[4] *Bank Secrecy Act Regulations –Definitions and Other Regulations Relating to Money Services Businesses*, 76 FR 43585 (July 21, 2011) (the "MSB Rule"). This defines an MSB as "a person wherever located doing business, whether or not on a regular basis or as an organized or licensed business concern,

wholly or in substantial part within the United States, in one or more of the capacities listed in paragraphs (ff)(1) through (ff)(7) of this section. This includes but is not limited to maintenance of any agent, agency, branch, or office within the United States." 31 CFR § 1010.100(ff).

[5] *Final Rule –Definitions and Other Regulations Relating to Prepaid Access*, 76 FR 45403 (July 29, 2011),

[6] These terms are used for the exclusive purpose of this regulatory guidance. Depending on the type and combination of a person's activities, one person may be acting in more than one of these capacities.

[7] How a person engages in "obtaining" a virtual currency may be described using any number of other terms, such as "earning," "harvesting," "mining," "creating," "auto-generating," "manufacturing," or "purchasing," depending on the details of the specific virtual currency model involved. For purposes of this guidance, the label applied to a particular process of obtaining a virtual currency is not material to the legal characterization under the BSA of the process or of the person engaging in the process.

¶1240

tions.[8] Such activity, in and of itself, does not fit within the definition of "money transmission services" and therefore is not subject to FinCEN's registration, reporting, and recordkeeping regulations for MSBs.[9]

Administrators and Exchangers of Virtual Currency

An administrator or exchanger that (1) accepts and transmits a convertible virtual currency or (2) buys or sells convertible virtual currency for any reason *is* a money transmitter under FinCEN's regulations, unless a limitation to or exemption from the definition applies to the person.[10] FinCEN's regulations define the term "money transmitter" as a person that provides money transmission services, or any other person engaged in the transfer of funds. The term "money transmission services" means "the acceptance of currency, funds, or other value that substitutes for currency from one person *and* the transmission of currency, funds, or other value that substitutes for currency to another location or person by any means."[11]

The definition of a money transmitter does not differentiate between real currencies and convertible virtual currencies. Accepting and transmitting anything of value that substitutes for currency makes a person a money transmitter under the regulations implementing the BSA.[12] FinCEN has reviewed different activities involving virtual currency and has made determinations regarding the appropriate regulatory treatment of administrators and exchangers under three scenarios: brokers and dealers of e-currencies and e-precious metals; centralized convertible virtual currencies; and decentralized convertible virtual currencies.

a. E-Currencies and E-Precious Metals

The first type of activity involves electronic trading in e-currencies or e-precious metals.[13] In 2008, FinCEN issued guidance stating that as long as a broker or dealer in real currency or other commodities accepts and transmits funds solely for the purpose of effecting a *bona fide* purchase or sale of the real currency or other commodities for or with a customer, such person is not acting as a money transmitter under the regulations.[14]

However, if the broker or dealer transfers funds between a customer and a third party that is not part of the currency or commodity transaction, such transmission of funds is no longer a fundamental element of the actual transaction necessary to execute the contract for the purchase or sale of the currency or the other commodity. This scenario is, therefore, money transmission.[15] Examples include, in part, (1) the transfer of funds between a customer and a third party by permitting a third party to fund a customer's account; (2) the transfer of value from a customer's currency or commodity position to the account of another customer; or (3) the closing out of a customer's currency or commodity position, with a transfer of proceeds to a third party. Since the definition of a money transmitter does not differentiate between real currencies and convertible virtual currencies, the same rules apply to brokers and dealers of e-currency and e-precious metals.

b. Centralized Virtual Currencies

The second type of activity involves a convertible virtual currency that has a centralized repository. The administrator of that repository will be a money transmitter to the extent that it allows transfers of value between persons or from one location to another. This conclusion applies, whether the value is denominated in a real currency or a convertible virtual currency. In addition, any exchanger that uses its access to the convertible virtual currency services provided by the administrator to accept and transmit the convertible virtual currency on behalf of others, including transfers intended to pay a third party for

---

[8] As noted above, this should not be interpreted as a statement about the extent to which the user's activities comport with other federal or state statutes, rules, regulations, or orders. For example, the activity may still be subject to abuse in the form of trade-based money laundering or terrorist financing. The activity may follow the same patterns of behavior observed in the "real" economy with respect to the purchase of "real" goods and services, such as systematic over- or under-invoicing or inflated transaction fees or commissions.

[9] 31 CFR § 1010.100(ff)(1-7).

[10] FinCEN's regulations provide that whether a person is a money transmitter is a matter of facts and circumstances. The regulations identify six circumstances under which a person is not a money transmitter, despite accepting and transmitting currency, funds, or value that substitutes for currency. 31 CFR § 1010.100(ff)(5)(ii)(A)–(F).

[11] 31 CFR § 1010.100(ff)(5)(i)(A).

[12] Ibid.

[13] Typically, this involves the broker or dealer electronically distributing digital certificates of ownership of real currencies or precious metals, with the digital certificate being the virtual currency. However, the same conclusions would

apply in the case of the broker or dealer issuing paper ownership certificates or manifesting customer ownership or control of real currencies or commodities in an account statement or any other form. These conclusions would also apply in the case of a broker or dealer in commodities other than real currencies or precious metals. A broker or dealer of e-currencies or e-precious metals that engages in money transmission could be either an administrator or exchanger depending on its business model.

[14] *Application of the Definition of Money Transmitter to Brokers and Dealers in Currency and other Commodities,* FIN-2008-G008, Sept. 10, 2008. The guidance also notes that the definition of money transmitter excludes any person, such as a futures commission merchant, that is "registered with, and regulated or examined by . . . the Commodity Futures Trading Commission."

[15] In 2011, FinCEN amended the definition of money transmitter. The 2008 guidance, however, was primarily concerned with the core elements of the definition – accepting and transmitting currency or value – and the exemption for acceptance and transmission integral to another transaction not involving money transmission. The 2011 amendments have not materially changed these aspects of the definition.

virtual goods and services, is also a money transmitter.

FinCEN understands that the exchanger's activities may take one of two forms. The first form involves an exchanger (acting as a "seller" of the convertible virtual currency) that accepts real currency or its equivalent from a user (the "purchaser") and transmits the value of that real currency to fund the user's convertible virtual currency account with the administrator. Under FinCEN's regulations, sending "value that substitutes for currency" to another person or to another location constitutes money transmission, unless a limitation to or exemption from the definition applies.[16] This circumstance constitutes transmission *to another location*, namely from the user's account at one location (e.g., a user's real currency account at a bank) to the user's convertible virtual currency account with the administrator. It might be argued that the exchanger is entitled to the exemption from the definition of "money transmitter" for persons involved in the sale of goods or the provision of services. Under such an argument, one might assert that the exchanger is merely providing the service of connecting the user to the administrator and that the transmission of value is integral to this service. However, this exemption does not apply when the only services being provided are money transmission services.[17]

The second form involves a *de facto* sale of convertible virtual currency that is not completely transparent. The exchanger accepts currency or its equivalent from a user and privately credits the user with an appropriate portion of the exchanger's own convertible virtual currency held with the administrator of the repository. The exchanger then transmits that internally credited value to third parties at the user's direction. This constitutes transmission *to another person*, namely each third party to which transmissions are made at the user's direction. To the extent that the convertible virtual currency is generally understood as a substitute for real currencies, transmitting the convertible virtual currency at the direction and for the benefit of the user constitutes money transmission on the part of the exchanger.

c. De-Centralized Virtual Currencies

A final type of convertible virtual currency activity involves a de-centralized convertible virtual currency (1) that has no central repository and no single administrator, and (2) that persons may obtain by their own computing or manufacturing effort.

A person that creates units of this convertible virtual currency and uses it to purchase real or virtual goods and services is a user of the convertible virtual currency and not subject to regulation as a money transmitter. By contrast, a person that creates units of convertible virtual currency and sells those units to another person for real currency or its equivalent is engaged in transmission to another location and is a money transmitter. In addition, a person is an exchanger and a money transmitter if the person accepts such de-centralized convertible virtual currency from one person and transmits it to another person as part of the acceptance and transfer of currency, funds, or other value that substitutes for currency.

Providers and Sellers of Prepaid Access

A person's acceptance and/or transmission of convertible virtual currency cannot be characterized as providing or selling prepaid access because prepaid access is limited to real currencies.[18]

Dealers in Foreign Exchange

A person must exchange the currency of two or more countries to be considered a dealer in foreign exchange.[19] Virtual currency does not meet the criteria to be considered "currency" under the BSA, because it is not legal tender. Therefore, a person who accepts real currency in exchange for virtual currency, or *vice versa*, is not a dealer in foreign exchange under FinCEN's regulations.

* * * * *

Financial institutions with questions about this guidance or other matters related to compliance with the implementing regulations of the BSA may contact FinCEN's Regulatory Helpline at (800) 949-2732.

---

[16] See footnote 11 and adjacent text.

[17] 31 CFR § 1010.100(ff)(5)(ii)(F).

[18] This is true even if the person holds the value accepted for a period of time before transmitting some or all of that value at the direction of the person from whom the value was originally accepted. FinCEN's regulations define "prepaid access" as "access to funds or the value of funds that have been paid in advance and can be retrieved or transferred at some point in the future through an electronic device or vehicle, such as a card, code, electronic serial number, mobile identification number, or personal identification number." 31 CFR § 1010.100(ww). Thus, "prepaid access" under FinCEN's regulations is limited to "access to funds or the value of funds." If FinCEN had intended prepaid access to cover funds denomi-

nated in a virtual currency or something else that substitutes for real currency, it would have used language in the definition of prepaid access like that in the definition of money transmission, which expressly includes the acceptance and transmission of "other value that substitutes for currency." 31 CFR § 1010.100(ff)(5)(i).

[19] FinCEN defines a "dealer in foreign exchange" as a "person that accepts the currency, or other monetary instruments, funds, or other instruments denominated in the currency, of one or more countries in exchange for the currency, or other monetary instruments, funds, or other instruments denominated in the currency, of one or more other countries in an amount greater than $1,000 for any other person on any day in one or more transactions, whether or not for same-day delivery." 31 CFR § 1010.100(ff)(1).

¶1240

¶ 1250 Application of FinCEN's Regulations to Virtual Currency Mining Operations

Department of the Treasury

Financial Crimes Enforcement Network

FIN-2014-R001

Issued: January 30, 2014

Subject: Application of FinCEN's Regulations to Virtual Currency Mining Operations

Dear [ ]:

This responds to your letter of June 1, 2013, seeking an administrative ruling from the Financial Crimes Enforcement Network ("FinCEN") on behalf of [the Company], about [the Company]'s possible status as a money services business ("MSB") under the Bank Secrecy Act ("BSA"). Specifically, you ask whether certain ways of disposing of the Bitcoins mined by [the Company] would make [the Company] a money transmitter under the BSA.

You state that [the Company] mines Bitcoins. You further state that the Bitcoins that [the Company] has mined have not yet been used or transferred, but that [the Company] may decide to use this virtual currency to purchase goods or services, convert the virtual currency into currency of legal tender and use the currency to purchase goods and services, or transfer the virtual currency to the owner of the company. You ask in your letter whether any of these transactions would make [the Company] a money transmitter under the BSA.

On July 21, 2011, FinCEN published a Final Rule amending definitions and other regulations relating to MSBs (the "Rule").[1] The amended regulations define an MSB as "a person wherever located doing business, whether or not on a regular basis or as an organized business concern, wholly or in substantial part within the United States, in one or more of the capacities listed in paragraphs (ff)(1) through (ff)(6) of this section. This includes but is not limited to maintenance of any agent, agency, branch, or office within the United States."[2]

BSA regulations, as amended, define the term "money transmitter" to include a person that provides money transmission services, or any other person engaged in the transfer of funds. The term "money transmission services" means the acceptance of currency, funds, or other value that substitutes for currency from one person *and* the transmission of currency, funds, or other value that substitutes for currency to another location or

person by any means.[3] The regulations also stipulate that whether a person is a money transmitter is a matter of facts and circumstances, and identifies circumstances under which a person's activities would not make such person a money transmitter.[4]

On March 18, 2013, FinCEN issued guidance on the application of FinCEN's regulations to transactions in virtual currencies (the "guidance").[5] FinCEN's regulations define currency (also referred to as "real" currency) as "the coin and paper money of the United States or of any other country that [i] is designated as legal tender and that [ii] circulates and [iii] is customarily used and accepted as a medium of exchange in the country of issuance."[6] In contrast to real currency, "virtual" currency is a medium of exchange that operates like a currency in some environments, but does not have all the attributes of real currency. In particular, virtual currency does not have legal tender status in any jurisdiction. The guidance addresses "convertible" virtual currency. This type of virtual currency either has an equivalent value in real currency, or acts as a substitute for real currency.

For purposes of the guidance, FinCEN refers to the participants in generic virtual currency arrangements, using the terms "exchanger," "administrator," and "user." An *exchanger* is a person engaged as a business in the exchange of virtual currency for real currency, funds, or other virtual currency. An *administrator* is a person engaged as a business in issuing (putting into circulation) a virtual currency, and who has the authority to redeem (to withdraw from circulation) such virtual currency. A *user* is a person that obtains virtual currency to purchase goods or services on the user's own behalf.

The guidance makes clear that an administrator or exchanger of convertible virtual currencies that (1) accepts and transmits a convertible virtual currency or (2) buys or sells convertible virtual currency in exchange for currency of legal tender or another convertible virtual currency for any reason (including when intermediating between a user and a seller of goods or services the user is purchasing on the user's behalf) is a money transmitter under FinCEN's regulations, unless a limitation to or exemption from the definition applies to the person.[7] The guidance also makes clear that "a user who obtains convertible virtual currency and uses it to purchase real or virtual goods or services is **not** an MSB under FinCEN's regula-

---

[1] Bank Secrecy Act Regulations – Definitions and Other Regulations Relating to Money Services Businesses, 76 FR 43585 (July 21, 2011).

[2] 31 CFR § 1010.100(ff).

[3] 31 CFR § 1010.100(ff)(5)(i)(A) and (B).

[4] 31 CFR § 1010.100(ff)(5)(ii).

[5] FIN-2013-G001, "Application of FinCEN's Regulations to Persons Administering, Exchanging, or Using Virtual Currencies," March 18, 2013.

[6] 31 CFR § 1010.100(m).

[7] The definition of "money transmitter" in FinCEN's regulations defines six sets of circumstances – variously referred to as limitations or exemptions – under which a person is not a money transmitter, despite accepting and transmitting currency, funds, or value that substitutes for currency. 31 CFR § 1010.100(ff)(5)(ii)(A)-(F).

tions." FinCEN understands your letter to amount to a request to elaborate on this last statement in the specific context of a user that obtains the convertible virtual currency Bitcoin by mining.

How a user obtains a virtual currency may be described using any number of other terms, such as "earning," "harvesting," "mining," "creating," "auto-generating," "manufacturing," or "purchasing," depending on the details of the specific virtual currency model involved. The label applied to a particular process of obtaining a virtual currency is not material to the legal characterization under the BSA of the process or of the person engaging in the process to send that virtual currency or its equivalent value to any other person or place. What is material to the conclusion that a person is not an MSB is not the mechanism by which a person obtains the convertible virtual currency, but what the person uses the convertible virtual currency for, and for whose benefit.

FinCEN understands that Bitcoin mining imposes no obligations on a Bitcoin user to send mined Bitcoin to any other person or place for the benefit of another. Instead, the user is free to use the mined virtual currency or its equivalent for the user's own purposes, such as to purchase real or virtual goods and services for the user's own use. To the extent that a user mines Bitcoin and uses the Bitcoin solely for the user's own purposes and not for the benefit of another, the user is *not* an MSB under FinCEN's regulations, because these activities involve neither "acceptance" nor "transmission" of the convertible virtual currency and are not the transmission of funds within the meaning of the Rule. This is the case whether the user mining and using the Bitcoin is an individual or a corporation, and whether the user is purchasing goods or services for the user's own use, paying debts previously incurred in the ordinary course of business, or (in the case of a corporate user) making distributions to shareholders. Activities that, in and of themselves, do not constitute accepting and transmitting currency, funds or the value of funds, are activities that do not fit within the definition of "money transmission services" and therefore are not subject to FinCEN's registration, reporting, and recordkeeping regulations for MSBs.[8]

From time to time, as your letter has indicated, it may be necessary for a user to convert Bitcoin that it has mined into a real currency or another convertible virtual currency, either because the seller of the goods or services the user wishes to purchase will not accept Bitcoin, or because the user wishes to diversify currency holdings in anticipation of future needs or for the user's own investment purposes. In undertaking such a conversion transaction, the user is not acting as an exchanger, notwithstanding the fact that the user is accepting a real currency or another convertible virtual currency and transmitting Bitcoin, so long as the user is undertaking the transaction solely for the user's own purposes and not as a business service performed for the benefit of another. A user's conversion of Bitcoin into a real currency or another convertible virtual currency, therefore, does not in and of itself make the user a money transmitter.[9]

FinCEN therefore concludes that, under the facts you have provided, [the Company] would be a user of Bitcoin, and not an MSB, to the extent that it uses Bitcoin it has mined: (a) to pay for the purchase of goods or services, pay debts it has previously incurred (including debts to its owner(s)), or make distributions to owners; or (b) to purchase real currency or another convertible virtual currency, so long as the real currency or other convertible virtual currency is used solely in order to make payments (as set forth above) or for [the Company]'s own investment purposes. Any transfers to third parties at the behest of sellers, creditors, owners, or counterparties involved in these transactions should be closely scrutinized, as they may constitute money transmission. (See footnotes 8 and 9 above.) And of course, should [the Company] engage in any other activity constituting acceptance and transmission of either currency of legal tender or virtual currency, it may be engaged in money transmission activities that would be subject to the requirements of the BSA.

This ruling is provided in accordance with the procedures set forth at 31 CFR Part1010 Subpart G. In arriving at the conclusions in this administrative ruling, we have relied upon the accuracy and completeness of the representations you made in your communications with us. Nothing precludes FinCEN from arriving at a different conclusion or from taking other action should circumstances change or should any of the information you have provided prove inaccurate or incomplete. We reserve the right, after redacting your name and address, and similar identifying information for your clients, to publish this letter as guidance to financial institutions in accordance with our regulations.[10] You have fourteen days from the date of this letter to identify any other information you

---

[8] However, a user wishing to purchase goods or services with Bitcoin it has mined, which pays the Bitcoin to a third party at the direction of a seller or creditor, may be engaged in money transmission. A number of older FinCEN administrative rulings, although not directly on point because they interpret an older version of the regulatory definition of MSBs, discuss situations involving persons that would have been exempted from MSB status, but for their payments to third parties not involved in the original transaction. *See* FIN-2008-R004 (Whether a Foreign Exchange Consultant is a Currency Dealer or Exchanger or Money Transmitter -

05/09/2008); FIN-2008-R003 (Whether a Person That is Engaged in the Business of Foreign Exchange Risk Management is a Currency Dealer or Exchanger or Money Transmitter - 05/09/2008); FIN-2008-R002 (Whether a Foreign Exchange Dealer is a Currency Dealer or Exchanger or Money Transmitter - 05/09/2008).

[9] As noted in footnote 8 above, however, a user engaging in such a transaction, which pays the Bitcoin to a third party at the direction of the counterparty, may be engaged in money transmission.

[10] 31 CFR §§ 1010.711-717.

believe should be redacted and the legal basis for redaction.

If you have questions about this ruling, please contact FinCEN's regulatory helpline at (703) 905-3591.

Sincerely,

//signed//

Jamal El-Hindi

Associate Director

Policy Division

¶ 1260 Application of FinCEN's Regulations to Virtual Currency Software Development and Certain Investment Activity

Department of the Treasury

Financial Crimes Enforcement Network

FIN-2014-R002

Issued: January 30, 2014

Subject: Application of FinCEN's Regulations to Virtual Currency Software Development and Certain Investment Activity

Dear []:

This responds to your letters of May 21, 2013 and July 10, 2013, seeking an administrative ruling from the Financial Crimes Enforcement Network ("FinCEN") regarding the status of [ ] (the "Company") as a money services business ("MSB") under the Bank Secrecy Act ("BSA"). Specifically, you ask whether the periodic investment of the Company in convertible virtual currency, and the production and distribution of software to facilitate the Company's purchase of virtual currency for purposes of its own investment, would make the Company a money transmitter under the BSA.

In your May 21, 2013 letter, you state that the Company intends to produce a piece of software that will facilitate the Company's purchase of virtual currency from sellers, by automating the collection of the virtual currency and the payment of the equivalent in currency of legal tender. The seller would initiate the process via the software's interface, offering its virtual currency to the Company, choosing among several options for a means of receiving the equivalent in currency of legal tender (check, credit to a designated credit, debit, or prepaid card, or payment processed through a third-party money transmitter), and paying a transaction fee. The software would not be sold or provided to any third party for resale, and it would be reserved for the sole use of the Company's counterparties.

Your addendum of July 10, 2013 clarifies that the Company intends to limit its activities to investing in convertible virtual currencies for its own account, purchasing virtual currency from sellers and reselling the currency at the Company's discretion, whenever such purchases and sales make investment sense according to the Company's business plan. The seller would offer its virtual currency to the Company via the software discussed above, and the Company would sell all or part of its virtual currency at a virtual currency exchange after receipt from the

seller, at a time of the Company's choosing based on the Company's own investment decisions.

BSA Obligations of the Company as a Software Provider

On July 21, 2011, FinCEN published a Final Rule amending definitions and other regulations relating to MSBs (the "Rule").[1] The amended regulations define an MSB as "a person wherever located doing business, whether or not on a regular basis or as an organized business concern, wholly or in substantial part within the United States, in one or more of the capacities listed in paragraphs (ff)(1) through (ff)(6) of this section. This includes but is not limited to maintenance of any agent, agency, branch, or office within the United States."[2]

BSA regulations, as amended, define the term "money transmitter" to include a person that provides money transmission services, or any other person engaged in the transfer of funds. The term "money transmission services" means the acceptance of currency, funds, or other value that substitutes for currency from one person *and* the transmission of currency, funds, or other value that substitutes for currency to another location or person by any means.[3] The regulations also stipulate that whether a person is a money transmitter is a matter of facts and circumstances, and identifies circumstances under which a person's activities would not make such person a money transmitter.[4]

The production and distribution of software, in and of itself, does not constitute acceptance and transmission of value, even if the purpose of the software is to facilitate the sale of virtual currency. As a result, the Company's production and distribution of its contemplated software would not make the Company a money transmitter subject to BSA regulation.[5]

BSA Obligations of the Company as an Investor in Virtual Currencies

On March 18, 2013, FinCEN issued guidance on the application of FinCEN's regulations to transactions in virtual currencies (the "guidance").[6] FinCEN's regulations define currency (also referred to as "real" currency) as "the coin and paper money of the United States or of any other country that [i] is designated as legal tender and that [ii] circulates and [iii] is customarily used and accepted as a medium of exchange in the country

---

[1] Bank Secrecy Act Regulations – Definitions and Other Regulations Relating to Money Services Businesses, 76 FR 43585 (July 21, 2011).

[2] 31 CFR § 1010.100(ff).

[3] 31 CFR § 1010.100(ff)(5)(i)(A) and (B).

[4] 31 CFR § 1010.100(ff)(5)(ii).

[5] A number of older FinCEN administrative rulings, although not directly on point because they interpret an older version of the regulatory definition of MSBs, explain the

application of our definitions in comparable situations. *See, e.g.,* FIN-2009-R001, "Whether Certain Operations of a Service Provider to Prepaid Stored Value Program Participants is a Money Services Business," January 22, 2009, available at *http://www.fincen.gov/statutes_regs/guidance/pdf/fin-2009-r001.pdf.*

[6] FIN-2013-G001, "Application of FinCEN's Regulations to Persons Administering, Exchanging, or Using Virtual Currencies," March 18, 2013.

¶1260

of issuance."[7] In contrast to real currency, "virtual" currency is a medium of exchange that operates like a currency in some environments, but does not have all the attributes of real currency. In particular, virtual currency does not have legal tender status in any jurisdiction. The guidance addresses "convertible" virtual currency. This type of virtual currency either has an equivalent value in real currency, or acts as a substitute for real currency.

For purposes of the guidance, FinCEN refers to the participants in generic virtual currency arrangements, using the terms "exchanger," "administrator," and "user." An *exchanger* is a person engaged as a business in the exchange of virtual currency for real currency, funds, or other virtual currency. An *administrator* is a person engaged as a business in issuing (putting into circulation) a virtual currency, and who has the authority to redeem (to withdraw from circulation) such virtual currency. A *user* is a person that obtains virtual currency to purchase goods or services on the user's own behalf.

The guidance makes clear that an administrator or exchanger of convertible virtual currencies that (1) accepts and transmits a convertible virtual currency or (2) buys or sells convertible virtual currency in exchange for currency of legal tender or another convertible virtual currency for any reason (including when intermediating between a user and a seller of goods or services the user is purchasing on the user's behalf) is a money transmitter under FinCEN's regulations, unless a limitation to or exemption from the definition applies to the person.[8] The guidance also makes clear that "a user who obtains convertible virtual currency and uses it to purchase real or virtual goods or services is **not** an MSB under FinCEN's regulations."

How a user engages in obtaining a virtual currency may be described using any number of other terms, such as "earning," "harvesting," "mining," "creating," "auto-generating," "manufacturing," or "purchasing," depending on the details of the specific virtual currency model involved. The label applied to a particular process of obtaining a virtual currency is not material to the legal characterization under the BSA of the process or of the person engaging in the process to send that virtual currency or its equivalent value to any other person or place. What is material to the conclusion that a person is not an MSB is not the mechanism by which person obtains the convertible virtual currency, but what the person uses the convertible virtual currency for, and for whose benefit. Activities that, in and of themselves, do not constitute accepting and transmitting currency, funds or the value of funds do not fit within the definition of "money transmission services" and therefore are not subject to FinCEN's registration, reporting, and recordkeeping regulations for MSBs.[9]

To the extent that the Company purchases and sells convertible virtual currency, paying and receiving the equivalent value in currency of legal tender to and from counterparties, all exclusively as investments for its own account, it is not engaged in the business of exchanging convertible virtual currency for currency of legal tender for other persons. In effect, when the Company invests in a convertible virtual currency for its own account, and when it realizes the value of its investment, it is acting as a user of that convertible virtual currency within the meaning of the guidance. As a result, to the extent that the Company limits its activities strictly to investing in virtual currency for its own account, it is not acting as a money transmitter and is not an MSB under FinCEN's regulations. However, any transfers to third parties at the behest of the Company's counterparties, creditors, or owners entitled to direct payments should be closely scrutinized, as they may constitute money transmission. (See footnote 10 to this ruling.)

If the Company were to provide services to others (including investment-related or brokerage services) that involved the accepting and transmitting of convertible virtual currency, or the exchange of convertible virtual currency for currency of legal tender or another convertible virtual currency, of course, additional analysis would be necessary to determine the Company's regulatory status and obligations with respect to such activity.[10] In addition, should the Company

---

[7] 31 CFR § 1010.100(m).

[8] The definition of "money transmitter" in FinCEN's regulations defines six sets of circumstances – variously referred to as limitations or exemptions – under which a person is not a money transmitter, despite accepting and transmitting currency, funds, or value that substitute for currency. 31 CFR § 1010.100(ff)(5)(ii)(A)-(F).

[9] However, a user wishing to purchase goods or services with a convertible virtual currency it has obtained, which pays the convertible virtual currency to a third party at the direction of a seller or creditor, may be engaged in money transmission. A number of older FinCEN administrative rulings, although not directly on point because they interpret an older version of the regulatory definition of MSBs, discuss situations involving persons that would have been exempted from MSB status, but for their payments to third parties not involved in the original transaction. *See* FIN-2008-R004 (Whether a Foreign Exchange Consultant is a Currency

Dealer or Exchanger or Money Transmitter - 05/09/2008); FIN-2008-R003 (Whether a Person That is Engaged in the Business of Foreign Exchange Risk Management is a Currency Dealer or Exchanger or Money Transmitter - 05/09/2008); FIN-2008-R002 (Whether a Foreign Exchange Dealer is a Currency Dealer or Exchanger or Money Transmitter - 05/09/2008).

[10] For example, providing specific brokerage-related services might require the Company to be registered with the Securities and Exchange Commission (SEC) or the Commodities and Futures Trading Commission (CFTC), in which case the Company would be covered under the BSA as a securities broker-dealer or a commodities or futures trader. If the Company did not fall under SEC or CFTC supervision, then the extent to which its money transmission activities were integral to the non-money transmission services it provided would need to be considered in order to determine whether the Company could claim an exemption from the money transmit-

begin to engage as a business in the exchange of virtual currency against currency of legal tender (or even against other convertible virtual currency), the Company would become a money transmitter under FinCEN's regulations. Under such circumstances, the Company would have to register with FinCEN, implement an effective, risk-based anti-money laundering program, and comply with the recordkeeping, reporting, and transaction monitoring requirements applicable to money transmitters.

This ruling is provided in accordance with the procedures set forth at 31 CFR Part1010 Subpart G.[11] In arriving at the conclusions in this administrative ruling, we have relied upon the accuracy and completeness of the representations you made in your communications with us. Nothing precludes FinCEN from arriving at a different conclusion or from taking other action should circumstances change or should any of the information

you have provided prove inaccurate or incomplete. We reserve the right, after redacting your name and address, and similar identifying information for your clients, to publish this letter as guidance to financial institutions in accordance with our regulations.[12] You have fourteen days from the date of this letter to identify any other information you believe should be redacted and the legal basis for redaction.

If you have questions about this ruling, please contact FinCEN's regulatory helpline at (703) 905-3591.

Sincerely,

//signed//

Jamal El-Hindi

Associate Director

Policy Division

(Footnote Continued)

ter definition under 31 CFR § 1010.100(ff)(5)(ii)(F), or would qualify as a money transmitter under FinCEN's regulations.

[11] Your subsequent e-mail communication of September 24, 2013 has informed us that you received a subpoena from the New York State Department of Financial Services on August 9, 2013 regarding the Company's activities. Although you have not informed us, and we have not by other means

become aware, of the substance of any investigation to which this subpoena may relate, we have waived the requirement in our regulations that you certify that the question at issue in this administrative ruling is not applicable to any ongoing investigation. *See* 31 CFR § § 1010.711(a)(4).

[12] 31 CFR § § 1010.711-717.

¶ 1270 Application of Money Services Business Regulations to the Rental of Computer Systems for Mining Virtual Currency

Department of the Treasury

Financial Crimes Enforcement Network

FIN-2014-R007

Issued: April 29, 2014

Subject: Application of Money Services Business regulations to the rental of computer systems for mining virtual currency

Dear [ ]:

This responds to your letter mailed to us on February 26, 2014, seeking an administrative ruling from the Financial Crimes Enforcement Network ("FinCEN") regarding the status of [ ] (the "Company") as a money services business ("MSB") under the Bank Secrecy Act ("BSA"). Specifically, you ask whether the rental of computer systems for mining virtual currency would make the Company an administrator of virtual currency or a money transmitter under the BSA. Based on the following analysis of the facts and circumstances described in your letter, FinCEN finds that the Company is not functioning as an administrator of virtual currency and that the Company's renting of mining computer systems to third parties does not make the Company a money transmitter under BSA regulations.

You state that the Company has developed a computer system that mines crypto currencies. At times, the company rents this system to third parties in exchange for a payment based on the rental period, which may range from 24 hours to 30 days. The third party will furnish the Company with limited information about its mining pool, which the Company will enter into the system so the third party benefits directly and exclusively from the mining work. All virtual currency mined by the third party remains the third party's property, and the Company has no access to the third party wallet, nor receives or pays virtual currency on the third party's behalf.

On July 21, 2011, FinCEN published a Final Rule amending definitions and other regulations relating to MSBs (the "Rule").[1] The amended regulations define an MSB as "a person wherever located doing business, whether or not on a regular basis or as an organized business concern, wholly or in substantial part within the United States, in one or more of the capacities listed in paragraphs (ff)(1) through (ff)(6) of this section. This includes but is not limited to maintenance of any agent, agency, branch, or office within the United States."[2]

BSA regulations, as amended, define the term "money transmitter" to include a person that pro-

vides money transmission services, or any other person engaged in the transfer of funds. The term "money transmission services" means the acceptance of currency, funds, or other value that substitutes for currency from one person *and* the transmission of currency, funds, or other value that substitutes for currency to another location or person by any means.[3]

On March 18, 2013, FinCEN issued guidance on the application of FinCEN's regulations to transactions in virtual currencies (the "guidance").[4] FinCEN's regulations define currency (also referred to as "real" currency) as "the coin and paper money of the United States or of any other country that [i] is designated as legal tender and that [ii] circulates and [iii] is customarily used and accepted as a medium of exchange in the country of issuance."[5] In contrast to real currency, "virtual" currency is a medium of exchange that operates like a currency in some environments, but does not have all the attributes of real currency. In particular, virtual currency does not have legal tender status in any jurisdiction. The guidance addresses "convertible" virtual currency. This type of virtual currency either has an equivalent value in real currency, or acts as a substitute for real currency.

For purposes of the guidance, FinCEN refers to the participants in generic virtual currency arrangements, using the terms "user," "exchanger," and "administrator." A *user* is a person that obtains virtual currency to purchase goods or services on the user's own behalf. FinCEN has determined that users are not money transmitters. An *exchanger* is a person engaged as a business in the exchange of virtual currency for real currency, funds, or other virtual currency. An *administrator* is a person engaged as a business in issuing (putting into circulation) a virtual currency, and who has the authority to redeem (to withdraw from circulation) such virtual currency. Both exchangers and administrators may operate as money transmitters depending on the specific facts and circumstances. According to your letter, the Company does not engage in the activities of an exchanger or administrator. Instead, the Company provides a rental service to those interested in using your computer system for mining virtual currencies administered by other entities. As such, FinCEN finds that the Company is not functioning as an administrator of virtual currency.

Further, FinCEN regulations stipulate that whether a person is a money transmitter is a matter of facts and circumstances, and identifies circumstances under which a person's activities would not make such person a money transmitter.

---

[1] Bank Secrecy Act Regulations – Definitions and Other Regulations Relating to Money Services Businesses, 76 FR 43585 (July 21, 2011).

[2] 31 CFR § 1010.100(ff).

[3] 31 CFR § 1010.100(ff)(5)(i)(A) and (B).

[4] FIN-2013-G001, "Application of FinCEN's Regulations to Persons Administering, Exchanging, or Using Virtual Currencies," March 18, 2013.

[5] 31 CFR § 1010.100(m).

The rental of computer systems to third parties is not an activity covered by FinCEN regulations. The regulations specifically exempt from money transmitter status a person that only provides the delivery, communication, or network data access services used by a money transmitter to supply money transmission services.[6] Based on this exemption, and on the description of the service offered by the Company, we find that, even if the Company rents a computer system to third parties that will use it to obtain convertible virtual currency to fund their activities as exchangers, such rental activity, in and of itself, would not make the Company a money transmitter subject to BSA regulation.[7]

This ruling is provided in accordance with the procedures set forth at 31 CFR Part 1010 Subpart G. In arriving at the conclusions in this administrative ruling, we have relied upon the accuracy and completeness of the representations you made in your communications with us. Nothing precludes FinCEN from arriving at a different conclusion or

from taking other action should circumstances change or should any of the information you have provided prove inaccurate or incomplete. We reserve the right, after redacting your name and address, and similar identifying information for your clients, to publish this letter as guidance to financial institutions in accordance with our regulations.[8] You have fourteen days from the date of this letter to identify any other information you believe should be redacted and the legal basis for redaction.

If you have questions about this ruling, please contact FinCEN's regulatory helpline at (703) 905-3591.

Sincerely,

//signed//

Jamal El-Hindi

Associate Director

Policy Division

---

[6] 31 CFR § 1010.100(ff) (5) (ii) (A).

[7] A number of older FinCEN administrative rulings, although not directly on point because they interpret an older version of the regulatory definition of MSBs, explain the application of our definitions in comparable situations. *See, e.g.,* FIN-2009-R001, "Whether Certain Operations of a Service Provider to Prepaid Stored Value Program Participants is a Money Services Business," January 22, 2009, available at *http://www.fincen.gov/statutes_regs/guidance/pdf/fin-2009-r001.pdf.*

[8] 31 CFR § § 1010.711-717.

¶ 1280 Request for Administrative Ruling on the Application of FinCEN's Regulations to a Virtual Currency Trading Platform

UNITED STATES DEPARTMENT OF THE TREASURY

FinCEN

FINANCIAL CRIMES ENFORCEMENT NETWORK

FIN-2014-R011

Issued: October 27, 2014

Subject: Request for Administrative Ruling on the Application of FinCEN's Regulations to a Virtual Currency Trading Platform

Dear [ ]:

This responds to your letter of December 3, 2013, seeking an administrative ruling from the Financial Crimes Enforcement Network ("FinCEN") on behalf of [ ] (the "Company"), about the Company's possible status as a money services business ("MSB") under the Bank Secrecy Act ("BSA"). Specifically, you ask whether the convertible virtual currency trading and booking platform that the Company intends to set up (the "Platform") would make the Company a money transmitter under the BSA. Based on the following analysis of the description of the Platform as presented in your letter, FinCEN finds that the Company would be a money transmitter pursuant to our regulations.

You state in your letter that the Company wishes to set up a Platform that consists of a trading system (the "System") to match offers to buy and sell convertible virtual currency for currency of legal tender ("real currency"), and a set of book accounts in which prospective buyers or sellers of one type of currency or the other ("Customers") can deposit funds to cover their exchanges. The Company will maintain separate accounts in U.S. dollars and a virtual wallet, both segregated from the Company's operational accounts and protected from seizure by the Company's creditors (the "Funding Accounts"), in which Customers will deposit their U.S. dollars or convertible virtual currency to fund the exchanges. The Company will maintain the funding received from each Customer in its separate book entry account (the "Customer Account").

Once the exchange is funded, the Customer will submit an order to the Company to purchase or sell the currency deposited at a given price. The Platform will automatically attempt to match each purchase order of one currency to one or more sell orders of the same currency. If a match is found, the Company will purchase from the Customer acting as seller and sell to the Customer acting as buyer, without identifying one to the other. If a match is not found, the Customer may

elect to withdraw the funds or keep them in its Customer Account to fund future orders.

According to your letter, the Company will not allow inter-account transfers, third-party funding of a Customer Account, or payments from one Customer Account to a third party. Payments to or from the Customer are sent or received by credit transmittals of funds through the Automatic Clearinghouse (ACH) system or wire transfers from U.S. banks. In addition, you note that the Platform will not allow any Customer to know the identity of another Customer, and Customers must conduct transactions exclusively through their formal agreements with the Company.

In your letter, you state that the Company is already registered with FinCEN as a money transmitter and a dealer in foreign exchange. However, you assert that the Company should not be regulated as a money transmitter for the following reasons:

- The Company acts in a similar manner to securities or commodities exchanges, and there is no money transmission between the Company and any counterparty.

- If FinCEN were to find that the Company is engaged in money transmission, then such activity would be integral to the Company's business or eligible for the payment processor exemption.

- Lastly, should FinCEN find that the above exemptions do not apply, the Company fits the definition of "user" rather than "exchanger" or "administrator" pursuant to FinCEN's guidance.[1]

This letter first will address the application of the definition of money transmission and its exemptions to the Company's activities, and then address whether the Company should be considered a user rather than an exchanger or administrator of virtual currency.

FinCEN's definition of money transmission and existing exemptions

In your letter, you reference language from FinCEN's definition of money transmitter that existed prior to FinCEN's 2011 amendments to the MSB definition. On July 21, 2011, FinCEN published a Final Rule amending definitions and other regulations relating to MSBs (the "Rule").[2] Amended regulations define an MSB as "a person wherever located doing business, whether or not on a regular basis or as an organized or licensed business concern, wholly or in substantial part within the United States, in one or more of the capacities listed in paragraphs (ff)(1) through (ff)(7) of this section. This includes but is not

---

[1] FIN-2013-G001, "Application of FinCEN's Regulations to Persons Administering, Exchanging, or Using Virtual Currencies," March 18, 2013 (the "Guidance").

[2] Bank Secrecy Act Regulations – Definitions and Other Regulations Relating to Money Services Businesses, 76 FR 43585 (July 21, 2011).

limited to maintenance of any agent, agency, branch, or office within the United States."[3]

The Rule defines the term "money transmitter" to include a person that provides money transmission services, or any other person engaged in the transfer of funds. The term "money transmission services" means the acceptance of currency, funds, or other value that substitutes for currency from one person *and* the transmission of currency, funds, or other value that substitutes for currency to another location or person by any means.[4] The regulations also stipulate that whether a person is a money transmitter is a matter of facts and circumstances, and identifies circumstances under which a person's activities would not make such person a money transmitter.[5]

You argue that the Platform renders exchanges anonymous among Customers in the same way open exchanges for publicly traded equities keep the identity of each member's counterparty confidential. At this time, your analogy to the securities and futures industries and their traditional methods for buying and selling securities and commodities is not relevant for analysis of the Company's obligations under the BSA. FinCEN's guidance issued on a product or service under one set of specific facts and circumstances should only be relied upon when applied to another product or service that shares the same specific facts and circumstances.

As explained in the Guidance, a person is an exchanger and a money transmitter if the person accepts convertible virtual currency from one person and transmits it to another person as part of the acceptance and transfer of currency, funds, or other value that substitutes for currency.[6] We disagree with your contention that there is no money transmission when the instructions of the Customers are issued subject to the condition of finding an offsetting match. The regulatory definition of money transmission does not contain any element of conditionality before it applies. A person that accepts currency, funds, or any value that substitutes for currency, with the intent and/or effect of transmitting currency, funds, or any value that substitutes for currency to another person or location if a certain predetermined condition established by the transmitter is met, is a money transmitter under FinCEN's regulations. The fact that such a transmission sometimes may not occur in your business model if no match is found does not remove the Company from the scope of the regulations for those transactions that do occur.

You state that if money transmission occurs at all, it occurs between the Customer that sells and the Customer that purchases virtual currency. Your letter clearly describes the Company's Platform as consisting of two parts: an electronic matching book for offers of buying and selling virtual currency and a set of book accounts that pre-fund the transactions ordered by Customers that want to exchange virtual currency for real currency (and, on the other hand, by Customers that want to exchange real currency for virtual currency). You state that a key feature of the Platform is that Customers are never identified to each other, even after the buyer and the seller are matched. The fact that Customers are never identified to each other does not affect FinCEN's analysis of the transactions. FinCEN finds that in each trade conducted through the Platform, two money transmission transactions occur: one between the Company and the Customer wishing to buy virtual currency, and another between the Company and the Customer wishing to sell such virtual currency at the same exchange rate.

With regard to whether the money transmission is integral to the provision of the Company's service, and thus potentially eligible for exemption, FinCEN has concluded that the money transmission that takes place within the System does not qualify for the exemption. There are three fundamental conditions that must be met for the exemption to apply:

- The money transmission component must be part of the provision of goods or services distinct from money transmission itself.

- The exemption can only be claimed by the person that is engaged in the provision of goods or services distinct from money transmission.

- The money transmission component must be integral (that is, necessary) for the provision of the goods or services.

In FinCEN's view, the payment service that the Company intends to offer meets the definition of money transmission. The Company is facilitating the transfer of value, both real and virtual, between third parties. Such money transmission is the sole purpose of the Company's System, and is not a necessary part of another, non-money transmission service being provided by the Company. Although rendered before the 2011 modifications to MSB definitions and in some cases involving a different type of MSB, FinCEN reached the same conclusion in several administrative rulings that apply to this particular point.[7]

---

[3] 31 CFR § 1010.100(ff).

[4] 31 CFR § 1010.100(ff) (5) (i) (A).

[5] 31 CFR § 1010.100(ff) (5) (ii).

[6] *See* FIN-2013-G001.

[7] *See* FIN-2008-R007 ("Whether a Certain Operation Protecting On-line Personal Financial Information is a Money Transmitter" - 06/11/2008); FIN-2008-R004 ("Whether a For-

eign Exchange Consultant is a Currency Dealer or Exchanger or Money Transmitter" - 05/09/2008); FIN-2008-R003 ("Whether a Person That is Engaged in the Business of Foreign Exchange Risk Management is a Currency Dealer or Exchanger or Money Transmitter" -05/09/2008); FIN-2008-R002 ("Whether a Foreign Exchange Dealer is a Currency Dealer or Exchanger or Money Transmitter" -05/09/2008).

As you noted in your letter, FinCEN stipulates four conditions for the payment processor exemption to apply to a particular business pattern:[8]

(a) the entity providing the service must facilitate the purchase of goods or services, or the payment of bills for goods or services (other than money transmission itself);

(b) the entity must operate through clearance and settlement systems that admit only BSA-regulated financial institutions;

(c) the entity must provide the service pursuant to a formal agreement; and

(d) the entity's agreement must be at a minimum with the seller or creditor that provided the goods or services and receives the funds.

Despite your assertion that this exemption would apply to the Platform, the Company fails to meet two of the conditions for the exemption. Specifically, the Customer is not receiving payment as a seller or creditor from a buyer or debtor for the provision of non-money transmission related goods or services (FinCEN does not consider providing virtual currency for real currency or vice versa as a non-money transmission related service), and the Company is not operating through a clearing and settlement system that only admits BSA-regulated financial institutions as members. Although, according to your letter, payments to or from the Customer Accounts may take place in part using a clearing and settlement system such as EPN, FedACH, or FedWire, the Platform itself is not a clearance and settlement system that admits only BSA-regulated financial institutions, and the payments of convertible virtual currency to and from the Customers, by definition, take place outside such a clearance and settlement system.

For the above reasons, FinCEN has determined that the Company is engaged in money transmission, and such activity is not covered by either the integral exemption or the payment processor exemption.

FinCEN's Virtual Currency Guidance

On March 18, 2013, FinCEN issued guidance on the application of FinCEN's regulations to transactions in virtual currencies (the "Guidance").[9] FinCEN's regulations define currency as "the coin and paper money of the United States or of any other country that is designated as legal tender and that circulates and is customarily used and accepted as a medium of exchange in the country of issuance."[10] In contrast to real currency, "virtual" currency is a medium of exchange that operates like a currency in some environments, but does not have all the attributes of real currency. In

particular, virtual currency does not have legal tender status in any jurisdiction. The Guidance addresses "convertible" virtual currency. This type of virtual currency either has an equivalent value in real currency, or acts as a substitute for real currency.

For purposes of the Guidance, FinCEN refers to the participants in generic virtual currency arrangements, using the terms "exchanger," "administrator," and "user." An *exchanger* is a person engaged as a business in the exchange of virtual currency for real currency, funds, or other virtual currency. An *administrator* is a person engaged as a business in issuing (putting into circulation) a virtual currency, and who has the authority to redeem (to withdraw from circulation) such virtual currency. A *user* is a person that obtains virtual currency to purchase goods or services on the user's own behalf

The Guidance makes clear that an administrator or exchanger of convertible virtual currencies that accepts and transmits a convertible virtual currency, or buys or sells convertible virtual currency in exchange for currency of legal tender or another convertible virtual currency for any reason is a money transmitter under FinCEN's regulations, unless a limitation to or exemption from the definition applies to the person.[11] The guidance also makes clear that "a user who obtains convertible virtual currency and uses it to purchase real or virtual goods or services is not an MSB under FinCEN's regulations."

How a user engages in obtaining a virtual currency may be described using any number of other terms, such as "earning," "harvesting," "mining," "creating," "auto-generating," "manufacturing," or "purchasing," depending on the details of the specific virtual currency model involved. The label applied to a particular process of obtaining virtual currency is not material to its characterization under the BSA. Whether a person is deemed to be an MSB depends on how that person uses the convertible virtual currency, and for whose benefit. The mechanism by which the virtual currency is obtained is not material in determining MSB status.

FinCEN does not accept the Company's argument that it should be considered a user and not an exchanger, because "a true virtual currency exchange would have its own reserve of virtual currency and dollars that it would buy and sell in order to fund exchanges with its users." As explained in the Guidance and indicated above, a person is an exchanger and a money transmitter if the person accepts convertible virtual currency from one person and transmits it to another person as part of the acceptance and transfer of cur-

[8] FIN-2013-R002 ("Whether a Company that Offers a Payment Mechanism Based on Payable-Through Drafts to its Commercial Customers is a Money Transmitter" -11/13/2013).

[9] *See* footnote 1.

[10] 31 CFR § 1010.100(m).

[11] The definition of "money transmitter" in FinCEN's regulations defines six sets of circumstances – variously referred to as limitations or exemptions – under which a person is not a money transmitter, despite accepting and transmitting currency, funds, or value that substitutes for currency. 31 CFR § 1010.100(ff)(5)(ii)(A)-(F).

rency, funds, or other value that substitutes for currency. The method of funding the transactions is not relevant to the definition of money transmitter. An exchanger will be subject to the same obligations under FinCEN regulations regardless of whether the exchanger acts as a broker (attempting to match two (mostly) simultaneous and offsetting transactions involving the acceptance of one type of currency and the transmission of another) or as a dealer (transacting from its own reserve in either convertible virtual currency or real currency). Therefore, FinCEN finds that the Company is acting as an exchanger of convertible virtual currency, as that term was described in the Guidance.

When engaging in convertible virtual currency transactions as an exchanger, a person must register with FinCEN as a money transmitter, assess the money laundering risk involved in its non-exempt transactions, and implement an anti-money laundering program to mitigate such risk. In addition, the Company must comply with the recordkeeping, reporting, and transaction monitoring requirements under FinCEN regulations. Examples of such requirements include the filing of Currency Transaction Reports (31 CFR § 1022.310) and Suspicious Activity Reports (31 CFR § 1022.320), whenever applicable, general recordkeeping maintenance (31 CFR § 1010.410), and recordkeeping related to the sale of negotiable instruments (31 CFR § 1010.415). Furthermore, to the extent that any of the Company's transactions constitute a "transmittal of funds" (31 CFR § 1010.100(ddd)) under FinCEN's regulations, then the Company must also comply with the "Funds Transfer Rule" (31 CFR § 1010.410(e)) and the "Funds Travel Rule" (31 CFR § 1010.410(f)).[12]

This ruling is provided in accordance with the procedures set forth at 31 CFR Part 1010 Subpart G. In arriving at the conclusions in this administrative ruling, we have relied upon the accuracy and completeness of the representations you made in your communications with us. Nothing precludes FinCEN from arriving at a different conclusion or from taking other action should circumstances change or should any of the information you have provided prove inaccurate or incomplete. We reserve the right, after redacting your name and address, and similar identifying information for your clients, to publish this letter as guidance to financial institutions in accordance with our regulations.[13] You have fourteen days from the date of this letter to identify any other information you believe should be redacted and the legal basis for redaction.

If you have questions about this ruling, please contact FinCEN's regulatory helpline at (703) 905-3591.

Sincerely,

//signed//

Jamal El-Hindi

Associate Director

Policy Division

---

[12] For example, the definition of transmittal of funds involves unconditional transmittal orders. Please note that FinCEN does not consider some predetermined conditions (such as "at market") to exempt a series of transactions involving the acceptance and transmission of currency, funds, or value that substitutes for currency from a transmitter to a recipient from the definition of transmittal of funds and its related recordkeeping requirements.

[13] 31 CFR §§ 1010.711-717.

¶ 1290 Request for Administrative Ruling on the Application of FinCEN's Regulations to a Virtual Currency Payment System

UNITED STATES DEPARTMENT OF THE TREASURY

FinCEN

FINANCIAL CRIMES ENFORCEMENT NETWORK

FIN-2014-R012

Issued: October 27, 2014

Subject: Request for Administrative Ruling on the Application of FinCEN's Regulations to a Virtual Currency Payment System

Dear [ ]:

This responds to your letter of January 6, 2014, seeking an administrative ruling from the Financial Crimes Enforcement Network ("FinCEN") on behalf of [ ] (the "Company"), about the Company's possible status as a money services business ("MSB") under the Bank Secrecy Act ("BSA"). Specifically, you ask whether the convertible virtual currency payment system the Company intends to set up (the "System") would make the Company a money transmitter under the BSA. Based on the following analysis of the description of the System to provide payments to merchants who wish to receive customer payments in Bitcoin, FinCEN finds that, if the Company sets up the System, the Company would be a money transmitter and should comply with all risk management, risk mitigation, recordkeeping, reporting, and transaction monitoring requirements corresponding to such status.

You state in your letter that the Company wishes to set up a System that will provide virtual currency-based payments to merchants in the United States and (mostly) Latin America, who wish to receive payment for goods or services sold in a currency other than that of legal tender in their respective jurisdictions. The Company would receive payment from the buyer or debtor in currency of legal tender ("real currency"), and transfer the equivalent in Bitcoin to the seller or creditor, minus a transaction fee. The current intended market for the System is the hotel industry in four Latin American countries where, because of currency controls and extreme inflation, merchants face substantial foreign exchange risks when dealing with overseas customers.

According to your letter, a merchant will sign up with the Company to use the System, and incorporate the Company's software into its website. Customers purchasing the merchant's goods or services (e.g., hotel reservations) will pay for the purchase using a credit card. Instead of the credit card payment going to the merchant, it will

go to the Company, which will transfer the equivalent in Bitcoin to the merchant. The Company pays the merchant using the reserve of Bitcoin it has acquired from wholesale purchases from virtual currency exchangers at the Company's discretion (thus the Company assumes any exchange risk that occurs during the time between the Company's wholesale purchases and its payment to a merchant). The Company has no agreement with the customer and will only make payment to the merchant.

You maintain that the Company should not be regulated as a money transmitter because it does not conform to the definition of virtual currency exchanger, due to the fact that the Company makes payments from an inventory it maintains, rather than funding each individual transaction. You also maintain that, should the Company be considered an exchanger of convertible virtual currency, the Company's business should be covered under an exemption that applies to certain payment processing activities,[1] and/or the Company's transmissions should be deemed integral to the transaction and thereby covered under another exemption from money transmission.[2]

FinCEN's Virtual Currency Guidance

On March 18, 2013, FinCEN issued guidance on the application of FinCEN's regulations to transactions in virtual currencies (the "Guidance").[3] FinCEN's regulations define "currency" as "[t]he coin and paper money of the United States or of any other country that is designated as legal tender and that circulates and is customarily used and accepted as a medium of exchange in the country of issuance."[4] In contrast to real currency, "virtual" currency is a medium of exchange that operates like a currency in some environments, but does not have all the attributes of real currency. In particular, virtual currency does not have legal tender status in any jurisdiction. The Guidance addresses "convertible" virtual currency. This type of virtual currency either has an equivalent value in real currency, or acts as a substitute for real currency.

For purposes of the Guidance, FinCEN refers to the participants in generic virtual currency arrangements, using the terms "exchanger," "administrator," and "user." An *exchanger* is a person engaged as a business in the exchange of virtual currency for real currency, funds, or other virtual currency. An *administrator* is a person engaged as a business in issuing (putting into circulation) a virtual currency, and who has the authority to redeem (to withdraw from circulation) such virtual currency. A *user* is a person that obtains

---

[1] 31 CFR § 1010.100(ff) (5) (ii) (B).
[2] 31 CFR § 1010.100(ff) (5) (ii) (F).

[3] FIN-2013-G001 ("Application of FinCEN's Regulations to Persons Administering, Exchanging, or Using Virtual Currencies," March 18, 2013).
[4] 31 CFR § 1010.100(m).

virtual currency to purchase goods or services.[5] Under the Guidance, both exchangers and administrators are considered to be money transmitters unless a limitation or exemption from the definition of money transmitter applies to that person.[6]

FinCEN disagrees with your position that the Company does not convert the customer's real currency into virtual currency because the Company purchases and stores large quantities of Bitcoin that the Company then uses to pay the merchant. As described above, the Company is an exchanger under the Guidance because it engages as a business in accepting and converting the customer's real currency into virtual currency for transmission to the merchant. The fact that the Company uses its cache of Bitcoin to pay the merchant is not relevant to whether it fits within the definition of money transmitter. An exchanger will be subject to the same obligations under FinCEN regulations regardless of whether the exchanger acts as a broker (attempting to match two (mostly) simultaneous and offsetting transactions involving the acceptance of one type of currency and the transmission of another) or as a dealer (transacting from its own reserve in either convertible virtual currency or real currency).

FinCEN concludes that the Company would be a money transmitter, specifically because it is acting as an exchanger of convertible virtual currency, as that term was described in the Guidance. Additionally, you then ask, if FinCEN determines that the Company is an exchanger, whether either an exemption for certain payment processing activities or an exemption for transactions integral to the sale of other goods or services would apply.

FinCEN's definition of money transmission and existing exemptions

On July 21, 2011, FinCEN published a Final Rule amending definitions and other regulations relating to MSBs (the "Rule").[7] The amended regulations define an MSB as "a person wherever located doing business, whether or not on a regular basis or as an organized or licensed business concern, wholly or in substantial part within the United States, in one or more of the capacities listed in paragraphs (ff)(1) through (ff)(7) of this section. This includes but is not limited to maintenance of any agent, agency, branch, or office within the United States."[8]

BSA regulations, as amended, define the term "money transmitter" to include a person that provides money transmission services, or any other person engaged in the transfer of funds. The term "money transmission services" means the acceptance of currency, funds, or other value that substitutes for currency from one person *and* the transmission of currency, funds, or other value that substitutes for currency to another location or person by any means.[9] The regulations also stipulate that whether a person is a money transmitter is a matter of facts and circumstances, and identifies circumstances under which a person's activities would not make such person a money transmitter.[10]

FinCEN stipulates four conditions for the payment processor exemption to apply to a particular business pattern:

(a) the entity providing the service must facilitate the purchase of goods or services, or the payment of bills for goods or services (other than money transmission itself);

(b) the entity must operate through clearance and settlement systems that admit only BSA-regulated financial institutions;

(c) the entity must provide the service pursuant to a formal agreement; and

(d) the entity's agreement must be at a minimum with the seller or creditor that provided the goods or services and receives the funds.[11]

The Company fails to satisfy one of these conditions. The Company is not operating through clearing and settlement systems that only admit BSA-regulated financial institutions as members. According to your letter the real currency payments from the consumer take place within a clearing and settlement system that only admits BSA-regulated financial institutions as members (specifically, a credit card network), however, the payment of the Bitcoin equivalent to the merchant, by definition, takes place outside such a clearing and settlement system, either to a merchant-owned virtual currency wallet or to a larger virtual currency exchange that admits both financial institution and non-financial institution members, for the account of the merchant.

With regard to whether the money transmission is integral to the provision of the Company's service, and thus potentially eligible for exemption, FinCEN has concluded that the money transmission that takes place within the System does not qualify for the exemption. There are three fundamental conditions that must be met for the exemption to apply:

---

[5] FIN-2014-R001 "Application of FinCEN's Regulations to Virtual Currency Mining Operations" -01/30/2014, clarified that a *user* is a person that obtains virtual currency to purchase goods or services *on the user's own behalf. (emphasis added)*

[6] *See* FIN-2013-G001.

[7] Bank Secrecy Act Regulations – Definitions and Other Regulations Relating to Money Services Businesses, 76 FR 43585 (July 21, 2011).

[8] 31 CFR § 1010.100(ff).

[9] 31 CFR § 1010.100(ff)(5)(i)(A).

[10] 31 CFR § 1010.100(ff)(5)(ii).

[11] *See* 31 CFR § 1010.100(ff)(5)(ii)(B); *see also* FIN-2013-R002 ("Whether a Company that Offers a Payment Mechanism Based on Payable-Through Drafts to its Commercial Customers is a Money Transmitter" - 11/13/2013). FIN-2013-R002 clarifies that for the payment processor exemption to apply, the entity must use a clearance and settlement system that intermediates solely between BSA regulated institutions.

a) The money transmission component must be part of the provision of goods or services distinct from money transmission itself;

b) The exemption can only be claimed by the person that is engaged in the provision of goods or services distinct from money transmission;

c) The money transmission component must be integral (that is, necessary) for the provision of the goods or services.

In FinCEN's view, the payment service that the Company intends to offer meets the definition of money transmission. Such money transmission is the sole purpose of the Company's System, and is not a necessary part of another, non-money transmission service being provided by the Company. Although rendered before the 2011 modifications to MSB definitions and in some cases involving a different type of MSB, FinCEN reached the same conclusion in several administrative rulings that apply to this particular point.[12]

For the above reasons, FinCEN has determined that the Company is engaged in money transmission, and such activity is not covered by either the payment processor or the integral exemption. Please note that FinCEN would reach the same conclusions if payments were made in virtual currencies other than Bitcoin. As a money transmitter, the Company will be required to (a) register with FinCEN, (b) conduct a comprehensive risk assessment of its exposure to money laundering,[13] (c) implement an Anti-Money Laundering Program based on such risk assessment, and (d) comply with the recordkeeping, reporting and transaction monitoring obligations set down in Parts 1010 and 1022 of 31 CFR Chapter X. Examples of such requirements include the filing of Currency Transaction Reports (31 CFR § 1022.310) and Suspicious Activity Reports (31 CFR § 1022.320), whenever applicable, general recordkeeping maintenance (31 CFR § 1010.410), and recordkeeping related to the sale of negotiable instruments (31 CFR § 1010.415). Furthermore, to the extent that any of the Company's transactions constitute a "transmittal of funds" (31 CFR § 1010.100(ddd)) under FinCEN's regulations, then the Company must also comply with the "Funds Transfer Rule" (31 CFR § 1010.410(e)) and the "Funds Travel Rule" (31 CFR § 1010.410(f)).

This ruling is provided in accordance with the procedures set forth at 31 CFR Part 1010 Subpart G. In arriving at the conclusions in this administrative ruling, we have relied upon the accuracy and completeness of the representations you made in your communications with us. Nothing precludes FinCEN from arriving at a different conclusion or from taking other action should circumstances change or should any of the information you have provided prove inaccurate or incomplete. We reserve the right, after redacting your name and address, and similar identifying information for your clients, to publish this letter as guidance to financial institutions in accordance with our regulations.[14] You have fourteen days from the date of this letter to identify any other information you believe should be redacted and the legal basis for redaction.

If you have questions about this ruling, please contact FinCEN's regulatory helpline at (703) 905-3591.

Sincerely,

//signed//

Jamal El-Hindi

Associate Director

Policy Division

---

[12] *See* FIN-2008-R007 ("Whether a Certain Operation Protecting On-line Personal Financial Information is a Money Transmitter" - 06/11/2008); FIN-2008-R004 ("Whether a Foreign Exchange Consultant is a Currency Dealer or Exchanger or Money Transmitter" - 05/09/2008); FIN-2008-R003 ("Whether a Person That is Engaged in the Business of Foreign Exchange Risk Management is a Currency Dealer or Exchanger or Money Transmitter" - 05/09/2008); and FIN-2008-R002 ("Whether a Foreign Exchange Dealer is a Currency Dealer or Exchanger or Money Transmitter" - 05/09/2008).

[13] We caution the Company about incorporating into its comprehensive risk assessment the delicate balance between helping merchants avoid losses due to the fluctuation of their currencies of legal tender because of inflationary trends or devaluation, on the one hand, and collaboration with their potential evasion of foreign exchange control regulations applicable in their jurisdictions, on the other.

[14] 31 CFR §§ 1010.711-717.

¶ 1300 Application of FinCEN's Regulations to Persons Issuing Physical or Digital Negotiable Certificates of Ownership of Precious Metals

UNITED STATES DEPARTMENT OF THE TREASURY

FinCEN

FINANCIAL CRIMES ENFORCEMENT NETWORK

RULING

FIN-2015-R001

Issued: August 14, 2015

Subject: Application of FinCEN's Regulations to Persons Issuing Physical or Digital Negotiable Certificates of Ownership of Precious Metals

Dear [ ]:

This responds to your letter of July 15, 2014, seeking an administrative ruling from the Financial Crimes Enforcement Network ("FinCEN") on behalf of [ ] (the "Company"), regarding FinCEN's money services business ("MSB") regulations under the Bank Secrecy Act ("BSA"). Specifically, you ask for FinCEN's determination as to whether the operations and transaction services offered by the Company make it a money transmitter as defined under the BSA. Based on the following analysis of the description of the Company's activities as presented in your letter, FinCEN finds that the Company would be a money transmitter and a dealer in precious metals, precious stones, or jewels pursuant to our regulations.

You state in your letter that the Company engages in three complementary but distinct types of activities:

a) The Company provides Internet-based brokerage services between buyers and sellers of precious metals. Buyers pay sellers directly by check, wire transfer, or bitcoin.

b) The Company buys and sells precious metals on its own account.

c) The Company holds precious metals in custody for buyers that purchase this service ("Customers"), opening a digital wallet for the Customer and issuing a digital proof of custody (a "digital certificate") that can be linked to the Customer's wallet on the Bitcoin blockchain ledger. The Customer then can trade or exchange its precious metals holdings at the Company by any means it could trade or exchange bitcoin via the rails of the blockchain ledger.

The Company derives its income from charging a transaction fee on transfers of digital certificates by Customers and a custody fee for precious metals held in custody.

FinCEN's definition of money transmission and existing exemptions; relationship to the Company's activities as a broker and an issuer of freely transferable digital gold certificates

On July 21, 2011, FinCEN published a Final Rule amending definitions and other regulations relating to MSBs (the "Rule").[1] The amended regulations define an MSB as "[A] person wherever located doing business, whether or not on a regular basis or as an organized or licensed business concern, wholly or in substantial part within the United States, in one or more of the capacities listed in paragraphs (ff)(1) through (ff)(7) of this section. This includes but is not limited to maintenance of any agent, agency, branch, or office within the United States."[2]

The Rule defines the term "money transmitter" to include a person that provides money transmission services, or any other person engaged in transfer of funds. The term "money transmission services" means the acceptance of currency, funds, or other value that substitutes for currency from one person *and* the transmission of currency, funds, or other value that substitutes for currency to another location or person by any means.[3] The regulations also stipulate that whether a person is a money transmitter is a matter of facts and circumstances, and identifies circumstances under which a person's activities would not make such person a money transmitter.[4] The regulations specifically exempt from money transmitter status a person that only provides the delivery, communication, or network data access services used by a money transmitter to supply money transmission services.[5] To the extent the only type of brokerage services offered by the Company are those in which the buyer makes payment directly to the seller, the Company would meet this exemption and FinCEN would not deem the Company a money transmitter.

On March 18, 2013, FinCEN issued guidance on the application of FinCEN's regulations to transactions in virtual currencies (the "guidance").[6] FinCEN's regulations define currency (also referred to as "real" currency) as "[t]he coin and paper money of the United States or of any other country that [i] is designated as legal tender and that [ii] circulates and [iii] is customarily used and accepted as a medium of exchange in the country

---

[1] Bank Secrecy Act Regulations – Definitions and Other Regulations Relating to Money Services Businesses, 76 FR 43585 (July 21, 2011).

[2] 31 CFR § 1010.100(ff).

[3] 31 CFR § 1010.100(ff)(5)(i)(A).

[4] 31 CFR § 1010.100(ff)(5)(ii).

[5] 31 CFR § 1010.100(ff)(5)(ii)(A).

[6] FIN-2013-G001, "Application of FinCEN's Regulations to Persons Administering, Exchanging, or Using Virtual Currencies," March 18, 2013.

of issuance."[7] In contrast to real currency, "virtual" currency is a medium of exchange that operates like a currency in some environments, but does not have all the attributes of real currency. In particular, virtual currency does not have legal tender status in any jurisdiction. The guidance addresses "convertible" virtual currency. This type of virtual currency either has an equivalent value in real currency, or acts as a substitute for real currency.

For purposes of the guidance, FinCEN refers to the participants in generic virtual currency arrangements, using the terms "user," "exchanger," and "administrator." A *user* is a person that obtains virtual currency to purchase goods or services on the user's own behalf. FinCEN has determined that users are not money transmitters. An *exchanger* is a person engaged as a business in the exchange of virtual currency for real currency, funds, or other virtual currency. An *administrator* is a person engaged as a business in issuing (putting into circulation) a virtual currency, and who has the authority to redeem (to withdraw from circulation) such virtual currency. Both exchangers and administrators may operate as money transmitters depending on the specific facts and circumstances.

The guidance describes three common business models (types of activity) to illustrate the application of the money transmission definition. The first type of activity involves electronic trading in e-currencies or e-precious metals.[8] In 2008, FinCEN issued guidance stating that as long as a broker or dealer in real currency or other commodities accepts and transmits funds solely for the purpose of effecting a *bona fide* purchase or sale of the real currency or other commodities for or with a customer, such person is not acting as a money transmitter under the regulations. However, if the broker or dealer transfers funds between a customer and a third party that is not part of the currency or commodity transaction, such transmission of funds is no longer a fundamental element of the actual transaction necessary to execute the contract for the purchase or sale of the currency or the other commodity.[9] This scenario is, therefore, money transmission.[10] Examples include, in part, (1) the transfer of funds between a customer and a third party by permitting a third party to fund a customer's account; (2) the transfer of value from a customer's currency or commodity position to the account of another customer; or (3) the closing out of a customer's currency or commodity position, with a transfer of proceeds to a third party. Since the definition of a money transmitter does not differentiate between real currencies and convertible virtual currencies, the same rules apply to brokers and dealers of e-currency and e-precious metals.

The Company does not fall under the e-currencies or e-precious metals trading exemption from money transmission because, when the Company issues a freely transferable digital certificate of ownership to buyers, it is allowing the unrestricted transfer of value from a customer's commodity position to the position of another customer or a third-party, and it is no longer limiting itself to the type of transmission of funds that is a fundamental element of the actual transaction necessary to execute the contract for the purchase or sale of the currency or the other commodity. FinCEN finds that, as the Company is going beyond the activities of a broker or dealer in commodities and is acting as a convertible virtual currency administrator (with the freely transferable digital certificates being the commodity-backed virtual currency), the Company falls under the definition of money transmitter.

FinCEN's definition of dealer in precious metals, precious stones, or jewels; application to the Company's activities as a direct seller of precious metals

Dealers and certain retailers engaging in the purchase and sale of precious metals, precious stones, or jewels are financial institutions under FinCEN regulations. FinCEN defines a dealer as "a person engaged within the United States as a business in the purchase and sale of covered goods and who, during the prior calendar or tax year (i) purchased more than $50,000 in covered goods; and (ii) received more than $50,000 gross proceeds from the sale of covered goods."[11] FinCEN includes in the definition of "dealer" those persons ". . . engaged within the United States in the business of sales primarily to the public of covered goods . . . who during the prior calendar or tax year . . . purchased more than $50,000 in covered goods from persons other than dealers or other retailers (such as members of the

---

[7] 31 CFR § 1010.100(m).

[8] Typically, this involves the broker or dealer electronically distributing digital certificates of ownership of real currencies or precious metals, with the digital certificate being the virtual currency. However, the same conclusions would apply in the case of the broker or dealer issuing paper ownership certificates or manifesting customer ownership or control of real currencies or commodities in an account statement or any other form. These conclusions would also apply in the case of a broker or dealer in commodities other than real currencies or precious metals. A broker or dealer of e-currencies or e-precious metals that engages in money transmission could be either an administrator or exchanger depending on its business model.

[9] *Application of the Definition of Money Transmitter to Brokers and Dealers in Currency and other Commodities,* FIN-2008-G008, Sept. 10, 2008. The guidance also notes that the definition of money transmitter excludes any person, such as a futures commission merchant, that is "registered with, and regulated or examined by . . . the Commodity Futures Trading Commission."

[10] In 2011, FinCEN amended the definition of money transmitter. The 2008 guidance, however, was primarily concerned with the core elements of the definition – accepting and transmitting currency or value – and the exemption for acceptance and transmission integral to another transaction not involving money transmission. The 2011 amendments have not materially changed these aspects of the definition.

[11] 31 CFR § 1027.100(b).

general public or foreign sources of supply."[12] The term "covered goods" includes precious metals as listed in 31 CFR § 1027.100(d). Based on your letter, and subject to the monetary threshold and type of supplier considerations explained above, the purchases and sales the Company entered into on its own account would make the Company a dealer in precious metals, and therefore a financial institution subject to FinCEN regulations.

When acting as either a money transmitter or a dealer in precious metals, precious stones, or jewels, the Company must assess the money laundering risk involved in its non-exempt transactions, and implement an anti-money laundering program to mitigate such risk. In addition, the Company must comply with the recordkeeping, reporting, and transaction monitoring requirements under FinCEN regulations. Examples of such requirements include the filing of reports relating to currency in excess of $10,000 received in a trade or business (31 CFR § 1027.330) whenever applicable, general recordkeeping maintenance (31 CFR § 1027.410), and recordkeeping related to the sale of negotiable instruments (31 CFR § 1010.415). Furthermore, to the extent that any of the Company's transactions constitute a "transmittal of funds" (31 CFR § 1010.100(ddd)) under FinCEN's regulations, then the Company must also comply with the "Funds Transfer Rule" (31 CFR § 1010.410(e)) and the "Funds Travel Rule" (31 CFR § 1010.410(f)). Additionally, as a money transmitter, the Company must register with FinCEN within 180 days of starting to engage in convertible virtual currency transactions as an exchanger (31 CFR § 1022.380).

This ruling is provided in accordance with the procedures set forth at 31 CFR Part 1010 Subpart G. In arriving at the conclusions in this administrative ruling, we have relied upon the accuracy and completeness of the representations you made in your communications with us. Nothing precludes FinCEN from arriving at a different conclusion or from taking other action should circumstances change or should any of the information you have provided prove inaccurate or incomplete. We reserve the right, after redacting your name and address, and similar identifying information for your clients, to publish this letter as guidance to financial institutions in accordance with our regulations.[13] You have fourteen days from the date of this letter to identify any other information you believe should be redacted and the legal basis for redaction.

If you have questions about this ruling, please contact FinCEN's regulatory helpline at (703) 905-3591.

Sincerely,

//signed//

Robert Gerardi

Acting Associate Director

Policy Division

---

[12] 31 CFR § 1027.100(b)(2)(i).

[13] 31 CFR §§ 1010.711-717.

¶ 1310 Statement of Jennifer Shasky Calvery, Director Financial Crimes Enforcement Network
United States Department of the Treasury

Statement of Jennifer Shasky Calvery,
Director Financial Crimes Enforcement
Network United States Department of the
Treasury

Before the United States Senate Committee on
Homeland Security and Government Affairs

November 18, 2013

Chairman Carper, Ranking Member Coburn, and distinguished Members of the Committee, I am Jennifer Shasky Calvery, Director of the Financial Crimes Enforcement Network (FinCEN), and I appreciate the opportunity to appear before you today to discuss FinCEN's ongoing role in the Administration's efforts to establish a meaningful regulatory framework for virtual currencies that intersect with the U.S. financial system. We appreciate the Committee's interest in this important issue, and your continued support of our efforts to prevent illicit financial activity from exploiting potential gaps in our regulatory structure as technological advances create new and innovative ways to move money. I am also pleased to be testifying with my colleagues from the Departments of Justice and Homeland Security. Both play an important role in the global fight against money laundering and terrorist financing, and our collaboration on these issues greatly enhances the effectiveness of our efforts.

FinCEN's mission is to safeguard the financial system from illicit use, combat money laundering and promote national security through the collection, analysis, and dissemination of financial intelligence and strategic use of financial authorities. FinCEN works to achieve its mission through a broad range of interrelated strategies, including:

- Administering the Bank Secrecy Act (BSA) - the United States' primary anti-money laundering (AML)/counter-terrorist financing (CFT) regulatory regime;

- Sharing the rich financial intelligence we collect, as well as our analysis and expertise, with law enforcement, intelligence, and regulatory partners; and,

- Building global cooperation and technical expertise among financial intelligence units throughout the world.

To accomplish these activities, FinCEN employs a team comprised of approximately 340 dedi-cated employees with a broad range of expertise in illicit finance, financial intelligence, the financial industry, the AML/CFT regulatory regime, technology, and enforcement. We also leverage our close relationships with regulatory, law enforcement, international, and industry partners to increase our collective insight and better protect the U.S. financial system.

What is Virtual Currency?

Before moving into a discussion of FinCEN's role in ensuring we have smart regulation for virtual currency that is not too burdensome but also protects the U.S. financial system from illicit use, let me set the stage with some of the definitions we are using at FinCEN to understand virtual currency and the various types present in the market today. Virtual currency is a medium of exchange that operates like a currency in some environments but does not have all the attributes of real currency. In particular, virtual currency does not have legal tender status in any jurisdiction. A *convertible* virtual currency either has an equivalent value in real currency, or acts as a substitute for real currency. In other words, it is a virtual currency that can be exchanged for real currency. At FinCEN, we have focused on two types of convertible virtual currencies: centralized and decentralized.

Centralized virtual currencies have a centralized repository and a single administrator. Liberty Reserve, which FinCEN identified earlier this year as being of primary money laundering concern pursuant to Section 311 of the USA PATRIOT Act, is an example of a centralized virtual currency. Decentralized virtual currencies, on the other hand, and as the name suggests, have no central repository and no single administrator. Instead, value is electronically transmitted between parties without an intermediary. Bitcoin is an example of a decentralized virtual currency. Bitcoin is also known as cryptocurrency, meaning that it relies on cryptographic software protocols to generate the currency and validate transactions

There are a variety of methods an individual user might employ to obtain, spend, and then "cash out" either a centralized or decentralized virtual currency. The following illustration shows a typical series of transactions in a centralized virtual currency, such as Liberty Reserve:

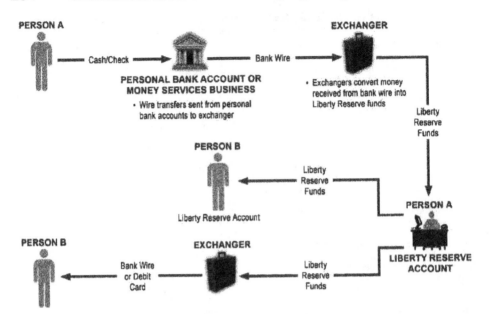

By way of comparison, the next illustration shows a very similar series of transactions in a decentralized virtual currency such as Bitcoin:

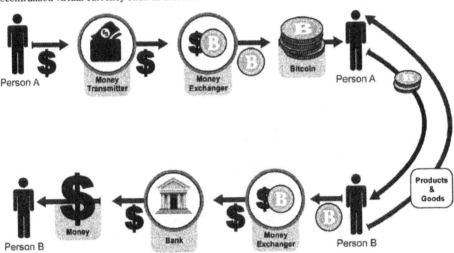

From a "follow the money" standpoint, the main difference between these two series of transactions is the absence of an "administrator" serving as intermediary in the case of Bitcoin. This difference does have significance in FinCEN's regulatory approach to virtual currency, and that approach will be addressed further during the course of my testimony today.

Money Laundering Vulnerabilities in Virtual Currencies

Any financial institution, payment system, or medium of exchange has the potential to be ex-

ploited for money laundering or terrorist financing. Virtual currency is not different in this regard. As with all parts of the financial system, though, FinCEN seeks to understand the specific attributes that make virtual currency vulnerable to illicit use, so that we can both employ a smart regulatory approach and encourage industry to develop mitigating features in its products.

Some of the following reasons an illicit actor might decide to use a virtual currency to store and transfer value are the same reasons that legitimate users have, while other reasons are more nefari-

¶1310

ous. Specifically, an illicit actor may choose to use virtually currency because it:

- Enables the user to remain relatively anonymous;

- Is relatively simple for the user to navigate;

- May have low fees;

- Is accessible across the globe with a simple Internet connection;

- Can be used both to store value and make international transfers of value;

- Does not typically have transaction limits;

- Is generally secure;

- Features irrevocable transactions;

- Depending on the system, may have been created with the intent (and added features) to facilitate money laundering;

- If it is decentralized, has no administrator to maintain information on users and report suspicious activity to governmental authorities;

- Can exploit weaknesses in the anti-money laundering/counter terrorist financing (AML/CFT) regimes of various jurisdictions, including international disparities in, and a general lack of, regulations needed to effectively support the prevention and detection of money laundering and terrorist financing.

Because any financial institution, payment system, or medium of exchange has the potential to be exploited for money laundering, fighting such illicit use requires consistent regulation across the financial system. Virtual currency is not different from other financial products and services in this regard. What is important is that financial institutions that deal in virtual currency put effective AML/CFT controls in place to harden themselves from becoming the targets of illicit actors that would exploit any identified vulnerabilities.

Indeed, the idea that illicit actors might exploit the vulnerabilities of virtual currency to launder money is not merely theoretical. We have seen both centralized and decentralized virtual currencies exploited by illicit actors. Liberty Reserve used its centralized virtual currency as part of an alleged $6 billion money laundering operation purportedly used by criminal organizations engaged in credit card fraud, identity theft, investment fraud, computer hacking, narcotics trafficking, and child pornography. One Liberty Reserve co-founder has already pleaded guilty to money laundering in the scheme. And just recently, the Department of Justice has alleged that customers of Silk Road, the largest narcotic and contraband marketplace on the Internet to date, were required to pay in bitcoins to enable both the operator of Silk Road and its sellers to evade detection and launder hundreds of millions of dollars. With money laundering activity already valued in the billions of dollars, virtual currency is certainly worthy of FinCEN's attention.

That being said, it is also important to put virtual currency in perspective as a payment system. The U.S. government indictment and proposed special measures against Liberty Reserve allege it was involved in laundering more than $6 billion. Administrators of other major centralized virtual currencies report processing similar transaction volumes to what Liberty Reserve did. In the case of Bitcoin, it has been publicly reported that its users processed transactions worth approximately $8 billion over the twelve-month period preceding October 2013; however, this measure may be artificially high due to the extensive use of automated layering in many Bitcoin transactions. By way of comparison, according to information reported publicly, in 2012 Bank of America processed $244.4 trillion in wire transfers, PayPal processed approximately $145 billion in online payments, Western Union made remittances totaling approximately $81 billion, the Automated Clearing House (ACH) Network processed more than 21 billion transactions with a total dollar value of $36.9 trillion, and Fedwire, which handles large-scale wholesale transfers, processed 132 million transactions for a total of $599 trillion. This relative volume of transactions becomes important when you consider that, according to the United Nations Office on Drugs and Crime (UNODC), the best estimate for the amount of all global criminal proceeds available for laundering through the financial system in 2009 was $1.6 trillion. While of growing concern, to date, virtual currencies have yet to overtake more traditional methods to move funds internationally, whether for legitimate or criminal purposes.

Mitigating Money Laundering Vulnerabilities in Virtual Currencies

FinCEN's main goal in administering the BSA is to ensure the integrity and transparency of the U.S. financial system so that money laundering and terrorist financing can be prevented and, where it does occur, be detected for follow on action. One of our biggest challenges is striking the right balance between the costs and benefits of regulation. One strategy we use to address this challenge is to promote consistency, where possible, in our regulatory framework across different parts of the financial services industry. It ensures a level playing field for industry and minimizes gaps in our AML/CFT coverage.

Recognizing the emergence of new payment methods and the potential for abuse by illicit actors, FinCEN began working with our law enforcement and regulatory partners several years ago to study the issue. We understood that AML protections must keep pace with the emergence of new payment systems, such as virtual currency and prepaid cards, lest those innovations become a favored tool of illicit actors. In July 2011, after a public comment period designed to receive feedback from industry, FinCEN released two rules that update several definitions and provide the needed flexibility to accommodate innovation in the payment systems space under our preexisting regulatory framework. Those rules are: (1) Definitions and Other Regulations Relating to Money Services Businesses; and (2) Definitions and Other Regulations Relating to Prepaid Access.

The updated definitions reflect FinCEN's earlier guidance and rulings, as well as current business operations in the industry. As such, they have been able to accommodate the development of new payment systems, including virtual currency. Specifically, the new rule on money services businesses added the phrase "other value that substitutes for currency" to the definition of "money transmission services." And since a convertible virtual currency either has an equivalent value in real currency, or acts a substitute for real currency, it qualifies as "other value that substitutes for currency" under the definition of "money transmission services." A person that provides money transmission services is a "money transmitter," a type of money services business already covered by the AML/CFT protections in the BSA.

As a follow-up to the regulations and in an effort to provide additional clarity on the compliance expectations for those actors involved in virtual currency transactions subject to FinCEN oversight, on March 18, 2013, FinCEN supplemented its money services business regulations with interpretive guidance designed to clarify the applicability of the regulations implementing the BSA to persons creating, obtaining, distributing, exchanging, accepting, or transmitting virtual currencies. In the simplest of terms, FinCEN's guidance explains that administrators or exchangers of virtual currencies must register with FinCEN, and institute certain recordkeeping, reporting and AML program control measures, unless an exception to these requirements applies. The guidance also explains that those who use virtual currencies exclusively for common personal transactions like buying goods or services online are users, not subject to regulatory requirements under the BSA. In all cases, FinCEN employs an activity-based test to determine when someone dealing with virtual currency qualifies as a money transmitter. The guidance clarifies definitions and expectations to ensure that businesses engaged in such activities are aware of their regulatory responsibilities, including registering appropriately. Furthermore, FinCEN closely coordinates with its state regulatory counterparts to encourage appropriate application of FinCEN guidance as part of the states' separate AML compliance oversight of financial institutions.

It is in the best interest of virtual currency providers to comply with these regulations for a number of reasons. First is the idea of corporate responsibility. Legitimate financial institutions, including virtual currency providers, do not go into business with the aim of laundering money on behalf of criminals. Virtual currencies are a financial service, and virtual currency administrators and exchangers are financial institutions. As I stated earlier, any financial institution could be exploited for money laundering purposes. What is important is for institutions to put controls in place

to deal with those money laundering threats, and to meet their AML reporting obligations.

At the same time, being a good corporate citizen and complying with regulatory responsibilities is good for a company's bottom line. Every financial institution needs to be concerned about its reputation and show that it is operating with transparency and integrity within the bounds of law. Legitimate customers will be drawn to a virtual currency or administrator or exchanger where they know their money is safe and where they know the company has a reputation for integrity. And banks will want to provide services to administrators or exchangers that show not only great innovation, but also great integrity and transparency.

The decision to bring virtual currency within the scope of our regulatory framework should be viewed by those who respect and obey the basic rule of law as a positive development for this sector. It recognizes the innovation virtual currencies provide, and the benefits they might offer society. Several new payment methods in the financial sector have proven their capacity to empower customers, encourage the development of innovative financial products, and expand access to financial services. We want these advances to continue. However, those institutions that choose to act outside of their AML obligations and outside of the law have and will continue to be held accountable. FinCEN will do everything in its regulatory power to stop such abuses of the U.S. financial system.

As previously mentioned, earlier this year, FinCEN identified Liberty Reserve as a financial institution of primary money laundering concern under Section 311 of the USA PATRIOT Act. Liberty Reserve operated as an online, virtual currency, money transfer system conceived and operated specifically to allow – and encourage – illicit use because of the anonymity it offered. It was deliberately designed to avoid regulatory scrutiny and tailored its services to illicit actors looking to launder their ill-gotten gains. According to the allegations contained in a related criminal action brought by the U.S. Department of Justice, those illicit actors included criminal organizations engaged in credit card fraud, identity theft, investment fraud, computer hacking, narcotics trafficking, and child pornography, just to name a few. The 311 action taken by FinCEN was designed to restrict the ability of Liberty Reserve to access the U.S. financial system, publicly notify the international financial community of the risks posed by Liberty Reserve, and to send a resounding message to other offshore money launderers that such abuse of the U.S. financial system will not be tolerated and their activity can be reached through our targeted financial measures.

Sharing Our Knowledge and Expertise on Virtual Currency

As the financial intelligence unit for the United States, FinCEN must stay current on how money is being laundered in the United States, including

¶1310

through new and emerging payment systems, so that we can share this expertise with our many law enforcement, regulatory, industry, and foreign financial intelligence unit partners, and effectively serve as the cornerstone of this country's AML/CFT regime. FinCEN has certainly sought to meet this responsibility with regard to virtual currency and its exploitation by illicit actors. In doing so, we have drawn and continue to draw from the knowledge we have gained through our regulatory efforts, use of targeted financial measures, analysis of the financial intelligence we collect, independent study of virtual currency, outreach to industry, and collaboration with our many partners in law enforcement.

In the same month we issued our guidance on virtual currency, March 2013, FinCEN also issued a Networking Bulletin on crypto-currencies to provide a more granular explanation of this highly complex industry to law enforcement and assist it in following the money as it funnels between virtual currency channels and the U.S. financial system. Among other things, the bulletin addresses the role of traditional banks, money transmitters, and exchangers that come into play as intermediaries by enabling users to fund the purchase of virtual currencies and exchange virtual currencies for other types of currency. It also highlights known records processes associated with virtual currencies and the potential value these records may offer to investigative officials. The bulletin has been in high demand since its publication and the feedback regarding its tremendous value has come from the entire spectrum of our law enforcement partners. In fact, demand for more detailed information on crypto-currencies has been so high that we have also shared it with several of our regulatory and foreign financial intelligence unit partners.

One feature of a FinCEN Networking Bulletin is that it asks the readers to provide ongoing feedback on what they are learning through their investigations so that we can create a forum to quickly learn of new developments, something particularly important with a new payment method. Based on what we are learning through this forum and other means, FinCEN has issued several analytical products of a tactical nature to inform law enforcement operations.

Equally important to our ongoing efforts to deliver expertise to our law enforcement partners is FinCEN's engagement with our regulatory counterparts to ensure they are kept apprised of the latest trends in virtual currencies and the potential vulnerabilities they pose to traditional financial institutions under their supervision. FinCEN uses its collaboration with the Federal Financial Institutions Examination Council (FFIEC) BSA Working Group as a platform to review and discuss FinCEN's regulations and guidance, and the most recent and relevant trends in virtual currencies. One such example occurred just recently, when several FinCEN virtual currency experts gave a comprehensive presentation on the topic to an audience of Federal and state bank examiners at an FFIEC Payment Systems Risk Conference. The presentation covered an overview of virtual currency operations, FinCEN's guidance on the application of FinCEN regulations to virtual currency, enforcement actions, and ongoing industry outreach efforts.

FinCEN also participates in the FBI-led Virtual Currency Emerging Threats Working Group, the FDIC-led Cyber Fraud Working Group, the Terrorist Financing & Financial Crimes-led Treasury Cyber Working Group, and with a community of other financial intelligence units. We host speakers, discuss current trends, and provide information on FinCEN resources and authorities as we work with our partners in an effort to foster an open line of communication across the government regarding bad actors involved in virtual currency and cyber-related crime.

Finally, FinCEN has shared its strategic analysis on money laundering through virtual currency with executives at many of our partner law enforcement and regulatory agencies, and foreign financial intelligence units, as well as with U.S. government policy makers.

Outreach to the Virtual Currency Industry

Recognizing that the new, expanded definition of money transmission would bring new financial entities under the purview of FinCEN's regulatory framework, shortly after the publication of the interpretive guidance and as part of FinCEN's ongoing commitment to engage in dialogue with the financial industry and continually learn more about the industries that we regulate, FinCEN announced its interest in holding outreach meetings with representatives from the virtual currency industry. The meetings are designed to hear feedback on the implications of recent regulatory responsibilities imposed on this industry, and to receive industry's input on where additional guidance would be helpful to facilitate compliance.

We held the first such meeting with representatives of the Bitcoin Foundation on August 26, 2013 at FinCEN's Washington, DC offices and included attendees from a cross-section of the law enforcement and regulatory communities. This outreach was part of FinCEN's overall efforts to increase knowledge and understanding of the regulated industry and how its members are impacted by regulations, and thereby help FinCEN most efficiently and effectively work with regulated entities to further the common goals of the detection and deterrence of financial crime. To further capitalize on this important dialogue and exchange of ideas, FinCEN has invited the Bitcoin Foundation to provide a similar presentation at the next plenary of the Bank Secrecy Act Advisory Group (BSAAG) scheduled for mid-December. The BSAAG is a Congressionally-chartered forum that brings together representatives from the financial industry, law enforcement, and the regulatory community to advise FinCEN on the functioning of our AML/CFT regime.

Conclusion

The Administration has made appropriate oversight of the virtual currency industry a priority, and as a result, FinCEN's efforts in this regard have increased significantly over recent years through targeted regulatory measures, outreach to regulatory and law enforcement counterparts and our partners in the private sector, and the development of expertise. We are very encouraged by the progress we have made thus far. We are dedicated to continuing to build on these accomplishments by remaining focused on future trends in the virtual currency industry and how they may inform potential changes to our regulatory framework for the future. Thank you for inviting me to testify before you today. I would be happy to answer any questions you may have.

¶ 1320 Supporting Responsible Innovation in the Federal Banking System: An OCC Perspective

Office of the Comptroller of the Currency

Washington, D.C.

March 2016

Preface by the Comptroller of the Currency

Innovation has been a hallmark of the national banking system since its founding in 1863 by President Lincoln. That innovative spirit has been especially evident in recent decades as national banks and federal savings associations have led the way in developing and adapting products, services, and technology to meet the changing needs of their customers.

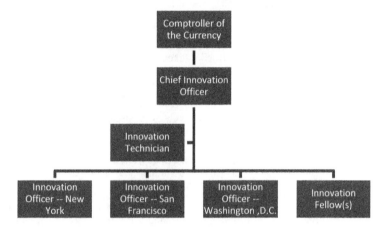

Figure 1. Office of Innovation Organization

While banks continue to innovate, rapid and dramatic advances in financial technology (fintech) are beginning to disrupt the way traditional banks do business. As the prudential regulator of the federal banking system, we want national banks and federal savings associations to thrive in this environment and to continue fulfilling their vital role of providing financial services to consumers, businesses, and their communities.

Our diverse system of banks has many advantages in developing and adapting financial innovations. Federally chartered institutions have stable funding sources, capital, and extensive customer relationships. They also have a long history of risk management that has led to enhanced information security capabilities, mature credit modeling and underwriting processes, and compliance programs that help protect consumers. These capabilities lay a foundation for innovation in the 21st century, and are major reasons the federal banking system still serves as a source of strength for the nation after 153 years.

At the Office of the Comptroller of the Currency (OCC), we are making certain that institutions with federal charters have a regulatory framework that is receptive to responsible innovation along with the supervision that supports it.

Innovation holds much promise. Technology, for example, can promote financial inclusion by expanding services to the underserved. It can provide more control and better tools for families to save, borrow, and manage their financial affairs. It can help companies and institutions scale operations efficiently to compete in the marketplace, and it can make business and consumer transactions faster and safer.

Innovation is not free from risk, but when managed appropriately, risk should not impede progress. Indeed, effective risk management is essential to responsible innovation. Banks and regulators must strike the right balance between risk and innovation.

This paper describes the OCC's vision for responsible innovation in the federal banking system and discusses the principles that will guide the development of our framework for evaluating new and innovative financial products and services. We welcome your feedback.

'At the OCC, we are making certain that institutions with federal charters have a regulatory framework that is receptive to responsible innovation along with the supervision that supports it.' – Comptroller of the Currency Thomas J. Curry

OCC Innovation Initiative

In August 2015, Comptroller of the Currency Thomas J. Curry announced an initiative to develop a comprehensive framework to improve the OCC's ability to identify and understand trends and innovations in the financial services industry, as well as the evolving needs of consumers of financial services.[1] This framework is intended to improve how the OCC evaluates innovative products, services, and processes that require regulatory approval and identifies potential risks associated with them. Even when approval of an innovation is not necessary, enhancing the agency's understanding will enable it to be a more effective resource to institutions, particularly community banks and thrifts, interested in innovation. The framework also will help clarify lines of communication between the agency and the industry regarding emerging technology and new products, services, and processes.

As part of that initiative, the OCC formed a team of policy experts, examiners, lawyers, and other agency staff members to gain a better understanding of emerging technology and new approaches in financial services and then use that information to design the OCC's framework for evaluating financial innovation. To obtain a broad perspective, the team met with a variety of groups to discuss the changes in the financial services industry and the opportunities and challenges for banks to participate fully in this evolving landscape. These discussions included bankers from community, midsize, and large banks; innovators in various fields; consumer groups; academics; other regulators; and OCC employees.

Some common themes emerged from these meetings as well as from other research the OCC team conducted. For example, many participants, including both banks and nonbanks, suggested that the "rules of the road" governing the development of innovative products and services are unclear. Banks, particularly smaller ones, also expressed uncertainty about the OCC's expectations regarding partnerships with nonbanks and third parties. Many nonbanks also indicated a desire to understand regulatory requirements and the supervisory environment as they seek to expand their relationships with banks.

Opportunities and Challenges for National Banks and Federal Savings Associations

The financial services industry in the United States is undergoing rapid technological change aimed at meeting evolving consumer and business expectations and needs. Mobile payment services and mobile wallets are changing the way consumers make retail payments. New distributed ledger technology has the potential to transform how transactions are processed and settled. New technology services offer the prospect of a banking relationship that exists only on a smartphone, tablet, or personal computer. Marketplace lending has the potential to change how loans are underwritten and funded. In addition, automated systems are competing with traditional financial advisors, and crowdfunding sites are raising equity capital for new and existing companies.

Many of these innovations are taking place outside the banking industry, often in unregulated or lightly regulated fintech companies. Fintech companies are growing rapidly in number, and they are attracting increasing investment. In 2015, the number of fintech companies in the United States and United Kingdom increased to more than 4,000,[2] and investment in fintech companies since 2010 has surpassed $24 billion worldwide.[3]

---

[1] See Remarks by Thomas J. Curry, Comptroller of the Currency, Before the Federal Home Loan Bank of Chicago. August 7, 2015 (http://www.occ.gov/news-issuances/speeches/2015/pub-speech-2015-111.pdf).

[2] "The Fintech Boom and Bank Innovation," *Forbes.* December 14, 2015 (http://www.forbes.com/sites/falgu-

nidesai/2015/12/14/the-fintech-revolution/#2715e4857a0b502b478836da).

[3] "Is the Fintech Sector Overheating?" *American Banker.* September 25, 2015 (http://www.americanbanker.com/news/bank-technology/is-the-fintech-sector-overheating-1076982-1.html).

Demographic changes also are influencing customer needs and expectations in dramatic ways. One of the most important changes in the United States involves the millennial generation, which includes nearly 80 million people. Millennials have the majority of their financial lives ahead of them, and they have demonstrated great receptivity to technical innovation in financial services.[4]

National banks and federal savings associations are seizing the opportunities and meeting these challenges in different ways. Some are working in their own laboratories and technology incubators to develop innovative ways to improve services and make their operations more efficient. Others are combining forces through consortiums and other collaborative arrangements to share the cost of developing and acquiring new technologies. Some banks are investing in fintech firms or new financial technology, and a growing number of banks are partnering with leading fintech companies and start-ups to develop the applications of tomorrow—applications that could eventually be revolutionary in their own ways.

In today's financial services environment, banks and fintech companies have different advantages when it comes to innovation. Banks have large and often loyal customer bases that contribute to diverse and stable funding that most fintech companies do not have. Banks also have capital that enables them to deal with losses and continue serving their customers throughout the fluctuations of an economic cycle. Banks often have extensive customer information, networks of physical locations, access to the payment system, and sophisticated underwriting, modeling, and risk management capabilities. Many banks benefit from name recognition, well-established marketing functions, and enterprise-wide compliance frameworks. They also have experience operating in complex regulatory environments.

Fintech companies and other nonbank innovators have their own advantages. Start-ups with few investors and one or two big ideas often can sometimes move faster than larger and more established organizations. They can focus their energy and resources on a single opportunity. Start-ups do not have legacy technology systems or large brick-and-mortar infrastructures that can be costly to maintain or change. Nonbank innovators also may have specialized technical knowledge, experience, and skills with respect to emerging technology and trends.

By employing their respective advantages, banks and nonbank innovators can benefit from collaboration. Through strategic and prudent collaboration, banks can gain access to new technologies, and nonbank innovators can gain access to funding sources and large customer bases.

The OCC Perspective on Responsible Innovation

The OCC's mission is to ensure that national banks and federal savings associations operate in a safe and sound manner, provide fair access to financial services, treat customers fairly, and comply with applicable laws and regulations. Supporting a financial system that innovates responsibly is central to the OCC's mission.

Definition of Responsible Innovation

While innovation has many meanings, the OCC defines responsible innovation to mean:

> *The use of new or improved financial products, services, and processes to meet the evolving needs of consumers, businesses, and communities in a manner that is consistent with sound risk management and is aligned with the bank's overall business strategy.*

This definition recognizes the importance of banks' receptivity to new ideas, products, and operational approaches to succeed in meeting the needs of consumers, businesses, and communities in the rapidly changing financial environment.

The definition also emphasizes effective risk management and corporate governance. As we learned in the financial crisis, not all innovation is positive. The financial crisis was fueled in part by innovations such as option adjustable rate mortgages, structured investment vehicles, and a variety of complex securities that ultimately resulted in significant losses for financial institutions and their customers and threatened the entire financial system. The OCC will support innovation that is consistent with safety and soundness, compliant with applicable laws and regulations, and protective of consumers' rights.

Guiding Principles for the OCC's Approach to Responsible Innovation

---

[4] "The 2014 ICBA American Millennials and Community Banking Study," Independent Community Bankers of America. October 2014 (https://www.icba.org/files/ ICBASites/PDFs/ ICBAMillennialsandCommunityBankingStudyWhitePaper.pdf).

The agency has formulated eight principles to guide the development of its framework for understanding and evaluating innovative products, services, and processes that OCC-regulated banks may offer or perform. These principles call for the OCC to:

1. Support responsible innovation.

2. Foster an internal culture receptive to responsible innovation.

3. Leverage agency experience and expertise.

4. Encourage responsible innovation that provides fair access to financial services and fair treatment of consumers.

5. Further safe and sound operations through effective risk management.

6. Encourage banks of all sizes to integrate responsible innovation into their strategic planning.

7. Promote ongoing dialogue through formal outreach.

8. Collaborate with other regulators.

Each principle is discussed below more fully.

1. Support responsible innovation.

To support responsible innovation, the OCC is considering various reforms to improve its process for understanding and evaluating innovative financial products, services, and processes. The goal is an improved process that will provide a clear path for banks and other stakeholders to seek the agency's views and guidance. To meet its goal, the OCC is exploring changes to coordinate decision making more effectively within the OCC and expedite review whenever possible, while ensuring a thoughtful assessment of associated risks.

Currently, banks and nonbanks use a variety of formal and informal entry points to communicate with the OCC. For example, a bank interested in an innovative process to speed payments may approach its examiners with a proposal, request a legal opinion from the OCC, file any required application with the appropriate licensing office, or contact one of the agency's experts on credit, compliance, payments, cybersecurity, or modeling. While providing flexibility, the current process can result in some inconsistencies and inefficiencies.

To address this concern, one possible approach is to create a centralized office on innovation. The office could serve as a forum to vet ideas before a bank or nonbank makes a formal request or launches an innovative product or service. Other responsibilities could include holding meetings with interested stakeholders and appropriate OCC officials and coordinating among OCC examiners and experts to identify supervisory, policy, legal or precedent-setting issues, or concerns early in the process. To maintain an ongoing understanding of financial industry innovation, the office also could hold regular meetings with fintech innovators. In addition, the office could develop educational materials on innovation for banks and OCC personnel.

Alternatively, the OCC could adopt a less formal process where an existing unit within the OCC assumes the responsibility as the agency's central point of contact on innovation. That unit could be responsible for ensuring appropriate OCC staff and experts are involved early when considering innovative proposals by banks and nonbanks.

To be effective, the improved process should clarify agency expectations. Banks and nonbanks suggested a need for more guidance, particularly with respect to third-party relationships, including partnerships between banks and nonbanks.

To clarify these expectations and promote better understanding of the regulatory regime, the OCC will evaluate existing guidance on new product development and third-party risk management and assess whether additional guidance is appropriate to address the needs of banks and their customers in the rapidly changing environment.

To expedite decision making, the OCC is evaluating whether it can streamline some of its licensing procedures, where appropriate, or develop new procedures where existing procedures may not work for certain innovative activities.

Another idea touted by banks and nonbanks is to allow banks to test or pilot new products and services on a small scale before committing significant bank resources to a full rollout. Such a program could entail board approval and appropriate limitations that would protect consumers and would not involve giving banks a safe harbor from consumer laws and regulations during the testing phase of a new product. By analogy, the OCC recently issued guidance permitting banks to offer loans that exceed supervisory loan-to-value limits in communities targeted for revitalization

¶1320

under certain circumstances. Although that guidance did not involve technological innovation, the OCC recognized that supporting long-term community revitalization could benefit from innovative lending programs.

2. Foster an internal culture receptive to responsible innovation.

A key component of a successful framework is an agency culture that is receptive to responsible innovation. When researching this project, the OCC gathered perspectives from OCC-supervised institutions and others in the financial services industry and conducted focus groups with agency employees. Many employees shared an interest in a culture that is more receptive to responsible innovation. The common perceptions about the agency that emerged from those discussions include 1) a low risk tolerance for innovative products and services; 2) a deliberate and extended vetting process that can discourage innovation inadvertently; 3) a need for increased awareness and education; and 4) a desire by employees for additional expert resources and easier access to those resources.

The OCC will evaluate its policies and processes, define roles and responsibilities with respect to evaluating innovation, identify and close knowledge and expertise gaps, and enhance communication within the agency and with outside stakeholders. The agency has taken several steps to foster a more receptive culture and to improve the awareness and knowledge of financial innovations. For example, the OCC has established a dedicated Payment Systems Policy Group that provides examination support, training, and guidance to examiners and acts as a resource to OCC-supervised institutions on innovative and traditional payment structures. Additionally, the OCC has formed an internal working group on marketplace lending to monitor developments in that sector.

The agency will develop or augment existing training to reinforce the agency's receptiveness to responsible innovation and develop additional expertise to evaluate the opportunities and risks related to specific types of innovation. The OCC is considering establishing dedicated internal Web pages describing resources and training opportunities on innovation for all employees.

3. Leverage agency experience and expertise.

The OCC will rely heavily on the breadth and depth of knowledge of existing staff in implementing its responsible innovation framework. The agency's examiners, policy and compliance experts, legal staff, information technology professionals, and economists have a deep understanding of the financial system and a growing understanding of the emerging technology that can bring innovative products, services, and processes to businesses and consumers. The agency will continue to develop expertise in this important area.

Examiners are often the first and primary points of contact for banks considering new products or services, and they play a critical role in supporting responsible innovation. The OCC assigns a designated examiner or team of examiners to every institution under its supervision depending on its size and complexity. Examiners develop a robust understanding of each bank's activities, business strategies and goals, and risk appetite. That knowledge guides the OCC's supervisory strategy for that bank. The examiner also understands the local economy and the operating conditions in specific markets. As banks progress into new products or services, examiners can be important sources of information.

Ongoing communication with OCC examining staff provides the opportunity for banks to discuss the most recent trends and information that may affect the institution. These discussions include the introduction of new products, services, third-party relationships, changes in risk management or audit activities, and other planned corporate activities. These activities and ongoing dialogue help ensure effective supervision and early identification of evolving opportunities and risks. They also help resolve supervisory concerns as early as possible.

Industry stakeholders also benefit from the agency's expertise in other areas. OCC compliance policy experts support agency examiners and assist the banks they supervise on issues related to a variety of consumer protection and banking laws, such as the Bank Secrecy Act (BSA). Community reinvestment experts advise supervised institutions on community development issues. The OCC's Payments Systems Policy Group provides expertise in payments systems including traditional bank payments systems and distributed ledger technologies. Legal staff interprets banking laws and rules. Technology professionals help assess bank technology systems and cyber risks facing the industry. Economists provide expertise on modeling and quantitative analysis that assists in evaluating the effects of emerging technology and new programs and services and their implications for banking policy. All these experts play important roles in helping banks and nonbanks interested in innovation navigate the complex regulatory environment.

The OCC also will consider designating lead experts on responsible innovation who could support bank supervision and provide advice based on a broad view of innovation trends and developments across the federal banking system. The agency has an effective lead expert program in retail and commercial credit, compliance, bank information technology, asset management, and operational risk to support examiners and supervised banks.

In addition, the OCC will regularly evaluate whether it has the appropriate resources to supervise innovation within the federal banking system.

4. Encourage responsible innovation that provides fair access to financial services and fair treatment of consumers.

Responsible innovation among banks should help them fulfill their public purpose by promoting fair access to financial services and fair treatment of consumers. Current innovations in the financial industry hold great promise for increasing financial inclusion of underserved consumers, who represent more than 68 million people and spend more than $78 billion annually.[5] Data suggest underserved communities are more likely to use mobile banking technology than fully banked communities.[6] Social media use, in particular, appears disproportionately popular among demographic groups likely to be underserved, including young adults, low- and moderate-income consumers, and minorities compared with the population as a whole.[7]

Brick-and-mortar branches are a stabilizing force in low-income neighborhoods, and innovative technology should not be seen as a substitute for a physical presence in those communities. However, the OCC believes there is great potential for responsible innovation to broaden access to financial services by delivering more affordable products and services on suitable terms to unbanked, underbanked, and low- to moderate-income consumers. Examples of products cited by some that could help address unmet financial services needs of the unbanked and underbanked include

- online and mobile banking, saving, budgeting, and financial management tools.
- small dollar, unsecured consumer loans.
- small business loans.
- credit consolidation or refinancing of consumer or student loans.
- use of behavioral models to improve automated underwriting models that could expand the pool of eligible consumers.
- improved payment services.

Innovations in lending are not limited to digital services and could include new ways to extend credit or provide other types of financial services. Social responsibility funds, for example, can expand opportunities in affordable housing and community or economic development.

Innovation also can encourage fair access by spurring small business and community investment that improves services and provides community redevelopment resources. Small business investment funds can attract capital for start-ups and businesses located in low- and moderate-income communities. Mortgage- or asset-backed securities backed by Community Reinvestment Act-qualified investments can provide liquidity for loans that benefit low- and moderate-income individuals or small businesses. Tax credit programs can promote investment in renewable energy, historic preservation, economic development, and affordable housing.

To encourage responsible innovations that provide fair access to financial services and fair treatment, the OCC plans to share success stories describing how national banks and federal savings associations have innovated to increase access to unbanked and underbanked populations; to increase the speed, efficiency, effectiveness, and transparency of financial transactions; and to lend and invest in ways designed to address the credit needs of low- and moderate-income individuals and communities.

The OCC may also issue guidance on its expectations related to products and services designed to address the needs of low- to moderate-income individuals and communities and may

---

[5] "Financial Technology Trends in the Underbanked Market," Center for Financial Services Innovation. May 2013.

[6] "Assessing the Economic Inclusion Potential of Mobile Financial Services," Federal Deposit Insurance Corporation. June 30, 2014 (https://www.fdic.gov/consumers/community/mobile/Mobile-Financial-Services.pdf).

[7] "Financial Technology Trends in the Underbanked Market," Center for Financial Services Innovation. May 2013.

¶1320

encourage innovative approaches to financial inclusion by promoting awareness of other activities that could qualify for Community Reinvestment Act consideration.

5. Further safe and sound operations through effective risk management.

Effective risk management and good corporate governance are fundamental for banks to develop new products, services, and processes successfully. The OCC's framework must consider how national banks and federal savings associations identify and address risks resulting from emerging technology.

The OCC's research found that banks, nonbanks, and bank customers believe that cyber risk is one of the most significant risks facing the financial industry as it implements new technologies. In addition, risk to customer data through data aggregation and third-party use is increasing. Innovating through in-house development, third-party collaboration, or business combinations also presents different risks that require effective corporate governance, due diligence, risk identification and measurement, and internal controls.

Banks of all sizes should ensure that effective corporate governance and risk management meet supervisory expectations when considering new products, services, and processes. This includes expectations described in OCC guidance related to strategic planning, evaluating new products and services,[8] using models,[9] operational risk, cybersecurity,[10] and managing third-party relationships.[11]

The OCC also will continue to improve its ability to understand and monitor emerging risks in the financial industry. Over the past several years, the OCC has improved its internal governance and risk identification capabilities through enhancements to the OCC's National Risk Committee and several committees focused on particular risks such as credit, operational, and compliance. The National Risk Committee structure is designed to assess current and emerging risks and to communicate that information to examiners and banks. The National Risk Committee also publishes the OCC's *Semiannual Risk Perspective*[12] on current and emerging risks in the federal banking system. The OCC is considering ways to leverage the work of the National Risk Committee in its responsible innovation framework.

6. Encourage banks of all sizes to integrate responsible innovation into their strategic planning.

The agency's framework for evaluating new and innovative financial products and services must consider how banks integrate innovation in their strategic planning processes. Sound strategic decisions are essential for any bank to achieve its business goals and successfully meet the needs of the consumers, businesses, and communities it serves.

A bank's decision to offer innovative products and services should be consistent with the bank's long-term business plan rather than following the latest fad or industry trend. Pursuit of emerging technology and other innovation should align with customer needs and the bank's strategic plan as well as its risk management capabilities. A bank collaborating with a nonbank to offer innovative products and services should also consider whether such a partnership helps the bank achieve its strategic objectives.

When discussing innovation, banks are reminded that traditional strategic planning criteria such as those listed below still apply:

- Consistency with the bank's corporate governance, business plan, and risk appetite.
- Realistic financial projections.
- Adequate staff, both in number and expertise.
- Technology support.

---

[8] See OCC Bulletin 2004-20, "Risk Management of New, Expanded, or Modified Bank Products and Services." May 10, 2004 (http://www.occ.gov/news-issuances/bulletins/2004/bulletin-2004-20.html).

[9] See OCC Bulletin 2011-12, "Supervisory Guidance on Model Risk Management." April 4, 2011 (http://www.occ.gov/news-issuances/bulletins/2011/bulletin-2011-12.html).

[10] See OCC Bulletin 2015-31, "FFIEC Cybersecurity Assessment Tool." June 30, 2015 (http://www.occ.gov/news-issuances/bulletins/2015/bulletin-2015-31.html).

[11] See OCC Bulletin 2013-29, "Third-Party Relationships." October 30, 2013 (http://www.occ.gov/news-issuances/bulletins/2013/bulletin-2013-29.html).

[12] See http://www.occ.gov/publications/publications-by-type/other-publications-reports/index-semiannual-risk-perspective.html.

- Consideration of all applicable risks, including reputation and compliance, and appropriate risk management systems and practices.
- Exit strategies.

7. Promote ongoing dialogue through formal outreach.

Outreach is a key component of encouraging and supporting responsible innovation, and the OCC intends to incorporate formal outreach into its framework. An ongoing dialogue with all stakeholders, including banks, nonbank innovators, and consumer groups, will enable the agency to

- stay abreast of current trends and developments, including new products, services, process improvements, and partnerships.
- understand the underlying reasons and customer needs that drive such developments.
- promote awareness and understanding of its expectations related to responsible innovation.
- identify opportunities to improve its ability to respond more quickly, efficiently, and effectively to inquiries regarding new products and services, including licensing requests.
- serve as a more effective resource to institutions interested in innovation.
- solicit feedback on how its actions encourage or impede responsible innovation.

As part of its ongoing outreach activities, the OCC plans to bring together banks, nonbanks, and other stakeholders through a forum and a variety of workshops and meetings to discuss responsible innovation in the financial industry. The agency also intends to host "innovator fairs" to bring together banks and nonbank innovators with OCC experts to discuss regulatory requirements and supervisory expectations in the financial services industry. In addition, the OCC will provide resources, information, and guidance through its Web sites, including OCC.gov and BankNet.gov, which may include links to future papers and other resources on responsible innovation for those who want to engage with the OCC.

8. Collaborate with other regulators.

Supervision of the financial services industry involves regulatory authorities at the state, federal, and international levels. Exchanging ideas and discussing innovation with other regulators are important to promote a common understanding and consistent application of laws, regulations, and guidance. Such collaborative supervision can support responsible innovation in the financial services industry.

The OCC will work with agencies like the Consumer Financial Protection Bureau (CFPB) on innovations promoted by or affecting banks subject to OCC and CFPB supervision. Because the missions of the CFPB, the OCC, and other bank regulatory agencies intersect and agencies share the goal of minimizing unnecessary regulatory burden, the agencies implemented a number of memorandums of understanding that describe how to interact and work with one another to supervise industry participants. Such coordination gives banks greater confidence that regulators who share responsibilities will consider innovative ideas consistently.

The banking agencies already collaborate successfully on a number of issues and could create additional workgroups to further that coordination and increase communication about this important topic. Collaboration on responsible innovation should include the following actions:

- Establish regular channels of communication.
- Identify information to share on an ongoing basis or upon request.
- Provide other agencies with such advance notice as is reasonably possible regarding upcoming innovation activities that may be of common interest.
- Use best efforts to avoid inconsistent communications with supervised entities.

Conclusion and Request for Comments

As the OCC continues to develop its framework to support responsible innovation in the federal banking system, it seeks feedback on all aspects of this paper. The OCC also solicits responses to the questions below. The OCC requests that respondents provide written comments on these questions and other topics presented in this paper by May 31, 2016. Submissions should be e-mailed to innovation@occ.treas.gov.

1. What challenges do community banks face with regard to emerging technology and financial innovation?

2. How can the OCC facilitate responsible innovation by institutions of all sizes?

¶1320

3. How can the OCC enhance its process for monitoring and assessing innovation within the federal banking system?

4. How would establishing a centralized office of innovation within the OCC facilitate more open, timely, and ongoing dialogue regarding opportunities for responsible innovation?

5. How could the OCC provide guidance to nonbank innovators regarding its expectations for banks' interactions and partnerships with such companies?

6. What additional tools and resources would help community bankers incorporate innovation into their strategic planning processes?

7. What additional guidance could support responsible innovation? How could the OCC revise existing guidance to promote responsible innovation?

8. What forms of outreach and information sharing venues are the most effective?

9. What should the OCC consider with respect to innovation?

¶ 1330 Recommendations and Decisions for Implementing a Responsible Innovation Framework

Office of the Comptroller of the Currency

Washington, D.C.

October 2016

Executive Summary

As the prudential regulator of the federal banking system, the Office of the Comptroller of the Currency (OCC) supports the ability of national banks and federal savings associations (collectively, banks) to fulfill their role of providing financial services to consumers, businesses, and their communities through responsible innovation that is safe and sound, consistent with applicable law, and protective of consumer rights.

Building on the OCC's innovation initiatives over the last year, the agency's Innovation Framework Development Team developed a comprehensive set of recommendations that the Comptroller of the Currency and Executive Committee accepted in early October 2016. The recommendations cover the following areas:

Key Takeaways From the OCC's Decisions

— *Provide value to stakeholders*

— *Support responsible innovation*

— *Align to guiding principles*

— *Leverage existing practices and expertise*

— *Be responsive to feedback*

— *Preserve existing decision-making functions*

— *Integrate activities across the agency*

- **Create an Office of Innovation to Implement the Framework**
- **Establish an Outreach and Technical Assistance Program**
- **Conduct Awareness and Training Activities**
- **Encourage Coordination and Facilitation**
- **Establish an Innovation Research Function**
- **Promote Interagency Collaboration**

This paper contains a summary of the financial services landscape and the OCC's innovation initiatives, followed by a discussion of the approved recommendations for the OCC's Framework for Responsible Innovation, including the Office of Innovation and other key elements.

Background

Financial Services Landscape

Technological advances, together with evolving consumer preferences, are reshaping the financial services industry at an accelerated pace. Over the last several years, a large and growing number of nonbank financial technology companies (fintechs) have emerged to provide financial products and services through alternative platforms and delivery channels. Venture capital investment in these companies has increased dramatically. Today, fintechs engage in the traditional banking functions of consumer lending, payments, wealth management, and settlements. Fintechs also are leveraging new technologies and processes, such as cloud computing, application programming interfaces, distributed ledgers, artificial intelligence, and big data analytics.

Consumer preferences for financial products and services are also changing rapidly. Emerging innovations give consumers increased access and product options, control over choices, and the ability to tailor products to meet their individual needs. In addition, nonbanks have raised consumer expectations by expediting decisions and offering real-time, cross-channel capabilities and a more seamless experience. As a result, consumers are more willing to use multiple channels and providers to meet their needs. New entrants into the market must not engage in unfair and deceptive practices or discriminatory activities.

These changes challenge traditional banking business models. Although banks have a long history of adapting to new technology and introducing innovative products and services, it is

¶1330

imperative for them to understand the impact of the evolving landscape on their business strategies and leverage their unique advantages so they can continue to meet the needs of their customers, businesses, and communities.

OCC-supervised institutions are currently in various stages of developing and implementing innovation strategies. For example, some banks have proactively launched their own innovation labs. Many larger banks have also provided venture capital funding and completed acquisitions of fintech firms. Other institutions are taking more of a watch and follow approach. Banks of all sizes are increasingly partnering with fintechs, as both banks and fintechs recognize the benefits of collaboration. Some community banks, however, have not developed an innovation strategy.

OCC Innovation Initiatives

In 2015, the OCC launched an initiative focused on innovation to better understand the evolving financial services landscape and determine what actions the OCC might take in response. OCC working group members conducted extensive research of the financial innovators, the evolving needs of consumers and small businesses, and the innovation-related activities of OCC-supervised banks. Team members met with community, midsize, and large banks; fintechs; consultants; academics; community and consumer groups; and other regulators. In addition, they conducted a series of focus groups to gain the perspective of OCC staff and established an internal staff advisory group to serve as an ongoing sounding board.

The group's research informed agency executives' decision to develop a framework to support responsible innovation. The OCC summarized the themes that emerged from the research in a white paper published in March 2016.[1] The white paper defined responsible innovation and detailed eight principles to guide the OCC's development of its framework.

- **Responsible Innovation:** The use of new or improved financial products, services, and processes to meet the evolving needs of consumers, businesses, and communities in a manner consistent with sound risk management and aligned with the bank's overall business strategy.

- **Guiding Principles:**

  — Support responsible innovation;

  — Foster an internal culture receptive to responsible innovation;

  — Leverage agency experience and expertise;

  — Encourage responsible innovation that provides fair access to financial services and fair treatment of consumers;

  — Further safe and sound operations through effective risk management;

  — Encourage banks of all sizes to integrate responsible innovation into their strategic planning;

  — Promote ongoing dialogue through formal outreach; and

  — Collaborate with other regulators.

The white paper also requested comment on nine questions and other topics presented in the paper. The OCC received 63 comments from a broad cross section of stakeholders. The comments informed the recommendations included in this report.

Following the publication of the white paper, the OCC formed a dedicated team to develop recommendations for implementing a framework for responsible innovation. The Innovation Framework Development Team was launched in June 2016 and includes representatives from Midsize and Community Bank Supervision, Large Bank Supervision, the Office of the Chief National Bank Examiner, the Chief Counsel's Office, and Compliance and Community Affairs. In developing the project plan, the team combined the eight guiding principles into five objectives covering outreach, awareness and education, timely and transparent processes, interagency communication, and organizational structure.

The scope of work consisted of extensive information gathering and analysis, including interviews with key internal stakeholders, a detailed analysis of the comments received on the white paper, and review of the research completed previously. The team also considered feedback from ongoing meetings with external stakeholders and the OCC Forum on Responsible Innova-

---

[1] See *Supporting Responsible Innovation in the Federal Banking System: An OCC Perspective.* March 2016 (https:/ /occ.gov/topics/bank-operations/innovation/index-innovation.html).

tion held in June 2016.[2] In addition, the team sought employee feedback on preferred delivery channels for OCC news, job-related information, and training, as well as familiarity with the fintech products and services that are currently available to consumers. The team then incorporated all of the information gathered into an assessment of relevant existing programs and processes, ultimately leading to the development of the recommendations that follow.

Create an Office of Innovation to Implement the Framework

The team recommends establishing a stand-alone Office of Innovation (office). The office would provide appropriate internal and external visibility and have the greatest likelihood of fulfilling the following core functions:

- Serve as a central point of contact and facilitate responses to inquiries and requests;
- Conduct outreach and provide technical assistance;
- Enhance awareness, culture and education;
- Monitor the evolving financial services landscape; and
- Collaborate with domestic and international regulators.

The team used the following principles to evaluate each option:

- Ensure efficient and effective execution of core functions;
- Leverage OCC expertise;
- Preserve existing decision-making functions;
- Develop resources on innovation for internal and external stakeholders; and
- Provide credible challenges to processes and decision making.

The team considered the comments received in response to the white paper and feedback from internal stakeholders. External commenters overall supported the creation of a stand-alone office. Stakeholders favored an office that facilitates discussion, promotes consistency and efficiency, develops OCC expertise, and enables the OCC to provide timely guidance to examiners and the industry. However, commenters opposed an office that resulted in another regulatory hurdle or a silo. Commenters also emphasized a need to preserve interactions with local supervisory staff. OCC management and employees supported a centralized clearinghouse for innovation activities, but did not support an additional or separate decision maker.

Based on an evaluation of the principles described above and feedback received, the team determined that a stand-alone office reporting directly to the Comptroller's Office would be the most effective option for implementing the framework. The office would be in a position to manage the core functions, promote consistent and timely decisions, and provide insight independent of other business units within the OCC, clear ownership, and accountability.

The office would rely on existing expertise, systems, and processes to achieve its mission, whenever possible.

DECISION: Approved.

Staffing and roles

The team recommends that the office consist of a Chief Innovation Officer (CINO), Innovation Officers, an Innovation Technician, and potentially a small number of Innovation Fellows. The CINO would be responsible for carrying out the core functions of the office and providing updates and reports to the Executive Committee and applicable business units. The team recommends that the CINO be a member of the National Risk Committee (NRC) and that Innovation Officers be members of applicable NRC subcommittees to provide perspective based on the work of the office.

Similar to the Office of the Chief Accountant fellowship program, Innovation Fellows would enable the office to leverage the experience and knowledge of academics, consumer and community advocates, and the private sector and share and transfer OCC knowledge on regulation and supervision to the fellows. The team recommends using fellows to study and research innovation trends and analyze the effects of emerging innovations on banks, consumers of financial services, and the federal banking system. Fellows could also advise OCC management and staff on innovation practices and developments. Fellows should report to the CINO or through an

---

[2] See https://occ.gov/topics/bank-operations/innova-tion/innovation-forum-videos.html.

¶1330

Innovation Officer. The OCC should also consider using secondments by other regulators, both foreign and domestic, to the office, as well as sending OCC employees to other regulators for a period to learn more about how other regulators approach innovation.

DECISION: Approved.

Locations

The team proposes that the OCC place Innovation Officers in various geographic locations. The CINO and a small staff should be located in the OCC Headquarters to ensure that the office can successfully perform its core functions, particularly the need to collaborate with other OCC business lines; serve as a resource, both internally and externally; and facilitate the proposed decision-making and pilot processes.

The team recommends that Innovation Officers initially be located in San Francisco and New York City, as well as Headquarters. A number of commenters suggested that the OCC consider positioning staff in financial technology hubs, such as Silicon Valley and New York. While many cities are experiencing significant growth in financial technology startups, New York and San Francisco stand out, as they are already home to OCC offices. Additionally, the local presence in technology hubs will facilitate "office hours"[3] and face-to-face interactions among OCC staff, banks, and nonbanks, allowing the office to stay attuned to local trends, recruit fellows and skilled staff, and participate in local outreach events.

The OCC should also consider conducting outreach events and "office hours" in other technology hubs (e.g., Austin, Texas; Boulder, Colorado; Raleigh-Durham, North Carolina; and Seattle, Washington), but the team does not recommend locating permanent staff in these locations at this time.

DECISION: Approved.

Create a Responsible Innovation Committee to Advise the Office

The team recommends establishing a committee of OCC staff from across the agency to advise the office and promote collaboration across agency business units. The Responsible Innovation Committee would include Deputy Comptrollers or Directors from OCC business units. It would provide cross-functional advice and facilitate two-way communication. The creation of the committee also would help build support for the framework and related activities throughout the agency and enable the office to disseminate information regarding innovation throughout the agency. The committee would assist the CINO in determining which stakeholders should be consulted on particular matters and ensure that responses from business lines, when required, are timely and complete.

DECISION: Approved.

Framework for Responsible Innovation

In addition to recommending the establishment of a stand-alone Office of Innovation, the team recommends actions in the following five areas: Outreach and Technical Assistance; Awareness and Training; Coordination and Facilitation; Research; and Interagency Collaboration. Recommendations in these areas comprise the core components of the agency's Framework for Responsible Innovation.

Establish an Outreach and Technical Assistance Program

The team recommends establishing a robust program of outreach and technical assistance to maintain agency awareness of innovation trends and activities and support banks and fintechs in their pursuit of responsible innovation affecting the federal banking system.

Ongoing dialogue with all stakeholders, including banks, nonbanks, and community and consumer groups, enables the OCC to stay abreast of current trends and developments, better understand the evolving needs of consumers of financial products and services, and solicit stakeholder feedback. Outreach also enables the agency to serve as a more effective resource and promote awareness and understanding of OCC expectations.

---

[3] "Office hours" are listening sessions with a single party (e.g., fintech, bank, or community group) held at an OCC office or other location, advertised in advance, and booked by appointment. Office hours are used by other regulators including the Consumer Financial Protection Bureau.

Commenters widely supported the development of an outreach program focused on innovation. External and internal feedback indicated that the OCC's willingness to engage in a dialogue was a key step to changing the perception that the agency is not always receptive to innovation.

The team acknowledges that the OCC's lines of business already conduct extensive outreach to banks and community and consumer groups. Staff throughout the agency organize meetings, present at conferences, organize and participate in banker roundtables and workshops, and participate in interagency, industry, and consumer and community group events. However, currently there is no formal channel to reach nonbank companies providing financial services, seeking to partner with banks, or seeking to become banks.

Research also indicated that many banks, particularly smaller institutions, seek to understand how the OCC views the application of existing rules and guidance regarding innovation. For example, many banks are partnering with fintechs to provide cost-effective solutions to meet customer needs. As a result, banks seek assistance to understand how OCC expectations for third-party risk management apply to such relationships. Nonbank fintechs also seek ways to learn directly from the regulators how to operate effectively in a highly regulated environment.

Based on its review, the team recommends the following to build an effective outreach and technical assistance program for responsible innovation:

Develop and implement a formal innovation outreach strategy

The team recommends that the OCC develop a formal outreach strategy related to innovation. The office, working with Public Affairs, should develop a strategy that includes all stakeholders and uses a wide variety of channels. A wide-reaching outreach program would enable the OCC to maintain a broad understanding of industry trends as well as the needs of consumers of financial services from all stakeholder perspectives. While the innovation outreach strategy can leverage existing agency avenues for outreach with banks and community and consumer groups, a formal outreach program for nonbanks would need to be developed.

The team recommends that the office serve as the focal point for fintech outreach. The outreach strategy should use a wide variety of channels, including

- holding "office hours";

- organizing innovation workshops and roundtables on specific topics;

- leveraging existing OCC-sponsored outreach events, such as banker roundtables and consumer and community events, when appropriate;

- sponsoring a periodic Responsible Innovation Forum; and

- participating, when appropriate, in non-OCC-sponsored events.

Additionally, the team recommends that the OCC develop targeted communication tools, including a dedicated external-facing web page. The web page should be designed as a "one-stop shop" and contain resource materials and technical information. In addition, the web page should provide links to relevant OCC speeches, papers, and other materials. Finally, the web page could be used to solicit feedback on issues related to innovation, as needed.

Meeting the evolving communication expectations of industry stakeholders, consumer and community advocates, and the public necessitates increased flexibility and agility by the OCC in adopting new communication tools. The team recommends that the OCC consider, in the longer term, adopting mobile apps and other communication methods to better reach targeted audiences.

DECISION: Approved.

Provide technical assistance to banks and nonbanks

Banks regularly seek information and assistance on how to manage third-party relationships, and some smaller banks with limited resources seek information on how to develop and implement an effective innovation strategy.

Fintechs are increasingly reaching out to regulators to understand regulatory expectations, and how to operate in a heavily regulated environment. Many fintechs recognize that to develop successful partnerships with banks, they must thoroughly understand applicable regulatory expectations. Well-informed fintechs also benefit the banks with which they partner. In addition, some fintechs desire these types of resources as they evaluate whether to become banks or pursue partnerships with banks.

¶1330

The team recommends that the OCC provide technical assistance to banks and fintechs, when appropriate, as part of the agency's innovation outreach strategy. Technical assistance would include

- creating resource material for banks and nonbanks on regulatory principles, processes, and expectations;
- designing "rules of the road" material for nonbanks; and
- sharing success stories and lessons learned.

Resources for community institutions should include suggestions on how to develop an innovation strategy and manage third-party risk. The team recommends that the agency leverage its collaboration paper[4] and provide examples of how community banks can collaborate on third-party due diligence and ongoing monitoring of fintech partners. In addition, "office hours" and other meetings could be used to provide banks and fintechs with meaningful information about how to effectively and responsibly engage in innovation.

DECISION: Approved.

Conduct Awareness and Training Activities

The team recommends the following actions to build an effective awareness and training program to ensure adequate evaluation and supervision of new products, services, and processes by a well-informed staff.

Improve staff awareness of industry innovations and developing trends

The team identified a need for greater awareness and expertise regarding industry innovations among OCC staff. While the agency has some information on certain industry developments, more is needed. Further, when information and expertise are available, they are not always easily located and accessible to staff who need them most. To improve awareness by OCC staff, the team recommends that the agency provide additional resources that are available to all employees, expand information delivery channels, establish an Innovation Networking Group, and create other means to promote awareness of industry innovations among staff.

The team recommends that the OCC develop additional materials that describe the fundamentals of emerging products, services, processes, and technology. The OCC should create and maintain an internal web page that provides OCC staff a "one-stop shop" to access information on industry trends and innovative products, services, and processes. Examples of the types of materials that could be available on the web page include

- resources on specific types of innovations and industry trends;
- training materials and presentations; and
- applicable guidance or policy statements.

As the agency continues to enhance its communication, it should incorporate new and innovative information delivery channels when appropriate. These channels could improve the agency's ability to provide "just in time" training and appeal to a diverse workforce.

To promote awareness and information sharing within the OCC, the team also recommends the creation of an Innovation Networking Group. Similar to lead expert networking groups already in place, the group could expand the knowledge base and perspective of interested employees. The group could help

- identify employees with interest or expertise in specific industry innovations;
- promote consistent, high-quality supervision;
- establish two-way communication between staff and the office;
- discuss trends in innovation in the federal banking system;
- consider emerging risks and opportunities; and
- share success stories and lessons learned.

The team recommends that the group be cross-functional, with representation from the field and Headquarters, and that it include examiners and non-examiners. In addition to the group,

---

[4] See, *An Opportunity for Community Banks Working Together Collaboratively.* January 2015 (https://occ.gov/publications/publications-by-type/other-publications-re-ports/pub-other-community-banks-working-collaborately.pdf).

knowledge sharing among employees and managers on innovation-related topics should be included routinely in business unit calls and meetings. The office should participate in these meetings and share information that it learns through its research and outreach so that staff understands the benefits and risks of innovation.

DECISION: Approved.

Create additional training content necessary to evaluate and understand industry innovations

The financial services industry increasingly relies on technology to deliver products and services to customers in an efficient and timely manner. In addition, payments systems are undergoing rapid change. To supervise the federal banking system effectively, OCC staff members should have a foundational understanding of technology and payments systems.

The team recommends that the OCC develop a process to review and update training content continuously to address rapidly changing industry trends and new products and services.

DECISION: Approved.

Broaden and increase OCC expertise in areas related to innovation

The rapid technological and engineering developments in the financial industry also raise important questions about whether the OCC has sufficient expertise to understand and supervise some emerging developments. Skill sets such as technology and mathematics are becoming more important in bank supervision as the financial industry offers more technology-driven products and services.

The team recommends that the OCC expand recruiting to reach individuals with a broader variety of skills than traditionally used by the agency. Examples of expanded skills include engineering, advanced information technology, systems development, cybersecurity, statistics, and mathematical modeling. In addition, the OCC should recruit specialists and use the office fellowship program to supplement expertise in specific areas. The OCC should enhance its specialty skills program through additional functions related to innovation and technologies (e.g., cloud-based computing, distributed ledger technology, and model risk management) and expand the current list of OCC-sponsored certifications to encourage staff to build expertise related to innovation.[5] Finally, the team recommends the agency use short-term rotational assignments, on-the-job training, and additional training to increase staff knowledge.

DECISION: Approved.

Encourage Coordination and Facilitation

Given that inquiries and requests related to innovation may be new and potentially novel, it is important that the OCC have well-coordinated, consistent, and timely responses wherever possible. In addition, inquiries and requests related to new products, services, and processes can be complex and involve the expertise of multiple OCC business lines.

Further, as the industry evolves, external stakeholders look for earlier and potentially different engagement from regulators. For example, some in the industry and in the regulatory community are seeking the creation of regulatory sandboxes or pilot programs to enable regulators to be involved in testing new products and technologies. Determining OCC engagement in such pilots requires significant coordination and facilitation.

The team recommends the following actions regarding coordination and facilitation.

Improve the timeliness and transparency of OCC decision-making

Lack of transparency and timeliness in decision-making related to innovative products, services, and processes was a consistent theme in agency research, comment letters, and internal stakeholder interviews.

External commenters stated that regulatory uncertainty, lack of transparency, and inconsistency deter innovation. The feedback further indicated that the absence of a streamlined review process for innovation, with a fixed response time, acts as a disincentive for institutions to expend

---

[5] Examples of such certifications include Accredited ACH Professional, Certified Third-Party Risk Professional, and Certification in Finance and Technology.

requisite time and resources. Employees also identified opportunities to improve OCC decision-making processes.

To improve decision-making related to innovation, the team recommends

- establishing specific response and disposition expectations for innovation inquiries and requests, including communication standards for written and verbal inquiries and requests for technical assistance;

- using a standard workflow to manage inquiries and requests for new products, processes, and services, including process steps with specific time frames and responsible parties; and

- implementing an inquiry and request tracking process.

The team developed a proposed workflow that incorporates the above recommendations. The team recommends that the office be responsible for managing the proposed workflow, coordinating the involvement of appropriate business units, and monitoring the timeline. While the office would be responsible for managing the process, it would not have a decision-making role. Decisions would continue to reside with the responsible business unit.

Establishing clear response expectations, time frames, and workflows would provide more consistent, transparent, and timely processes and facilitate disposition of inquiries and proposals. In addition, implementing the team's recommendations would clearly define responsibilities and establish accountability for responses and decisions related to innovative products, services, and processes. Improving the transparency and timeliness of OCC decision-making related to innovation would also align with industry expectations.

DECISION: Approved.

Develop and implement an optional program for OCC participation in bank-run pilots

Banks have historically tested new products and services before implementation, largely without the involvement of regulators. However, given the rapid pace of technological change, there is a growing demand for regulators to create a "safe place" for experimentation. The OCC received numerous external comments regarding development of a pilot program—also referred to as a "sandbox," "safe space," or "incubator."

Commenters were overwhelmingly in favor of a process to test innovative products, services, and processes. They noted that a pilot program would facilitate adoption of new solutions and enhancement of risk management by permitting testing and discovery before full-scale commitment and rollout. Some commenters expressed concerns about the potential for consumer harm and suggested that a pilot framework balance flexibility with consumer protection.

OCC stakeholders expressed general support for a pilot program but emphasized that participation in a pilot program must be voluntary and would not provide a safe harbor from consumer protection requirements.

The team recommends that the OCC develop and implement an optional program for agency participation in bank-run pilots that meet at least one of the following objectives:

- Fosters responsible innovation by OCC-supervised banks;

- Furthers the OCC's understanding of innovative products, services, processes, or technologies; or

- Facilitates OCC policy objectives.

Eligible participants for the program would include OCC-supervised banks and significant service providers, fintechs in partnership with an OCC-supervised bank or significant service provider, and other regulators as applicable.

DECISION: Approved with additional development needed.

Conduct Research

Given the rapid and dramatic advances in fintech, it is important that the OCC improve its ability to identify and understand trends and innovations in the financial services industry. This includes not only understanding the new products and services offered and processes implemented by banks, but also the evolving needs of consumers of financial products and services and demographics driving the changes in the financial industry. The pace, magnitude, and volume of change means that regulators need to learn and understand the changes as they occur, in a manner that allows them to anticipate the impact to the federal banking system.

In addition, staying attuned to changes in the industry enables the OCC to adjust and clarify expectations in a timely manner. Finally, staying abreast of technological developments and their effects on consumers may also improve the OCC's capabilities for supervising the federal banking system and managing its internal operations. The team recommends the following to build an effective research function.

Conduct industry innovation research

Several commenters on the white paper encouraged the agency to develop real-time research and monitoring capabilities. These capabilities could benefit the OCC by improving risk identification and understanding of industry innovations and benefit banks and fintechs that seek agency views on issues and concerns as they consider engaging in certain innovations. OCC staff also expressed a need for ongoing research on emerging innovations to enable the agency to stay ahead of the curve on industry developments.

The team recommends that the OCC develop a research function within the office to

- collect information on specific innovations and industry technology trends;
- analyze how innovation affects individual banks, bank segments, and the federal banking system as a whole; and
- obtain information on customer needs, demographics, and financial inclusion.

The office would provide research to applicable business lines for use in risk identification, policy development, and supervision. A more robust research capability would enable the OCC to develop more timely background material on emerging issues to promote awareness and knowledge throughout the agency.

Use research and dialogue with industry, consumer, and community groups to inform policy and guidance

In its March paper on responsible innovation, the OCC specifically asked how the agency could revise or clarify existing guidance to promote responsible innovation and whether additional guidance was needed. In response, commenters indicated a desire for principles-based guidance that would not stifle innovation. In addition, commenters submitted more specific recommendations to update, modernize, or clarify a range of guidance documents. The most common areas related to third-party risk management, partnerships, collaboration, and the Community Reinvestment Act. The team recommends that the applicable business units prioritize and initiate updates and clarifications to existing guidance as appropriate. On an ongoing basis, the OCC should continue to use the research and outreach conducted by the office and others to identify future gaps so that OCC guidance remains current and responsive to evolution in the industry.

DECISION: Approved.

Promote Interagency Collaboration

Exchanging ideas and discussing innovation with other regulators promotes common understanding and consistency. Coordination with other agencies can be critical, for example, where agencies have overlapping jurisdiction. Comments on the white paper supported collaboration among domestic and international regulators.

The team recommends the following:

Leverage existing interagency channels

The OCC already has well-developed channels for collaborating on a variety of topics at all levels of the agency. The OCC routinely collaborates with the other federal banking agencies as well as many other agencies. For example, the OCC collaborates with the Consumer Financial Protection Bureau on consumer-related matters, and the OCC is an active member of many of the Department of the Treasury's working groups and committees, including one on marketplace lending. Internationally, the agency participates in committees and task forces with many international regulators. The OCC's Director of Bank Information Technology, for instance, co-chairs the Basel Committee's Task Force on Financial Technology (TFFT).[6] Collaboration with other international regulators also occurs through policy groups, supervisory colleges, formal bilateral meetings, examinations, and secondments.

---

[6] The TFFT's mandate is to foster financial stability through the assessment of risks and supervisory challenges associated with innovation and technological changes affecting banking.

The team recommends that the OCC leverage these channels to discuss innovation in the industry. The focus of collaboration should be to share information to increase knowledge, develop consistent approaches, where appropriate, and provide a clear message to the industry. The OCC should also continue to leverage relationships it has with international regulators, such as the United Kingdom's Prudential Regulatory Authority and Financial Conduct Authority, and continue to take a leadership role, as appropriate, in international working groups. The office could also liaise with counterparts of other agencies and international regulators.

DECISION: Approved.

Develop an OCC-led information-sharing group

As noted in external and internal feedback, there is a desire for the OCC to assume a leadership role in this area. Therefore, the team recommends the agency establish an OCC-led innovation information-sharing group consisting of domestic and international regulators. The group would meet periodically to share information and promote responsible innovation.

DECISION: Approved.

Conclusion

The approved recommendations described in this report provide a framework to improve the agency's ability to identify, understand, and respond to innovations, emerging trends, and related risks in the financial services industry. The approved recommendations also provide a core foundation for support of responsible innovation in the federal banking system.

¶ 1340 Exploring Special Purpose National Bank Charters for Fintech Companies

Office of the Comptroller of the Currency

Washington, D.C.

December 2016

Preface by the Comptroller of the Currency

When President Abraham Lincoln signed the law creating the national banking system and the Office of the Comptroller of the Currency (OCC), the very notion of establishing a national bank charter was itself innovative. Our country's leaders provided the Comptroller with the authority to grant a national charter because they recognized the public value of a robust, unified, and nationwide system of banks.

The national banking system became a source of strength for the nation and our economy. National banks and, later, federal savings associations became anchors of their communities and the predominant providers of financial services for consumers and businesses. The system flourished because it enabled and encouraged national banks and federal savings associations to adapt to the changing needs of their customers and the market.

More than 150 years later, we have a diversified and evolving financial services industry. New technology makes financial products and services more accessible, easier to use, and much more tailored to individual consumer needs. At the same time, consumer preferences and demands are evolving, driven by important demographic changes: for example, the entry of 85 million millennials into the financial marketplace in the United States. Responding to those market forces are thousands of technology-driven nonbank companies offering a new approach to products and services. Five years ago these services either were available only from traditional banks or not available at all. Initially, many of these nonbank providers of financial services viewed themselves as competitors of banks. Now, some financial technology—or fintech—companies are considering whether to become banks.

These industry developments raise fundamental policy questions. Is the nation better served when banking products are provided by institutions subject to ongoing supervision and examination? Should a nonbank company that offers banking-related products have a path to become a bank? And, what conditions should apply if a nonbank company becomes a national bank?

I challenged staff at the OCC to explore these important questions when I asked them to examine the agency's authority to grant special purpose national bank charters to fintech companies and the conditions under which we might do so. This paper summarizes that work, describes the OCC's legal authority to grant a special purpose charter, and articulates what the OCC considers to be necessary conditions if the OCC is to exercise that authority. It makes clear that if we decide to grant a national charter to a particular fintech company, that institution will be held to the same high standards of safety and soundness, fair access, and fair treatment of customers that all federally chartered institutions must meet.

Public comment will help inform our consideration of these issues. We welcome your feedback on all of the issues raised in this paper and on the specific questions included at the end.

Introduction

The OCC's chartering authority includes the authority to charter special purpose national banks. In fact, many special purpose national banks are operating today—primarily trust banks and credit card banks. A question raised by technological advances in financial services and evolving customer preferences is whether it would be appropriate for the OCC to consider granting a special purpose national bank charter to a fintech company. For a number of reasons, the OCC believes it may be in the public interest to do so.

First, applying a bank regulatory framework to fintech companies will help ensure that these companies operate in a safe and sound manner so that they can effectively serve the needs of customers, businesses, and communities, just as banks do that operate under full-service charters. Second, applying the OCC's uniform supervision over national banks, including fintech companies, will help promote consistency in the application of law and regulation across the country and ensure that consumers are treated fairly. Third, providing a path for fintech companies to become national banks can make the federal banking system stronger. The OCC's oversight not only would help ensure that these companies operate in a safe and sound manner, it would also

¶1340

encourage them to explore new ways to promote fair access and financial inclusion and innovate responsibly. Fintech companies vary widely in their business models and product offerings. Some are marketplace lenders providing loans to consumers and small businesses, others offer payment-related services, others engage in digital currencies and distributed ledger technology, and still others provide financial planning and wealth management products and services.

If the OCC decides to grant a charter to a particular fintech company, the institution would be held to the same rigorous standards of safety and soundness, fair access, and fair treatment of customers that apply to all national banks and federal savings associations. The OCC acknowledges, however, that to approve a fintech charter the agency may need to account for differences in business models and the applicability of certain laws. For example, a fintech company with a special purpose national charter that does not take deposits, and therefore is not insured by the Federal Deposit Insurance Corporation (FDIC), would not be subject to laws that apply only to insured depository institutions.

Where a law does not apply directly, the OCC may, nonetheless, work with a fintech company to achieve the goals of a particular statute or regulation through the OCC's authority to impose conditions on its approval of a charter, taking into account any relevant differences between a full-service bank and special purpose bank. In this way, the OCC could advance important policy objectives, such as enhancing the ways in which financial services are provided in the 21st century, while ensuring that new fintech banks operate in a safe and sound manner, support their communities, promote financial inclusion, and protect customers.

This paper explores these and other issues related to the OCC's consideration of charter applications from fintech companies. The OCC welcomes comments about how it can foster responsible innovation in the chartering process while continuing to provide the robust oversight that its mandate requires.

Background

The OCC's responsible innovation work to date

In August 2015, the OCC began an initiative to better understand innovation occurring in the financial services industry and to develop a framework supporting responsible innovation. To gain a broad perspective, the OCC conducted extensive research and had discussions with fintech companies, banks, community and consumer groups, academics, and other regulators. This work led to the publication of a white paper in March 2016 that outlined clear principles to guide the development of a framework to support responsible innovation in the federal banking system.[1] In October 2016, the OCC announced plans to implement its framework for responsible innovation, including the establishment of an Office of Innovation to serve as the central point of contact and clearinghouse for requests and information related to innovation.[2] The office also will conduct outreach and provide technical assistance and other resources for banks and nonbanks on regulatory expectations and principles.

Chartering authority

The OCC has authority to grant charters for national banks and federal savings associations under the National Bank Act and the Home Owners' Loan Act, respectively.[3] That authority includes granting charters for special purpose national banks. A special purpose national bank may limit its activities to fiduciary activities or to any other activities within the business of banking. A special purpose national bank that conducts activities other than fiduciary activities must conduct at least one of the following three core banking functions: receiving deposits, paying checks, or lending money.[4]

---

[1] "Supporting Responsible Innovation in the Federal Banking System: An OCC Perspective" can be found at https://www.occ.gov/publications/publications-by-type/other-publications-reports/pub-responsible-innovation-banking-system-occ-perspective.pdf.

[2] "Recommendations and Decisions for Implementing a Responsible Innovation Framework" can be found at https://www.occ.gov/topics/bank-operations/innovation/recommendations-decisions-for-implementing-a-responsible-innovation-framework.pdf.

[3] See 12 USC 1 et seq. and 1461 et seq. The OCC also has authority, under the International Banking Act, 12 USC 3102, to license a foreign bank to operate a federal branch or agency in the United States.

[4] See 12 CFR 5.20(e)(1). This paper focuses on the national bank charter, because it has more flexibility than the federal savings association charter. Federal savings associations are subject to asset and investment limitations and are required to have deposit insurance. See 12 CFR 160.30 and 5.20(e)(3).

Special purpose national bank charters have been in use for some time. The most common types of these charters are trust banks (national banks limited to the activities of a trust company) and credit card banks (national banks limited to a credit card business).[5] Though the focus of this paper is on fintech companies in particular, there is no legal limitation on the type of "special purpose" for which a national bank charter may be granted, so long as the entity engages in fiduciary activities or in activities that include receiving deposits, paying checks, or lending money. As the next section describes, the OCC has the legal authority to construe these activities to include bank-permissible, technology-based innovations in financial services.

Features and attributes of a national bank charter

Corporate structure

A national bank charter is a federal form of corporate organization that authorizes a bank to conduct business on a nationwide basis and subjects the bank to uniform standards and rigorous federal oversight. All national banks, including special purpose national banks, are organized under, and governed by, the National Bank Act. The corporate organization and structure provisions of the National Bank Act (e.g., classes of shares, voting rights, number of directors, and term of office) govern the corporate structure of a special purpose national bank.

Bank-permissible activities

A special purpose national bank may engage only in activities that are permissible for national banks. Bank-permissible activities are identified in statutes, in the OCC's regulations, and in legal opinions and corporate decisions that the OCC regularly publishes.[6] The OCC and the courts that have considered the scope of bank-permissible activities also recognize that the business of banking develops over time as the economy and business methods evolve.[7]

Consistent with legal precedent, the OCC views the National Bank Act as sufficiently adaptable to permit national banks—full-service or special purpose—to engage in new activities as part of the business of banking or to engage in traditional activities in new ways.[8] For example, discounting notes, purchasing bank-permissible debt securities, engaging in lease-financing transactions, and making loans are forms of lending money. Similarly, issuing debit cards or engaging in other means of facilitating payments electronically are the modern equivalent of paying checks. The OCC would consider on a case-by-case basis the permissibility of a new activity that a company seeking a special purpose charter wishes to conduct.

Rules and standards applicable to a special purpose national bank

In general, a special purpose national bank is subject to the same laws, regulations, examination, reporting requirements, and ongoing supervision as other national banks. Statutes that by their terms apply to national banks apply to all special purpose national banks, even uninsured national banks. These laws include, for example, statutes and regulations on legal lending limits and limits on real estate holdings.[9]

Other laws that apply to special purpose banks include the Bank Secrecy Act (BSA), other anti-money laundering (AML) laws, and the economic sanctions administered by the U.S. Department of the Treasury's Office of Foreign Assets Control (OFAC). In addition, special purpose national banks generally are subject to the prohibitions on engaging in unfair or deceptive acts or practices under section 5 of the Federal Trade Commission Act and unfair, deceptive, or abusive acts or practices under section 1036 of the Dodd-Frank Wall Street Reform and Consumer Protection Act (Dodd-Frank). The OCC's chartering regulation and licensing policies and procedures also would apply to a special purpose national bank. The established charter policies and

---

[5] The OCC also has chartered other special purpose national banks including bankers' banks, community development banks, and cash management banks.

[6] See OCC Interpretations and Actions at https://www.occ.gov/topics/licensing/interpretations-and-actions/index-interpretations-and-actions.html.

[7] See generally NationsBank of North Carolina, N.A. v. Variable Life Annuity Co., 513 U.S. 251 (1995); M&M Leasing Corp. v. Seattle First National Bank, 563 F.2d 1377 (9th Cir. 1977), cert. denied, 436 U.S. 987 (1978); OCC Conditional Approval No. 267 (January 12, 1998).

(certification authority and repository and key escrow are part of the business of banking); OCC Interpretive Letter No. 494 (December 20, 1989) (allowing national banks to purchase and sell financial futures for their own account).

[8] See, e.g., 12 CFR 7.5002 (OCC regulation authorizing national banks to use electronic means to conduct activities they are otherwise authorized to conduct, subject to appropriate safety and soundness and compliance standards and conditions).

[9] See 12 USC 84 and 12 CFR 32 (lending limits) and 12 USC 29 and 12 CFR 7.1000 (limits on holding real estate).

procedures are set forth in 12 CFR Part 5 and the "Charters" booklet of the *Comptroller's Licensing Manual* and are discussed in the Chartering process section below.[10]

A special purpose national bank also has the same status and attributes under federal law as a full-service national bank.[11] State law applies to a special purpose national bank in the same way and to the same extent as it applies to a full-service national bank. Limits on state visitorial authority also apply in the same way. A special purpose national bank would look to the relevant statutes (including the preemption provisions added to the National Bank Act by Dodd-Frank), regulations (including the OCC's preemption regulations), and federal judicial precedent to determine if or how state law applies. For example, under these statutes, rules, and precedents, state laws would not apply if they would require a national bank to be licensed in order to engage in certain types of activity or business. Examples of state laws that *would* generally apply to national banks include state laws on anti-discrimination, fair lending, debt collection, taxation, zoning, criminal laws, and torts. In addition, any other state laws that only incidentally affect national banks' exercise of their federally authorized powers to lend, take deposits, and engage in other federally authorized activities are not preempted. Moreover, the OCC has taken the position that state laws aimed at unfair or deceptive treatment of customers apply to national banks.[12]

Many other federal statutes apply to any bank, financial institution, or other type of entity based on the activities in which the entity engages. For example, banks that engage in residential real estate lending must comply with the Truth in Lending Act, Real Estate Settlement Procedures Act, Home Mortgage Disclosure Act, Equal Credit Opportunity Act, Fair Credit Reporting Act, Fair Housing Act, Servicemembers Civil Relief Act, and Military Lending Act.

Some statutes, however, apply to a national bank only if it is FDIC-insured and, therefore, would not apply to an uninsured special purpose national bank. For example, certain provisions in the Federal Deposit Insurance Act (FDIA), such as section 1831p-1 (safety and soundness standards) and section 1829b (retention of records), only apply to insured depository institutions.[13] In addition, if a national bank is not insured, the provisions in the FDIA governing the receivership of insured depository institutions would not apply. The OCC recently issued a proposed rule that would address this regulatory gap by establishing a framework for the receivership of an uninsured national bank under the receivership provisions in the National Bank Act.[14] The proposed rule primarily focuses on uninsured national trust banks, but specifically contemplates application to other special purpose national banks. The Community Reinvestment Act (CRA) is an example of another law that only applies to insured institutions.[15]

As discussed in the Chartering process section below, the OCC could impose requirements on an uninsured special purpose bank as a condition for granting a charter that are similar to certain statutory requirements applicable to insured banks, if it deems the conditions appropriate based on the risks and business model of the institution.[16]

Coordination among regulators

The OCC is the primary prudential regulator and supervisor of national banks. Depending on the structure of the bank and the activities it conducts, other regulators will have oversight roles as well. A fintech company considering a special purpose national bank charter likely would need to engage with other regulators in addition to the OCC. The OCC traditionally coordinates with other banking regulators on charter-related activities and would continue to coordinate and

---

[10] See 12 CFR Part 5 and the "Charters" booklet of the *Comptroller's Licensing Manual* (September 2016), https://www.occ.gov/publications/publications-by-type/licensing-manuals/charters.pdf.

[11] A special purpose national bank has the same charter as a full-service national bank. It limits its activities through the bank's articles of association or through OCC-imposed conditions for approving the charter.

[12] The OCC looks to the substantive content of the state statute and not its title or characterization to determine whether it falls within this category.

[13] While certain provisions of the FDIA do not apply to uninsured national banks, the OCC can address unsafe or unsound practices, violations of law, unsafe or unsound conditions, or other practices under its other supervisory

and enforcement authorities. The FDIA's principal enforcement section, 12 U.S.C. 1818, generally would apply to any national banking association, including an uninsured national bank. See 12 USC 1818(b)(5).

[14] The proposed rule was published in the Federal Register at 81 Fed. Reg. 62835 (September 13, 2016) and is available at https://www.occ.gov/news-issuances/news-releases/2016/nr-occ-2016-110a.pdf.

[15] 12 USC 2901 et seq. See also 12 CFR Part 25 (OCC CRA regulations).

[16] Such conditions are conditions imposed in writing by the OCC in connection with any action on any application, notice, or other request under 12 USC 1818(b)(1). As such they are enforceable under 12 CFR 1818.

communicate where appropriate with other regulators in the case of an application by a fintech company for a special purpose national bank charter.

Federal Reserve: With rare exceptions, all national banks, including insured and uninsured trust banks and other special purpose national banks, are required to be members of the Federal Reserve System.[17] National banks become member banks by subscribing for the stock of the appropriate Federal Reserve Bank.[18] Since most special purpose national banks would be member banks, the statutes and regulations that apply to member banks also would apply to them.[19] These statutes and regulations are administered by the Board of Governors of the Federal Reserve System (Federal Reserve Board) and the Federal Reserve Banks.

In addition, the Federal Reserve Board administers and interprets the scope and requirements of the Bank Holding Company Act (BHCA). If a fintech company interested in operating as a special purpose national bank has or plans to have a holding company that would be the sole or controlling owner of the bank (and investors would, in turn, own shares in the holding company), the BHCA could apply. A national bank is a "bank" for purposes of the BHCA if (A) it is either (i) an FDIC-insured bank or (ii) a bank that both accepts demand deposits and engages in the business of making commercial loans and (B) it does not qualify for any of the exceptions from the definition of "bank" in the BHCA.[20]

Federal Deposit Insurance Corporation: A fintech company that proposes to accept deposits other than trust funds would be required to apply to, and receive approval from, the FDIC. Generally, a bank must be engaged in the business of receiving deposits other than trust funds for the FDIC to consider granting deposit insurance.[21] For example, some national trust banks engage only in fiduciary and related activities and do not engage in the business of receiving deposits other than trust funds. As a result, they are not FDIC-insured.[22] If the OCC chartered another type of special purpose national bank that did not receive deposits other than trust funds, such as a fintech company, that new bank also would not be eligible for FDIC insurance.

Consumer Financial Protection Bureau: A special purpose national bank that engages in an activity that is regulated under a federal consumer financial law, as defined by Dodd-Frank, may also be subject to oversight by the Consumer Financial Protection Bureau (CFPB). A special purpose national bank that is an insured depository institution generally would be supervised by either the CFPB or the OCC for purposes of all federal consumer financial laws based on its asset size.[23] Under Dodd-Frank, the CFPB would supervise an uninsured special purpose national bank engaged in certain activities for compliance with federal consumer financial law.[24]

Baseline supervisory expectations

All national banks are required to meet high supervisory standards. Consistent with the OCC's mission, these standards include safety and soundness requirements, as well as requirements to provide fair access to financial services, treat customers fairly, and comply with all applicable laws and regulations. The OCC tailors these standards based on the bank's size, complexity, and risks. As a national bank, a special purpose national bank also would be expected to meet these high standards, tailored to its size, complexity, and risks.

---

[17] See 12 USC 222. National banks located in territories and insular possessions of the United States are not required to be member banks. See 12 USC 466.

[18] See 12 USC 282; 12 CFR 209.2(b).

[19] For example, the Federal Reserve Act imposes quantitative and qualitative restrictions on a member bank's transactions with its affiliates. 12 USC 371c, 371c-1. These restrictions are implemented by the Federal Reserve Board. See 12 CFR Part 223.

[20] See 12 USC 1841.

[21] See 12 USC 1815(a). The FDIC's regulations provide that an institution is engaged in the business of receiving deposits other than trust funds if it maintains one or more non-trust deposit accounts in the minimum aggregate amount of $500,000. 12 CFR 303.14(a).

[22] There are several FDIC-insured trust banks. Currently, four national trust banks have FDIC insurance.

[23] The CFPB has exclusive supervisory authority and primary enforcement authority over special purpose national banks that are insured depository institutions and have assets greater than $10 billion. See 12 CFR 5515. The OCC generally has exclusive supervisory and enforcement authority over special purpose national banks that are insured depository institutions and have assets of $10 billion or less. See 12 USC 5516, 5581(c)(1)(B).

[24] See 12 USC 5514. Section 5514(a) defines the "scope of coverage" for the CFPB's supervisory authority over nondepository covered persons, which does not include all activities governed by a federal consumer financial law. Instead, the "scope of coverage" set forth in subsection (a) includes specified activities (e.g., offering or providing: origination, brokerage, or servicing of consumer mortgage loans; payday loans; or private education loans) as well as a means for the CFPB to expand the coverage through specified actions (e.g., a rulemaking to designate "larger market participants"). 12 USC 5514(a).

The OCC has identified the following baseline supervisory expectations for any entity seeking a national charter. These baseline expectations stress the importance of a detailed business plan, governance, capital, liquidity, compliance risk management, financial inclusion, and recovery and resolution planning. As with other applicants seeking a national bank charter, applicants for a special purpose charter are strongly encouraged, prior to filing an application, to meet with the OCC to discuss these baseline expectations in detail and how the expectations (and any others arising from the particular proposal) apply to their proposed bank. Those meetings enable the OCC to work with the applicant to develop and tailor supervisory standards to each applicant based on the applicant's circumstances including its size, business model, complexity and risk profile.

Robust, well-developed business plan

A well-developed business plan is a key component of any charter proposal.[25] The OCC expects a company seeking any type of national bank charter to clearly articulate why it is seeking a national bank charter and provide significant detail about the proposed bank's activities. The business plan is a written summary of how the proposed bank will organize its resources to meet its goals and objectives and how it will measure progress. As such, the business plan should be comprehensive, reflecting in-depth planning by the organizers, Board of Directors, and management.

The plan should clearly define the market the proposed bank plans to serve and the products and services it will provide.[26] In addition, it should realistically forecast market demand, economic conditions, competition, and the proposed bank's customer base. The plan also must demonstrate a realistic assessment of risk, describing management's assessment of all risks inherent in the proposed products and services, including risks relating to BSA/AML requirements, consumer protection, fair lending requirements, and the design of related risk management controls and management information systems. Additionally, the plan should describe the experience and expertise of proposed management, including the Board, to manage the proposed bank.

The business plan should cover a minimum of three years and provide a full description of proposed actions to accomplish the primary functions of the proposed bank. The description should provide enough detail to demonstrate that the proposed bank has a reasonable chance for success, will operate in a safe and sound manner, and will have adequate capital to support its risk profile. The OCC expects a proposed bank's business plan to outline the plans for initial and future capital contributions, as well as to provide specific information on how the proposed bank intends to maintain and monitor appropriate capital levels. The plan should also identify external sources available to bolster capital levels, if needed. Additionally, the business plan should include comprehensive alternative business strategies to address various best-case and worst-case scenarios (e.g., financial performance, revenue growth, market share). The business plan also should include the organizing group's knowledge of and plans for serving the community, if applicable.

Governance structure

The OCC expects the governance structure for any proposed special purpose national bank to be commensurate with the risk and complexity of its proposed products, services, and activities, as it is for other national banks. The OCC sets high standards for governance and for risk management systems that identify, monitor, manage, and control risk in national banks. The OCC expects national banks to have the expertise, financial acumen, and risk management framework to promote safety and soundness oversight. The Board of Directors must have a prominent role in the overall governance structure by participating on key committees and guiding the risk management framework. Board members also must actively oversee management, provide credible challenge, and exercise independent judgment.

Capital

The OCC's evaluation of a bank's capital is important, not only to assess the strength of an individual bank, but also to evaluate the safety and soundness of the entire federal banking system. Bank capital, among other things, helps to ensure public confidence in the stability of individual banks and the banking system; supports the volume, type, and character of the business conducted; and provides for the possibility of unexpected loss.

---

[25] See the "Charters" booklet of the *Comptroller's Licensing Manual* for more information on business plan requirements.

[26] For example, the business plan for a proposed bank that will engage in payments activities should address how the bank proposes to access various payment systems.

Minimum and ongoing capital levels need to be commensurate with the risk and complexity of the proposed activities (including on-and off-balance sheet activities). The OCC's evaluation of capital adequacy (initial and ongoing) consider the risks and complexities of the proposed products, services, and operating characteristics, taking into account both quantitative and qualitative factors. Key qualitative elements that influence the determination of capital adequacy include the scope and nature of the bank's proposed activities, quality of management, funds management, ownership, operating procedures and controls, asset quality, earnings and their retention, risk diversification, and strategic planning. In addition to assessing the quality and source of capital, the OCC also considers on- and-off balance sheet composition, credit risk, concentration, and market risks.

Special purpose national bank charter applicants whose business activities may be off-balance sheet would be subject to the OCC's minimum regulatory capital requirements, but the minimum capital levels required may not adequately reflect the risks associated with off-balance sheet activities.[27] To account for this gap, applicants are expected to propose a minimum level of capital that the proposed bank would meet or exceed at all times. For example, national trust banks typically have few assets on the balance sheet, usually composed of cash on deposit with an insured depository institution, investment securities, premises and equipment, and intangible assets. Because these banks do not make loans or rely on deposit funding, the OCC typically requires them to hold a specific minimum amount of capital, which often exceeds the capital requirements for other types of banks. Similarly, the OCC would consider adapting capital requirements applicable to a fintech applicant for a special purpose national bank charter as necessary to adequately reflect its risks and to the extent consistent with applicable law.

Liquidity

The OCC's evaluation of liquidity focuses on a bank's capacity to readily and efficiently meet expected and unexpected cash flows and collateral needs at a reasonable cost, without adversely affecting either daily operations or the financial condition of the bank. As with capital, minimum and ongoing liquidity (both operating and contingent obligations) for a special purpose national bank need to be commensurate with the risk and complexity of the proposed activities. In assessing the liquidity position of a proposed bank, the OCC considers a proposed bank's access to funds as well as its cost of funding. Some key areas of consideration include projected funding sources, needs, and costs; net cash flow and liquid asset positions; projected borrowing capacity; highly liquid asset and collateral positions (including the eligibility and marketability of such assets under a variety of market environments); requirements for unfunded commitments; and the adequacy of contingency funding plans. All aspects of liquidity should address the impact to earnings and capital, and incorporate planned and unplanned balance sheet changes, as well as varying interest rate scenarios, time horizons, and market conditions.[28]

Compliance risk management

The OCC expects all national banks to manage compliance risks effectively. A strong compliance infrastructure contributes to a national bank's safe and sound operation, as well as the provision of fair access to financial services, fair treatment of customers, and compliance with applicable laws.

An applicant seeking a special purpose national bank charter, like any applicant for a national bank charter, is expected to demonstrate a culture of compliance that includes a top-down, enterprise-wide commitment to understanding and adhering to applicable laws and regulations and to operating consistently with OCC supervisory guidance. In addition, the applicant would need appropriate systems and programs to identify, assess, manage and monitor the compliance process (e.g., policies and procedures, practices, training, internal controls, and audit), and a commitment to maintain adequate compliance resources.

Appropriate compliance risk management includes a well-developed compliance management system that is commensurate with the risks to the proposed bank and includes:

- a compliance program designed to ensure and monitor compliance with the requirements imposed by the BSA, other AML statutes, and related regulations, as well as OFAC economic sanctions obligations; and

---

[27] The OCC's capital requirements are set forth at 12 CFR Part 3.

[28] See the "Liquidity" booklet of the *Comptroller's Handbook* for more information. https://www.occ.gov/publications/publications-by-type/comptrollers-handbook/liquidity.pdf.

¶1340

- a consumer compliance program designed to ensure fair treatment of customers and fair access to financial services, as well as compliance with Section 5 of the Federal Trade Commission Act, the unfair, deceptive, or abusive acts or practices prohibitions of Dodd-Frank, and all other applicable consumer financial protection laws and regulations.

The OCC expects any applicant seeking a special purpose national bank charter to provide a sufficient description of the proposed bank's activities for the OCC to fully understand the BSA/AML and compliance risks the proposed bank faces, how it intends to assess, manage, and monitor these risks, and how it would comply with relevant laws, regulations, and requirements.

As with any national bank, the compliance risk management system appropriate for a specific bank should consider the nature of the company's business, its size, and the diversity and complexity of the risks associated with its operations. While this general standard is consistent across all national banks, applying the standard to a fintech company's business model could raise novel considerations. The OCC would consider and address in its evaluation of a fintech charter application whether and how innovative elements of a business model may affect the proposed bank's compliance risk profile.

Financial inclusion

The OCC's statutory mission includes ensuring that national banks treat customers fairly and provide fair access to financial services.[29] This part of the OCC's mission is directly related to financial inclusion.[30] For insured depository institutions, this mission is advanced, in part, through the CRA framework, under which the OCC assesses an institution's record of helping meet the credit needs of its entire community, including low- and moderate-income neighborhoods, individuals, and underserved geographic areas. Special purpose national banks that are not insured depository institutions, however, are not subject to the CRA.[31]

Distinct from any direct CRA obligation, the OCC is guided by certain principles in determining whether to approve a charter application to establish a national bank. These principles include "encouraging" the national bank "to provide fair access to financial services by helping to meet the credit needs of its entire community" and "promoting fair treatment of customers including efficiency and better service."[32] The OCC expects an applicant seeking a special purpose national bank charter that engages in lending activities to demonstrate a commitment to financial inclusion that supports fair access to financial services and fair treatment of customers. The nature of the commitment would depend on the entity's business model and the types of loan products or services it intends to provide.

The OCC's chartering regulation generally requires an applicant for a national bank charter to submit a business plan that demonstrates how the proposed bank plans to respond to the needs of the community, consistent with the safe and sound operation of the bank.[33] Although this element of the business plan is not mandatory for all special purpose banks, the OCC expects a special purpose bank engaged in lending to explain its commitment to financial inclusion in its business plan. In developing the financial inclusion component of its business plan, a proposed special purpose bank engaged in lending should consider the following elements:

- an identification of, and method for defining, the relevant market, customer base, or community;

- a description of the nature of the products or services the company intends to offer (consistent with its business plan), the marketing and outreach plans, and the intended delivery mechanisms for these products or services;

---

[29] See 12 USC 1.

[30] The problem of financially unserved and underserved sectors of society is a global issue. The World Bank has described "financial inclusion" to mean that "individuals and businesses have access to useful and affordable financial products and services that meet their needs—transactions, payments, savings, credit and insurance—delivered in a responsible and sustainable way." See the World Bank Financial Inclusion Overview page at http://www.worldbank.org/en/topic/financialinclusion/overview. Separately, recent final guidance from the Basel Committee on Banking Supervision addresses financial inclusion, focusing on unserved and underserved customers. See Guidance on the application of the Core Principles for Effective Banking Supervision to the regulation and supervision of institutions relevant to financial inclusion (September 2016) at http://www.bis.org/bcbs/publ/d383.pdf.

[31] See 12 USC 2902 (defining "regulated financial institution" to mean an "insured depository institution"). See also 12 CFR 25.12 (defining "bank" as a national bank with federally insured deposits).

[32] See 12 CFR 5.20(f)(1)(ii) and (iv).

[33] See 12 CFR 5.20(h)(5).

- an explanation of how such products and services, marketing plans, and delivery mechanisms would promote financial inclusion (e.g., provide access to underserved consumers or small businesses); and

full information regarding how the proposed bank's policies, procedures, and practices are designed to ensure products and services are offered on a fair and non-discriminatory basis. For example, the OCC may ask an applicant that plans to extend credit to provide the terms on which it plans to lend, including a description of the protections it plans to provide to individuals and small business borrowers.

As with other elements of the applicant's business plan, the OCC may require a company to obtain approval, or no-objection, from the OCC if it departs materially from its financial inclusion plans.

Recovery and exit strategies; resolution plan and authority

As noted above, the OCC expects a proposed bank's business plan to include alternative business and recovery strategies to address various best-case and worst-case scenarios. Simply put, the OCC expects business plans to articulate specific financial or other risk triggers that would prompt the Board and management's determination to unwind the operation in an organized manner. These strategies must provide a comprehensive framework for evaluating the financial effects of severe stress that may affect an entity and options to remain viable under such stress. The business plan must address material changes in the institution's size, risk profile, activities, complexity, and external threats, and be integrated into the entity's overall risk governance framework. Plans must be specific to that entity, aligned with the entity's other plans, and coordinated with any applicable parent or affiliate planning. A plan should include triggers alerting the entity to the risk or presence of severe stress, a wide range of credible options an entity could take to restore its financial strength and viability, and escalation and notification procedures. While the objective of these business and recovery strategies is to remain a viable entity, the OCC may also require a company to have a clear exit strategy.

Chartering process

The OCC's standard process for reviewing and making decisions about charter applications would apply to applications from fintech companies for a special purpose national bank charter. Charter applications are reviewed and processed through the OCC's Licensing Department. The "Charters" booklet of the *Comptroller's Licensing Manual*[34] contains detailed information about that process, which consists of four stages:

- The prefiling stage, in which potential applicants engage with the OCC in formal and informal meetings to discuss their proposal, the chartering process, and application requirements. At this stage, applicants also prepare a complete application, including a business plan.

- The filing stage, in which the organizers submit the application. Organizers also must publish notice of the charter application as soon as possible before or after the date of the filing.

- The review and evaluation stage, in which the OCC conducts background and field investigations, and reviews and analyzes the application to determine whether the proposed bank: has a reasonable chance of success; will be operated in a safe and sound manner; will provide fair access to financial services; will ensure compliance with laws and regulations; will promote fair treatment of customers; and will foster healthy competition.

- The decision stage, which includes three phases:

  ○ The preliminary conditional approval phase, when the OCC decides whether to grant preliminary conditional approval;

  ○ The organization phase, when the bank raises capital, prepares for opening, and the OCC conducts a preopening examination; and

  ○ The final approval phase, when the OCC decides whether the bank has met the requirements and conditions for opening.

The OCC imposes a number of standard requirements on a bank when it grants preliminary conditional approval, such as the establishment of appropriate policies and procedures and the adoption of an internal audit system appropriate to the size, nature, and scope of the bank's activities. The OCC may impose additional conditions for a variety of reasons, including for

---

[34] See the "Charters" booklet of the *Comptroller's Licensing Manual.*

¶1340

example to ensure the newly chartered bank does not change its business model from that proposed in the application without prior OCC approval; to mandate higher capital and liquidity requirements; or to require the bank to have a resolution plan to sell itself or wind down if necessary. In addition, in the case of an uninsured bank, the OCC may impose requirements by way of conditions similar to those that apply by statute to an insured bank, to the extent appropriate given the business model and risk profile of a particular applicant. The OCC likely would impose additional conditions in connection with granting a special purpose national bank charter requested by a fintech company based on the fintech company's business model and risk profile.[35]

The OCC recognizes it also may need to tailor some requirements that apply to a full-service national bank to address the business model of a special purpose national bank. The OCC has experience in adapting legal requirements to different types of business models. For example, as noted above, the OCC has modified capital requirements for certain trust banks.[36] Similarly, the OCC would consider adapting requirements applicable to a fintech applicant for a special purpose national bank charter to the extent consistent with applicable law.

The OCC recommends that potential applicants carefully review the OCC chartering regulation and the "Charters" booklet of the *Comptroller's Licensing Manual* for a full description of the charter application process and requirements. The OCC also strongly urges groups or individuals interested in a special purpose national bank charter to engage with the OCC well in advance of filing an application to ensure they understand the requirements. In addition, interested parties are advised to consult the *Comptroller's Handbook* for additional information on how the OCC supervises and examines national banks.[37] The Office of Innovation also can be an important resource to fintech companies interested in exploring the possibility of a special purpose national bank charter. Contact information for the Licensing Department and the Office of Innovation may be found on the OCC's website.

Request for comment

As the OCC considers the granting of special purpose national bank charters to fintech companies, it seeks feedback on all aspects of this paper. The OCC also solicits responses to the following questions. Respondents should provide written comments by January 15, 2017 (45 days from this paper's publication). Submissions should be sent to specialpurposecharter@occ.treas.gov.

1. What are the public policy benefits of approving fintech companies to operate under a national bank charter? What are the risks?

2. What elements should the OCC consider in establishing the capital and liquidity requirements for an uninsured special purpose national bank that limits the type of assets it holds?

3. What information should a special purpose national bank provide to the OCC to demonstrate its commitment to financial inclusion to individuals, businesses and communities? For instance, what new or alternative means (e.g., products, services) might a special purpose national bank establish in furtherance of its support for financial inclusion? How could an uninsured special purpose bank that uses innovative methods to develop or deliver financial products or services in a virtual or physical community demonstrate its commitment to financial inclusion?

4. Should the OCC seek a financial inclusion commitment from an uninsured special purpose national bank that would not engage in lending, and if so, how could such a bank demonstrate a commitment to financial inclusion?

5. How could a special purpose national bank that is not engaged in providing banking services to the public support financial inclusion?

---

[35] An applicant may be required, as a condition of approval, to enter into an "operating agreement" with the OCC containing the substantive charter conditions. The special purpose charters section of the "Charters" booklet of the *Comptroller's Licensing Manual* has additional information on operating agreements and other documents used for some special purpose national trust banks.

[36] The OCC is funded through assessments and fees charged to the institutions it supervises. See 12 USC 16. Consistent with this authorization, the OCC has modified the assessments it charges an independent trust bank or a credit card bank to account for the scope and activities of the entity and the amount and type of assets that the entity holds. The OCC would determine assessments for a fintech special purpose national bank to account for similar factors.

[37] *The Comptroller's Handbook* is a collection of booklets that contain the concepts and procedures established by the OCC for the examination of banks. It is available at www.occ.gov.

6. Should the OCC use its chartering authority as an opportunity to address the gaps in protections afforded individuals versus small business borrowers, and if so, how?

7. What are potential challenges in executing or adapting a fintech business model to meet regulatory expectations, and what specific conditions governing the activities of special purpose national banks should the OCC consider?

8. What actions should the OCC take to ensure special purpose national banks operate in a safe and sound manner and in the public interest?

9. Would a fintech special purpose national bank have any competitive advantages over full-service banks the OCC should address? Are there risks to full-service banks from fintech companies that do not have bank charters?

10. Are there particular products or services offered by fintech companies, such as digital currencies, that may require different approaches to supervision to mitigate risk for both the institution and the broader financial system?

11. How can the OCC enhance its coordination and communication with other regulators that have jurisdiction over a proposed special purpose national bank, its parent company, or its activities?

12. Certain risks may be increased in a special purpose national bank because of its concentration in a limited number of business activities. How can the OCC ensure that a special purpose national bank sufficiently mitigates these risks?

13. What additional information, materials, and technical assistance from the OCC would a prospective fintech applicant find useful in the application process?

¶ 1350 OCC Summary of Comments and Explanatory Statement: Special Purpose National Bank Charters for Financial Technology Companies

Office of the Comptroller of the Currency

Washington, D.C.

March 2017

Introduction

The Office of the Comptroller of the Currency (OCC) has considered whether it is in the public interest to entertain applications for a special purpose national bank (SPNB) charter from financial technology (fintech) companies that engage in banking activities and meet the standards applicable to national banks. The OCC has carefully considered the issues outlined in and the comments received on the OCC's paper *Exploring Special Purpose National Bank Charters for Fintech Companies* (SPNB Paper). This summary of comments and explanatory statement addresses key issues raised by commenters and explains the OCC's decision to issue for public comment a draft supplement to the *Comptroller's Licensing Manual* (Supplement) providing guidance to any fintech company that may wish to file a charter application.

The OCC will accept comments on the Supplement through close of business April 14, 2017. Comments should be submitted to specialpurposecharter@occ.treas.gov.

OCC Support for Responsible Innovation

The OCC has long supported innovation in the national banking system. Federally chartered institutions have continually sought new approaches to meet the needs of customers and an evolving marketplace. It has been and remains the OCC's role to encourage and support institutions' efforts to engage in responsible innovation to meet the needs of consumers, businesses, and communities. The OCC's decision to issue the draft Supplement is consistent with that support. It is also one component of an initiative that began in 2015, when Comptroller of the Currency Thomas J. Curry announced[1] the agency's efforts to better understand innovation occurring in the financial services industry and to develop a framework to support responsible innovation in the federal banking system. To gain a broad perspective, the OCC conducted extensive research and held numerous discussions with fintech companies, banks, community and consumer groups, academics, and other regulators. This work led to the publication of a paper, *Supporting Responsible Innovation in the Federal Banking System: An OCC Perspective*,[2] outlining principles to guide the OCC's development of a responsible innovation framework. A wide range of stakeholders provided comments on that paper, including some who suggested the OCC consider issuing federal charters to fintech companies. Charter discussions continued at the OCC's June 2016 Forum on Responsible Innovation. Since then, there has been significant and growing interest in federal bank charters for fintech companies.

Work also has continued on the development of the OCC's framework to support responsible innovation. In October 2016, the OCC established a stand-alone Office of Innovation (Office) to serve as a clearinghouse for innovation-related matters and a central point of contact for OCC staff, banks, and nonbanks. The Office conducts outreach to a variety of financial services stakeholders and provides technical assistance and other resources for banks and nonbanks on the OCC's expectations and guiding principles regarding responsible innovation. The Office also promotes awareness of industry developments among OCC staff and other regulators.

SPNB Paper and SPNB Licensing Manual Draft Supplement

In December 2016, Comptroller Curry announced that the OCC would move forward with considering applications from fintech companies to become SPNBs. The OCC published and requested public comment on the SPNB Paper describing the issues associated with offering national bank charters to fintech companies.[3] The paper described the OCC's legal authority to grant a national bank charter to companies with limited purposes and articulated what the OCC considers the requirements for obtaining a charter. In particular, the paper made clear that if the

---

[1] Remarks by Thomas J. Curry, Comptroller of the Currency, Before the Federal Home Loan Bank of Chicago, August 7, 2015.

[2] OCC, *Supporting Responsible Innovation in the Federal Banking System: An OCC Perspective*, March 2016.

[3] OCC, *Exploring Special Purpose National Bank Charters for Fintech Companies* (PDF), December 2, 2016.

OCC grants a national charter to a particular fintech company, the agency will hold that institution to the same high standards of safety and soundness, fair access, and fair treatment of customers that all federally chartered institutions must meet.

The Comptroller also asked staff to develop the draft Supplement to provide guidance for evaluating fintech charter applications and to ensure that the agency considers safety and soundness, risk management, financial inclusion, and compliance with applicable consumer protection and other laws and regulations were it to entertain applications from fintech companies. The draft Supplement, informed by the comments received on the SPNB Paper, explains how the OCC would evaluate applications from fintech companies and the conditions for approving such charters. The OCC welcomes additional comments on the draft Supplement.

While the term "special purpose national bank" is used elsewhere in the OCC's rules and policies to refer to a number of types of special purpose national banks, for purposes of the draft Supplement and this statement, "SPNB" means a national bank that engages in a limited range of banking activities, including one of the core banking functions, but does not take deposits and is not insured by the Federal Deposit Insurance Corporation (FDIC). The draft Supplement applies specifically to the OCC's consideration of applications from fintech companies to charter an SPNB and does not apply to other types of special purpose banks described in current the *Comptroller's Licensing Manual*.[4]

OCC Responses to Comments on SPNB Paper

The OCC received more than 100 comment letters on the SPNB Paper. After considering those comments, the OCC states that in evaluating applications from fintech companies for an SPNB charter, the agency would be guided by certain threshold principles that inform the draft Supplement:

- The OCC will not allow the inappropriate commingling of banking and commerce.

- The OCC will not allow products with predatory features nor will it allow unfair or deceptive acts or practices.

- There will be no "light-touch" supervision of companies that have an SPNB charter. Any fintech companies granted such charters will be held to the same high standards that all federally chartered banks must meet.

Aligned with those principles, the OCC believes that making SPNB charters available to qualified fintech companies would be in the public interest. An SPNB charter provides a framework of uniform standards and robust supervision for companies that qualify. Applying this framework to fintech companies would help ensure that they operate in a safe and sound manner and fairly serve the needs of consumers, businesses, and communities. In addition, the OCC believes supervision by a federal regulator would promote consistency in the application of federal laws and regulations across the country.

Further, making charters available to qualifying fintech companies supports a robust dual banking system by providing these companies the option of offering banking products and services under a federal charter and operating under federal law, while ensuring essential consumer protections. This is the same choice Congress has made available to companies that deliver banking products and services in traditional ways.

Moreover, providing a path for fintech companies to become national banks can make the financial system stronger by promoting growth, modernization, and competition. The OCC believes that denying fintech companies this option could make the federal banking system less capable of adapting to evolving business and consumer needs. Additionally, the OCC's supervision of fintech companies chartered as SPNBs would deepen the agency's expertise in the emerging technologies that will be crucial to delivering banking products and services in the future.

Finally, the OCC believes innovation has the potential to broaden access to financial services. Many fintech companies state that they offer products and services that reach consumers who have had limited access to banks in the past. Chartering fintech companies increases the potential to reach consumers and thereby promote financial inclusion.

General Comments

---

[4] For example, the draft Supplement would not apply to a fintech company that intends to engage in fiduciary activities and otherwise meets the requirements of a trust bank.

Many commenters supported the OCC's decision to consider charter applications from fintech companies and noted many of the same public benefits cited by the OCC. For example, many agreed that a national charter would provide fintech companies with uniform, clear, and consistent supervision and regulation. Numerous commenters also viewed the national bank charter as a means to empower consumers and provide greater access to credit in underserved communities. Others said the availability of a national charter would spur innovation and encourage competition. One commenter pointed out that a federal charter would give the OCC a better-informed, direct view of innovations that are reshaping the financial system. Several commenters also noted that having a national bank charter would eliminate the need for state-by-state licenses, thereby reducing regulatory burdens and costs and facilitating growth.

Other commenters warned of possible risks of permitting fintech companies to operate as national banks. Some expressed concern about the potential for consumer harm, noting that a fintech company chartered as an SPNB could avoid consumer protections granted by state laws or federal laws that only apply to deposit-taking banks. Other commenters warned that the OCC has not limited SPNB charters to fintech companies, and thus the charters could be used by payday lenders.

In addition, several commenters expressed concern that the OCC's supervision of fintech companies chartered as national banks would be less stringent than the supervision fintech companies receive from state regulators today. Others were concerned SPNBs might receive less rigorous supervision than full-service national banks.

In contrast, some commenters were concerned that a rigid regulatory framework could stifle innovation and urged the OCC to provide flexible regulation tailored to the fintech company's business model and risks. Moreover, some argued that imposing standards that only the largest fintech companies could meet could lead to industry consolidation and ultimately less innovation.

Certain commenters opposed to the charter challenged the OCC's chartering authority and suggested that a national bank charter for fintech companies could undermine the separation of banking and commerce.

Charter proponents and critics alike urged the OCC to establish clear supervisory standards in advance and to make the charter approval process transparent. Many commenters supported requiring fintech banks to demonstrate a commitment to financial inclusion.

The following sections of this statement address these and other key issues raised by commenters.

Consumer Protection

Several commenters expressed concern that granting a national bank charter to a fintech company would allow such a company to avoid state laws designed to protect consumers. Other commenters argued that federal preemption of state law could encourage charter shopping. In particular, some commenters expressed concern that SPNBs would not be subject to state laws prohibiting unfair or deceptive acts or practices. Further, some commenters stated that granting a national bank charter to fintech companies would weaken states' ability to enforce consumer protection laws by removing their visitorial oversight, thereby making it more difficult to investigate and prosecute potential violations of law.

The OCC disagrees. Consumer protection laws and enforcement activities vary from state to state. A fintech company that is approved for a national bank charter would be subject to consistent federal consumer protection standards and federal supervision and regulation.

With the passage of the Dodd–Frank Wall Street Reform and Consumer Protection Act of 2010 (Dodd–Frank Act), Congress expanded federal protections for consumers through the Consumer Financial Protection Act and the establishment of the Consumer Financial Protection Bureau (CFPB).[5] Other federal laws also contain extensive protections for consumers. The Federal Trade Commission Act (FTC Act) provides that "unfair or deceptive acts or practices in or affecting commerce" are unlawful.[6] The OCC enforces the FTC Act with respect to both insured

---

[5] For example, in addition to prohibiting unfair or deceptive acts or practices, the Dodd–Frank Act prohibits "abusive" acts or practices as well. Dodd–Frank, section 1031, codified at 12 USC 5531. The Dodd-Frank Act also generally preserves any state law that affords consumers greater protection than Title X of the Act, including with respect to unfair, deceptive, or abusive acts or practices. The Dodd–Frank Act, section 1041(a)(2), codified at 12 USC 5551(a)(2). Title X, section 1011(a), codified at 12 USC 5491(a), created the CFPB.

[6] See 15 USC 45(a)(1) and 15 USC 45(n). See also "FTC Policy Statement on Unfairness," Federal Trade

and uninsured national banks[7] and has taken a number of public enforcement actions against national banks for unfair or deceptive acts or practices.[8] Many state laws prohibiting unfair or deceptive acts or practices borrow FTC Act language and explicitly reference FTC standards and related judicial precedents. Consequently, OCC enforcement actions under the FTC Act often address the same conduct as is covered under the state "mini-FTC Acts."[9]

Congress has also carefully considered the OCC's use of federal preemption, and the Dodd-Frank Act clarified the standards and scope of the OCC's application of federal preemption for national banks and federal savings associations. The OCC acts in accordance with those provisions, which would also apply to the OCC's regulation of SPNBs. Thus, state law applies to an SPNB in the same way and to the same extent as it applies to other national banks. For example, state laws that address anti-discrimination, fair lending, debt collection, taxation, zoning, crime, and torts, generally apply to national banks and would also apply to SPNBs. In contrast to commenters' assertions, state laws that prohibit unfair or deceptive acts or practices, for example, business conduct laws that address consumer protection concerns such as material misrepresentations and omissions about products and services in billing, disclosure, and marketing materials, generally would apply to national banks, including SPNBs. The OCC understands that this would be the result even when the language of the state statute does not specifically refer to banks. Moreover, to the extent that a state law prohibiting unfair or deceptive acts or practices applies to a national bank and provides consumers with the right to bring a lawsuit against the bank, that remedy would be available against an SPNB. In addition, to the extent that a state law prohibiting unfair or deceptive acts or practices applies to a national bank and authorizes the state attorney general to enforce the law through judicial action, the state attorney general could bring an action in court against an SPNB for violation of the law.[10]

In addition to concerns regarding consumer protection laws, certain commenters expressed concerns that state laws establishing interest rate caps would be preempted for federally chartered banks. In particular, commenters warned that preemption and the availability of a fintech national bank charter could open the door for predatory lenders.

The OCC shares commenters' concerns about predatory lending and has taken significant steps to eliminate predatory, unfair, or deceptive practices in the federal banking system. For example, the OCC requires national banks engaged in lending to take into account the borrower's ability to repay the loan according to its terms.[11] Additionally, the OCC has cautioned national banks about lending activities that may be considered predatory, unfair, or deceptive, and notes

---

(Footnote Continued)

Commission (December 17, 1980); "FTC Policy Statement on Deception," Federal Trade Commission (October 14, 1983).

[7] See 12 USC 1818(b). OCC regulations regarding non-real estate and real estate lending, as well as the OCC's enforceable "Guidelines for Residential Mortgage Lending Practices," expressly reference the FTC standards. See 12 CFR 7.4008(c); 12 CFR 34.3(c); 12 CFR 30, appendix C. Further, OCC guidance also directly addresses unfair or deceptive acts or practices with respect to national banks. See OCC Advisory Letter 2002-3, "Guidance on Unfair or Deceptive Acts or Practices" (March 22, 2002); OCC Advisory Letter 2003-2, "Guidelines for National Banks to Guard Against Predatory and Abusive Lending Practices" (February 21, 2003) (OCC Advisory Letter 2003-2); OCC Advisory Letter 2003-3, "Avoiding Predatory and Abusive Lending Practices in Brokered and Purchased Loans" (February 21, 2003) (OCC Advisory Letter 2003-3); OCC Bulletin 2013-40, "Deposit Advance Products: Final Supervisory Guidance" (December 26, 2013) (OCC Bulletin 2013-40); OCC Bulletin 2014-37, "Risk Management Guidance: Consumer Debt Sales" (August 4, 2014) (OCC Bulletin 2014-37); and "Interagency Guidance Regarding Unfair or Deceptive Credit Practices" (August 22, 2014).

[8] For example, OCC actions have addressed national banks' failure to: provide sufficient information to allow consumers to understand the terms of the product or service being offered; adequately disclose when significant fees or similar material prerequisites are imposed in order to obtain the particular product or service being offered; and adequately disclose material limitations affecting the product or service being offered.

[9] Moreover, as explained in this statement, generally state laws prohibiting unfair or deceptive acts or practices are not preempted by either the FTC Act or the National Bank Act.

[10] See *Cuomo v. Clearing House Assn., LLC*, 557 U.S. 519 (2009).

[11] See, e.g., 12 CFR 7.4008(b) (secured consumer lending); 12 CFR 34.3(b) (secured consumer real estate lending). In addition, insured depository institutions must consider, as part of prudent credit underwriting practices, "the borrower's overall financial condition and resources . . . and the borrower's character and willingness to repay as agreed." See 12 CFR 30, appendix A, "Safety and Soundness Standards." As described in the draft Supplement, the OCC could impose special conditions on SPNBs that are similar to certain laws that apply by statute to only insured banks, to the extent appropriate given the business model and risk profile of the applicant.

that many of these lending practices already are unlawful under existing federal laws and regulations, including the FTC Act, and otherwise present significant safety and soundness and other risks. The highlighted practices include those that target prospective borrowers who cannot afford credit on the terms being offered, provide inadequate disclosures of the true costs and risks of transactions, involve loans with high fees and frequent renewals, or constitute loan "flipping" (frequent refinancings that result in little or no economic benefit to the borrower that are undertaken with the primary or sole objective of generating additional fees).[12] The OCC's policies establish that such practices conflict with the high standards expected of national banks and also present significant safety and soundness, reputation, and other risks.

The OCC does not approve charter applications from any company that plans to offer financial products and services with predatory, unfair, or deceptive features and so would not approve any such application from a fintech company. Further, the OCC takes appropriate supervisory action to ensure compliance with applicable laws, address unsafe or unsound banking practices, and prevent practices that harm consumers.[13]

Finally, it is important to remember that although a national bank can export the usury laws of the state in which it is located,[14] Congress provided this same benefit to state-chartered banks in 1980, by giving insured state banks the same ability as national banks to extend credit under their home state usury rules.

Small Business Protections

In addition to consumer protections, many commenters urged the OCC to address gaps in protection for small business customers. Some commenters suggested that the OCC look to the Small Business Borrowers' Bill of Rights, an agreement by certain online lenders to provide certain disclosures to small business borrowers. Others suggested that the OCC impose consumer protections whenever an individual may be held personally liable for the loan.

Some commenters argued against the OCC's imposition of small business borrower protections, however, noting that Congress has not extended consumer borrower protections to small businesses. They noted that Congress has repeatedly recognized important distinctions between individuals and small businesses, such as their level of sophistication. Some commenters warned that imposing any such requirements could impede the flow of capital to more sophisticated borrowers.

Other commenters argued that small business lending is regulated sufficiently by such laws as the Fair Credit Reporting Act, the Equal Credit Opportunity Act, and the FTC Act, and, thus, additional protections are not required. Some commenters urged the OCC to rely on industry developed standards and not impose standards of its own.

The OCC would take appropriate supervisory action to ensure compliance with all applicable laws,[15] including laws that address unfair or deceptive practices[16] that affect small business borrowers.[17] In addition, the OCC would expect an SPNB involved in lending to provide sufficient disclosures and clear information to ensure that all borrowers, including consumers and small businesses, can make informed credit decisions. The OCC recognizes the efforts by some companies in the online lending community to address this important issue. The OCC would look favorably on an applicant's commitment to educate small business borrowers about their rights and responsibilities.

Financial Inclusion

---

[12] See OCC Advisory Letter 2000-7, "Abusive Lending Practices" (July 25, 2000); OCC Advisory Letter 2000-10, "Payday Lending" (November 27, 2000); OCC Advisory Letter 2003-2; OCC Advisory Letter 2003-3; OCC Bulletin 2013-40; OCC Bulletin 2014-37.

[13] Federal consumer financial laws are supervised and enforced by either the OCC or CFPB as set forth in Title X of the Dodd–Frank Act.

[14] See 12 USC 85.

[15] Applicable laws include for example the Equal Credit Opportunity Act, the Fair Credit Reporting Act, and section 5 of the FTC Act.

[16] The FTC Act, by its terms, does not limit the prohibition against unfair or deceptive acts or practices to individual consumers. 15 USC 45(a) (". . . unfair or deceptive acts or practices in or affecting commerce, are hereby declared unlawful").

[17] As previously noted, federal consumer financial laws are enforced by either the OCC or CFPB, as set forth in Title X of the Dodd–Frank Act.

The OCC's statutory mission includes ensuring that national banks provide fair access to financial services and treat customers fairly.[18] To fulfill that mission, the OCC is guided by certain principles in determining whether to approve a charter application to establish a national bank. These principles include encouraging a national bank "to provide fair access to financial services by helping to meet the credit needs of its entire community" and "promoting fair treatment of customers, including efficiency and better service."[19]

The OCC requires an applicant for a traditional national bank charter to submit a business plan that demonstrates how the proposed bank plans to respond to the needs of the community, consistent with the safe and sound operation of the bank.[20] As outlined in appendix B to the draft Supplement, the OCC also would expect an applicant for an SPNB charter that intends to engage in lending or provide financial services to consumers or small businesses to include a financial inclusion plan as a component of its business plan. The nature of the commitment would depend on the entity's business model and the types of products or services it intends to provide.

The OCC received many comments on whether it should seek a financial inclusion commitment from SPNBs and how these institutions could promote financial inclusion. Many commenters argued that SPNBs can provide valuable services to underserved communities and should make a commitment to financial inclusion. They urged the OCC to require financial inclusion plans that include measurable goals and are formulated with input from the community. Without requiring a financial inclusion commitment, one commenter warned, many individuals and communities could remain underserved.

Other commenters were opposed to requiring such a commitment. Some commenters suggested that fintech companies naturally promote financial inclusion, and therefore no formal commitment is necessary.

Many commenters urged the OCC to be flexible in evaluating how different SPNBs promote financial inclusion. Some commenters proposed specific activities SPNBs could engage in to demonstrate their commitment. For example, a number of commenters suggested that SPNBs could establish financial literacy programs or provide funding for credit building and credit counseling services in low- and moderate-income communities. Other commenters viewed partnerships and investments as promising means for SPNBs to promote financial inclusion. Some commenters specifically identified Community Development Financial Institutions as potential partners or investments for SPNBs.

The OCC agrees that many fintech companies have significant potential to expand access to financial services. To help ensure that this potential is realized, the OCC would expect a formal commitment to, and plan for, financial inclusion from SPNBs engaged in lending activities or providing financial services to consumers or small businesses.

The OCC also agrees that there are many different activities SPNBs could engage in to promote financial inclusion. The OCC encourages the development of innovative products or services designed to address the needs of low- and moderate-income individuals and communities. SPNBs could also demonstrate their commitment to financial inclusion in more traditional ways. For example, the OCC has supported national banks' participation in programs, such as financial literacy and credit counseling services, that improve individuals' understanding of the financial products and services that meet their needs. Investments in certain funds or organizations may also be part of an effective financial inclusion plan. The OCC looks forward to working with potential SPNB applicants on both new and conventional ways to promote financial inclusion.

Regulatory and Supervisory Standards

The OCC has been clear that it would hold companies granted SPNB charters to the same high standards of safety, soundness, and fairness that all other federally chartered banks must meet. As it does for all banks, the OCC would tailor these requirements based on the bank's size, complexity, and risk, consistent with applicable law. While most commenters agreed with that standard, some commenters urged the OCC to be flexible in its regulation and supervision of fintech companies that become national banks. For example, certain commenters questioned whether start-up fintech companies would be able to meet the OCC's standards, even when tailored to the companies' size, risk, and complexity. These commenters asked whether the OCC would consider adapting its standards for fintech start-ups, with some suggesting that the OCC consider separate, more lenient standards for start-ups.

---

[18] See 12 USC 1(a).

[19] See 12 CFR 5.20(f)(1)(ii) and (iv).

[20] See 12 CFR 5.20(h)(5).

The OCC is sensitive to commenters' concerns regarding the need for appropriate standards. As the prudential regulator for approximately 1,400 national banks and federal savings associations, including nearly 1,200 community banks and savings associations, the OCC is experienced in evaluating whether a proposed bank would be able to meet the criteria to become an SPNB. Size alone is not a disqualifying factor. As explained in the draft Supplement, there are, however, certain minimum statutory and regulatory standards an institution must meet to qualify for a national bank charter. For example, an applicant must demonstrate that the bank has a reasonable chance of success, will operate in a safe and sound manner, and will foster healthy competition. In evaluating whether an institution meets those standards, the OCC considers, among other factors, whether the organizers and proposed management have the appropriate skills and experience to operate as a national bank. Further, banks must maintain sufficient liquidity and adequate capital. Additional criteria are outlined in the draft Supplement and the "Charters" booklet of the *Comptroller's Licensing Manual.*

Other commenters emphasized the need for flexibility to give SPNBs the ability to innovate rapidly. For example, some commenters expressed concern that the OCC may require SPNBs to obtain the OCC's approval before making significant deviations from their business plans and that such a requirement could make them less nimble. Specifically, these commenters referred to the condition imposed on all de novo banks to provide notice and obtain a supervisory non-objection letter from the OCC before making significant deviations from their approved business plans.

The OCC recognizes that certain deviations may be necessary and desirable to meet changes in market conditions or to introduce technological innovations that improve the customer experience. As explained in appendix F of the "Charters" booklet, however, new banks are particularly vulnerable to significant internal and external risks until they achieve a certain level of stability and profitability. The significant deviation condition provides the OCC with the opportunity to evaluate whether a proposed change could significantly increase a bank's risk profile and whether the bank can properly manage any increased risk.

It is also important to understand that the condition does not apply to all changes, just those changes that constitute significant deviations from a bank's business plan.[21] For example, a bank may decide to significantly reduce its emphasis on its targeted niche (e.g., consumer or small business lending) in favor of expanding into another area (e.g., payments processing). In that case, the bank would need to obtain the OCC's supervisory non-objection before undertaking changes to its business plan or operations. The significant deviation condition, however, would not preclude limited testing or piloting of new products or services, provided the bank has put in place appropriate internal controls and protections for targeted customers.

Capital and Liquidity Requirements

Commenters also addressed potential capital and liquidity requirements for SPNBs. Some commenters felt strongly that capital and liquidity requirements should be as consistent with current national bank chartering requirements as possible. They argued that without consistent requirements, fintech companies chartered as special purpose national banks would have a competitive advantage. Others held that capital and liquidity requirements should be commensurate with the scope of activities contemplated in the company's charter application. Some commenters recommended that a fintech company chartered as a special purpose national bank only be required to have the capital and liquidity necessary to wind down its business plan without harming customers in the event of failure. Along these lines, some suggested that companies with simpler business models or a narrower range of services, such as an online lending platform, should have lower capital requirements than full-service national banks.

Capital

Like all national banks, SPNBs would be subject to the leverage and risk-based capital requirements in 12 CFR 3. As commenters pointed out, however, for any entities that have few on-balance-sheet exposures, it will be necessary to tailor an SPNB's capital requirements to capture the different risks associated with limited balance sheets or nontraditional strategies. The OCC acknowledges that the minimum capital requirements set forth in 12 CFR 3, which measure

---

[21] See appendix F, "Significant Deviations After Opening," of the *Comptroller's Licensing Manual,* "Charters," pp. 105-06. The "Charters" booklet defines "significant deviation" as a "material variance from the bank's business plan or operations, or introduction of any new product, service, or activity or change in market that was not part of the approved business plan." Significant deviations may include, but are not limited to, significant deviations in the bank's projected growth, business strategy, lines of business, or funding sources.

regulatory capital levels relative to an entity's assets and off-balance-sheet exposures, may not be sufficient for measuring capital adequacy for some SPNBs. In those cases, the OCC will use alternative approaches to determine the appropriate capital requirement. As noted in the draft Supplement, the OCC has considerable experience imposing individual capital and liquidity requirements when appropriate.

Beyond those minimum requirements, capital levels must be commensurate with the risk and complexity of the bank's proposed activities (including on- and off-balance-sheet activities). The OCC's evaluation of capital adequacy considers the risks and complexities of the proposed products, services, and operating characteristics, taking into account factors such as the scope and nature of the bank's proposed activities, quality of management, and stability or volatility of sources of funds. The OCC also considers on- and off-balance-sheet composition, credit risk, concentration, and market risk.

Liquidity

As with capital, the OCC would consider any applicant's specific business model when evaluating its liquidity profile and liquidity risk management. For other types of special purpose national banks, the OCC has imposed tailored requirements to ensure adequate liquidity. Such requirements could include entering into a liquidity maintenance agreement with a parent company or maintaining a certain amount of high-quality liquid assets.

Some commenters urged the OCC to require SPNBs to assess their liquidity needs over various periods and scenarios, including normal and stressed conditions. They highlighted that many fintech companies emerged during a period of strong credit conditions and have not yet been tested throughout a full credit cycle. One commenter suggested that fintech companies chartered as national banks engaged in lending be required to have adequate funds to meet a specified level of future loan originations, to ensure lending continues during a liquidity crisis.

The OCC is aware that many companies and business models have not yet operated in stressed conditions. As a result, the OCC expects any charter applicant to consider and address, among other items, projected borrowing capacity under normal and adverse market conditions. For instance, a fintech bank could establish a minimum number of months of current projected operating expenses to maintain adequate liquidity. In addition, the OCC believes SPNBs should establish comprehensive contingency funding plans, just as other national banks do.

Charter Application Process

While many commenters wanted flexible and tailored regulation, they also advocated for a clear understanding of the standards that would apply during the chartering process. In particular, they urged the OCC to make the application process transparent by establishing at the outset the conditions a fintech company would be required to meet. Other commenters advised the OCC to adopt a clear definition of "fintech" and identify the types of companies the OCC views as eligible for an SPNB charter.

Commenters also expressed concern that having the OCC make chartering decisions on a case-by-case basis could lead to inconsistent treatment. Certain commenters were concerned that exercising such broad discretion could put the OCC in the position of picking winners and losers. To ensure consistent treatment, a number of commenters urged the OCC to outline the criteria for charter approval clearly, limit the use of charter conditions and operating agreements, and make chartering decisions, including applicable conditions, publicly available.

The OCC strives to make the charter application process clear, understandable, and transparent. The OCC provides detailed information about this process in its charter regulation at 12 CFR 5.20 and in the "Charters" booklet. These materials list the OCC's criteria and requirements for charter approvals of national banks, including special purpose national banks. As discussed above, the OCC is also issuing for public comment a draft Supplement to the *Comptroller's Licensing Manual* for any fintech companies seeking an SPNB charter. In addition, applicants would have an opportunity to ask questions about the process, including the conditions for approval, through multiple prefiling meetings with OCC Licensing and supervisory staff. The OCC's Office of Innovation also is available to facilitate the application process.

The decision to impose special conditions for approval of a charter application is made on the basis of many factors, including the applicant's business plan, proposed management, and relevant experience. Conditions may be imposed directly in the preliminary approval letter, or the OCC may require as a condition of approval that the applicant enter into an operating agreement. The operating agreement may impose safeguards to address certain aspects of a bank's operations, including growth, capital, or liquidity. The OCC publishes all conditional approvals, which disclose the existence of an operating agreement.

As the prudential regulator for national banks and federal savings associations, the OCC must exercise its judgment in deciding whether to approve a national bank charter to a particular company. As explained in the "Charters" booklet and the draft Supplement, the OCC's decision to approve a charter is guided by its mission to promote a vibrant and diverse banking system that benefits consumers, communities, businesses, and the U.S. economy. In general, the OCC would approve applications to charter an SPNB from any companies that have a reasonable chance of success, will provide fair access to financial services, will ensure compliance with applicable laws and regulations, and will promote fair treatment of customers and foster healthy competition.[22]

Coordination Among Regulators

Many commenters urged the OCC to coordinate with other federal and state regulators to provide consistency and clarity regarding the regulation of fintech companies. Some commenters suggested this coordination could be achieved by the creation of an interagency working group or a special subcommittee of the Federal Financial Institutions Examination Council (FFIEC).

The OCC agrees with commenters that coordination among federal and state regulators is essential to fostering responsible financial innovation. The OCC will continue to engage with other regulators in a collaborative way regarding financial technology to promote a common understanding and consistent application of laws, regulations, and guidance. The OCC regularly coordinates with other state and federal banking regulators through its participation in the FFIEC. For example, the OCC participated in the FFIEC's cybersecurity initiative to raise financial institutions' awareness of cybersecurity concerns and strengthen the oversight of cybersecurity readiness.[23] The OCC also currently chairs the FFIEC Task Force on Consumer Compliance. In addition, the OCC collaborates with the CFPB on consumer-related matters, and the OCC is an active member of many of the U.S. Department of the Treasury's working groups and committees, including one for marketplace lending. The OCC also co-chairs the Basel Committee's Task Force on Financial Technology (TFFT).[24] The OCC will continue to leverage these channels of communication to collaborate and share information regarding the chartering and supervision of SPNBs.

Depending on the structure of a fintech bank and the activities it conducts, other regulators may have oversight roles as well. As a result, any fintech company considering an SPNB charter likely will need to engage with other regulators in addition to the OCC. In considering applications, the OCC would coordinate as appropriate with other federal regulators with jurisdiction over the SPNB, including to facilitate simultaneous consideration of any applications or approvals that may be required by those regulators.

Ongoing Supervision

Commenters questioned how the OCC would supervise fintech companies that become national banks. Several commenters asserted that SPNBs should be subject to the same oversight and regular examination as traditional banks. Specifically, commenters noted the importance of having regular, rigorous examinations to ensure compliance with requirements regarding safety and soundness, Bank Secrecy Act/anti-money laundering (BSA/AML) provisions, financial inclusion, fair lending, and other applicable laws. Other commenters asserted that the OCC did not have the resources or expertise necessary to properly supervise fintech companies that would become SPNBs.

As discussed in appendix A of the draft Supplement, an SPNB would be subject to the same oversight and supervision as other national banks. The OCC's supervisory process for all national banks and federal savings associations establishes minimum supervisory standards, reflects the unique characteristics of each institution, and is responsive to changes within individual institutions and the markets where they compete. Consistent with the OCC's supervision of other national banks, the OCC's supervisory strategy for SPNBs would be tailored to each bank's

---

[22] The charter regulation, 12 CFR 5.20(e), *Comptroller's Licensing Manual*, "Charters," and the draft Supplement outline the factors the OCC considers in reviewing a charter application.

[23] FFIEC Cybersecurity Awareness Initiative, available at https://www.ffiec.gov/cybersecurity.htm.

[24] The TFFT fosters financial stability through the assessment of the risks and supervisory challenges associated with innovation and technological changes affecting banking. The TFFT's work is currently focused on the impact that fintech has on banks and banks' business models, and the implications this has for supervision.

business model and include on-site and off-site supervisory activities conducted by an experienced, knowledgeable examination team.

The OCC has technical expertise in a number of areas that would likely be relevant for a newly chartered SPNB, including compliance with capital, liquidity, risk management, and consumer protection requirements. As it does with any other de novo charter, the OCC would leverage those examiners who have expertise appropriate for the bank's business model and activities. Likewise, dedicated licensing specialists, economists, other subject matter experts (e.g., those specialized in credit risk, compliance, financial inclusion, BSA/AML, operational risk, cybersecurity, or information technology), lawyers, and other staff would be assigned to individual charters, as appropriate, to support their supervision. For example, the examination team for a fintech company specializing in payment processing technology would be assisted by the OCC's Payments Systems Policy Group, whose expertise includes the latest innovations in payments systems, including distributed ledger technology. In addition, the OCC has significant experience assisting national banks in their assessment and management of risks associated with technology service providers and other third-party relationships.[25] Further, to ensure consistency in OCC supervision, a dedicated Assistant Deputy Comptroller would oversee any SPNB.

Other commenters noted the importance of ensuring that SPNBs maintain robust compliance and risk management programs. As detailed in the draft Supplement, the OCC would require any SPNB to establish and maintain well-developed, robust compliance and risk management programs that address, among other things, BSA/AML, consumer protection, third-party risk management, and data and information security requirements. The OCC expects a bank's risk management systems to be commensurate to the size, complexity, and risks of its activities. Regardless of the risk management program's design, it should address the following: risk identification, risk measurement, risk monitoring, and risk control. For example, the OCC would expect SPNBs to have a rigorous cybersecurity framework in place to assess cybersecurity risks and respond to, manage, and defend against cyber attacks.

Some commenters recommended that the OCC develop and deploy technology to modernize its approach to regulation and supervision. The OCC is committed to broadening and increasing its expertise in areas related to innovation. As part of its Responsible Innovation initiative, the OCC is open to considering ways current procedures and processes can be improved through the use of technology.

Chartering Authority

Some commenters questioned the OCC's authority to charter SPNBs that are not authorized to offer FDIC-insured deposits. They asserted that the OCC could only charter non-deposit-taking banks when expressly authorized by statute, as is the case for trust banks, bankers' banks, and credit card banks. In these commenters' view, to be chartered as a national bank under the National Bank Act, the bank must engage in the "business of banking," which they suggest requires, at a minimum, taking deposits.

Under the National Bank Act, the OCC has broad authority to grant charters for national banks to carry on the "business of banking." The OCC has interpreted the "business of banking" to include any of the three core banking functions of receiving deposits, paying checks, or lending money. The Act does not require that a bank take deposits in order to be engaged in the "business of banking." Rather, under the Act, performing only one of these three activities is sufficient to be performing core banking functions. This is reflected in the OCC's regulation 12 CFR 5.20, which provides that, to be eligible for a national bank charter, a special purpose bank must either be engaged in fiduciary activities or conduct at least one of three core banking functions: receiving deposits, paying checks, or lending money.

Separation of Banking and Commerce

Some commenters expressed concern that granting a national bank charter to a non-depository fintech company could erode the traditional separation of banking and commerce. As noted in the draft Supplement and above, the OCC will not approve charter proposals that would result in the inappropriate commingling of banking and commerce. Such proposals could introduce into the banking system risks associated with nonbanking commercial activities, interfere with the efficient allocation of credit throughout the U.S. economy, and foster anti-competitive effects and undesirable concentrations of economic power.

---

[25] See OCC Bulletin 2013-29, "Third-Party Relationships: Risk Management Guidance" (October 30, 2013).

Conclusion

The OCC appreciates the suggestions, issues, and concerns raised in the more than 100 comment letters that we received in response to the SPNB Paper. These comments informed our development of the draft Supplement, which explains how the OCC would evaluate applications from fintech companies for SPNB charters. For more information about the envisioned application process for fintech companies seeking an SPNB charter, please refer to the draft *Comptroller's Licensing Manual Supplement: Evaluating Charter Applications From Financial Technology Companies.*

The OCC will accept comments on the Supplement through close of business April 14, 2017. Comments should be submitted to specialpurposecharter@occ.treas.gov.

¶ 1360 Exploring Special Purpose National Bank Charters for Fintech Companies

January 13, 2017

Office of the Comptroller of the Currency (OCC)

Legislative and Regulatory Activities Division

400 7th Street SW, Suite 3E-218

Mail Stop 9W-11 Washington, DC 20219

Re: Exploring Special Purpose National Bank Charters for Fintech Companies

Dear Comptroller Curry,

The Conference of State Bank Supervisors appreciates the opportunity to comment on the white paper, titled *Exploring Special Purpose National Bank Charters for Fintech Companies*, announcing the Office of the Comptroller of the Currency's (hereinafter "OCC" or "Comptroller") intention to "move forward with chartering financial technology companies that offer bank products and services."

CSBS is the nationwide organization of state banking and financial services regulators from all 50 U.S. states, the District of Columbia, Guam, Puerto Rico, and the U.S. Virgin Islands. For more than a century, CSBS has given state bank and financial services regulators a national forum to coordinate bank and nondepository supervision and to develop regulatory policy. As the chartering, licensing and supervisory authorities for over 75% of the banks in the United States and over 20,000 nondepository financial services providers, State regulators are charged with protecting consumers, ensuring safety and soundness, and encouraging economic prosperity in their states.

As stated in our November 2016 comment letter to the OCC[1], state bank regulators oppose the creation of a special purpose national bank charter for financial technology (fintech) and other nondepository companies because:

    1. The OCC lacks statutory authority to issue such a charter;

    2. Such a charter will distort the marketplace for financial services, with a federal agency arbitrarily picking winners and losers;

    3. The issuance of such a charter creates tremendous uncertainty and risks pertaining to access to critical government resources, including the payments system and the federal safety net; and

    4. The preemptive effect of this charter nullifies the states' ability to protect consumers.

This comment letter will provide an overview of the reasons underlying our opposition to the OCC creating a special purpose national bank charter for fintech and other nondepository companies (hereinafter "special purpose national nonbank charter" or "special purpose national nonbank"). Additionally, we have attached a Legal and Policy Assessment that provides a more in-depth discussion of the unlawful and invalid nature of a special purpose national nonbank charter, the many unsettling policy implications resulting from the Comptroller acting outside the confines of its statutory chartering authority, the many legal uncertainties and policy issues stemming from the unlawful nature of a special purpose nonbank charter, and the dangerous consequences stemming from the preemption of state laws through such a charter.

I. The OCC's proposed special purpose "fintech" charter is inconsistent with the letter and intent of the National Bank Act.

The OCC claims, citing its chartering regulations, that it has the authority to charter a special purpose bank to conduct any activity within the business of banking so long as it engages in receiving deposits, lending money, or paying checks. Consequently, the OCC claims to have the statutory authority to charter a special purpose national nonbank—that is, a special purpose bank that does not engage in deposit-taking and only engages in lending money or paying checks.

---

[1] CSBS's previous comment letter on the OCC's proposed rule establishing a framework to govern receiverships for uninsured national banks is available at: CSBS   Comment Letter on Proposed Rule on Receiverships for Uninsured National Banks.

However, as CSBS has set out in previous comments to the OCC and reiterates with this letter, the OCC lacks any statutory authority to charter a special purpose national nonbank.

A. Special purpose national nonbanks cannot lawfully be formed under any type of special purpose bank charter.

Courts have held and Congress has made clear that the Comptroller is prohibited from chartering a national bank that does not engage in deposit-taking, unless the charter is for a special purpose bank expressly authorized in statute.[2] The special purpose banks expressly authorized by Congress are trust banks, bankers' banks, and credit card banks. Since Congress has not expressly authorized the Comptroller to issue a special purpose nonbank charter, any attempt to grant a special purpose national bank charter to such an institution would be unlawful and invalid.

B. Special purpose national nonbanks cannot lawfully be formed under a full-service bank charter.

According to the white paper, the Comptroller proposes that these newly chartered entities would have "the same charter as a full-service national bank." However, since a special purpose national nonbank would not be engaged in deposit-taking, the Comptroller is prohibited from granting it a full-service national bank charter.[3] Full-service national banks are chartered to engage in the "business of banking". Engaging in the "business of banking" under the National Bank Act, as a matter of law[4] and as a matter of common sense, requires engaging in deposit-taking. Thus, any attempt to grant a full-service national bank charter to a special purpose national nonbank would be unlawful and invalid.

C. Special purpose national nonbank charters would be unlawful and invalid.

Therefore, since (1) the granting of a special purpose nonbank charter has not been expressly authorized by Congress, and since (2) a special purpose nonbank would not engage in deposit-taking, the Comptroller lacks the authority to charter a special purpose nonbank. Accordingly, regardless of what the Comptroller's regulations provide, any attempt by the Comptroller to charter a special purpose nonbank would be unlawful and invalid.[5] State regulators urge the Comptroller to avoid taking the unlawful action contemplated in the white paper, for the creation of a national nonbank charter would be an unauthorized and unprecedented expansion of the Comptroller's chartering authority, distorting the purpose for which the national banking system was established.

II. The OCC's proposed "fintech" charter destabilizes banking's legal and regulatory structure.

A. Most federal banking laws will not apply to the OCC's proposed special purpose nonbanks.

The special purpose national nonbank that the OCC proposes to charter would not be subject to the clear majority of federal banking laws. For instance, these special purpose nonbanks would be exempt from many of the statutes and regulations that apply to insured depository institutions, including prompt corrective action requirements, source of strength requirements, restrictions on management interlocks, generally applicable prudential safeguards, community reinvestment act requirements, and uniform accounting standards. This notable absence of generally applicable federal banking laws covering special purpose nonbanks clearly evidences that Congress has not contemplated the creation of a special purpose national nonbank charter.

---

[2] For a more in-depth analysis of the applicable precedent and applicable federal statutes, see Part I.B.2. of the Assessment.

[3] While the Comptroller may claim that a special purpose nonbank would receive a full-service charter and voluntarily refrain from receiving deposits, such a legal machination does not escape the rule that a charter recipient must exercise the power to receive deposits for the Comptroller to have the authority to grant a full-service national bank charter. Additionally, such a chartering structure places an improper reliance on the OCC's enforcement authority to bolster its chartering authority, as discussed in Part I.B.2. of the Assessment, and will have

numerous unsettling policy implications, as discussed in Part II of the Assessment.

[4] See *Independent Bankers Ass'n of America v. Conover*, 1985 U.S. Dist. LEXIS 22529, at *34 -*36 (M.D. Fla. Feb. 15, 1985) (*IBAA v. Conover*).

[5] The chartering of a special purpose nonbank would not be the first time that the OCC has attempted to charter a special purpose institution which it lacks the authority to charter. For a discussion of the history of the OCC's special purpose chartering authority and Congressional reactions to the OCC's unlawful chartering attempts, see Part I.B.1. of the Assessment.

The OCC has intentionally structured the special purpose nonbank charter to evade the application of certain federal banking laws. For instance, a special purpose nonbank is specifically designed to avoid being classified as a "bank" for purposes of the Bank Holding Company Act. Evading this Act means that special purpose nonbanks would not be subject to consolidated supervision by the Federal Reserve and the parent companies of special purpose nonbanks would not be subject to the anti-tying rules, restrictions on proprietary trading, and restrictions on affiliations with commercial companies.

Even under the National Bank Act—the enabling statute that purportedly authorizes the grant of nonbank charters—the treatment of special purpose nonbanks is uncertain. For instance, the scope of the incidental powers granted to a special purpose nonbank cannot be clearly delineated, given that the currently authorized incidental powers were permitted on the basis that they would be exercised by institutions that exercise all the express powers granted under the National Bank Act. There is similar uncertainty surrounding how branching requirements will apply.

Furthermore, whether a special purpose nonbank would be required to be a Federal Reserve member and the consequences of membership for a special purpose nonbank are also unclear. Moreover, it is uncertain whether a special purpose nonbank would be eligible for access to Federal Reserve services, including gaining access to the payments systems and the discount window. As discussed more fully in Part II.B. of the Assessment, state regulators believe it would be unwise to provide unfettered access to Federal Reserve services, particularly the payments systems, to special purpose national nonbanks because they refrain from engaging in the business of receiving deposits.

B. The OCC proposes an ad-hoc, confidential regulatory framework that will create an unlevel playing field.

Even more unsettling is the regulatory and supervisory framework proposed by the OCC to compensate for the legal chasm in which special purpose nonbanks will operate. In the white paper, the OCC states that it will incorporate otherwise inapplicable rules or impose equivalent requirements by entering into operating agreements with charter recipients which are enforceable under the OCC's enforcement authority. In the absence of generally applicable federal banking laws to govern the operations of special purpose nonbanks, the OCC will have absolute discretion as to whether and to what extent otherwise inapplicable rules will be made applicable through operating agreements.

The white paper makes clear that the operating agreements will be completely individualized to the business model of the charter recipient. This lack of transparency and certainty leaves the general public and potential applicants completely in the dark as to the rules and requirements in key areas such as the Community Reinvestment Act, capital, liquidity, and other "baseline supervisory expectations." Furthermore, charter recipients and the industry generally will have no assurance that rules will be applied and enforced in a uniform, impartial manner, and, because the operating agreements will not be made publicly available, no means of verifying any assurances given.

As fully discussed in Part II.A of the Assessment, the inevitable result of the OCC's proposed supervisory framework will be an unlevel playing field to the disadvantage of traditional, full-service banks. Equally important, due to the ad-hoc, opaque nature of the operating agreements, the OCC will have the unchecked power to favor certain applicants over others, thereby picking winners and losers. Most startups do not have profitable business plans, and only a limited number of established financial technology firms have annual profits. These are not the companies who will enjoy the benefits of the proposed charter. Additionally, the lack of transparency and absence of objective requirements in the proposed supervisory framework for special purpose nonbanks will have a deleterious effect on the ability of new financial innovation to emerge going forward. In short, the special purpose nonbank charter proposed by the OCC will benefit large incumbent firms with established business model and create a barrier to entry for the vast majority of emerging fintech firms.

C. Special purpose nonbanks may be exempt from the OCC's enforcement authority under federal securities laws.

The treatment of special purpose national nonbanks under federal securities laws, although not discussed in the white paper, is an issue of major importance. As discussed in more detail in Part III.D. of the Assessment, while special purpose nonbanks will enjoy exemptions under several federal securities laws, there are serious questions as to whether the enforcement authority delegated to the Comptroller under such laws is sufficient to enable the Comptroller to apply and enforce these laws to institutions that refrain from engaging in the business of receiving deposits.

D. Special purpose national nonbanks will not be subject to federal consumer financial laws to the same extent as full-service banks.

Lastly, the applicability of federal consumer financial law to special purpose nonbanks chartered by the Comptroller while relatively less uncertain is telling in that it demonstrates how the Comptroller will generally apply and enforce otherwise inapplicable laws through the proposed operating agreements. The white paper discusses how only a handful of federal consumer financial laws will apply to special purpose nonbanks, namely, those that apply to nondepository covered persons. However, as discussed more fully in Part III.E. of the Assessment, the Comptroller fails to acknowledge and apparently refuses to utilize the broader authority granted to the OCC under the Dodd-Frank Act to apply and enforce the totality of federal consumer financial law under its general enforcement authority. State regulators believe that the OCC's failure to use its enforcement authority to its fullest extent in the consumer protection context does not bode well for the uniform application and robust enforcement of otherwise inapplicable federal banking, securities, and consumer protection laws.

III. The OCC's proposed "fintech" charter eliminates states' consumer protection authority.

State regulators have witnessed OCC preemption determinations hurt consumers through the preemption of anti-predatory lending laws, adjustable rate mortgage restrictions, and state oversight of national bank operating subsidiaries. This consistent effort by the OCC to preempt state consumer protection laws created the legal foundation for the mortgage crisis and prevented states from having the opportunity to respond to lending practices that hurt consumers. Congress recognized this in the Dodd-Frank Act, repealing the OCC's preemption of state supervision of national bank operating subsidiaries, requiring the CFPB to determine whether OCC preemption determinations are tenable, and lowering the agency deference available to the OCC on preemption challenges. Unilateral chartering decisions by the OCC defies the requirements imposed on the OCC by Congress.

In addition to supervising approximately 4,790 state-chartered banks, most state banking departments also regulate a variety of nondepository financial services providers, including money transmitters, mortgage lenders, and consumer lenders. Based on the OCC's description of the "fintech" charter, any of these 20,000 plus companies would qualify for a national bank charter because they pay checks or lend money. Time and again, Congress has made the conscious decision to reserve the licensure and supervision of institutions engaged in these nondepository activities to the states, choosing to pass activity-based laws like the Electronic Funds Transaction Act, not federal chartering laws.

States require nondepositories to meet safety and soundness requirements and conform to both state and federal consumer protection laws through a state licensing process. Multi-state nondepository companies are examined on a collaborative basis with multi-state teams, reducing regulatory burden and improving allocation of resources among states. As proposed, and without any discussion, a special purpose national bank charter will preempt this regulatory framework for any charter recipient.

IV. Conclusion

State bank regulators appreciate the opportunity to comment on the OCC's white paper announcing their intention to charter a special purpose nonbank through an unprecedented expansion of their chartering authority. As discussed above and in the attached Legal and Policy assessment, state regulators have several significant concerns with how the OCC's existing statutory chartering authority could provide any valid basis for the OCC to charter a special purpose nonbank engaged exclusively in nondepository core banking functions. Additionally, state bank supervisors believe significant risks and costs are likely to result from an expansive, unprecedented use of the OCC's chartering authority. Contrary to the OCC's assertions, a level-playing field between the proposed charter type and the financial services industry is not feasible given the lack of both transparency and impartiality inherent in the proposed chartering framework.

As fellow chartering and regulatory authorities, the members of CSBS take great pride in our long history of promoting the strength and vitality of the dual-banking system. As state regulators continue to work with each other and our federal regulatory counterparts to foster a regulatory and supervisory environment that promotes innovative practices in the delivery of financial services, we encourage the Comptroller to respect the balance of federal and state authority in the regulation of financial services and to avoid undermining the effectiveness and impairing the vitality of the dual-banking system.

Sincerely,

John W. Ryan

President & CEO

Attachment: CSBS Legal and Policy Assessment

CONFERENCE OF STATE BANK SUPERVISORS

CSBS Legal and Policy Assessment

CSBS has attached this legal and policy assessment to our comment letter to discuss, in greater detail, our perspective as to how the Comptroller's unauthorized expansion of its chartering authority will create a multitude of hazards for consumers, the financial services industry, and the broader regulatory community.

In Part I, CSBS discusses the unprecedented and unauthorized nature of the special purpose charter proposed in the white paper in the context of the history and limits of the Comptroller's chartering authority. Part II discusses the unsettling policy implications that State regulators believe are prompted by the Comptroller's proposed expansion of its chartering authority, including the inevitability of an unlevel playing field in favor of the proposed special purpose charter. In Part III, CSBS discusses the tremendous legal uncertainty surrounding the treatment of the proposed type of special purpose charter under federal banking law, federal securities law, and federal consumer protection law. Lastly, in Part IV, State bank regulators share our perspective on the dangers of preempting state laws, including state consumer protection law.

I. Statutory Limits of the OCC's Chartering Authority

In the OCC's white paper, the Comptroller has asserted the authority to charter a new type of special purpose institution, which would not carry on the business of banking and which has not been specifically authorized by Congress. This Part will demonstrate that the Comptroller has no statutory authority under the NBA or other federal banking laws to approve any new type of special purpose charter, and the Comptroller has no authority to issue any regulation that would expand the limits of the chartering authority established by Congress. In the sections that follow, we set out that (1) the Comptroller lacks the requisite statutory authority to charter institutions whose activities are limited to lending money and/or paying checks or functionally similar activities (hereinafter "special purpose nonbank charters" or "special purpose nonbanks"), and (2) due to this insufficient statutory authority, the Comptroller has no power to bootstrap his chartering authority through an unauthorized, unprecedented, and arbitrary reliance on the agency's enforcement authority.

A. National banks must be chartered either to carry on the business of banking, or to engage exclusively in a special purpose activity expressly authorized by Congress.

1. Full-service national banks may be formed only to engage in the business of banking which includes, at minimum, engaging in deposit-taking.

Since the enactment of the National Bank Act (NBA) in 1863, the Comptroller has been authorized to charter "associations for carrying on the business of banking" (hereinafter "full-service national banks"). In the NBA, the phrase "business of banking" not only refers to the enumerated and incidental powers of national banks, but also serves to limit what constitutes a valid exercise of the Comptroller's chartering authority.[1] While the business of national banks has evolved and fluctuated over time, it remains as true today as it did in 1863 that an institution cannot carry on the "business of banking" under the NBA unless it is endowed with and actually exercises the power to receive deposits.

Unlike the many other enumerated powers of national banks, the receiving of deposits has always been recognized as the minimum essential element of, and the necessary condition to carry on, the "business of banking" under the NBA. A private company could conceivably carry on every other activity within the business of banking without obtaining a bank charter. However, when such a company supplements any of those activities by engaging in the business of receiving

---

[1] *See* 12 U.S.C. §§ 21, 26-27.

deposits, the entire character of the institution's business is transformed, for its business thereby becomes intimately connected with the public interest and, accordingly, it is required to obtain a bank charter.[2]

Most importantly, as a necessary condition for "carrying on the business of banking", granting the power to receive deposits to a national bank is a necessary condition for the valid exercise of the Comptroller's chartering authority, in the absence of a specific grant of congressional authority for chartering a special purpose national bank.

2. Special purpose national banks may be formed only to engage in special purpose activities expressly authorized by Congress.

When, as today, the Comptroller has attempted to charter institutions that intend to refrain from receiving deposits, it has been held that specific statutory authorization is required to charter such institutions. Courts have declared that the Comptroller is not empowered by the NBA to charter nondepository institutions that do not carry on the business of banking, unless specifically authorized by Congress. As detailed in this Part, Congress, through narrowly-drawn amendments to the NBA and the Bank Holding Company Act (BHC Act), has specifically authorized the Comptroller to charter certain special purpose institutions that could not otherwise be chartered by the Comptroller because they do not carry on the "business of banking", including trust banks, bankers' banks, and credit card banks.

3. A new type of special purpose charter not expressly authorized by Congress may not be created through the grant of a full-service charter.

In the white paper, the OCC asserts the authority to grant charters to special purpose national banks that limit their activities to any activity within the business of banking as long as they conduct at least one of the following three core banking functions: receiving deposits, paying checks, or lending money. According to the OCC, it has statutory authority to charter special purpose nonbanks, that is, institutions which refrain from accepting deposits and exclusively engage in the nondepository core banking functions of paying checks or lending money (or functionally similar activities). Presumably, the OCC bases this asserted authority on the false premise that the authority to charter full-service national banks to carry on the business of banking implies the authority to charter special purpose national banks, including special purpose nonbanks. Put differently, the Comptroller incorrectly asserts that an implicit grant of special purpose chartering authority can be derived from its traditional, full-service chartering authority.

B. OCC's special purpose chartering authority is limited in scope and distinct from its full-service chartering authority.

The OCC's framing of its chartering authority fundamentally misconstrues the relationship between its full-service chartering authority and its special purpose chartering authority. This rationale neglects the very essence of the agency's full-service chartering authority and the historical development of its special purpose chartering authority. Since the OCC has repeatedly neglected to outline the nature and limits of its special purpose chartering authority, an overview of the history of the Comptroller's special purpose chartering authority follows.

The historical overview below demonstrates that (1) the OCC's special purpose chartering authority is a separate and distinct grant of explicit chartering authority and cannot be implied from the OCC's full-service chartering authority, and (2) the Comptroller lacks the special purpose chartering authority to charter special purpose nonbanks except for trust banks, bankers' banks, and credit card banks. After outlining the historical development of the OCC's authority to charter special purpose national banks, we will discuss how the Comptroller lacks the authority to use its full-service chartering authority to create a new type of special purpose charter for institutions which do not accept deposits, unless specifically authorized by Congress.

1. The historical development of the OCC's special purpose chartering authority demonstrates its distinct legislative origin and limited nature.

For over a century, the Comptroller's chartering authority was limited to the authority to charter full-service national banks organized for the purpose of "carrying on the business of banking", including the acceptance of deposits. At various points since the mid-1970s, the OCC has attempted to charter institutions that would not carry on the business of banking. Instead, such institutions were chartered to engage in activities that either were not within the business of banking as originally defined in the National Bank Act of 1864 (such as the fiduciary activities of

---

[2] *See* 12 U.S.C. 378.

national trust banks) or activities that did not include receiving of deposits from the general public (such as the activities of bankers' banks and credit card banks). The Comptroller's attempts to charter such institutions gave rise to several legal controversies regarding the minimum essential characteristics of the "business of banking" under the NBA. Those earlier controversies have reemerged today as the Comptroller unlawfully asserts in the white paper the authority to charter special purpose nonbanks.

Two federal courts struck down the OCC's attempts to charter institutions that were not engaged in the business of banking, holding that the OCC's chartering of special purpose institutions exceeded the limits of its chartering authority.[3] As a consequence of these legal defeats, the OCC persuaded Congress to authorize or ratify the chartering of special purpose national banks through targeted, narrowly drawn amendments to the NBA or BHC Act.[4] These carefully-targeted legislative grants of authority empowered the Comptroller to charter narrowly defined categories of special purpose national banks that do not carry on the business of banking. Congress' carefully limited grants of chartering authority for special purpose national banks make clear that the OCC's authority to charter special purpose institutions is completely separate and distinct from the Comptroller's traditional authority to charter full-service national banks that accept deposits and engage in "the business of banking."

   a. National trust banks and credit card banks were originally unlawfully chartered and subsequently ratified by Congress.

The creation of the OCC's special purpose chartering authority for national trust banks is illustrative of this pattern. In 1977, the Comptroller issued to City Trust Services a certificate of authority (i.e. charter) to carry on the business of banking as a national bank despite the fact that City Trust's articles of association declared that its activities would be limited to the fiduciary services provided by a trust company.[5] When the proposed charter was challenged, a federal district court held that the charter was invalid because the Comptroller lacked authority to charter an institution that would engage only in fiduciary activities and would not engage in the business of banking, including the acceptance of deposits.[6]

Following this defeat, the Comptroller requested an amendment to the NBA that would specifically authorize the Comptroller to charter national trust banks.[7] Congress adopted the requested amendment in 1978 and thereby gave specific authority for the creation of national trust banks, the first type of special purpose chartering authority conferred upon the OCC.[8] Similar events, in which the OCC exceeded its statutory chartering authority and persuaded Congress to ratify new types of special purpose charters, took place with respect to credit card banks. In each case, Congress gave the OCC a carefully-limited authority to charter a narrowly-defined category of limited-purpose financial institutions, as shown by 12 U.S.C. 27(a), 27(b), 1841(c)(2)(D), and 1841(c)(2)(F).

Today, the Comptroller is once again attempting to usurp the legislative prerogatives of Congress by asserting an unfounded authority to charter a new, broadly-defined class of special purpose national nonbanks for fintech and other nondepository institutions. The OCC has taken this unlawful action in spite of the fact that Congress has not only not authorized, but actually intended to prohibit the chartering of special purpose national nonbanks, whether for fintech companies or any other nondepository.[9]

   b. Nonbank banks were unlawfully chartered and subsequently prohibited by Congress.

---

[3] *See Independent Bankers Ass'n of America v. Conover,* 1985 U.S. Dist. LEXIS 22529, at *34 -*36 (M.D. Fla. Feb. 15, 1985) (*IBAA v. Conover*) (special purpose "nonbank banks" were held unlawful). See also *National State Bank of Elizabeth v. Smith,* No. 76-1479 (D.N.J. September 16, 1977) (special purpose trust banks were held unlawful prior to Congress' specific grant of statutory authorization for such institutions), rev'd on other grounds, 591 F.2d 223 (3d Cir. 1979)

[4] *See* Financial Institutions Regulatory and Interest Rate Control Act of 1978 (FIRIRCA), Pub. L. No. 95-630, § 1504, 92 Stat. 3641 (1978) (codified at 12 U.S.C. § 27(a) (national trust banks); Garn-St. Germain Depository Institutions Act of 1982, Pub. L. No. 97-320, § 404, 96 Stat. 1511

(1982) (codified at 12 U.S.C. § 27(b)(1)) (bankers' banks); Competitive Equality in Banking Act of 1987 (CEBA), Pub. L. No. 100-86, § 101, 101 Stat. 552, 554 (1987), codified at 12 U.S.C. § 1841(c) (credit card banks).

[5] *See National State Bank of Elizabeth v. Smith,* supra note 3.

[6] *See id.*

[7] *See IBAA v. Conover,* at *34, supra note 3.

[8] *See* 12 U.S.C. 27(a), enacted as part of FIRIRCA, supra note 4.

[9] *See IBAA v. Conover,* supra note 3. See also CEBA, supra note 4.

In the 1980s, the Comptroller was rebuffed by a federal court and by Congress when the Comptroller made a similar attempt to issue national bank charters to special purpose institutions that only engaged in lending and did not accept deposits. A federal district court struck down the Comptroller's attempt as unlawful in *Independent Bankers Ass'n of America v. Conover*.[10] In that case, the court held that the Comptroller lacked the authority to charter such special purpose "nonbank banks" because those special purpose institutions (1) did not accept deposits and thus would not carry on the business of banking and (2) were not otherwise specifically authorized by the NBA or federal banking law.

In 1987, with the passage of CEBA, Congress effectively ratified the court's decision by redefining the term "bank" in the BHC Act to include any institution that either (1) accepts deposits subject to withdrawal on demand or by check and also makes commercial loans, or (2) accepts deposits that are insured by the Federal Deposit Insurance Corporation. The term "bank," as so defined, does not include a special purpose institution that makes loans but does not accept deposits.

As indicated above, the first basis for the court's decision in *Independent Bankers Ass'n of America v. Conover* was that the Comptroller may not validly approve a full-service national bank charter unless the power to receive deposits is conferred and exercised by the chartered institution, because the acceptance of deposits is required in order to carry on "the business of banking" under the National Bank Act. That holding finds clear, indisputable support in applicable judicial precedents and federal banking statutes.[11] The second basis for the court's decision—that the Comptroller could not approve limited purpose charters for "nonbank banks"—relied on the canon of statutory interpretation known as *expressio unius est exlusio alterius* (the expression of one or more items of a class implies that those not identified are to be excluded). Applying that canon, the court reasoned that, since Congress included specific grants of authority in the NBA and the BHC Act that enable the Comptroller to issue special-purpose charters for trust companies and banker's banks, Congress must have intended to prohibit the OCC from chartering other types of special-purpose national banks that were not expressly authorized.[12]

After *IBAA v. Conover*, Congress did not confer the requisite special purpose chartering authority for "nonbank banks" that the OCC had unsuccessfully asserted.[13] On the contrary, as

---

[10] *See IBAA v. Conover*, supra note 3.

[11] *See IBAA v. Conover*, at *25-*26, supra note 3 (citing *Mercantile National Bank v. Mayor*, 121 U.S. 139 (1887); U.S. v. *Philadelphia National Bank*, 374 U.S. 321 (1963)). *See e.g.*, *Opinion of the Attorney General* (March 31, 1915) ("The power to receive deposits, expressly granted to every national bank is, of course, indispensable to the conduct of the business of banking: and the extent of its exercise is in a degree the measure of the success of the bank."); *Warren v. Shook*, 91 U.S. 704 (1875) ("Having a place of business where deposits are received *and* paid out on checks, *and* where money is loaned upon security, is the substance of the business of a banker."); *People v. Utica Insurance Co.*, 15 Johns. 538 (1819) ("The principal attributes of a bank are the right to issue negotiable notes, discount notes *and* receive deposits.").

The court also held that the BHC Act and the NBA should be read together *in pari materia* because they constitute a "joint regulatory scheme". Specifically, the court found that the definition of "bank" in the BHC Act should be construed as a limit on the Comptroller's full-service chartering authority which would prohibit the Comptroller from using this authority to charter an institution which refrained from either receiving deposits or making loans. *See IBAA v. Conover*, at *32, supra note 3; 12 U.S.C. 1841(c)(1) (defining "bank" for purposes of the BHC Act). *See also*, 12 U.S.C. § 22 (requiring organization certificate to specify "place where its operation of discount and deposit are to be carried on."); 12 U.S.C. 378

(prohibiting all persons other than chartered depository institutions from accepting deposits).

[12] For similar decisions striking down unauthorized actions of the Comptroller under the same canon of statutory constructions, see *First National Bank in St. Louis v. Missouri*, 263 U.S. 640 (1923) (holding, prior to the enactment of the McFadden Act in 1927, that the Comptroller could not give to national banks a general power of establishing branches in view of the narrowly-defined grants of branching authority made by Congress); *Independent Ins. Agents of America v. Hawke*, 211 F.3d 638 (D.C. Cir. 2000) (holding that the Comptroller could not give national banks a broad power to act as insurance agents in view of the narrowly-defined grants of insurance agency authority made by Congress).

[13] Earlier iterations of CEBA in the 1980s would have authorized the Comptroller to charter "consumer banks," but the pertinent language was omitted prior to enactment by Congress. More recently, legislation has been proposed which would provide the OCC with the authority to charter special purpose nondepository institutions, but such legislation has never been enacted by Congress. See FFSCC Charter Act of 2011, H.R. 1909, 112th Cong. (2011); Consumer Credit Access, Innovation, and Modernization Act, H.R. 6139, 112th Cong. (2012). Nevertheless, the fact that proposed legislation was introduced in order to authorize the OCC to charter a special purpose nonbank underscores the need for Congressional authorization with respect to the special purpose nonbank charter currently under consideration.

noted above, Congress precluded the Comptroller from chartering special purpose "nonbank banks" by enacting the Competitive Equality in Banking Act of 1987 (CEBA), which closed the "nonbank bank" loophole and made clear that financial institutions that do not accept deposits are not "banks."[14] In fact, despite the many major financial services reforms promulgated by Congress in the years and decades that followed, including many amendments to the NBA and the BHC Act, Congress has never given the OCC a general authority to charter special purpose nonbanks.

c. Despite being unlawful and prohibited, the OCC rehabilitated the nonbank bank charter through an invalid regulation.

In the absence of Congressional authorization, the Comptroller decided instead, in 2003, to amend its chartering regulations to enable the chartering of a nondepository institution that " . . . limits its activities . . . to any other activities within the business of banking."[15] When CSBS and other organizations objected to this unauthorized expansion of the Comptroller's chartering authority, the Comptroller added in the final rule the following requirement: "A special purpose bank that conducts activities other than fiduciary activities must conduct at least one of the following three core banking functions: Receiving deposits; paying checks; or lending money."[16] This unprecedented and unauthorized regulatory expansion of the OCC's special purpose chartering authority continued to lie dormant until the OCC issued its white paper announcing the OCC's intention to create a new special purpose national bank charter for a wide range of nondepository institutions, including fintech firms.

d. The historical development of the OCC's special purpose chartering authority demonstrates that the OCC's chartering regulations are invalid.

Several conclusions can be drawn from the historical development of the Comptroller's chartering authority. First, carrying on the "business of banking" under the NBA—and thereby qualifying for a full-service national bank charter—requires, at a minimum, being empowered to and actually exercising the power to receive deposits. Second, the OCC's authority to charter special purpose national banks is separate and distinct from its authority to charter full-service national banks to carry on the business of banking. The OCC's authority to charter special purpose national banks has been carefully limited by Congress through a series of specific, narrowly drawn legislative authorizations for trust banks, bankers' banks and credit card banks. Finally, Congress has never conferred upon the OCC any type of broad power to grant special purpose nonbank charters for institutions that only lend money or pay checks without accepting deposits.

Based on these conclusions, it is clear that the regulation on which the OCC now relies, 12 C.F.R. 5.20(e)(1)(i), to charter a special purpose nonbank exceeds the statutory bases of the OCC's chartering authority. The chartering regulation does not implement a statute enabling the chartering of special purpose nonbanks—because no such statute exists. Thus, the regulation has no basis in the OCC's special purpose chartering authority. Furthermore, the chartering regulation is not a rational implementation of the OCC's statutory authority to charter full-service banks, because it enables the OCC to charter an institution to refrain from engaging in deposit-taking—a function which is indispensable to the business of banking. Thus, Section 5.20(e)(1)(i) is in excess of statutory authority and, accordingly, invalid.

2. The OCC intends to use its enforcement authority in an unauthorized manner to create an unlawful and invalid special purpose nonbank charter.

(Footnote Continued)

See also, Peter J. Wallison, *Reform Bills Don't Go Far Enough*, American Enterprise Institute, Oct. 22, 1999 (stating that, absent further legislative reform, *"IBAA v. Conover* would prevent the Comptroller from chartering federal banks as nonbank banks").

[14] *See* CEBA, supra note 4 (amending 12 U.S.C. 1841(c)). There is considerable evidence in the several hearings held on the issue of nonbank banks, that advocates of closing the nonbank bank loophole considered the CEBA amendments to make permanent the ruling of the court in *IBAA v. Conover*. See, e.g., Sen. Rept. No. 99-15 (statements of the Federal Reserve Board, Conference of State Bank Supervisors, Independent Bankers

Association of America, National Conference of State Legislatures, U.S. League of Savings Institutions, Association of Bank Holding Companies, the National Small Business Association, and the National Federation of Independent Businesses).

[15] *See* Rules, Policies, and Procedures for Corporate Activities; Bank Activities and Operations; Real Estate Lending and Appraisals, 68 Fed. Reg. 6363, 6371 (Feb. 7, 2003) (proposed rule).

[16] *See* Rules, Policies, and Procedures for Corporate Activities; Bank Activities and Operations; Real Estate Lending and Appraisals, 68 Fed. Reg. 70122, 70126 (Dec. 17, 2003) (final rule).

National banks are authorized and created by the Congress pursuant to the NBA. While authority has been delegated to the Comptroller to grant corporate charters to national banks, Congress retains absolute authority over the National Bank Act and the specific statutory conditions under which the business of national banks may be carried on. The OCC has no authority to issue regulations or orders that expand the powers or immunities of national banks beyond the limits established by Congress.[17] In view of the white paper's assertion of a broad power to grant special purpose charters to national nonbanks, the Comptroller is clearly attempting to usurp authority that has not been granted to him by Congress. The Comptroller has no prerogative to create a special purpose chartering system that lacks any basis in the National Bank Act and other federal statutes and is contrary to the long history of the national banking system.

As mentioned above, the OCC's white paper claims that the authority to charter full-service national banks includes an implicit authority to charter special purpose nonbanks that voluntarily agree to refrain from engaging in deposit-taking or other aspects of the "business of banking." Specifically, the OCC asserts that a special purpose national bank operates under the same charter as a full-service national bank but "voluntarily" agrees to limit its activities by entering into an operating agreement with the OCC. The OCC contends that such an operating agreement is enforceable based on the OCC's general enforcement authority under the Federal Deposit Insurance Act (FDIA).[18]

In addition to the deeply alarming policy implications created by this unlawful method of chartering special purpose nonbanks, discussed more fully in Part II, the OCC's reliance on its enforcement authority to expand the statutory limits of its chartering authority ignores judicial precedent that forbids this method of chartering and contradicts the clear intent of Congress in enacting the enforcement authority upon which the OCC now relies.

a. Requiring a full-service national bank to refrain from engaging in deposit-taking has been held to be unlawful and invalid.

In *IBAA v. Conover*, after the court concluded that engaging in deposit-taking was essential to the chartering of national banks under the National Bank Act (except for the specially authorized categories of trust banks and bankers' banks), the Comptroller argued, as it does today, that " . . . even if associations must have the power to accept demand deposits and make commercial loans, the charters [issued] to nonbank banks qualify fully. They are full charters, and [the Comptroller] has placed no conditions on them. If the nonbank banks have relinquished any of their powers, they have done so through voluntary agreement . . . ".[19] The court specifically rejected this argument and held that the OCC cannot condition the approval of a charter to carry on the business of banking by arranging for the applicant to agree to refrain from exercising a power essential to carrying on the business of banking (namely, deposit-taking). According to the court, it was immaterial that the proposed limits on permissible bank activities were contained in operating agreements rather than the approved charters, because, as the court stated, "the substantive effect is the same as if the charters contained terms limiting them."[20]

The court's reasoning is consistent with a fundamental principle of corporate law, which holds that a corporation's authority to amend its charter does not allow the corporation to add provisions that would not be permissible in its original charter.[21] Thus, amendments to corporate charters are generally void if they could not have lawfully been made part of the original charters. Such a principle is intended to prevent usurpations of power by chartering authorities or chartered institutions. For a chartering authority to condition the approval of a charter on the recipient agreeing not to fulfill the purpose for which the charter was granted is an unlawful and blatant attempt to circumvent the statutory limits on the power of the chartering authority itself.

In attempting to enlarge its special purpose chartering authority through an unauthorized reliance on its alleged authority to enforce operating agreements, the Comptroller would allow applicants to organize national banks for a purpose that the Comptroller cannot itself sanction (namely, to engage exclusively in a nondepository business outside the categories that Congress has expressly authorized). The Supreme Court has recently and strongly warned the OCC that it

---

[17] *See, e.g., Cuomo v. Clearing House Ass'n*, 557 U.S. 519 (2009); *First National Bank of Logan v. Walker Bank & Trust Co.*, 385 U.S. 252 (1966); *First National Bank in St. Louis v. Missouri*, 263 U.S. 640 (1923); *Independent Ins. Agents of America v. Hawke*, 211 F.3d 638 (D.C. Cir. 2000).

[18] *See* 12 USC § 1818(b)(1),(5).

[19] *See IBAA v. Conover*, at *38, supra note 3.

[20] *See id.*

[21] *See Henry v. Markesan State Bank*, 68 F.2d 554 (C.C.A. 8th Cir. 1934). See generally *Proprietors of Charles River Bridge v. Proprietors of Warren Bridge*, 36 U.S. 420 (1837).

cannot expand its supervisory authority by asserting enforcement powers that have not been granted by Congress and impair the historic public safety and consumer protection functions of the states.[22]

b. Requiring a full-service national bank to enter into an operating agreement to refrain from engaging in deposit-taking would constitute an unauthorized use of the OCC's enforcement authority.

Since, as outlined above, the OCC lacks any statutory authority to charter special purpose nonbanks, the OCC places considerable reliance on Section 8 of the FDI Act to create a new, unauthorized type of special purpose charter. Specifically, the OCC claims that it will grant a full-service national bank charter to a prospective special purpose nonbank and then, in the chartering process, condition the approval of the charter on the applicant entering into an "operating agreement" with the OCC in which the applicant commits to "voluntarily" limit its activities to certain nondepository core banking functions, such as lending money and/or paying checks. This agreement, according to the OCC, is enforceable as a "condition imposed in writing" under Section 8(b)(1) and is authorized with respect to uninsured national banks under Section 8(b)(5).[23]

This framing of the OCC's special purpose chartering authority is premised upon an interpretation of the OCC's enforcement authority which defies the legislative intent underlying the relevant provisions of Section 8 of the FDI Act. The reference to "uninsured associations" in Section 8(b)(5) of the FDI Act was added in 1982 with the passage of the Garn-St. Germain Depository Institutions Act, based on Congress's concerns regarding the Comptroller's lack of explicit enforcement authority with respect to the newly sanctioned but carefully limited categories of special purpose national banks—namely, trust banks and bankers' banks. Based on the clear legislative intent underlying Section 8(b)(5), the FDI Act's principal enforcement provision was extended to cover special purpose national banks to fill an existing gap in the OCC's enforcement authority relative to its newly created special purpose chartering authority, and not to authorize the OCC to create new types of special purpose charters not specifically authorized by Congress.

II. Policy Issues with the Proposed Supervisory Framework.

As described in Part I, because the Comptroller lacks any statutory authority to charter special purpose nonbanks, the Comptroller intends to use its enforcement authority in an unauthorized manner to expand its special purpose chartering authority beyond the carefully defined limits established by Congress. In addition to the unlawful and invalid nature of a special purpose national nonbank charter, many significant policy considerations counsel strongly against the OCC attempting to create new types of special purpose charters which Congress has not specifically authorized. As discussed in this Part, the OCC's proposed system of regulating special purpose nonbanks through individualized operating agreements not only highlights the benefits of the activities-based focus of State law but also creates great concerns about the near impossibility of maintaining and assuring a level playing field, assuring the protection of consumers, and upholding a safe and sound financial system.

A. The OCC's proposed approach of regulation by operating agreement creates an opaque legal and regulatory framework inconsistent with federal banking law.

1. Significant federal banking laws would not apply to the proposed special purpose nonbank.

As stated above, the business of national banks has been considered so intimately connected with the public interest that Congress prescribes, through statute, the conditions under which it may be carried on. However, because the OCC now intends to exceed the confines of its statutory authority by chartering a broad range of special purpose nonbanks, there is an almost complete absence of generally applicable rules prescribing the conditions under which the business of such special purpose nonbanks may be conducted. For instance, special purpose nonbanks would be exempt from many of the rules that apply to insured depository institutions, including prompt corrective action requirements, source of strength requirements, restrictions on management interlocks, generally applicable prudential safeguards, community reinvestment act requirements and uniform accounting standards.

Furthermore, if such special purpose nonbanks are not members of the Federal Reserve System (FRS) they will be exempt from major prudential policies, including restrictions on affiliate transactions, restrictions on insider loans, and generally applicable safety and soundness standards. The fact that such institutions would not be covered by most federal banking laws should

---

[22] *See Cuomo v. Clearing House Ass'n, supra.*   [23] *See* 12 USC § 1818(b)(1),(5).

not be surprising as Congress did not confer upon the Comptroller the requisite authority to charter special purpose nonbanks and thus did not contemplate their existence in enacting federal banking laws.

2. The OCC's proposed approach of incorporating otherwise inapplicable rules by agreement on an ad-hoc, confidential basis creates an unlevel playing field.

To fill these major gaps, the OCC gives its assurance that it can "impose requirements . . . that are similar to certain statutory requirements applicable to insured banks" by incorporating such requirements into the operating agreement entered into with the special purpose nonbank. However, the OCC gives no assurance that such requirements will be uniform across special purpose nonbanks or comparable to the requirements applicable to full-service national banks. Indeed, the white paper states that the OCC will only incorporate otherwise "inapplicable" rules into an operating agreement for a special purpose national nonbank "if it deems the conditions appropriate based on the risks and business model of the institution". While state regulators agree that tailoring regulatory and supervisory requirements to the size, risk, and complexity of regulated institutions is an important priority, we also believe that the extent of the tailoring planned by the OCC is so extreme and confidential as to raise serious concerns regarding equal treatment, fair competition, and administrative impartiality.

3. The lack of transparency regarding specific regulatory requirements nullifies any promise of a level playing field.

The OCC's white paper provides no meaningful standards or guidelines for determining the circumstances under which the OCC will, or will not, require special purpose national nonbanks to comply with the rules that apply to full-service national banks and competing state banks.

Even if the OCC were to commit to imposing similar requirements on similarly-situated applicants, such a commitment would be a poor substitute for generally applicable rules enacted by Congress and implemented through proper notice-and-comment rulemaking procedures. A special purpose nonbank applicant would have no assurance that the otherwise inapplicable rules incorporated through its operating agreement are incorporated to the same extent as in the operating agreements of other special purpose nonbanks. Such assurance is unobtainable because the OCC will not publicly disclose these operating agreements—despite arguably being required to do so under Section 8 of the FDI Act.[24] Moreover, this lack of transparency means that state regulators and consumers will have no means of verifying that special purpose nonbanks are lawfully entitled to exercise powers purportedly granted in these operating agreements.

Although the OCC may attempt to provide, by means of informal guidance, the requirements or standards that will apply to proposed special purpose nonbanks, any such bank would have no assurance that the OCC will not deviate from such ad hoc requirements or standards. Any such assurance would be illusory because the OCC would be acting outside the authority granted to it by Congress and could not be held accountable for deviations from its informal guidance to the same extent as it could for failing to comply with governing federal statutes.

For decades, the OCC has been criticized for a lack of transparency in its chartering process; to now graft onto that opaque process an informal, ad hoc standard-setting function in which the OCC negotiates every rule governing the operation of the proposed special purpose national nonbank precludes any possibility of maintaining a level playing field.[25] Special purpose national nonbanks, and the banking industry in general, will be required to merely trust, without any means for verification, that the OCC is actually maintaining a level playing field between special purpose nonbanks themselves as well as between special purpose nonbanks and full-service national banks.

B. Activities-based state licensing encourages and enables financial innovation.

The lack of generally applicable law and the lack of uniformity and transparency in the OCC's regulatory and supervisory expectations underscore the benefits of maintaining the viability of the transaction-oriented focus embodied in State laws governing providers of financial services. In the regulation of financial services, three broad regulatory models are recognized: transactional regulation, institutional regulation, and individuated regulation.[26]

---

[24] *See* 12 U.S.C. § 1818(u).

[25] *See* generally Scott, *In Quest of Reason: The Licensing Decisions of the Federal Banking Agencies*, 42 U. Chi. L. Rev. 235 (1975).

[26] *See* Governor Daniel K. Tarullo, *Pedagogy and Scholarship in a Post-Crisis World* (Oct. 21, 2016).

Transactional regulation generally regulates any persons that engage in a particular type of transaction (subject to *de minimis* exemptions) without regard to their status as a particular type of financial intermediary. State licensing of nonbank financial services providers is a type of transactional regulation. Banks—whether state or national and whether commercial or thrift—are generally subject to institutional regulation which imposes a uniform set of rules on institutions with substantially similar business models. Finally, individuated regulation is regulation that applies not because of the business model of the regulated institution, but rather because of the particular, unique characteristics of that institution. Institutions subject to individuated regulation include institutions designated systemically important and, as has been made apparent in the white paper, prospective special purpose nonbanks.

Transactional, activities-based regulation, such as state licensing, is generally more transparent, and more impartial and equitable than individuated regulation. The impartial nature of transactional regulation involved in state licensing of financial services is, in part, what has enabled the emergence of the tremendous financial innovations we are witnessing today. The degree of flexibility accorded state-licensed financial service providers with respect to their business models is precisely what has enabled such institutions to more effectively meet and adapt to the evolving needs of consumers of financial services. Additionally, the transactional focus of state licensing has maintained a level playing field in the financial services industry and thereby has ensured that emerging and innovative financial services providers are not excluded from the market by high barriers to entry erected by large, entrenched industry incumbents.

By contrast, the individuated regulation the Comptroller intends to impose on special purpose national nonbanks will be significantly less transparent and less impartial than the transactional, activities-based approach extant at the state level. The OCC's approach provides no assurance or method of verifying that such charters will be or are granted in an equitable, impartial manner. It is highly probable, as a former OCC senior official recently noted, that only the largest nonbank financial services providers will succeed in obtaining special purpose national nonbank charters,[27] fundamentally distorting the competitive environment for companies seeking to develop and offer innovative financial services. In the end, despite the OCC's assurance that the charter will technically be voluntary, it will be effectively mandatory and the Comptroller will have established his office as the ultimate and final arbiter of financial innovation as well as the self-appointed umpire, effectively picking winners and losers in the fintech industry.

III. Legal Uncertainty and Special Purpose Nonbank Charters.

Given that Congress has not granted to the OCC any authority to issue special purpose national nonbank charters, there is significant uncertainty surrounding the applicability of many federal laws to an institution operating under such a charter, including federal banking law, federal securities law, and federal consumer financial law. The white paper addresses a few of the applicable legal issues in a perfunctory manner, such as the discussion of membership in the FRS, access to Federal Reserve services, and the jurisdiction of the Consumer Financial Protection Bureau (CFPB). In this Part, we will provide the State regulators' perspective on these issues and many other legal uncertainties that the OCC has failed to address.

A. The uncertain scope of the incidental powers conferred through a special purpose national nonbank charter raises significant safety and soundness concerns.

The general powers of full-service national banks are expressly delineated in various sections of Title 12 of the U.S. Code, primarily in 12 U.S.C. 24. Section 24(Seventh) expressly authorizes national banks:

> "[t]o exercise by its board of directors or duly authorized officers or agents, subject to law, all such incidental powers as shall be necessary to carry on the business of banking; by discounting and negotiating promissory notes, drafts, bills of exchange, and other evidences of debt; by receiving deposits; by buying and selling exchange, coin, and bullion; by loaning money on personal security; and by obtaining, issuing, and circulating notes according to the provisions of title 62 of the Revised Statutes."

In Section 24(Seventh), the "business of banking" is represented by the series of express powers mentioned. However, the first clause, the so-called incidental powers clause, grants banks

---

[27] *See* Zach Fox, *OCC's fintech charter unlikely to kill bank partnerships*, SNL Financial, (Dec. 2, 2016) (quoting former Deputy Comptroller of the Currency, Jo Ann Barefoot: "I do not expect a stampede of small fintechs into national bank charters . . . I don't think they would try and — even if they do — I don't think they would succeed.").

the power to conduct activities incidental to the business of banking. The "incidental powers" concept has often been used by the Comptroller to justify new powers that might not intuitively be thought of as banking powers. In attempting to craft some sort of limiting principle as to what constitutes an incidental power, courts have generally held that an incidental power must either be "directly related to one or another of a national bank's express powers" or "convenient and useful in connection with the performance of one of [a] bank's established activities".[28] This requirement that a "functional equivalence" be identified between express statutory powers and claimed incidental powers, presents novel issues with respect to special purpose national nonbanks.

As discussed above, the Comptroller claims that a special purpose national nonbank receives the same charter as a full-service national bank, but, as a condition for approving the charter, agrees to refrain from exercising certain enumerated powers in Section 24(Seventh). The question thus arises as to whether a special purpose nonbank that is not authorized to exercise an express power within the business of banking would be authorized to exercise any incidental power that is directly related to the prohibited express power. For instance, if the OCC charters a special purpose national nonbank that agrees to refrain from exercising the express power to receive deposits, there would be no legal basis for such an institution to exercise any incidental power that is related to the express deposit-taking power that has been abdicated.

The legal uncertainty as to the scope of incidental powers that a special purpose national nonbank may exercise presents a serious safety and soundness concern that the OCC has not, to date, addressed. Many of the incidental powers authorized by the Comptroller and sanctioned by the courts since the passage of the NBA were granted on the premise that they would be exercised by a full-service national bank endowed with all the express powers and limitations contemplated by the NBA. State regulators believe that allowing special purpose national nonbanks to exercise incidental powers deemed functionally equivalent to express powers not conferred upon the institution would be irresponsible. State regulators request that the OCC clarify how it intends to ensure that special purpose national nonbanks will refrain from exercising incidental powers that have been permitted only for full-service national banks that operate with entirely different business models.

B. The uncertain status of special purpose nonbanks in the Federal Reserve System raises significant public policy concerns.

Pursuant to the Federal Reserve Act, a special purpose national nonbank chartered by the OCC would generally be required to become a member of the FRS.[29] The membership of special purpose national nonbanks in the FRS would raise several legal and policy concerns, including whether membership is or should be required and whether such institutions would be subject to regulation by the FRS and would have access to services offered by the FRS, including the discount window and the payments system. These concerns are addressed in the sections that follow.

1. The OCC's proposal lacks clarity on the membership of special purpose nonbanks in the Federal Reserve System.

After stating that national banks are generally required to be members of the FRS, the OCC notes an exception to the membership requirement for national banks located in territories and insular possessions of the United States. While it is unclear whether this reference should be taken as an indication that the OCC intends to charter special purpose nonbanks in territories and insular possessions in order to avoid the membership requirement, such an arrangement would certainly present a number of complications. For instance, despite not being members in the FRS, national banks located in dependencies and insular possessions are generally subject to a reserve requirement under 12 U.S.C. § 143 requiring that such banks have on hand, at all times, an amount equal to 15 percent of the aggregate amount of its deposits.[30]

State regulators believe that the OCC should clarify whether it intends to charter special purpose nonbanks in territories and insular possessions of the United States to avoid the requirement that national banks be members of the FRS. Furthermore, State regulators request that the OCC clarify how a national nonmember bank located in a dependency or insular possession would comply with such a requirement, particularly, for an institution which refrains from engaging in a deposit-taking function.

---

[28] *Compare* Arnold Tours, Inc. v. Camp, 472 F.2d 427 (1st Cir. 1972) *with* M & M Leasing Corp. v. Seattle First Nat'l Bank, 563 F.2d 1377 (9th Cir. 1977).

[29] *See* 12 U.S.C. 222.

[30] *See* 12 U.S.C. § 143.

2. The OCC's proposal lacks clarity on the access of special purpose nonbanks to the federal safety net and critical public resources.

In addition to the membership status of potential special purpose national nonbanks, the issue of whether such institutions qualify as "depository institutions" under the Federal Reserve Act will have very significant consequences due to the bearing that such a designation would have on their access to Federal Reserve services, including access to the Federal Reserve payments systems and access to the discount window. In general, special purpose national banks are prohibited from accessing or significantly limited in their access to such services. Congress intended for access to Federal Reserve services to be a privilege enjoyed by those engaged in the business of receiving deposits, not by nondepository institutions whose activities bear some resemblance to a deposit-taking function but who are ultimately dependent upon the deposit-taking services of institutions *truly* engaged in the business of banking.

The subsections that follow discuss whether a special purpose nonbank of the type contemplated in the white paper would have access to Federal Reserve services and the policy issues pertaining to allowing such institutions to gain access.

a. The uncertain degree of access afforded special purpose national nonbanks to the FRS payments system raises significant public policy concerns.

Although not susceptible to precise definition, the term "payments system" generally refers to the clearing and settlement services that are provided by the FRS through the regional Federal Reserve Banks, and by other clearing and settling organizations that interact with the FRS and carry on their activities under the guidance of the operating rules and procedures established by the Board of Governors of the FRS. Many significant functions are performed by the payments system, including the traditional clearing and settlement of paper checks through the FRS and regional clearinghouses, and the electronic clearance and settlement of the transfer of funds (principally large dollar transfers) through automated clearinghouses or electronic funds transfer services such as the FRS's FedWire.

Generally, direct access to the payments systems has been limited to "depository institutions", including member banks and nonmember banks. Since they do not accept deposits, nonbanks are generally not permitted to have direct access to the FRS payments services, but must instead use these services indirectly as customers of depository institutions. The term "depository institution" is defined in Section 19 of the Federal Reserve Act to mean, in relevant part, " . . . any insured bank as defined in section 3 of the Federal Deposit Insurance Act or any bank which is eligible to make application to become an insured bank under section 5 of such Act; . . . ".[31] To be eligible to apply to become an insured bank, a bank must be "engaged in the business of receiving deposits". Given that the OCC seems to indicate in the white paper that it intends to charter a special purpose nonbank that *does not* accept deposits, such a special purpose nonbank would not be engaged in the business of receiving deposits and therefore would not be eligible to apply to become an insured bank. This ineligibility would entail that the special purpose nonbank would not be a "depository institution" and thus would not be permitted direct access to the FRS payments systems.

The legal barrier preventing special purpose national nonbanks from directly accessing the FRS payments systems due to their nondepository nature accords with legitimate regulatory concerns. Chief among such concerns is the principle that access to the payments systems should be limited to financial institutions that conduct their activities in such a manner as to ensure the proper functioning and safety and soundness of that system. Essential to the willingness of economic actors to accept payment in mediums other than cash is the confidence that, when requested, cash will be received in a timely manner. Were this confidence to be shaken by a disruption to the normal functioning of the payments system—for instance, if a payments systems participant were to default on their obligations or fall victim to a security breach which spread throughout the system—a severe disruption in the normal flow of commerce and finance could ensue.

The likelihood of such disruption is greatly amplified by permitting institutions to directly access the payments systems when they are not subject to the same heightened prudential and safety and soundness regulatory and supervisory framework to which depository institutions are subject. In light of the legal barriers to allowing nonbanks direct access to the FRS payments

---

[31] *See* 12 U.S.C. § 461(b)(1)(A)(i).

¶1360

system and the strong policy rationales for limiting access, State regulators are opposed to allowing special purpose national nonbanks to directly access the FRS payments systems.

b. The proposed special purpose national nonbank's potential access to the discount window raises significant public policy concerns.

As with access to the FRS payment systems, the issue as to whether a special purpose national nonbank would have access to the Federal Reserve discount window is a matter of significant consequence. The concern here is whether a special purpose national nonbank will enjoy the same discounting and borrowing privileges enjoyed by full-service banks under the normal lending authority of the Federal Reserve Banks. The issue, again, is whether these special purpose nonbanks will be members of the FRS, and, if not, whether they will be "depository institutions".

If a special purpose nonbank is either a member of the FRS or a nonmember "depository institution", then it will enjoy the same discounting and borrowing privileges traditionally enjoyed by full-service national member banks. However, as discussed above, the special purpose national nonbanks discussed in the white paper will most likely not be "depository institutions" under the Federal Reserve Act provided that the OCC requires such institutions to refrain from exercising a deposit-taking function. A special purpose nonbank which is not a member of the FRS and is not a depository institution will still be eligible to borrow from Federal Reserve Banks, but as a nonmember nonbank will be subject to the relatively more demanding collateral requirements applicable to nonbank entities.[32] State regulators believe that, for special purpose national nonbanks that refrain from deposit-taking, providing such institutions with the same borrowing and discounting privileges conferred upon member and nonmember depository institutions would be unwarranted and inequitable.

C. The OCC's proposed special purpose nonbank charter is structured to evade the coverage of the Bank Holding Company Act.

The OCC has intentionally structured the special purpose nonbank charter to avoid being classified as a "bank" for purposes of the Bank Holding Company Act. Evading this Act means that special purpose nonbanks would not be subject to consolidated supervision by the Federal Reserve and the parent companies of special purpose nonbanks would not be subject to the anti-tying rules, restrictions on proprietary trading, and restrictions on affiliations with commercial companies. Accordingly, the OCC intends, without discussion, to simply violate the fundamental policy goals of Congress in enacting the BHC Act, namely to maintain a separation between banking and commerce.

1. The OCC's proposal runs afoul of the principle of separation of banking and commerce.

In originally establishing a wall between banking and commerce, Congress explicitly relied on the business of banking concept[33], precisely because economic neutrality ought to be required in the exercise of banking powers. If the OCC charters an institution which engages exclusively in nondepository core banking functions, the fact that the institution is characterized as, in itself, conducting the business of banking should warrant the separation of its credit granting and credit exchange functions from general commercial enterprises. However, because the novel charter type would be exempt from coverage under the BHCA, there would be no federal mechanism to ensure that its activities remain divorced from ownership or control by commercial enterprises.

Accordingly, if an institution that engages exclusively in nondepository core banking functions thereby engages in the business of banking under the NBA, then, state regulators believe, the fundamental principle mandating the separation of banking and commerce is in jeopardy. Thus, state regulators urge the Comptroller to avoid relying upon an expansive interpretation of its chartering authority to create novel, unprecedented charter types that dilute the very meaning of the business of banking and thereby undermine the wall established by Congress between banking and commerce.

2. The OCC's proposal creates the opportunity for regulatory capital arbitrage.

Since a special purpose nonbank would qualify as a depository institution under the generally applicable risk-based capital rules, bank holding companies would likely be able to arbitrage the capital requirements by maintaining a special purpose nonbank as an unconsolidated subsidiary. If special purpose nonbanks are not consolidated with their parent holding company for reporting

---

[32] *Compare* 12 U.S.C. § 347c (corporation, partnerships, and individuals) *with* 12 U.S.C. § 347 (member banks).

[33] *See* 12 U.S.C. § 1843(c)(8).

purposes, and the parent company only maintains a minority interest in the subsidiary, the parent holding company will only be required to maintain capital for its equity investment in the subsidiary despite being financially responsible for the totality of the subsidiary's liabilities. Alternatively, if the special purpose nonbank is consolidated with its parent holding company for reporting purposes, then it will be permitted to count the equity investments in its nonbank subsidiary (likely funded by debt issued and guaranteed by the parent) towards its own capital requirements, and thereby mask the double leverage inherent in the parent-subsidiary structure.

The largest bank and financial holding companies would experience the largest benefit from maintaining a special purpose nonbank as a subsidiary, since they generally employ the advanced approaches methodology for calculating risk-based capital. Specifically, since a special purpose nonbank would be a "regulated financial institution" for the purposes of the risk-based capital rule, an advanced approaches holding company would generally not be subject to the increased asset value correlation factor for wholesale exposures to unregulated financial institutions and large regulated financial institutions, and, accordingly, not be held to the same stringent capital requirements applicable absent the existence of a special purpose nonbank. Put simply, the creation of the special purpose nonbank charter will be a means for bank holding companies to reduce the quality and quantity of capital they are required to hold under the risk-based and leverage capital rules. The benefits of this arbitrage enabled through the structuring of transactions with special purpose nonbank charters will accrue to the greatest extent to the largest institutions. A similar type of arbitrage under the liquidity rules applicable to advanced approach institutions will also likely be made possible through the creation of special purpose nonbanks.

State bank regulators believe that maintaining a high quantity and quality of capital is the cornerstone of bank regulation and supervision—a belief edified through the experiences of the recent financial crisis. For this reason, we urge the OCC to refrain from creating new types of institutions which will enable the largest institutions to engage in regulatory arbitrage in a manner that would lead to a lower quality and quantity of capital.

D. The OCC's proposal lacks clarity on the applicability of federal securities laws to special purpose nonbanks.

1. The proposed special purpose nonbanks will be exempt from the enforcement authority of the Securities and Exchange Commission.

Although the OCC discusses how it intends to collaborate with various federal banking regulators in the regulation and supervision of the proposed special purpose nonbanks, the OCC does not discuss how such an institution would be governed under the federal securities regulatory framework. To a varying degree, banks enjoy exemptions from federal securities laws and the authority to enforce federal securities laws is generally the responsibility of the institution's federal banking regulator rather than the Securities Exchange Commission. As discussed in this section, the fact that Congress did not contemplate the OCC chartering a special purpose nonbank creates uncertainty not only as to whether such institutions will be exempt from various requirements under federal securities laws but also as to which agency is responsible for the enforcement of federal securities laws.

A special purpose nonbank would likely qualify for the exemption for banks under the Securities Act of 1933, Securities Exchange Act of 1934, the Investment Company Act of 1940, and the Investment Advisers Act of 1940. The exemptions for banks in federal securities laws is generally predicated upon such institutions being subject to substantially similar registration, disclosure and antifraud rules by their primary federal banking regulator and the requisite enforcement authority being delegated to these agencies to ensure compliance with these requirements.

2. The OCC lacks the authority to enforce federal securities laws against special purpose nonbanks.

Section 12(i) of the Securities Exchange Act delegates to the OCC "the powers, functions, and duties" vested in the SEC to administer and enforce various enumerated sections of the Act, including rulemaking powers, a delisting power, a trading suspension power, a power to issue orders, an investigatory power, and a litigating power.[34] However, based on the plain meaning of Section 12(i), this enforcement authority is not delegated to the OCC with respect to special purpose nonbanks. Specifically, Section 12(i) only delegates the powers, functions and duties of

---

[34] *See* 15 U.S.C. § 78l(i).

the SEC "[i]n respect of any securities issued by banks ... the deposits of which are insured in accordance with the Federal Deposit Insurance Act."[35]

Accordingly, with respect to special purpose national nonbanks which refrain from receiving deposits, the Comptroller will lack the requisite authority to enforce the requirements of the Securities Exchange Act. Nevertheless, since they will qualify as "banks" under the federal securities laws, special purpose national nonbanks will be exempt from the requirements of that Act and the enforcement authority of the SEC. Thus, in addition to enjoying an exemption from the requirements of federal securities law and the jurisdiction of the SEC, special purpose national nonbanks that refrain from receiving deposits will also not be subject to the requirements of federal securities law imposed by or the enforcement authority delegated to the OCC.

State regulators believe that an exemption of this magnitude would be unprecedented and should counsel against the OCC using its chartering authority in such a manner as to create types of special purpose institutions clearly not contemplated by Congress. State regulators request that the OCC clarify how and on what legal basis the OCC will ensure compliance with the requirements of the Securities Exchange Act.

E. The OCC's proposal lacks clarity on the applicability of federal consumer financial laws to special purpose nonbanks.

1. The proposed special purpose nonbanks would not be subject to federal consumer protection laws to the same extent as full-service banks.

In outlining the extent to which the Consumer Financial Protection Bureau (CFPB) will oversee special purpose national nonbanks, the OCC discusses how federal consumer financial law will apply to such institutions. Specifically, the OCC notes that the "CFPB would supervise an uninsured special purpose national bank *engaged in certain activities* for compliance with federal consumer financial law" (emphasis added). The OCC qualifies the extent to which federal consumer financial law will apply to special purpose nonbanks because such institutions will not be subject to the entirety of federal consumer financial law, as would an insured depository institution, but rather only to the limited set of rules which apply to nondepository covered persons and only if they qualify as larger participants.[36]

2. The OCC is shirking its authority to apply federal consumer financial laws to special purpose nonbanks to the same extent as full-service banks.

To avoid creating an unlevel playing field in favor of special purpose nonbanks, State regulators believe it is imperative that special purpose national nonbanks be required to comply with federal consumer financial law to the same extent as full-service national banks. In transferring authority to the CFPB, the Dodd-Frank Act expressly enabled the OCC to use its enforcement authority under Section 8 of the FDIA to subject special purpose national nonbanks to the requirements of federal consumer financial law to the same extent as full-service national banks.[37]

The fact that the OCC refrains from using its enforcement authority in this respect to ensure a level playing field between banks and nonbanks fails to instill any confidence that the Comptroller will be even-handed in the use of its enforcement authority in the operating agreements entered into in chartering special purpose nonbanks. Likewise, the OCC's abdication of its authority under 12 U.S.C. 5581 does not bode well for other federal and state laws the applicability of which is left to the discretion of the Comptroller, including state laws on anti-discrimination, fair lending, and debt collection.

State regulators believe that, for the Comptroller's commitment to "high supervisory standards" to be anything more than a hollow platitude, the OCC must use its enforcement authority under the Consumer Financial Protection Act to subject special purpose nonbanks to the requirements of federal consumer financial law to the same extent as full-service national banks. Any measure short of full incorporation of federal consumer financial law (verifiable through the public availability of the operating agreements between the OCC and special purpose nonbanks) ought to cast doubt as to the commitment of the Comptroller to maintaining a level playing field while also ensuring compliance with any purportedly applicable federal and state laws.

IV. Preemption of State Law

---

[35] *See* id.

[36] *See* 12 U.S.C. § 5514.

[37] *See* 12 U.S.C. § 5581(c)(2)(C).

In the wake of the financial crisis, there is a plethora of evidence that broad preemption is simply not good public policy. Understanding local markets and business practices requires a strong presence in the community. While financial technologies are deployed on a national and international basis, consumer interaction still occurs at a local level that requires local oversight. The Constitution established a federalist system to balance local and national priorities, and the emergence of financial technology does not change the fact that a balanced State-federal regulatory structure is vital to the strength of our financial system.[38]

A. The proposed special purpose nonbank will entitle fintech and other nondepository companies to federal preemption to the detriment of consumers.

Experience has shown the States not to trust the OCC when it seeks to expand its power.[39] Policymakers needn't look further than the mortgage crisis for an illustration of the disastrous results of the OCC's preemption of locally identified needs and priorities.[40]

In 1982, the OCC nullified state restrictions on adjustable rate mortgages, eliminating the ability of states to respond to lending practices that hurt consumers.[41] This laid the groundwork for predatory lending practices, culminating in state action to protect consumers where federal regulators refused to act. In 1999, North Carolina became the first State to enact a comprehensive anti-predatory law. Other states followed suit as the devastating results of predatory mortgage lending became apparent through increased foreclosures and disinvestment.

Unfortunately, rather than supporting these anti-predatory lending laws, federal regulators preempted them. In 1996, the OCC's predecessor for federal thrifts – the Office of Thrift Supervision ("OTS") – preempted all state lending laws. The OCC followed suit in 2003 with a determination that the Georgia Fair Lending Act did not apply to national banks.[42] A 2004 rule followed, exempting all national banks from state lending laws, including anti-predatory lending laws like those of Georgia and North Carolina. At a hearing on the OCC's preemption rule, Comptroller Hawke acknowledged, in response to questioning from Senator Sarbanes, that one reason Hawke issued the preemption rule was to attract additional charters, which helps to bolster the budget of the OCC.[43]

These actions removed an extra layer of regulatory protection. State officials have a unique expertise in local banking practices and local markets, which makes them uniquely situated to recognize and act upon consumer financial protection issues. Licensure is one of the key tools available to state regulators under the police powers preserved to the States by the Constitution. However, in 2006, the OCC supported an interpretation of the National Bank Act that led to the preemption of state licensing laws for operating subsidiaries of national banks.[44]

As a result of 25 years of policy that swept state responses under the rug, the mortgage crisis emerged. National bank subsidiaries offered abusive products while state regulators were powerless to enforce laws state legislators enacted to stop harm. While the OCC and supporters of the national bank system have suggested the cause was unregulated nonbank mortgage companies,[45]

---

[38] For more information on the traditional role of the States in licensing nondepository financial services providers and its constitutional underpinnings, see CSBS's previous comment letter on the OCC's proposed rule establishing a framework to govern receiverships for uninsured national banks, available at: CSBS Comment Letter on Proposed Rule on Receiverships for Uninsured National Banks.

[39] Past Comptrollers have gone as far as saying that national bank preemption "may operate in some cases to the disadvantage of consumers," and that losing market share [charters] "is a matter of concern to us." Jess Bravin & Paul Beckett, Friendly Watchdog: Federal Regulator Often Helps Banks Fighting Consumers, WALL ST. J., Jan. 28, 2002, at A1 (summarizing and quoting from an interview with Comptroller Hawke).

[40] See Di Maggio, Marco and Kermani, Amir and Korgaonkar, Sanket, *Partial Deregulation and Competition: Effects on Risky Mortgage Origination*, Columbia Business School Research Paper No. 15-47 (November 17, 2016)

(finding "national banks' supply of loans with prepayment penalties and longer prepayment terms increased significantly" after state anti-predatory lending laws were preempted). Available at SSRN: https://ssrn.com/abstract=2591434 or http://dx.doi.org/10.2139/ssrn.2591434.

[41] See Conference of State Bank Supervisors v. Conover, 710 F.2d 878 (D.C. Cir. 1983).

[42] See Preemption Determination and Order, 68 Fed. Reg. 46264 (August 5, 2003) (preempting "the provisions of the [Georgia Fair Lending Act] affecting national banks' real estate lending" in response to a request from National City).

[43] See Senate Banking Committee Hearing, *Review of the National Bank Preemption Rules* (June 7, 2004).

[44] See Watters v. Wachovia Bank, N.A., 127 S.Ct. 1559 (2007).

[45] See Jesse Stiller, *Banking Modern America: Studies in Regulatory History* (2016).

there can be no logical support for this argument when reviewing the evidence, which even includes abuses of financial technology.

Wachovia Mortgage Loan Trust, Series 2006-AMN1 is a mortgage backed security issued in 2006.[46] The loans backing the security were originated by American Mortgage Network ("AmNet"), "an indirect wholly owned subsidiary of Wachovia Bank and Wachovia Corporation."[47] AmNet originated Alt-A mortgages through branches and "over the Internet."[48] These Alt-A loans were originated with "reduced documentation programs," including a "'No Income/No Assets/No Employment' program, where there is no verification of income, assets or employment."[49] To CSBS's knowledge, the OCC never examined this company as an operating subsidiary of Wachovia Bank, N.A.

The lending "programs" used by AmNet would have been illegal under many state laws, and examination of nonbank subsidiaries would have revealed the predatory loans. However, the OCC's preemption determinations prevented the states from examining AmNet and stopping lending practices known to local governments as predatory and counter to sound financial dealings.

B. The OCC's proposed special purpose nonbank charter will preempt the States' activities-based nondepository licensing and regulatory regimes.

Distressingly, the OCC white paper makes no reference to the state regulatory system and disingenuously suggests that entities potentially eligible for the special purpose nonbank charter are currently subject to no regulation. Equally disingenuous is the OCC's claim in the white paper that certain state laws will generally apply to national banks including laws on anti-discrimination, fair lending, and debt collection. Because the OCC is not, as a public servant, charged with the enforcement of these state laws, it is questionable whether they will "apply" as the OCC claims. In the end, these state laws will apply only at the discretion of the Comptroller which is a prerogative the OCC has tended to employ to defeat, rather than enforce, the application of state law.

In addition to supervising approximately 4,790 state-chartered banks,[50] most state banking departments also regulate a variety of nondepository financial services providers, including money transmitters, mortgage lenders, and consumer lenders. According to the OCC white paper, any of these 20,000 plus companies would qualify for a national bank charter because they send money or lend.[51] Like state banks, nondepositories licensed by state regulators are required to meet safety and soundness requirements and conform to both state and federal consumer protection laws. This is accomplished by licensing and subsequently examining nondepository companies on a regular basis. Examination of multi-state entities is performed on a collaborative basis with multi-state teams, reducing regulatory burden and improving allocation of resources among states.[52]

As proposed, and without any discussion, a special purpose national bank charter will preempt this regulatory framework for any charter recipient. The only likely charter recipients will be those financial technology firms and nondepository companies with sufficient legal resources to navigate and comply with the OCC's opaque, unarticulated chartering requirements and supervisory standards. In the end, the proposed chartering and supervisory framework will benefit large, entrenched incumbents and create a larger barrier to entry for the vast majority of financial technology firms.

---

[46] See Prospectus Supplement, Wachovia Mortgage Loan Trust, Series 2006-AMN1 (May 23, 2006). Available at https://www.sec.gov/Archives/edgar/data/1326845/000128269506000309/e65745_424b5.htm.

[47] See id. at S-30.

[48] See id. AmNet was later rolled into Wachovia Securities. See http://www.prnewswire.com/news-releases/american-mortgage-network-and-wachovia-third-party-lending-rebranded-to-create-vertice-51630642.html.

[49] See id. at 31.

[50] See FDIC Statistics on Depository Institutions as of Year End 2015. Available at https://www.fdic.gov/bank/statistical/.

[51] As of year end 2015, there were 20,440 state licensed entities on the Nationwide Multi-State Licensing System. See 2015 Annual Report, State Regulatory Registry. Available at http://mortgage.nationwidelicensingsystem.org/about/Documents/SRR_2015AR_Web.pdf.

[52] See Multi-state Mortgage Committee Report to State Regulators (2015) available at https://www.csbs.org/news/presentations/annualreports/Documents/MMC%202015%20Annual%20Report_FINAL_0505.pdf; Multi-state MSB Examination Taskforce Report to State Regulators (2015) available at https://www.csbs.org/news/presentations/annualreports/Documents/2015%20MMET%20Annual%20Report.pdf.

DEPARTMENT OF THE TREASURY

Office of the Comptroller of the Currency

12 CFR Part 51

[Docket ID OCC-2016-0017]

RIN 1557-AE07

AGENCY: Office of the Comptroller of the Currency, Treasury.

ACTION: Final rule.

SUMMARY: The Office of the Comptroller of the Currency (OCC) is adopting a final rule addressing the conduct of receiverships for national banks that are not insured by the Federal Deposit Insurance Corporation (FDIC) (uninsured banks) and for which the FDIC would not be appointed as receiver. The final rule implements the provisions of the National Bank Act (NBA) that provide the legal framework for receiverships of such institutions. The final rule adopts the rule as proposed without change.

DATES: This final rule is effective on [INSERT DATE 30 DAYS FROM DATE OF PUBLICATION IN FEDERAL REGISTER].

FOR FURTHER INFORMATION CONTACT: Mitchell Plave, Special Counsel, Legislative and Regulatory Activities Division, (202) 649-5490, or for persons who are deaf or hard of hearing, TTY, (202) 649–5597, or Richard Cleva, Senior Counsel, Bank Activities and Structure Division, (202) 649-5500, Office of the Comptroller of the Currency, 400 7th Street, SW.,

Washington, DC 20219.

SUPPLEMENTARY INFORMATION:

I. Introduction

On September 13, 2016, the OCC published a proposed rule to implement the provisions of the NBA that provide the legal framework for receiverships for uninsured banks,[1] 12 U.S.C. 191 – 200, with comments due by November 14, 2016.[2] The OCC received 11 comments concerning the proposal. For the reasons discussed in section III of the SUPPLEMENTARY INFORMATION, the OCC is adopting the rule as proposed, without change.

II. Background

As of December 2, 2016, the OCC supervised 52 uninsured banks, all of which are national trust banks.[3] Uninsured national trust banks have fundamentally different business models compared to commercial and consumer banks and savings associations and therefore face very different types of risks. National trust banks typically have few assets on the balance sheet, usually composed of cash on deposit with an insured depository institution, investment securities, premises and equipment, and intangible assets. These banks exercise fiduciary and custody powers, do not make loans, do not rely on deposit funding, and consequently have simple liquidity management programs. In view of these differences, the OCC typically requires these banks to hold capital in a specific minimum amount; as a result they hold capital in amounts that exceed substantially the "well capitalized" standard that applies when national banks calculate their capital pursuant to the OCC's rules in 12 CFR part 3.

The business model of national trust banks is to generate income in the form of fees by offering fiduciary and custodial services that generally fall into one or more of a few broad categories. Some national trust banks focus on institutional asset management, providing trust and custodial services for investment portfolios of pension plans, foundations and endowments, and other entities, often with an investment management component. A few other national trust banks serve primarily as a fiduciary and custodian to facilitate the establishment of Individual Retirement Accounts by customers of an affiliated mutual fund complex or broker-dealer firm. Some national trust banks provide custodial services, such as corporate trust accounts, under which the bank performs services for others in connection with their issuance, transfer, and registration of debt or equity securities. Other custody accounts may be a holding facility for customer securities, where the bank assists institutional customers with global settlement and safekeeping of the customer's securities.

---

[1] All Federal savings associations (FSAs), including trust-only FSAs, are required to be insured. For this reason, this final rule does not apply to FSAs, given that receiverships for FSAs would be conducted by the FDIC.

[2] Receiverships for Uninsured National Banks, 81 FR 62835 (September 13, 2016) (Proposed Rule).

[3] The OCC may charter national banks whose operations are limited to those of a trust company and related activities (national trust bank). *See, e.g.,* 12 U.S.C. 27(a); 12 CFR 5.20(*l*).

Many of the uninsured national trust banks are subsidiaries or affiliates of a full-service insured national bank or are affiliates of an insured state bank. Other uninsured national trust banks are not affiliated with an insured depository institution, but are affiliated with an investment management firm or other financial services firm. Still other uninsured national trust banks have no affiliation with a larger parent company.[4]

The OCC appoints and oversees receivers for uninsured banks under the provisions of the NBA[5] and the substantial body of case law applying the statutory provisions and common law receivership principles to national bank receiverships.[6] The FDIC is the required receiver only for an insured national (or state) bank.[7] Based on the statutory history of the NBA and FIRREA, it is likely that the Federal Deposit Insurance Act (FDIA) would not apply to an OCC receivership of an uninsured bank conducted by the OCC, and that such a receivership would be governed exclusively by the NBA, the common law of receivers, and cases applying the statutes and common law to national bank receiverships. While FIRREA and the Federal Deposit Insurance Corporation Improvement Act of 1991 (FDICIA) greatly expanded the FDIC's powers in resolving failed insured depository institutions, the OCC believes that those additional powers are not available to the OCC as receiver of uninsured banks under the NBA.

The OCC has not appointed a receiver for an uninsured bank since shortly after the Congress established the FDIC in response to the banking panics of 1930-1933. National trust banks face very different types of risks because of the fundamentally different business model of national trust banks compared to commercial and consumer banks and savings associations. These risks include operational, compliance, strategic, and reputational risks without the credit and liquidity risks that additionally affect the solvency of commercial and consumer banks. While any of these risks can result in the precipitous failure of a bank or savings association, from a historical perspective, trust banks have been more likely to decline into a weakened condition, allowing the OCC and the institution the time needed to find other solutions for rehabilitating the institution or to successfully resolve the institution without the need to appoint a receiver.

The OCC believes it would nevertheless be beneficial to financial market participants and the broader community of regulators for the OCC to clarify the receivership framework for uninsured banks. Although the OCC conducted 2,762 receiverships pursuant to this framework in the years prior to the creation of the FDIC,[8] and the associated legal issues are the subject of a robust body of published judicial precedents, the details have not been widely articulated in recent jurisprudence or legal commentary. This final rule may also facilitate synergies with the ongoing efforts of U.S. and international financial regulators since the financial crisis to enhance our readiness to respond effectively to the different critical financial distresses that could manifest themselves unexpectedly in the diverse types of financial firms presently operating in the market.

II. Public Comments on the Proposed Rule

The OCC received 11 comments from the public in response to the OCC's notice of proposed rulemaking and the alternatives the OCC discussed therein. The commenters included individuals, a state trust company, and a think tank, as well as representatives of consumer groups, financial reform advocacy groups, state banking regulators, banking institutions, and bitcoin firms. These submissions offered issues and viewpoints about selected portions of the proposed rule's regulatory provisions for the OCC's consideration; these are discussed in connection with the discussion of the OCC's rationale for issuing the associated portions of the final rule, in Section III of this **SUPPLEMENTARY INFORMATION**.

As part of the notice of proposed rulemaking, the OCC also asked for the public's input on a number of specific questions and received comments on two of these questions. One question was whether any unique considerations would be raised by applying the proposed rule's framework for receivership of uninsured national banks, which are all national trust banks at present, to other uninsured banks that would be organized to engage in the delivery of banking services in new and innovative ways, such as special purpose national banks engaged in financial technology (fintech) activities.[9]

---

[4] For additional discussion of the business model of uninsured national trust banks, *see* Proposed Rule, 81 FR at 62836–62837.

[5] 12 U.S.C. 191–200.

[6] For a discussion of the statutory history relating to receiverships of national banks conducted by the OCC, under the NBA, and by the FDIC, pursuant to the Financial Institutions Reform, Recovery and Enforcement Act of 1989 (FIRREA), *see* Proposed Rule, 81 FR at 62836.

[7] Section 11(c)(2)(A)(ii) of the FDIA provides that the FDIC "shall" be appointed receiver, and "shall" accept such appointment, whenever a receiver is appointed for the purpose of liquidation or winding up the affairs of an insured Federal depository institution by the appropriate Federal banking agency, notwithstanding any other provision of Federal law. 12 U.S.C. 1821(c)(2)(A)(ii). The term "Federal depository institution" includes national banks. 12 U.S.C. 1813(c)(4).

[8] *Annual Report of the Comptroller of the Currency for the Year Ended October 31, 1934* at 33 (discussing the status of active and closed receiverships under the jurisdiction of the Comptroller between 1865 and 1934).

[9] *See* Proposed Rule, 81 FR at 62837 (discussing the OCC's initiative on responsible innovation in the Federal banking system, and the OCC's authority to charter special purpose

On this receivership framework question, two commenters expressed concerns that the earlier-established legal regime for receiverships under the NBA and associated judicial precedent does not include select elements subsequently created for insured depository institutions under FIRREA and FDICIA, and thus might not be as effective outside the trust bank sphere in application to the receivership of special purpose national banks engaged in fintech activities. These commenters said the OCC should refrain from chartering these special purpose national banks until the law changes to address this difference. One commenter expressed concern that the rule's incorporation of the NBA's priority requirements for payment of receivership claims, which include no preference for consumer claims over other general creditors, might have the effect of distorting incentives among debt investors across special purpose national banks, and more broadly contribute to moral hazard.

The OCC understands these comments to be urging, in effect, changes in the statutory receivership provisions underlying the rule. Absent Congressional action to do so, however, the current provisions of the NBA are the ones that would govern should it become necessary to appoint a receiver for an uninsured national bank. The OCC believes it is best to be clear, through a regulation implementing those NBA provisions, about the framework that would apply in order to avoid clouding the ongoing discussion about the chartering of special purpose national banks engaged in fintech activities with uncertainty about how uninsured institutions are resolved.

More broadly, some commenters said the OCC should consider receivership and cost issues in deciding whether to charter special purpose national banks engaged in fintech activities, or the terms on which they could be chartered. Two commenters said the nature of a fintech firm's business diverges widely from banks, and that creditor loss rates in a receivership for an uninsured special purpose national bank engaged in fintech activities may exceed levels that are tolerable in the resolution of a chartered bank. These commenters said this was a contraindication for chartering such banks, but one of the commenters further elaborated that the OCC can and should exercise particularly close supervision of these firms and thereby reduce the risk of receiverships ever taking place. Another commenter said that fintech firms do not have national trust banks' track record for remaining solvent and avoiding receivership, and the OCC should mitigate potential concerns about receivership costs by imposing capital support agreements and similar obligations in chartering special purpose national banks that engage in fintech activities.

In contrast to these views about the uniqueness of special purpose national banks engaged in fintech activities, one commenter said that a fintech firm, such as a digital currency exchange, performs a function comparable to a national trust bank that obtains payments on behalf of customers and provides security for those funds, and therefore such institutions do not pose unique considerations for the receivership framework. Another commenter said the functions of special purpose national banks that engage in fintech activities could be even simpler than a national trust bank, such as a special purpose national bank that provides fintech payment services where each customer transaction is brief and segregated. For special purpose national banks engaged in fintech activities involving lending, this commenter stated the customer relationships are somewhat longer but still discrete, and that the OCC could adequately eliminate concerns about the impact of a receivership by ensuring the bank's plans for back-up servicing and orderly wind-up were robust.

Some commenters discussed additional topics not touching on the receivership issues covered by the notice of proposed rulemaking, but more germane to the desired framework for creating, regulating, and supervising special purpose national banks that engage in fintech activities or uninsured national trust banks. These broader comments do not pertain to the OCC's adoption of the final rule for uninsured banks and many of them implicate issues that the OCC would need to evaluate on a case-by-case basis in connection with a decision on whether to charter a particular special purpose national bank that engages in fintech activities. The OCC has recently published and invited comment on a paper discussing these issues.[10] We will consider the broader comments on fintech chartering submitted as part of this rulemaking together with those we receive in response to the paper.

In the second question asked in the preamble to the Proposed Rule, the OCC asked for alternatives that would take into account the cost considerations that could arise for the OCC if the administrative expenses of an uninsured national bank receivership exceeded the assets in the receivership.[11] In response to this question, one commenter urged the OCC not to impose assessment costs for special purpose national banks that engage in fintech activities on insured national banks, and another

---

(Footnote Continued)

banks that engage in selected core non-depository services within the business of banking).

[10] See Exploring Special Purpose National Bank Charters for Fintech Companies (Dec. 2016), available at https://www.occ.gov/topics/bank-operations/innovation/special-purpose-national-bank-charters-for-fintech.pdf.

[11] See Proposed Rule, 81 Fed. Reg. at 62838 (discussing the receiver's priority claim to liquidation proceeds for administrative expenses, the OCC's potential direct expenses for its receivership functions, and funding alternatives, such as building resources to defray these costs through the OCC's regulations governing the OCC's collection of assessments from uninsured national banks).

commenter further urged the OCC not to impose assessment costs for such banks on uninsured national trust banks. The OCC continues to consider what approach to assessments would be appropriate should it approve charters for special purpose national banks engaged in fintech activities. Any resulting modification to the OCC's assessment structure would be proposed for public comment in a separate rulemaking.

IV. The Final Rule

Overview

The final rule incorporates the framework set forth in the NBA for the Comptroller to appoint a receiver for an uninsured bank, generally under the same grounds for appointment of the FDIC as receiver for insured national banks. The uninsured bank may challenge the appointment in court, and the NBA affords jurisdiction to the appropriate United States district court for this purpose. The OCC will provide the public with notice of the appointment, as well as instructions for submitting claims against the uninsured bank in receivership. The Comptroller may appoint any person as receiver, including the OCC or another government agency. The receiver carries out its duties under the direction of the Comptroller.

The final rule also follows the statutory framework under the NBA with respect to claims, under which persons with claims against an uninsured bank in receivership will file their claims with the receiver for the failed uninsured bank, for review by the OCC. In the event the OCC denies the claim, the only remedy available to the claimant is to bring a judicial action against the uninsured bank's receivership estate and assert the claim *de novo*. A person is also free to initiate a claim by bringing an action against the receivership estate in court for adjudication and then submit the judgment to the OCC to participate in ratable dividends of liquidation proceeds along with other approved and adjudicated claims.[12]

Approved or adjudicated claims are paid solely out of the assets of the uninsured national bank in receivership. This reflects the legal distinction between the OCC as regulatory agency and the OCC acting in a receivership capacity. In the former, the OCC oversees national banks, FSAs, and Federal branches and Federal agencies, supervising them under the charge of assuring the safety and soundness of, and compliance with laws and regulations, fair access to financial services, and fair treatment of customers by, the institutions and other persons subject to its jurisdiction. As receiver, the OCC appoints and oversees receivers for uninsured national banks, thereby facilitating the winding down of bank operations, assets, and accounts while minimizing disruptions to customers and creditors of the institution. Under the "separate capacities" doctrine, which has long been recognized in litigation involving the FDIC, it is well established that the agency, when acting in one capacity, is not liable for claims against the agency acting in its other capacity.[13]

As provided in the final rule, the receiver liquidates the assets of the uninsured bank, with court approval, and pays the proceeds into an account as directed by the OCC. The categories of claims and the priority thereof for payment are set out in the final rule. The final rule also clarifies certain powers held by the receiver.

Section-by-Section Analysis

Section 51.1 of the final rule identifies the purpose and scope of the final rule and clarifies that the rule applies to receiverships conducted by the OCC under the NBA for national banks that are not insured by the FDIC.[14] The final rule does not extend to receiverships for uninsured Federal branches, although elements of the framework may be similar for uninsured Federal branch receiverships, which would also be resolved under provisions of the NBA.

Section 51.2 of the final rule is based on 12 U.S.C. 191 and 192 and concerns appointment of a receiver. The final rule sets out the Comptroller's authority to appoint any person, including the OCC or another government agency, as receiver for an uninsured bank and provides that the receiver performs its duties subject to the approval and direction of the Comptroller.[15] If the Comptroller were to appoint the OCC as

---

[12] *See First Nat'l Bank of Bethel v. Nat'l Pahquioque Bank,* 81 U.S. 383, 401 (1871).

[13] For a discussion of the separate capacities doctrine and related case law, *see* Proposed Rule, 81 FR at 62838.

[14] A nationwide organization of state regulators requested clarity on how the NBA receivership framework for uninsured national banks and the OCC's proposed rule thereunder would interact with the processes established for debtors and creditors pursuant to the U.S. Bankruptcy Code. The OCC is not aware of any opinion of a U.S. Bankruptcy Court, or any

other U.S. court, finding that an uninsured national bank is eligible to be a debtor subject to a petition under the Code.

[15] *But see* 12 U.S.C. § 1821(c)(6) (Comptroller may appoint the FDIC as conservator or receiver and the FDIC has discretion to accept such appointment); *id.* section 1821(c)(2)(C) (FDIC "not subject to any other agency" when acting as conservator or receiver"). Read together, these provisions likely mean that the provision in §51.2 concerning oversight of the receiver by the Comptroller would not apply to the FDIC acting as conservator or receiver for an uninsured institution, should the Comptroller appoint the FDIC and the FDIC accept such an appointment.

receiver, the OCC would act in a receivership capacity with respect to the uninsured bank in receivership, rather than in the OCC's supervisory capacity.

As discussed earlier, this dual capacity (OCC as supervisor versus OCC as receivership sponsor for an uninsured bank) recognizes that, while the NBA makes the receivership oversight and claims review functions of the Comptroller part of the OCC's responsibilities, the receivership oversight role is unique and distinct from the OCC's role as a Federal regulatory agency and supervisor of national banks and FSAs. This is comparable to the dual capacity of the FDIC's receivership function for insured depository institutions pursuant to the FDIA.

Section 51.2 of the final rule also provides that the Comptroller may require the receiver to post a bond or other security and the receiver may hire staff and professional advisors, with the approval of the Comptroller, if needed to carry out the receivership. This section also identifies the grounds for appointment of a receiver for an uninsured bank and notes that uninsured banks may seek judicial review of the appointment pursuant to 12 U.S.C. 191.

Section 51.3 of the final rule provides that the OCC will provide notice to the public of the appointment of a receiver for the uninsured bank. The final rule specifies that one component of this notice will include publication in a newspaper of general circulation selected by the OCC for three consecutive months, as required by 12 U.S.C. 193. As a component of the OCC's notice to the public about the receivership, the OCC will also provide instructions for creditors and other claimants seeking to submit claims with the receiver for the uninsured bank.

As noted in the proposed rule, the OCC believes that the purpose of section 193 may be better served by publication through means in addition to the statutorily required publication in a newspaper. For example, the OCC could provide direct notice to customers and creditors of the uninsured bank to the extent the uninsured bank's records included current contact information. The OCC could also arrange to provide notice through electronic channels that customers would typically use to contact the uninsured bank, such as the uninsured bank's website. The OCC believes that an effective set of notice protocols would best be established on a case-by-case basis, in light of a specific uninsured bank's fiduciary and custodial activities, the types of customers served by the bank, coordination with other notice protocols under way for any related entity that is also undergoing resolution activity, and similar factors. The OCC requested comment on alternative means of communicating with customers of uninsured banks.

One commenter, a trade association for banks, suggested that the OCC employ notice mechanisms that are consistent with the way in which the failed bank typically communicates with its clients and counterparties. The commenter suggested, for example, that a receiver for an institution with clients in other countries should communicate with those clients in the language typically used by the institution in its communications with those clients. The OCC agrees that this approach would be appropriate in such cases and reiterates that effective forms of notice, beyond the statutorily required notice in a newspaper, will be evaluated on a case-by-case basis.

Section 51.4 of the final rule addresses the submission of claims to the receiver for an uninsured bank. Under § 51.4(a), a person with a claim against the receivership may submit a claim to the OCC, which will consider the claim and make a determination concerning its validity and approved amount. This process reflects the provisions in 12 U.S.C. 193 and 194 regarding presentation of claims and payment of dividends on claims that are proved to the satisfaction of the Comptroller. Section 51.4 also provides that the Comptroller will establish a deadline for filing claims with the receiver, which could not be earlier than 30 days after the three-month publication of notice required by § 51.3. This provision reflects NBA case law that permits the Comptroller to establish a date for filing claims against the receiver for a failed bank.[16]

Section 51.4(b) of the final rule clarifies that persons with claims against an uninsured bank in receivership may present their claims to a court of competent jurisdiction for adjudication in addition to, or as an alternative to, filing a claim with the OCC. If successful in court, such persons will be required to submit a copy of the final judgment to the OCC to participate in ratable dividends of liquidation proceeds along with claims against the bank in receivership submitted to, and approved by, the OCC. The final rule requires submission of a copy of the court's final judgment to the OCC. This provision is based on 12 U.S.C. 193 and 194.

In this regard, the receivership regime established by the NBA differs somewhat from the approach set out in other resolution regimes, such as the bankruptcy provisions of the United States Code and the receivership provisions of the FDIA. Under those resolution regimes, creditors and claimants must generally submit their claims to the receivership estate for centralized administration and disposition, and claims that are not submitted by the claims deadline are barred from any participation in liquidation payments. The NBA provisions are different in that claimants are provided the opportunity to submit

---

[16] *See Queenan v. Mays*, 90 F.2d 525, 531 (10th Cir. 1937).

claims to the OCC for evaluation, but are not foreclosed from pursuing judicial resolution by filing litigation (or continuing a pre-existing lawsuit) in a court of competent jurisdiction against the uninsured bank in receivership.

The claims filing deadline established by the Comptroller pursuant to § 51.4(a) of the final rule is the date by which claimants seeking review under the OCC's claims process must make their submission. Nevertheless, a claimant that has not made a submission to the OCC by the deadline is not barred from initiating judicial claims against the uninsured bank in receivership solely by virtue of missing the claims deadline.[17]

The NBA's receivership provisions are like the receivership regime established by the FDIC under the FDIA, however, in that the avenue available to a party whose claim has been denied by the FDIC or OCC, when performing the agencies' receivership claims functions, is to file (or continue) a *de novo* judicial action asserting the facts and legal theory of the claim against the receivership of the bank. The NBA does not contemplate or support further action by the claimant in an administrative or judicial forum against the OCC seeking review of the claim determination.

Section 51.4(c) of the final rule provides that if a person with a claim against an uninsured bank in receivership also has an obligation owed to the bank, the claim and obligation will be set off against each other and only the net balance remaining after set-off will be considered as a claim. To this end, § 51.4(a) also includes language referring to claims for set- off. The right of set-off where parties have mutual obligations has long been recognized as an equitable principle.[18] Well-settled case law has held that a receivership creditor's or other claimant's equitable right to a set-off is not precluded by the ratable distribution requirement of the NBA, provided such set-off is otherwise legally valid.[19] If, after set-off, an amount is owed to the creditor, the creditor may file a claim for the net amount remaining as any other general creditor. Conversely, if, after set-off, an amount is owed to the bank, the creditor does not have a claim and the net amount remaining is an asset of the uninsured bank, which the receiver may obtain in connection with marshalling the assets (as described further in § 51.7(a) of the final rule).

The OCC requested comment on whether there are additional characteristics of set-offs or other situations in which set-off may arise that should be included in the rule. One commenter, a trade association for banks, said that the administration of set-offs may be complex, given that the trust and fiduciary business is a fee-based industry. The commenter offered the example of instances in which fees have been accrued or are otherwise in the process of payment to one or more service providers at the time of receivership. The commenter suggested that the final rule acknowledge that a given resolution may involve bespoke, fact-specific set-off situations that would need to be carefully considered, while also serving the need for the receiver or a successor fiduciary to be in a position to continue providing fiduciary services during the receivership.

The OCC believes that, on balance, it is not necessary to make this kind of an addition to the language of the final rule. Section 51.4 as a whole is designed to make the basic framework of claim submission transparent to creditors of the uninsured bank, and set-off is included as an element of this framework. As the commenter states, the OCC's determination of particular claims will require consideration of fact-specific situations prior to reaching a disposition, and this extends to considerations of set-offs. The final rule is designed to accommodate with flexibility the consideration of such factors in the context in which each claim is postured.

Section 51.5 of the final rule sets out the order of priorities for payment of administrative expenses of the receiver and claims against the uninsured bank in receivership. Under this section, the OCC will pay these expenses and claims in the following order: (1) administrative expenses of the receiver; (2) unsecured creditors, including secured creditors to the extent their claim exceeds their valid and enforceable security interest; (3) creditors of the uninsured bank, if any, whose claims are subordinated to general creditor claims; and (4) shareholders of the uninsured bank. The order is based on case law and, in the case of the first priority for administrative expenses, on 12 U.S.C. 196.[20]

---

[17] *See First Nat'l Bank of Bethel v. Nat'l Pahquioque Bank,* 81 U.S. 383, 401 (1871); *Queenan v. Mays,* 90 F.2d 525, 531 (10th Cir. 1937). As noted earlier, it is incumbent on a claimant that pursues the judicial route and ultimately obtains judicial relief to submit the final judicial determination and award to the OCC, in order to participate in the OCC's periodic ratable dividends of liquidation proceeds of the receivership estate. Except with respect to a valid and enforceable security interest in specific property of the uninsured bank established as part of a final judicial determination, there are no assets or funds available to a successful judicial claimant other than that the ratable dividend process set out in 12 U.S.C. 194 and described in § 51.8 of the final rule.

[18] *See, e.g., Scammon v. Kimball,* 92 U.S. 362 (1876); *Blount v. Windley,* 95 U.S. 173, 177 (1877); *Carr v. Hamilton,* 129 U.S. 252 (1889).

[19] *See Scott v. Armstrong,* 146 U.S. 499, 510 (1892); *InterFirst Bank of Abilene, N.A. v. FDIC,* 777 F.2d 1092, 1095-1096 (5th Cir. 1985); *FDIC v. Mademoiselle of California,* 379 F.2d 660, 663 (9th Cir. 1967).

[20] *See Ticonic Nat'l Bank v. Sprague,* 303 U.S. 406, 410-411 (1938); *Merrill v. Nat'l Bank of Jacksonville,* 173 U.S. 131, 146 (1899); *Scott v. Armstrong,* 146 U.S. 499, 510 (1892); *Bell v. Hanover Nat'l Bank,* 57 F. 821, 822 (C.C.S.D.N.Y. 1893).

A creditor or other claimant with a security interest that was valid and enforceable as to its terms prior to the appointment of the receiver is entitled to exercise that security interest, outside the priority of distributions set out in the final rule.[21] If the collateral value exceeds the amount of the claim as it was immediately prior to the receiver's appointment, the surplus remains an asset of the uninsured bank, and the receiver may obtain it in connection with marshalling the assets (as further described in § 51.7(a) of the final rule).[22]

Liens arising from judicial determinations after the initiation of the receivership, as well as contractual liens that are triggered due to the appointment of a receiver or other post- appointment events, are not enforceable. This is because recognition of these liens would afford these claimants a priority that is not recognized under the established legal priorities described in § 51.5 of the final rule. Similarly, a secured creditor is not entitled to a priority distribution of any portion of the claim that is not covered by the value of the collateral because the creditor is in the position of a general unsecured creditor for that portion of the claim and must participate in ratable liquidation distributions on par with other unsecured creditors.[23]

Assets held by the uninsured bank at the time of the receiver's appointment in a fiduciary or custodial capacity, as identified on the bank's books and records, are not general assets of the bank. Section 51.8(b) of the final rule reiterates this point. In the same vein, the claim of the customer for the return of the customer's fiduciary or custodial assets is separate from, and not subject to, the priority set out in § 51.5. Fiduciary and custodial customers of the bank have direct claims on those assets pursuant to their fiduciary or custodial account contracts. However, the priority of a fiduciary or custodial customer's other claims against the bank, if any, would remain subject to the priority described in § 51.5. For example, a fiduciary customer's claim for a refund of prepaid investment management fees that were attributable to periods after the receiver returned the fiduciary assets to the customer generally would be a general unsecured claim covered by § 51.5(b). The claims process described in § 51.4(b) is available to a fiduciary customer, for both a direct claim for the return of fiduciary assets, as well as a receivership claim for amounts the customer believes it is owed by the bank.

The OCC requested comment on whether there are other Federal statutes regarding specific types of claims that may be applicable to a receivership of an uninsured bank under the NBA and that would give certain claims a different priority, such as claims owed to the Federal government. One commenter, a coalition that advocates for reform in the financial services industry, agreed that customer assets held by a bank in a fiduciary capacity should not be considered assets of the bank, but questioned why other claims of the customer, such as a claim for a refund of prepaid investment management fees that were attributable to periods after the receiver returned the fiduciary assets to the customer, would be treated as a unsecured general creditor claim. The commenter suggested that such customer funds would have less protection in a receivership for an uninsured bank than they would under certain modern receivership and bankruptcy statutes that set forth claim priorities which include preference to customer claims over other general creditor claims.

The OCC is required, by statute, to pay claims on a ratable basis. As discussed in connection with the description of § 51.8 of the final rule, this requirement has been interpreted by the courts as requiring the OCC to make distributions on OCC-approved claims and judicial awards on an equal footing, determining the amount of each creditor's claim as it stands at the point of insolvency. As a result, the controlling ratable payment statute does not support a rule that makes distinctions in distribution priority between customer and general creditor claimants.

Section 51.6 of the final rule provides that all administrative expenses of the receiver for an uninsured bank will be paid out of the assets of the receivership before payment of claims against the receivership. This reflects the requirements in 12 U.S.C. 196. The final rule also states that receivership expenses will include pre-receivership and post-receivership obligations that the receiver determines are necessary and appropriate to facilitate the orderly liquidation or other resolution of the uninsured bank in receivership. To further illustrate the kinds of expenses that § 196 affords a first priority claim on the uninsured bank's receivership assets, § 51.6 enumerates examples of such administrative expenses, such as wages and salaries of employees, expenses for professional services, contractual rent pursuant to an existing lease or rental agreement, and payments to third-party or affiliated service providers, when the receiver determines these expenses are of benefit to the receivership.

Section 51.7 of the final rule contains provisions describing the powers and duties of the receiver and the disposition of fiduciary and custodial accounts. As described in § 51.7, the receiver will take over the assets and operation of the uninsured bank, take action to realize on debts owed to the uninsured bank, sell the property of the bank, and liquidate the assets of the uninsured bank for payment of claims

---

[21] *Ticonic Nat'l Bank v. Sprague*, 303 U.S. 406, 410-411 (1938); *Bell v. Hanover Nat'l Bank*, 57 F. 821, 822 (C.C.S.D.N.Y. 1893).

[22] *Bell v. Hanover Nat'l Bank*, 57 F. 821, 822 (C.C.S.D.N.Y. 1893).

[23] *Merrill v. Nat'l Bank of Jacksonville*, 173 U.S. 131, 146 (1899).

against the receivership. Section 51.7(a)(1)-(5) lists some of the major powers and duties for the receiver set out in 12 U.S.C. 192 and clarified by the courts, including taking possession of the books and records of the bank, collecting on debts and claims owed to the bank, selling or compromising bad or doubtful debts (with court approval), and selling the bank's real and personal property (also with court approval).

Section 51.7(b) of the final rule provides for the receiver to close the uninsured bank's fiduciary and custodial appointments, or transfer such accounts to a successor fiduciary or custodian under 12 CFR 9.16 or other applicable Federal law. The uninsured banks currently in existence focus on fiduciary and custodial services, so this function of the receiver will be of primary importance. This provision recognizes that the receiver's power to wind up the affairs of the uninsured bank in receivership, acting with court approval to make disposition of bank assets, should properly encompass the power to transfer fiduciary or custodial appointments and any associated assets in appropriate circumstances.

Transfer of fiduciary appointments may occur under the terms of the instrument creating the relationship, if it provides for transfer, or under a fiduciary transfer statute, if one is applicable. The OCC believes there are strong public policy interests in endeavoring to replace fiduciaries and custodians expeditiously, without an interruption in service to their customers, if transfer can be arranged to a qualified successor, maintaining the same duties and standards of care with respect to the customers that previously pertained to their accounts at the uninsured bank in receivership. The alternative, given that the uninsured bank must be wound down and cannot provide services in the future, is to stop managing and reinvesting the customer's assets, stop responding to directions to transfer or receive assets in custody, close the accounts, and seek instructions from the account holders or the courts regarding return of associated assets. For institutional customers, this is likely to cause significant interruption of the intricate machinery of their financial operations. For individuals, it can potentially result in loss of asset value in adverse markets, or loss of income due to foregone reinvestments.

Across the United States, there are disparate and often conflicting legal rules restricting or conditioning transfers of an appointment of a fiduciary for a beneficiary residing within the state. Depending on the geographic area across which the uninsured bank has established fiduciary relationships with its customers, and the standardization of its fiduciary account agreements or appointing instruments, it may be practicable for the receiver to transition an uninsured bank's fiduciary and custody accounts to a qualified successor through the mechanisms provided by applicable local law. On the other hand, if faced with dispersed customers, diverse account agreements or appointments of different vintage, or even the absence of an applicable law of transfer for customers in certain states, reliance on these methods may be so cumbersome as to effectively prevent accomplishment of the transfers in a timely way.

In order to address these potential problems, the OCC, relying on the support of existing case law, is including language in the final rule to make it clear that the uninsured bank receiver's power under 12 U.S.C. 192 to sell, with court approval, the real and personal property of the bank includes the power to transfer the bank's fiduciary accounts and related assets, subject to the approval of the court exercising jurisdiction over the receiver's efforts to transfer the bank's assets. The final rule is consistent with case law recognizing that a receiver for a national bank may properly arrange asset purchase and liability assumption transactions to move the business of a failed bank to a successor on an integrated basis, as part of the power to transfer assets, as well as analogous case law concerning the transfer of fiduciary and custodial assets by the FDIC, acting as receiver of failed insured depository institutions.[24]

Section 51.7(c) of the final rule incorporates, in general terms, the powers, duties, and responsibilities of receivers for national banks under the NBA and under judicial precedents determining the authorities and responsibilities of receivers for national banks. Examples of these powers include: (1) the authority to repudiate certain contracts, including: (a) purely executory contracts, upon determining that the contracts would be unduly burdensome or unprofitable for the receivership estate,[25] (b) contracts that involve fraud or misrepresentation,[26] and (c) in limited cases, non-executory contracts that are contrary to public policy;[27] (2) the authority to recover fraudulent transfers;[28] and (3) the authority to enforce collection of notes from debtors and collateral, regardless of the existence of side arrangements that would otherwise defeat the collectability of such notes.[29]

Section 51.7(d) of the final rule requires the receiver to make periodic reports to the OCC concerning the status and proceedings of the receivership.

---

[24] See NCNB Texas National Bank v. Cowden, 895 F.2d 1488 (5th Cir. 1990) (holding that the FDIC, as receiver of insolvent bank, had authority to transfer fiduciary appointments to a bridge bank prior to the Financial Institutions Reform, Recovery, and Enforcement Act of 1989).

[25] Bank One Texas v. Prudential Life Ins. Co., 878 F. Supp. 943, 964-66 (N.D. Tex. 1995).

[26] A. Corbin, Corbin on Contracts § 228 at 320 (1952) (addressing contracts voidable for fraud, duress, or mistake).

[27] Cf. Fidelity Deposit Co. of Md. v. Conner, 973 F.2d 1236, 1241 (5th Cir. 1992).

[28] See Peters v. Bain, 133 U.S. 670 (1890) (applying state substantive law to determine whether to void a transfer); Rogers v. Marchant, 91 F.2d 660, 663 (4th Cir. 1937).

[29] D'Oench, Duhme & Co., Inc. v. FDIC, 315 U.S. 447, 458 (1942). A. Corbin, Corbin on Contracts, § 228 at 320 (1952) (addressing contracts voidable for fraud, duress or mistake).

Section 51.8 of the final rule contains provisions regarding the payment of dividends on claims against the uninsured bank and the distribution of any remaining proceeds to shareholders. This section provides that, after administrative expenses of the receivership have been paid, the OCC will make ratable dividends from available receivership funds based on the priority of claims in proposed § 51.5 for claims that have been proved to the OCC's satisfaction or adjudicated in a court of competent jurisdiction, as provided in 12 U.S.C. 194. The OCC will make payment of dividends, if any, periodically, at the discretion of the OCC, as the receiver liquidates the assets of the uninsured bank.

The final rule's inclusion of the "ratable dividend" requirement is designed to incorporate the associated standards about the proper application of this statutory directive, which the judiciary has articulated over the years. The ratable dividend requirement directs the OCC to make distributions on OCC-approved claims and judicial awards on an equal footing, determining the amount of each creditor's claim as it stands at the point of insolvency. As one example, a court's award of interest on an unpaid debt to the date of a judgment rendered in the plaintiff's favor after the receiver was appointed does not increase the amount of the plaintiff's claim for purposes of making ratable dividends. As another example, the ratable dividend requirement generally restricts claims against the bank receivership for debts that were not due and owing at the appointment of the receiver and arose for the first time as a consequence of the appointment or a post-appointment event.

The OCC requested comment on alternatives to the proposed rule's approach to paying dividends on claims, under which the OCC would exercise its discretion under section 194 to determine the timing of the distributions on established claims. Under one alternative presented in the proposed rule, the OCC would refrain from paying any dividends until all claims have been submitted and validated, with final allowed claim amounts established. As we noted in the proposal, this approach presents the possibility that proven claims may be delayed for a significant amount of time pending more protracted resolution of other claims. Under a second option presented in the proposed rule, the OCC would make ongoing dividends on proven claims, subject to the receiver's retaining a percentage of the funds on hand at the time of the distribution as a pool of dividends for catch-up distributions to a successful plaintiff later.

The OCC did not receive comments on these alternative approaches for making ratable distributions on claims against a receivership. For this reason, and because the proposed rule's approach to payment of dividends provides the OCC with the discretion to tailor the dividend process to facts and circumstances of a particular receivership, the final rule adopts § 51.8 as proposed.

Section 51.8(a)(2) of the final rule recognizes the basic legal premise under the NBA receivership provisions and judicial interpretations thereof that any dividend payments to creditors and other claimants of an uninsured bank will be made solely from receivership funds, if any, paid to the OCC by the receiver after payment of the expenses of the receiver. This provision is also consistent with the established dichotomy of the OCC's supervisory and receivership capacities in the NBA, as discussed earlier.

Section 51.8(b) of the final rule similarly recognizes that assets held by an uninsured national bank at the time of the receiver's appointment in a fiduciary or custodial capacity, as designated on the bank's books and records, are not part of the bank's general assets and liabilities held in connection with its other business and will not be considered a source for payment for unrelated claims of creditors and other claimants. This provision is intended to make clear that the receiver will segregate identified fiduciary and custodial assets and either transfer those assets to other fiduciaries or custodians as described in connection with § 51.7(b), or close the accounts and endeavor to make the associated assets available to the account holders or their representatives through other means.

One commenter, a trade association for banks, agreed with the treatment of fiduciary assets in the proposed rule, but questioned whether § 51.8(b) indicates with sufficient clarity that fiduciary assets will not be treated as assets of the bank in receivership. As stated in the final rule, fiduciary and custodial assets "will not be considered as part of the bank's general assets . . .". The OCC reiterates that, under this section, assets held by an uninsured bank in a fiduciary or custodial capacity, as designated on the bank's books and records, are not part of the bank's general assets and liabilities held in connection with its other business and will not be a source for payment for unrelated claims of creditors and other claimants.

Section 51.8(d) of the final rule provides that, after all administrative expenses and claims have been paid in full, any remaining proceeds will be paid to shareholders in proportion to their stock ownership, also as provided in 12 U.S.C. 194.

Section 51.9 of the final rule contains provisions for termination of receiverships in which there are assets remaining after all administrative expenses and all claims had been paid. This is the scenario addressed by 12 U.S.C. 197. In such a case, section 197 requires the Comptroller to call a meeting of the shareholders of the bank at which the shareholders would decide whether to continue oversight by the Comptroller, or whether to end the receivership and appoint a liquidating agent to continue the liquidation of the remaining assets, under the direction of the board of directors and shareholders, as in a liquidation that had commenced under 12 U.S.C. 181.

There may be other circumstances under which termination would take place, such as when there are no receivership assets remaining after completion of receivership activities. Under this scenario, the receiver for an uninsured bank has liquidated all of the bank's assets, closed or transferred all fiduciary accounts to a successor fiduciary, paid all administrative expenses, and either paid creditor claims in full and distributed the remaining proceeds to shareholders, as provided in § 51.8(c) of the final rule, or made ratable dividends of all remaining proceeds to creditors as provided in § 51.8(a), but no additional assets remain in the estate. Under these circumstances, the provisions in 12 U.S.C. 197 for termination would not apply.

V. Regulatory Analysis

A. *Paperwork Reduction Act*

Under the Paperwork Reduction Act (PRA) of 1995 (44 U.S.C. 3501 *et seq.*), the OCC may not conduct or sponsor, and, notwithstanding any other provision of law, a person is not required to respond to, an information collection unless the information collection displays a valid Office of Management and Budget (OMB) control number. The final rule contains no information collection requirements under the PRA.

B. *Regulatory Flexibility Act*

The Regulatory Flexibility Act (RFA), 5 U.S.C. 601 *et seq.*, generally requires that, in connection with a rulemaking, an agency prepare and make available for public comment a regulatory flexibility analysis that describes the impact of the rule on small entities. However, the regulatory flexibility analysis otherwise required under the RFA is not required if an agency certifies that the rule will not have a significant economic impact on a substantial number of small entities (defined in regulations promulgated by the Small Business Administration (SBA) to include commercial banks and savings institutions, and trust companies, with assets of $550 million or less and $38.5 million or less, respectively) and publishes its certification and a brief explanatory statement in the **Federal Register** together with the rule.

The OCC currently supervises approximately 1,032 small entities. The scope of the final rule extends to uninsured banks. The maximum number of OCC-supervised small uninsured banks that could be subject to the receivership framework described in the final rule is approximately 18.[30] Accordingly, the OCC certifies that the final rule will not have a significant economic impact on a substantial number of small entities.

OCC Unfunded Mandates Reform Act of 1995 Determination

The OCC has analyzed the final rule under the factors in the Unfunded Mandates Reform Act of 1995 (UMRA) (2 U.S.C. 1532). Under this analysis, the OCC considered whether the final rule includes a Federal mandate that may result in the expenditure by state, local, and tribal governments, in the aggregate, or by the private sector, of $100 million or more in any one year (adjusted annually for inflation). As detailed in the **SUPPLEMENTARY INFORMATION,** the OCC currently supervises 52 uninsured banks, all of which are uninsured trust banks, and has not appointed a receiver for an uninsured bank since 1933. Unlike commercial and consumer banks and savings associations, which generally face credit and liquidity risks, national trust banks primarily face operational, reputational, and strategic risks. While any of these risks could result in the precipitous failure of a bank or savings association, from a historical perspective, trust banks have been more likely to decline into a weakened condition, allowing the OCC and the institution the time needed to find other solutions for rehabilitating the institution or to successfully resolve the institution without the need to appoint a receiver. As such, we believe the OCC is unlikely to place an uninsured trust bank into receivership. For this reason, and because the final rule does not impose any implementation requirements, the OCC concludes that the final rule will not result in an expenditure of $100 million or more by state, local, and tribal governments, or by the private sector, in any one year.

List of Subjects in 12 CFR Part 51

Administrative practice and procedure, Banks, Banking, National banks, Procedural rules,

Receiverships.

Authority and Issuance

---

[30] Consistent with the General Principles of Affiliation 13 CFR 121.103(a), the OCC counts the assets of affiliated financial institutions when determining if we should classify an institution we supervise as a small entity. We used December 31, 2015, to determine size because a financial institution's assets are determined by averaging the assets reported on its four quarterly financial statements for the preceding year. *See* footnote 8 of the U.S. SBA's *Table of Size Standards.*

For the reasons set forth in the preamble and under the authority of 12 U.S.C. 16, 93a, 191-200, 481, 482, 1831c, and 1867 the Office of the Comptroller of the Currency adds part 51 to chapter I of title 12, Code of Federal Regulations to read as follows:

PART 51 — RECEIVERSHIPS FOR UNINSURED NATIONAL BANKS

Sec.

51.1 Purpose and scope.

51.2 Appointment of receiver.

51.3 Notice of appointment of receiver.

51.4 Claims.

51.5 Order of priorities.

51.6 Administrative expenses of receiver.

51.7 Powers and duties of receiver; disposition of fiduciary and custodial accounts.

51.8 Payment of claims and dividends to shareholders.

51.9 Termination of receivership.

Authority: 12 U.S.C. 16, 93a, 191-200, 481, 482, 1831c, and 1867.

§ 51.1 Purpose and scope.

(a) *Purpose.* This part sets out procedures for receiverships of national banks conducted by the Office of the Comptroller of the Currency (OCC) under the receivership provisions of the National Bank Act (NBA). These receivership provisions apply to national banks that are not insured by the Federal Deposit Insurance Corporation (FDIC).

(b) *Scope.* This part applies to the appointment of a receiver for uninsured national banks (uninsured banks) and the operation of a receivership after appointment of a receiver for an uninsured bank under 12 U.S.C. 191.[31]

§ 51.2 Appointment of receiver.

(a) *In general.* The Comptroller of the Currency (Comptroller) may appoint any person, including the OCC or another government agency, as receiver for an uninsured bank. The receiver performs its duties under the direction of the Comptroller and serves at the will of the Comptroller. The Comptroller may require the receiver to post a bond or other security. The receiver, with the approval of the Comptroller, may employ such staff and enter into contracts for professional services as are necessary to carry out the receivership.

(b) *Grounds for appointment.* The Comptroller may appoint a receiver for an uninsured bank based on any of the grounds specified in 12 U.S.C. 191(a).

(c) *Judicial review.* If the Comptroller appoints a receiver for an uninsured bank, the bank may seek judicial review of the appointment as provided in 12 U.S.C. 191(b).

§ 51.3 Notice of appointment of receiver.

Upon appointment of a receiver for an uninsured bank, the OCC will provide notice to the public of the receivership, including by publication in a newspaper of general circulation for three consecutive months. The notice of the receivership will provide instructions for creditors and other claimants seeking to submit claims with the receiver for the uninsured bank.

§ 51.4 Claims.

(a) *Submission of claims for consideration by the OCC.* (1) Persons who have claims against the receivership for an uninsured bank may present such claims, along with supporting documentation, for consideration by the OCC. The OCC will determine the validity and approve the amounts of such claims.

(2) The OCC will establish a date by which any person seeking to present a claim against the uninsured bank for consideration by the OCC must present their claim for determination. The deadline for filing such claims will not be less than 30 days after the end of the three-month notice period in § 51.3.

(3) The OCC will allow any claim against the uninsured bank received on or before the deadline for presenting claims if such claim is established to the OCC's satisfaction by the information on the

---

[31] This part does not apply to receiverships for uninsured Federal branches or uninsured Federal agencies.

uninsured bank's books and records or otherwise submitted. The OCC may disallow any portion of any claim by a creditor or claim of a security, preference, set-off, or priority which is not established to the satisfaction of the OCC.

(b) *Submission of claims to a court.* Persons with claims against an uninsured bank in receivership may present their claims to a court of competent jurisdiction for adjudication. Such persons must submit a copy of any final judgment received from the court to the OCC, to participate in ratable dividends along with other proved claims.

(c) *Right of set-off.* If a person with a claim against an uninsured bank in receivership also has an obligation owed to the bank, the claim and obligation will be set off against each other and only the net balance remaining after set-off shall be considered as a claim, provided such set-off is otherwise legally valid.

§51.5 Order of priorities.

The OCC will pay receivership expenses and proved claims against the uninsured bank in receivership in the following order of priority:

(a) Administrative expenses of the receiver;

(b) Unsecured creditors of the uninsured bank, including secured creditors to the extent their claim exceeds their valid and enforceable security interest;

(c) Creditors of the uninsured bank, if any, whose claims are subordinated to general creditor claims; and

(d) Shareholders of the uninsured bank.

§51.6 Administrative expenses of receiver.

(a) *Priority of administrative expenses.* All administrative expenses of the receiver for an uninsured bank shall be paid out of the assets of the bank in receivership before payment of claims against the receivership.

(b) *Scope of administrative expenses.* Administrative expenses of the receiver for an uninsured bank include those expenses incurred by the receiver in maintaining banking operations during the receivership, to preserve assets of the uninsured bank, while liquidating or otherwise resolving the affairs of the uninsured bank. Such expenses include pre-receivership and post-receivership obligations that the receiver determines are necessary and appropriate to facilitate the orderly liquidation or other resolution of the uninsured bank in receivership.

(c) *Types of administrative expenses.* Administrative expenses for the receiver of an uninsured bank include:

(1) Salaries, costs, and other expenses of the receiver and its staff, and costs of contracts entered into by the receiver for professional services relating to performing receivership duties; and

(2) Expenses necessary for the operation of the uninsured bank, including wages and salaries of employees, expenses for professional services, contractual rent pursuant to an existing lease or rental agreement, and payments to third-party or affiliated service providers, that in the opinion of the receiver are of benefit to the receivership, until the date the receiver repudiates, terminates, cancels, or otherwise discontinues the applicable contract.

§51.7 Powers and duties of receiver; disposition of fiduciary and custodial accounts.

(a) *Marshalling of assets.* In resolving the affairs of an uninsured bank in receivership, the receiver:

(1) Takes possession of the books, records and other property and assets of the uninsured bank, including the value of collateral pledged by the uninsured bank to the extent it exceeds valid and enforceable security interests of a claimant;

(2) Collects all debts, dues and claims belonging to the uninsured bank, including claims remaining after set-off;

(3) Sells or compromises all bad or doubtful debts, subject to approval by a court of competent jurisdiction;

(4) Sells the real and personal property of the uninsured bank, subject to approval by a court of competent jurisdiction, on such terms as the court shall direct; and

(5) Deposits all receivership funds collected from the liquidation of the uninsured bank in an account designated by the OCC.

(b) *Disposition of fiduciary and custodial accounts.* The receiver for an uninsured bank closes the bank's fiduciary and custodial appointments and accounts or transfers some or all of such accounts to successor fiduciaries and custodians, in accordance with 12 CFR 9.16, and other applicable Federal law.

(c) *Other powers.* The receiver for an uninsured bank may exercise other rights, privileges, and powers authorized for receivers of national banks under the NBA and the common law of receiverships as applied by the courts to receiverships of national banks conducted under the NBA.

(d) *Reports to OCC.* The receiver for an uninsured bank shall make periodic reports to the OCC on the status and proceedings of the receivership.

(e) *Receiver subject to removal; modification of fees.* (1) The Comptroller may remove and replace the receiver for an uninsured bank if, in the Comptroller's discretion, the receiver is not conducting the receivership in accordance with applicable Federal laws or regulations or fails to comply with decisions of the Comptroller with respect to the conduct of the receivership or claims against the receivership.

(2) The Comptroller may reduce the fees of the receiver for an uninsured bank if, in the Comptroller's discretion, the Comptroller finds the performance of the receiver to be deficient, or the fees of the receiver to be excessive, unreasonable, or beyond the scope of the work assigned to the receiver.

§51.8 Payment of claims and dividends to shareholders.

(a) *Claims.* (1) After the administrative expenses of the receivership have been paid, the OCC shall make ratable dividends from time to time of available receivership funds according to the priority described in §51.5, based on the claims that have been proved to the OCC's satisfaction or adjudicated in a court of competent jurisdiction.

(2) Dividend payments to creditors and other claimants of an uninsured bank will be made solely from receivership funds, if any, paid to the OCC by the receiver after payment of the expenses of the receiver.

(b) *Fiduciary and custodial assets.* Assets held by an uninsured bank in a fiduciary or custodial capacity, as designated on the bank's books and records, will not be considered as part of the bank's general assets and liabilities held in connection with its other business, and will not be considered a source for payment of unrelated claims of creditors and other claimants.

(c) *Timing of dividends.* The payment of dividends, if any, under paragraph (a) of this section, on proved or adjudicated claims will be made periodically, at the discretion of the OCC, as the receiver liquidates the assets of the uninsured bank.

(d) *Distribution to shareholders.* After all administrative expenses of the receiver and proved claims of creditors of the uninsured bank have been paid in full, to the extent there are receivership assets to make such payments, any remaining proceeds shall be paid to the shareholders, or their legal representatives, in proportion to their stock ownership.

§51.9 Termination of receivership.

If there are assets remaining after full payment of the expenses of the receiver and all claims of creditors for an uninsured bank and all fiduciary accounts of the bank have been closed or transferred to a successor fiduciary and fiduciary powers surrendered, the Comptroller shall call a meeting of the shareholders of the uninsured bank, as provided in 12 U.S.C. 197, for the shareholders to decide the manner in which the liquidation will continue. The liquidation may continue by:

(a) Continuing the receivership of the uninsured bank under the direction of the Comptroller; or

(b) Ending the receivership and oversight by the Comptroller and replacing the receiver with a liquidating agent to proceed to liquidate the remaining assets of the uninsured bank for the benefit of the shareholders, as set out in 12 U.S.C. 197.

Date: December 15, 2016

Thomas J. Curry,

Comptroller of the Currency.

[FR Doc. 2016-30666 Filed: 12/19/2016 8:45 am; Publication Date: 12/20/2016]

Appendix F—State Materials

¶ 1380 Application Forms For: License to Engage in Virtual Currency Business Activity

New York State Department of Financial Services

INSTRUCTIONS

For License to Engage in Virtual Currency Business Activity

I. INTRODUCTION

The following instructions are for filing an application pursuant to the provisions of 23 NYCRR 200 for a license to engage in Virtual Currency Business Activity.

II. DEFINITIONS

As used in this document, the following definitions apply:

i. *Affiliate* means any Person that directly or indirectly controls, is controlled by, or is under common control with, another Person;

ii. *Person* means an individual, partnership, corporation, association, joint stock association, trust, or other entity, however organized;

iii. *Principal Officer* means an executive officer of an entity, including, but not limited to, the chief executive, financial, operating, and compliance officers, president, general counsel, managing partner, general partner, controlling partner, and trustee, as applicable;

iv. *Principal Stockholder* means any Person that directly or indirectly owns, controls, or holds with power to vote ten percent or more of any class of outstanding capital stock or other equity interest of an entity or possesses the power to direct or cause the direction of the management or policies of the entity; and

v. *Principal Beneficiary* means any Person entitled to ten percent or more of the benefits of a trust.

vi. *Virtual Currency Business Activity* means the conduct of any one of the following types of activities involving New York or a New York Resident:

1. receiving virtual currency for transmission or transmitting virtual currency, except where the transaction is undertaken for non-financial purposes and does not involve the transfer of more than a nominal amount of virtual currency;

2. storing, holding, or maintaining custody or control of virtual currency on behalf of others;

3. buying and selling virtual currency as a customer business;

4. performing exchange services as a customer business; or .

5. controlling, administering, or issuing a virtual currency.

The development and dissemination of software in and of itself does not constitute Virtual Currency Business Activity.

III. GENERAL APPLICATION PROCEDURES

i. The license application shall be made, to the extent applicable, upon forms issued by the Superintendent of Financial Services of the State of New York. The application forms are available on the Department's website.

ii. All parts of the application, including documents submitted with the application, must be in the English language.

iii. The Application Form, Individual Questionnaires and other related forms shall be filled under oath or affirmation.

iv. A separate Application Form is required for each new (de novo) operation seeking to engage in activity under the provisions of 23 NYCRR 200.

v. All forms are to be printed or typed and fully completed. Type "none" or "not applicable" where appropriate. If additional space is required, prepare and annex a signed rider.

vi. Full names and addresses must be given, including zip codes and counties, where requested.

vii. To the extent that information or documents requested below have previously or concurrently been submitted to the Department in connection with an application for a money transmission license, the applicant may provide a cross-reference to the already submitted material in lieu of re-submitting the same information or material in response to the below requests. Cross-references must refer to the specific date and title of the referenced submission and, to the extent applicable, the specific portion of the prior or concurrent submission that addresses the requested information (*e.g.*, exhibit number or page number).

viii. The competed application shall be submitted together with any required fees to:

New York State Department of Financial Services

Virtual Currency Applications

One State Street

New York, NY 10004-1511

IV. *Application Processing*

Upon receipt, each application is reviewed by the Department to determine if it is substantially complete. Applicants/licensees submitting incomplete applications will receive written notification of the reason(s) their application was found incomplete and an itemized list of its deficiencies. In cases where the deficiencies are substantial, the entire application package, except for the application fee, will be returned to the applicant.

In addition to the application materials and information discussed below, the Superintendent may require additional information deemed necessary to adequately and efficiently assess the applicant within the intent of 23 NYCRR 200.

V. Contents

In addition to a completed application form, the application must include the information and documents discussed below.

A. *Information Regarding Corporate Matters*

i. Provide the exact name of the applicant, including any doing business as name, the form of organization, the date of organization, and the jurisdiction where organized or incorporated. Attach a copy of applicant's Articles of Incorporation (or equivalent documentation if the applicant is not a corporation) as amended to the date of filing the application, certified by the applicable agency of the applicant's domiciliary jurisdiction. Attach a copy of the applicant's By-Laws, certified as current and accurate by the corporate secretary, or equivalent documentation if the applicant is not a corporation.

1. If the applicant is a corporation organized under New York Law, submit a copy of the Certificate of Incorporation certified by the Secretary of State of New York, or equivalent documentation if the applicant is not a corporation.

2. Foreign entities must submit a copy of their Application for Authority and Foreign Bid Certificate, certified by the Secretary of State of New York, as proof of their qualification to do business in this State.

ii. Provide the name, mailing address, telephone number and facsimile telephone number for: (a) the applicant's head office; (b) the office where applicant's books and records are kept; and (c) each subsidiary or affiliated company engaged in Virtual Currency Business Activity.

iii. Provide the name and title of: (a) the individual to whom all communications from the Department should be addressed; and (b) the individual to whom all consumer inquiries and complaints should be addressed.

iv. In the case of any Person who has made a commitment to extend credit to the applicant and such commitment is outstanding, identify such Person(s) and the terms of the commitment(s).

v. Provide a list of all of the applicant's Affiliates and an organization chart illustrating the relationship among the applicant and such Affiliates;

vi. Provide a verification from the New York State Department of Taxation and Finance that the applicant is compliant with all New York State tax obligations.

¶1380

B. Fees

A non-refundable check, payable to the order of the Superintendent of Financial Services, for the $5,000 application fee must be sent with each new license application.

C. Information Regarding History and Business

i. A description of the proposed, current, and historical business of the applicant and all Affiliates, including detail on the products and services provided and to be provided, all associated website addresses, the jurisdictions in which the applicant and its Affiliates are engaged in business, the principal place of business, the primary market of operation, the projected customer base, any specific marketing targets, and the physical address of any operation in New York.

ii. If the applicant or its Affiliates have been or currently are engaged in Virtual Currency Business Activity without first obtaining a license to do so from the Superintendent, provide details as to: (a) the length of time engaged in such activity; (b) the amount and number of virtual currency transactions transmitted, exchanged, or held; and (c) the reason for not obtaining a license.

iii. Provide a list of the jurisdictions in which the applicant is licensed or otherwise authorized to engage in virtual currency-related activity, money transmission, or other financial services activity and the amount of any bond or deposit furnished in each such jurisdiction. In each case, please also specify the type of activity for which the applicant is licensed or otherwise authorized.

iv. List all jurisdictions, both domestic and foreign, in which the applicant or any Affiliate of the applicant has applied for a license or other authorization to engage in virtual currency-related activity, money transmission, or other financial services activity and has not been issued such license or authorization. State the reason(s) provided for why such license or authorization was not or has not yet been issued.

v. List all jurisdictions, both domestic and foreign, in which the license or other authorization of the applicant or its Affiliate to engage in virtual currency-related activity, money transmission, or other financial services was revoked, suspended, or refused renewal. State the reason(s) provided for why the revocation, suspension, or refusal occurred.

vi. Indicate whether the applicant or any Affiliate of the applicant has ever been the subject of a regulatory or enforcement action in any jurisdiction. If answered in the affirmative, describe the nature, and outcome, of all such regulatory or enforcement action(s).

vii. Provide, as applicable, a copy of any insurance policies maintained for the benefit of the applicant, its directors or officers, or its customers.

D. Information Regarding Directors, Principal Officers, Principal Stockholders and Principal Beneficiaries

i. Provide a list of, and detailed biographical information for, each individual applicant and each director, Principal Officer, Principal Stockholder, and Principal Beneficiary of the applicant, as applicable, including such individual's name, citizenship, title, social security number or alien identification number, as applicable, and physical and mailing addresses.

ii. Describe the amount and type of equity interests of the applicant owned by each Director, Principal Officer, Principal Stockholder, and Principal Beneficiary. Complete a sworn statement of ownership form for the applicant.

iii. For each Principal Stockholder and Principal Beneficiary who is a natural Person, and each director and Principal Officer, describe all material occupations, positions, offices or employment during the preceding 15 years. Include: (a) the name, address, and principal activities of any business, corporation, or other entity in which each occupation, position, office or employment was carried on; (b) the starting and ending dates of each; and (c) a statement as to whether within such period s/he was discharged from such occupation, position, office or employment and, if so, for what reason. Such information must be accompanied by a form of authority, executed by such individual, to release information to the Department.

iv. In the case any Person other than a natural Person is a Principal Stockholder or Principal Beneficiary of the applicant, provide the name, address, and date and place of incorporation or organization of any such Person. Also provide an organization chart to show the beneficial ownership relationship between the parties.

v. In the case of any owner that is not a natural Person but an investment company or equity fund, provide the following.

For each investment company, provide: (a) a general description of the company; (b) a listing of all funds managed by the company; (c) a listing of all directors and officers of the company; and (d) audited financial statements for the past two years. If audited financial statements are not available, provide a statement explaining why they are not required.

For each fund managed by an investment company, provide: (a) a general description of the Fund, the date formed, and the purpose of the fund; (b) a statement of whether the fund is opened or closed to new investors; (c) a list of any investors in the fund who hold more than a 10% interest; (d) a list of any investors in the fund who have any control over the management or policies of the fund; (e) indication of whether the investors in the fund are indirect, passive owners and, if so, attach a copy of the applicable pages from the investment agreement evincing said restriction; (f) a listing of all directors and officers of the fund; and (g) the BSA/AML and compliance policies in place for the screening of all potential investors in the fund.

vi. Describe the amount and type of equity interests of applicant, owned, either directly or indirectly through ownership of another entity, by any such Person or the Person's associates.

vii. Indicate whether any director, Principal Officer, Principal Stockholder, or Principal Beneficiary of the applicant ever applied for a license or other authorization, in this State or otherwise, to engage in virtual currency-related activity, money transmission, or other financial services activity. If answered in the affirmative, state whether such license was granted. If granted, state whether such license was ever suspended, revoked, or refused renewal.

viii. The exhibits marked "Questionnaire" and "Litigation Affidavit" in the enclosed material must be completed by each director, Principal Officer, Principal Stockholder, and Principal Beneficiary of the applicant.

ix. Provide an organization chart, including the applicant and all Affiliates. Indicate Principal Stockholders and Principal Beneficiaries.

E. Information Regarding Operations

i. List the jurisdictions in which the applicant proposes to operate. If applicable, list the locations in other countries in which the applicant proposes to engage in virtual currency-related activities. List any other virtual currency, money transmitter, or other entities routinely used to facilitate transactions.

ii. Provide an organization chart of the applicant and its management structure, including its Principal Officers or senior management, indicating lines of authority and the allocation of duties among its principal officers or senior management.

iii. Describe, in detail, the proposed operations for conducting the Virtual Currency Business Activity. This description should include information on the staffing and internal organization of the applicant, its systems and procedures, and details of all banking arrangements. Include letters from bank compliance officers that the bank is aware that the applicant's accounts are being used to facilitate virtual currency-related activity.

iv. Provide an explanation of the methodology used to calculate the value of virtual currency in fiat currency.

v. Provide a specimen form of all agreements, documents, receipts, disclosures, and contracts that the applicant plans to issue or use with customers in this State.

vi. Provide a flow of funds narrative, including a flow chart, specifying all flows of funds that will occur in the normal operation of the applicant. Specify who directs the flow and how it is done; the name and address of each entity the funds flow through; the title of each account; ownership or control of the accounts and addresses and who or what entity is liable for the funds at all points.

F. Information Regarding Other Agreements

Provide copies of any other agreements the applicant has entered into (or will enter into) in anticipation of Virtual Currency Business Activity.

G. Information Regarding Legal Proceedings

Describe (a) any criminal action brought against the applicant or any director, Principal Officer, Principal Stockholder or Principal Beneficiary of the applicant; (b) any civil action brought against the applicant or any director, Principal Officer, Principal Stockholder or Principal Beneficiary of the applicant (excluding any civil action in which the amount in controversy was less than $25,000 or which terminated more than 15 years prior to submission of this application); and (c) any proceeding brought to declare the applicant, or any director, Principal Officer, Principal

Stockholder or Principal Beneficiary of the applicant, bankrupt and the disposition of such action or proceeding.

H. Information Regarding Financial Statements

i. Provide a current audited financial statement for the applicant prepared by an independent certified public accountant and a projected balance sheet and income statement for the following year of the applicant's operation. The projected balance sheet and income statement must include the assumptions used in making the projections. If audited financial statements are unavailable, include an explanation of why. If the applicant's fiscal year ends more than 60 days prior to the date of application, provide a supplemental financial statement for a period ending not more than 60 days prior to the date of application (which may be prepared by applicant). All financial statements must include a balance sheet, profit and loss statement, and a statement of retained earnings. Where the applicant has wholly owned subsidiaries, financial statements for applicant alone, as well as consolidated financial statements, must be filed. Any exhibited losses must be explained and a projected date for the return to or achieving profitability must be included.

ii. Applicants that are not able to provide current financial statements must provide a pro forma balance sheet and profit and loss statement. Include retained earnings for the business as of the close of each of the first two years of operation. Include the assumptions used in making the projections. Any projected losses must be explained and an estimate of time to achieve profitability should be given.

iii. Financial statements of foreign-owned applicants must be presented in both the applicable foreign currency and in United States Dollars. The date and basis of conversion must be stated.

iv. Complete the enclosed Personal Financial Statement for each director, Principal Officer, Principal Stockholder and Principal Beneficiary of the applicant. Alternatively, a different format may be used provided it contains substantially similar information; but in either case the statement must be dated and certified as complete and correct by the party submitting it.

v. Provide audited financial statements for the most recent two fiscal years of any Person, other than a natural person, which directly or indirectly owns 10% or more of the equity interests of the applicant. Such financial statements must include a balance sheet, profit and loss statement, and a statement of retained earnings. Any exhibited losses must be explained and a projected date for the return to or achieving profitability must be included.

I. Required Affidavits

Provide affidavits describing any pending or threatened administrative, civil, or criminal action, litigation, or proceeding before any governmental agency, court, or arbitration tribunal against the applicant or any of its directors, Principal Officers, Principal Stockholders, and Principal Beneficiaries, as applicable, including the names of the parties, the nature of the proceeding, and the current status of the proceeding.

J. Anti-Money Laundering (BSA/AML)

i. Provide written BSA/AML policies and procedures that meet the requirements set forth in 23 NYCRR 200.15, including the applicant's risk assessment.

ii. Identify the individual or individuals who will be responsible for coordinating and monitoring day-to-day compliance with the applicant's anti-money laundering program and provide background information and materials demonstrating that the identified individual(s) is qualified to carry out such functions.

K. Surety Bond or Trust Account

i. Indicate how the applicant proposes to comply with the requirements of 23 NYCRR 200.9(a), including the general manner, the proposed amount of the bond or trust account, and why the applicant believes such an amount is sufficient for the protection of customers.

ii. To the extent the applicant purposes to use a trust account, identify the qualified custodian at which the account will be maintained.

L. Fingerprints

Applicants must provide, for each individual applicant; for each Principal Officer, Principal Stockholder, and Principal Beneficiary of the applicant, as applicable; and for all individuals to be employed by the applicant who have access to any customer funds, whether denominated in fiat currency or virtual currency:

i. a set of completed fingerprints, or a receipt indicating the vendor at which, and the date when, the fingerprints were taken, for submission to the State Division of Criminal Justice Services and the Federal Bureau of Investigation; and

ii. two portrait-style photographs of each such individual measuring not more than two inches by two inches.

iii. fingerprints must be submitted according to the procedures available on our website at http://www.dfs.ny.gov/banking/iafpplfs.htm.

M. Background Investigation Reports

Provide an investigative background report prepared by an independent investigatory agency for each individual applicant, and each Principal Officer, Principal Stockholder, and Principal Beneficiary of the applicant, as applicable. It is the responsibility of the applicant (and its, Principal Officers, Principal Stockholders, and Principal Beneficiaries, as applicable) to order such reports at their own expense, from an independent licensed private investigation company.

All background investigation reports must be provided directly to the Department by the licensed private investigation company. Note that the failure to promptly order the reports may delay application processing.

These reports should be sent to:

New York State Department of Financial Services

Virtual Currency Applications

One State Street, 20th Floor

New York, NY 10004-1511

The following list specifies information that must be included in a submitted background report. No background report will be considered complete unless all the information requested below is included in the investigation report.

i. Comprehensive credit report/history (include the actual report as well as summary).

ii. Civil Court and Bankruptcy Court records for the past 10 years. Include federal, state, and local courts. Such reports shall contain, at a minimum, court dates from courts located in counties in which the applicant both worked and resided and all counties contiguous to those counties.

iii. Criminal records, including felonies, misdemeanors, and violations. Include federal, state, and local courts. Such reports shall contain, at a minimum, court dates from courts located in counties in which the applicant worked and/or resided and all counties contiguous to those counties.

iv. Education records.

v. Employment history.

vi. Personal and professional references (at least three of each, excluding relatives), which must be furnished in writing.

vii. Media history, if applicable (include electronic search of national and local newspapers, wire services, and business publications).

viii. Regulatory history, if applicable (HUD, FREDDIE MAC, State Regulators, OCC, FINRA, etc.).

ix. Department of Motor Vehicles records.

x. All judgments and liens filed with the county clerk (within the past ten years) (such reports shall contain, at a minimum, information on judgments and liens filed with the county clerk in counties where the applicant worked and resided and all counties contiguous to those counties).

xi. Licenses granted by any governmental agency or judicial body (indicate if they are still in good standing).

xii. Listing of all credit relationships by the applicant (such as revolving credit and established credit facilities) and indication of any credit extensions, including loans, on which the applicant is in default (more than 90 days past due).

N. FinCEN Registration

¶1380

To the extent applicable, the applicant is required to submit evidence that it has registered with FinCEN as a Money Service Business. A copy of FinCEN's confirmation or acknowledgment letter will be sufficient. If the applicant believes it is not required to register with FinCEN, the applicant must provide an explanation and supporting documentation for that conclusion.

O. Written Policies and Procedures

Provide copies of all written policies and procedures required by, or related to, the requirements of 23 NYCRR 200, including but not limited to policies and procedures addressing:

    i. compliance;

    ii. anti-fraud;

    iii. cyber security;

    iv. privacy and information security;

    v. business continuity and disaster recovery;

    vi. complaints and complaint resolution.

P. Miscellaneous

Provide the name, address, telephone number and facsimile telephone number of applicant's counsel and independent certified public accountant, to the extent applicable.

VI. Filed Applications

For any questions concerning the preparation and filing of an application, submit questions to VCLicenseQuestions@dfs.ny.gov. Question submissions should include contact information that the Department may use to contact you regarding your question.ENCLOSURES

For a License to Engage in Virtual Currency Business Activity

As applicable, the following individual forms must be filled out by the applicant and submitted with the application:

- Authority to Release Information
- Background Report Certification
- Personal Financial Statement
- Litigation Affidavit - Individual
- Litigation Affidavit - Licensee/Applicant
- Questionnaire
- Statement of Ownership
- Taxpayer ID

These forms are provided below.

AUTHORITY TO RELEASE INFORMATION

TO WHOM IT MAY CONCERN:

I hereby authorize any duly authorized representative of the New York State Department of Financial Services (DFS) bearing this release, or copy thereof, within one year of its date, to obtain any information in your files pertaining to any professional license awarded to me (including any grievance records), employment, military, educational records (including, but not limited to academic achievement, attendance, athletic, personal history, and disciplinary records), credit records, and law enforcement records (including, but not limited to any record of charge, prosecution or conviction for criminal or civil offenses). I hereby direct you to release such information upon request to the bearer. This release is executed with full knowledge and understanding that the information is for the official use of the DFS. Consent is granted for the DFS to furnish such information, as is described above, to third parties in the course of fulfilling its official responsibilities. I hereby release you, as the custodian of such records, your employers, officers, employees, and related personnel, both individually and collectively, from any and all liability for damages of whatever kind, which may at any time result to me, my heirs, family or associates because of compliance with this authorization and request to release information, or any attempt to comply with it. I am furnishing my Social Security Account Number on a voluntary basis with the understanding such is not required by statute or regulation. I understand that the DFS will use the number only to assist the Superintendent of Financial Services in making a determination as to whether I meet the standards set forth pursuant to the Financial Services Law and regulations for receiving the license for which I am applying. Should there be any question as to the validity of this release, you may contact me as indicated below:

I have read the above release and agree to the terms and conditions therein.

Social Security Account Number: _____

Date of Birth: _____

Signature of Parent or Guardian (if required): _____

Date: _____

Current Address: _____

Telephone Number: _____

CPA/Bar Membership(s) State: _____

Registration Number: _____

Full Name (Signature): _____

Full Name (Typed or Printed): _____

(Include maiden and any other previously-used name(s)): _____

STATE OF _____} ss.:

COUNTY OF _____}

Before me, a Notary Public in and for said County and State, personally appeared the above-named who acknowledged that s/he did sign the foregoing instrument and that the same is his/her free and voluntary act and deed. IN TESTIMONY WHEREOF, I have hereunto set my hand and official seal at, _____ this _____ day of _____, 20 _____.

_____

Notary Public

¶ 1390 Illinois Blockchain and Distributed Ledger Task Force Final Report to the General Assembly
House Joint Resolution 25
January 31, 2018

Task Force Members

Co-Chairman: State Representative Michael J. Zalewski – 23st District
Co-Chairman: Ari Sharg – Edelson PC
State Representative Jaime M. Andradre Jr. – 40th District
State Representative Keith R. Wheeler – 50th District
State Senator Tom Rooney – 27th District State Senator John F. Curran – 41st District
Jennifer M. O'Rourke – Illinois Department of Commerce and Economic Opportunity
Michael Wons – Illinois Department of Innovation and Technology
Cab Morris – Illinois Department of Financial and Professional Regulation
Bryan A. Schneider – Illinois Department of Financial and Professional Regulation
Fred Moore – Illinois Department of Insurance
Mike Standley – Illinois Secretary of State
John Mirkovic – Cook County Recorder of Deeds
Kevin McDermott – Cook County Clerk's Office
Shamlan Siddiqi – NTT Data
Manuel Flores – Glass Mountain Capital, LLC
John Karantonis – Geopay.me

Report Authors

Cab Morris – Illinois Department of Financial and Professional Regulation
John Mirkovic – Cook County Recorder of Deeds
Jennifer M. O'Rourke – Illinois Department of Commerce and Economic Opportunity
Special thanks to Carie Cycholl – Illinois Department of Innovation and Technology

Contents

¶**1390**

Dear Chamber Leaders and Members of the General Assembly:

We are pleased to deliver to you the attached Final Report of the Illinois General Assembly Blockchain and Distributed Ledger Task Force.

This Report is the first official government report in Illinois to be permanently certified in a public blockchain, a small gesture that we believe will demonstrate our desire to see government begin to use this technology. Though the mathematics behind the unique digital fingerprint assigned to this Report may be difficult to understand, it is clear that distributed ledgers can begin a transition to a smarter, cheaper and safer way to administer government.

On DATE, this Task Force was charged by HJR 25 with studying: 1) opportunities and risks associated with using blockchain and other distributed ledger technologies, 2) the different types of blockchains, public and private, 3) projects and use cases in other states/nations that Illinois could consider, 4) how current state laws could be modified to support this technology, 5) encryption technology, including Illinois' digital signature infrastructure, and 6) official reports and recommendations from the Illinois Blockchain Initiative. The attached Report will provide more detail in each of these areas, and we urge you to read it and contact any member of the Task Force if you would like to learn more.

To broadly summarize our findings, this Task Force believes that blockchain technology and its built-in encryption can facilitate highly-secure methods for interacting with government and keeping paperless records, increasing data accuracy and providing better cybersecurity protections for Illinois residents. Though the technology still needs refinement, government has an opportunity to help shape and adopt innovative solutions before they become costly software subscriptions.

As you may know, the State of Illinois has a strong reputation as a leader in supporting blockchain and distributed ledger technologies, and maintaining a "light touch" and progressive regulatory approach. Our ongoing studies and pilot programs through the Illinois Blockchain Initiative are talked about across the globe. We believe our unique intergovernmental partnerships demonstrate how all layers of government can work together to jointly develop this "digital infrastructure" and build resilient networks that protect each other's data and share the cost of hardware and software.

Make no mistake, blockchain technology must improve its scalability and smart contract security before government adoption becomes widespread. But, we must remember that every day more and more Illinoisans are losing time and money due to hacks of their personal data, and government owes it to its taxpayers to lead a shift away from centralized servers full of sensitive data to a decentralized network that is more secure and easier to administer.

Sincerely,

Members of the Blockchain and Distributed Ledger Task Force

The Next Generation of the Internet

The first digital revolution brought endless innovations as the internet, social media, mobile and big data have changed nearly every aspect of our lives. Though the internet may have revolutionized communication, it has not necessarily transformed business and commerce in terms of trust.

Establishing identity and transacting value online still requires verification from a trusted third party (banks, governments, big technology companies).

While intermediaries fill a vital role in transacting value, relying too heavily on them often comes at the expense of inclusive prosperity. Intermediaries add costs and frictions to our economy for both businesses and consumers. They monetize vast amounts of data privacy and leave over a quarter of the world's population out of the global economy.

The Internet of Value

Enter the blockchain, the first "native" digital medium for peer to peer value exchange.

Anything of value, money, titles, deeds and identity attributes can be exchanged, stored, and managed securely and privately. Trust is not established exclusively by powerful intermediaries, but through network consensus, cryptography and code.

The Promise of Blockchains

Blockchains as peer-to-peer digital economies have the capability to address fundamental societal issues:

- They create a secure platform that enables immutable, irrevocable digital identities.

- They have the ability to provide universal access to financial services and government benefits

- They spur a stronger economy and create social stability through greater economic participation

Blockchains are rapidly becoming the foundation of the Fourth Industrial Revolution:

- They are being used to create distributed market structures to address security risks and eliminate single points of infrastructure failure.

- Supplying regulators with real time data on financial flow and asset class risks, they stand poised to improve the oversight of international markets.

- They are integrating granular provenance tracking, identity management and concepts of digital scarcity horizontally and vertically through global supply chains.

- In a 2015 World Economic Forum survey of global business and government leaders 58% of respondents believe that 10% of global gross domestic product (GDP) will be stored on blockchain technology.

The Unanswered Questions

Although blockchain technology may prove to be one of the most disruptive innovations of the 21st century, it currently is discussed as if it were more mature than it actually is. Many implementation hurdles at the technical, regulatory and governance level continue to hinder widespread adoption for both open and private blockchain networks. Blockchains are inherently a "network" technology meaning that without wide-scale collaboration and coordination, their power to improve society will never be realized.

Few Impactful Implementations

Since 2015, banks, regulators, tech giants and startups all over the world have raised billions of dollars to explore the promise of the blockchain. Despite the exuberance for the technology to date, Bitcoin still stands to be the only successful, scalable implementation of blockchain and distributed ledger technology.

The Limits of Open Governance

Contrary to popular belief, open and decentralized governance does not automatically mean fair and equitable rule of law. Democracy cannot be reduced to majority rule and consensus is a complex construct that requires concepts such as minority rights, equal access to decision making and legitimacy of procedure. Bitcoin's recent scaling debate and Ethereum's Decentralized Autonomous Organization or DAO scandal have brought to light the notion that "code is not law" and that a 51% majority does not always equal democracy.

Decentralized Market Structures are Untested

Blockchains and decentralized market structures are relatively untested in our global economy, which could either (a) be less preferable than "trust taxes" or (b) introduce fundamentally new risks into the global economy. By displacing intermediaries who policymakers have historically relied on to implement regulatory safeguards, it is unclear who or how broader systemic policy changes can get implemented when necessary.

Charting a Path Forward

Although government appear to be the antithesis of a technology that decentralizes economies and places trust in code over law, it is incumbent on the public sector to help catalyze the growth of this technology. Furthermore, the greatest risk may be letting of blockchain technology's potential fade, stagnate in its fractured status quo or be implemented in a non-inclusive way. Ultimately, code, algorithms, policy and rule of law are all artefacts of human design. Technology alone does not create prosperity, people do.

In Illinois, we believe it is imperative for government to take affirmative steps to harness the tremendous opportunities and minimize the risks of blockchain technologies during this critical period of development. In doing so, the state of Illinois will be able to:

1. Catalyze an Ecosystem for Growth and Collaboration

Although, the long-term benefits of blockchain are clear, blockchains and DLTs are still very much nascent technology. Governments can play a role in catalyzing its maturity as a technology by supporting grassroots developer innovation and encouraging collaboration among enterprises, countries and entrepreneurs.

2. Rethink Governance for a Distributed Economy

Effective governance in a distributed economy will require legislative agility beyond what rules and regulations can provide. Modern governance will need to carefully balance a combination of broad policy principles, technology standards and "code".

3. Create Hyperconnected Services for a Highly Efficient Government

A "hyperconnected" government enables unprecedented integration and efficiency, where services are tailored to each individual's needs. Blockchains will be used to connect disparate entities within and across regional, municipal, and state entities around citizens, businesses and assets.

What is Blockchain?

In simple terms, a blockchain is a type of database that is replicated over a peer-to peer (P2P) network. However, this definition could also apply to other types of distributed databases that have no central database manager. So, what makes a blockchain special?

The principal way in which a blockchain is different from other distributed databases is that a blockchain is designed to achieve consistent and reliable agreement over a record of events (often referred to as the "state") between independent participants who may have different motivations and objectives. Put in a slightly different way, participants in a blockchain network reach consensus about changes to the state of the shared database (i.e., transactions amongst participants) without needing to trust the integrity of any of the network participants or administrators.

The agreement between blockchain network participants over the state of the database is achieved through a consensus mechanism, which ensures that each participant's view of the shared database matches the view of all other participants. The combination of the consensus mechanism with a specific data structure allows blockchains to solve the so-called 'double spending' problem.

All participants have a consistent view of the shared database state. As a result, any improper alteration of the data (e.g., tampering by a malicious actor) will be immediately detected and rejected by all participants.

Components of Blockchains and Distributed Ledgers

Blockchains and distributed ledgers generally have the following five components:

1. Cryptography	Use of a variety of cryptographic techniques including cryptographic one-way hash functions, Merkle trees and public key infrastructure
2. P2P Network	Network for machine-readable data discovery and replicated peer-to-peer data sharing
3. Consensus Mechanism	Algorithm that determines the ordering of transactions in an adversarial environment (assuming not every participant is honest)
4. Ledger	List of cryptographically linked transactions (e.g. bundled in "blocks" for blockchains, direct acyclic graph DAG in IOTA)
5. Validity Rules - Access and Validation	Common set of rules of the network (i.e., what transactions are considered valid, how the ledger gets updated, etc.)

Types of Distributed Ledgers

Generally, a blockchain or distributed ledger can be either **public** or **private** and *permissionless* or *permissioned.*

		Validation	
		Permissionless	**Permissioned**
Access	Public	Bitcoin IOTA Ethereum	Sovrin
	Private	Hyperledger Sawtooth	Hyperledger Fabric R3 Corda Quorum

Permissionless

A permissionless blockchain or distributed ledger generally refers to a ledger where anyone may operate a validator node, i.e., a node that participates in the consensus protocol to validate transactions.

Permissioned

A permissioned blockchain or distributed ledger refers to a ledger where permission from some governing entity is required to operate a validator node.

Public

A public blockchain or distributed ledger refers to a ledger that is "open to the public" for usage, i.e., anyone can create transactions on the ledger

Private

A private blockchain or distributed ledger refers to a ledger where permissions to write entries are restricted to a single organization and read permissions can be either public or restricted.

Consensus Mechanisms

A consensus mechanism is the process in which a majority (or in some cases all) of network validators come to agreement on the state of a ledger. It is a set of rules and procedures that allows maintaining coherent set of facts between multiple participating nodes.

Proof of Work

A proof-of-work (PoW) protocol generally involves proving that some resource has been expended (typically processing time by a computer). It is a method to deter an abuse of service (i.e. denial of service attacks, spam, double spending) by requiring some form of "work". In a public blockchain, such as Bitcoin, PoW removes the need for trust amongst anonymous actors by reducing the likelihood of an attack by a single malicious actor. In this case, PoW aims to prevent one party from holding a majority of computational resources at one given time. Examples include:

Bitcoin	Ethereum	Dash
IOTA	Z-Cash	Monero

Proof of Stake

Proof of stake is a newer consensus mechanism designed to be less resource intensive. The key motivation for proof of stake is that consensus is performed by stakeholders who have the strongest incentive to be good and honest stewards of the system. Put differently, the nodes that validate transactions have 'skin in the game.' The major benefit of this consensus mechanism, as compared to proof of work, is that there is a large reduction in energy consumption resulting from a decreased need for hashing power.

Tezos	Ethereum (Casper Release)	NEO
Qtum	Nxt	Cardano

Majority Voting (Variants of Practical/Federated Byzantine Fault Tolerance) In majority voting systems, consensus is determined by a 2/3rds majority vote, designed to achieve byzantine fault

¶1390

tolerance for smaller networks where actors or participants are known and generally trusted. Examples include:

Hyperledger Fabric	Tendermint	Hashgraph
Ripple	Quorum	Stellar
Zilliqa	Sovrin	Corda

Benefits and Opportunities

Transaction = Reconciliation

Reconciliation is the process of ensuring that two sets of records agree. Particularly in the financial industry, the reconciliation of transaction records is critical to the accounting process. Bank A engages in a transaction with Bank B, and each bank records an entry in its respective ledger. At some point in the future, the entries are reconciled to ensure accuracy. The need for reconciliation extends beyond finance, and can include any data set or record that is maintained by more than one party.

Blockchain technology addresses data reconciliation by requiring network participants to share data points. In the banking example above, instead of Bank A and Bank B maintaining separate entries for a single transaction, they would share a single entry maintained on a shared ledger, eliminating the need to reconcile entries later.

Another subtle, but powerful impact of blockchain technology is the standardization of data and transactions formats. When users join a blockchain network, they (and their computers) agree to a protocol – a format for transmitting data between nodes on a network. By virtue of their participation, users are bound by the data and transaction formats of the network. Not only are the parties communicating in the same "language", they are sharing a place of record.

Immutability and Data Integrity

The permanent and persistent storage of transactions on blockchains, it's "immutability", is particularly useful for trusted governance, evidentiary or audit purposes. For example, forensic analysis and legal discovery processes could be conducted without the need for special methods, expensive technologies, or significant resources being employed. The clear benefit here is reduced court costs where a jurisdiction recognizes the facts in the distributed ledger as admissible. These reduced costs would could also create positive externalities such as improved behaviors, like honesty, encouraged by the transparency and immutability of the ledger.

Blockchains present opportunities for regulators to access high integrity records of transactions in real or near-real time. A persistent and machine-readable history of transactions would allow regulators a macro-view of an institution's compliance with assurance that no transactions had been tampered with. This unprecedented view into regulated industries would open pathways to productivity gains and risk management if managed appropriately.

Distributed ledger systems are transparent in that all transactions are traceable, and permanently stored by the network of participants. While a private distributed ledger network may add restrictions to who can write or read transactions, it preserves the feature of stakeholders having common access to their set of common transactions. The moment anyone starts transacting on the system, a history of all interactions is immediately logged in the system. This high level of transparency and reliability is an important factor in building trust in the integrity of the network not just from a regulatory oversight perspective, but can also reduce counterparty risk for participants in the network.

Improving Resilience and Security in Transactional Systems

Blockchains have the potential to increase the resilience of systems and data storage due to its distributed nature and its lack of a central point of. The ledger is owned by all participating parties which means that in the event of failure everyone can keep their own copy of data and transactions. This form of resilience and security provides the opportunity to create new identity systems where users own the data, which remains universally consistent and cannot be destroyed. Minimizing single points of failure in transactional systems is thus a key differentiator when compared with existing or legacy systems which often have centralized mechanisms of verification and security.

Challenges and Risks

Energy Consumption and Computer Processing Power

The proof-of-work competition also has the added cost of the wasted computational power and energy used by all the miners involved in the process. The snapshot below depicts the Bitcoin miners as currently consuming over 11 Terra Watt hours per year. To put this in context, Bitcoin mining currently accounts for 0.05% of the world's energy consumption, which could power over a million households in the United States of America.

Scalability and Performance

As ledgers are designed to retain all previous transactions, the ledger's size will increase. This increase in size will continually need to be forecast against both the capabilities of the network and the future behavior of the users. For example, the increasing popularity of Bitcoin is having an exponential influence on the size of that blockchain. Sometimes referred to as "network bloat" has the potential to detract from the technology's utility if the size becomes too great for everyday participants to readily use in a cost-effective way.

Interoperability

To realize the full benefits of distributed ledger technology, it will be critical for ledgers to be able to exchange information with other ledgers and with legacy IT systems. In the short and medium term, it is unclear whether businesses would be prepared to overhaul their existing operations.

Though blockchains may be designed for decentralized control but not for decentralized semantics. Blockchains don't have the equivalent of JSON or HTTP for Blockchains. They are highly specific to their application area and lack the flexibility required for a variety of different storage and provenance models. They possess no mechanism for extending their data model in a self-discoverable or machine-readable way. This makes tuning the existing monolithic blockchain designs to meet new use cases a challenging, if not financially and technically prohibitive, undertaking.

Currently there are hundreds of fragmented blockchains competing, each with their proprietary, non-interoperable standards and protocols. Wider adoption for blockchains depends on enabling seamless interaction, not just between blockchain-based systems, but also between current IT infrastructure.

Assuming there will be many different types of blockchains and distributed ledgers, then it follows that a generalized format for expressing and accessing these ledgers is desirable and a requirement for interoperability. To find the balance between a few large and many small blockchains, blockchains will need to be able to split and merge over time. Transactions on blockchains will need to have stable URLs and an equivalent of HTTP redirection to point to updated locations. Further standardization efforts are needed to create URL schemes for blockchain transactions.

Privacy and Correlation

If illegal, personal, classified or otherwise objectionable data is entered onto a public blockchain ledger, it is there forever. This means that situations may arise where information is recorded inappropriately or illegally, and cannot be removed. The potential impacts of the permanence and persistence of this information could potentially impact the privacy of individuals.

These potential privacy challenges will require thoughtful design and good governance to be prevented and managed. Even improper use of simple metadata, can have unintended consequences on privacy, allowing anyone to correlate data about an individual in a publicly discoverable way. Strong governance models and controls around data security and privacy will have to be examined carefully and have been demonstrated to be problematic. Information security would need to consider the potential for breaches where previous responses and mitigations are no longer effective.

1. Catalyzing an Ecosystem for Growth and Collaboration

Essential Questions

- What role should government play in developing an ecosystem?
- What unique areas of opportunity can we capitalize on in Illinois?

The State of Illinois as a Catalyst for Growth

Illinois regards its role in the development of the blockchain eco-system as one which supports the distinct needs of the respective eco-system stakeholders: entrepreneurs, capital providers, developers, governments, and academics to support and encourage the creation and growth of blockchain companies in Illinois. To accomplish this mission the Illinois Blockchain Initiative created the role of the State of Illinois Blockchain Business Liaison, which is responsible for the engagement of these stakeholders within the eco-system to identify and conclusively work to resolve their respective needs. As noted in the Tapscott Group's 2017 Blockchain Corridor Report: "many entrepreneurs are seeing a healthy dialogue with government, and a focus on governance more broadly, as a good thing. Companies like Coinbase, Circle and Gemini have joined trade organizations, and some even maintain close relations emerging governance institutions".

Reciprocally, the Illinois Blockchain Initiative has taken the unique step of directly joining blockchain industry participants in membership within industry organizations and blockchain consortiums such as the Chamber of Digital Commerce, R3, Hyperledger, Enterprise Ethereum Alliance and the Chicago Blockchain Center. The access to current market knowledge and highly regarded subject matter participants, which these industry organizations and consortium memberships provide, ensure the Illinois Blockchain Initiative is highly informed and thus well positioned to execute effective strategy to catalyze an ecosystem for growth and collaboration.

Areas of Opportunity for Illinois

Illinois is uniquely positioned to take a leadership role in the development of blockchain technology companies due to the critical mass of industries leveraging blockchain technology located in Illinois (Financial Services, Insurance, Supply Chain and Logistics), access to talent, support of entrepreneurship, and collaboration with enterprises.

Further supporting Illinois exceptional position to become the home of blockchain technology, Deloitte's 2017 Global FinTech Hub Ranking Report placed Chicago as a top five global fintech hub, outperforming cities like Hong Kong, Zurich and Sydney: "Chicago acts as the epicenter for all FinTech activity in the Midwest, representing well over 20,000 financial institutions. It is home to two fifths of the top business universities in the US and over 6% of the Chicago workforce are focused on the financial ecosystem contributing to its already significant talent pool.

With government support, Chicago companies are able to quickly innovate to create groundbreaking technology". Notably the Deloitte report explicitly articulated the Illinois government's support of blockchain technology: "over the next 12 months, we expect to see state and local government partnering with the private sector and NGOs to pursue greater adoption of blockchain as well as creating an innovation friendly environment.

Fostering a Talent Pipeline

Ensuring that businesses have access to the right employees and skill sets, a pipeline, is strategically important because it has a long-term talent-supply focus, which means that critical jobs can be filled faster and with higher quality and more interested prospects. The cost of talent is the largest expense for most firms, and the quality of that tech talent is becoming one of the most important considerations.

In a 2017 CBRE Report: Scoring Tech Talent in North America, noted that the Chicago area is the fourth-ranked market in the country for tech degrees, with 7,866 degree completions from 2014-2015, demonstrating a growth of 15.6 percent from 2011-2015, trailing only New York, Washington, D.C. and Los Angeles. Furthermore, Chicago was among the best value markets for tech talent, due to its moderate labor costs (averaging $95,180 for software developers) and "very-high"-quality labor pool.

Blockchain technology talent pools will require education in computer science and engineering. The University of Illinois system graduates more computer science and computer engineering students than CalTech, MIT, Stanford and Berkley combined. Furthermore, University of Illinois Urbana Champaign is ranked as the #5 top undergraduate schools for computer engineering by US News College Rankings. Although Illinois is well positioned to leverage its world class academic institutions, the Illinois Blockchain Initiative can provide additional bespoke blockchain education and programming outside of academia to supplement the talent pool.

The Illinois Blockchain Initiative has been and is positioned to continue to be an effective mechanism to facilitate educational workshops and conferences in which experienced practitioners and experts provide knowledge, specific insight and practical application and fosters grassroots innovation through hackathons national challenges, boot camps, and accelerators. Looking forward, the Illinois Blockchain Initiative will partner with educational institutions to incorporate blockchain curriculum into schools and colleges and to support blockchain workforce development.

Supporting Entrepreneurship

The government is well placed to support blockchain technology entrepreneurship by providing fiscal and educational resources to startups. The State of Illinois currently provides fiscal resources such as the recently renewed Angel Investment Tax Credit and R&D Tax Credit programs. It also provides educational resources such as the Small Business Development Center network, and has funded collaborative spaces which ease entrance into entrepreneurship such as 1871, MATTER and UILabs/DMDII. The Illinois Blockchain Initiative is a founding member of the Chicago Blockchain Center, created in June 2017, where services are focused on providing bespoke programming and education to the various segments of the local blockchain community.

Even as the government supports blockchain entrepreneurs' efforts to advance the technology, there is still a need to come up with new applications that will broaden the technology's appeal. The Illinois Blockchain Initiative will play a supporting role in the identification of the most important applications and opportunities for blockchain technology in business and government. In doing so, the Illinois Blockchain Initiative will build relationships with entrepreneurs and leaders that will in turn foster a supportive environment for startups and investment in the blockchain community.

Collaborating with Enterprises

The collaboration between corporations and startups has become crucial. Corporates collaborate with startups to fast-track disruptive, game-changing products and services and startups leverage corporates advantages in procurement, distribution, manufacturing, and sales and marketing. With 37 Fortune 500 companies headquartered in Illinois, Illinois is well positioned to connect the startup community residing in the network of over 100 incubators, accelerators, co-working spaces and academic labs (such as Built in Chicago, Clean Energy Trust, Energy Foundry, iBIO Institute, the Illinois Technology Association, and facilities such as 1871, MATTER, mHUB, and TechNexus) to these world class corporate partners.

2. Governance, Law and Distributed Economies

Essential Questions

- How can legislators ensure distributed ledger systems balance enduring policy goals while also mitigating new or unforeseen risks?

- Why might current regulatory and legal systems be redundant in a fully distributed economy?

Governing Distributed Ledger Technology

Effectively governing blockchain and distributed ledger technology will require finding an optimum balance between governance, regulation, legal code and technical code and will require a unique mix of skills and perspectives from a variety of stakeholders, including lawyers, mathematicians, business experts and computer scientists. For purposes of analysis governance, regulation, legal code and technical code are defined below:

- Governance: Rule-making by the owners or participants of a system with the purpose of safeguarding private interests.

- Regulation: Rule-making by an outside authority tasked with representing the broader interests of the public.

- Legal Code: Rules consisting of legal obligations set by either statute, administrative code or regulatory guidance.

- Technical Code: Rules defined in systems and code, executed and enforced by software and protocols.

Legislative Recommendations

Illinois' lack of "blockchain legislation" to date should not be viewed as a failure to act, but rather, as a recognition that many activities, transactions, agreements and events facilitated by the technology are probably already legal, so long as they are performed in good faith, without deception, and can be proven. For example, the state statutes governing county land records offices (55 ILCS 5/3-5005.2) provide that " . . . The Recorder shall have the right to select the computer or micrographic system to be used for document storage and retrieval." The Cook County Recorder of Deeds interprets this to mean that if the office so chooses, it can implement a blockchain or distributed database to store records without need for a state law to authorize it.

¶1390

Illinois has instead chosen a more restrained regulatory path, actively studying design principles rather than simply envisioning every possible use case and affirming its "legality." It can also be tempting to make a list of all the things the private sector *can't or shouldn't* do with blockchain in the name of consumer protection, but it seems that such a heavy-handed approach is more likely to send the message that Illinois is not friendly towards this technology.

Recommendations that follow will thus reflect necessary changes to the way information is submitted, stored and transmitted.

The recommendations available in appendix A are heavily focused in the areas of state law that affect property law and public recording, mainly because that is the area most heavily studied in Illinois thus far (*see Cook County Recorder of Deeds Blockchain Final Report, May 31, 2017*). It is the opinion of the Task Force that because property law continues to rely on archaic standards and paper-based regulatory guidance, that an overhaul of these sections could provide impetus and direction to lawmakers interested in carrying similar updates into other Sections of law.

It is beyond the abilities and mandate of this Task Force to analyze every corner of the Illinois Compiled Statutes and every opportunity. It is also important to remember that the purpose of this Task Force is to analyze opportunities and risks *for government usage*, which means this report will not directly consider legislation that is tangential to the delivery of government services.

3. Creating a Hyperconnected Government

Essential Questions

- How can distributed ledger technology help governments deliver more responsive, trusted and integrated public services?

- How can these technologies be utilized with other emerging technologies to radically rethink how government services are delivered?

Building a Hyperconnected Government with Blockchains

An important function of government is to maintain trusted information about individuals, organizations, assets, and activities. Local, regional and national agencies are charged with maintaining records that include, for instance, birth and death dates or information about marital status, business licensing, property transfers, or criminal activity. Managing and using these data can be complicated, even for advanced governments. Some records exist only in paper form, and if changes need to be made in official registries, citizens often must appear in person to do so. Individual agencies tend to build their own silos of data and information-management protocols, which preclude other parts of the government from using them. And, of course, these data must be protected against unauthorized access or manipulation, with no room for error.

Blockchain technology could simplify the management of trusted information, making it easier for government agencies to access and use critical public-sector data while maintaining the security of this information. At a high level blockchain and distributed ledger-enabled technologies enable government efficiencies in three ways:

- Integrating government services with distributed identity
- Efficiently and effectively managing the flow of digitized assets
- Combining blockchain with other emerging technologies to "reinvent public services"

Integrating Government Services with Identity

What is Identity?

Identity is a collection of attributes about a person which can relate to their preferences, personality or information that might be more sensitive such as their biometrics, healthcare records or criminal history. These attributes can be collected and used for a particular purpose, such as verifying that a person is who they say they are, and granting access to goods and services based on those attributes. For example, to buy certain goods, such as alcohol, a person needs to prove they are over 21, which is an attribute of their identity. Identity attributes can be broadly categorized into three groups: inherent, accumulated and assigned. Some identity attributes rarely change while others change frequently.

The Role of Identity in Government

Government has an important role to play in the development of any digital identity ecosystem. Identity is not only foundational to nearly every government service, but is the basis for trust and legitimacy in the public sector. It is the starting point of trust and confidence in interactions between the public and government and is a critical enabler of service delivery, security, privacy, and public safety activities. How identity attributes are collected, used, managed, and secured is and will continue to be of critical interest to leaders in the public sector charged with protecting the rights of citizens, ensuring privacy, and ensuring national security and public safety.

In government, various pieces of data (i.e. identity attributes) used to verify a person's identity and allow them to interact with and gain access to government services. This data can vary depending on the government service. (add how governments are the first register of identity information) Government identities are often siloed in databases across agencies, increasing opportunities for fraud, security breaches and errors.

Government identity attributes can be organized into four categories based on their general characteristics and types of services they enable:

Core Identity Attributes

Inherent or assigned personal identity attributes that are generally, but not always registered through a public sector identity register maintained by entities such as the post office or vital records office.

Legal Name (First, Middle, Last, Suffix)	Spouse(Marriage or Civil Union)	Birth Certificate
Date of Birth	Mother/Father/Sibling	Death Certificate
Physical and Mailing Address	Email(s)	Organ Donor
Gender	Phone Number(s)	Criminal History

Service Identifiers

Identifiers assigned to individuals after receiving access to certain government services, mandatory enrollment in government programs, or to exercise legally ordained rights and obligations such as paying taxes or voting.

Medicaid/Medicare number	Unemployment Insurance ID	Passport (Citizenship)
Social Security Number	Voter ID	Prisoner/Correctional ID
Tax ID	Veteran ID	Student ID

Ownerships

Legal rights afforded individuals or legal entities (e.g. businesses) to track manage and maintain possession and ownership of a high value physical asset. Ownerships and transfer of ownership is generally maintained by relevant federal, state and local governments in asset registries.

Land Title	Vehicle Title (Car/Boat)	Firearm Owner's ID (FOID)

Attestations

Information corroborated or certified by a government service or agency. Attestations either (1) provide individuals permission to perform certain tasks within government or outside of government or (2) provide proof to substantiate certain events occurred, or that particular qualifications were achieved.

Driver's License (Other Vehicles)	Concealed Carry Firearm Permit	Fishing License
Professional/Occupational License	Academic Credential	Travel Visa
Continuing Education Certifications	Pilot License	Military Service

Illinois' PKI Infrastructure

At a high level, Public Key Infrastructure (PKI) is a set of requirements that allow (among other things) the creation of digital signatures. Through PKI, each digital signature transaction includes a pair of keys: a private key and a public key. The private key, is not shared and is used only by the signer to electronically sign documents. The public key is openly available and used by those who need to validate the signer's electronic signature. PKI enforces additional requirements, such as the Certificate Authority (CA), a digital certificate, end-user enrollment software, and tools for managing, renewing, and revoking keys and certificates.

In 2001, the State of Illinois received certification as a self-signed Public Key Infrastructure (PKI) Certificate Authority (CA) and Registration Authority (RA) following an independent audit. Currently the Department of Innovation and Technology (DoIT), by legislative directive, is the sole source of digital certificates for State of Illinois agencies, boards, commissions, universities municipal government and business partners.

Illinois' public key infrastructure (PKI) is used today to assist with determining the identity of different people, devices and services. PKI goes beyond the use of user ID and password by employing cryptographic technology such as digital certificates and digital signatures which create unique credentials that are validated by a third party. Illinois' PKI is governed by roles, policies and procedures to ensure the appropriate management of digital certificates and public-key encryption. Illinois' PKI functions through the creation and issuance of cryptographic keys by the Illinois Certificate Authority (CA) which provides a public key for distribution throughout the user base and a secret key for private use by the entity (or individual) to which it belongs. The private key is typically used for decryption or digital signatures.

Despite the incremental benefits that PKI affords government services, it cannot be viewed as a cure all data security and identity management solution, rather it is one piece of the puzzle.

Why Decentralized identity Management on Blockchains?

Related to innovations in blockchain and distributed ledger technologies, decentralized public key infrastructure (DPKI) leveraging blockchains as a machine-readable key-value store is rapidly emerging as a more resilient form of managing public key infrastructure.

The blockchain-enabled identity model relies on the combination of four important standards: decentralized identifiers (DIDs), DID documents, verifiable claims and blockchain/distributed ledgers. *decentralized identifiers (DIDs)* are stored on a *blockchain or distributed ledger* with a corresponding DID document where collectively they form a key-value pair relationship **(not to be confused with a cryptographic key but rather linked data items: a key, which is a unique identifier for some item of data, and the value, which is either the data that is identified or a pointer to the location of that data).

The DID acts as a globally unique index and the a DID document contains a number of essential items including (1) a public key, (2) service endpoint (3) authentication mechanism (how a user cryptographically asserts they are the owner or controller of the DID/DID Document) and (4) ways in which keys can be revoke, rotated or replaced.

Decentralized public key infrastructure affords two improvements over existing public key infrastructure:

Decentralized Resilience

It does not rely on any single Certificate Authority to check for validity of public keys, rather it uses a globally available blockchain ledger for verification. This has the capability to reduce Man in the Middle (MITM) attacks that are difficult to detect and reduces the risk of a single Certificate Authority being a single point of failure.

Embedding PKI in Each Transaction

DPKI also leverages blockchains to make public key infrastructure more usable. Blockchains by nature require a built-in public key infrastructure mechanism which requires users to use public key infrastructure for every transaction, and if "wrapped" in a well-designed user experience, invisible to the end user. Furthermore, the key pair is pseudonymous, not revealing the actor's actual identity. However, supplemental information, such as name, contact information or professional credentials can be associated with these pairwise unique public-private key pair, merging on-chain and off-chain identity.

A Framework for Government-led Decentralized Identity

A citizen-centric digital identity model based on distributed ledger technologies could be used to consolidate disparate data that currently exists across multiple agencies and layers of government into a network centered around a citizen's or business' credentials, licenses and identity attributes. It would enable citizens to view their public service identity via an identity app on their smartphone and share relevant data with government to access public services.

This new model would reimagine the relationship between state and individual, as government would become the verifier, rather than the custodian, of people's public service identity. Government would move from providing data storage to verifying identity, allowing users to store access to personal data securely on devices.

Protecting personal data in this manner makes it increasingly difficult and economically disadvantageous to hack because each citizen's data stored in encrypted in the cloud with the only keys to unlock the data stored on each citizen's personal device. An attack on this model would require hackers to simultaneously gain access to person data in the cloud, blockchain and a majority of the citizen's devices.

The distributed nature of blockchain means that all departments on the network agree to 'one version of the truth when information is added. Furthermore, if designed well, distributed ledgers have the potential to provide answers that do not present a risk to user privacy. These ledgers allow citizens to share selectively share verified attributes of an identity along with the provenance of the verification or source document.

Efficiently and Effectively Managing Digital Assets

Government plays an important role in the distribution and administration of benefit and entitlement programs for citizens who meet certain eligibility requirements. Examples of programs include health care, welfare, unemployment, and housing assistance. Government could leverage blockchain and distributed ledger technology distribute benefits more efficiently, reducing entitlement fraud and increasing asset transparency for taxpayers. Effectively managing assets in government can be thought of in two ways:

- Digitizing physical assets to (sometimes referred to as tokenizing assets) increase asset transparency, improve liquidity and policy outcomes for incentive programs or titled assets.

- Managing revenue collection, or benefit and incentive distribution on a shared ledger with smart contracts to provide more granular control and real-time insight and transparency over complex administrative processes.

Digitizing Assets

Smart contract enabled distributed ledgers provide a standard for digitizing assets, dematerializing assets onto the blockchain. Representing items such as shares, cars, property, or tax credits as tokens on a blockchain allows assets to be transacted and spent as currency.

In this model, all users, transactions and data are digitally signed on the blockchain, creating an immutable record. The irrefutable record can dramatically reduce the cost and complexity of auditing, reconciliation and issue resolution as there is a clear and traceable audit trail of transactions, data and user interactions. Not only can this can lead to a material reduction in paperwork and more efficient asset transfer processes, but by significantly reducing transaction costs, blockchains could help public sector open up credit and securities markets for whole new classes of lower-value or non-traditional assets.

There is also a unique opportunities to create liquid secondary securities markets where assets can be fractionalized and traded as futures, options, or shares similar to oil, corn or other commodities.

Examples of public sector assets that could be digitized include:

Loyalty Rewards	Pension Liabilities	Tax Credits
Digital Currencies or Tokens	Municipal Bonds	Unclaimed Property
Prison Commissary Funds	Affordable Housing Vouchers	Highway Tolls

Use Case Snapshot: Tokenizing Tax Credits

Tax credits could be categorically "tokenized" on a blockchain to improve market visibility and ensure asset provenance. Government could also open an exchange where the "tax credit tokens" could be traded, improving their liquidity and ensuring the efficacy of the policy goal that the credit incentivizes. A blockchain-based system of management also allows aggregators granularly pool credit (or derivatives of) while maintaining direct visibility into its initial issuance.

Social Benefits and Incentive Program Distribution

¶1390

The State could also consider creating a blockchain platform to increase efficiencies and reduce costs for companies to comply with the State's workers compensation system. With the State's creation of a private permissioned blockchain consortium for workers compensation, all transactions are logged, including information on the date, time and participants, as well as the amount of every single transaction in an immutable record. Each party in the network would be party to a complete copy of the blockchain, and the transactions are verified using advanced cryptographic algorithms. This is the equivalent of a free notary present at each transaction. The employer's workers compensation insurance companies pay for workers compensation healthcare expenses to certified medical practitioners in the system.

In the case of the workers compensation blockchain consortium, whether someone actually follows the rules about medical visits and their corresponding payments as a result is no longer verified in a bureaucratic (and often fax or email driven) process afterward. The workers compensation program establishes these rules for compliance and transactions into the blockchain for the parties to participate. This has potential to reduce fraud and reduce processing costs in workers compensation transitions and ultimately lower workers compensation rates for Illinois companies.

Similarly, many government grants and incentives programs are eligibility based. That is, based on eligibility criteria, a grant is either approved or denied to an individual or entity based on the meeting of certain requirements. The difficulty in this process arises due to the data being held within disparate government and private entities, making the eligibility process time consuming and resource intensive to get right. Rolling up all of these systems into one distributed ledger simplifies the eligibility process. Upon eligibility, a smart-contract can trigger a grant payment to the recipient instantly.

A distributed ledger is an ideal technology to supplement the Medicaid enrollment and eligibility process. In this scenario, the State of Illinois maintains a distributed roster (ledger) of eligible Medicaid members. Data is fed into this ledger from various sources, including the member's employer or former employer and records from the federal and state government. This allows the eligibility status of a member to stay in constant sync. Should a member fall out of coverage once they find a stable job, a smart-contract would automatically terminate their enrollment in the program. A distributed ledger solution simplifies the system by rolling up the currently siloed databases and connecting them to shared eligibility ledger.

SNAP/TANF	Student Loans	Housing Support
Medicaid/Medicare	Disaster Recovery Grants	Tax Collection
Unemployment Insurance	Research Grants	Municipal Grants
Worker's Compensation	Agricultural Price Support	Conservation Grants

Social Benefits Distribution Use Case Snapshot

An interesting application could be an "entitlements digital currency" for benefit programs such as food stamps. Providing a digital identity verification would help the program accurately verify applicants and reduce fraud. Smart contracts could precisely determine eligibility efficiently and effectively. An additional "healthy eating token" incentive system could be offered to achieve ancillary health policy goals, providing additional cost savings for other health benefits systems.

Convergence: Reimagining Public Services

Illinois could also explore the feasibility of integrating other emerging technologies such as IoT or Artificial Intelligence with blockchain to (1) develop new products and (2) reinvent traditional services. New products could include peer-to-peer service marketplaces that monetize non-traditional datasets. Reinventing govt. services could involve using a combination of AI and smart contracts to automate complex eligibility processes or to re-engineer social benefits programs so that funds are pre-distributed to recipients.

For example, an interesting application of a blockchain-enabled public service application would be a sharing economy public transit service provided by the State of Illinois. With autonomous vehicles on the horizon, it is entirely possible to have a state-operated on-demand vehicle service that is hosted on a distributed ledger. In fact, private companies such as Arcade City are already providing rides to consumers by using a distributed ledger.

Use Case Snapshot - Device Marketplace for Waste Management

By combining blockchain, IoT, and big data, governments could create demand-based marketplaces for tasks such as waste management, recycling services, or snow removal. Sensors data could be fed into a blockchain system, where it interacts with smart contracts to determine demand autonomously. Price would be determined by sensors and service providers are sourced automatically based on conditions in the smart contract.

Use Case Snapshot – Disaster Recovery Grant Distribution

Many grants are based on eligibility criteria and are approved or denied based on a person or entity meeting pre-defined requirements. Rolling up all systems into smart-contracts managed by a distributed ledger could radically simplify the eligibility process. Upon eligibility, a smart-contract could trigger a grant payment instantly. For example, disaster recovery "smart contracts" could use a combination of computer vision data and IoT sensor data from drones providing an "oracle" to automate the disaster recovery eligibility process.

Blockchain in Government Pilot Database

Over the past year, the Illinois Blockchain Initiative has compiled a database of over 200 blockchain and distributed ledger technology pilots, projects and strategies announced by public sector entities. The database is an overview of how government at various levels globally are employing blockchain technology in their efforts to govern, improve the competitiveness of their economy and also deliver high-quality services in a more efficient manner.

The public sector is one of the most active blockchain sector's exploring the technology for a wide variety of use cases. Adoption of the technology in the public section is accelerating at an extraordinary pace.

The database can be found at the following link: http://bit.ly/govt-tracker-database

Appendix A: Legislative Recommendations

Reconcile State Digital Signature Laws With UETA

The Uniform Law Commission created the Uniform Electronic Transactions Act in 1999, which provides standards for retention of electronic records and the validity and use of electronic signatures. Though Illinois has some statutory language allowing electronic signatures, a push towards a blockchain-based system is an opportunity to again review whether Illinois should make an effort to fully join the rest of the nation and place itself on a path towards more efficient and secure paperless recordkeeping.

Modernization of Notarial Statutes

The Uniform Law Commission has created the Revised Uniform Law on Notarial Acts (RULONA) to reflect the changing nature of technology. A shift towards allowing electronic or video notarizing, perhaps tracked and verified on a public blockchain, would help modernize Illinois law in a clear direction towards electronic commerce and away from the ease of fraud that can be committed by paper-and-stamp methods. A holistic look at state notary laws should include an analysis of remote video notarization enablement, biometric based notarization as well as other technology enabled methods which would be a move that would better facilitate electronic transactions.

Self-Notarization of Documents

One of the basic functions a blockchain can provide is proving that a specific computer file or document existed at a certain point in time (akin to a "poor man's copyright"). Allowing documents that have had their hash values permanently timestamped and embedded into a known, trusted and public blockchain to be admitted as evidence in state courts would create efficiencies by removing the need for a lawyer to visit an office, purchase paper, then have that office expend taxpayer resources to physically mark that printout as "certified." This is also a step towards streamlining Illinois' public land record to be a record of text-data, as opposed to a registry of PDF scans of legal instruments that must be independently verified and inspected each time they are used. A specific instrument's SHA 256 hash fingerprint could be included in the public record as a way to avoid having government foot the expense of storing terabytes of bulky PDF or TIFF files.

Clarity to "Pure Notice" Conveyance and Recording Statute

A central issue in the legality and validity of property records centers on whether a state is a "race to the courthouse" state, a "notice" state, or a "race-notice" state. This refers to how competing disputes by "subsequent purchasers" as to ownership of a property are resolved, focusing on whether ownership claims that are unrecorded and thus unknown to subsequent purchasers adversely affect these bona fide purchasers who took title in good faith with no knowledge of previous claims or interest. It is the opinion of this Task Force that the case law that has misinterpreted the plain language of Illinois' "pure notice" statute (ILCS XXXXXXX) to be a "race-notice" should be invalidated by clear instructions of the General Assembly, simply by adding a clarifying statement to the existing statute.

Require Claims Against Real Estate to be Publicly Recorded

Though clarifying the notice requirements and effects in Illinois will go a long way towards shaping a logical public record and maximizing its benefit, allowing valid claims to remain unrecorded (including those by local governments) is something that should be re-examined in our modern age of computers, electronic recording, and overnight mail. It is no longer a burden for a person with a valid claim to simply place that claim in the public record, and it must be examined whether allowing uncertainty to exist in property records is truly serving the interests of taxpayers and property owners. This will make Illinois' public land record a true record that can be easily agreed upon, and not simply a record of those interests claimants felt like recording. A single record of claims will make title research easier and cheaper, and make a transition to a distributed ledger more attainable and valuable.

Reproduction Versus Storage

If the goal of a public land record is an accurate description of events between private parties, a system that manually recreates those records does not achieve this goal. Section 3-5010 of the Recorders Act, entitled "Duties of recorder", refers to duties related to "instruments in writing." This Section heavily focuses on reproducing written submissions and implies that a recorder must always "reproduce" what has already been created. This leads to inefficiencies and errors. A possible update to this section could allow for direct submission of plain-text data that was used to create the transaction into the public record, which would technically not be a "reproduction," but would provide 100% accuracy in the record of what actually occurred. As a background, recorder's office manually create indices of submitted records, a process that is vulnerable to human error and results in discrepancies that must be "insured" at the taxpayers' own expense. Such an update would not preclude private parties, through their settlement agents or attorneys, from providing hash-values for the lengthy contracts used in the transaction, allowing them to be used for evidentiary purposes in the future without requiring that costly client-server storage models be used to maintain millions of pages of unnecessary information.

Omnibus Real Estate Records Submission Modernization

Though Illinois law allows documents to be electronically submitted, industry conventions, and in some cases, the plain language of the law, confines practice to paper-based methods. For example, in outlining some duties of a Recorder, the law states " . . . No recorder shall record any instrument affecting title to real estate unless the name and address of the person who prepared and drafted such instruments is printed, typewritten or stamped on the face thereof in a legible manner . . . " (5/3-5022). A focused effort to update these laws to allow text-only records that have no "face" but still contain the needed information would be a great facilitator of blockchain-based recordkeeping. This inquiry should also focus on the Conveyances Act, and any section that specifically states how a record must be worded and constructed. For example, language such as " . . . the name and address of the preparer shall accompany any record affecting title to real estate . . . " would begin a shift away from paper-based modes of document submission and retention.

Statewide Unique Real Property Parcel Numbering System

For a blockchain-based property registry to work, every parcel of real estate must have a unique number to identify it (much like the interstate and international VIN system for automobiles). Earlier this year, the Real Estate Standards Organization (RESO), issued guidance for creating a universal Property Unique Identifier for real estate, similar to the VIN number for a vehicle. It combines ISO Country and FIPS County codes and incorporates the local unique identifier to create a system to uniquely number and identify parcels across a state. Legislation could simply adopt this standard and require counties to report whether they use a unique numbering system and adopt one if it does not.

Appendix B: Citations

1. Demirgüç-Kunt, A., Klapper, L. F., Singer, D., & Van Oudheusden, P. (2015). The global findex database 2014: Measuring financial inclusion around the world. http://docu-

ments.worldbank.org/mwg-internal/de5fs23hu73ds/progress?id=s8O3-TIkaKpsnQM78IysThFLxTdntJyQH1Fzpama0nM.

2. Tapscott, Don, and Alex Tapscott. Blockchain Revolution: How the Technology Behind Bitcoin Is Changing Money, Business, and the World. 2016.

3. Schwab, Klaus. "The Fourth Industrial Revolution: what it means, how to respond." World Economic Forum (2016). https://www.weforum.org/agenda/2016/01/the-fourth-industrial-revolution-what-it-means-and-how-to-respond.

4. Maupin, Julie A. "Blockchains and the G20: Building an Inclusive, Transparent and Accountable Digital Economy." CIGI Online (2017). https://www.cigionline.org/sites/default/files/documents/PB%20no.101.pdf.

5. World Economic Forum. Global Agenda. "Top 10 Emerging Technologies of 2016." (2016). https://www.weforum.org/reports/top-10-emerging-technologies-of-2016.

6. Atzori, Marcella. "Blockchain Governance and the Role of Trust Service Providers: The Trustedchain® Network." (2017). https://papers.ssrn.com/sol3/papers.cfm?abstract_id=2972837.

7. Atzori, Marcella. "Blockchain technology and decentralized governance: Is the state still necessary?" (2015). https://papers.ssrn.com/sol3/papers.cfm?abstract_id=2709713.

8. Tapscott, Alex, and Karen Gifford. "This is the technology that could help us make globalization work for everyone". Quartz (2017).

https://www.weforum.org/agenda/2017/02/this-is-the-technology-that-could-help-us-make-globalization-work-for-everyone.

9. Hexayurt.Capital, and ConsenSys. "Building the Hyerconnected Future on Blockchains". World Government Summit (2017). http://internetofagreements.com/files/WorldGovernment-Summit-Dubai2017.pdf.

10. Walport, M. G. C. S. A. "Distributed ledger technology: beyond block chain." UK Government Office for Science (2016). https://www.gov.uk/government/uploads/system/uploads/attachment_data/file/4929_72/gs-16-1-distributed-ledger-technology.pdf.

11. Australia Post and Boston Consulting Group. A frictionless future for identity management a practical solution for Australia's identity challenge. December 2016. https://auspostenterprise.com.au/content/dam/corp/ent-gov/documents/digital-identity-white-paper.pdf.

12. Hileman, Garrick, and Michel Rauchs. "2017 Global Blockchain Benchmarking Study." (2017). https://www.jbs.cam.ac.uk/faculty-research/centres/alternative-finance/publications/global-blockchain/#.Wg34KoQrIdU.

13. Hanson RT, Reeson A, Staples M. "Distributed Ledgers, Scenarios for the Australian economy over the coming decades" (2017). http://www.data61.csiro.au/en/Our-Work/Safety-and-security/Secure-Systems-and-Platforms/Blockchain.

14. Torgesen, Cory. "The Illinois Conveyances Act: A 200-Year-Old Labyrinth Whose Changing Walls Continue to Provide Inadequate Protection for Subsequent Purchasers." Southern Illinois University Law Journal (2013) http://www.law.siu.edu/_common/documents/law-journal/articles-2013/12%20-%20Torgesen%20Comment%20-%20final%20redo.pdf

15. Real Estate Standards Organization, PUID Working Group. https://www.reso.org/wp-content/uploads/2016/11/RESO-PUID-Workgroup-Meeting_Mark-Bessett.pdf

16. https://www.hyperledger.org/wp-content/uploads/2017/08/Hyperledger_Arch_WG_Paper_1_Consensus.pdf

17. http://www.un.org/esa/ffd/wp-content/uploads/2017/10/15STM_Blockchain-101.pdf

18. http://www.europarl.europa.eu/RegData/etudes/IDAN/2017/581948/EPRS_IDA(2017)5_81948_EN.pdf

19. http://dontapscott.com/BlockchainCorridorReport.pdf_pg.26

20. https://illinoisblockchain.tech/illinois-announces-initiative-to-grow-innovation-sector-ccf13e460287

21. https://www2.deloitte.com/content/dam/Deloitte/uk/Documents/Innovation/deloitte-uk-connecting-global-fintech-hub-federation-innotribe-innovate-finance.pdf

22. https://www.cbre.us/about/media-center/chicago-ranks-15-on-cbre-annual-tech-talent-scorecard

23. https://www.usnews.com/best-colleges/rankings/engineering-doctorate-computer

24. http://fortune.com/fortune500/list/filtered?statename=Illinois

25. http://www3.weforum.org/docs/
WEF_GAC15_Technological_Tipping_Points_report_2015.pdf

¶ 1400 Uniform Regulation of Virtual-Currency Businesses Act

drafted by the

NATIONAL CONFERENCE OF COMMISSIONERS

ON UNIFORM STATE LAWS

and by it

APPROVED AND RECOMMENDED FOR ENACTMENT

IN ALL THE STATES

at its

ANNUAL CONFERENCE

MEETING IN ITS ONE-HUNDRED-AND-TWENTY-SIXTH YEAR

SAN DIEGO, CALIFORNIA

JULY 14 - JULY 20, 2017

WITH PREFATORY NOTE AND COMMENTS

Copyright © 2017

By

NATIONAL CONFERENCE OF COMMISSIONERS

ON UNIFORM STATE LAWS

October 9, 2017

ABOUT ULC

The **Uniform Law Commission** (ULC), also known as National Conference of Commissioners on Uniform State Laws (NCCUSL), now in its 126th year, provides states with non-partisan, well-conceived and well-drafted legislation that brings clarity and stability to critical areas of state statutory law.

ULC members must be lawyers, qualified to practice law. They are practicing lawyers, judges, legislators and legislative staff and law professors, who have been appointed by state governments as well as the District of Columbia, Puerto Rico and the U.S. Virgin Islands to research, draft and promote enactment of uniform state laws in areas of state law where uniformity is desirable and practical.

- ULC strengthens the federal system by providing rules and procedures that are consistent from state to state but that also reflect the diverse experience of the states.

- ULC statutes are representative of state experience, because the organization is made up of representatives from each state, appointed by state government.

- ULC keeps state law up-to-date by addressing important and timely legal issues.

- ULC's efforts reduce the need for individuals and businesses to deal with different laws as they move and do business in different states.

- ULC's work facilitates economic development and provides a legal platform for foreign entities to deal with U.S. citizens and businesses.

- Uniform Law Commissioners donate thousands of hours of their time and legal and drafting expertise every year as a public service, and receive no salary or compensation for their work.

- ULC's deliberative and uniquely open drafting process draws on the expertise of commissioners, but also utilizes input from legal experts, and advisors and observers representing the views of other legal organizations or interests that will be subject to the proposed laws.

- ULC is a state-supported organization that represents true value for the states, providing services that most states could not otherwise afford or duplicate.

DRAFTING COMMITTEE ON UNIFORM REGULATION OF VIRTUAL-CURRENCY BUSINESSES ACT

The Committee appointed by and representing the National Conference of Commissioners on Uniform State Laws in preparing this Act consists of the following individuals:

FRED MILLER, 80 S. 8th Street, 2000 IDS Center, Minneapolis, MN 55402-2274, *Chair*

BORIS AUERBACH, 5715 E. 56th St., Indianapolis, IN 46226

THOMAS J. BUITEWEG, 3025 Boardwalk St., Suite 120, Ann Arbor, MI 48108

WILLIAM H. CLARK, JR., One Logan Square, 18th and Cherry St., Philadelphia, PA 19103- 2757

THOMAS E. HEMMENDINGER, 362 Broadway, Providence, RI 02909-1434

KIERAN MARION, 430 W. Allegan St., 4th Floor, Lansing, MI 48933

H. KATHLEEN PATCHEL, 5715 E. 56th St., Indianapolis, IN 46226

KEITH A. ROWLEY, University of Nevada Las Vegas, William S. Boyd School of Law, 4505 S. Maryland Pkwy., Box 451003, Las Vegas, NV 89154-1003

EDWIN E. SMITH, 1 Federal St., Boston, MA 02110-1726

CHARLES A. TROST, Nashville City Center, 511 Union St., Suite 2700, Nashville, TN 37219- 1760

SUZANNE B. WALSH, 185 Asylum St., Hartford, CT 06103-3469

V. DAVID ZVENYACH, 707 10th St. NE, Washington, DC 20002

SARAH JANE HUGHES, Indiana University Bloomington, Maurer School of Law, Baier Hall, 211 S. Indiana Ave., Bloomington, IN 47405, *Reporter*

EX OFFICIO

RICHARD T. CASSIDY, 1233 Shelburne Rd., Suite D5, South Burlington, VT 05403-7753, *President*

CAM WARD, 124 Newgate Rd., Alabaster, AL 35007, *Division Chair*

AMERICAN BAR ASSOCIATION ADVISOR

STEPHEN T. MIDDLEBROOK, Atlantic Station, 271-17th Street, N.W., # 2400, Atlanta, GA 30363, *ABA Advisor*

AMERICAN LAW INSTITUTE ADVISOR

RICHARD FIELD, 755 Anderson Avenue, #4, Cliffside Park, NJ 07010, *ALI Advisor*

EXECUTIVE DIRECTOR

LIZA KARSAI, 111 N. Wabash Ave., Suite 1010, Chicago, IL 60602, *Executive Director*

Copies of this Act may be obtained from:

NATIONAL CONFERENCE OF COMMISSIONERS

ON UNIFORM STATE LAWS

111 N. Wabash Ave., Suite 1010

Chicago, IL 60602

312/450-6600

www.uniformlaws.org

UNIFORM REGULATION OF VIRTUAL-CURRENCY BUSINESSES ACT

TABLE OF CONTENTS

PREFATORY NOTE

Purpose of the Act

The purpose of this act is to create a statutory structure for regulating the "virtual currency business activity" of persons offering services or products to residents of enacting states. This act does not regulate virtual currency as such and should not be interpreted as doing so.

"Virtual-currency business activity" covered by this act is similar to services whose providers are already subject to licensure and prudential regulation by "money transmitter" or "money services" statutes in many states. In particular, the act would require licensure of and impose prudential regulations and customer protection requirements on businesses whose products and services include

(1) the exchange of virtual currencies for cash, bank deposits, or other virtual currencies;

(2) the transfer from one customer to another person of virtual currencies; or

(3) certain custodial or fiduciary services in which the property or assets under the custodian's control or under management include property or assets recognized as "virtual currency."

The underlying assumption motivating this act is that regulations that are predictable and tailored to virtual-currency businesses will provide assurance to persons using virtual-currency products and services and to providers that they will in fairness be regulated like other providers of financial services and products. Accordingly, this act regulates providers of "virtual-currency business services" and certain issuers of "virtual currency" in a manner similar to the manner that states that enacted the Uniform Money Services Act regulate money transmitters, check cashers, and similar businesses, and to the manner in which prudential regulators of banks and similar providers are developing regulatory regimes, such as the Conference of State Bank Supervisors'(CSBS) September 2015 Framework, for regulating virtual-currency businesses. This act also should serve to clarify which state laws - those regulating "money transmission" or general "money services" or this specialty virtual-currency business law - will govern the licensure, prudential regulation, and customer protection requirements placed on those engaged in "virtual-currency business activity." Clarity about which regulatory regime will govern virtual-currency business activity will assist virtual-currency businesses in many states and the greater legitimacy that uniform acts can bring to industry sectors will enhance the ability of these types of businesses to attract investment and customers.

The key factors for determining which providers of virtual-currency products and services are subject to this act are found in two definitions in section 102 - the definitions of the terms "virtual currency" and "virtual-currency business activity." In addition, this act contains numerous complete exemptions from its provisions. These exemptions are similar to those found in the Uniform Money Services Act or in other state "money transmitter" statutes, as well as others found in guidance published by the Department of the Treasury's Financial Crimes Enforcement Network ("FinCEN") since March 2013. The exemptions are found in section 103 of this act.

This act has some novel features designed to modernize even relatively recent uniform laws to meet contemporary regulatory issues. Features of this act that distinguish it from the many state "money services" or "money transmitter" statutes include:

(1) a three-tier system for determining which providers are exempt from the act consisting of persons engaging in only minor activity, an intermediate registration status that is modeled as an "on-ramp" or "regulatory sandbox" that is designed to facilitate innovations in virtual-currency businesses with more modest regulatory requirements, and full licensure for providers with specified business volumes;

(2) the provisions of Section 502 that (a) require the virtual-currency business with "control" over virtual currency that belongs to residents of the enacting state to maintain an amount of each type of virtual currency sufficient to satisfy the aggregate entitlements of the persons to each type of virtual currency for the benefit of its resident customers, and (b) favor the interests of persons who place virtual currency under the control of a licensee or registrant over the interests of creditors of the licensee or registrant. Because the licensee or registrant will not have rights in the collateral, the balance sheets of licensees and registrants should not show the virtual currency under their control. To clarify the rights of persons that place their virtual currency under the control of virtual-currency businesses and of the virtual-currency businesses themselves, the Uniform Law Commission is developing an act that will provide, when approved and enacted, a substitute for Section 502 of this act that instead adopts UCC Article 8's more balanced approach to this matter. This act is expected to be ready for enactment in 2018;

(3) a heightened focus on enabling cross-state "reciprocal licensure" for providers to enable providers to provide new products to more customers at lower regulatory costs. These features are described in greater detail below; and

(4) more flexible provisions on net worth and reserve requirements than have been found in money transmitter acts that are related to the inclusion of Section 502's mandate that virtual-currency businesses with control over other persons' virtual currency must maintain virtual currency in the types and values of those they have in custody and also protect customers' virtual-currency assets from the reach of the provider's creditors.

This act is modeled after the licensing and prudential safeguards found in the Commission's Uniform Money Services Act and also adheres to the contours of FinCEN's published guidance and the Framework issued by the Conference of State Bank Supervisors. FinCEN's guidance, as issued from March 2013 to the present, focuses on which types of "virtual currency" are covered by its "prepaid access" regulations promulgated under the Bank Secrecy Act, and which are not. FinCEN's guidance thus clarifies which providers of services and products are required to register with FinCEN as "money services businesses" in order to comply with the Bank Secrecy Act and to avoid being in violation of 18 U.S.C. § 1960.

This Prefatory Note and Comments to this act explain in more detail how the Uniform Money Services Act, FinCEN regulations and guidance, and the CSBS Framework influenced this act' provisions.

It is not common for the Uniform Law Commission to sponsor drafting projects for industries as young as the virtual-currency business industry. Some of the driving factors behind this act have been mentioned above, but there are two additional important reasons for regulating virtual-currency businesses now. The first of these additional reasons for this project, and a reason for states to enact this act, is that for innovators to succeed they need customers. Customers want to know how new products and services work, and are likely in the financial services "space" to know whether the business has been vetted by a financial services regulator. This act addresses the needs of these future customers.

The second reason is that virtual-currency businesses need banking relationships and credit opportunities as well as early-round investors to succeed. This act is intended to put virtual-currency businesses more firmly on the public radar so as to afford these businesses banking services and greater regulatory certainty and supervision behind them.

What is Virtual Currency and How is it Used?

What is Virtual Currency?

Virtual currency is intangible. Its "manifestation" is in the form of lengthy computer addresses referred to as the private key and the public key. At this time, in order to transfer the value that the addresses represent, one needs to have access to both the public and private keys. The value of virtual currency is a function of what the market will bear, not a value decreed by a government or determined by an international organization. Thus, virtual-currency values are capable of fluctuations more like commodities than many government-dictated "exchange" values even if the exchange values "float."

Transfers of virtual currency operate much like sending an electronic mail ("email") message over the Internet. The sender sends a message to the addressee; the message contains the addresses that represent the value to be transferred. A "node" system of moving the messages that closely resembles the operation of the Internet is employed. If the virtual currency is centrally issued, the issuer may track the transfer of ownership. If the virtual currency is not centrally issued, such as with bitcoins, the address of the transferee will be added to a distributed ledger that holds records of value issued or earned and of transfers of interests in that value.

Virtual currencies currently are in one of two forms - they emanate, as described above, from a centralized issuer or they result from the work of a person solving a puzzle with the virtual currency being "issued" as a reward for the work expended. The former are referred to as centralized; the latter are decentralized.

The distributed ledger (or asset registry) that records the issuance or earning of virtual currencies and the transfers of interests can be public or private. These ledgers are often called "blockchains" because of the algorithms employed and the manner in which changes are recorded, as additions to the earlier blocks of information stored by the ledger. In centralized systems, a single operator manages the issuance and transfers. In decentralized systems, a group of managers work to maintain the integrity of the registry. In Bitcoin, the form of virtual currency created by "Satoshi Nakamoto," the group of problem-solver managers are known as "miners." Centralized issuers of virtual currencies do not require miners to help create units or record their transfers.

Virtual currencies are a subset of cryptocurrencies. As media of exchange, they offer a communications technology that facilitates peer-to-peer (P2P) transactions that is the equivalent of paying cash - irreversible and not dependent on a third-party (*i.e.*, a bank) to carry out the transaction. That does not mean, however, that users do not use third party custodians or intermediaries to perform transaction execution or facilitate storage of virtual-currency assets.

¶1400

A key feature of some virtual currencies is that peer-to-peer transactions operate through pseudonyms or the addresses mentioned above. It is possible to reconstruct a series of transfers affecting one unit of value, but not necessarily to identify the person owning the unit or initiating the transfer.

How is Virtual Currency Defined for this Act's Purposes?

Virtual currency, as defined in § 102(23),

    (A) means a digital representation of value that:

        (1) is used as a medium of exchange, unit of account, or store of value; and

        (2) is not legal tender, whether or not denominated in legal tender; and

    (B) does not include:

        (1) a transaction in which a merchant grants, as part of an affinity or rewards program, value that cannot be taken from or exchanged with the merchant for legal tender, bank credit, or virtual currency; or

        (2) a digital representation of value issued by or on behalf of a publisher and used solely within an online game, game platform, or family of games sold by the same publisher or offered on the same game platform.

The term "legal tender" is defined in Section 102(8) of this act. Although "virtual currency" is not "legal tender" under the definition, virtual currency is used as a substitute for "money" between an obligor and obligee that have agreed to transact business as if a barter transaction is occurring, that is, where the transaction is not subject to laws that specify when the discharge of the "debt" occurs.

To be covered by this act, the transaction must involve "virtual currency" and "virtual-currency business activity," which is defined in Section 102(25), a definition that relies on active verbs - control, exchange, store, and transfer.

Section 102(3)(A) defines the term "control" of virtual currency itself - as opposed to control of an entity - as:

"Control" means:

(A)When used in reference to a transaction or relationship involving virtual currency, power to execute unilaterally or prevent indefinitely a virtual-currency transaction; . . .

    . . .

Section 102(5) defines the term "exchange" as:

. . . to assume control of virtual currency from or on behalf of a resident, at least momentarily, to sell, trade or convert:

(A) virtual currency for legal tender, bank credit, or for one or more forms of virtual currency; or

(B) legal tender or bank credit for one or more forms of virtual currency.

The terms "storage" and "transfer" are defined in sections 102(20) and (21) as:

(20) "Store," except in the phrase "store of value," means to maintain control of virtual currency on behalf of a resident by a person other than the resident. "Storage" and "storing" have corresponding meanings.

(21) "Transfer" means to assume control of virtual currency from or on behalf of a resident and to:

(A) credit the virtual currency to the account of another person;

(B) move the virtual currency from one account of a resident to another account of the same resident; or

(C) relinquish control of virtual currency to another person.

What Types of Virtual-currency Business Activities Does this Act Cover?

There are three factors that determine whether this act will apply to a particular provider of a product or service that relates to virtual currency. The first factor is whether the product or service deals with "virtual currency" as defined in section 102 of this act. The second factor is whether the product or service qualifies as "virtual-currency business activity" under section 102 of this act. This factor depends on the four definitions mentioned above - control, exchange, storage, and transfer.

The term "virtual-currency business activity" in section 102(25) means:

(A) exchanging, transferring, or storing virtual currency or engaging in virtual-currency administration, whether directly or through an agreement with a virtual-currency control-services vendor;

(B) holding electronic precious metals or electronic certificates representing interests in previous metals on behalf of another person or issuing shares or electronic certificates representing interests in precious metals; or

(C) exchanging one or more digital representations of value used within one or more online games, game platforms, or family of games for

(i) virtual currency offered by or on behalf of the same publisher from which the original digital representation of value was received, or

(ii) legal tender or bank credit outside the online game, game platform, or family of games offered by or on behalf of the same publisher from which the original digital representation of value was received.

The third factor is whether the provider is exempt from this act under section 103. Section 103 contains 14 specific types of exemptions from this act's coverage. Many are commonly found in "money services" and "money transmitter" statutes enacted by the states. A few derive from guidance that FinCEN has issued to date, such as the exemption for "dealers in foreign exchange."

A few examples illustrate how these three factors work together in Section 102(25).

"Control" is intended to signal a case in which the "owner" of virtual currency gives power to another person who engages in virtual-currency business activity that permits the second person to unilaterally transact or permanently prevent transactions with the "owner's" virtual currency. To effectuate this, the "owner" gives both the public and private keys that enable transactions in the virtual currency. If the "owner" gives less than the power to transact without more or to prevent transactions, "control" is not present. There is a product or service known in that community as "multi sig." In "multi sig" situations, a provider may have one of several private keys and two or more of these keys are needed to allow transactions to take place. A "multi sig" provider that has no ability alone to transact or prevent transactions does not have "control."

"Transfer" is comparable to a transaction execution under ordinary systems involving "money services" or "money transmission" or, indeed, one that "pushes" or "pulls" in a wire transfer or check collection operation, respectively. The provider merely agrees to take funds or value on one end of the transaction and to deliver them to the designated person on the other end. The virtual-currency business subject to this act would need to possess sufficient credentials to be recognized in its community as having the power to act, and also verifiable virtual currency to "transfer." The definitions of the terms "control," "exchange," "store," and "transfer" are crucial to the operation of this act.

To illustrate, assume A wants to transfer a virtual currency "coin" or "token" identified by a specific address and value to B. A is identified only by a computer code known only to A and contacts the server running the distributed ledger and directs transfer to B, who also is identified only by a computer code known to A and B. The server updates the ledger, and from then on the "coin" or "token" belongs to B. If A tries to spend this coin again by sending it to C, the server will detect that and refuse as A no longer owns it.

Transactions, such as using a debit or credit card to buy a cup of coffee - are tied to a bank. If you have enough money in your account, or credit on the card, the bank authorizes the transaction and you get your coffee. If you bought the same cup of coffee with bitcoins, you could proceed as follows: You could simply transfer ownership to the coffee house in a direct person-to-business transaction via an instruction to update the ledger to show the coffee house as the new owner, and you would be finished. The ledger would validate the transaction and, if valid, record the change of ownership on the public ledger without the bank or any other financial institution (and all their transaction fees) being involved. The merchant gets its money and you get your coffee.

"Virtual-currency business activity" under the various definitions in this act replaces the P2P transaction to the coffee house just described with a transaction that uses an intermediary that holds itself out to the public as an entity worthy of trust. Thus, this act is focused on intermediary providers of virtual-currency products and services - not on the virtual currency itself or on the "owner" of virtual currency that has the requisite tools to effect that payment for coffee on its own behalf. Person-to-person ("P2P") transactions are exempt from the coverage of this act under subsection 103(b)(7).

"Store" is analogous to deposit-taking and holding, or to safe deposit business. The virtual-currency provider has the capacity to receive particular forms of virtual currency or many of the extant forms, and to offer safekeeping services to its clientele. Storage of virtual currency is likely to involve the "owner" of the virtual currency giving some credentials to the "storage" company, and it is highly likely that the credentials would enable the storage company to return the virtual currency to the "owner" or its designee. Thus, storage is similar to placing a deposit of funds with a bank. Storage in the world of virtual currency may be on an "electronic wallet" or in another form.

¶1400

When the person wants to spend virtual currency it has stored with a third-party virtual-currency business, it sends a message to the virtual-currency business to transfer some or all of the stored virtual currency to the seller of the goods, services, or real estate. This virtual-currency payment instruction is comparable to one involving a bank intermediary, except that the former may be faster, is not generally subject to countermand, and at least theoretically is more secure than the latter.

Does this act cover multiple forms of virtual currency?

The baseline answer to this question is "yes." This act is drafted to capture as many of the possible types of virtual currency, whether issued on a centralized or decentralized basis, which are currently in the marketplace. It also covers contemporary equivalents of "e-Gold," a system that issued against holdings of precious metals, certificates that could be transferred by agreement from one owner to another.

A final point also may assist understanding: one can make payments by delivering cash. The point here is not that the transfer of virtual currency is superior in most respects to payment in cash, as indeed is true for most modern payment methods, but why the merchant agrees to receiving cash (ignore the legal rule there is no choice where legal tender is involved). It is not because the paper money has intrinsic value, or can be exchanged for gold (which also has no intrinsic value), but because people perceive value in dollar bills because of the governments and legal rules that govern them. Likewise for virtual currency-people see value in using payment methods when the legal rules for it are clear and workable, and the act will enhance that perception of value since present "money transmission" rules that could be applied to govern virtual-currency business transactions are at best not designed to do so or are unclear in application. It also is critical that the rules, since the act will be state law, be uniform for businesses operating across state lines, and that is what the products of the Uniform Law Commission are designed to be.

Why should the regulation of virtual-currency businesses occur now?

Despite all of the media attention, pro and con, for virtual currency, it is important to appreciate (1) the intrinsic opportunities that virtual currency and blockchain technologies offer - for faster, cross-border or long-distance, and inexpensive transactions, and (2) the basis for development that a balanced regulatory system can provide.

Blockchain technology is an ingenious computer code, stored entirely by computers, that forms the underlying architecture for thousands of payment systems and also shows great promise in extending beyond the realm of just currency, such as to the transfer of records, securities, and more. The blockchain provides a permanent record of all transactions that have ever happened, a history that normally within an hour is unalterable. In the case of bitcoin millions of independent computers record transactions. That is the important value - the mathematical verification by millions of computers reaching a consensus that they witnessed the same thing at the same time.

Distributed ledgers are mutual, shared ledgers. They create a single record of transactions among multiple parties. Consequently, parties do not need to maintain their own copies and reconcile with each other. Distributed ledgers are append-only databases that maintain audit trails of who did what and when they did it. Trust is a product of the blockchain, and regulation fosters that trust.

Continuing with the reasons for acting now, the value of virtual currency arises from demand by people for the attributes it has, such as the absence of an expensive middleman such as a bank, the blockchain serving that purpose instead (which banks do in more traditional systems); the speed and certainty of transactions in virtual currency; and the security of such transactions, even when balanced against a number of risks since, unlike in the case of a bank account or a securities account, there is no government insurance against insolvency.

A virtue of blockchain technology is its ability to put a person's security and online identity into their own hands. Databases filled with personal information are under attack from nation-states and organized crime. Hackers who target governments, cause data breaches at large department stores and even credit reporting agencies, are the result of the same problem: criminal elements breaking through cybersecurity to their prize; databases filled with valuable personal information. Blockchain technology offers a secure alternative to consumers who do not wish to see their personal information fall prey on the Internet. It offers the ability to transact on the Internet without sharing their personal information with third parties whose databases make targets for hackers. Instead, blockchain technology gives consumers the power to provide their own hack-proof online security. The security offered by blockchain technology on the Internet has a flip side, however. The anonymity it provides presents an opportunity for criminals and terrorists to send and receive money over the internet, nearly anonymously, without a third party. Thus money laundering, terrorist financing, and tax evasion are risks inherent in technology and therefore a certain amount of regulation to ameliorate these issues also is prudent. Article 6 of this act requires virtual-currency businesses to establish and implement compliance programs aimed at deterring money laundering and the financing of terrorist activity. The transfer is fast as the transactions are grouped in blocks every 10 minutes but many can be instantaneous; generally transactions cannot be cancelled or reversed so there is virtual finality of payment.

Another reason, mentioned briefly elsewhere in this Prefatory Note, is the risk that some virtual-currency businesses will be subject to prosecution under 18 U.S.C. § 1960 for engaging in business without being properly licensed under existing money services or money transmitter statutes. It is important to address this risk from several perspectives that include compliance with federal and state requirements for licensure and registration as a "money service business" with FinCEN for anti-money-laundering and counter-terrorism-finance purposes, and provision to the states of which businesses are entering into business relationships with residents of that state whether or not that state's money services or money transmitter statute clearly covers the particular form of business. Thus, regulatory uncertainty is a major risk to individuals, to virtual-currency businesses, and to government agencies. This act should reduce that type of uncertainty to a considerable extent.

A final reason for acting now is that individual states are beginning to act as described below. Because virtual-currency transactions and businesses are not limited to a few states, a uniform act is desirable to avoid duplicative or undue burdens that may arrest development and cause innovative businesses to move to states with more certain or suitable regulatory environments. This act was drafted with the experience of New York State's BitLicense regulation and its critics in mind. This act represents solid solutions to each of these problems in the current marketplace and regulatory environment across the United States.

Legal Efforts to Establish Relevant Law

Various states are examining regulatory structures, such as New York and California. The New York Department of Financial Services (DFS), has announced final regulations for BitLicenses. *See* 37 N.Y. Reg. 7 (2015). New York's regulatory plan includes: (1) licensing rules and compliance provisions; (2) capital requirements; (3) custody and protection of consumer assets and other consumer protection provisions including a complaint procedure; (4) notices of material changes in business and of control and of mergers and acquisitions; (5) books and records; (6) examinations; and (7) the establishment and maintenance of anti-money laundering, cybersecurity, business continuity and disaster recovery programs. A release by DFS dated November 9, 2015, emphasized details for a cybersecurity program including: (1) information security, access controls and identity management, systems and network security and customer data privacy among other areas; (2) third party service provider management, including the use of multi-factor authentication to limit access to sensitive data and systems and the use of encryption to protect such data in transit and at rest; and (3) employment of a cybersecurity officer and adequate personnel to manage the cybersecurity risks and perform core functions, providing for an annual audit, and notice of cybersecurity incidents. New York also issued a trust company license in May 2015 that allows the company to serve as a custodian for customers' assets, including bitcoins.

The Conference of State Bank Supervisors (CSBS) has put forth the model regulatory framework of principles that defines virtual currency, mentioned above, as

a digital representation of value used as a medium of exchange, a unit of account, or a store of value, but does not have legal tender status as recognized by the United States government (so called "fiat currency"). Virtual currency does not include the software or protocols governing the transfer of the digital representation of value. Virtual currency does not include stored value redeemable exclusively in goods or services limited to transactions involving a defined merchant, such as rewards programs.

The framework addressed the following activities:

1. transmission;

2. exchanging "fiat" currency (money) for virtual currency or virtual currency for fiat currency; virtual currency for virtual currency; and

3. services that facilitate the third party exchange, storage, and/or transmission of virtual currency (e.g., wallets, vaults, kiosks, merchant acquirers, or payment processors).

The CSBS regulatory framework encouraged licensing requirements with a so-called "on ramp" to facilitate startup businesses, regulating financial strength and stability and permissible investments, providing consumer protections including disclosures and notice of risks, cybersecurity and auditing, compliance with anti-money laundering and procedures for detecting and monitoring fraud and other illegal activity, and required books and records.

The act being created by the Uniform Law Commission is a uniform statute for prudential regulation of virtual currency business activity. The act, completed in 2017, requires examinations, reports and records, enforcements, has user protections, and requires policies and procedures to detect and deter money-laundering and financing of terrorist activities, and to provide for cybersecurity, business continuation and disaster recovery programs. The act defines an appropriate level of prudential regulation of virtual-currency businesses. Its requires a license for any person wherever located that engages in or holds itself out as engaging in virtual-currency business activity with a resident of the enacting state, with certain exclusions, such as a person chartered as a bank to avoid double or overlapping regulation.

Development of the Act

The essence of creating a uniform state law is to obtain a sufficient consensus as a result of striking a balance among the interests of the various constituencies that will be affected by the act when enacted into law by the state legislatures. In short, each interest must see more benefit than detriment for them in the act's provisions. If this is achieved, it is likely that universal and uniform adoption by the legislatures of all 50 states will occur. Another critical consideration is that the law's provisions must be seen to reflect good policy and be workable rules to guide aspects of the present operations of the businesses that the act will govern.

To achieve that, the practice of the Uniform Law Commission is to announce the drafting undertaking and circulate that announcement widely, usually after a meeting of all identified interested parties has disclosed in general the appropriate direction for the proposed effort, and determined that the effort is worthwhile. Those interests that wish to be involved then are invited to participate in considering the drafts as the act develops. Since all uniform acts when completed are submitted to the American Bar Association (ABA) for approval, one or more advisors from the ABA are designated by the ABA to attend drafting committee meetings and to solicit input from all parts of the ABA and its members who may have an interest in the subject.

The Uniform Law Commission and Drafting Committee solicited and received comments from a broad range of governmental, industry and non-profit organizations, as well as some individuals. Stakeholders such as these who contributed to meetings or submitted written comments, included:

The U.S Department of the Treasury

The Conference of State Bank Supervisors

CoinCenter

American College of Commercial Finance Lawyers

The Digital Chamber of Commerce

J. Dax Hansen and Dana Syracuse, Perkins Coie, Seattle and New York

The Texas Department of Banking

The California Department of Business Oversight

The Department of Banking of the State of Washington

Ripple Labs, Inc.

The Electronic Freedom Frontier

Coinbase, Inc.

The Entertainment Software Association

Carol Van Cleef, Baker Law, Washington, D.C.

Rebecca Simmons, Sullivan & Cromwell, New York City

Ryan Strauss, Dorsey & Whitney, Seattle

Texas A&M School of Law

Tom Brown, Paul Hastings, San Francisco

The Bitcoin Foundation

Théo Chino, a member of The Bitcoin Foundation

Other participants included The Clearing House, the Federal Reserve Bank of New York, and PayPal. Dozens of other stakeholders signed in as Observers and we thank all of them for their attention.

The ULC also acknowledges the work of the Reporter, the dedication and attention of the ABA Advisor Stephen T. Middlebrook, the Commissioner members of the drafting committee, and, last but not least, the Observers to the committee who gave of their time and knowledge and, while articulating the views of the interests they represented, also recognized the need in any legislation for compromise to achieve the overall public good.

Balances Achieved

A. **Owners of Virtual Currency**. Owners of virtual currency benefit from the act by receiving a strong regulatory structure that (1) provides clear rules, (2) guards against risks, both economic and from abusive conduct, (3) provides important information allowing evaluation of participation and prospective transactions, (4) provides effective remedies if nonetheless matters turn sour, and (5) requires the adoption and maintenance of policies and programs to reduce risk from fraud and improper activity.

B. **Persons involved in virtual-currency business activity**. Persons who wish to engage in the virtual-currency business (1) obtain a balanced and reasonable regulatory structure that should validate good business practice and thus enhance trust for users of virtual currency, and may lead to SEC approval of virtual-currency offerings, (2) obtain flexibility in entering the business through a testing process of registration, (3) have regulatory examinations to catch problems before matters go too far wrong, (4) are helped in keeping their businesses workable by requirements to guard against insolvency and other risks and to better ensure that changes in the business do not impair its operations, (5) when operating, particularly in several jurisdictions, have reciprocity and other protections against undue burdens, and have protection for confidential information, (6) have protection against the potential for divergent results in private actions while still being subject to strong administrative action, (7) receive by incorporation of an existing structure for financing, the ability to overcome present difficulties to obtain adequate credit, and (8) receive by virtue of a supervised regulatory structure greater access to banking relationships for business operations.

[ARTICLE] 1 GENERAL PROVISIONS

Sec. 101 SHORT TITLE.

This [act] may be cited as the Uniform Regulation of Virtual-Currency Businesses Act.

Sec. 102 DEFINITIONS.

In this [act]:

(1) "Applicant" means a person that applies for a license under this [act].

(2) "Bank" means a federally-chartered or state-chartered depository institution or holder of a charter granted by the Office of the Comptroller of the Currency to a person engaged in the business of banking other than deposit-taking. The term does not include:

(A) an industrial loan company, state-chartered trust company, or a limited-purpose trust company unless the department has authorized the company to engage in virtual-currency business activity; or

(B) a trust company or limited-purpose trust company chartered by a state with which this state does not have a reciprocity agreement governing trust-company activities.

(3) "Control" means:

(A) when used in reference to a transaction or relationship involving virtual currency, power to execute unilaterally or prevent indefinitely a virtual-currency transaction; and

(B) when used in reference to a person, the direct or indirect power to direct the management, operations, or policies of the person through legal or beneficial ownership of voting power in the person or under a contract, arrangement, or understanding.

(4) "Department" means the [name of state agency implementing this [act]].

(5) "Exchange," used as a verb, means to assume control of virtual currency from or on behalf of a resident, at least momentarily, to sell, trade, or convert:

(A) virtual currency for legal tender, bank credit, or one or more forms of virtual currency; or

(B) legal tender or bank credit for one or more forms of virtual currency.

(6) "Executive officer" means an individual who is a director, officer, manager, managing member, partner, or trustee of a person that is not an individual.

(7) "Insolvent" means:

(A) having generally ceased to pay debts in the ordinary course of business other than as a result of a bona fide dispute;

(B) being unable to pay debts as they become due; or

(C) being insolvent within the meaning of federal bankruptcy law.

(8) "Legal tender" means a medium of exchange or unit of value, including the coin or paper money of the United States, issued by the United States or by another government.

(9) "Licensee" means a person licensed under this [act].

(10) "Person" means an individual, partnership, estate, business or nonprofit entity, [public corporation, government or governmental subdivision, agency, or instrumentality,] or other legal entity. [The term does not include a public corporation, government or governmental subdivision, agency, or instrumentality.]

(11) "Reciprocity agreement" means an arrangement between the department and the appropriate licensing agency of another state which permits a licensee operating under a license granted by the other state to engage in virtual-currency business activity with or on behalf of a resident.

(12) "Record" means information that is inscribed on a tangible medium or that is stored in an electronic or other medium and is retrievable in perceivable form.

(13) "Registrant" means a person that has registered with this state under Section 207 to conduct virtual-currency business activity.

(14) "Registration" means the ability under Section 207 to conduct virtual-currency business activity.

(15) "Registry" means the Nationwide Multistate Licensing System and Registry.

(16) "Resident":

    (A) means a person that

        (i) is domiciled in this state;

        (ii) is physically located in this state for more than 183 days of the previous 365 days; or

        (iii) has a place of business in this state; and

    (B) includes a legal representative of a person that satisfies subparagraph (A).

(17) "Responsible individual" means an individual who has managerial authority with respect to a licensee's or registrant's virtual-currency business activity with or on behalf of a resident.

(18) "Sign" means, with present intent to authenticate or adopt a record:

    (A) to execute or adopt a tangible symbol; or

    (B) to attach to or logically associate with the record an electronic

symbol, sound, or process.

(19) "State" means a state of the United States, the District of Columbia, Puerto Rico, the United States Virgin Islands, or any territory or insular possession subject to the jurisdiction of the United States.

(20) "Store," except in the phrase "store of value," means to maintain control of virtual currency on behalf of a resident by a person other than the resident. "Storage" and "storing" have corresponding meanings.

(21) "Transfer" means to assume control of virtual currency from or on behalf of a resident and to:

    (A) credit the virtual currency to the account of another person;

    (B) move the virtual currency from one account of a resident to another account of the same resident; or

    (C) relinquish control of virtual currency to another person.

(22) "U.S. Dollar equivalent of virtual currency" means the equivalent value of a particular virtual currency in United States dollars shown on a virtual-currency exchange based in the United States for a particular date or period specified in this [act].

(23) "Virtual currency":

    (A) means a digital representation of value that:

        (i) is used as a medium of exchange, unit of account, or store of value; and

        (ii) is not legal tender, whether or not denominated in legal tender; and

    (B) does not include:

        (i) a transaction in which a merchant grants, as part of an affinity or rewards program, value that cannot be taken from or exchanged with the merchant for legal tender, bank credit, or virtual currency; or

        (ii) a digital representation of value issued by or on behalf of a publisher and used solely within an online game, game platform, or family of games sold by the same publisher or offered on the same game platform.

(24) "Virtual-currency administration" means issuing virtual currency with the authority to redeem the currency for legal tender, bank credit, or other virtual currency.

(25) "Virtual-currency business activity" means:

(A) exchanging, transferring, or storing virtual currency or engaging in virtual-currency administration, whether directly or through an agreement with a virtual-currency control-services vendor;

(B) holding electronic precious metals or electronic certificates representing interests in precious metals on behalf of another person or issuing shares or electronic certificates representing interests in precious metals; or

(C) exchanging one or more digital representations of value used within one or more online games, game platforms, or family of games for:

(i) virtual currency offered by or on behalf of the same publisher from which the original digital representation of value was received; or

(ii) legal tender or bank credit outside the online game, game platform, or family of games offered by or on behalf of the same publisher from which the original digital representation of value was received.

(26) "Virtual-currency control-services vendor" means a person that has control of virtual currency solely under an agreement with a person that, on behalf of another person, assumes control of virtual currency.

Legislative Note: If a state includes state-chartered trust companies under the definition of "bank," that state should consider adding a sentence at the end of the definition that expresses the type of state-chartered trust company that is eligible for the exemption for "bank" in Section 103(b).

The definition of the term "person" is drawn from the Uniform Law Commission's Drafting Rules. The bracketed material is the optional text available as a substitute for the definition as the enacting state may deem appropriate to the scope of this act it determines to enact.

Comment

1. "Virtual Currency." The term "virtual currency" covers any unit of value or exchange (whether or not the unit is denominated in U.S. dollars) that is not "legal tender" as issued by the United States or by another government. Whether a unit of virtual currency is denominated in U.S. dollars or Yen is immaterial to the question of whether the person, other than a government, who issues it or holds themselves out as providing services connected to a transfer, exchange, or storage of such virtual currency should be regulated under this act, or should remain subject to regulation under a state money services or money transmission statute or be regulated as an insured depository institution or other form of trusted intermediary. (For additional information, see Comment 7, "Legal Tender.") So long as the virtual currency is not issued by the United States or by another government, it is virtual currency for purposes of this act - if it otherwise meets the definition of "virtual currency" in Section 102 of this act. The decision by a non-government issuer of "virtual currency" to denominate its exchange value in a particular fashion (USD, Yen, or Euros) also is not the controlling factor in determining coverage of the business entity or the transaction by this act.

The definition of "virtual currency" purposefully excludes certain merchants' affinity or rewards programs and the equivalent sorts of value in online games and online game platforms if the same game or platform publisher is involved to the extent that the accounting units cannot be converted into cash, bank credit, or other virtual currencies. Merchants' rewards or online game units that can be converted to cash, bank credit, or other virtual currency are within the scope of the definition of "virtual currency." This bright line between non-cash-out and cash-out possibilities is consistent with guidance FinCEN issued in 2016 on what does not and does qualify as "money transmission." Fin. Crimes Enf. Network, No-action Letter, April 2016 (unpublished; copy on file with the Uniform Law Commission) provided by the Entertainment Software Association with its April 2016 comment on URVCBA Draft.

The exclusion of retail rewards or affinity programs from this act also is consistent with the exclusion of loyalty card programs from the Revised Uniform Unclaimed Property Act approved at the ULC's 2016 Annual Meeting. The exclusions in both Acts apply only to the extent that these rewards cannot be monetized into legal tender, bank credit, or other virtual currencies.

The definition of "virtual currency" also closely follows the definition used by the Conference of State Bank Supervisors ("CSBS") in its September 15, 2015, Framework, which had the support of the bank commissioners in office when the Framework was approved. Thus, the definition of "virtual currency" is designed to promote uniform enactment and compliance ease, as well as to cover and exclude specific activities.

The definition tracks guidance offered by the U.S. Treasury Department's Financial Crimes Enforcement Network (FinCEN) since March 2013 on the question of what types of virtual-currency transactions qualified as "prepaid access" and thus would constitute "money transmission." Fin. Crimes Enf. Network, Application of FinCEN's Regulations to Persons Administering, Exchanging, or Using Virtual Currencies, FIN-2013-G001 (March 18, 2013). FinCEN's guidance also defines when persons engaged in money transmission need to register as "money services businesses with FinCEN to avoid potential criminal liability under 18 U.S.C. § 1960 for failure to be registered with FinCEN.

FinCEN defines the distinctions between "currency" or "real currency" and "virtual currency" with the former being " . . . the coin and paper money of the United States or of any other country that [i] is designated as legal tender and that [ii] circulates and [iii] is customarily used and accepted as a medium of exchange in the country of issuance." 31 C.F.R. § 1010.100(m).

FinCEN defines the term "virtual currency" to be "a medium of exchange that operates like a currency in some environments, but does not have all the attributes of real currency." FIN-2013-G001, supra. *FinCEN's* definition carved out digital representations of bank money as may be loaded onto electronic travelers' checks or credit cards in part because providers of those services are subject to longstanding regulation. The distinction between "virtual currency" and digital representations of "legal tender" as the terms are defined in this act lies in the fact that traditional demand deposit accounts are representations of legal tender or other "hard assets" in a manner that makes the account holder a creditor of a federally insured depository institution under the Federal Deposit Insurance Act. 12 U.S.C. § 1813(l) (2013).

The definition of "virtual currency" includes electronic precious metals ("e-precious metals,") and "electronic certificates for precious metals"- commonly called "e-certificates"— that can be transferred from one owner to another. In August 2015, FinCEN extended its March 2013 guidance concerning what types of business activity with virtual currency render the business a "money services business" for the purposes of federal AML requirements under 31 C.F.R. Part X. Fin. Crimes Enf. Network, Application of FinCEN's Regulations Pertaining to Persons Issuing Physical or Digital Negotiable Certificates of Ownership of Precious Metals, FIN-2015-R001, August 14, 2015, https://www.fincen.gov/news_room/rp/rulings/pdf/ FIN-2015-R001.pdf (hereinafter "FinCEN Precious Metals Certificate Guidance"). The 2015 guidance concluded that e-precious metals and e-certificates for precious metals were "virtual currency" and persons offering them were engaged in "money transmission" for two reasons. The first is that e-precious metals are units of value held by intermediaries on behalf of others and are not units of "legal tender." Thus, they are representations of value that underlie the virtual currency owned by another person. E-certificates for precious metals are similar to warehouse receipts in some ways, and are "negotiable" or transferable by one person to another, by one person from an account to another account that person owns, or by one jurisdiction to another.

The definition of what is or is not "legal tender" is a complex question and is likely to grow more complex if other governments issue their own forms of digitized "legal tender." The solution in this act is incomplete because issuance of a virtual currency by a sovereign could complicate the ability of regulators to distinguish between legal tender and virtual currency. Thus, for now, the definitions of "virtual currency" and "legal tender" in Section 102 of this act and the exemption for "dealers in foreign currency" in Section 103 of this act set the boundaries between what the United States government deems to be "legal tender" (by issuing it) and what "dealers in foreign exchange" deal in. What another sovereign government deems to be "legal tender" also falls under FinCEN's March 2013 guidance as "foreign exchange" to which distinct FinCEN regulations apply. *See,* FIN-2013-G001, *supra* at 5.

To the extent that a state department with rule-writing authority under this act requires greater certainty over what qualifies as "virtual currency," it could issue a clarification by rule or guidance.

2. "Virtual-currency Business Activity." This term is designed to capture those activities with sufficient similarity to money transmission or other regulated money services activities as to become proper subjects for regulation under this act. The definition restricts the subject activity to that performed with or on behalf of residents of the jurisdiction that seeks to license the provision of such activities in a jurisdiction in the United States.

The term is intended to limit the scope of this act to providers of products and services that are comparable to: (1) money transmission, issuance of virtual currencies from a centralized administration or source, exchange of virtual-currency for other virtual currencies, bank credit or legal tender, and (2) custodianships similar in nature to a securities entitlement subject to Article 8 of the Uniform Commercial Code. It is not intended to cover relationships in which the provider offers a service or product that is limited and the provider cannot transact or prevent transactions unilaterally. Thus, arrangements that the virtual-currency community refers to as "multi-sig" -that is, arrangements that require more than one credential-equivalent to be used to effect transactions are not covered. "Multi-sig" services operate on the basis that more than one third-party entity may hold a key to virtual-currency that can be used to effect exchanges or transfers of virtual-currency only when used in combination with one or more other keys. The exclusion for "multi-sig" proceeds from the definition of the term "control," which requires that the provider subject to the act have power to transact unilaterally or prevent on a permanent basis transactions in that virtual-currency. If an owner of virtual-currency stored one of several keys needed to transfer virtual-currency to a third party with a "multi-sig" firm, and two such keys were required to transact business in that virtual-currency, the "multi-sig" party would lack the power to transact unilaterally and the power to prevent use of the other keys and, so, to prevent the transaction.

The definition works with the definition of "control of virtual-currency" to cover only those providers whose products and services have (1) the power unilaterally to transact, convert or redeem, or (2) the power to prevent such transactions permanently.

Three active verbs - Exchange, Transfer, and Store - cover the core concepts animating what constitutes "virtual-currency business activity." To qualify as a virtual-currency business activity, the activity must be between a provider and an end-user (either a consumer or a business user), and the user must provide to the virtual-currency business sufficient information to allow the provider on a unilateral basis either to transact or prevent transactions without further participation by the end-user.

For consistency with the "money services" and "end-user-facing" scope of the Uniform Money Services Act and other state-enacted "money transmitter" statutes, the term does not cover non-currency uses of the technologies underlying virtual currencies today. This definition, thus, excludes a new class of technologies at an enterprise or business-wide level that are not end-user-facing and are designed to perform functions, such as "enabling existing currencies to be exchanged more efficiently." A specific exemption for this type of "enterprise solution" used by persons otherwise exempt from this act appears in Section 103.

This act does not adopt a "facts and circumstances" approach to determining which products and services should be included in the definition of "virtual-currency business activity." FinCEN uses such a test it in its 2013 guidance on what constitutes "money services" activities that trigger its regulations governing federal registration of "money services" businesses. A "facts and circumstances" approach is not as workable in a licensure and prudential regulatory scheme as it may be in determining liability for failure to register with FinCEN. A second reason for departing from FinCEN's "facts and circumstances" approach is that this act established two pre-licensure stages (a full exemption in Section 103 and "registration" under Section 207) and a licensure requirement. Each of these stages needs to operate on lines as bright as possible to provide certainty and uniformity - and to protect persons in the two early stages from civil or criminal liability for not being fully licensed.

Although bitcoins are "mined" (a process yielding a "bitcoin" that is a form of payment or reward for solving a difficult puzzle), other virtual currencies are issued by a centralized authority in exchange for legal tender or other virtual currencies to a user who seeks to obtain goods or services, other virtual currency, or legal tender in exchange. Centralized issuers of virtual currency at the moment of issuance are engaged in virtual-currency business activity because they hold themselves out to others as the equivalent of issuers of prepaid cards (also known as "prepaid value") or offer other forms of trusted and intermediated financial services that this act covers. Miners not engaged in offering services to third parties (other than the clearing and verification roles they play in the Bitcoin blockchain) are not engaged in virtual-currency business activity, and are exempt from this act under Section 103.

3. "Bank." Entities meeting this definition are exempt from the provisions of this act. Others are not. For example, this act excludes trust companies from the definition of the term "bank." Thus, trust companies seeking to engage in virtual-currency business activities would need to comply with the provisions of this act. State statutes authorizing trust companies vary as do states' attitudes about the ability of out-of-state trust companies to engage with residents of their states if the trust company does not hold a trust company charter from their state. This issue rose in prominence when New York State issued a trust company charter to ItBit in 2015. ItBit's ability to engage in transactions with residents of other states was challenged by other states. In April 2016, ItBit withdrew from offering its services to residents of Texas. Since then, there has been no additional information about whether the states will insist on their own charters for trust companies engaging in virtual-currency business activity.

This act also excludes industrial loan companies from the definition of the term "bank." ILC's are regulated for many purposes as banks, but the scope of their permissible activities are not the same as banks and many states do not charter ILCs. Exemption from this act for industrial loan companies - a result that their inclusion in the definition of the term "bank" would accomplish — might complicate state regulation of the activities of virtual-currency businesses and the licensing reciprocity provisions in Article 2.

4. "Control." The term "control" is a concept ordinarily used in the context of mergers and acquisitions, and in the implementation and enforcement of federal banking laws. The term is used for two purposes in this act. First, the act looks at the use of the word in statutes governing the provision of financial services - attributing "control" to the ability to make decisions and direct policy and procedures over a regulated entity. The persons with "control" are normally investigated closely by state agencies that issue licenses to engage in the provision of financial services. Some persons may not be the type of person the state's department issuing licenses normally would allow to perform trusted intermediary or money services business activities. Changes in the identity of persons exercising, or capable of exercising, "control" may affect the operation of a business adversely, and federal and state laws regulating trusted intermediaries often define terms such as "control" for this reason. This concept primarily applies to Articles 2 and 3 of this act.

This act also defines the term "control" to include the power to transact in virtual currency for customers unilaterally or to prevent transactions indefinitely without the cooperation or action of the owner of the virtual currency involved. The second, transactional definition of "control" is one of the major innovations that this act offers over other state efforts to regulate virtual-currency businesses.

5. *"Exchange."* The definition of the term "exchange" covers cases in which the exchanger, at a specific time, has "control" of the virtual currency being exchanged. This term is not intended to cover an individual that operates equipment to perform a function or service on the individual's own virtual currency. Thus, in order to maintain a distinction between businesses that offer "virtual-currency business" services and products to others and persons managing their own virtual-currency holdings, if the intermediary virtual-currency business lacks control of virtual currency, as the term "control" is defined in Section 102(3)(A), then that person is not engaged in the "exchange" of virtual currency for purposes of this act.

The verb "exchange" covers any sale or barter of virtual currency for other virtual currency, or "real world" goods or services other than by "miners." "Miners" in the Bitcoin system use computing power to expand the extant number of bitcoins in a decentralized currency (such as Bitcoin) and are also exempt under FinCEN's March 2013 guidance. Miners are not compensated directly by the persons for whom they perform ledger-registration services on the blockchain. Thus, miners do not engage as known trusted intermediaries with third parties except to maintain the blockchain's record of transfers of virtual currencies. Miners who mine bitcoins for their own purposes or who use virtual currencies to pay for goods or services are also exempt from FinCEN's regulations.

6. *"Executive officer."* This definition is intended to be entity-neutral.

7. *"Legal tender."* This act defines "legal tender" as opposed to the term "money." The definition limits what qualifies as "legal tender" to that issued by the United States government or another government. Note that "dealers in foreign exchange" are exempt from this act under Section 103(b)(5). As a result, if another government issues or recognizes a form of virtual currency as "legal tender" for purposes of tax collection or discharge of debts inside that government's domain, the result would be "foreign exchange" - not "legal tender" that is acceptable inside the United States.

Dealers in foreign exchange should consult FinCEN's guidance on their obligations under the federal statutes and regulations that FinCEN enforces.

8. *"Registrant" and "Registration."* The virtual-currency community is composed of many types of businesses at many stages of business maturity. The act identifies a space for start-up businesses to test their products and operate on a small scale without being required to become fully licensed before offering any services to residents of the state. This status is denominated "registration" and the persons or entities holding this status are "registrants."

This act separates providers of virtual-currency business services and products into three categories. First, those businesses with aggregate activity volumes with residents of an enacting state is at $5,000 or less are exempt from any requirements of this act in Section 103. Second, those with aggregate activity levels with residents of an enacting state is more than $5,000 and less than $35,000 for virtual-currency business may register as "registrants" under Section 207. Those whose volumes of activity with residents of an enacting state exceed $35,000 in U.S. dollar equivalency should have licenses or should have applied to the enacting state for licenses.

Registrants under Section 207, although they do not need to undergo and wait for full licensure, have responsibilities for compliance with basic user protections, cybersecurity, and anti-money laundering requirements that the act imposes on fully licensed persons. Registrants under this act must register with FinCEN as "money services businesses" to comply with this act's "registration" requirements and to avoid federal Bank Secrecy Act liability as mentioned above.

The act's provisions on small-volume providers and "registrants" are among the most important in the act to the virtual-currency community and are among its most innovative.

9. *"Reciprocity Agreement."* Some state banking departments and money transmitter regulators have signed on to a reciprocity framework created by the CSBS and may use the services provided by its subsidiary, the NMLS Registry. The lack of reciprocity is frequently mentioned by businesses seeking licensure as "money transmitters" as a major obstacle to the growth of their businesses.

This act sought to facilitate reciprocity in licensure among the states to enable businesses to operate in the growing spheres of internet- and mobile-enabled payments and custodial services and products. Reciprocity may be authorized on a bilateral or multi-lateral basis in any enacting state or by adoption of the Registry operating under the auspices of the CSBS in its current form or a later version of that Registry.

10. "Transfer." The term "transfer" does not include movement of fiat currency (legal tender) from one user to another, or from one user to another account of the same user, or from one jurisdiction to another because such fiat currency transfers "money transmission" and are not "virtual-currency transmission." If a transaction involved both fiat currency and virtual-currency, that transaction involves an "exchange" not a transfer.

11. "U.S. Dollar equivalent of virtual-currency." The three-tier structure in this act - a full exemption for annual volumes of activity less than $5,000, a registration option for providers with transaction volumes more than $5,000 and less than $35,000, and a full licensure requirement for transaction volumes above $35,000— made it necessary to specify how those threshold amounts would be calculated.

In this act, the term "U.S. Dollar equivalent of virtual-currency" means the equivalent value of a particular virtual-currency in United States dollars shown on a virtual-currency exchange based in the United States for a particular date or period specified in this act. A decision to require that the virtual-currency exchange be based in the United States means that the September 2017 decision by the People's Republic of China to close all virtual-currency exchanges or any similar decision does not keep this act from being fully operational.

12. "Virtual-currency administration." The definition of "virtual-currency administration" follows definitions set forth in the Financial Crimes Enforcement Network's March 18, 2013 guidance on virtual-currency and money transmission: "An *administrator* is a person engaged as a business in issuing (putting into circulation) a virtual-currency, and who has the authority to redeem (to withdraw from circulation) such virtual currency." Fin. Crimes Enf. Network, Application of FinCEN's Regulations to Persons Administering, Exchanging, or Using Virtual Currencies, FIN-2013-G001, https://www.fincen.gov/statutes_regs/guidance/pdf/FIN-2013-G001.pdf.

13. "Virtual-currency control-services vendor". These service providers to persons or entities that themselves deal with end-users of virtual-currency business products and services are exempt from this act under Section 103. Only virtual-currency businesses that deal directly with the public are virtual-currency businesses under this act.

Sec. 103 SCOPE.

(a) Except as otherwise provided in subsection (b) or (c), this [act] governs the virtual-currency business activity of a person, wherever located, that engages in or holds itself out as engaging in the activity with or on behalf of a resident.

(b) This [act] does not apply to the exchange, transfer, or storage of virtual currency or to virtual-currency administration to the extent the Electronic Fund Transfer Act of 1978, 15 U.S.C. Sections 1693 through 1693r [,as amended], the Securities Exchange Act of 1934, 15 U.S.C. Sections 78a through 78oo [,as amended], the Commodities Exchange Act of 1936, 7 U.S.C. Sections 1 through 27f [,as amended], or [insert citation to "blue sky" laws of this state] govern the activity. This [act] does not apply to activity by:

(1) the United States, a state, political subdivision of a state, agency or instrumentality of federal, state, or local government, or a foreign government or a subdivision, department, agency or instrumentality of a foreign government;

(2) a bank;

(3) a person engaged in money transmission that:

(A) holds a license under [insert citation to money-services or money-transmission statute of this state];

(B) is authorized by the department to engage in virtual-currency business activity; and

(C) complies with [Articles] 2, 3, 5, and 6;

(4) a person whose participation in a payment system is limited to providing processing, clearing, or performing settlement services solely for transactions between or among persons that are exempt from the licensing or registration requirements of this [act];

(5) a person engaged in the business of dealing in foreign exchange to the extent the person's activity meets the definition in 31 C.F.R. Section 1010.605(f)(1)(iv) [, as amended];

(6) a person that:

(A) contributes only connectivity software or computing power to a decentralized virtual currency, or to a protocol governing transfer of the digital representation of value;

(B) provides only data storage or security services for a business engaged in virtual-currency business activity and does not otherwise engage in virtual-currency business activity on behalf of another person; or

(C) provides only to a person otherwise exempt from this [act] virtual currency as one or more enterprise solutions used solely among each other and has no agreement or relationship with a resident that is an end-user of virtual currency;

(7) a person using virtual currency, including creating, investing, buying or selling, or obtaining virtual currency as payment for the purchase or sale of goods or services, solely:

(A) on its own behalf;

(B) for personal, family, or household purposes; or

(C) for academic purposes;

(8) a person whose virtual-currency business activity with or on behalf of residents is reasonably expected to be valued, in the aggregate, on an annual basis at $5,000 or less, measured by the U.S. Dollar equivalent of virtual currency;

(9) an attorney to the extent of providing escrow services to a resident;

(10) a title insurance company to the extent of providing escrow services to a resident;

(11) a securities intermediary, as defined in [insert citation to U.C.C. Section 8-102 of this state], or a commodity intermediary, as defined in [insert citation to U.C.C. 9-102 of this state], that:

(A) does not engage in the ordinary course of business in virtual-currency business activity with or on behalf of a resident in addition to maintaining securities accounts or commodities accounts and is regulated as a securities intermediary or commodity intermediary under federal law, law of this state other than this [act], or law of another state; and

(B) affords a resident protections comparable to those set forth in Section 502;

(12) a secured creditor under [insert citation to U.C.C. Article 9 of any state] or creditor with a judicial lien or lien arising by operation of law on collateral that is virtual currency, if the virtual-currency business activity of the creditor is limited to enforcement of the security interest in compliance with [insert citation to U.C.C. Article 9 of any state] or lien in compliance with the law applicable to the lien;

(13) a virtual-currency control-services vendor; or

(14) a person that:

(A) does not receive compensation from a resident for:

(i) providing virtual-currency products or services; or

(ii) conducting virtual-currency business activity; or

(B) is engaged in testing products or services with the person's own funds.

(c) The department may determine that a person or class of persons, given facts particular to the person or class, should be exempt from this [act], whether the person or class is covered by requirements imposed under federal law on a money-service business.

Legislative Note: *If a state adjusts the U.S. Dollar Equivalent for the exemption provided in this act under subsection (b)(8) to a figure higher than $5,000, the state should consider adding to the obligations of the person compliance with Section 502.*

In states in which the constitution, or other law, does not permit the phrase "as amended" when federal statutes are incorporated into state law, the phrase "as amended" should be deleted from subsection (b).

Comment

1. The goal of this act is not to regulate "virtual currencies" as such. Rather, it is to regulate persons that issue virtual currencies or that provide services that allow others to transfer virtual currencies, provide "virtual-currency" exchange services to the public, or offer to take custody of virtual currency for other persons. The goal is to regulate these persons in a manner that affords suitable licensure, supervision, and user protections. Accordingly, this act is intended to govern persons that hold themselves out as providing services to owners of virtual currency comparable to service that would be deemed "money transmission" under the Uniform Money Services Act or other state "money transmission" statute.

2. Section 103 also identifies exemptions from this act. The majority of the exemptions will be familiar to persons familiar with the Uniform Law Commission's Uniform "Money Services Act" and with guidance published by the U.S. Department of Treasury's Financial Crimes Enforcement Network ("FinCEN") since March 2013.

Section 103 exempts persons who use virtual currencies for personal purposes (including uses for investment purposes or in the purchase of goods or services) or businesses that receive virtual currencies from sales of goods or services in the ordinary course of business. These persons are not engaged in the equivalent of money transmission. FinCEN laid out this distinction in published guidance beginning with its March 2013 guidance, *see supra*. Other activities that are exempt include investing in virtual currencies and later sale of virtual currencies from one's own portfolio, purchasing virtual currencies in order to pay for goods or services, and engaging in research with virtual currencies and related technologies.

This act provides a permanent exemption for a person experimenting with a virtual-currency technology and whose volume of testing, etc. with residents of an enacting state runs less than $5,000.

This act also exempts entities that do not charge for services or receive other forms of compensation.

Beyond that permanent exemptions for tiny volumes of activity and for entities that do not charge for services or receive other forms of compensation is a new status in the form of an "on-ramp" for entities between the permanent exemption and a higher figure that still controls consumer risk, a status that this act refers to as "registration." These independent exemptions craft a licensure and prudentially "lite" regulatory scheme for virtual-currency businesses that facilitates innovation by virtual-currency businesses. Businesses in this group must comply with other obligations set forth in this act, including user protections and establishment and implementation of anti-money laundering and cyber-security programs.

Registrants will be expected to have registered with both the regulators in jurisdictions offering this "on-ramp," and with FinCEN to the degree that their activities meet the tests for "money service" businesses under FinCEN guidance. Separating the application of this act into three stages does not alter the businesses' need to follow FinCEN's regulations and guidance pertaining to which types of activities are "money services" for purposes of Bank Secrecy Act and anti-money laundering compliance. (It also will not excuse any business from compliance with statutes and regulations enforced by Treasury's Office of Foreign Asset Control (OFAC).) FinCEN's regulations impose a "registration" requirement on all businesses that offer money services to the general public. The obligation to register with FinCEN as a "money services business" remains regardless of what this act provides. Thus, this act is not intended to derogate from any of these federal compliance requirements: businesses that are exempt from this act or on the "on ramp" should register with FinCEN to avoid penalties for non-registration imposed by FinCEN to the extent their business activities align with FinCEN's interpretations of the Bank Secrecy Act's requirements.

This act sets the full-licensure threshold at an annual transaction volume of $35,000 or more in the U.S. Dollar equivalent with residents of an enacting state. This figure is intended to allow some "in the wild" testing of the products and services in the enacting state. When aggregated with the same threshold in other states that enact this act, this threshold is intended to allow room for market-and function- testing virtual-currency products or services involved on a modest basis in more than one enacting state without first needing to hold a license from each of those states.

A virtual-currency business that exceeds the $5,000 threshold — below which it is exempt under this Section from obligations under this act — must register in accordance with Section 207 or cease operating in the enacting state.

A virtual-currency business whose transaction volume in U.S. Dollar equivalency is approaching the $35,000 threshold under which it can operate under a registration must file a full license application under this act or cease operations in the enacting state. Additionally, if the department does not approve an application from a virtual-currency business, the virtual-currency business must halt and promptly unwind its virtual-currency business activity in the enacting state.

The "registrant" also must file an application for a full license under Section 202 as the second anniversary of its registration approaches, or cease doing business in the state involved.

For businesses whose U.S. Dollar equivalent in business volume exceeds $35,000 in an enacting state, Article 2 of this act requires full licensure under Section 202 or a reciprocal license under Section 203.

The provisions of Article 2 that pertain to licensure, renewal, and periodic reporting are modeled on the Uniform Law Commission's Uniform Money Services Act. To the extent that provisions of Article 2 differ from the Uniform Money Services Act, the two acts reflect the differences between long-established businesses handling legal tender and new-age businesses handling virtual currency that is not legal tender.

Exemptions are not readily susceptible to a "facts and circumstances" approach. Without precise parameters that businesses, state regulators, and law enforcement agencies can look to, this act will not achieve the certainty and predictability intended or the goal of uniformity in this market will be frustrated.

Besides encouraging innovators, both the limited full exemption and the "registration" on-ramp are intended to protect start-up businesses from inadvertently engaging in activity that should be licensed in order

¶1400

to avoid prosecution as an unlicensed money transmitter under 18 U.S.C. Section 1960. As such, the on-ramp is central to the goal of encouraging innovators in the virtual-currency business community and, as their businesses expand, of bringing them under state licensure and supervision.

3. This act exempts dealers in foreign exchange. FinCEN refined the definition of the term "currency dealer or exchanger" for purposes of 31 C.F.R. Part X in 2011 to "a dealer in foreign exchange" to capture the exchange of money instruments as well as of funds or other instruments denominated in foreign currency. See Bank Secrecy Act Regulations: Definitions and Other Regulations Relating to Money Services Businesses, 76 Fed. Reg. 43585, 43589 & 43596 (July 21, 2011).

4. This act also exempts lawyers and title insurance companies engaged in offering to their customers escrow services involving virtual currency only to the extent of that activity, and lien creditors or foreclosing secured parties so long as their activity is limited to enforcement of their lien or security interests.

5. The term "bank" is defined in Section 102. Banks are exempt from this act to preclude duplicate and possibly conflicting regulation.

As previously noted, an issue in the exemption for banks relates to the treatment of state-chartered trust companies and limited-purpose trust companies. If the enacting state decided to exempt these categories of trust companies, it needs to adjust the definition of the term "bank" and of "trust company" in Section 102.

The Office of the Comptroller of the Currency has announced plans for issuing "special purpose national bank charters" to certain "fintech" companies, a category that might include some virtual-currency businesses. OCC-chartered special purpose national banks would be entitled to whatever preemption of state laws and licensure requirements that the final rule that the OCC may adopt provides. Thus, it is unclear to what extent the OCC's plans overlap with operating authority that might be granted to license applicants under this act. However, it is clear that this act's exemptions and on-ramp/registration provisions will allow innovators acting under this act to operate even though the OCC might not be willing to grant start-ups special purpose national bank charters, or the OCC might impose stiff "conditions" on their operations.

In the end, the OCC's plans generally increase the need for this act, the on-ramp for start-up providers, and other exemptions this act currently provides because of the likelihood that only the best-capitalized and managed "brand" names in the fintech industry (as yet undefined by the OCC) will qualify for the OCC's special purpose national bank charters. In other words, the vast majority of fintech companies that do not receive OCC charters will require the uniformity and certainty that a uniform act offers. The definition of the term "bank" in Section 102 will include entities to which the OCC has granted fintech "special purpose national bank charters," a category that as currently proposed by the OCC would not be deposit-taking entities requiring federal deposit insurance.

6. Persons holding licenses as money transmitters or money services businesses in the licensing state are exempt from this act if they meet two additional requirements. First, they must have permission from the state regulatory agency to engage in virtual-currency business activity. Second, they must comply with the provisions of this act that differ substantially from those imposed on money transmitters or money services businesses under the law of that state. The only state currently requiring both licenses for "money transmission" and "virtual-currency" business activities is New York, which has adopted comprehensive licensure and prudential regulation provisions for both types of businesses.

7. The last exemption allows the state regulatory agency to issue discretionary exemptions for particular use cases that may vary over time and place.

Sec. 104 SUPPLEMENTARY LAW.

Unless displaced by the particular provisions of this [act], the principles of law and equity supplement its provisions.

[ARTICLE] 2 LICENSURE

Sec. 201 CONDITIONS PRECEDENT TO ENGAGING IN VIRTUAL-CURRENCY BUSINESS ACTIVITY.

A person may not engage in virtual-currency business activity, or hold itself out as being able to engage in virtual-currency business activity, with or on behalf of a resident unless the person is:

    (1) licensed in this state by the department under Section 202;

    (2) licensed in another state to conduct virtual-currency business activity by a state with which this state has a reciprocity agreement and has qualified under Section 203;

    (3) registered with the department and operating in compliance with Section 207; or

    (4) exempt from licensure or registration under this [act] by Section 103(b) or (c).

Comment

1. Unless one of the exemptions in Section 103 applies, and only to the extent of the exemption, a person that engages in virtual-currency business activity with a resident of the enacting state is subject to this act.

2. The act's coverage is not dependent on whether the business has a physical location in the enacting state including a virtual-currency "automated-teller-machine" (ATM) kiosk, and includes all forms of purposeful engagement with residents of a state. An advertisement, solicitation, or other holding out that appears in a newspaper or on a website or by telephone, electronic mail, or other mail received by a resident regardless of whether the resident saw or received the information, suffices as contact with the enacting state to trigger the need for a license unless this state and another state have a reciprocity agreement that covers the person's activities in this state, the transaction is consummated while the resident is physically present in another state, or the person has filed a registration in this state as provided in Section 207 of this act.

3. Pursuant to Section 208, no license issued by this state or registration filed with this state may be assigned or transferred except pursuant to law, including the provisions of Article 3 of this act, and then only so long as the relevant state or federal regulator does not disapprove the assignment or transfer. Sections 306 and 307 of this act set forth the requirements for changes in control, or merger, consolidation or acquisition of substantially all of the assets of a licensee or registrant operating in this state under this act. If a person applies to assume control over a registrant or licensee under this act, and the department does not approve the change in control application, the person must not proceed with the proposed change in control or promptly must cease doing virtual-currency business activity in this state. Similarly, if a person seeks to acquire or merge or consolidate with a licensee or registrant governed by this act, and the department does not approve, the person must not proceed with the merger or acquisition or promptly must cease doing virtual-currency business activity in this state.

4. This act does not require that, as a condition or operations, a licensee or registrant be incorporated in this state, or that the licensee or registrant maintain a physical location in this state while the licensee or registrant engages in virtual-currency business activities with residents of this state.

5. A person that has applied for "reciprocal licensure" under Section 203 may engage in virtual-currency business activity under that section during the pendency of the licensure process in this state.

6. This act does not give holders of licenses from this state to operate under this state's Money Services Act or Money Transmitter Act any preference.

7. Registration does not convey a property right to the person engaged in virtual-currency business activities in this state.

Sec. 202 LICENSE BY APPLICATION.

(a) Except as otherwise provided in Section 203, an application for a license under this [act]:

(1) must be made in a form and medium prescribed by the department or the registry;

(2) except as otherwise provided in subsection (b), must provide the following information relevant to the applicant's proposed virtual-currency business activity:

(A) the legal name of the applicant, each current or proposed business United States Postal Service address of the applicant, and any fictitious or trade name the applicant uses or plans to use in conducting its virtual-currency business activity with or on behalf of a resident;

(B) the legal name, any former or fictitious name, and the residential and business United States Postal Service address of each executive officer and responsible individual of the applicant, and each person that has control of the applicant;

(C) a description of the current and former business of the applicant for the five years before the application is submitted or if the business has operated for less than five years, for the time the business has operated, including its products and services, associated website addresses and social media pages, principal place of business, projected user base, and specific marketing targets;

(D) the name, United States Postal Service address, and telephone number of a person that manages each server the applicant expects to use in conducting its virtual-currency business activity with or on behalf of a resident and a copy of any agreement with that person;

(E) a list of:

(i) each money-service or money-transmitter license the applicant holds in another state;

(ii) the date the license expires; and

(iii) any license revocation, license suspension, or other disciplinary action taken against the licensee in another state and any license applications rejected by another state;

(F) a list of any criminal conviction, deferred prosecution agreement, and pending criminal proceeding in any jurisdiction against:

(i) the applicant;

(ii) each executive officer of the applicant;

(iii) each responsible individual of the applicant;

(iv) each person that has control over the applicant; and

(v) each person over which the applicant has control;

(G) a list of any litigation, arbitration, or administrative proceeding in any jurisdiction in which the applicant, or an executive officer or a responsible individual of the applicant has been a party for the five years before the application is submitted, determined to be material in accordance with generally accepted accounting principles and, to the extent the applicant would be required to disclose the litigation, arbitration, or administrative proceeding in the applicant's audited financial statements, reports to equity owners, and similar statements or reports;

(H) a list of any bankruptcy or receivership proceeding in any jurisdiction for the 10 years before the application is submitted in which any of the following was a debtor:

(i) the applicant;

(ii) each executive officer of the applicant;

(iii) each responsible individual of the applicant;

(iv) each person that has control over the applicant; and

(v) each person over which the applicant has control;

(I) the name and United States Postal Service address of each bank in which the applicant plans to deposit funds obtained by its virtual-currency business activity;

(J) the source of funds and credit to be used by the applicant to conduct virtual-currency business activity with or on behalf of a resident and documentation demonstrating that the applicant has the net worth and reserves required by Section 204;

(K) the United States Postal Service address and electronic mail address to which communications from the department may be sent;

(L) the name, United States Postal Service address, and electronic mail address of the registered agent of the applicant in this state;

(M) a copy of the certificate, or a detailed summary acceptable to the department, of coverage for each liability, casualty, business-interruption or cyber-security insurance policy maintained by the applicant for itself, an executive officer, a responsible individual, or the applicant's users;

(N) if applicable, the date on which and the state where the applicant is formed and a copy of a current certificate of good standing issued by that state;

(O) if a person has control of the applicant and the person's equity interests are publicly traded in the United States, a copy of the audited financial statement of the person for the most recent fiscal year or most recent report of the person filed under Section 13 of the Securities Exchange Act of 1934, 15 U.S.C. Section 78m [,as amended];

(P) if a person has control of the applicant and the person's equity interests are publicly traded outside the United States, a copy of the audited financial statement of the person for the most recent fiscal year of the person or a copy of the most recent documentation similar to that required in subparagraph (O) filed with the foreign regulator in the domicile of the person;

(Q) if the applicant is a partnership or a member-managed limited-liability company, the names and United States Postal Service addresses of general partners or members;

(R) if the applicant is required to register with the Financial Crimes Enforcement Network of the United States Department of the Treasury as a money-service business, evidence of the registration;

(S) a set of fingerprints for each executive officer and responsible individual of the applicant;

(T) if available, for each executive officer and responsible individual of the applicant, for the five years before the application is submitted:

(i) employment history; and

(ii) history of any investigation of the individual or legal proceeding to which the individual was a party;

(U) the plans through which the applicant will meet its obligations under [Article] 6; and

(V) other information the department reasonably requires by rule; and

(3) must be accompanied by a nonrefundable fee in the amount [required by law of this state other than this [act] or specified by the department by rule].

(b) For good cause, the department may waive a requirement of subsection (a) or permit the applicant to submit other information instead of the required information.

(c) An application for a license under this section is not complete until the department receives all information required by this [act] and completes its investigation under subsection (d).

(d) On receipt of a completed application:

(1) the department shall investigate:

(A) the financial condition and responsibility of the applicant;

(B) the relevant financial and business experience, character, and general fitness of the applicant; and

(C) the competence, experience, character, and general fitness of each executive officer, each responsible individual, and any person that has control of the applicant; and

(2) the department may conduct an investigation of the business premises of an applicant.

(e) Not later than 30 days after an application is complete, the department shall send the applicant notice of its decision to approve, conditionally approve, or deny the application. If the department does not send the applicant notice of its decision within 31 days of completion of the application, the application is deemed denied. If the department does not receive notice from the applicant that the applicant accepts conditions specified by the department within 31 days following the department's notice of the conditions, the application is deemed denied.

(f) A license takes effect on the later of:

(1) the date on which the department issues the license; or

(2) the date the licensee provides the security required by Section 204.

(g) An applicant shall pay the reasonable costs of the department's investigation under this section.

Legislative Note: In a state that does not delegate the setting of fees to departmental discretion, the state should specify the amount of an initial fee for a license under this act. In a state that allows the department charged with supervising and enforcing laws similar to this act to set fees, the department should set the fees for licenses under this act. This note applies to the fee that must accompany an application under subsection (a)(3) and any fee to be paid before the issuance of a license under this act.

In states in which the constitution, or other law, does not permit the phrase "as amended" when federal statutes are incorporated into state law, the phrase should be deleted in subsection (a)(2)(O).

Sec. 203 LICENSE BY RECIPROCITY.

Alternative A

(a) Instead of an application required by Section 202, a person licensed by another state to conduct virtual-currency business activity in that state may file with the registry an application under this section.

(b) When an application under this section is filed with the registry, the applicant shall notify the department in a record that the applicant has submitted the application to the registry and shall submit to the department:

(1) a certification of license history from the agency responsible for issuing a license in each state in which the applicant has been licensed to conduct virtual-currency business activity;

(2) a nonrefundable reciprocal licensing application fee in the amount [required by law of this state other than this [act]or specified by the department by rule];

(3) documentation demonstrating that the applicant complies with the security and net worth reserve requirements of Section 204; and

(4) a certification signed by an executive officer of the applicant affirming that [
will conduct its virtual-currency business activity with or on behalf of a resident i~ ~
with this [act].

(c) The department may permit conduct of virtual-currency business activity by an applicant that complies with this section.

Alternative B

(a) A person licensed by another state to engage in virtual-currency business activity in that state may engage in virtual-currency business activity with or on behalf of a resident to the same extent as a licensee if:

(1) the department determines that the state in which the person is licensed has in force laws regulating virtual-currency business activity which are substantially similar to, or more protective of rights of users than, this [act];

(2) at least 30 days before the person commences virtual-currency business activity with or on behalf of a resident, the person submits to the department:

(A) notice containing:

(i) a statement that the person will rely on reciprocal licensing;

(ii) a copy of the license to conduct virtual-currency business activity issued by the other state; and

(iii) a certification of license history from the agency responsible for issuing the license to conduct virtual-currency business activity in the other state;

(B) a nonrefundable reciprocal license fee in the amount [required by law of this state other than this [act] or specified by the department by rule];

(C) documentation demonstrating that the applicant complies with the security and net worth reserve requirements of Section 204; and

(D) a certification signed by an executive officer of the applicant affirming that the applicant will conduct its virtual-currency business activity with or on behalf of a resident in compliance with this [act];

(3) subject to subsection (b), the department does not deny the application not later than [15] days after receipt of the items submitted under paragraph (2); and

(4) subject to subsection (b), the applicant does not commence virtual-currency business activity with or on behalf of a resident until at least 31 days after complying with paragraph (2).

(b) For good cause, the department may modify a period in this section.

End of Alternatives

Legislative Note: *Alternative A is applicable only if the department has agreed to participate in the registry operated by a subsidiary of the Conference of State Bank Supervisors. If the state already participates in the registry, Alternative A would be enacted and Alternative B should be deleted. If the state elects not to participate in the registry, then Alternative B should be enacted.*

An enacting state should not waive any requirement that the applicant have sufficient reserves or security to cover expenses sufficient to wind up its business with a resident and to complete any transaction a resident has instructed the licensee to complete.

Comment

1. This act encourages reciprocal licensing either through the processes supervised by the Conference of State Bank Supervisors and its National Multistate Licensing System and Registry ("Registry") or through discretionary authority granted to the department in this act.

2. Alternative A relies on use of the Registry to facilitate reciprocal licensure or recognition of licensure by states other than the first state that licensed a virtual-currency business.

3. Alternative B allows the department to ascertain the nature of the licensing scheme in another state compared with its own and to grant reciprocity on a discretionary basis without reference to the Registry.

4. The NMLS and Registry operated by a subsidiary of the Conference of State Bank Supervisors is the recommended mechanism for the submission and management of reciprocal licensure applications under this act.

5. This act does not use the reciprocity protocols of the Uniform Law Commission's Athlete Agents Act, because State banking agencies are already familiar with the CSBS' Registry and non-depository providers of financial services also are likely to be familiar with the CSBS' NMLS and Registry.

Sec. 204 SECURITY, NET WORTH, AND RESERVES.

(a) Before a license is issued under this [act]:

(1) an applicant must deposit with the department funds or investment property, a letter of credit, a surety bond, or other security satisfactory to the department that:

(A) secures the applicant's faithful performance of its duties under this [act]; and

(B) is in an amount the department specifies based on the nature and extent of risks in the applicant's virtual-currency business model;

(2) the department may not require a surety bond as security under this [act] unless a surety bond is generally available in the state at a commercially reasonable cost;

(3) security deposited under this section must be payable to this state for the benefit of a claim against the licensee on account of the licensee's virtual-currency business activity with or on behalf of a resident;

(4) security deposited under this section must cover claims for the period the department specifies by rule and for an additional period the department specifies after the licensee ceases to engage in virtual-currency business activity with or on behalf of a resident;

(5) for good cause, the department may require the licensee to increase the amount of security deposited under this section, and the licensee shall deposit the additional security not later than [15] days after the licensee receives notice in a record of the required increase;

(6) for good cause, the department may permit a licensee to substitute or deposit an alternate form of security satisfactory to the department if the licensee at all times complies with this section;

(7) a claimant does not have a direct right to recover against security deposited under this section; and

(8) only the department may recover against the security, and the department may retain the recovery for no longer than [five] years and may process claims and distribute recoveries to claimants in accordance with rules adopted by the department under [insert citation to uniform money-services act or money-transmitters act of this state].

(b) In addition to the security required under subsection (a), a licensee and a registrant, at the time of the application for a license under this act or filing of registration, shall submit to the department evidence of and maintain:

(1) a minimum net worth of $[25,000]; and

(2) sufficient unencumbered reserves for winding down the licensee's or registrant's operations as agreed to by the department considering the nature and size of expected virtual-currency business activity with or on behalf of residents.

(c) A licensee or registrant may include in its calculation of net worth virtual currency, measured by the average value of the virtual currency in U.S. Dollar equivalent over the prior six months, other than the virtual currency over which it has control for a resident entitled to the protections under Section 502.

(d) For good cause, the department may require a licensee or registrant to increase the net worth or reserves required under this section. The licensee or registrant shall submit to the department evidence that it has the additional net worth or reserves not later than [15] days after the licensee or registrant receives notice in a record of the required increase.

Legislative Note: *In subsection (a)(8), the state should specify the period it believes represents a reasonable period for an aggrieved party to discover the party's claim and file it with the department and for the department to determine whether the claim is valid and process the claim.*

Comment

1. Surety bonds and letters of credit are not readily available to virtual-currency business start-ups at this time. Accordingly, the security described in Section 204 does not require surety bonds or letters of credit because such a requirement effectively would prevent some start-up virtual-currency businesses from being licensed at this time. Although surety bonds or letters of credit are commonly required for other forms of non-depository financial services licensees such as money transmitters, there is no point in requiring as all or part of the security that licenses must offer any form of security that is not readily available in the marketplace.

2. The market may improve as surety bond companies and banks are more familiar with the operations of virtual-currency businesses and as states clarify their positions on licensure and regulation of virtual-currency businesses and the relationship of virtual-currency businesses to traditional money services and money transmission that states otherwise regulate.

3. This act allows the department to accept funds, investment property, surety bonds, letters or credit or other security from the licensee or registrant as evidence of the licensee's or registrant's ability to conduct operations and have sufficient funding available to wind up its operations in this state as may occur. The primary reason is that, although virtual-currency business may find it easier to obtain a letter of credit than a surety bond, banks have their own credential requirements for issuing letters of credit. The requirements of this act should not convey a sense that there is something wrong with a virtual-currency business if it cannot obtain a particular form of security, such as a letter of credit or surety bond, because the market is immature.

4. The amount of security required may be minimal depending on the scope of activities that the applicant presents as its business model in a given state. This is particularly true because of the inclusion in this act of an analogue to U.C.C. section 8-503 that specifies that the provider does not have a property interest in the virtual currency it controls or has custody over for its customers, and that the virtual currency is not subject to claims of the provider's creditors.

5. Forms of security may include virtual currency of the type in which the provider transacts business with residents (a term limited under Section 102's definition to residents of the enacting state), a guarantee or, possibly, even a letter asserting compliance. The regulators' ability to hold security after the licensee ceases to engage in virtual-currency business activity is common in non-depository financial services regulation. Because of this need for security to be available during a winding-up period, bonds - if available - would be problematic for licensees.

6. Surety bonds run with the person or entity that first acquired them. In the virtual-currency community, one expects innovators to merge or be acquired by others with more frequency than might have applied to other forms of non-depository providers of financial services. Any requirement that the security to survive a merger or acquisition necessarily requires a form of security that is not entity-dependent, which is an important consideration and likely a complication with some forms of security that are typically used in non-depository licensure schemes.

Sec. 205 ISSUANCE OF LICENSE; APPEAL.

(a) Absent good cause, the department shall issue a license to an applicant if the applicant complies with this [article] and pays the costs of the investigation under Section 202(g) and the initial licensee fee under Section 202(a)(3) in an amount required by law or specified by the department by rule.

(b) An applicant may appeal a denial of its application under Section 202 or 203, under [cite state administrative procedure act] not later than 30 days after:

1. the department notifies the applicant of the denial; or

2. the application is deemed denied.

Comment

The addition of the phrase "absent good cause" to subsection (a) grants discretion to the department to deny an application if the applicant has been allegedly engaged in violations of other laws, such as federal anti-money-laundering or other regulations.

Sec. 206 RENEWAL OF LICENSE.

(a) Subject to subsection (g), not later than 15 days before the anniversary date of issuance of its license under this [act], a licensee may apply for renewal of the license by:

(1) paying a renewal fee [in an amount required by law of this state other than this [act] or specified by the department by rule]; and

(2) submitting to the department a renewal report under subsection (b).

(b) A renewal report required by subsection (a)(2) must be submitted in a form and medium prescribed by the department. The report must contain:

(1) a copy of the licensee's most recent:

(A) reviewed annual financial statement if the licensee's virtual-currency business activity in this state was $[insert amount state uses for corporate activity auditing purposes] or less for the fiscal year ending before the anniversary date of issuance of its license under this [act]; or

(B) audited annual financial statement if the licensee's virtual-currency business activity in this state amounted to more than $[insert the figure state employs for corporate activity auditing purposes] for the fiscal year ending before the anniversary date;

(2) if a person other than an individual has control of the licensee, a copy of the person's most recent:

(A) reviewed annual financial statement if the person's gross revenue was $[insert amount state uses for corporate activity auditing purposes] or less in the previous fiscal year, measured as of the anniversary date of issuance of its license under this [act]; or

(B) audited consolidated annual financial statement if the person's gross revenue was more than $[insert amount state uses for corporate activity auditing purposes] in the previous fiscal year, measured as of the anniversary date of issuance of its license under this [act];

(3) a description of any:

(A) material change in the financial condition of the licensee;

(B) material litigation involving the licensee or an executive officer, or responsible individual of the licensee;

(C) license suspension or revocation proceeding commenced, or other action taken, involving a license to conduct virtual-currency business activity issued by another state on which reciprocal licensing is based;

(D) federal or state investigation involving the licensee; and

(E) data security breach involving the licensee;

(4) information or records required by Section 305 the licensee has not reported to the department;

(5) the number of virtual-currency business activity transactions with or on behalf of residents for the period since, subject to subsection (g), the later of the date the license was issued or the date the last renewal report was submitted;

(6) the:

(A) amount of U.S. Dollar equivalent of virtual currency in the control of the licensee at, subject to subsection (g), the end of the last month that ends not later than 30 days before the date of the renewal report; and

(B) total number of residents for whom the licensee had control of U.S. Dollar equivalent of virtual currency on that date;

(7) evidence that the licensee continues to satisfy Section 502;

(8) evidence that the licensee continues to satisfy Section 204;

(9) a list of each location where the licensee operates its virtual-currency business activity; and

(10) the name, United States Postal Service address, and telephone number of each person that manages a server used by the licensee in conducting its virtual-currency business activity with or on behalf of a resident.

(c) If a licensee does not timely comply with subsection (a), the department may use enforcement measures provided under [Article] 4. Notice or hearing is not required for a suspension or revocation of a license under this [act] for failure to pay a renewal fee or file a renewal report.

(d) If the department suspends or revokes a license under this [act] for noncompliance with subsection (a), the department may end the suspension or rescind the revocation and notify the licensee of the action if, subject to subsection (g), not later than 20 days after the license was suspended or revoked, the licensee:

(1) files a renewal report and pays a renewal fee; and

(2) pays any penalty assessed under Section 404.

(e) The department shall give prompt notice to a licensee of the lifting of a suspension or rescission of a revocation after the licensee complies with subsection (d).

(f) Suspension or revocation of a license under this section does not invalidate a transfer or exchange of virtual currency for or on behalf of a resident made during the suspension or revocation and does not insulate the licensee from liability under this [act].

(g) For good cause, the department may extend a period under this section.

¶1400

(h) The department shall review the renewal of a license issued under Section 203 to ensure that the state that issued the original license has not suspended, revoked, or limited the license.

(i) A licensee that does not comply with this section shall cease operations with or on behalf of a resident on or before the anniversary date of issuance of its license under this [act].

(j) A licensee shall pay the reasonable and necessary costs of the department's investigation under this section.

Legislative Note: If a state delegates the setting of fees under subsection (a) (1) to the department, this section should be revised to grant authority to set fees and to establish any minimum or maximum fee levels the department is required to observe. If the state does not permit delegation, the enacting state should set the fees required under this section.

Comment

1. Small entities may not be required by state law to submit audited financial statements as part of their licensure renewal programs. In these cases, state law instead may require that the entity to have a "reviewed" financial statement and that the entity should provide it in lieu of a fully audited financial statement.

2. Any change in a license issued by another state or jurisdiction that was the basis for reciprocal licensure under this act should be disclosed in the renewal report, if not previously disclosed to the state regulatory authority in this state.

Sec. 207 REGISTRATION IN LIEU OF LICENSE.

(a) A person whose volume of virtual-currency business activity in U.S. Dollar equivalent of virtual currency will not exceed $35,000 annually may engage in virtual-currency business activity with or on behalf of a resident under a registration without first obtaining a license under this [act] if the person:

(1) files with the department a notice in the form and medium prescribed by the department of its intention to engage in virtual-currency business activity with or on behalf of a resident;

(2) provides the information for an investigation under Section 202;

(3) states the anticipated virtual-currency business activity for its next fiscal quarter;

(4) pays the department a registration fee in the amount [required by law of this state other than this [act] or specified by the department by rule];

(5) if required to register with the Financial Crimes Enforcement Network of the United States Department of the Treasury as a money-service business, provides the department evidence of the registration;

(6) provides evidence that the person has policies and procedures to comply with the Bank Secrecy Act, 31 U.S.C. Section 5311 et seq. [, as amended], and other applicable laws;

(7) describes the source of funds and credit to be used by the person to conduct virtual-currency business activity with or on behalf of a resident and provides evidence of and agrees to maintain the minimum net worth and reserves required by Section 204 and sufficient unencumbered reserves for winding down operations;

(8) provides the department with evidence that the person has in place policies and procedures to comply with [Articles] 3, 5, and 6 and other provisions of this [act] designated by the department; and

(9) provides the department with a copy of its most recent financial statement, whether reviewed or audited.

(b) Before the virtual-currency business activity of a registrant with or on behalf of residents exceeds $35,000 annually in U.S. Dollar equivalent of virtual currency, the registrant shall file an application for a license under this [act] and may continue to operate after the activity exceeds $35,000 annually while its application for license is pending.

(c) For good cause, the department may suspend or revoke a registration without a prior hearing or opportunity to be heard.

(d) A registrant shall cease all virtual-currency business activity with or on behalf of residents:

(1) if the department denies the registrant's application for a license under this [act], one day after the registrant receives notice in a record that the department has denied the application;

(2) if the department suspends or revokes the registration, one day after the department sends notice of the suspension or revocation to the registrant in a record by a means reasonably selected for the notice to be received by the recipient in one day, to the address provided for receiving communications from the department;

(3) if the virtual-currency business activity of the registrant with or on behalf of residents exceeds $35,000 annually in U.S. Dollar equivalent of virtual currency and the registrant has not filed an application for a license under this [act]; or

(4) on the second anniversary date of the registration.

Legislative note: In a state that does not delegate the setting of fees to departmental discretion, the state should specify the amount of an initial fee for a registration under this act. In a state which allows the department charged with supervising and enforcing laws similar to this act to set fees, the department should set the fees for registration. This note applies to the fee that must accompany a registration filing that the registrant must pay along with its filing.

In states in which the constitution, or other law, does not permit the phrase "as amended" when federal statutes are incorporated into state law, the phrase should be deleted in subsection (a) (6).

Comment

1. Section 207 is designed to allow an intermediate status between full exemption under Section 103 and full licensure under Section 202.

2. Section 207 offers some advantages both the public and to the business entity. For example, it instructs the entity wishing to take advantage of this in-between status to register with the U.S. Department of the Treasury's Financial Crimes Enforcement Network (FinCEN) to the extent that FinCEN's regulations and guidance mandate registration. It also provides notice to the states enacting this act when a start-up company with actual or expected transaction volumes exceed the $5,000 figure for full exemption comes into the state to start serving residents. In this fashion, it gives the states the opportunity to follow the newcomers' activities with the residents of each enacting state.

3. For the virtual-currency business, registration provides an "on-ramp" to doing business within a new state, clear requirements for what the business must do to retain its status as a registrant and for the point in its history when it must file a full-fledged application for licensure. In this manner, this act intends to allow start-up businesses and those testing new products in states in which it does not have a full license a transition period with protection from potential violation of 18 U.S.C. 1960.

4. State money-services and money-transmitter statutes do not have thresholds: they require full licensure on the first day of operation. Thus, the thresholds in this act are a departure from the status-quo in state statutes. They are designed to implement important goals - that is, promotion of innovation and allowance for both academic research and beta testing to occur without the necessity of full licensure. They are, however, suitable to prevent significant risks to users.

Additionally, the full exemption in Section 103 for activity of $5,000 or less and the provisions allowing for "registration" in Section 207 are designed to eliminate risks to virtual-currency businesses of being prosecuted for engaging in unlicensed money transmission or prepaid access activity under state laws or 18 U.S.C. Section 1960.

This act's thresholds operate on a per-state basis. Thus, a virtual-currency business could have aggregate activity of much more than $35,000 if the virtual-currency business is operating in more than one state. So long as its activity volume in each state that does not exceed $5,000 or that exceeds $5,000 but is less than $35,000, the respective thresholds between the full exemption and threshold before the business must have applied for a license, the business does not need a license in states that enact this act. Virtual-currency businesses operating in more than one state could engage in a significant amount of market- and product-testing without needing a full license if they restrict their operations to states that have enacted this act.

Sec. 208 LICENSE OR REGISTRATION NOT ASSIGNABLE OR TRANSFERABLE.

A license or registration under this [act] is not transferable or assignable.

Comment

It is not customary for licenses issued to money-services businesses or money-transmitters to be assignable or transferable except on application to and approval by the state regulatory agencies that issue such licenses. Thus, in this act, neither licenses nor registrations should be assignable or transferable at will. Provisions governing changes in control and mergers and acquisitions of licensees or registrants are found in Sections 306 and 307 of this act.

Sec. 209 RULES AND GUIDANCE.

The department may adopt rules to implement this [act] and issue guidance as appropriate.

[ARTICLE] 3 EXAMINATION; EXAMINATION FEES; DISCLOSURE OF INFORMATION OBTAINED DURING EXAMINATION

Sec. 301 AUTHORITY TO CONDUCT EXAMINATION.

(a) The department may conduct an annual examination of a licensee or registrant. For good cause, the department may conduct an additional examination. The department may examine a licensee or registrant without prior notice to the licensee or registrant.

(b) A licensee or registrant shall pay the reasonable and necessary costs of an examination under this section.

(c) Information obtained during an examination under this [Article] may be disclosed only as provided in Section 304.

Sec. 302 RECORDS.

(a) A licensee or registrant shall maintain, for all virtual-currency business activity with or on behalf of a resident five years after the date of the activity, a record of:

(1) each transaction of the licensee or registrant with or on behalf of the resident or for the licensee's or registrant's account in this state, including:

(A) the identity of the resident;

(B) the form of the transaction;

(C) the amount, date, and payment instructions given by the resident; and

(D) the account number, name, and United States Postal Service address of the resident, and, to the extent feasible, other parties to the transaction;

(2) the aggregate number of transactions and aggregate value of transactions by the licensee or registrant with or on behalf of the resident and for the licensee's or registrant's account in this state, expressed in U.S. Dollar equivalent of virtual currency for the previous 12 calendar months;

(3) each transaction in which the licensee or registrant exchanges one form of virtual currency for legal tender or another form of virtual currency with or on behalf of the resident;

(4) a general ledger posted at least monthly that lists all assets, liabilities, capital, income, and expenses of the licensee or registrant;

(5) each business-call report the licensee or registrant is required to create or provide to the department or registry;

(6) bank statements and bank reconciliation records for the licensee or registrant and the name, account number, and United States Postal Service address of each bank the licensee or registrant uses in the conduct of its virtual-currency business activity with or on behalf of the resident;

(7) a report of any dispute with the resident; and

(8) a report of any virtual-currency business activity transaction with or on behalf of a resident which the licensee or registrant was unable to complete.

(b) A licensee or registrant shall maintain records required by subsection (a) in a form that enables the department to determine whether the licensee or registrant is in compliance with this [act], any court order, and law of this state other than this [act].

(c) If a licensee or registrant maintains records outside this state that pertain to transactions with or on behalf of a resident, the licensee or registrant shall make the records available to the department not later than three days after request, or, on a determination of good cause by the department, at a later time.

(d) All records maintained by a licensee or registrant are subject to inspection by the department.

Sec. 303 RULES; COOPERATION; AND DATA-SHARING AUTHORITY.

(a) Subject to Section 304 and law of this state other than this [act] concerning privacy, consumer financial privacy, data protection, privilege, and confidentiality, the department may cooperate, coordinate, jointly examine, consult, and share records and other information with the appropriate regulatory agency of another state, a self-regulatory organization, federal or state regulator of banking or non-depository providers, or a regulator of a jurisdiction outside the United States, concerning the affairs and conduct of a licensee or registrant in this state.

(b) The department shall:

(1) establish or participate in, with another state that enacts a law substantially similar to this [act], a central depository for filings required by law of this state other than this [act];

(2) cooperate in developing and implementing uniform forms for applications and renewal reports and the conduct of joint administrative proceedings and civil actions;

(3) formulate joint rules, forms, statements of policy, and guidance and interpretive opinions and releases; and

(4) develop common systems and procedures.

(c) The department may not establish or participate in a central commercial depository that contains nonpublic personally identifiable information which does not comply with Section 502(e)(5) or (8) of the Gramm-Leach-Bliley Act, 15 U.S.C. Section 6802(e)(5) or (8) [, as amended], or with the Federal Right to Financial Privacy Act, 18 U.S.C. Section 3401 et seq. [, as amended].

(d) In deciding whether and how to cooperate, coordinate, jointly examine, consult, or share records and other information under subsection (a), the department shall consider:

(1) maximizing effectiveness and uniformity of regulation, examination, implementation, and enforcement for the benefit of residents and licensees and registrants; and

(2) minimizing burdens on licensees and registrants without adversely affecting protection for residents.

Legislative note: In states in which the constitution, or other law, does not permit the phrase "as amended" when federal statutes are incorporated into state law, the phrase "as amended" should be deleted from subsection (c).

Comment

Enacting states may wish to provide a list of its statutes that impose obligations such as those mentioned in the text. These may include state data or transactional privacy laws, state data security/breach notification laws, and provisions of federal law such as Title V of the Gramm-Leach-Bliley Financial Services Modernization Act of 1999 and the Fair Credit Reporting and Fair and Accurate Credit Transactions Act.

Sec. 304 CONFIDENTIALITY.

(a) Except as otherwise provided in subsection (b) or (c), information not contained in a report otherwise available to the public or reports obtained by the department from an applicant, licensee, or registrant, information contained in or related to an examination, investigation, or operating or condition report prepared by, on behalf of, or for the use of the department, and other financial and operating information, is not subject to disclosure under [insert citation to open records law of this state]. If the department determines the information or records are confidential under the open records law of a reciprocal-licensing state, the information or records may not be disclosed.

(b) A trade secret of an applicant, a licensee, or a registrant is confidential and is not subject to disclosure under [insert citation to open records law of this state]. If the department determines a trade secret is confidential under the open records law of a reciprocal-licensing state, the trade secret may not be disclosed.

(c) Subsection (a) does not prohibit disclosure of:

(1) general information about a licensee's or registrant's virtual-currency business activity with or on behalf of a resident;

(2) a list of persons licensed or registered under this [act]; or

(3) aggregated financial data concerning licensees or registrants in this state.

Sec. 305 INTERIM REPORT.

(a) Each licensee and registrant shall file with the department a report of:

(1) a material change in information in the application for a license under this act or a registration or the most recent renewal report of the licensee under this [act] or for the registrant;

(2) a material change in the licensee's or registrant's business for the conduct of its virtual-currency business activity with or on behalf of a resident; and

(3) a change of an executive officer, responsible individual, or person in control of the licensee or registrant.

(b) Absent good cause, a report required by subsection (a) must be filed not later than 15 days after the change.

Comment

For a useful guide of what is "material" for the purposes described in this Section, one may refer to the provisions of the Securities Exchange Act of 1934 and regulatory guidance and judicial determinations made under it.

Sec. 306 CHANGE IN CONTROL OF LICENSEE OR REGISTRANT.

(a) In this section, "proposed person to be in control" means the person that would control a licensee or registrant after a proposed transaction that would result in a change in control of the licensee or registrant.

(b) The following rules apply in determining whether a person has control over a licensee or registrant:

(1) There is a rebuttable presumption of control if the person's voting power in the licensee or registrant constitutes or will constitute at least 25 percent of the total voting power of the licensee or registrant.

(2) There is a rebuttable presumption of control if:

(A) the person's voting power in another person constitutes or will constitute at least 10 percent of the total voting power of the other person; and

(B) the other person's voting power in the licensee or registrant constitutes at least 25 percent of the total voting power of the licensee or registrant.

(3) There is no presumption of control solely because an individual is an executive officer of the licensee or registrant.

(c) At least 30 days before a proposed change in control of a licensee or registrant, the proposed person to be in control shall submit to the department in a record:

(1) an application in a form and medium prescribed by the department;

(2) the information and records that Section 202 would require if the proposed person to be in control already had control of the licensee;

(3) a license application under Section 202 by the proposed person to be in control;

(4) in the case of a registrant, the information that Section 207 would require if the proposed person to be in control already had control of the registrant; and

(5) in the case of a registration, a registration under Section 207 by the proposed person to be in control.

(d) The department, in accordance with Section 202, shall approve, approve with conditions, or deny an application for a change in control of a licensee or registrant. The department, in a record, shall send notice of its decision to the licensee or registrant and the person that would be in control if the department had approved the change in control. If the department denies the application, the licensee or registrant shall abandon the proposed change in control or cease virtual-currency business activity with or on behalf of residents.

(e) If the department applies a condition to approval of a change in control of a licensee or registrant and the department does not receive notice of the applicant's acceptance of the condition specified by the department not later than 31 days after the department sends notice of the condition, the application is deemed denied. If the application is deemed denied, the licensee or registrant shall abandon the proposed change in control or cease virtual-currency business activity with or on behalf of residents.

(f) Submission in good faith of records required by subsection (c) relieves the proposed person to be in control from any obligation imposed by this section other than subsections (d), (e), and (h) until the department has acted on the application.

(g) The department may revoke or modify a determination under subsection (d), after notice and opportunity to be heard, if, in its judgment, revocation or modification is consistent with this [act].

(h) If a change in control of a licensee or registrant requires approval of an agency of this state or another state with which this state has a reciprocity agreement and the action of the other agency conflicts with that of the department, the department shall confer with the other agency. If the proposed change in control cannot be completed because the conflict cannot be resolved, the licensee or registrant shall abandon the change in control or cease virtual-currency business activity with or on behalf of residents.

Comment

Sections 306 and 307 are the logical extensions of Section 208, which provides that neither licenses nor registrations are assignable or transferable at will. In Sections 306 and 307, a licensee or registrant that wishes to allow a new party to be in control of its business or wishes to merge with, consolidate with, or acquire another business will need approval from the department before proceeding. Sections 306 and 307 also provide that, in the event the department is unable to approve the change in control, merger, consolidation, or acquisition, the licensee or registrant has a choice. It can opt not to proceed with the change, merger, consolidation, or acquisition, or it can cease doing business with residents of the state whose department will not approve the change.

A similar choice may be presented to a licensee that obtained its license in this state through a reciprocity agreement. If the department in this state and the state regulatory agency in the other state do not agree on approval of the proposed change, merger, consolidation, or acquisition, the licensee is forced to choose between abandonment of the change, etc., or cessation of business with residents of the state that does not approve.

Sec. 307 MERGER OR CONSOLIDATION BY LICENSEE OR REGISTRANT.

(a) At least 30 days before a proposed merger or consolidation of a licensee or registrant with another person, the licensee or registrant shall submit to the department in a record:

(1) an application in a form and medium prescribed by the department;

(2) the plan of merger or consolidation in accordance with subsection (e);

(3) in the case of a licensee, the information required by Section 202 concerning the person that would be the surviving entity in the proposed merger or consolidation; and

(4) in the case of a registrant, the information required by Section 207 concerning the person that would be the surviving entity in the proposed merger or consolidation.

(b) If a proposed merger or consolidation would change the control of a licensee or registrant, the licensee or registrant shall comply with Section 306 and this section.

(c) The department, in accordance with Section 202, shall approve, conditionally approve, or deny an application for approval of a merger or consolidation of a licensee or registrant. The department, in a record, shall send notice of its decision to the licensee or registrant and the person that would be the surviving entity. If the department denies the application, the licensee or registrant shall abandon the merger or consolidation or cease virtual-currency business activity with or on behalf of residents.

(d) The department may revoke or modify a determination under subsection (c), after notice and opportunity to be heard, if, in its judgment, revocation or modification is consistent with this [act].

(e) A plan of merger or consolidation of a licensee or a registrant with another person must:

(1) describe the effect of the proposed transaction on the licensee's or registrant's conduct of virtual-currency business activity with or on behalf of residents;

(2) identify each person to be merged or consolidated and the person that would be the surviving entity; and

(3) describe the terms and conditions of the merger or consolidation and the mode of carrying it into effect.

(f) If a merger or consolidation of a licensee or registrant and another person requires approval of an agency of this state or another state with which this state has a reciprocity agreement and the action of the other agency conflicts with that of the department, the department shall confer with the other agency. If the proposed merger or consolidation cannot be completed because the conflict cannot be resolved, the licensee or registrant shall abandon the merger or consolidation or cease virtual-currency business activity with or on behalf of residents.

(g) The department may condition approval of an application under subsection (a). If the department does not receive notice from the parties that the parties accept the department's condition not later than 31 days after the department sends notice in a record of the condition, the application is deemed denied. If the application is deemed denied, the licensee or registrant shall abandon the merger or consolidation or cease virtual-currency business activity with or on behalf of residents.

(h) If a licensee or registrant acquires substantially all the assets of a person, whether or not the person's license was approved by or registration was filed with the department, the transaction is subject to this section.

(i) Submission in good faith of the records required by subsection (e) relieves the proposed surviving entity from any obligation imposed by this section, other than subsections (c), (f), and (g), until the department has acted on the application.

[ARTICLE] 4 ENFORCEMENT

Sec. 401 ENFORCEMENT MEASURE.

In this [article], "enforcement measure" means an action to:

(1) suspend or revoke a license or a registration under this [act];

¶1400

(2) order a person to cease and desist from doing virtual-currency business activity with or on behalf of a resident;

(3) request the court to appoint a receiver for the assets of a person doing virtual-currency business activity with or on behalf of a resident;

(4) request the court to issue temporary, preliminary, or permanent injunctive relief against a person doing virtual-currency business activity with or on behalf of a resident;

(5) assess a penalty under Section 404;

(6) recover on the security under Section 204 and initiate a plan to distribute the proceeds for the benefit of a resident injured by a violation of this [act] or law of this state other than this [act] which applies to virtual-currency business activity with or on behalf of a resident; or

(7) impose necessary or appropriate conditions on the conduct of virtual-currency business activity with or on behalf of a resident.

Comment

1. This comment sets forth the enforcement measures that the department may utilize to ensure compliance with the provisions of this act. Some of these measures the department may take on its own subject to the due process requirements provisions in Section 403 or existing state law. These include suspension or revocation of a license or registration. For other enforcement measures, such as obtaining a receivership for the licensee or registrant, the department must request the aid of an appropriate court.

2. This Article does not employ the criminal law as an enforcement measure. It also does not authorize the department to remove officers or directors of licensees or registrants.

3. This Article does not provide, with the exception of Section 407, for a private right of action to enforce the act in the beliefs that (a) administrative action can be more effective than private action where the burden is on an individual or individual users of the licensee's or registrant's services, and (b) administrative action will produce more uniform enforcement efforts in and among states enacting this act (for example, under Section 303). Moreover, more even application of this act may assist licensees and registrants as well as users of their services compared with individual actions inconsistent in result and that may take years to conclude.

Sec. 402 DEPARTMENT AUTHORITY TO USE ENFORCEMENT MEASURES.

(a) The department may take an enforcement measure against a licensee, registrant, or person that is neither a licensee nor registrant but is engaging in virtual-currency business activity with or on behalf of a resident if:

(1) the licensee, registrant, or person materially violates this [act], a rule adopted or order issued under this [act], or law of this state other than this [act] which applies to virtual-currency business activity of the violator with or on behalf of a resident;

(2) the licensee, registrant, or person does not cooperate substantially with an examination or investigation by the department, fails to pay a fee, or fails to submit a report or documentation;

(3) the licensee, registrant, or person, in the conduct of its virtual-currency business activity with or on behalf of a resident, engages in:

(A) an unsafe or unsound act or practice;

(B) an unfair or deceptive act or practice;

(C) fraud or intentional misrepresentation;

(D) another dishonest act; or

(E) misappropriation of legal tender, virtual currency, or other value held by a fiduciary;

(4) an agency of the United States or another state takes an action against the licensee, registrant, or person which would constitute an enforcement measure if the department had taken the action;

(5) the licensee, registrant, or person is convicted of a crime related to its virtual-currency business activity with or on behalf of a resident or involving fraud or felonious activity that, as determined by the department, makes the licensee, registrant, or person unsuitable to engage in virtual-currency business activity; or

(6) the licensee, registrant, or person:

(A) becomes insolvent;

(B) makes a general assignment for the benefit of its creditors;

(C) becomes the debtor, alleged debtor, respondent, or person in a similar capacity in a case or other proceeding under any bankruptcy, reorganization, arrangement, readjustment, insolvency, receivership, dissolution, liquidation, or similar law, and does not obtain from the court, within a reasonable time, confirmation of a plan or dismissal of the case or proceeding; or

(D) applies for or permits the appointment of a receiver, trustee, or other agent of a court for itself or for a substantial part of its assets; or

(7) the licensee, registrant, or person makes a material misrepresentation to the department.

(b) On application and for good cause, the department may:

(1) extend the due date for filing a document or report under subsection (a)(2); or

(2) waive to the extent warranted by circumstances, such as a bona fide error notwithstanding reasonable procedures designed to prevent error, an enforcement measure under subsection (a) if the department determines that the waiver will not adversely affect the likelihood of compliance with this [act].

(c) In an enforcement action related to operating without a license under this [act] or registration in this state, it is a defense to the action that the person has in effect a customer- identification program reasonably designed to identify whether a customer is a resident, which failed to identify the particular customer as a resident.

(d) A proceeding under this [act] is subject to the [insert citation to state's administrative procedure act].

Comment

1. This section sets out the circumstances under which the department may take the enforcement measures authorized under Section 401 against a licensee, a registrant, or a person that should be licensed or registered but is not. Minor violations as opposed to material violations are not subject to the enforcement measures of Section 401. What is a material violation is to be determined by the department, and a pattern or practice of the same or similar minor violations may be treated as a material violation of this act. The same principles apply to Subsection 402(a)(3), with the possible exception of some types of dishonest acts, which may be considered material violations.

2. An enforcement measure may be involved for activity that does not per se constitute a violation of this act, such as a failure to cooperate with an examination, committing a crime related to the virtual-currency business activity of the person, or the person becoming insolvent.

3. Proceedings by the department are subject to the administrative procedures act of the enacting jurisdiction.

4. This section expressly provides for certain defenses for licensees and registrants. One of these is a bona fide error notwithstanding reasonable procedures designed, implemented, and maintained to prevent errors. Reliance on and compliance in good faith with a rule or guidance issued or provided by the department even though the rule or guidance is later invalidated normally will constitute a bona fide error, but reliance on opinion of counsel even in good faith will not constitute a bona fide error if the opinion turns out to be incorrect. A similar defense normally exists for a person that should be licensed or registered but is not.

5. In connection with subsection (a)(3), a list of examples of felonies involving bank fraud or other activity that would make a person unsuitable for a position of trust in virtual-currency business activity could be inserted. An example of such a list from Texas Fin. Code 151.202(d) and (e) covers:

• Money transmission or other money services, including a reporting, recordkeeping or registration requirement of the Bank Secrecy Act, the USA Patriot Act, or comparable provisions of state law;

• Money laundering, structuring, or a related financial crime;

• Drug trafficking;

• Terrorist funding; or,

• A similar law of a foreign country unless it is demonstrated to the satisfaction of the department that the conviction was based on extenuating circumstances unrelated to the person's reputation for honesty or obedience to the law.

[Sec. 403 NOTICE AND OPPORTUNITY FOR HEARING.

(a) Except as otherwise provided in subsection (b), the department may take an enforcement measure only after notice and opportunity for a hearing appropriate in the circumstances.

(b) The department may take an enforcement measure other than the imposition of a civil penalty under Section 404:

(1) without notice if the circumstances require action before notice can be given;

(2) after notice and without a prior hearing if the circumstances require action before a hearing can be held; or

(3) after notice and without a hearing if the person conducting virtual-currency business activity with or on behalf of a resident does not timely request a hearing.

(c) If the department takes action under subsection (b)(1) or (2), the person subject to the enforcement measure has the right to an expedited post-action hearing by the department unless the person has waived the hearing.]

Legislative Note: *If the state's administrative procedure act does not set out due process rights, the enacting state should enact Section 403. If the department would not be subject to the state's administrative procedure [act], the administrative procedure act should be amended to apply to the department for purposes of this [act].*

Sec. 404 CIVIL PENALTY.

(a) If a person other than a licensee or registrant engages in virtual-currency business activity with or on behalf of a resident in violation of this [act], the department may assess a civil penalty against the person in an amount not to exceed $[50,000] for each day of violation.

(b) If a licensee or registrant materially violates a provision of this [act], the department may assess a civil penalty in an amount not to exceed $[10,000] for each day of violation.

(c) A civil penalty under this section continues to accrue until the earlier of:

(1) the date the violation ceases; or

(2) a date specified by the department.

Legislative Note: *If state law or practice does not allow a state agency to both prosecute and adjudicate a civil penalty, the enacting state should amend this section to reflect its law or practice.*

Comment

1. This section allows the department to impose a civil penalty in an appropriate amount depending on the nature and duration of the violation against the violating licensee or registrant. A person who should be licensed or registered but is not is subject to the most potentially severe penalty of up to $50,000 per day, depending on the reason for the violation.

2. Other material violations of this act incur a lesser potential penalty, which may range from a small amount for an inadvertent technical violation to the maximum amount for a serious violation committed with reckless disregard or with intent.

3. A minor violation in isolation is not subject to a civil penalty under this section. A minor violation, if repeated so as to become material, may be subject to a civil penalty under this section.

Sec. 405 EFFECTIVE PERIOD OF REVOCATION, SUSPENSION, OR CEASE AND DESIST ORDER.

(a) Revocation of a license under this [act] is effective against a licensee one day after the department sends notice in a record of the revocation to the licensee, by a means reasonably selected for the notice to be received by the recipient in one day, to the address provided for receiving communications from the department.

(b) Suspension of a license under this [act], suspension of a registration, or an order to cease and desist is effective against a licensee, registrant, or other person one day after the department sends notice in a record of the suspension or order to the licensee, registrant, or other person, by a means reasonably selected for the notice to be received by the recipient in one day, to the address provided for receiving communications from the department or, if no address is provided, to the recipient's last known address. A suspension or order to cease and desist remains in effect until the earliest of:

(1) entry of an order by the department under the [state administrative procedure act] setting aside or limiting the suspension or order;

(2) entry of a court order setting aside or limiting the suspension or order to cease and desist; or

(3) a date specified by the department.

(c) If, without reason to know of the department's notice sent under subsection (a) or (b), a licensee, registrant, or other person does not comply in accordance with the notice until the notice is actually received at the address provided, the department may consider the delay in compliance in imposing a sanction for the failure.

Sec. 406 CONSENT ORDER.

The department may enter into a consent order with a person regarding an enforcement measure. The order may provide that it does not constitute an admission of fact by a party.

Sec. 407 SCOPE OF RIGHT OF ACTION.

(a) Except as otherwise provided in this section, a person does not have a right of action for violation of this [act].

(b) The department may bring an action for restitution on behalf of a resident if the department proves economic injury due to a violation of this [act].

(c) This section does not preclude an action by a resident to enforce rights under Section 502 or law of this state other than this [act].

Comment

1. As explained in Comment 2 to Section 401, this act does not afford a private right of action for a violation. There are two exceptions to this principle. The first is for a violation of Section 502. Section 502 is derived from Uniform Commercial Code ("UCC") Section 8-503; UCC Article 8 does provide for private rights of action if a person in the capacity of a securities intermediary violates UCC Section 8-503. It is, therefore, logical that an individual should have a similar right of action for a violation of Section 502 of this act, which is modeled on UCC Section 8-503.

2. The other exception to the rule against private rights of action for violations of this act would afford an individual a right of action for conduct that violates or is related to Section 502 of this act, such as fraudulently covering up a failure to maintain the required amount of virtual currency under control, or converting for the virtual-currency business' own use the virtual currency under its control for other persons.

3. When a class action may be brought to enforce individual rights of action is not specifically addressed by this section. In some circumstances, such as those described in comment 2 to this section, a class action may be warranted. In others, such as where only a particular owner's virtual currency is converted, no class action would be warranted.

4. A failure by a virtual-currency business to perform as directed by a customer, such as by use of a customer's virtual currency directly or as collateral for an obligation of the virtual-currency business, or otherwise, could give rise to a private right of action under subsection (c) of this section. Because a customer's directions are specific to the transaction and the virtual-currency business's obligations to that customer, allowing a limited private right of action normally should not add, and is not intended to add, a risk of class-action claims.

5. Nothing in this Article is intended to preclude an enforcement action by the department seeking recovery for customers of the virtual-currency business and subsection (b) specifically provides the department authority to do so.

[ARTICLE] 5 DISCLOSURES AND OTHER PROTECTIONS FOR RESIDENTS

Sec. 501 REQUIRED DISCLOSURES.

(a) A licensee or registrant shall provide to a resident who uses the licensee's or registrant's products or service the disclosures required by subsection (b) and any additional disclosure the department by rule determines reasonably necessary for the protection of residents. The department shall determine by rule the time and form required for disclosure. A disclosure required by this section must be made separately from any other information provided by the licensee or registrant and in a clear and conspicuous manner in a record the resident may keep. A licensee or registrant may propose for the department's approval alternate disclosures as more appropriate for its virtual-currency business activity with or on behalf of residents.

(b) Before establishing a relationship with a resident, a licensee or registrant shall disclose, to the extent applicable to the virtual-currency business activity the licensee or registrant will undertake with the resident:

(1) a schedule of fees and charges the licensee or registrant may assess, the manner by which fees and charges will be calculated if they are not set in advance and disclosed, and the timing of the fees and charges;

(2) whether the product or service provided by the licensee or registrant is covered by:

(A) a form of insurance or is otherwise guaranteed against loss by an agency of the United States:

(i) up to the full U.S. Dollar equivalent of virtual currency placed under the control of or purchased from the licensee or registrant as of the date of the placement or purchase, including the maximum amount provided by insurance under the Federal Deposit Insurance Corporation or otherwise available from the Securities Investor Protection Corporation; or

(ii) if not provided at the full U.S. Dollar equivalent of virtual currency placed under the control of or purchased from the licensee or registrant, the maximum amount of coverage for each resident expressed in the U.S. Dollar equivalent of the virtual currency; or

(B) private insurance against theft or loss, including cyber theft or theft by other means;

(3) the irrevocability of a transfer or exchange and any exception to irrevocability;

(4) a description of:

(A) liability for an unauthorized, mistaken, or accidental transfer or exchange;

(B) the resident's responsibility to provide notice to the licensee or registrant of the transfer or exchange;

(C) the basis for any recovery by the resident from the licensee or registrant;

(D) general error-resolution rights applicable to the transfer or exchange; and

(E) the method for the resident to update the resident's contact information with the licensee or registrant;

(5) that the date or time when the transfer or exchange is made and the resident's account is debited may differ from the date or time when the resident initiates the instruction to make the transfer or exchange;

(6) whether the resident has a right to stop a pre-authorized payment or revoke authorization for a transfer and the procedure to initiate a stop-payment order or revoke authorization for a subsequent transfer;

(7) the resident's right to receive a receipt, trade ticket, or other evidence of the transfer or exchange;

(8) the resident's right to at least 30 days' prior notice of a change in the licensee's or registrant's fee schedule, other terms and conditions of operating its virtual-currency business activity with the resident and the policies applicable to the resident's account; and

(9) that virtual currency is not legal tender.

(c) Except as otherwise provided in subsection (d), at the conclusion of a virtual-currency transaction with or on behalf of a resident, a licensee or registrant shall provide the resident a confirmation in a record which contains:

(1) the name and contact information of the licensee or registrant, including information the resident may need to ask a question or file a complaint;

(2) the type, value, date, precise time, and amount of the transaction; and

(3) the fee charged for the transaction, including any charge for conversion of virtual currency to legal tender, bank credit, or other virtual currency.

(d) If a licensee or registrant discloses that it will provide a daily confirmation in the initial disclosure under subsection (c), the licensee or registrant may elect to provide a single, daily confirmation for all transactions with or on behalf of a resident on that day instead of a per-transaction confirmation.

Comment

1. Section 501 specifies the types of disclosures that a licensee and registrant should be able to make in its dealings with or on behalf of residents of this state. Subparagraph 501(b)(2) requires a licensee or registrant to disclose to its customers whether the product or service provided is covered by a form of insurance or otherwise is guaranteed against loss by an agency of the United States, and the degree of coverage - whether coverage is up to the full U.S. dollar equivalent of the virtual currency or the maximum amount of coverage that the licensee or registrant makes available.

2. Uniform acts commonly employ two approaches to "level the playing field" when "consumers" of services and products deal with "merchants." One is to provide disclosures to provide consumers adequate knowledge that they might not otherwise have to enable them to protect their own interests. The other, to address unequal bargaining power, is to prohibit certain practices and terms or conditions in agreements. This act employs both approaches, the former in Section 501 and the latter in Section 502. It also employs a third approach in Article 6

that mandates the establishment and maintenance of specified policies and procedures to reduce or eliminate the designated problems that might otherwise arise. This approach allows policies and procedures appropriate for specific business plans, rather than regulating a "one size fits all" statutory mandate. The disclosures are required even if the person receiving them is a business. Many persons engaging in virtual-currency business activities are unsophisticated, and, even if they are knowledgeable, trying to define which persons are knowledgeable and which are not is not desirable because the disclosures do not harm and requiring the virtual-currency business to make such a determination opens the door to errors in compliance.

3. Section 501 requires a number of disclosures while allowing flexibility to design disclosures for particular types of services or products and circumstances. The specified disclosures are mandated before a resident of an enacting state establishes a relationship with the virtual-currency business and are appropriate to that context, such as the schedule of fees and charges, whether the provider offers any insurance against loss, procedures if a resident questions a transaction as unauthorized, mistaken, or accidental, other error-resolution rights, and any right to stop the transaction, among others.

4. The form for, and delivery of, the information required to be disclosed is covered, the latter to assure that the information is not lost in a complex, lengthy form. The department's authority to issue regulations and guidance under Article 2 is available to be employed here.

Sec. 502 PROPERTY INTERESTS AND ENTITLEMENTS TO VIRTUAL CURRENCY.

(a) A licensee or registrant that has control of virtual currency for one or more persons shall maintain in its control an amount of each type of virtual currency sufficient to satisfy the aggregate entitlements of the persons to the type of virtual currency.

(b) If a licensee or registrant violates subsection (a), the property interests of the persons in the virtual currency are pro rata property interests in the type of virtual currency to which the persons are entitled, without regard to the time the persons became entitled to the virtual currency or the licensee or registrant obtained control of the virtual currency.

(c) The virtual currency referred to in this section is:

(1) held for the persons entitled to the virtual currency;

(2) not property of the licensee or registrant; and

(3) not subject to the claims of creditors of the licensee or registrant.

Comment

1. This section is based on Uniform Commercial Code ("UCC") Sections 8-503 and 8-504 and protects the owner of virtual currency that is entrusted to a licensee or registrant for a purpose governed by this act. Enforcement is by the department, but also by private rights of action under this section as mentioned in Section 407. In essence, this section takes the virtual currency under the control of a licensee or registrant off the balance sheet of the virtual-currency business and beyond the business' right to deal with it as their own property. This formulation reduces the need for greater net worth and reserves than Section 204 requires without sacrificing user protection.

2. This section favors the interests of persons who place virtual currency under the control of a licensee or registrant over the interests of a licensee's or registrant's creditors. Section 502 (a) requires the virtual-currency business with "control" over virtual currency that belongs to residents of the enacting state to maintain an amount of each type of virtual currency sufficient to satisfy the aggregate entitlements of the persons to each type of virtual currency for the benefit of its resident customers, and (b) favors the interests of persons who place virtual currency under the control of a licensee or registrant over the interests of creditors of the licensee or registrant. To clarify the rights of persons that place their virtual currency under the control of virtual-currency businesses and of the virtual-currency businesses themselves, the Uniform Law Commission is developing an act that will provide, when approved and enacted, a substitute for Section 502 of this act that instead adopts UCC Article 8's more balanced approach to this matter. This act is expected to be ready for enactment in 2018.

[ARTICLE] 6 POLICIES AND PROCEDURES

Sec. 601 MANDATED COMPLIANCE PROGRAMS AND MONITORING.

(a) An applicant, before submitting an application, and registrant, before registering, shall create and, during licensure or registration, maintain in a record policies and procedures for:

(1) an information-security and operational-security program;

(2) a business-continuity program;

(3) a disaster-recovery program;

¶1400

(4) an anti-fraud program;

(5) an anti-money-laundering program;

(6) a program to prevent funding of terrorist activity; and

(7) a program designed to:

(A) ensure compliance with this [act], law of this state other than this [act], and federal law, which are relevant to the virtual-currency business activity contemplated by the licensee or registrant with or on behalf of residents; and

(B) assist the licensee or registrant in achieving the purposes of law of this state other than this [act] and federal law if violation of that law has a remedy under this [act].

(b) Each policy required by subsection (a) must be in a record and designed to be adequate for a licensee's or registrant's contemplated virtual-currency business activity with or on behalf of residents, considering the circumstances of all participants and the safe operation of the activity. Each policy and implementing procedure must be compatible with other policies and the procedures implementing them and not conflict with policies or procedures applicable to the licensee or registrant under law of this state other than this [act]. A policy and implementing procedure may be one in existence in the licensee's or registrant's virtual-currency business activity with or on behalf of residents.

(c) A licensee's or registrant's policy for detecting fraud must include:

(1) identification and assessment of the material risks of its virtual-currency business activity related to fraud;

(2) protection against any material risk related to fraud identified by the department or the licensee or registrant; and

(3) periodic evaluation and revision of the anti-fraud procedure.

(d) A licensee's or registrant's policy for preventing money laundering and financing of terrorist activity must include:

(1) identification and assessment of the material risks of its virtual-currency business activity related to money laundering and financing of terrorist activity;

(2) procedures, in accordance with federal law or guidance published by federal agencies responsible for enforcing federal law, pertaining to money laundering and financing of terrorist activity; and

(3) filing reports under the Bank Secrecy Act, 31 U.S.C. Section 5311 et seq. [,as amended], or 31 C.F.R. Part X [,as amended], and other federal or state laws pertaining to the prevention or detection of money laundering or financing of terrorist activity.

(e) A licensee's or registrant's information-security and operational-security policy must include reasonable and appropriate administrative, physical, and technical safeguards to protect the confidentiality, integrity, and availability of any non-public personal information or virtual currency it receives, maintains, or transmits.

(f) A licensee or registrant is not required to file with the department a copy of a report it makes to a federal authority unless the department specifically requires filing.

(g) A licensee's or registrant's protection policy under subsection (e) for residents must include:

(1) any action or system of records required to comply with this [act] and law of this state other than this [act] applicable to the licensee or registrant with respect to virtual- currency business activity with or on behalf of a resident;

(2) a procedure for resolving disputes between the licensee or registrant and a resident;

(3) a procedure for a resident to report an unauthorized, mistaken, or accidental virtual-currency business activity transaction; and

(4) a procedure for a resident to file a complaint with the licensee or registrant and for the resolution of the complaint in a fair and timely manner with notice to the resident as soon as reasonably practical of the resolution and the reasons for the resolution.

(h) After the policies and procedures required under this section are created and approved by the department and the licensee or registrant, the licensee or registrant shall engage a responsible individual with adequate authority and experience to monitor each policy and procedure, publicize it as appropriate, recommend changes as desirable, and enforce it.

(i) A licensee or registrant may:

(1) request advice from the department as to compliance with this section; and

(2) with the department's approval, outsource functions, other than compliance, required under this section.

(j) Failure of a particular policy or procedure adopted under this section to meet its goals in a particular instance is not a ground for liability of the licensee or registrant if the policy or procedure was created, implemented, and monitored properly. Repeated failures of a policy or procedure are evidence that the policy or procedure was not created or implemented properly.

(k) Policies and procedures adopted under this section must be disclosed separately from other disclosures made available to a resident, in a clear and conspicuous manner and in the medium through which the resident contacted the licensee or registrant.

Legislative Note: In states in which the constitution, or other law, does not permit the phrase "as amended" when federal statutes or regulations are incorporated into state law, the phrase should be deleted in subsection (d)(3).

Comment

1. As explained in Comment 1 to Section 501, this section and Section 602 require that a licensee and registrant establish and maintain policies and procedures covering the items listed in this section that are intended to reduce or eliminate problems that may arise in the operation of the businesses of trusted intermediaries, such as virtual-currency business licensees and registrants. The specific policies and procedures include information and operational security (often referred to colloquially as "cybersecurity"), anti-fraud protections such as the "Red Flags" requirements imposed by the Fair Credit Reporting Act and federal agency regulations implementing them, anti-money-laundering and counter-terrorist-financing statutes and regulations, and compliance with other relevant federal or state laws. This approach allows policies and procedures to be designed to fit particular business models rather than taking a statutory "one-size-fits-all" approach.

2. Subparagraph (1)(a) speaks to the need of what has been referred to colloquially as a "cyber-security" policy or program. Cyber-security includes both information security and operational security and, accordingly, this act uses the more contemporary fulsome descriptions in Section 601 to describe the obligations imposed on licensees and registrants under this act.

3. The department is authorized to assist through advice in the development of required policies and procedures, and to allow outsourcing of the operation of certain programs rather than requiring the virtual-currency business to engage a third party with adequate experience and facilities to do so. The disclosure requirement allows persons engaging the services of a licensee or registrant to be aware of the policies and procedures intended for their benefit.

4. There is no requirement in this act for the licensee or registrant to make filings with the department that would duplicate filings they must make to federal agencies and departments under the federal Bank Secrecy Act or regulations enforced by the Department of the Treasury's FinCEN or Office of Foreign Assets Control ("OFAC") agencies.

Sec. 602 MANDATED COMPLIANCE POLICY OR PROCEDURE.

(a) An applicant, before submitting its application, and a registrant, before registering, shall establish and maintain in a record a policy or procedure designed to ensure compliance with:

(1) this [act]; and

(2) law of this state other than this [act] if:

(A) the other law is relevant to the virtual-currency business activity contemplated by the licensee or registrant or the scope of this [act]; or

(B) this [act] could assist in the purpose of the other law because violation of the other law has a remedy under this [act].

(b) A policy or procedure under subsection (a):

(1) must be compatible, and not conflict, with requirements applicable to a licensee or registrant under law of this state other than this [act] and under federal law; and

(2) may be a policy or procedure in existence for the licensee's or registrant's virtual-currency business activity with or on behalf of a resident.

(c) After the policies and procedures required under this section are created by the licensee or registrant and approved by the department, the licensee or registrant shall engage a responsible individual with adequate authority and experience to monitor each policy or procedure, publicize it as appropriate, recommend changes as desirable, and enforce it.

(d) A licensee or registrant may:

(1) request advice from the department as to compliance with this section; and

(2) with the department's approval, outsource functions, other than compliance, required under this section.

(e) Failure of a particular policy or procedure adopted under this section to meet its goals in a particular instance is not a ground for liability of the licensee or registrant if the policy or procedure was created, implemented, and monitored properly. Repeated failures of a policy or procedure are evidence that the policy or procedure was not created or implemented properly.

[ARTICLE] 7 MISCELLANEOUS PROVISIONS

Sec. 701 UNIFORMITY OF APPLICATION AND CONSTRUCTION.

In applying and construing this uniform [act], consideration must be given to the need to promote uniformity of the law with respect to its subject matter among the states that enact it.

Sec. 702 RELATION TO ELECTRONIC SIGNATURES IN GLOBAL AND NATIONAL COMMERCE ACT.

This [act] modifies, limits, or supersedes the Electronic Signatures in Global and National Commerce Act, 15 U.S.C. Section 7001, et seq., but does not modify, limit, or supersede Section 101(c) of that act, 15 U.S.C. Section 7001(c), or authorize electronic delivery of any of the notices described in Section 103(b) of that act, 15 U.S.C. Section 7003(b)).

Sec. 703 SAVING AND TRANSITIONAL PROVISIONS.

(a) A license issued under [insert citation to state's Money Services Act or Money Transmitter Act] which is in effect immediately before [the effective date of this [act]] remains in effect as a license for its duration unless revoked or suspended by the licensing authority that issued it. A person licensed under [insert citation to state's Money Services Act or Money Transmitter Act] which does not intend to engage in virtual-currency business activity is not required to inform the department of its intention.

(b) If the department denies, suspends, or revokes a license under this [act] or suspends, or revokes a registration to conduct virtual-currency business activity with or on behalf of a resident, the denial, suspension, or revocation may not be used as a ground for suspension or revocation of a license granted under [insert citation to state's Money Services Act or Money Transmitter Act] unless that [act] independently provides a basis for action against the licensee or registrant.

(c) This [act] applies to virtual-currency business activity with or on behalf of a resident on or after [the effective date of this [act]].

(d) A person is deemed to be conducting unlicensed virtual-currency business activity with or on behalf of a resident in violation of this [act] if the person engages in virtual-currency business activity on or after [the effective date of this [act]] and the person does not hold a license issued or recognized under this [act], is not exempt from this [act], and has not applied for a license or filed a registration. This subsection includes a person that:

(1) has obtained a license under [insert citation to state's Money Services Act or Money Transmitter Act], whether or not that [act] covers virtual-currency business activity, or holds a charter as a trust company from this state; and

(2) does not have permission to engage in virtual-currency business activity with or on behalf of a resident.

Legislative Note: A state that allows a state-chartered bank with trust powers or a non-bank trust company or limited-purpose trust company to engage in activities that would be governed by this [act], only if it has received a separate permit or approval, or otherwise conditions its exercise of powers governed by this [act], should add a separate savings or transitional subsection to this [article]. The new subsection should specify any limitations on the powers of the trust company or limited-purpose trust company as well as the state's preference on reciprocal licensing of a trust company or limited-purpose trust company, or of recognizing cross-border activities of a chartered trust company or limited-purpose trust company not domiciled in the state.

[Sec. 704 SEVERABILITY CLAUSE.

If any provision of this [act] or its application to any person or circumstance is held invalid, the invalidity does not affect other provisions or application of this [act] which can be given effect without the invalid provision or application, and to this end the provisions of this [act] are severable.]

Legislative Note: Include this section only if this state lacks a general severability statute or a decision by the highest court of this state stating a general rule of severability.

Sec. 705 REPEALS; CONFORMING AMENDMENTS.

    (a) ....

    (b) ....

    (c) ....

Legislative Note: *An enacting state should modify or repeal any other law regulating virtual-currency business activity with or behalf of a resident, if the state regulates virtual-currency business activities as money transmission.*

Sec. 706 EFFECTIVE DATE.

This [act] takes effect ....

GLOSSARY

GLOSSARY OF TERMS

Anti-money-laundering rules:

Rules to help detect and report suspicious activity including the predicate offenses to money laundering and terrorist financing, such as securities fraud and market manipulation. In the United States, the main AML law is the Bank Secrecy Act.

Binary option:

A type of option that returns a payoff of either a fixed amount or zero. For example, there could be a binary option that pays $100 if a hurricane makes landfall in Florida before a specified date and zero if it does not.

Bitcoin:

Bitcoin is the world's first decentralized currency utilizing peer-to-peer blockchain technology. Envisioned in a 2008 white paper titled *Bitcoin: A Peer-to-Peer Electronic Cash System*, published by an anonymous person (or group of people) going by the name of Satoshi Nakamoto.

BitLicense:

New York's framework for the licensing and regulation of businesses transmitting virtual currency. Anyone transmitting virtual currency; storing, holding, or maintaining custody or control of virtual currency on behalf of others; buying and selling virtual currency as a customer business; performing exchange services as a customer business; or controlling, administering, or issuing a virtual currency must obtain a BitLicense.

Block:

A set of data on the blockchain ledger representing a given transaction.

Blockchain:

A type of distributed ledger on a peer-to-peer, networked database that digitally records transactions via a series of blocks of transactional data that are chronologically and cryptographically linked to one another. A blockchain can be used in the context of virtual currencies and typically relies on miners to solve mathematically complex problems to achieve consensus about which blocks of transactions should be added to the blockchain. A blockchain also can be forked into alternative chains at the urging of the blockchain's participants.

Blue sky law:

A state law delineating standards for buying and selling of securities, particularly when the security is not listed on an exchange. Blue sky laws typically provide both criminal and civil prescriptions on fraud and misrepresentations regarding securities, and they create private actions for recovery of losses under covered transactions.

Broker-dealer:

A broker-dealer is an agent engaged in the business of effecting transactions in securities for others, or itself, acting as principal.

Chain:

The process of securing and linking a block on a blockchain with prior blocks.

Chamber of Digital Commerce:

A trade association established in 2014 that represents the digital asset and blockchain industry. Its stated mission is to promote the acceptance and use of digital assets and blockchain-based technologies.

Commodity Exchange Act:

The 1936 Commodity Exchange Act as amended, 7 USC 1, et seq., provides for the federal regulation of commodity futures and options trading.

Consensus:

The process of verifying transactions before they are validated and written to a blockchain ledger.

Cryptocurrency:

Virtual currency that relies on cryptographic software protocols to create the currency and track and validate ownership transfers.

Denial-of-service attack:

A malicious attack on a computer or network intended to disrupt the service, typically by overloading the target with requests. In a distributed denial-of-service (DDoS) attack, the requests derive from multiple sources, making it more difficult for the victim to stop the attack.

Derivative:

A financial instrument, traded on or off an exchange, the price of which is directly dependent upon (i.e., "derived from") the value of one or more underlying securities, equity indices, debt instruments, commodities, other derivative instruments, or any agreed upon pricing index or arrangement (e.g., the movement over time of the Consumer Price Index or freight rates). They are used to hedge risk or to exchange a floating rate of return for fixed rate of return. Derivatives include futures, options, and swaps. For example, futures contracts are derivatives of the physical contract and options on futures are derivatives of futures contracts.

Designated Contract Market (DCM):

A board of trade or exchange designated by the Commodity Futures Trading Commission to trade futures or options under the Commodity Exchange Act. A contract market can allow both institutional and retail participants and can list for trading futures contracts on any commodity, provided that each contract is not readily susceptible to manipulation.

Distributed Ledger Technology (DLT):

A database that has multiple copies of data on many nodes (computers) in a network. DLT can utilize either a public or private network. A blockchain is one specific type of distributed ledger that adds changes to the ledger via a series of blocks of transactional data that are chronologically and cryptographically linked to one another.

Glossary

Electronic Fund Transfer Act (EFTA):

Establishes the basic rights, liabilities, and responsibilities of consumers who use electronic fund transfer and remittance transfer services and of financial institutions or other persons that offer these services. The EFTA is implemented by Reg. E—Electronic Funds Transfer (12 CFR Part 1005).

Enterprise Ethereum Alliance Legal Industry Working Group:

A group that seeks to leverage open-source Ethereum technology by bringing together leading law firms and individuals to explore building enterprise-grade applications on Ethereum.

European Securities and Markets Authority (ESMA):

An independent European Union regulatory agency that contributes to safeguarding the stability of the EU's financial system by enhancing the protection of investors and promoting stable and orderly financial markets.

Financial Crimes Enforcement Network (FinCEN):

A bureau of the Treasury Department with the principal statutory duties of collecting, analyzing, and distributing information on money laundering and other financial system abuses. It also has the authority to adopt regulations to implement the Bank Secrecy Act.

Futures contract:

An agreement to purchase or sell a commodity for delivery in the future: (1) at a price that is determined at initiation of the contract; (2) that obligates each party to the contract to fulfill the contract at the specified price; (3) that is used to assume or shift price risk; and (4) that may be satisfied by delivery or offset.

Global Legal Blockchain Consortium:

An organization consisting of major law firms, corporations, and technology vendors with the mission of organizing and aligning the stakeholders in the global legal industry with regard to the use of blockchain technology.

Hash:

A cryptographic algorithm utilized in blockchain technology which makes it extremely difficult to modify, misrepresent, or hack transactions once confirmed by the system.

Hype cycle:

A representation of the maturity and adoption of technologies and applications which incorporates key phases of a technology's life cycle.

Immutability:

A characteristic of blockchain which describes the unchanging nature of the ledger once a transaction is confirmed.

Initial coin offering:

An initial coin offering (ICO) is a fundraising device, much like crowdfunding, in which the issuer offers a digital coin or token in exchange for consideration in the form of virtual and/or fiat currency. An ICO is the blockchain analog to an initial public offering (IPO) of traditional shares in a company, although an ICO can be very different from an IPO and may or may not involve an investment interest that is a security. Coins or tokens issued via an

ICO may be traded in secondary markets via online platforms or virtual currency exchanges. The issuing entity in an ICO typically publishes a white paper that explains the business goals and technical aspects of the ICO.

Know-your-customer:

A customer identification program for the opening of a customer account at a financial institution that enables law enforcement and supervisory agencies to identify accounts maintained by individuals suspected of terrorist activities.

Manipulation:

Any planned operation, transaction, or practice that causes or maintains an artificial price. Specific types of commodity manipulation include corners and squeezes as well as unusually large purchases or sales of a commodity or security in a short period of time in order to distort prices, or putting out false information in order to distort prices.

Miner:

A person or organization that verifies and secures a distributed ledger by contributing computing resources and solving cryptographic problems. A miner can be compensated by receiving newly minted coins or by receiving transaction fees.

Money services business:

For purposes of virtual currency regulation, either: a money transmitter or a seller of prepaid access, if (a) the prepaid access can be used before the buyer's identification can be verified or (b) the seller sells any single person prepaid access to more than $10,000 in a single day.

Money transmitter:

A person that accepts currency, funds, or other value that substitutes for currency and then transmits the value to another person or another location by any means, and that does not satisfy any of the regulatory exemptions.

Money transmitter law:

Every state except Montana has legislation governing entities in the business of transmitting money, which typically impose licensing and reporting requirements. Depending on the jurisdiction, these laws may or may not apply to those holding or transmitting virtual currencies.

National Securities Exchange:

An organization registered under Securities Exchange Act Section 6 that provides a marketplace or facility for bringing together purchasers and sellers of securities.

Payment, clearing, and settlement (PCS) systems:

Facilitates financial transactions and purchases of goods and services and the attendant movement of money at all levels of the U.S. economy—on behalf of individuals and institutions, buyers and sellers, consumers and businesses, investors and securities issuers.

Permissions (blockchain):

A permissioned blockchain is a closed system that limits access only to approved users, enabling finer controls over privacy and confidentiality. A permissionless blockchain, such as the one that underlies Bitcoin, is accessible to anyone, facilitating decentralization.

Ponzi scheme:

Named after Charles Ponzi, a man with a remarkable criminal career in the early 20th century, the term has been used to describe pyramid arrangements whereby an enterprise makes payments to investors from the proceeds of a later investment rather than from profits of the underlying business venture, as the investors expected, and gives investors the impression that a legitimate profit-making business or investment opportunity exists, where in fact it is a mere fiction.

Private key:

A designation of the blockchain public-key cryptography system given to a user which is private and typically maintained like a private password.

Public key:

A designation of the blockchain public-key cryptography system given to a user which is known to the world and often referred to as the Bitcoin address.

Public key cryptography:

A system for sending secured transmissions that consists of a public key that is a pseudonymous address used to identify an account on a distributed ledger or blockchain and a private key address that is used to sign transactions on a distributed ledger or blockchain. Unlike public keys, private keys are intended to be kept secret and anyone who holds a private key may use it to sign transactions.

Regulatory sandbox:

A regulatory accommodation allowing businesses to test innovative products and services without needing to comply with the full degree of regulations that would otherwise apply.

Responsible innovation:

In the banking context, the use of new or improved financial products, services and processes to meet the evolving needs of consumers, businesses, and communities in a manner that is consistent with sound risk management and is aligned with a bank's overall business strategy.

Retail customer:

A customer that does not qualify as an eligible contract participant under Section 1a (12) of the Commodity Exchange Act, 7 USC 1a (12). An individual with total assets that do not exceed $10 million, or $5 million if the individual is entering into an agreement, contract, or transaction to manage risk, would be considered a retail customer.

Security:

A security includes stock, debt instruments, warrants and other instruments commonly thought of as securities, including any investment contract or arrangement in which a person invests money in a common enterprise with the expectation of profiting from the efforts of others.

Smart contract:

Broadly, a legal contract with automated components, especially regarding the performance of operational terms contained in a contract. More narrowly, a type of computer code that can be programmed to perform a series of if-then statements when prompted.

Glossary

Special purpose national bank:

A bank chartered by the Office of the Comptroller of the Currency that has limited activities such as fiduciary powers or credit card operations.

Spot commodity:

(1) The actual commodity as distinguished from a futures contract;

(2) Cash commodities available for immediate delivery.

Swap:

In general, the exchange of one asset or liability for a similar asset or liability for the purpose of lengthening or shortening maturities, or otherwise shifting risks. This may entail selling one securities issue and buying another in foreign currency, or it may entail buying a currency on the spot market and simultaneously selling it forward. Swaps also may involve exchanging income flows; for example, exchanging the fixed rate coupon stream of a bond for a variable rate payment stream, or vice versa, while not swapping the principal component of the bond.

Swap Execution Facilities (SEFs):

Trading facilities that operate under the regulatory oversight of the CFTC pursuant to Section 5h of the Commodity Exchange Act, 7 USC 7b-3. SEFs were created by the addition of Section 5h by Section 733 of the Dodd-Frank Wall Street Reform and Consumer Protection Act for the trading and processing of swaps.

Token:

A digital representation of a product or service, a right, or an investment interest. Includes the term "utility token," which suggests a functional component separate from any investment interest such that, depending on the economic facts and circumstances, a token or utility token may or may not be a security.

Treasury Inspector General for Tax Administration (TIGTA):

An office of the Treasury Department that provides independent oversight of the Internal Revenue Service. TIGTA's focus is devoted entirely to tax administration and acts independently of the Department and all other Treasury offices and bureaus.

Truth in Lending Act (TILA):

A consumer protection law that is intended to ensure that credit terms are disclosed in a meaningful way so consumers can compare credit terms more readily and knowledgeably. TILA is implemented by Reg. Z—Truth in Lending (12 CFR Part 1026).

Virtual currency:

A digital representation of value that functions as a medium of exchange, a unit of account, and/or a store of value, although a virtual currency is not legal tender and it may have other characteristics that cause it to be accorded varying legal treatment depending on the context.

Wallet:

An online service that stores digital credentials allowing a user to access and transact in Bitcoin or other virtual currency.

Glossary

Topical Index

References are to paragraph (¶) numbers.